Classroom Assessment for Students in Special and General Education

SECOND EDITION

CATHLEEN G. SPINELLI
St. Joseph's University

PEARSON

Merrill
Prentice Hall

Upper Saddle River, New Jersey
Columbus, Ohio

Library of Congress Cataloging-in-Publication Data

Spinelli, Cathleen G.
   Classroom assessment for students in special and general education / Cathleen G. Spinelli.—2nd ed.
     p. cm.
   Rev. ed. of: Classroom assessment for students with special needs in inclusive settings. c2002.
   Includes bibliographical references and index.
   ISBN 0-13-119353-8 (paperback)
   1. Children with disabilities—Education—United States—Evaluation. 2. Inclusive education—United States—Evaluation. 3. Educational tests and measurements—United States. I. Spinelli, Cathleen G., 1951– Classroom assessment for students with special needs in inclusive settings. II. Title.
LC4031.S745 2006
371.9'046—dc22

2005045882

Vice President and Executive Publisher: Jeffery W. Johnston
Senior Editor: Allyson P. Sharp
Editorial Assistant: Kathleen S. Burk
Production Editor: Sheryl Glicker Langner
Production Coordination: GGS Book Services, Atlantic Highlands
Design Coordinator: Diane C. Lorenzo
Cover Designer: Bryan Huber
Cover Art: Corbis
Production Manager: Laura Messerly
Director of Marketing: Ann Castel Davis
Marketing Manager: Autumn Purdy
Marketing Coordinator: Brian Mounts

This book was set in Garamond by GGS Book Services, Atlantic Highlands. It was printed and bound by Hamilton Printing Company. The cover was printed by The Lehigh Press, Inc.

Photo Credits: Michael A. Spinelli, pp. 2, 44, 56, 81, 129, 150, 160, 218, 271, 310, 346, 358, 400, 446, 468, 500, 509; Julie Spinelli, pp. 33, 76, 178, 284, 400, 490; Laird Bindrim, p. 122; Drew Spinelli, pp. 192, 462

Pearson Prentice Hall™ is a trademark of Pearson Education, Inc.
Pearson® is a registered trademark of Pearson plc
Prentice Hall® is a registered trademark of Pearson Education, Inc.
Merrill® is a registered trademark of Pearson Education, Inc.

Pearson Education Ltd.,
Pearson Education Singapore Pte. Ltd.
Pearson Education Canada, Ltd.
Pearson Education—Japan

Pearson Education Australia Pty. Limited
Pearson Education North Asia Ltd.
Pearson Educación de Mexico, S.A. de C.V.
Pearson Education Malaysia Pte. Ltd.

10 9 8 7 6 5 4 3 2
ISBN: 0-13-119353-8

Preface

Classroom Assessment for Students in Special and General Education is written for future teachers and experienced educators who are interested in developing or expanding their understanding of effective and reflective assessment practices. It has been designed as a text for undergraduate and graduate education courses as well as for in-service and reaccredidation courses for practicing teachers, support staff, administration staff, and other personnel who provide services to students with diverse learning needs. The focus of this text is on inclusive practices and procedures, collaboration, and the relationship between assessment and instructional programming. This text can also serve as a supplementary text for educational psychology, tests and measures, methods, or consultation courses.

Most assessment texts focus on formal, standardized assessment. This text is different. It addresses all aspects of assessment but focuses primarily on informal, teacher-friendly, and classroom-relevant methods of measuring achievement, identifying strengths and weaknesses, and monitoring the progress of students with diverse learning needs. The goal of this book is to provide the educator with the skills necessary to effectively use an authentic, dynamic approach to understanding the needs of the whole child. This goal is accomplished by identifying how various factors—cultural, linguistic, medical, health, social-emotional and the home, school, and community environment—can affect the child's educational adjustment and progress in educational programs.

CHAPTER CONTENTS AND ORGANIZATION

Each chapter begins with key terms that direct and guide learning, followed by chapter objectives that provide a focus on the topics covered in the chapter. Chapters are divided into sections for easy reference. The book is organized according to general test procedural order. Clear explanations are provided for developing, administering, scoring, interpreting, graphing, and correlating individualized education plan (IEP) results into instructional goals. Also addressed are curriculum design and methods for reporting progress to parents, related services personnel, and support and administration staff.

Authentic case studies give readers examples of classroom scenarios that demonstrate how, when, and why particular assessment procedures are used and explain how to match needed accommodations or modifications to individual needs. Each chapter contains numerous illustrations, examples, models, and directions to guide teachers in correlating assessment measures with students' curriculum—and subsequently, assessment results to instructional programming. At the end of each chapter, summary points directly correlate with the chapter objectives, providing the reader with focus points for reflection and review. Chapter Check-Ups are higher order thinking questions and Practical Application Assessment Activities provide the reader with opportunities to test and apply their learning.

This book is organized into four parts. Part 1, Overview of the Assessment Process, consists of chapters 1, 2, and 3. These chapters cover the reasons for assessment, what the assessment process entails, and variables that can affect assessment results. Chapter 1 addresses the purpose of assessment, with an extensive description of the evaluation process—from the initial identification of a problem through the prereferral, referral, classification, program development, and placement decisions to progress monitoring. Chapter 2 covers standardized assessment tests and procedures, their strengths and weaknesses, the issues to consider when deciding which assessment method to use, how to administer assessments and what scores mean, the use of technology in assessment, and how to report test results. Chapter 3 deals with types of informal assessments; planning, constructing, administering, and scoring assessments; converting scores to grades; and guidelines for reporting progress to parents.

Part 2, Preliminary Assessment Issues, consists of chapters 4 and 5. This part deals with the legal, ethical, political, and accountability issues that must be considered during the assessment process. Chapter 4 covers the recent reforms of major professional educational associations and mandated legislative issues, with particular focus on the new 2004 Individuals with Disabilities Education Act Amendment (IDEA 2004) regulations that deal with the assessment of students with diverse educational needs. Additional issues address accountability; the impact of including students with disabilities in core curricular content assessments; and guidelines for using accommodations, modifications, or alternative assessments when assessing students with diverse educational needs. Chapter 5 deals with obtaining relevant preliminary assessment information, including parent, teacher, and student interviews; record reviews, work-sample analyses, and observations.

Part 3, Basic Skills and Content-Subject Assessment, consists of chapters 6 through 10. These chapters cover assessment in the basic skill and content area subjects, specifically oral language, ELL/bilingual, reading, written language, mathematics, science, and social studies. Also discussed are the factors that affect students with learning difficulties; the various techniques teachers can use to evaluate students individually, in small groups, or as a whole class in inclusive instructional settings; and methods of integrating assessment results into instructional/IEP planning and progress monitoring.

Part 4, Special Focus Assessment, consists of chapters 11 through 13 and covers areas beyond specific subject matter. Chapter 11 deals with study and test-taking skill assessment, including factors influencing work-study skills, test preparation and test-taking performance, and suggestions for helping students to become more effective test takers. Chapter 12 addresses psychosocial evaluation; topics covered include behavioral analysis procedures; direct observation and recording techniques; functional assessment, character education, evaluation strategies, and social skill assessment. Chapter 13 discusses transitions, from early childhood to secondary school and post-high-school options. Components to be evaluated, legislative mandates regulating the transition process, and assessment methods used for transition assessment are addressed. Also covered are individual student programming for preschoolers; the individualized family service plan; individualized transition plan development; career, self-determination, and situational and person-centered assessment. Issues related to transition assessments and planning, ranging from special to general education classes, and from a medical or residential facility back to school are also discussed.

ACKNOWLEDGMENTS

I am grateful to my family, friends, and colleagues who have encouraged and supported me through the revision of this second edition. It would not have been possible without the tremendous support and efforts of the members of my family, and I dedicate this book to them. Special appreciation goes to my ever-patient husband, Michael, for sharing his experience and expertise, suggestions, and direction, and for his gentle prodding that brought this dream to fruition. The love and ongoing support from my mother, Helen Gallagher, is also particularly appreciated, especially for her editorial assistance. Thanks also to our children—Eric, Julie, Drew, and especially Joan—who was always willing to help and dedicate her time and talent to the production of this revision.

My sincere gratitude goes to Allyson Sharp, senior editor, for her guidance, patience, and ongoing enthusiasm for this project. Many thanks also to Kathy Burk, editorial assistant, to Kelly Keeler from GGS Book Services, to Paula Grant for her copyediting, and to Sheryl Langner for overseeing this project and fine-tuning this text on its way to press. I also appreciate the efforts of the manuscript reviewers who provided thoughtful and insightful comments, Gerlinde G. Beckers, Southeastern Louisiana University; Sherrie Bettenhausen, College of Charlestown; Dorota Celinska, Roosevelt University; Lynne Chalmers, University of North Dakota; and Jane Mangum, Nicholls State University.

Special acknowledgment and appreciation go to two very bright and hard-working young women, Miriam Reynolds and Natalie Warren, who dedicated many hours to research the final product. I also want to thank Margie Crutchfield for her support and advice, Marsha Danser for her help and willingness to share resources, and all those who contributed to this text.

Cathleen G. Spinelli

About the Author

Cathleen G. Spinelli is an associate professor and Director of the Special Education Program at Saint Joseph's University in Philadelphia, Pennsylvania, where she teaches undergraduate and graduate classes in diagnosis and teaching techniques. She has extensive experience working in the public school system, evaluating students from preschool to adults, as a certified school psychologist and an educational diagnostician. She has enjoyed her years as both a special education teacher and a school administrator in the public school system. Readers may contact her at cathleen.spinelli@sju.edu. Please be sure to visit her Website at: www.sju.edu/cas/education/cathleen_spinelli

Educator Learning Center:
An Invaluable Online Resource

Merrill Education and the Association for Supervision and Curriculum Development (ASCD) invite you to take advantage of a new online resource, one that provides access to the top research and proven strategies associated with ASCD and Merrill—the Educator Learning Center. At **www.educatorlearningcenter.com**, you will find resources that will enhance your students' understanding of course topics and of current educational issues, in addition to being invaluable for further research.

HOW THE EDUCATOR LEARNING CENTER WILL HELP YOUR STUDENTS BECOME BETTER TEACHERS

With the combined resources of Merrill Education and ASCD, you and your students will find a wealth of tools and materials to better prepare them for the classroom.

Research

- More than 600 articles from the ASCD journal *Educational Leadership* discuss everyday issues faced by practicing teachers.
- A direct link on the site to Research Navigator™ gives students access to many of the leading education journals, as well as extensive content detailing the research process.
- Excerpts from Merrill Education texts give your students insights on important topics of instructional methods, diverse populations, assessment, classroom management, technology, and refining classroom practice.

Classroom Practice

- Hundreds of lesson plans and teaching strategies are categorized by content area and age range.
- Case studies and classroom video footage provide virtual field experience for student reflection.
- Computer simulations and other electronic tools keep your students abreast of today's classrooms and current technologies.

LOOK INTO THE VALUE OF EDUCATOR LEARNING CENTER YOURSELF

A four-month subscription to Educator Learning Center is $25 but is **FREE** when packaged with any Merrill Education text. In order for your students to have access to this site, you must use this special value-pack ISBN number **WHEN** placing your textbook order with the bookstore: 0-13-155988-5. Your students will then receive a copy of the text packaged with a free ASCD pincode. To preview the value of this website to you and your students, please go to www.educatorlearningcenter.com and click on "Demo."

Discover the *Merrill Resources for Special Education Website* Accompanying This Book

Technology is a constantly growing and changing aspect of our field that is creating a need for new content and resources. To address this emerging need, Merrill Education has developed an online learning environment for students, teachers, and professors alike to complement our products—the *Merrill Resources for Special Education* Website. This content-rich website provides additional resources specific to this book's topic and will help you—professors, classroom teachers, and students—augment your teaching, learning, and professional development.

Our goal is to build on and enhance what our products already offer. For this reason, the content for our user-friendly website is organized by topic and provides teachers, professors, and students with a variety of meaningful resources all in one location. With this website, we bring together the best of what Merrill has to offer: text resources, video clips, web links, tutorials, and a wide variety of information on topics of interest to general and special educators alike. Rich content, applications, and competencies further enhancing the learning process.

The *Merrill Resources for Special Education* Website includes:

RESOURCES FOR THE PROFESSOR—

- The **Syllabus Manager**™, an online syllabus creation and management tool, enables instructors to create and revise their syllabus with an easy, step-by-step process. Students can access your syllabus and any changes you make during the course of your class from any computer with Internet access. To access this tailored syllabus, students will just need the URL of the website and the password assigned to the syllabus. By clicking on the date, the student can see a list of activities, assignments, and readings due for that particular class.
- In addition to the **Syllabus Manager**™ and its benefits listed above, professors also have access to all of the wonderful resources that students have access to on the site.

RESOURCES FOR THE STUDENT—

- Video clips specific to each topic, with questions to help you evaluate the content and make crucial theory-to-practice connections.
- Thought-provoking critical analysis questions that students can answer and turn in for evaluation or that can serve as basis for class discussions and lectures.
- Access to a wide variety of resources related to classroom strategies and methods, including lesson planning and classroom management.
- Information on all the most current relevant topics related to special and general education, including CEC INTASC, and Praxis standards, IEPs, portfolios, and professional development.
- Extensive web resources and overviews on each topic addressed on the website.
- A message board with discussion starters where students can respond to class discussion topics, post questions and responses, or ask questions about assignments.
- A search feature to help access specific information quickly.

To take advantage of these and other resources, please visit the Merrill Resources for Special Education Website at:

http://www.prenhall.com/spinelli

Brief Contents

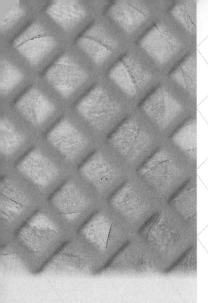

Contents

PART 3   Basic Skills and Content-Subject Assessment   177

Chapter 6   Oral and English Language Learner/Bilingual Assessment   178

NOTE: Every effort has been made to provide accurate and current Internet information in this book. However, the Internet and information posted on it are constantly changing, and it is inevitable that some of the Internet addresses listed in this textbook will change.

Overview of the Assessment Process

CHAPTER

1

The Process of Assessment

The Role of the Teacher

KEY TERMS AND CONCEPTS

- special education services
- related services
- compliance
- Individuals with Disabilities Education Act (IDEA)
- screening process
- early intervening services
- overidentification
- intervention plan
- Section 504 of the Rehabilitation Act of 1973
- auxiliary aids
- multidisciplinary team
- IEP team
- surrogate parent
- state education agency (SEA)
- local education agency (LEA)
- parental rights booklet
- informed consent
- consent form
- evaluation plan
- comprehensive educational evaluation
- nondiscriminatory evaluation
- classification eligibility
- independent educational evaluation (IEE)
- developmental delay
- individual education plan (IEP)
- least restrictive environment (LRE)
- supplemental instruction
- replacement instruction
- assistive technology device
- assistive technology service
- annual review
- declassification
- mediation
- impartial due process hearing

CHAPTER OBJECTIVES

After reading this chapter, you should be able to:

- Identify the five primary reasons for assessment
- Describe the purpose of early intervening services
- Explain Section 504 of the Rehabilitation Act of 1973 and how this Section provides services for students
- Describe the referral process
- Describe the components of a comprehensive educational evaluation
- Explain parental rights in the assessment process
- Identify classification categories
- Describe the components of an individualized education plan (IEP)
- Identify various related services
- Compare and contrast mediation and due process

3

Introduction to the Process of Assessment

All teachers—both general and special education—will have children in their classes who are experiencing learning problems, behaviorial problems, or both. As professional educators, we have sound knowledge of content and pedagogy but, of course, no one has all the answers. There will be students who, despite our best efforts, require more or different interventions than we can provide. In order to provide the best education program to our students, we need to know how to intervene with the appropriate intervention and support services. Many schools have intervention teams or other general education resources to ameliorate students' problems. Sometimes, however, even with the best interventions, students need the next step: referral to the individualized education plan (IEP) multidisciplinary team. The referral may be needed to determine whether **special education services** (provided to students to facilitate their achievement in school), **related services** (support or therapeutic services that are not part of the education program), or both are needed.

The special education decision-making and programming system is a complex and often confusing process for both parents and school personnel. Both general and special education teachers need to understand the process. They also need to be familiar with legislative mandates regarding special education services and requirements for **compliance**; that is, how to operate within the federal regulations—specifically, Public Law 94–142, the Education for All Handicapped Children Act; and Public Law 101–476, the **Individuals with Disabilities Education Act (IDEA)**, and its amendments. Finally, they must be ready to be a knowledgeable and contributing member of the decision-making team. This chapter provides a detailed overview of our system of identifying, planning for, and implementing appropriate educational services for students who have special educational needs; specifically: how students qualify for a specific classification; who does the testing; what tests are used; how tests are administered; how test results are interpreted; and how the results factor into eligibility, placement, and programming decisions.

THE DECISION TO ASSESS

The primary purpose of assessments is to obtain information to facilitate effective decision making. In the educational system, assessments help teachers, administrators, psychologists, and parents make at least five kinds of decisions: (1) screening, (2) identifying strengths and weaknesses, (3) determining eligibility and making diagnoses, (4) doing instructional and program planning, and (5) determining program planning effectiveness (Salvia & Ysseldyke, 2004). Each type of decision requires collecting various data on students' backgrounds, interests, and abilities, as well as on the environmental conditions and expectations of their families and the school. Academic achievement data—such as scores on standardized achievement tests, results from informal evaluation procedures, grades, class observations, work-sample analyses, and behavior rating data—can be helpful in making any of the five kinds of decisions.

There are systematic procedures to facilitate the process—from the initial identification of a student's problem, to the placement of the student, to the programming of the student's education for specialized instruction and services. The process is described in the next section and a graphic of the process model is provided in Figure 1–1.

Figure 1–1 Special Education Services Process Model

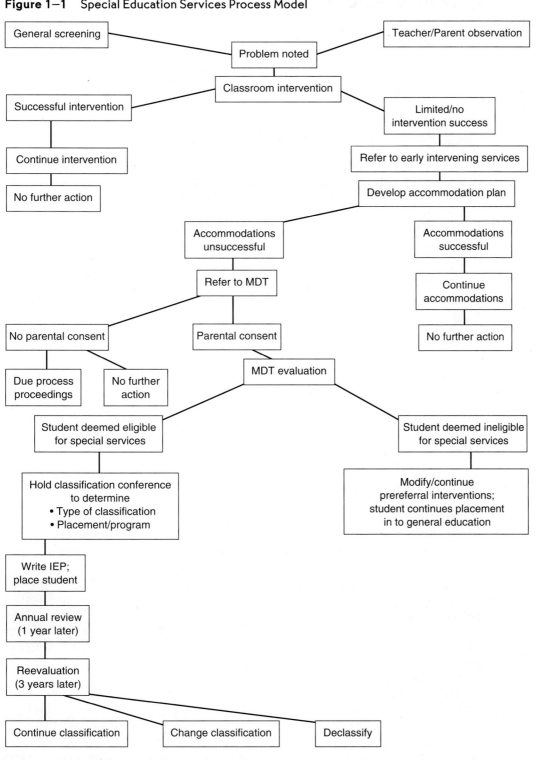

SECTION 1: THE PREREFERRAL PROCESS

Identifying the Problem

Concerns about a student's progress or adjustment may surface early in the school year, or they may emerge over a period of months. Frequently, teachers observe that particular students are not adjusting well to the class routine and procedures, are unable to complete assignments, do poorly on tests, or are not getting along with their teachers or peers. When academic or behavioral adjustment problems do not subside after a few weeks, teachers need to begin screening.

Classroom Scenario: What Do You Do?

September 25: In your third week of teaching your second-grade class, you notice that Cindy seems to be confused and falling behind with class work. She is a friendly and cooperative child, who appears to be trying to do her best, but her basic skills seem to be limited, she has difficulty following both oral and written directions, and she has not been handing in homework assignments. What do you do?

FYI: You closely observe Cindy's performance, keep a record of your concerns, try interventions, and document the results of those interventions. You also consult with Cindy's parents.

Screening is the first step in the overall assessment process. The purpose of the **screening process** is to collect data to determine whether more intensive or additional assessments should be conducted by educational, psychological, or medical specialists (Salvia & Ysseldyke, 2004).

Individual Screening Procedures

Teachers first focus on the individual student who is presenting concerns. They determine the student's areas of strengths and weaknesses by reviewing class work and homework; noting the student's work-study skills and classroom adjustment; and monitoring the student's work samples, attention, time on task, work pace, attention to detail, and work quality. The teacher must also determine whether the student's functioning is significantly different from that of his or her classmates. Ascertaining whether the student has a history of school problems; whether the intensity of those problems has increased and, if so, over what period of time; and whether the problems are more evident in particular circumstances or settings, at particular times, and/or with certain people is important.

Informal diagnostic assessment for individual students may include teacher-made tests, skill inventories, behavioral checklists, daily observations, and student interviews. These assessment measures are used to determine the identified student's ability to function in relation to age and grade norms and the degree to which the student is comprehending and retaining the skills and concepts presented in class. During this initial assessment it is also important to identify any personal and/or environmental factors that may be inhibiting the student's classroom adjustment and to determine which types of instructional materials and methods seem to be most effective. In addition to academic and behavioral screening procedures by teachers, speech, vision, and hearing specialists are routinely involved in screening. All of these screening procedures are informal and therefore do not fall under the strict regulations mandated by IDEA.

Group Screening Procedures

Students can be screened individually or all students in an entire class can be screened. When individual students are screened, parental consent is required; however, when screening is conducted on a large-group basis, parental consent is not required.

Screening generally entails some form of assessment, which often consists of group testing administered to entire populations of students to determine whether they have the basic abilities and skills needed to succeed in general education settings. School districts conduct accountability testing at least once each year to measure academic growth, which can also function as a general screening. (See Chapter 4 for more discussion of accountability testing.) When tests are used as a screening device, the results can be used to determine the current functioning level of the student and to compare the current year's test results with the previous year's results in order to establish whether progress has been made.

Schools generally administer standardized group tests (e.g., the California Achievement Test-5 (CAT-5); the Terra Nova, second edition; or a specific state department of education test) to their elementary and secondary-level students to assess their performance in reading, math, written and oral language, science, social studies, and study skills. Test profiles of these screening tools provide national and local (district) percentiles, grade equivalencies, and stanine scores. Most school districts have set cutoff scores that serve as criteria for qualification for remedial services, and they may use the results to determine whether further, more comprehensive educational evaluation in all areas of suspected disability is needed.

Preschool and Kindergarten Screening for Students "At-Risk"

Children under age 5 are often referred for evaluation by parental request, by pediatrician referral, or from communitywide preschool screening (such as Child Find) to identify those who are experiencing developmental delays and require intervention before they start elementary school. These evaluations generally include a physical examination; a developmental history attained through a parental or guardian interview; vision and hearing acuity testing; and a general overview of the child's cognitive, physical, communicative, social-emotional, speech and language, fine and gross motor, self-help, and adaptive development. Children found to be "at risk" for educational problems are referred for more comprehensive evaluation to determine whether they qualify for early intervention (birth to age 2) or preschool (ages 3 to 5) special education services, therapeutic intervention, or both. Their progress is closely monitored.

Early Intervening Services

Although not mandated in every state, most state departments of education require school districts to have a formal process to address and document interventions that are attempted before the student is referred for formal testing in order to determine eligibility for classification and special education services. Many school districts have implemented an early intervening service in which teachers, school staff, and parents work together to support the teacher and ultimately help the student. This **early intervening team** of educators (often referred to as the school resource team, the teacher support committee, or the student assistance team) work together as problem-solvers.

Classroom Scenario: What Do You Do?

November 8: Over the last six weeks, you have tried several interventions with Cindy. Although parental support, peer assistance, modified assignments, and supportive teaching strategies have resulted in keeping Cindy on task, you have noted that the gap between average performance and her functioning level has increased.

FYI: Discuss your concerns and share your documentation and the results of the attempted interventions with the early intervening service team. Inform Cindy's parents of your intention to present your concerns to this support service team.

These teams make a systematic collaborative effort to assist general education teachers who experience difficulty dealing effectively with the at-risk students in their classrooms. The purpose of the services these teams provide is twofold: (1) to reduce the need for special education services by providing assistance to students in general education classrooms; and (2) to decrease the number of unnecessary evaluations, misdiagnoses, and subsequent **overidentification** of students placed in special education who are not actually disabled (Coutinho, Oswald, & Best, 2002; Donovan & Cross, 2002; Turnbull, Turnbull, Smith, & Leal, 2002). In addition professionals who provide early intervening services:

- Document difficulties the student may be having with instruction and determine possible reasons for the problem.
- Provide and document classroom modifications, strategies, or both.
- Assess interventions to ensure that they are appropriate and successful.
- Monitor the student's progress for a significant period of time.
- Identify students for whom the learning difficulty, behavior difficulty, or both persists in spite of suggested interventions (National Alliance of Black School Educators, & ILIAD Partnership, 2002).

Early intervening teams usually consist of school administrators (typically principals or their designees), school nurses, guidance counselors, remedial specialists, and several classroom teachers who have experience at various grade levels. The team convenes periodically to discuss the students who are referred to it and the difficulties these students are experiencing in the general education classroom. During these meetings, the team defines the key issues involved and suggests remedial strategies and services that can be implemented in the general education classroom in an attempt to reduce or eliminate the targeted problems. Possible interventions include behavior management systems, curricular and testing modifications, and instructional strategy adaptations. (See Chapter 4 for details on accommodations and modifications.) Progress is closely monitored and reviewed at each early intervening team meeting.

Early intervening teams have proven to be productive in several ways. At team meetings, the teacher has the opportunity to share with colleagues any concerns and

Tips for Teachers

Preparing for an early intervening service meeting involves asking yourself the following questions:

Have I . . .

_____ informed parents of the scheduled meeting and arranged a follow-up meeting to communicate results to them?

_____ determined language dominance and communication proficiency of the child and the child's family members?

_____ made arrangements for an interpreter or a translator if needed and modified written messages to facilitate communication?

_____ checked into the child's general health and for any family problems?

_____ had the child's visual and auditory acuity screened?

_____ checked the child's school records for history of attendance, grades, and discipline problems?

_____ kept a record of academic, behavioral, and social concerns?

_____ noted examples, dates, and times of incidents and outcomes?

_____ noted antecedents (conditions or environment) prior to any incidents?

_____ documented alternative strategies, curricula, and environmental accommodations that have been made?

frustrations regarding students' academic, behavioral, and social-emotional difficulties. In this safe, nonthreatening environment, the problems may become clearer and can be prioritized through the sharing process, as well as by the discussions that take place among team members. During the team meeting, the teacher explains the student's strengths and problem areas; identifies which instructional, curricular, and environmental modifications have been attempted; and reports on how successful or unsuccessful these modifications have been. The team brainstorms not only on the possible etiology of the problem but more importantly on possible solutions to it. Team members may have also experienced similar situations, or they may know about—or have successfully used—innovative remedial strategies that the teacher can try with the student. These suggestions are written into a plan of action, which is generally referred to as an **intervention plan** (or an accommodation plan). This plan should consist of recommended research-based interventions, strategies, and modifications that can be referred to for monitoring purposes. (See Figure 1–2 for a sample intervention plan.) Generally, one team member is assigned to support the teacher as interventions are implemented with the student in the classroom.

At times, early intervening service strategies result in successful management of the student, thus eliminating the need to initiate the referral process and, ultimately, special education placement (McLoughlin & Lewis, 2005). However, even when the most efficient and effective strategies and accommodations are used, these interventions may not be sufficient to effectively alleviate the problem. When this occurs, the referral process is initiated. The referral process involves comprehensive testing and may ultimately result in the student receiving special services according to IDEA criteria or Public Law 93–112, **Section 504 of the Rehabilitation Act**.

Figure 1–2   Student Intervention Plan

Student Intervention Plan

NAME: Jane Doe   **GRADE:** 7th
DATE OF BIRTH: 6/11/89   **DATE OF CONFERENCE:** 10/14/2005

1. Describe the present concerns:

Difficulty staying on task
Inattentiveness
Failure to complete assignments
Inability to follow oral or written directions
consistently

2. Describe the type of disorder (if known):   Attention deficit disorder (ADD)

3. List reasonable accommodations:

Move seat near teacher's desk
Provide a work space carrel
Modify assignments
Assign a student study buddy
Have homework assignment book signed

4. Designate classes where
   accommodation will be provided: All

Case manager: Mr. Black   Review/Reassessment Date: 11/2/2006

Participants:

Mrs. Smith	teacher
Ms. Clark	school nurse
Mr. Black	guidance counselor
Mr. Johnson	reading teacher
Dr. Adams	principal
Mr. and Mrs. Doe	parents

cc: Student's Cumulative File Attachment: Information Regarding Section 504 of the Vocational
Rehabilitation Act of 1973
Attachment: Information Regarding Section 504 of the Vocational Rehabilitation Act of 1973

Section 504 of the Rehabilitation Act

The purpose of Section 504 of the Rehabilitation Act of 1973 is defined in the act, which states that "no otherwise qualified handicapped individual . . . shall, solely by reason of his/her handicap, be excluded from participation in, be denied the benefits of, or be subject to discrimination under any program or activity receiving federal financial assistance." Under this section, even if the child does not qualify for special education or related services but is found to have "a physical or mental impairment which substantially limits a major life activity" (e.g., learning), the school must make an "individualized determination of the child's education needs for regular or special education or related aids and services." Section 504 also mandates that reasonable accommodations be provided within the general education classroom. Students who are disabled are classified according to IDEA criteria and are eligible to receive special services. However, many students do not fit one of the 13 IDEA classification categories (which are defined later in this chapter). Although not classifiable, these students may be entitled to special accommodations and modifications (Henderson, 2001). (See Figure 1–3 for a list of differences between IDEA and Section 504.)

Figure 1–3 Differences Between IDEA and Section 504

	IDEA	Section 504
Type/Purpose	Federal funding statute requiring public schools to provide free and appropriate education in the least restrictive environment appropriate to students' individual needs	Broad civil rights law protecting the rights of individuals with disabilities in programs and activities receiving federal financial assistance from the U.S. Department of Education
Eligibility	Children and youths 3 to 21 years Student is eligible in one or more of 13 classification categories; 3- to 9-year-olds with developmental delays; infants/toddlers (birth to 2 years) may be eligible for early intervention services with an individual family service plan	Any person qualified for military service, employment, or school services Student who (1) has a physical or mental impairment substantially limiting one or more major life activities, (2) has a record of such an impairment, or (3) is regarded as having such an impairment
Local Enforcer	District director of special education	Section 504 coordinator
Federal Enforcer	Office of Special Education Programs U.S. Department of Education Washington, DC 20202	Disability Rights Section-Civil Rights Office U.S. Department of Justice Washington, DC 20035-6738

Classroom Scenario: What Would You Do?

Cassandra and Katrina are children in your class. Cassandra has recently been in an accident and is now legally blind. Katrina has just been diagnosed as having attention deficit disorder (ADD). Both children's parents ask what educational services their daughters are eligible for. What do you say?

FYI: Cassandra should qualify for special education services, since she should be eligible for classification under IDEA. She should also be covered under Section 504 and under the Americans with Disabilities Act (ADA), since blindness is considered a physical impairment that substantially limits the major life function of seeing.

You should explain to Katrina's family that she will not be covered under IDEA (unless she meets criteria for a classification category, such as other health impairment or specific learning disability). However, Katrina is likely to be covered under Section 504 and ADA because ADD is an impairment that may substantially limit the major life activity of learning.

Often these students are diagnosed as having "disorders" or chronic medical conditions by professionals (e.g., physicians, private psychologists, neurologists, or psychiatrists) who use diagnostic systems, such as the *Diagnostic and Statistical Manual* fourth edition (*DSM–IV*) of the American Psychiatric Association. Common diagnoses that can affect the learning process but are generally not classifiable categories under IDEA criteria include attention deficit-hyperactivity disorder (ADHD), depression, epilepsy, dyslexia, asthma/severe allergies, diabetes, Tourette's syndrome, AIDS/HIV, sleep disorders, alcohol and drug dependency problems (if not currently engaging in the illegal use of drugs), mental illness, arthritis, and obesity. Students whose main problem is poor impulse control, antisocial behavior, or poor judgment generally are not covered under the IDEA. However, those who require modifications in the standard program in order to function in school may qualify for services under Section 504 (Sullivan, Lantz, & Zirkel, 2000).

Section 504 is a civil rights law that protects against discrimination and grants equal access for all. It affects all students who have a physical or mental impairment that substantially limits one or more major life functions. Because learning is considered to be a major life activity, educators are mandated to provide reasonable accommodations for students who are eligible for services under Section 504 (Office of Civil Rights, Senior Staff Memorandum, 1992). All students protected under IDEA are also protected under Section 504; however, all students who are eligible under Section 504 do not necessarily meet IDEA criteria to be classified. Under Section 504 mandates, accommodations are provided primarily in the general education classroom (Murdick, Gartin, & Crabtree, 2002). Although there is no official list of reasonable accommodations, the following academic adjustments are noted specifically in the law: (a) modifications to the method of instruction, (b) extended exam time, (c) alternative testing formats, and (d) increased time to complete a course. Also, **auxiliary aids**—such as calculators, tape recorders, word processors, and spell/grammar checks—may be considered reasonable accommodations (OCR Senior Staff Memorandum, 1992). This law also covers structural and environmental modifications, such as installing building ramps and widening access doors for students who use wheelchairs and furnishing air-conditioned classrooms for students with serious allergies. Section 504 protections extend to extracurricular and nonacademic activities (e.g., recess; team, club, and sports activities; field trips; and graduation ceremonies).

Section 504 has been used increasingly in schools as parents and teachers have become aware of the opportunities for accommodations it offers to students who have difficulty learning. School districts are implementing procedures to screen students who are brought to their attention, and frequently, the prereferral intervention team review is the screening option. Students who are eligible for accommodations under Section 504 are assessed in the school to determine what modifications or accommodations they need, and a detailed intervention program and schedule are developed and implemented. (Refer back to Figure 1–2.) Under Section 504, when parents disagree with the services recommended, or if the school does not provide an evaluation or services in a timely or an appropriate manner, the parents can file a complaint with the Office of Civil Rights (OCR) at the U.S. Department of Justice. If the school is found to be at fault, the school district is liable for civil damages and risks losing federal funding.

Section 504 also guarantees the right to accommodations for students with disabilities beyond their high school graduation, extending to students attending postsecondary educational programs (e.g., college and vocational training programs). Section 504 provisions apply if a student with a disability is excluded from public education, or from participating in, or denied the benefits of, or is subjected to discrimination under any program or activity on the basis of disability. Students with disabilities must have an equal opportunity to participate in, for example, health services, extracurricular activities, school clubs, and special interest groups, and recreational programs.

Critical Thinking and Reflection Activity

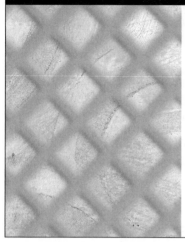

Bernardo, a middle school student who has a physical disability, wants to participate in an extracurricular activity. He has been placed in a school across town, since there is no special education class in his neighborhood school. He has to ride a bus to and from school, and because his afternoon bus ride is 30 minutes, he is not dropped off at his home until 3:30 P.M. All extracurricular activities at Bernardo's neighborhood school begin at 3:15 P.M. The school has refused to change the bus schedule. Bernardo is being excluded from a program because of his disability. Do you think this is a violation of IDEA or of Section 504?

SECTION 2: THE REFERRAL AND CLASSIFICATION PROCESS

Initiating the Referral Process

When teacher interventions and accommodations have been attempted and documented yet students continue to experience academic, behavioral, and/or social-emotional difficulties that are seriously affecting their school progress, a formal referral for evaluation to determine eligibility for classification and special services is made. The referral process is the initial phase in the evaluation procedure that ultimately determines (a) the existence of a disability, (b) the type and degree of disability in order to determine eligibility for special education and/or related services, and (c) the specific educational needs of the student with the disability. The referral process is generally initiated by the classroom teacher, the student's parents or guardians, or both, who define their concerns regarding the student's school difficulties.

Referral requests are directed to the school district's **multidisciplinary team**, who are members of the individualized education plan **(IEP) team**. This team of professionals from varying disciplines is referred to by various terms, including the child study team and the eligibility review team. Although referral requests generally lead to evaluation, the team may, after reviewing the referral documentation, decide not to conduct an evaluation if there is no reasonable basis to suspect that a disability exists. In such cases, the team may determine that the referral problem is not significant enough to warrant consideration for classification or that attempts at making modifications in the classroom were insufficient. When the team declines to evaluate a student who was referred by parental request, the parents must be given written

CLARIFYING TERMS

IDEA's definition of *parent* is broad. It focuses primarily on the child's legal guardian, and includes the child's natural or adoptive parent, or **surrogate parent**.

A surrogate parent is a person who is acting in the place of a parent (e.g., a grandparent or stepparent with whom the child lives, or a person who is legally responsible, often court appointed, for the child's welfare) (Section 300.20).

notification that the referral was denied, including the reason for the denial, and be notified of their legal rights under IDEA. (See the section on due process rights later in this chapter.)

Parental Safeguards and Protections

According to IDEA-2004, a copy of the procedural safeguards must be given to parents only 1 time a year, except that a copy also shall be given to the parents:

i. when the child is initially referred or if parents request an evaluation;
ii. the first time a complaint is filed; and
iii. when requested by the parent.

State education agencies (SEA) generally require the **local education agency (LEA)** to provide parents with a written copy of the procedural safeguards, known as the **parental rights booklet**. This booklet should be written in the family's primary language with necessary modifications (i.e., such as large-print or Braille versions) made to ensure that the information can be read and understood. A LEA may place a current copy of the procedural safeguard notice on its internet website (SECTION 615 (D) (1A)).

Parents' Right to Know

- School districts must notify parents of meetings related to their child's assessment for and placement in special education, and of their right to participate in these meetings (34 C.F.R. §300.501)
- Schools must notify parents in writing of any intent to initiate or change the identification, assessment, or placement of their child. The law specifies the types of information to be included in the notice. School districts must make sure that parents understand the content and language of the notice (34 C.F.R. §300.503(c)).
- Parents must provide **informed consent** for the referral, evaluation, and placement of their child in special education (34 C.F.R. §300.505). This means that the responsible adults in the student's life must have knowledge of the eligibility, classification, and placement process, be made aware of their due process rights, and sign a **consent form** indicating their permission for the referral process to be initiated. In the case of reevaluations, consent is required unless the school district can demonstrate that it has taken reasonable measures to obtain consent and the parent has failed to respond.
- Parents have the right to review all records related to evaluation, eligibility, and placement (34 C.F.R. §300.501).
- The assessment process should include evaluations and information provided by the parents (34 C.F.R. §300.532(b)) and must be reviewed by the school district personnel (34 C.F.R. §300.533(a)(2)).
- If parents disagree with the evaluation conducted by the district, they have the right to request an independent evaluation at no cost to them (34 C.F.R. §300.502(b)(1)).
- Decisions about eligibility and placement must be made with parental input. This means that parents must participate in any group that makes decisions about educational placements, and that school districts are responsible for

ensuring that parents understand and are able to participate in such meetings. For parents whose native language is not English, interpreters must be provided (34 C.F.R. §§300.501, 300.535).

- A copy of the evaluation report and documentation determining disability must be provided to the parents (34 C.F.R. §300.534(a)). Parents must be informed about the educational progress of their child, by such means as periodic report cards, at least as often as parents of nondisabled children.

Gathering Information for the Referral

Before referring a student who is experiencing academic, behavioral, or social-emotional problems to the school's professional evaluation staff for more comprehensive evaluation, teachers are expected to implement and document prereferral interventions; specifically, strategies and accommodations that attempt to ameliorate the problem. Documenting prereferral interventions provides (a) useful information for determining the etiology of the student's problem and for helping to establish factors that contribute to or alleviate the problem; (b) documentation to be given to parents of the attempts made to deal with the problem in the classroom and to further clarify the reason for the teacher's concern, which is resulting in the referral; and (c) a record of which interventions have or have not been successful and to what degree.

It is helpful for the teacher to keep a record of the student's daily progress, which includes the following information:

- Specific concerns about the student (e.g., academic, behavioral, social-emotional adjustment, work-study)
- Documentation regarding when (date and time), where (e.g., in the classroom during reading period), and what caused the problem to occur (e.g., while working in small group, cooperative activities)
- Modifications made, strategies used, and interventions implemented to resolve the problem, noting both those that have and have not been successful, and the subsequent adjustments made to increase their effectiveness
- Individuals (e.g., professional school staff, teacher assistants, parents, and the student's peers) who assisted in devising, implementing, and/or monitoring the intervention plan

In most cases, referrals lead to a full IEP team evaluation. According to federal regulations, informed consent must be obtained before the testing process can proceed and may be revoked at any time.

An important part of the informed consent is documentation of the reason for the referral (the identified problem) and the interventions used to ameliorate the problem before initiating the referral. (See Figure 1–4 for a sample referral form.) In cases where the parents refuse to allow their child to be evaluated and an agreement

Tips for Teachers

Be sure to contact parents as your concerns surface. Keep in contact with them regarding the interventions being used in order to gain their support and to inform them of your referral and the results of the early intervening services team meetings.

Figure 1–4   Sample IEP Multidisciplinary Team Referral Form

REFERRAL FORM

STUDENT INFORMATION

NAME: John Brown   DATE OF EVALUATION: 5/27/2005
DATE OF BIRTH: 12/26/94   AGE: 10–5 years
TEACHER: Mrs. Smith   GRADE: 5th

SCHOOL RECORD

Current Average Grades:
     Reading: 82   Math: 66   English: 74   Science: 62   Social Studies: 61

Standardized Test Scores:
     CAT/5 (4/2004):   Reading: 20%ile   Language: 28%ile   Math: 64%ile

CURRENT STATUS

John transferred to this district at the beginning of the 2003–2004 school year. Records indicate that he had been retained in grade 2 and has a history of below-average grades. John has been functioning below average in all subjects, he has not been completing assignments, and he has been easily frustrated. He was brought to the attention of the early intervening services team during the second marking period of this school year. Interventions were attempted but were not sufficient to ameliorate his problems.

NURSE'S REPORT

John does not wear his prescriptive glasses to class. His asthma condition is controlled by medication.

PRINCIPAL'S REPORT

John is in jeopardy of failing all five academic subjects at the third-quarter point of the final marking period. He has not been completing school or homework assignments. He seems to lack motivation, is easily frustrated, and has refused to participate in many class activities. Mr. and Mrs. Brown have been very concerned about their son's poor progress and have requested that John be evaluated by the IEP multidisciplinary team.

INTERVENTIONS ATTEMPTED

Worked with a peer
Homework assignment pad signed between parents and teacher
Provided extended time for tests
Provided extra support from the classroom aide
Modified assignments

                                                     _____
                                                     Principal's Signature

Has the parent been advised of the referral to the IEP multidisciplinary team, and been given a copy of the procedural safeguards. _____ Yes _____ No

I, the parent(s) of John Brown give permission for my son to be evaluated by the IEP multidisciplinary team.

                                                     _____
                                                     Parent's Signature

cannot be reached, the school district is required to initiate an impartial hearing at which a hearing officer can determine whether to waive parental consent and proceed with the evaluation (Murdick, Gartin, & Crabtree, 2002). Conversely, in cases where the parents request an evaluation and the school refuses, the parents may initiate mediation and due process procedures.

The Evaluation Process

Once the parents have signed and returned the referral form, the evaluation, eligibility, and placement decision-making process must be completed, and the initiation of special services must begin within a designated period of time. In general, an IEA has 60 days from receipt of parental consent for initial evaluation to determine eligibility (Council for Exceptional Children, 2005). The process begins with a meeting to map out a plan and to provide all parties with opportunities to express their concerns so that the testing is specific to the child's identified needs.

The Evaluation Plan

Since the implementation of IDEA-97, the IEP evaluation team is no longer the sole determinant of which areas are to be tested and which tests are to be used in the evaluation process. It is now required that parents be included in the development of the **evaluation plan**. This plan specifies the methods of evaluation—specifically, which tests, interviews, inventories, observations, and reviews will be done, and by which member of the IEP evaluation team—and what type of other evaluating specialists, if any, will be called on to complete the assessment process. (See Figure 1–5 for a sample evaluation plan.) When developing the evaluation plan, the following IDEA assessment guidelines must be followed:

a. The process must be comprehensive and multidisciplinary.
b. The team must include at least one teacher or specialist who is knowledgeable about the area of the child's suspected disability.
c. Assessments must be conducted by individuals trained to administer and interpret the tests and other assessment tools used.
d. The assessment must thoroughly investigate all areas related to the suspected disability.
e. The process must utilize a variety of valid assessment tools and observational data; no single procedure may be used as the sole criterion for determining the child's eligibility for special education or services.
f. All testing must be administered on an individual basis.
g. All assessments must be conducted in a nondiscriminatory way, and test content must not be racially or culturally discriminatory and must be free of bias.
h. All assessments must be administered in the child's primary language or mode of communication (e.g., using an interpreter) unless it is clearly not feasible to do so.
i. All tests must be validated for the specific use for which they are used.
j. The team must ensure that all measures are being used for the purpose designed and that the child's disability does not interfere with the his or her ability to take any test measuring specific abilities (e.g., an auditory

Figure 1–5   Sample Evaluation Plan

EVALUATION PLAN

The multidisciplinary team has met and developed the following evaluation plan for your child. If you have any questions about the evaluation plan, please contact the case manager designated below.

STUDENT'S NAME: Mary White
DATE OF BIRTH: 10/22/93
CHRONOLOGICAL AGE: 11–9 years
PARENT (S) NAME (S): Mr. & Mrs. Harry White

REFERRAL INFORMATION

Date of Referral: 11/5/2005   Person Making Referral: Parents and teacher

Summary of referral information: Mary is working below average in all academic areas.

STUDENT'S NATIVE LANGUAGE AND COMMUNICATION SKILLS

__x__ English   _____ Spanish   _____ Sign Language   _____ Other (Specify)

COMMENT ON STUDENT'S COMMUNICATION SKILLS: Satisfactory

INFORMATION/EVALUATIONS TO BE OBTAINED AND PROCEDURES TO BE USED

__x__ Health Appraisal	__x__ Individually Administered Tests
__x__ Psychological Assessment	__x__ Classroom Observation
__x__ Educational Assessment	__x__ Teacher Interview
__x__ Social History Assessment	__x__ Student Interview
_____ Speech & Language Assessment	__x__ Behavioral Checklist
_____ Psychiatric Evaluation	__x__ Informal Checklist
_____ Neurological Evaluation	__x__ Informal Assessment of Work Samples
_____ Audiological Evaluation	__x__ Examination by Physician
_____ Ophthalmological/Optometric Evaluation	_____ Evaluation by Specialists
_____ Other (Specify)	_____ Other (Specify)

   If other assessments are needed after a review of these data has been completed, the case manager will notify the parents to explain and gain consent for additional evaluations.

CASE MANAGER: Dee Glass, Counselor   _____
TELEPHONE: 222-3344   (CASE MANAGER'S SIGNATURE)
DATE: 11/15/2005

cc: Mr. and Mrs. Harry White
     Administration
     Student's file

      impairment affects the child's ability to follow oral directions or respond adequately to orally presented questions).

  k. The rights of the child and his or her parents must be protected during the assessment.

IDEA Requirements for Eligibility Evaluation

The common elements of a **comprehensive educational evaluation**—a complete assessment procedure that includes all areas of suspected disability—generally include the following:

  a. A psychological evaluation, which includes a standardized aptitude test that measures cognitive functioning, a clinical interview, observations, and as-needed social-emotional and adaptive behavior rating scales;

  b. A social history, which includes developmental, medical, and educational histories, and parent, teacher, and student interviews;

  c. An educational evaluation, which includes achievement testing, learning style inventory, and a classroom observation; and

  d. A medical evaluation/health appraisal, which includes a physical examination and visual and auditory acuity testing.

The exact assessment procedures and measures used depend on the individual concerns that initiated the referral process. When the student's profile suggests possible traumatic brain injury or central nervous system impairment, a neurological assessment may be conducted. In situations where emotional, social, or behavioral problems are evident, a psychiatric evaluation may be suggested. If communication problems are detected, a speech and language evaluation is necessary. When there is evidence of fine or gross motor developmental delays, an occupational or physical therapy evaluation may be needed. Pupils who have difficulty understanding orally presented information often require a central auditory processing evaluation. An assistive technology evaluation must be conducted if there is evidence that the student may require technological supports.

IEP Multidisciplinary Team Membership

IDEA mandates that a comprehensive and **nondiscriminatory evaluation** (i.e., a fair and objective evaluation) be completed with all areas of suspected disability assessed. (See Figure 1–6.) In addition to evaluating the student, members of the IEP multidisciplinary team decide whether the student is eligible for classification, determine which classification category is appropriate, develop the educational plan, and agree on appropriate placement and needed related services. (See Figure 1–7 for a list of the members required under IDEA–97 to be part of this decision-making team.)

    Each member of the IEP multidisciplinary team has a specific role and function. (See Figure 1–8 for a description of the responsibilities of individuals who may, depending on the student's individual needs, administer tests, provide assessment information, or be consulted to evaluate the student on an as-needed-basis.)

Classification Eligibility

The multidisciplinary team, which includes the referring teacher, and the parent(s) discuss the evaluation results and determine the student's **classification eligibility**. This decision is based on the information obtained during the evaluation process

Figure 1–6   Key IDEA Components of Nondiscriminatory Assessments

Teachers should consider the following questions when evaluating a student for suspected disability:

_____ Have various assessment measures been used as criteria for determining eligibility?

_____ Have technically sound instruments been used that assess cognitive, behavioral, physical, or developmental factors?

_____ Are the tests used in a nondiscriminating manner on both a racial and cultural basis?

_____ Are the test measures administered in the child's native language or other mode of communication, such as using sign language, an interpreter/translator, larger print, or Braille?

_____ Have the tests been administered by trained and knowledgeable personnel who follow exact instructions for administration and scoring?

_____ Have all standardized tests been validated for their intended purpose?

_____ Are the assessment procedures and tools appropriate for determining the student's specific educational needs; and does the disability of the child interfere with obtaining valid assessment results in any area?

_____ Does the evaluator have experience testing students with problems similar to those of the student being evaluated?

_____ Is the group on which the test was normed similar to the child being tested?

_____ Is the evaluator who will be conducting the tests familiar with the child's culture?

_____ Have the parents been involved by contributing background information, their perceptions, etc.?

_____ Have sufficient efforts been made to ensure that the student feels comfortable and performs optimally during the testing session? (Alliance, 2001).

Figure 1–7   Required Membership of the IEP Team

The IEP multidisciplinary team must consist of the following members:

(1) One or both parent(s) or guardian, if the child is a minor

(2) General education teacher, if the child is or may participate in the general education environment

(3) Special education teacher, if the student is or may be classified and receive special education services

(4) Representative from the school district who is qualified to provide or supervise specially designed instruction to meet the child's unique needs and is knowledgeable about the general curriculum and availability of resources

(5) Individual(s) who have evaluated the child and can interpret evaluation results (e.g., school psychologist, educational diagnostician, social worker, speech and language pathologist)

(6) Other participants at the discretion of the parents and school personnel, that is, individuals who have knowledge or special expertise regarding the child, including a child advocate, counselor, remedial or transition specialist, and/or related services personnel

(7) Student, as appropriate (if transition services are discussed, student must be present) (20 U.S.C. §1414(d)(1)(B)).

(e.g., test score data, information provided by teachers and parents, and observations). If it is determined that the student is not eligible for classification, then he or she remains in the general education classroom. The teacher can confer with the early intervening service team to get further information and suggestions on how to modify the student's programs to address the problem areas.

Figure 1–8 IEP Team Membership Roles

IEP Team Member	Membership Role
Parent(s)	(a) Requests and/or consents to an IEP multidisciplinary team evaluation; (b) provides input in the evaluation process; (c) supplies input from independent professional sources (e.g., private medical, psychological, or therapeutic evaluations or consultation reports); (d) contributes to the eligibility and placement decision-making process; (e) participates in writing program goals, and objectives; (f) takes an active part in the instructional program; (g) monitors progress; (h) seeks the services of an advocate when unsure of special education policy and procedures, is uncomfortable interacting with school personnel, or is concerned that the school district is not acting in their child's best interest; (i) proceeds with due process
Special education teacher	Administers educational assessment; recommends IEP goals and objectives; suggests educational programming, placement, support services, and educational interventions; monitors academic progress; and reviews and revises IEP
General education	Participates in developing, reviewing, and revising the IEP; and determines appropriate positive behavioral interventions/strategies, supplementary aides services, program modifications, and support school personnel
School psychologist	Administers individualized aptitude tests to obtain a full-scale intelligence quotient (IQ) score comprised of verbal and nonverbal abilities; and assesses social-emotional adjustment, adaptive, and self-help skills
Social worker	Acts as a liaison between home, school, and community. Social worker interviews consist of a developmental history, including any pre- or postnatal complications, developmental milestones, preschool and early school adjustment, significant medical or physical issues (e.g., surgeries, injuries, illnesses), critical family stressors (e.g., parental divorce/separation, job loss, changes in lifestyle), home environmental issues, extracurricular activities, peer influences, home responsibilities, adaptive behavior, etc.
Educational diagnostician	Evaluates students' academic functioning levels; administers (in many districts) the standardized educational assessments for word recognition and reading comprehension, mathematical calculation and applied problems, written language (including spelling, grammar, and writing samples), oral expression, general knowledge of science, social studies, and humanities, work-study skills, and perceptual processing (See Figure 1–10 for a sample educational evaluation.)
School physician	Conducts a basic physical examination assessing physical development, sensory abilities, medical problems, and central nervous system functioning. When specific medical problems are detected, a referral is made to the appropriate specialist.
School nurse	Monitors students' general health status, screens their vision and auditory acuity, and takes their weight and height measurements. Nurses can provide pertinent data regarding students' general health, school attendance, allergies, medical complaints, major accidents, and history of medications.
Speech-language pathologist	Evaluates speech and language development; specifically, expressive (speaking) and receptive (understanding) use of words, concepts,

Figure 1–8   (Continued)

	sentences, and stories, oral-motor examination, checking for physiological abnormalities—including atypical use of the muscles of the mouth, tongue, and throat that permit speech—and for unusual speech habits, such as breathiness in speaking or noticeable voice strains. Referral is made to an audiologist if auditory acuity is a concern.
Guidance-transition counselor	Provides pertinent information regarding students' overall adjustment, assists with career counselor planning, and can administer and interpret vocational interest and aptitude tests
Neurologist	Not a standard member of the MDT but is called on to evaluate students suspected of having central nervous system dysfunction. The neurological evaluation consists of a medical and developmental history and physiological testing that includes (a) cerebral functions (level of consciousness, intelligence, language usage, orientation, and emotional status); (b) cranial nerves (general speech, hearing and vision, facial muscle movement, and pupilar reflexes); (c) cerebellar functions (rapid alternating movements, heel-to-toe, finger-to-nose-to-finger, and standing with eyes opened and then closed); (d) motor functioning (muscle size and tone, reflexes and coordination); and (e) sensory nerves (superficial pain senses and tactile sense).
Psychiatrist	Not a standard member of the MDT, but may evaluate students who are experiencing mental, emotional, or social adjustment problems mainly through clinical interview with students and their parents. The psychiatrist relies on the American Psychological Association's *Diagnostic Statistical Manual*, 5th ed. (*DSM-IV*), which provides explicit criteria for diagnosis.
Occupational therapist	Evaluates students with fine motor problems, including upper extremities; fine motor abilities (cutting, pasting); self-help skills (e.g., buttoning, lacing, feeding), and handwriting
Physical therapist	Evaluates students experiencing gross motor problems, assessing lower extremities and large muscles, gait, strength, agility, and range of motion; also evaluates gross motor functioning as it relates to self-help skills, living skills, and job-related skills

In cases where students are determined to be eligible for classification, a classification conference report is written. (See Figure 1–9 for a sample classification conference report.) This report documents the eligibility decision and serves as the signed parental permission verifying consent. Copies are distributed to the parents and placed in the student's confidential file.

Eligibility Decision Conflicts

If the parents disagree with the results of an evaluation, they have the right to obtain an **independent educational evaluation** (IEE) at public expense. The IEE is conducted by a qualified evaluator not employed by the school, and the district must provide the parents with a list of evaluators. The IEE must be completed without unreasonable delay, and the district must consider the results when determining the

Figure 1–9 Sample Classification Conference Report

CONFIDENTIAL
The information in this report
is for professional use only and
not to be divulged to any
person or agency without
prior authority.

CLASSIFICATION CONFERENCE REPORT

NAME: Mary Brown   DATE OF BIRTH: 1/27/97
SCHOOL: Washington School   GRADE: 3rd
CLASSIFICATION: Specific Learning Disability   RECOMMENDED PLACEMENT: Resource
                                                                              Center w/ mainstreaming

Dates

Referral: 3/30/2005   IEP Conference: 5/12/2005
Classification: 5/12/2005   Annual Review: On or before 5/11/2006
Program Implementation: 5/30/2005

Classification Team Identification

Multidisciplinary Team	Evaluator	Evaluation Date
Psychologist	Barbara McDonald	4/30/2005
Social Worker	Joan Gallagher	4/20/2005
Educational Diagnostician	Helen McGann	4/24/2005
Speech/Language Therapist	Stuart Smith	4/29/2005

The members of the multidisciplinary team, the teacher, and the parent(s) met jointly and
determined the pupil to be eligible for special education programming and/or related services.

	Signature	Date
Psychologist	_____	
Social Worker	_____	
Educational Diagnostician	_____	
Teacher	_____	
Parent(s)	_____	
	_____	
Other (Speech/Language Therapist)	_____	

student's eligibility or IEP development; otherwise, the district must show (at an impartial due process hearing) that its evaluation is appropriate (The Alliance, 2001). (See Figure 1–10 for a sample educational evaluation.)

Classification Criteria

Teachers play a key role in deciding whether students are eligible to receive special services. They must be knowledgeable about the classification process, including the standards used to report standardized test scores and the interpretation of assessment

Figure 1–10   Sample Educational Evaluation

EDUCATIONAL EVALUATION

NAME: Ivan West   **SCHOOL**: Main Street Middle
DATE OF BIRTH: 7/27/92   **DATE OF EVALUATION**: 12/12/05
AGE: 14–5 years   **GRADE**: 7th

REASON FOR EVALUATION

Ivan was referred due to concern about his poor academic progress. His achievement is being assessed to determine whether he is eligible for special education and/or related services.

BACKGROUND INFORMATION

Ivan transferred to this district in October of this school year. He had been referred to the IEP multidisciplinary team while in his previous school district due to academic delays. He was evaluated but he was not classified at that time. This school year, Ivan has continued to experience academic difficulties. His first marking period grades were a C in English, Science, and Social Studies, and a D in Reading and Math. His English and Social Studies teachers had indicated that he displayed an active interest in class yet his general performance has been relatively poor. Ivan had been referred to early intervening services in October of 2004. It was suggested that a reading inventory be completed, which indicated below average performance, therefore, a IEP multidisciplinary team referral was recommended.

TESTING OBSERVATIONS

Ivan was a willing and cooperative participant throughout the testing session. He feels that he is beginning to adjust to school this year but admitted that he did better academically in his previous school, explaining that in his previous school, "I did good there . . . they gave notes and would explain." Ivan identified his best subject as Social Studies and his most difficult subject as Reading. He admits to having difficulties with Reading and Math, especially doing homework assignments in these subjects. He denies having any attention or behavioral problems. His extracurricular activity is playing basketball at school but he has no other involvements. His speech and language were adequate for testing and for conversational purposes and he worked at a moderate pace. Ivan does not wear prescriptive glasses and seems to have adequate auditory acuity. He is right handed and demonstrates adequate pencil grip.

CLASSROOM OBSERVATIONS

Ivan was observed during his Math class period. He sits in a desk in the middle of the room. The teacher was giving the students a quick review before a test to be administered during the period. Ivan cleared his desk as his teacher requested. Mrs. Jones discussed the key points the students were to know. Ivan laid his head down on his desk as he listened to the questions and answers that were discussed. When the test began, Ivan seemed to work steadily and was attentively throughout the period. Mrs. Jones reported that Ivan has inconsistent scores and his math skills are weak.

EVALUATION MEASURES

Woodcock-Johnson III – Tests of Achievement
Classroom Observation
Teacher Interview
Record Review

TEST RESULTS AND CONCLUSIONS

Broad reading skills are within the low-average range. His overall reading ability is comparable to the 16th percentile as he achieved a standard score of 85. His word identification skills are within the low-average range. Word attack skills are just within average limits as demonstrated by his ability to phonetically and structurally analyze words. Reading fluency is low-average demonstrated by his ability to quickly read simple sentences and determine whether the statement is true. Passage comprehension is a measure of his ability to understand what is being read during the process of reading. He functions within the low-average range when required to read a short passage and identify a missing key word that makes sense in the context of the passage.

Broad mathematical ability is within the low-average range as his overall math skills are developed to the 22nd percentile. He achieved a standard score of 88 when compared to his chronological age peers. His ability to solve written equations is just within the average range. Ivan is able to solve addition and subtraction equations requiring regrouping, and he can solve multiplication and division equations with up to two-digit multipliers and divisors. Ivan is able to add and subtract but not multiply or divide fractions with like-denominators or decimal numbers. He has not learned to convert improper fractions to mixed numbers. His mathematical fluency is within average norms. When presented with a series of word problems that are read orally by the evaluator, Ivan functions within the low-average range, as demonstrated by his ability to recognize the procedure to be followed, identify the relevant data, and then perform relatively simple calculation.

Broad written language skills are just within average limits as Ivan functions at the 25th percentile with a standard score of 90. His ability to take oral dictation is within the low-average range, as demonstrated by his written response to a variety of questions involving spelling, capitalization, punctuation, and word usage. Specific errors were noted in spelling ("anually" for annually and "fiffty one" for fifty-one), in punctuation (failure to separate city and state with a comma), and in capitalization (failure to capitalize city and state). His ability to write sentences in response to specific pictures is within the average range for content and fluency. These subtests evaluated written expressive skills and writing speed but do not penalize for errors in basic mechanics of writing, such as spelling or punctuation.

Broad knowledge of general knowledge is within the low-average limits. Ivan's basic fund of general information in science, social studies, and humanities is developed to the 10th percentile as he achieved a standard score of 81. His ability to respond to science questions related to the biological and physical sciences; his knowledge of history, government, economics, and other aspects of social studies; and his knowledge in various areas of art, music, and literature are below the average range.

SUMMARY

Ivan is a 14-year, 5-month-old, seventh-grade-level student. Test results indicate that his academic skills are mostly within the low-average range. He demonstrates relative strength in written expression and fluency. All recommendations regarding Ivan's placement and program will be made by the full multidisciplinary team after all interviews, assessments, and observations have been completed.

results. (See Chapter 2.) According to IDEA 2004, students may not be deemed eligible for special education services if they do not meet the eligibility criteria or if their eligibility is based on a lack of instruction in reading including the essential components of reading instruction and of instruction in math; or if they have limited English proficiency (SEC 614b (5A,B,C)). The teacher also needs to understand that the disability must adversely affect the child's educational performance and know the criteria for each classification category in order to contribute to the eligibility decision. The 13 classification categories are as follows:

Autism is a pervasive developmental disability that significantly affects verbal and nonverbal communication and social interaction and is generally manifested by age 3. Other characteristics often include engaging in repetitive activities or stereotyped movements, resisting changes in the environment or to routines, and having unusual responses to sensory experiences.

Deafness is a hearing impairment so severe that the child is unable to process linguistic information, with or without amplification.

Deaf-blindness is a simultaneous hearing and visual impairment that together causes such severe communication problems that children with this impairment cannot be accommodated in programs that are designed solely for children with deafness or blindness.

Hearing impairment is an impairment in hearing, whether permanent or fluctuating, that is not included under the definition of deafness.

Mental retardation is significantly below-average intellectual functioning, concurrent with deficits in adapted behavior manifested during the development period.

Multiple disabilities are the manifestation of two or more disabilities (e.g., mental retardation and deafness) that causes educational problems which cannot be accommodated in programs solely for one impairment (not including deaf-blindness).

Orthopedic impairment is a physical disability, including a congenital anomaly, impairments caused by disease, and impairments from other causes (e.g., an injury).

Other health impairment is an impairment resulting in limited strength, vitality, or alertness due to chronic or acute health problems (e.g., a heart condition, cancer, asthma).

Emotional disturbance is a disability characterized by emotional or behavior problems exhibited over a long period of time and to a marked degree. This classification may be characterized by unsatisfactory interpersonal relationships, inappropriate behavior or feelings, a general pervasive mood of unhappiness or depression, or a tendency to develop physical symptoms or fears associated with personal or school problems.

Specific learning disability is a disorder in one or more of the basic psychology processes involved in understanding or in using language, spoken or written, that may manifest itself in an imperfect ability to listen, think, speak, read, write, spell, or do mathematical calculations. According to IDEA-2004, when considering the classification of specific learning disability, the LEA is no longer required to take into consideration where a child has a severe discrepancy between achievement. The LEA may use a process that determines if the child responds to scientific, research-based intervention as a part of the evaluation procedures SEC 614b (6A-B).

Speech or language impairment is a communication disorder (e.g., stuttering, articulation, language, or voice impairment).

Traumatic brain injury is an acquired injury to the brain caused by an external physical force resulting in total or partial functional disability or psychosocial impairment, or both, but does not apply to brain injuries that are congenital, degenerative, or induced by birth trauma.

Visual impairment is a visual disorder that, even with correction, adversely affects the child's educational performance, including both partial sight and blindness.

The term, "child with a disability" may be used for children ranging in age from 3 through 9 (or any subset of that age range, including ages 3 through 5), at the discretion of the State and the LEA, include a child who is experiencing developmental delays in one or more of the following areas: physical development, cognitive development, communication development, social or emotional development, or adaptive development and therefore, needs special education and related services (SEC. 602 3B).

SECTION 3: IEP DEVELOPMENT AND EVALUATION PROCESS

Developing the Individualized Education Plan

Once eligibility is determined, the **individualized education plan** (IEP)—the prescriptive individualized education program—is developed by the IEP program team. This team is composed of the parents of a child with a disability; not less than 1 regular education teacher of the child who is or may be participating in the regular education environment; not less than 1 special education teacher, or where appropriate, not less than 1 special education provider of the child; a representative of the LEA who is qualified to provide, or supervise the specially designed instruction to meet the unique needs of the child, is knowledgeable about the general education curriculum and the availability of resources of the LEA; an individual who can interpret the instructional implications of evaluation results, who may be a member of the IEP team; and, when appropriate, the child (IDEA-2004 or P.L. 108–446; SEC 5). (614d Bi–vii).

In developing the IEP, the Team should consider the strengths of the child; the concerns of the parents for enhancing the education of their child; the results of the initial evaluation or most recent evaluation; and the academic, developmental, and functional needs of the child (IDEA-2004 or P.L. 108–446, SEC. 614d (3Ai–iv). Besides the basic IEP, there is an individualized special education plan that is developed for children from birth to 2 years is the Individualized Family Service Plan (IFSP) and an additional component of the IEP that addresses the educational transitional planning needs of students 16 years and older. Further detail about preschool and secondary level planning is provided in Chapter 13).

The IEP is based on the comprehensive assessment of the student's unique needs and must include relevant information about the student, such as the educational placement, expected outcomes, the curriculum, teacher and staff responsibilities, the specific program, service schedule, and methods and timelines of measuring success (Mercer & Mercer, 2005).

Information Required in the IEP

To ensure that critical issues are addressed in the development of the IEP, the teacher needs to understand how to include assessment results in each component. (See Figure 1–11 for a sample IEP.) IDEA requires that each IEP contain the following information.

1. Present level of academic achievement and functional performance
   —What the student can and cannot do compared to other children of a similar age. The present levels needs to include how the child's disability

Figure 1–11   Sample IEP

INDIVIDUAL EDUCATION PLAN

NAME: Ed U. Cate
SCHOOL: Main Street Elementary
PRIMARY LANGUAGE: English
PROGRAM TIMELINE: 9/5/2005–6/16/2006

DATE OF BIRTH: 4/10/96
GRADE: 4th
DATE OF MEETING: 6/15/2005
REVIEW DATE: 6/10/2006

PRESENT LEVEL OF ACADEMIC ACHIEVEMENT AND FUNCTIONAL PERFORMANCE

Ed is currently in the grade 4 resource center program. His overall academic progress has been good. *Reading:* Overall functioning at the beginning grade 3 level with weaknesses noted in comprehension (answering inferential questions and drawing conclusions), vocabulary, and decoding skills. *Math:* Overall functioning at the mid grade 4 level. He grasps concepts easily; mistakes are generally calculation errors and in multistep and word problems. *Language Arts:* Overall functioning at the mid grade 3 level. He does not apply skills learned into his daily writing; he has difficulty constructing sequentially organized paragraphs. *Cognitive Functioning:* Trouble retaining newly learned skills, especially in language arts; requires visual and auditory approach, difficulty formulating concepts; math is an area of strength; reading/language arts is poorly developed. *Personal/Social Development:* Quiet and cooperative child; willing to work with teacher; tardiness to school somewhat improved; frequently late with or missing assignments; needs to work on organization skills; monitoring of homework is needed. *Physical/Health Status:* Due to recurring kidney infections, may need to go to the bathroom frequently.

EDUCATIONAL PROGRAM/SCHEDULE OF SERVICES

Regular Education	Special Education	Related Arts Subjects
Science	Reading	Art
Social Studies	Language Arts	Music
	Math (In-class support)	Physical Education

RELATED SERVICES/SCHEDULE OF SERVICES/DURATION OF SERVICES

Times per Week	1x	2x	3x	4x	5x	Minutes per week	Duration From	To
Occupational therapy								
Physical therapy								
Speech therapy			Sm.			60	9/5/2005	6/15/2006
Counseling	Ind.					30	9/6/2005	6/16/2006
Adaptive P.E.								
Transportation (daily to and from school)							9/5/2005	6/15/2006
Other:								

Ind. – Denotes Individual Sessions   *Sm.* – Denotes Small Group   *Lg.* – Denotes Large Group

RATIONALE FOR PLACEMENT AND SERVICES

It is determined by the multidisciplinary team that Ed's educational needs can be best met in a resource room program due to his need for individualized instruction to ameliorate deficient skills; specifically, reading and written language skills. Placement in a general education class for mathematics (with in-class support), service and social studies and related arts subjects. The use of a computer, a tape recorder, and a notetaker, as well as test and assignment modifications, should help Ed function optimally in the general education classroom. Ed's self-concept and social skills should benefit from interaction with his general education peers. Speech and language therapy will help him improve his articulation skills and develop his expressive language skills. Counseling sessions will provide Ed with the social skill support necessary to improve his peer interactions.

ANNUAL GOAL — ACADEMIC

Ed will improve overall reading skills from a beginning grade 3 to the beginning grade 4 level.

PROGRESS POINTS	TYPE OF EVALUATION
After reading a passage at the appropriate level, the student:	
1. States six important facts.	Curriculum-based measurement
2. Arranges five events in correct sequence.	Work samples
3. Orally explains the main idea.	Oral responses
4. Orally explains at least one logical conclusion that can be drawn from the text.	**EVALUATOR:** Teacher

ANNUAL GOAL — FUNCTIONAL

Ed will improve overall work study functional skills from a mid-grade 3 to the mid-grade 4 level.

PROGRESS POINTS	TYPE OF EVALUATION
1. Using a homework sign-off notebook, Ed will complete all homework assignments 80% of the time.	Curriculum-based measurement Portfolio review
2. Working with a peer buddy, Ed will have his required assignments submitted on time 90% of the time.	**EVALUATOR:** Teacher

PROGRESS REPORTS: SENT TO PARENTS — Nov., Feb., April, June

ADAPTIVE DEVICES AND MODIFICATIONS

Ed will be provided with a computer and a tape recorder, and arrangements will be made for him to have a notetaker in his mainstreamed classes. He will be given test modifications, including extended time to take tests; he will be tested in a quiet room with minimal to no distractions; and he will have access to a computer and a word processing program for use in testing situations.

LANGUAGE OF INSTRUCTION: ENGLISH

IEP PARTICIPANTS

Committee Participants Signature(s)   Relationship/Role

Mrs. Andrea Cates	_____	Parent	_____
Mr. Harry Cates	_____	Parent	_____
Mr. John Byrd	_____	Teacher	_____
Ms. Ann Bate	_____	Speech Therapist	_____
Mr. Sam Masters	_____	Counselor	_____
Dr. Pat Smith	_____	Case Manager	_____

Parent(s) were _____ were not _____ members of the committee. (Please check appropriate response.)

I (We) agree with the Individual Education Program _____

I (We) disagree with the Individual Education Program _____

_____
Parents/Guardian Signature

affects the child's involvement and progress in the general education curriculum, and for preschool children how the disability affects the child's participation in appropriate activities. For children who take alternate assessments aligned to alternative assessment standards, a description of benchmarks or short-term objectives is needed.

2. Statement of measurable annual goals, including academic and functional goals —These goals should be designed to meet the child's needs resulting from their child's disability and enable the child to be involved in and make progress in the general education curriculum and other educational needs that result from the child's disability.

> Joan's math calculation skills will improve from the beginning 2nd grade to the beginning 3rd grade level.

3. Evaluation procedures and schedule—A description of how the child's progress toward meeting the annual goals will be measured and when these periodic progress reports (such as through the use of quarterly or other periodic reports, concurrent with the issuance of report cards) will be provided.

FYI

"Formative assessment is when the chef tastes the soup; summative assessment is when the customer tastes the soup."

AUTHOR UNKNOWN

Formative assessment is ongoing so that the student's progress is monitored regularly throughout the instructional period thereby allowing teachers to modify and adjust instruction. When assessment results indicate that progess has been poor, teachers will be informed that the student needs additional practice, more instructional time, a change in strategy, or a modification in instructional materials. Likewise, when progress is noted to exceed expectations or criteria, formative evaluation results provide the teacher with information to make curriculum adjustments and challenge the student at his or her appropriate level (zone of proximal development).

> Is the new instructional approach (or intervention) working? Has Joan made progress this week (or this unit)?

Summative assessment is a final assessment of progress, administered at the end of a period of instruction, such as a term, semester, or year (although more frequent evaluation of the student's progress in meeting the prescribed goals and objectives is highly recommended). This type of assessment determines how many skills or concepts a student has learned and retained over an extended period of time and can determine the overall effectiveness of an instructional program.

> Which intervention was most effective? Has Joan made progress this semester (or year) in reading fluency?

4. Statement of special education, related services, and supplementary aids and services, based on peer-reviewed research to the extent practicable, and a statement of the program modifications or supports for school personnel that will be provided for the child to advance appropriately toward meeting the annual goals.

5. An explanation of the extent, if any, to which the child will not participate with nondisabled children in the regular class and the curricular and extra-curricular activities.

6. Statement of any individual appropriate accommodations necessary to measure the academic achievement and functional performance of the child on state and district-wide assessments. Also, if the IEP team determines

The IEP Connection

Academic Subject	Condition	Behavior	Criterion
Reading Math Spelling Written expression	In (*number of weeks until annual review*) when given a randomly selected (*reading passage, or math problems, words, or story starter/topic section*) from (*level and name of reading, or math, or spelling series/or when given three minutes to write*)	Student will read aloud, or solve, or write	(*Number of words read correctly, or correct number of digits, or correct number of words/letter sequences*)

that the child shall take an alternative assessment on a particular state of district-wide assessment of student achievement, a statement of why the child cannot participate in the regular assessment and the particular alternate assessment selected is appropriate for the child.

7. Projected date for the beginning of the services and modifications as well as their anticipated frequency, location, and duration.

> Joan will receive individual speech therapy, scheduled two times per week for one-half-hour sessions.

8. Transition planning to prepare the student for post high school year must begin not later than the first IEP to be in effect when the child is 16, and updated annually thereafter. The IEP must include appropriate measurable post secondary goals based upon age appropriate transition assessments related to training, education, employment, and where appropriate, independent living skills and transition services. Beginning not later than 1 year before the child reaches the age of majority under state law, a statement must be included in the IEP that indicates that the child has been informed of his/her rights, if any, that will transfer to the child on reaching the age of majority.

Coordinating Assessment Results in IEP Development

Informal assessment methods are well suited to coordinating areas of instructional need, educational goals and objectives, and progress tracking. Teachers can identify students' competencies and deficiencies noted on curriculum-based, portfolio, or performance assessments, use task analyses and error analyses to break down individual skills needed to solve specific problems, and list these skills in hierarchial order of instructional need. Grade and subject scope and sequence lists that identify expected competencies can be matched directly to students' particular strengths and weaknesses. Teachers can develop skill checklists based directly on students' study and work skills, their disposition toward the subject area, and the instructional curriculum. Each skill or concept that is identified as emerging or as not mastered is converted directly into an instructional objective.

What is lacking in many assessment programs is the linkage between assessment and curriculum. This connection integrates students' developmental needs with program goals and activities. "It completes the instructional cycle, which includes assessing development, setting individual and program goals, planning and implementing curricular activities, monitoring progress, and making needed modifications" (Catron & Allen, 1999, p. 158). Working with assessment results, the IEP/IFSP/ITP goals and objectives can be developed. According to Davis, Kilgo, & Gamel-McCormick (1998), the steps to be followed in developing goals and establishing specific outcomes are as follows:

1. Begin by identifying skills that are partially acquired or that are demonstrated in some contexts but not others.
2. Identify skills that will permit the child to participate in routine daily activities within the natural environment and, therefore, increase the opportunities for interaction with peers.
3. Determine skills that would be instrumental in accomplishing the greatest number of other skills or functional tasks.
4. Identify skills that the child is highly motivated to learn and/or that the family wants him to learn.
5. Select skills that will increase participation in future environments (p. 2).

SECTION 4: THE PLACEMENT AND SERVICE DETERMINATION PROCESS

Placement Determination

One of the final steps in the special education process is to determine appropriate placement and services for the classified student. There is a continuum of educational placements, ranging from the highly integrated setting of the general education classroom to the highly segregated setting of the home or hospital. (See Figure 1–12). Placement decisions are based on the student's individual needs, skills, and abilities. The Education for All Handicapped Children Act mandates that students with disabilities

Figure 1–12   Educational Placement Options

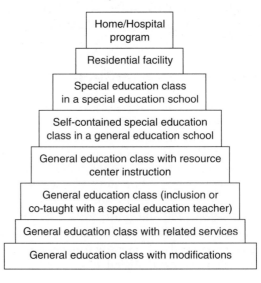

be placed in the **least restrictive environment (LRE)**, which means to the maximum extent appropriate, children with disabilities, including children in public or private institutions or other care facilities, are educated with children who are not disabled, and special classes, separate schooling, or other removal of children with disabilities from the regular educational environment occurs only when the nature or severity of the disability of a child is such that education in regular classes with the use of supplementary aids and services cannot be achieved (IDEA Section 612(a)(5)(A)).

The LRE does not necessarily refer to an inclusion class; it could mean residential placement for students with severe disabilities. Although many school districts use special education class placements, even for students with relatively mild disabilities, placement of students in this type of class is becoming less common as schools become more inclusive. Consideration of each type of educational setting is important not only when determining initial placement but also when reconsidering placement options at the annual review or triennial reevaluation meeting. For example, the student classified as having an emotional disturbance who has been placed in a self-contained special education class but, since making considerable improvement in self-control, may, at the annual review, be ready to be moved to a less restrictive placement, such as an inclusion class.

Optional Placement Considerations

The teacher needs to be familiar with the range of program options in order to participate in the placement decision. To do so, the teacher should ask the following key questions when considering if the placement is the most appropriate and in the least restrictive environment.

When making placement decisions, focus must be on determining the least restrictive classroom environment.

General education class with modifications

- Is the LRE an integrated general education program with accommodations or supports?
- In this setting does the student need adaptive devices, alternative instructional strategies, or both?

General education class with related services

- Is the LRE a mainstreamed program for all subject and school activities?
- What related services are required? How often and what type of sessions are required?

General education class (inclusion or co-taught with a special education teacher)

- Is the LRE a general education class in which both a general and a special education teacher work together to teach all students in the class while providing extra attention and support to students with disabilities?
- Are curriculum, instructional strategies or materials, behavior management, or work-study skill support required?

General education class with resource center instruction

- Is the LRE a general education class with specialized instruction from a special education teacher, either in the general education classroom or in a resource center?
- Should the resource center subject (e.g., reading) instruction be **supplemental instruction** so that primary reading instruction occurs in the general education class with additional reading instruction in the resource center, or should it be **replacement instruction** so that the primary reading instruction occurs in the resource center?

Self-contained special education class in a general education school

- Is the LRE a self-contained class in a general education neighborhood school?
- Will placement be exclusively in a self-contained special education class?
- Is general education placement being considered for related arts subjects (art, music, library, and physical education), for nonacademic activities (lunch, recess, bus travel), and for extracurricular school activities (field trips, assemblies, athletic activities, school clubs)?

Special education class in a special education school

- Is the LRE a self-contained class in a school exclusively for students with disabilities?
- Does the student have moderate-to-severe cognitive, emotional, social, and/or physical disabilities that require this restrictive placement?

Residential facility

- Is the LRE a live-in facility where 24-hour supervision and comprehensive medical and/or psychological services are provided?
- Does the student have severe cognitive, emotional, social, and/or physical disabilities such that this more restrictive placement is required?

Home/hospital program

- Is the LRE in the home, in a group home, or in a hospital setting?
- Does the student have serious and/or chronic physical or mental illnesses, an injury, or behavioral issues that put the student or others in jeopardy (e.g., hitting other students, starting fires)?

- Will instruction be provided by a homebound certified special education teacher or through distance learning?
- Will this placement be temporary or short-term?

Related Services Determination

Assessment results may indicate the need for specific therapy or auxiliary services in order to remediate an area of deficiency or to provide students with compensatory supports that allow them to function appropriately in the school setting. Students may be scheduled for special education placement with related services, or they may be included in general education classes and require related services to supplement their mainstreamed programs. In order to participate in placement and programming decisions, the referring teacher needs to be aware of the range and description of the related services available to the classified student. According to IDEA regulations, related services include "transportation and such developmental, corrective, and other supportive services (including speech-language pathology and audiology services; psychological services; physical and occupational therapy; recreation, including therapeutic recreation; social work services; school nurse services designed to enable a child with a disability to receive a free and appropriate public education as described in the individual education program of the child; counseling services, including rehabilitation counseling; orientation and mobility services; and medical services, except that such medical services shall be for diagnostic and evaluation purposes only) as may be required to assist a child with a disability to benefit from special education, and includes the early identification and assessment of disabling conditions in children. *Exception: The term does not include a medical device that is surgically implanted, or the replacement of such device*" (Section 602 (26)(A)(B)).

Assistive Technology Services and Devices

Assistive technology devices and services needs to be included in the IEP, when necessary, to ensure that students receive a free and appropriate education (FAPE) or to maintain them in the LRE through the provision of supplementary aids and services. When writing the IEP, a determination must be made whether students with disabilities, regardless of category, need assistive technology devices, services, or both.

An **assistive technology device** is any item, piece of equipment, or product system—whether acquired commercially off the shelf, modified, or customized—that is used to increase, maintain, or improve the functional capabilities of a child with a disability (Section 602(1)(A)).

Assistive technology service is any service that directly assists a child with a disability in the selection, acquisition, or use of an assistive technology device. This includes:

a. the evaluation of the needs of such child, including functional assessment of the child in his or her customary environment;
b. purchasing, leasing, or otherwise providing for the acquisition of assistive technology devices by such child;
c. selecting, designing, fitting, customizing, adapting, applying, retaining, repairing, or replacing of assistive technology devices;
d. coordinating and using other therapies, interventions, or services with assistive technology devices, such as those associated with existing education and rehabilitation plans and programs;

     e. training or technical assistance for such child, or, where appropriate, the family of such child; and

     f. training or technical assistance for professionals (including individuals providing education and rehabilitation services), employers, or other individuals who provide services to, employ, or are otherwise substantially involved in the major life functions of such child (Section 602(2)(A-F)).

SECTION 5: THE PROGRAM REVIEW PROCESS

Evaluating Progress

The program review process is a monitoring system to ensure that student educational programs remain appropriate, that their goals and objectives are being met, and that procedures exist for resolving disputes between parents and the school district (Friend & Bursuck, 2002). Students with disabilities need their prescriptive educational programs to be closely monitored so that adjustments can be made, if needed, in a timely manner. Legislative mandates require a formal review to be conducted only once each year (the annual review), but when teachers use a test-teach-test approach they can determine whether students are making sufficient progress to meet the projected goals in the IEP. Students with disabilities often need modifications and adjustments in standard curricular or instructional procedures, including more individualized attention, reinforcement, adaptations, special equipment, adjustments in how mastery is assessed (test modifications), and more structure or flexibility.

Experienced teachers may become quite accurate in projecting how far students will progress in a year. They also may be adept at selecting the right materials and methods for the student so that progress is steady and goals are attained. However, many teachers feel that predicting how far students will progress in a year is, at best, an "educated guess." When assessment procedures, such as curriculum-based assessment probes, are used on a regular basis, adjustments in the student's instructional program can be made before precious learning time is lost and so that progress can continue. Through ongoing assessment, the teacher can quickly identify when a student is responding well to his or her IEP program and when the goals need to be raised and the program made more challenging.

The Annual Review

The **annual review** process is the initial phase in the program evaluation process. The IEP team reviews the child's IEP periodically, but not less frequently than annually to determine whether the annual goals are being addressed. The IEP is revised, as needed, to address (i) any lack of expected progress toward the annual goal and in the general education curriculum; (ii) the results of any reevaluation; (iii) information about the child provided to or by the parents; (iv) the child's anticipated needs; (v) other matters (SEC 614d(4)(Ai–v)).

The purpose of the annual review is to ensure students' placements and IEP instructional programs are current and appropriate. However, according to IDEA-2004, the parent of the child with a disability and the LEA may agree not to convene an IEP meeting for the purposes of making such changes, and instead may develop a written document to amend or modify the child's current IEP. Upon request, the parent shall be provided with a revised copy of the amended IEP (SEC 614d(3)(D)(F)). The student is encouraged (when appropriate) to participate in developing the annual review IEP. The teacher most knowledgeable about the student's day-to-day functioning is also required to attend the annual review. This teacher may be the special education teacher, although, if the student is or will be attending a general education class, a general education teacher must also participate in the development of the IEP by contributing to the classroom perspective.

The role of the regular education teacher is, to the extent appropriate, to participate in the development of the IEP of the child, including the determination of appropriate positive behavioral interventions and supports, and other strategies, and the determination of supplementary aids and services, program modifications, and support for school personnel (SEC 614d(3)(C)).

Reevaluation

Theoretically, after several years of receiving special services, the students' needs change: They may need more, less, or different services, or may no longer require any special services. The reevaluation process is a safeguard designed to prevent students with disabilities from remaining in services or programs that are no longer appropriate for them.

Reevaluation is required if the LEA determines that educational or related needs, including improved academic and functional performance, is warranted. A reevaluation may not occur more than once a year, unless the parent(s) and LEA agree otherwise, but at least once every 3 years, unless parent and LEA agree otherwise (IDEA-2004, Sec. 614(a)(1)(B)(2a & b)). Reevaluation may also be completed earlier if the student has made significant progress and **declassification** is being considered. Students may be declassified if, through the evaluation process, it is determined that they no longer meet the criteria for classification and are therefore no longer eligible to receive special services. Reevaluation may be warranted before the mandated three-year period if parents, teachers, or school personnel are concerned about the student's slow progress or lack of progress and feel that the student's prescribed program needs to be revised. A student must also be reevaluated when the student has serious disciplinary problems and the school district is contemplating a long-term suspension of the student or his or her expulsion.

Informed parental consent is required for a school to perform a reevaluation. The one exception to this mandate is when the local educational agency (LEA) can demonstrate that it had taken reasonable measures to obtain such consent and the child's parent has failed to respond (IDEA-2004). This exception allows districts to continue providing high-quality special services to students whose parents are no longer actively involved in their child's education (Friend & Bursuck, 2002). At the time of the three-year reevaluation, students may be administered the same tests and assessments that were used during the initial eligibility assessment process, including the basic multidisciplinary team evaluations and any additional specialists' evaluations deemed necessary according to the student's individual profile. This means that most or all of the evaluation procedures (tests, interviews, rating scales, observations) will be repeated to determine how the student's achievement, skill levels, adjustment, and so on have changed since the last evaluation was completed. This comparison may be needed to determine whether the child continues to have a disability and educational needs; whether the child continues to need special education and related services; whether any additions or modifications to the special education and related services are needed to enable the child to meet the measurable annual goals set out in the individualized education program of the child and to participate, as appropriate, in the general education curriculum (IDEA-2004 SEC 614c) (Bi–iv). If parents and teachers feel that the student's progress has been adequate and that the student would benefit from a continuation of his or her present classification, placement, and program, they may agree to forgo all or part of the testing process and rely on data from observation, work samples, daily reports, and informal teacher assessment to justify the reevaluation. At the conclusion of the triennial evaluation process, a revised IEP must be written (The Alliance, 2001). This reevaluation IEP replaces the annual review IEP at the three-year mark. For the next two years an annual review IEP is written.

Mediation and Due Process

Parents who are dissatisfied with the services that their child is receiving may choose to pursue their due process rights. The due process procedures first involve mediation. **Mediation** is a process in which the parents or guardian and the school district personnel meet to discuss their concerns. At this meeting, an impartial person, called a mediator, from the state department of education tries to help both parties either compromise or agree on a way to resolve the issue. If no resolution is reached, the next level of intervention is an administrative hearing that involves a court case. An administrative judge hears both sides of the case, including statements from expert witnesses, before rendering a decision.

Due process is the set of procedures established by legislation for resolving disagreements between school district personnel and parents regarding the special education process for students with disabilities. The intent of due process is to protect the rights of parents to have input into their child's educational program and to take steps to resolve disagreements. This hearing is designed to allow an impartial third party—the hearing officer who is generally an administrative judge—to listen to both sides of a disagreement, examine the issues, and settle the dispute (Alliance Technical Assistance Alliance, 2001). The intent of Congress in instituting this type of adversarial system to settle disputes was to ensure that both parents and school officials have equal opportunity to present their case (Turnbull & Turnbull, 2000).

Parents may request an **impartial due process hearing** (a meeting held to resolve differences between the school and the parents) to contest a school's identification, evaluation, or educational placement process or the provision regarding the student's right to a free and appropriate education; or to question the information in their child's educational records (IDEA Regulations, 2004). Parents generally invoke their due process rights when they feel that the school district is not acting in the best interest of their child (Rothstein, 1999). Schools may also initiate due process when parents refuse to consent to an evaluation or a recommended placement.

SUMMARY POINTS

- There are at least five reasons for assessment: (1) screening, (2) identifying strengths and weaknesses, (3) determining eligibility and making diagnoses, (4) doing instructional and program planning, and (5) determining program effectiveness.

- Early intervening service teams are formed to assist general education teachers with the at-risk students in their classes, and to (1) reduce the need for special education services by providing recommendations for use in general education classrooms, and (2) decrease the number of unnecessary evaluations, misdiagnoses and subsequent overidentification of students.

- Students who have "a physical or mental impairment which substantially limits a major life activity," such as learning, and require modifications in the standard program to function in school may qualify for services under Section 504 of the Vocational Rehabilitation Act.

- A comprehensive educational evaluation is a complete assessment procedure that includes all areas of suspected disability.

- The referral to the IEP multidisciplinary team is the step in the process for determining whether special education services (provided to students to facilitate their achievement in school) and/or related services (support or therapeutic services not part of the education program) are needed.

- Parents have rights in the eligibility, placement, and programming decisions of their child. Parents must be included in this decision-making process, the information provided to them must be in their native language, the parents must provide informed consent, and they must be informed of their child's progress as least as often as are parents of nondisabled children.

- Students may be determined eligible for one of the 13 classification categories and qualify for special education services if they meet the eligibility criteria and if their eligibility is not based on a lack of instruction in reading, math, or limited English proficiency.

- IDEA-2004 requires that each IEP contain (a) present level of academic achievement and functional performance, (b) annual goals and short-term objectives, (c) evaluative procedures and schedule, (d) special education and services, (e) explanation of any non participating with nondisabled peers, (f) accomodations, (g) initiation and duration of services, (h) transition planning, ask as needed.

- Related services include transportation and such developmental, corrective, and other supportive services as are required to assist a child with a disability to benefit from special education.

- Mediation is a process in which an impartial person, called a mediator, from the state department of education attempts to help both parents and school personnel agree on a way to resolve the issue. If no resolution is reached, the next level of intervention is a due process hearing at which an administrative judge hears both sides of the case, including statements from expert witnesses, and renders a decision.

Chapter Check-Ups

1. How would you explain to a parent or a colleague the benefit of early intervening services?

2. Describe a scenario in which a student could receive Section 504 services but would not be eligible for IDEA services.

3. How would you explain the special education process to a parent? What are the special communication issues you need to consider when the parent is (a) a newly arrived immigrant, (b) illiterate, or (c) auditorily impaired/deaf?

4. What should a school district do if the parent of a child refused to sign an informed consent for initial eligibility testing? What rights do parents have if they disagree with the recommended classification or special education placement?

5. When discussing the referral of one of your students, what would you tell the parents in regards to their involvement in the assessment and placement decision-making process?

Practical Application Assessment Activities

1. Interview the educational professionals who specialize in the referral and evaluation process of students in local school districts. Refer to Figure 1–1 in the text for the sequence and components of the Special Education Process Model as you generate relevant questions for each aspect of the process. Ask these professionals to describe experiences that worked well and those that were marred by communication barriers or other problems. Have them identify how they minimized problems.

2. Select a few class members to depict a prereferral team conference meeting. Role-play the members of an early intervening services team conducting a discussion about a student who is experiencing academic, social-emotional, behavioral, and/or work-study problems. Group members will play the role of the referring teacher, the school administrator, nurse, counselor, one of the general education teachers, or remedial specialist. The referring teacher will discuss the strengths and weaknesses of the hypothetically referred child and identify what interventions have been used to attempt to deal with the presenting problems. The intervention team members will discuss the issues and make recommendations. Together draft an intervention plan for this child. Discuss this experience and how you would involve the child's parent(s).

3. Interview the parent(s) of a classified student to discuss their experiences with the referral, evaluation, classification and IEP process. Ask these parents to share their feelings about the special education system, to identify the strengths and weaknesses of the special education process from the parent's perspective, to tell what type of information they were asked to provide about their child during the evaluation process, and to suggest ways to make the process more "parent-friendly." Follow-up by compiling a list of best practices for involving parents in this process.

4. A group of class members role-play a multidisciplinary team staffing for a child recently assessed. Each class member should assume the role of either the parent(s), student, referring teacher, administrator or a member of the multidisciplinary team. Assessment result information will be provided to team members so that they can contribute to the discussion in their areas of expertise. The team will discuss test results and attempt to determine whether the child is eligible for classification, if so, what the classification category would be, and the child's specific special services needs (i.e., placement recommendations).

5. Attend a multi-disciplinary eligibility or IEP team conference. Following the meeting, interview the parent(s) and the teacher separately about their general impressions of the conference. Particular attention should be given to their impressions of the general atmosphere of the meeting, the effectiveness of the interactions, the clarity and sensitivity of the discussion, and the potential

effectiveness of the recommendations made. Compare and contrast their perspectives and perceptions.

Connection Between CEC, PRAXIS, and INTASC Standards and Chapter 1

The Council for Exceptional Children—Professional Standards

Standard 1 Foundations

1. Models, theories, and philosophies that form the basis for special education practice.
2. Laws, policies, and ethical principles regarding behavior management planning and implementation.
3. Relationship of special education to the organization and function of educational agencies.
4. Rights and responsibilities of students, parents, teachers, and other professionals, and schools related to exceptional learning needs.
5. Issues in definition and identification of individuals with exceptional learning needs, including those from culturally and linguistically diverse backgrounds.
6. Issues, assurances, and due process rights related to assessment, eligibility, and placement within a continuum of services.
7. Family systems and the role of families in the educational process.

Standard 10 Collaboration

2. Roles of individuals with exceptional learning needs, families, and school and community personnel in planning of an individualized program.
3. Concerns of families of individuals with exceptional learning needs and strategies to help address these concerns.
4. Culturally responsive factors that promote effective communication and collaboration with individuals with exceptional learning needs, families, school personnel, and community members.
5. Maintain confidential communication about individuals with exceptional learning needs.
6. Collaborate with families and others in assessment of individuals with exceptional learning needs.
7. Foster respectful and beneficial relationships between families and professionals.
8. Assist individuals with exceptional learning needs and their families in becoming active participants in the educational team.
9. Plan and conduct collaborative conferences with individuals with exceptional learning needs and their families.
10. Collaborate with school personnel and community members in integrating individuals with exceptional learning needs into various settings.
11. Use group problem solving skills to develop, implement and evaluate collaborative activities.
13. Communicate with school personnel about the characteristics and needs of individuals.

14. Communicate effectively with families of individuals with exceptional learning needs from diverse backgrounds.

CEC standards from The Council of Exceptional Children. Reprinted with Permission.

PRAXIS Standards for Special Education

Standard 1 Understanding Exceptionalities

3. Basic concepts in special education, including definitions of all major categories and specific disabilities; causation and prevention of disability; the nature of behaviors, including frequency, duration, intensity, and degrees of severity; and classification of students with disabilities, including classifications as represented in IDEA and labeling of students.

Standard 2 Legal and Societal Issues

1. Federal laws and landmark legal cases related to special education.
2. Issues related to school, family, and/or community, such as teacher advocacy for students and families, including advocating for educational change and developing students' self-advocacy; family participation and support systems; public attitudes toward individuals with disabilities; and cultural and community influences.

Standard 3 Delivery of Services to Students with Disabilities

2. Professional roles and responsibilities of teachers of students with disabilities (for example, teacher as a collaborator with other teachers, parents, community groups, and outside agencies); teacher as a multidisciplinary team member; teacher's role in selecting appropriate environments and providing appropriate services to students; knowledge and use of professional literature, research (including classroom research), and professional organizations and association; and reflecting on one's own teaching.
4. Placement and program issues (including continuum of services; mainstreaming; integration; inclusion; least restrictive environment; non-categorical, categorical, and cross-categorical programs; related services; early intervention; community-based training; transition of students into and within special education placements; post school transition; and access to assistive technology).
5. Curriculum and instruction, including the IEP/ITP process; instructional development and implementation (for example, instructional activities, curricular materials, resources and equipment, working with classroom personnel, tutoring and the use of technology); teaching strategies and methods (for example, direct instruction, cooperative learning, diagnostic-prescriptive method); instructional format and components (for example, individualized instruction, small- and large-group instruction, modeling, drill and practice); and areas of instruction (such as academics, study and learning skills, social, self-care, and vocational skills).

PRAXIS materials from Tests at a Glance: Special Education: Knowledge-Based Core Principles, 2004. Reprinted by permission of Educational Testing Service, the copyright owner.

Permission to reprint PRAXIS materials does not constitute review or endorsement by Educational Testing Service of this publication as a whole or of any other testing information it may concern.

INTASC Standards for Teacher Education

Standard 7

The teacher plans instruction based upon knowledge of subject matter, students, the community, and curriculum goals.

Standard 10

The teacher fosters relationships with school colleagues, parents, and agencies in the larger community to support students' learning and well-being.

The Interstate New Teacher Assessment and Support Consortium (INTASC) standards were developed by the Council of Chief State School Officers and member states.

Copies may be downloaded from the Council's website at http://www.ccsso.org.

Council of Chief State School Officers. (1992). Model standards for beginning teacher licensing, assessment, and development. A resource for state dialogue. Washington, DC: Author. http://www.ccsso.org/content/pdfs/corestrd.pdf.

CHAPTER 2

Standardized Assessment

Types, Scores, Reporting

KEY TERMS AND CONCEPTS

- formal, or standardized, assessments
- informal, or nonstandardized, assessments
- norm-referenced tests
- norm, or reference, group
- criterion-referenced tests
- group-administered assessments
- individually-administered assessments
- basal level
- ceiling level

- splintered score
- raw score
- standard score
- stanine
- percentile
- percentile rank
- standard error of measurement (SEM)
- confidence interval
- grade equivalent, or age equivalent, score

CHAPTER OBJECTIVES

After reading this chapter, you should be able to:

- Identify differences between formal and informal assessments
- Explain the criteria for standardization
- Identify the criteria for judging test integrity
- Discuss how norming groups are determined

- Identify and explain standardized test interpretation terms
- Explain considerations that are important when writing test result reports

Introduction to Standardized Assessment

Although the main focus of this text is informal assessment procedures, this chapter provides an overview of traditional standardized assessment procedures, also referred to as formal assessment methods. Since both special education and general education teachers are required to be active participants in the eligibility, classification, and placement decision-making processes, they need to understand how to administer, score, and interpret the standardized tests. Because each standardized test comes with an administration and scoring technical manual that describes what the test measures, as well as test administration and scoring instructions specific to the particular test, this chapter focuses on providing teachers with practical information; that is, what they need to know, rather than an extensive psychometric discussion better suited to an educational psychology text.

This chapter looks at how to follow standardized procedures; how test scores are derived; what the various types of scoring results mean; and how to read, interpret, compare, and contrast national and district-level normative data. It describes what each type of standardized measure indicates, the fundamental differences among the measures, the strengths and weaknesses of each, factors to consider when determining what kind of test to use for a particular student, as well as offering suggestions for reporting test results to parents and students.

Standardized assessment has an important role in determining whether students meet classification criteria and are eligible to receive special education, related services, or both. Standardized assessment is also used for accountability purposes; that is, to determine whether students have made overall progress from grade to grade and which students scored below the criteria established to qualify for funded remedial services. Local education agencies (LEAs) use these test results for No Child Left Behind (NCLB) accountability reporting.

Our goal in assessing students is to gather evidence about their level of achievement in a specific subject area so that we can make inferences based on that evidence to determine their skill acquisition, proficiency, generalization, and application. Educators must be able to assess individual student achievement otherwise it would be impossible to know whether a student's curriculum standards are being reached. In effect, assessment serves to undergird the standards movement. It is the "glue" that holds the standards framework together (Seaman, DePauw, Morton, & Omoto, 2003). Our assessment procedures should (1) reflect the subject content that is most important for students to learn, (2) enhance learning through a connection with instruction, (3) provide consistent (reliable) evidence of student performance, and (4) yield valid inferences about student learning (National Association for Sport & Physical Education, 1995).

FYI

Assessment and learning are two sides of the same coin. When students engage in assessments, they should learn from those assessments (National Research Council, 1999).

SECTION 1: TYPES OF FORMAL ASSESSMENTS

There are two general categories of assessments: formal and informal. The type of assessment used must match the purpose for administering the assessment. **Formal, or standardized, assessments** compare a student's performance with that of peers who are similar in age or grade level. **Informal, or nonstandardized, assessments,** which are more authentic, are often curriculum or performance-based, and are used primarily to describe performance and inform instruction. Formal assessments are data driven, and the data are mathematically computed and summarized. Scores, such as percentiles, stanines, or standard scores, are mostly commonly associated with this type of assessment. Informal assessments are not data driven but rather content and performance driven. For example, listening to a child read a text orally while assessing accuracy and speed is an informal assessment. Scores, such as the number of correct answers or the number of seconds it takes the child to read a passage, are commonly used for this type of assessment.

Standardized tests, whether aptitude or achievement, are objective and often multiple-choice, which provide broad indicators of a student's performance in particular skill areas. Standardized tests are rigorously developed by experts to be used with large populations of students. These tests are administered, scored, and interpreted according to specific standards. Standardized tests evaluate what a child has already learned (achievement) or predict what a child may be capable of doing in the future (aptitude).

There are primarily three basic criteria for judging the integrity of formal tests: "(1) standardization (on what group was the test standardized?); (2) reliability (are test results consistent?); and (3) validity (does the test measure what it claims to measure?)" (Lerner, 2003, p. 88). Most of the tests used to determine eligibility for learning disabilities are inadequate for these criteria (Salvia & Ysseldyke, 2001). Instead, these test results should be used in conjunction with multiple measures (e.g., observations, interviews, work-sample analyses, and curricula and performance-based assessments), and one single test score should not be overgeneralized (Lerner, 2003).

Tests of Aptitude

The aptitude test determines intelligence quotient (or IQ). Scores on aptitude tests are relatively good predictors of academic achievement. The Individuals with Disabilities Education Act (IDEA) requires the use of aptitude tests for the diagnosis and determination of eligibility for several classification categories. (See Figure 2-1 for commonly used, commercially published standardized aptitude tests.)

Tests of Achievement

The achievement battery of tests generally cover the basic academic skills. Achievement tests are administered to (a) determine eligibility for special education services, (b) identify students who need remedial services, (c) compare one group of students to another (district, state, or national norms), and (d) evaluate the effectiveness of the teacher, the curriculum, or both. (See Figure 2-2 for commonly used, commercially prepared standardized achievement tests.)

Norm-Referenced Tests

Formal assessments—the traditional test format—are standardized and generally provide norm-referenced statistical information and standardized directions and procedures that must be followed to ensure validity and reliability. **Norm-referenced tests** compare a student's performance with the performance of a comparison group (children of the same age and grade), referred to as the **norm**, or **reference, group**. Standardized test norms typically are established by administering the test to large numbers

Figure 2–1 Commonly Used Standardized Aptitude Tests of Intelligence and Cognitive Abilities

Test Name	Type	Age/Grade	Purpose	Publisher
Wechsler Preschool and Primary Scale of Intelligence	Individual	3 to 7-3 yrs.	To measure aptitude—three scores: verbal, performance, and full scale IQ	Harcourt Assessment
Wechsler Intelligence Scale for Children	Individual	6 to 6-11 yrs.	To measure aptitude—three scores: verbal, performance, and full-scale IQ	Harcourt Assessment
Wechsler Adult Intelligence Scale (3rd ed.)	Individual	16 to 74 yrs.	To measure aptitude—three scores: verbal, performance, and full scale IQ	Harcourt Assessment
Woodcock-Johnson III Tests of Cognitive Ability	Individual	2 to 90+ yrs.	To measure cognitive ability	Riverside Publishing
Stanford-Binet Intelligence Scale, 4th ed.	Individual	2 to adult yrs.	To measure IQ and four areas: verbal reasoning, quantitative reasoning, abstract-visual reasoning, and short-term memory	Riverside Publishing
Kaufman Assessment Battery for Children	Individual	2.5 to 12.5 yrs.	To classify mental abilities as either sequential processing or simultaneous processing	American Guidance Services

of individuals, the target population of the test, who have specifically defined characteristics, such as age and sex. The data are statistically analyzed, and performance standards, referred to as norms, are constructed based on this analysis. Norms are used to compare one individual's performance to the performance of similar individuals (Seaman, DePauw, Morton, & Omoto, 2003).

The Norming of Standardized Tests

National norming samples include students from various geographic regions across the United States; urban and rural schools of different sizes; and a balance of sexes, socioeconomic levels, and ethnic backgrounds. Similarly, regional and local norming samples are representative of these student populations. Most norm-referenced tests use a norming population that is correlated directly on national statistics, such as the census data that are revised each decade. When reviewing various norm-referenced tests to determine which test is most appropriate for a specific class or an individual student, it is important to consider the population on which the test was normed (Lerner, 2003).

Figure 2–2 Commonly Used Standardized Tests of Achievement

Test Name	Type	Age/Grade	Purpose	Publisher
Woodcock-Johnson III Tests of Achievement	Individual	age 2 to adulthood	To measure academic achievement	Riverside Publishing Co.
Wechsler Individual Achievement Test (2nd ed.)	Individual	grades K to 12	To assess reading, math, oral, and written language achievement	Harcourt Assessments
Peabody Individual Achievement Test (revised)	Individual	grades K to 12	To measure reading, math, written expression, spelling, and general information achievement	American Guidance Services
Kaufman Test of Educational Achievement	Individual	grades 1 to 12	To assess reading, math, and spelling achievement	American Guidance Services
California Achievement Test–5	Group	grades K to 12	To assess achievement in seven basic and content areas	McGraw Hill
Comprehensive Tests of Basic Skills	Group	grades K to 12	To screen, tests for basic skills	McGraw Hill
Brigance Diagnostic Comprehensive Inventory of Basic Skills	Individual, criterion-referenced	grades K to 9	To assess basic academic skills	Curriculum Associates
Diagnostic Achievement Battery–2	Individual	ages 6 to 14	To assess basic academic skills	Pro-Ed
Diagnostic Achievement Test for Adolescents–2	Individual	grades 7 to 12	To assess basic academic skills	Pro-Ed

The norm consists of sets of scores for age or grade-level peers based on the average scores of the subjects of that norm group, reported in percentiles, standard scores, and/or age or grade equivalence scores. For example, a student with a score of 40 percent on a standardized test would rank in the lowest 40 percent compared with the norm group of students. These tests consist of a limited number of questions at each grade level.

All norm-referenced tests are standardized, meaning that the test must be administered following certain criteria, ensuring that all students take the test using exactly the same administration and scoring procedures to ensure validity and reliability. The evaluation procedures must also abide by federal legislative mandates. These mandates require that the assessment measures used must (a) be technically adequate, (b) be free of racial and cultural bias, (c) be administered in the student's native language whenever possible, (d) bypass the student's disability, and (e) be comprehensive, focused on the student's specific area of need, and involve individuals who know the student, have an understanding of the student's disability and are qualified to conduct and interpret these assessments.

Although norm-referenced tests are generally used to determine eligibility for special education or remedial services, they are of little value for instructional planning purposes. Additional drawbacks to standardized testing is that it is normed to the national average, and since particular classroom norms can vary significantly nationwide, standardized testing does not provide teachers with useful information about how the student's skill level compares with the typical skill level of his or her classroom or district grade-level peers. Also, the test items intended to measure performance standards according to a national average often do not overlap with the local classroom curriculum. Thus, a poor performance may lead one to assume incorrectly that the student has made less progress than actually occurred. Another consideration is that standardized tests are administered rather infrequently, generally once a year. If the teacher were to rely on yearly test results, instituting needed changes in program structure or interventions may be delayed. Standardized tests also tend to be less sensitive to short-term gains in skill mastery.

Criterion-Referenced Tests

Although most standardized tests are norm-referenced, they can also be criterion-referenced. A primary difference in these two types of assessment is that norm-referenced tests *compare* one student's performance with that of other students whereas **criterion-referenced tests** *describe* student performance (Richek, Caldwell, Jennings, & Lerner, 2000). Teachers set the criteria score expected for each skill taught and tested. Scores are typically reported as simple numerical scores, percent of correct responses, letter grades, or graphic score reports. Simple numerical scores are the number of right and wrong answers on a test (e.g., indicated as 6/10 when the student answers six out of 10 possible responses). The percent of correct responses is determined by dividing the number of correct answers by the total number of items on the test. The pupil who correctly answers seven out of the 10 questions would receive a score of 70 percent. The typical letter grade is derived from a percent of correct responses in relation to a grading scale. The student whose percent score is between 90 and 100 percent would receive an A, the student whose percent score is between 80 and 90 percent would receive a B, and so on. Graph reports consist of a visual representation of the student's performance, specifying progress over a period of time, comparing different subjects and specific skills within a subject area. The differences between norm-referenced and criterion-referenced tests can perhaps be better clarified by relating it to another area of learning: riding a bicycle. (See FYI.)

Criterion-referenced tests can be either standardized or nonstandardized. Standardized tests have precise directions for administration and scoring procedures, and they can be administered individually or to a group. Criterion tests are not norm-based, although frequently criterion test results can be compared to norm-based test results. There are both published versions and teacher-made criterion-referenced tests.

SECTION 2: CHOOSING THE TYPE OF TEST TO USE

When deciding which standardized test to use to evaluate students, the evaluator—whether the teacher or the individualized education plan (IEP) multidisciplinary team member—needs to be informed about the reliability, validity, suitability, and

FYI

NORM VS. CRITERION

When referring to Juanita's bike-riding skills in norm-referenced terms, you would say that she rides her bicycle as well as the average 7-year-old. But if Juanita's biking skills are referred to in criterion-referenced terms, she is judged on the basis of certain accomplishments, such as balancing herself on a two-wheeled bike, turning corners, and braking quickly.

Figure 2–3   Criteria for Assessments

Assessments should

- Focus on the whole child and measure processes that deal with students' cognitive, academic, social, emotional, and physical development.
- Be efficient; easy to administer, score and interpret; and not be excessively long so that students' attention and interest can be maintained.
- Include a range of methods and be completed in a variety of natural settings to ensure a broad view of the student.
- Be culturally appropriate and sensitive to cultural and linguistic issues.
- Be valid, measuring what they are supposed to measure, so that the results can be used to make educational decisions.
- Be reliable, with results that can be consistently produced when the assessment procedure is repeated using the same students and under the same conditions.
- Involve repeated observations to provide the evaluator with patterns of behavior, so that decisions are not based on atypical student behavior.
- Occur in authentic settings (e.g., evaluating reading in a language-arts lesson as the child orally reads a text passage).
- Be continuous, so that students' progress can be compared to their individual progress over time rather than to the average performance and behavior of a group of students.

objectivity of the tests being considered. The evaluator must be able to evaluate whether the test to be administered is an appropriate measure for determining the information being sought. (See Figure 2–3 for a list of test criteria.)

Mental measurement yearbooks are a good resource for individuals who are evaluating students to consult when seeking a standardized test that best suits their purposes and that has been normed on a population similar to the students being tested. These yearbooks provide critical reviews of tests by authorities in the field of evaluating tests. Other resources include *Tests in Print, Tests: A Comprehensive Reference for Assessments in Psychology, Education, and Business,* and *Test Critiques* (Rubin, 1997).

Determining Which Type of Test Is Appropriate

Tests are administered to gather the information needed to make appropriate educational decisions about students. The type of test that a teacher uses depends on the reason for testing, which may be to (a) determine the proficiency or mastery of specific content, (b) compare the student's performance with that of other students, or (c) evaluate progress over time. It is also necessary to consider the type of information needed to determine which type of test is most appropriate: (a) standardized, norm-referenced, (b) criterion-referenced, or (c) alternative measures (e.g., curriculum-based, authentic, performance-based, portfolio).

Standardized testing is widely used by school systems for accountability and reporting purposes. It is used to determine how well the school district as a whole, individual schools within a district, and individual classes within a school are performing. It is also used to determine individual student's progress from year to year, for district reporting information, for reporting progress to parents, and for determining

ONLINE SUPPORTS

Test Reviews Online:
http://buros.unl.edu/ buros/jsp/search.jsp

Test Link: World's Largest Test Collection Database
http://www.ets.org/ testcoll/index.html

Figure 2–4   The Wise Selection of Standardized Tests

The wise selection of standardized tests is preceded by careful consideration of the following:

1. What is the purpose of the test?
2. What reliability and validity data are available?
3. Is the test designed for individual or group administration?
4. For what age person is the test intended?
5. Who will administer and score the test?
6. Are there other tests or assessments that will be administered in conjunction with this one?
7. How shall the scores be interpreted and by whom?
8. How will test results be used?
9. How much time does the test take to administer? to score?
10. What is the cost per test per pupil?
11. Are there individual benefits to be gained from taking the test?
12. Are there benefits to instruction to be gained?
13. What happens to students who "fail" the test?

Source: Authentic Assessments of the Young Child, by M. B. Puckett, & J. K. Black, © 2000. Reprinted by permission of Pearson Education, Inc., Upper Saddle River, NJ 07458.

whether a particular student is eligible for special education services. (See Figure 2–4.) The following are factors to consider when deciding what test measures to use (standardized vs. non-standardized).

Critical Thinking and Reflective Analysis

You are administering a norm-referenced test to your class of ethnically, racially, linguistically, and academically diverse second-graders who attend a large city neighborhood school. To ensure reliability, you need to check the test's norm-referenced group to make sure that the comparison population includes grade 2-level students, including those with disabilities and those who come from multicultural urban settings, to ensure accurate norming. Why is this important? How would you do that?

Standardized or Nonstandardized

Standardized, formal assessments are published tests that are generally developed by experts in the field. They have precise directions for administration and scoring procedures. Standardization requires that the procedures specified for these tests be followed exactly in order to ensure that all students take the test according to the same procedures followed by the population on whom the test was normed. Test directions are very specific, test administration procedures must be uniform, and the calculation of test scores must be clearly defined and explicitly executed in order to ensure that all students are tested and ranked under similar conditions. Those administering standardized tests need to be familiar with key terms and concepts necessary for test selection, administration, scoring, and interpretation. Generally, standardized results are reported in quantitative terms, such as numbers or statistics, including percentiles or stanines that compare the students' achievement and academic performances with their chronological age or grade-level peers.

Advantages of Standardized Assessment

The advantages of using standardized, norm-referenced testing measures are (a) many states use them to determine eligibility for special education; (b) the results from this type of assessment are considered easier to report (e.g., when using percentiles, students' performance can be compared to national, state, and local norms); and (c) these types of assessment measures have been more thoroughly researched with technical data. Standardized, group assessments tend to be more time and cost efficient, require less teacher involvement, and are useful for statewide and national administrative, policy-making, and reporting systems.

Disadvantages of Standardized Assessment

One problem with this more traditional type of assessment (i.e., norm-referenced, standardized) is the discrepancy between what is tested and what is covered in the curriculum. With so many textbook series and schools using a variety of curriculum models, it is very likely that the published, nationally normed test does not correlate closely with many of the skills and concepts covered in individual school districts' grade-level curricula. Additionally, the premise of norm-referenced testing is to compare one child with many others. Although the student may score well below average according to age or grade norms or percentiles, this one number score does not take into consideration relevant factors, such as the impact of the curriculum, teacher effectiveness, and environmental factors.

Critical Thinking and Reflective Analysis

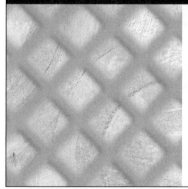

As a new teacher in the grade 3 inclusion class, you are concerned that your students do well on the end-of-the-year group achievement test. As you teach using the district's curriculum scope and sequence and focus on each student's IEP goals, you realize that you will not be teaching several major skills that are likely to be on the group test. You could switch the order of the curriculum sequence and skip a few IEP objectives so that you could cover the skills that will be covered on the test. What would you do?

Additional concerns regarding the use of standardized assessment from the teachers' perspective are that these tests do not provide enough information about students and may not assess what students are learning in class. They tend to emphasize segmented skills rather than higher order thinking skills, creativity, and problem solving (Lerner, 2003). Also, with the pressure to achieve high scores on these accountability tests, teachers feel they are forced to "teach to the test." Standardized testing provides minimal useful data for instructional planning (Salvia & Ysseldyke, 2004; Shinn, Collins, & Gallagher, 1998) and may not match the actual distribution of classroom achievement (Salvia & Ysseldyke, 2004). In addition, these tests are often culturally biased. Finally, because group tests are not administered on a frequent basis, their usefulness as a tool for evaluating day-to-day progress is limited.

Determining How Testing Should Be Administered

Group-administered assessments are specifically designed to be administered to a group of students at the same time. Although a group test can be administered to one student, a test designed and standardized for **individually-administered assessments** (e.g., the Woodcock-Johnson III) cannot be administered to a whole group at one time. Group achievement tests are not used to determine eligibility for special services. Although they provide information about how the student performs in relation to others of the same age or grade level, they do not identify an individual student's specific pattern but rather provide a broad overview of strengths and weaknesses. Compared with individual tests, group tests generally require less training to administer. Most, but not all, group tests are standardized. Because the format of these tests is generally multiple choice, the diagnostic information that can be obtained from them is limited.

Individually administered assessments require one-to-one administration and are therefore less efficient and economical for a school district. They may, however, be a more valid and reliable method of assessing a student's true capabilities and acquisition of skills and concepts. A group test can be administered to an individual student when (a) there is some inconsistency between the student's classroom behavior or academic potential and his or her scores on standardized tests, (b) the student's behavior during testing is significant and must be closely monitored (e.g., attention to task, ability to follow directions), or (c) the student requires test modifications or environmental accommodations. (See Chapter 4 for more discussion about test alternatives, modifications, and accommodations.)

Standardized, norm-referenced tests are administered individually to students as part of the eligibility determination procedure for special education, generally by a member of the school's individualized education plan (IEP) multidisciplinary team. The test battery consists primarily of standardized measures. To ensure that comprehensive assessment systems are in place and that multifaceted approaches are used, functional assessment measures—such as observations, teacher interviews, and so forth—are also a required part of the multidisciplinary team testing process. According to IDEA, various assessment tools and strategies must be used to gather a relevant and complete profile of the child, including information provided by the parent.

No Child Left Behind has made accountability testing a national mandate. Group standardized tests are generally used to meet local, state, and federal mandates for assessing whether core curriculum content standards have been mastered. They are also used by school districts for pre- and postevaluation of skill competency in these subject areas. Group-administered, standardized tests are generally given once each year to all students from kindergarten through grade 12 in most districts nationwide. These achievement tests are used for screening, accountability, and record-keeping purposes, with progress documented and compared from one year to the next.

Generally, federally funded remedial programming eligibility is based, at least in part, on these standardized test results. In addition, student progress is tested using group proficiency or aptitude tests at designated grade levels, generally midway through the elementary grades, when the student is entering the secondary level, and before the student is determined to be eligible to graduate from high school. In the past, students who are disabled were not required to take this standardized group testing if an exception statement had been written into their IEP. Now IDEA mandates that all students, including those who are receiving special education or related services, are to be included and their test results reported. Among the issues that need to be considered when using standardized group testing are the following:

1. During large-group test administration, directions are often read orally and may be incomprehensible for many students, such as those with processing problems. Another issue is that students are not allowed to ask questions or get clarification for written directions or test questions (Overton, 2003).

2. This type of assessment typically requires that each member of the group taking the test work independently. They are required to read the problems or questions and respond by writing or marking the correct answer, which may be difficult for students who do not work well independently; who have difficulty with word recognition, comprehending what they have read, or both; who are not proficient at putting thoughts on paper; or who have visual motor integration problems, fine motor coordination problems, or motor delays.

3. Pupils who are easily distracted, those with short attention spans, and those who have difficulty focusing or maintaining attention to the task when required to persevere through tedious writing tasks may have considerable difficulty with group-testing pencil-paper requirements.

4. Many students experience test anxiety, especially those who have had difficulty in school due to learning disorders. These students often feel particularly tense when taking tests with other students. They may be embarrassed by their physical manifestations of stress and be upset by time constraints—real or self-imposed—because they often take considerably longer to read, process, retrieve, and write the answers to test items that their classmates may quickly and easily respond to.

Determining Whether to Use Norm-Referenced or Criterion-Referenced Tests

Norm-referenced tests are generally used for accountability and record-keeping measures. They are also used for screening purposes and for pre- and posttesting to monitor individual and group progress. Each year school districts administer to all students from kindergarten through grade 12 norm-referenced tests. Often, federally funded remedial math programming eligibility is based, at least in part, on these standardized test results. Because the format of these tests is generally multiple choice, the diagnostic information that can be obtained is limited.

Norm-referenced testing provides little information that can be used to develop specific instructional programs. Whereas, criterion-referenced tests are designed to gain information about the specific behaviors and the various skill levels of students.

Criterion-referenced assessment is closely related to instruction; measures student knowledge on relatively small and discrete units; and is used to determine which skills have been mastered, which skills need to be reinforced, and which skills should be introduced next. Thus, criterion-referenced tests should be used when the intent is to measure mastery of a skill rather than to assign percentile rank, which would be reported in norm-referenced terms.

Critical Thinking and Reflective Analysis

Mr. Smith wants to determine whether his students understand the economic vocabulary they were just taught. Ms. Jones wants to know how her students' economic vocabulary knowledge compares to students nationally. Which type of test would you recommend for each of these teachers, and why?

SECTION 3: ADMINISTERING STANDARDIZED TESTS

Although some school districts require teachers to administer achievement tests, many rely primarily on the school psychologist, social workers, educational diagnosticians, and the remedial specialist to conduct the individually administered, standardized assessment to determine eligibility. In any case, all teachers, especially special educators are involved, to some extent, in the evaluation process when one of their students is referred for eligibility testing. Their contributions include providing

The school psychologist administers norm-referenced aptitude tests along with informal assessment measures such as behavior rating scales, adaptive functioning interviews, and observations.

valuable anecdotal records, perceptions of the student's functioning in the classroom, and academic and behavioral data provided by rating scales, checklists, and informal assessments.

Preparing for Testing

No matter who administers standardized tests, teachers need to understand the testing process. They need to know what is involved; how to follow standard testing procedures; and how to read and interpret test results so that they can actively participate in classification, placement, and program decisions. They should also be familiar with the terms used in standardized test administration, scoring, and interpretation.

Tips for Teachers

- Develop a rapport with the student before beginning the testing.
- Avoid correcting the student unnecessarily.
- Use positive, reaffirming terms, praise, and compliments.
- Provide opportunities for choice when possible (e.g., use of pencil or pen, when to take a break, the order of the tasks).

Determining Exact Chronological Age

Knowing the student's exact age is required in order to calculate test scores. This computation is accomplished by subtracting the birth date from the test date. The following example demonstrates how to calculate exact chronological age when regrouping is required.

Step 1: In the day column, since you cannot subtract 19 from 12, you need to borrow 30 days (one month) from the month column and add these days to the day column (12 + 30 = 42).

Step 2: Since you can not subtract 10 months from 6 months (remember one month was already subtracted and carried over to the day column), you have to borrow 12 months (one year) from the year column (reduce the year from 2005 to 2004) and move this one year (12 months) from the year column and add it to the month column (the month now becomes 6 + 12 = 18). After regrouping and applying simple subtraction, the student's chronological age is

	Year	Month	Day
	(2004)	(6 + 12 = 18)	(12 + 30 = 42)
Date of testing	2005	7[6]	12
Date of birth	1999	10	19
Chronological age	5	8	23

The Test Environment

According to the Standards for Educational and Psychological Testing (AERA, APA, & NCME, 1999), it is important to test the child in a quiet, comfortable room that has adequate ventilation and lighting. Ideally, the only individuals in the room should be the evaluator and the student, and all interruptions must be avoided. Test equipment should be readily available (e.g., stopwatch, headphones, testing materials). Rapport should be established before initiating the test. Encouragement should be provided, but the evaluator needs to be careful not to make comments that reveal whether the responses are correct or incorrect.

Prompts and Questioning

Often the student may not respond readily to the test question. This may be due to processing delays, difficulty in recalling information, a reluctance to respond when the student is unsure of the answer, or the student may have no idea how to answer and thus not say anything. It is important to allow the student time to process the question and formulate a response (Bos & Vaughn, 2002). The evaluator may offer encouragement without supplying cues or affirmation and may coax or encourage a response or clarification by asking "Can you tell me more?"

Standardized tests require specific responses that are acceptable as correct or partially correct. Most test manuals provide suggested wording for questioning and even acceptable prompt statements to obtain more information. Rephrasing questions or providing cues is not acceptable. It is important to remember that the norming was based on exact wording and specific guidelines for administration. Variation can invalidate test results. When the student asks for assistance, the evaluator can respond with a statement such as, "I'm not supposed to help you with that." When a student being tested asks if his or her response is correct, the evaluator should tell the student that evaluators are not supposed to provide answers and then reassure the student to simply do the best he or she can. When recording a student's responses or lack of responses, the following coding is generally used:

Q:	Question—	indicates the evaluator asked a question to clarify the response.
DK:	Don't Know—	indicates the student responded "I don't know."
NR:	No Response—	indicates the student did not respond to the question.
SC:	Self-Correction—	indicates the student correctly changed his or her original response.

Evaluating Test Behavior

An important aspect of the assessment is to note how the student responds to the evaluator and the testing situation. Student behaviors to observe include their attentiveness, cooperation, ability to follow directions, need for reassurance, willingness to attempt to guess when they are unsure of the answer, problem-solving skills, response time, and ability to transition to different types of tasks. The evaluator needs to focus on whether the student uses pencil and paper to come up with answers or can calculate mentally, the types of questions asked, the types of questions and tasks the student has difficulty with, and the student's activity level (e.g., fidgety, restless, lethargic). The evaluator should also note the student's expressive language skills, including the ability to use age-appropriate vocabulary and grammar, to converse fluently, to articulate clearly, to speak at an adequate pace and volume, and to respond with a direct answer to the question asked.

Administering the Test

Standardized test administration must be very precise to ensure that outcomes are the same for all students and not subjected to the judgment and biases of individual test examiners. Test conditions specified in each test manual must be closely followed. The administration of standardized tests has an established, sequential order of administration; many alternating between different formats (e.g., timed vs. untimed, verbal vs. nonverbal) to facilitate optimal attention and to maintain interest. If the test is timed, the evaluator must carefully follow specified guidelines.

Basal and Ceiling Levels

Most standardized tests require the administrator to start the test questions or items at a level of difficulty at which the student will succeed. Generally, test directions require that the student have a specific number of correct responses as a **basal level**, or baseline, before proceeding to the next item. The test administrator must continue asking questions until the student makes a specific number of incorrect responses, referred to as the **ceiling level**. Once the ceiling level is reached, the test is discontinued. Using basal and ceiling levels helps to ensure that the student's range of skills is covered.

> Joey's performance on a standard reading test (which has a basal of six items and a ceiling of six items for most subtests) suggests that at a certain level of difficulty, Joey clearly cannot answer correctly. (See Figure 2–5). However, Joey's test profile suggests that he has splintered skills. Although he nearly reached the ceiling numerous times with a series of up to five errors, he was able to respond correctly to the sixth item in the series, which required that he continue the test items until he reached a ceiling of six items answered incorrectly. This inconsistent pattern of correct and incorrect answers (often referred to as a **splintered score**) indicates that he may actually have greater potential than test scores indicate.

SECTION 4: SCORING AND INTERPRETING STANDARDIZED TESTS

Teachers must be familiar with how test (score) results are calculated and what the test scores mean in order to understand and interpret the information the scores provide. Individual tests have specific scoring standards and report different types of scores. (See Figure 2–6.) The following sections discuss commonly used scoring criteria.

Raw Score

The **raw score** is the number of items on a test that a student answers correctly. Raw scores are usually not reported in test profiles or interpretive reports because they do not convey meaningful information. In order to compare two or more test results, the tests must be on the same scale. Raw scores cannot be compared because the tests may differ in the number or level of difficulty of the items.

Figure 2–5   Sample Test: Basal/Ceiling Levels

Letter/Word Recognition Test

Basal: 6 lowest correct
Ceiling: 6 highest incorrect

Score 1, 0

1 ____ D		41 _0_ inside	
2 ____ S		42 _0_ minute	
		43 _0_ bottle	
3 ____ P		44 _0_ scramble	
4 ____ F		45 ____ merchant	
		46 ____ hinge	
5 ____ e		47 ____ balance	
6 ____ t		48 ____ character	
7 ____ B		49 ____ wharf	
8 ____ H		50 ____ ignore	
9 ____ U		51 ____ forge	
		52 ____ plastic	
10 ____ big		53 ____ bureau	
11 ____ n		54 ____ image	
12 ____ k		55 ____ voyage	
13 ____ r		56 ____ mineral	
14 ____ w		57 ____ distinguish	
15 _1_ cat		58 ____ advertise	
16 _1_ an		59 ____ boundary	
		60 ____ amazement	
17 _1_ of		61 ____ frantic	
18 _1_ his		62 ____ rhythm	
19 _1_ on		63 ____ prairie	
20 _1_ dig		64 ____ devour	
21 _1_ boy		65 ____ crisis	
22 _0_ run		66 ____ college	
23 _0_ man		67 ____ offense	
24 _0_ hurt		68 ____ specialist	
25 _0_ bean		69 ____ exploration	
26 _0_ foot		70 ____ tournament	
27 _1_ park		71 ____ investigation	
28 _0_ drop		72 ____ journal	
29 _0_ gone		73 ____ amateur	
30 _0_ fall		74 ____ reflection	
31 _0_ can't		75 ____ quarry	
32 _0_ harm		76 ____ embarrassed	
33 _1_ bridge			
34 _0_ church			
35 _0_ because			
36 _0_ visit			
37 _0_ shadow			
38 _1_ handle			
39 _0_ puppy			
40 _0_ surprise			

24	Number Correct (0–76)

Figure 2–6   Sample Woodcock-Johnson III Test Profile

Cluster/test	AE	Easy to Diff		PR	SS	Rating
Basic reading skills	11–2	9–9	12–11	73	109	Average
Math reasoning	8–3	7–7	9–1	26	91	Average
Academic skills	12–8	10–11	14–8	93	123	Superior
Academic applications	7–3	6–10	7–11	11	82	Low Average
Academic knowledge	7–5	6–5	8–7	18	86	Low Average
Letter-Word Identification	14–6	12–11	16–8	95	125	Superior
Calculation	10–10	9–9	12–4	84	115	High Average
Spelling	12–7	9–11	15–2	79	112	High Average
Passage comprehension	7–3	6–11	7–8	10	81	Low Average
Applied problems	7–9	7–1	8–5	18	86	Low Average
Writing samples	6–11	6–4	7–9	5	75	Low
Word attack	8–1	7–7	8–10	31	93	Average
Quantitative concepts	8–11	8–1	10–0	42	97	Average
Academic knowledge	7–5	6–5	8–7	18	86	Low Average

AE = Age Equivalent   PR = Percentile   SS = Standard Score

Raw scores must be converted to some type of derived score—such as a percentile rank, grade-equivalent score, or standard score—in order to make an accurate comparison.

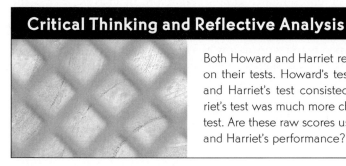

Critical Thinking and Reflective Analysis

Both Howard and Harriet received a raw score of 65 on their tests. Howard's test consisted of 100 items and Harriet's test consisted of 75 items. Also, Harriet's test was much more challenging than Howard's test. Are these raw scores useful to compare Howard and Harriet's performance?

Correct/Incorrect Possible Score

The correct/incorrect possible score is generally associated with informal, criterion-based tests and is most commonly used to inform instruction. The numbers of both correct and incorrect responses out of the total number of test items are reported. These scores are typically reported as a percent (e.g., 15 words correct out of 20 words on test = 75 percent).

Standard Score

A **standard score** is a term for a variety of scores that represent performance by comparing the deviation of an individual score with the mean or average score for students in a norm group of the same chronological age or grade level. These scores, which are generated from testing hundreds or thousands of students on a test, are statistically calculated. Standard scores allow comparison of performance across tests, which is useful for classification purposes because widely used aptitude and achievement tests have standard scores with means of 100 and standard deviations (SD) of 15. On most formal tests a standard score of 90 to 110 is average.

Critical Thinking and Reflective Analysis

When comparing the test scores of three students in your class who have average intelligence (100 to 105 standard score range on the IQ score), you find that Eugenia received a standard score of 100 on the standardized reading test, Tonya received a standard score of 120, and Ned had a standard score of 82. Did any of these students scores indicate that they have a discrepancy between their IQ and achievement scores.

Stanine

The term **stanine** is a combination of the words *standard* and *nine* based on the fact that the scores range from a low of 1 to a high of 9. These measures reflect a bell curve, although there are only 9 stanines. Stanines of 4 through 6 represent the average range, stanines of 3 or below are considered a below-average performance, and stanines of 7 to 9 are above the average range. Stanine scores are assigned so that the results represent a normal distribution (a representative sample). Therefore, in an average class, the stanine scores of most students are within the 4-to-6 range, with only a few receiving scores of 1 or 9. A major problem with stanine scores is that they are not precise (e.g., a stanine of 5 could have a percentile score as low as 41 or as high as 59) (Rubin, 2002). Stanines can be reported as national stanines (NS), which compare one student with students across the nation at a given grade level. Local stanines (LS) represent the average range for the school district at a given grade level. Figure 2–7 shows the correlation among stanines, percentages (PRs), and normal curve equivalents (NCEs). To help interpret stanines, the following descriptors can be helpful:

9 = Very superior	4 = Low average
8 = Superior	3 = Considerably below average
7 = Very good	2 = Poor
6 = Good	1 = Very poor
5 = Average	

CLARIFYING TERMS

Percentile vs. Percentage

PERCENTILE:

A test score of 35 percent is the same as or better than 35 percent of those in the norm group.

PERCENTAGE:

A test score of 35 percent indicates the percentage of items answered correct on a test.

Percentiles

A **percentile**, the most frequently used norm score, is used to describe how a student performs in comparison with others in the same age group or grade. Percentiles are expressed in numbers ranging from a low of 1 to a high of 99 and reflect a bell curve, with a 50 percentile being average. For example, a percentile of 70 means that 70 percent of the standardized sample scored at or below the examinee's score.

A **percentile rank** is the percentage of students who had scores the same as or lower than the student being tested and is useful for describing the student's relative

Figure 2–7   Correlation Among Stanines, Percentages and NCEs

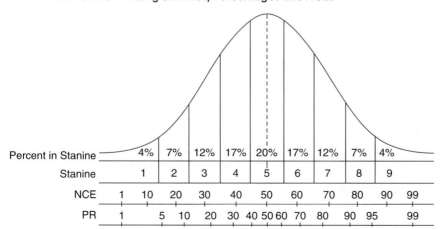

Percent in Stanine		4%	7%	12%	17%	20%	17%	12%	7%	4%	
Stanine		1	2	3	4	5	6	7	8	9	

NCE	1	10	20	30	40	50	60	70	80	90	99

| PR | 1 | | 5 | 10 | 20 | 30 | 40 | 50 | 60 | 70 | 80 | 90 | 95 | | 99 |

standing in the population. Since percentile ranks are not equal units, a percentile ranking of 70 does not mean that the student so ranked did twice as well as a student with a percentile rank of 35. Also, there is not a direct correlation between raw score points and percentiles. Many scores center around the mean, so there is often a noticeable difference between the 80th and 90th compared with the 50th and 60th percentiles. There is a constant relationship between stanines and percentiles, which means that the range of percentiles included within each stanine is always the same. (See Figure 2–8.)

Critical Thinking and Reflection Activity

Last year, one of your students scored in the 40th percentile on the end-of-the-year standardized reading test. He scored in the 40th percentile on the reading test at the end of this school year. Do these scores indicate that this student has made no progress?

FYI: The student has maintained the same percent, which implies that growth has occurred because the norm group is now a grade level higher.

Standard Error of Measurement

The **standard error of measurement** (SEM) is an estimate of how often errors of a given size in a student's score are expected. An SEM is closely related to reliability. A low SEM indicates high reliability, while a high SEM indicates low reliability.

Confidence Interval

A **confidence interval** is the range of scores in which a true score will fall within a given probability. For example, a confidence interval of 68 percent is 1 standard deviation (SD). The percentage that falls between −1 SD and +1 SD is 68 percent.

Figure 2–8   Group Test Profile

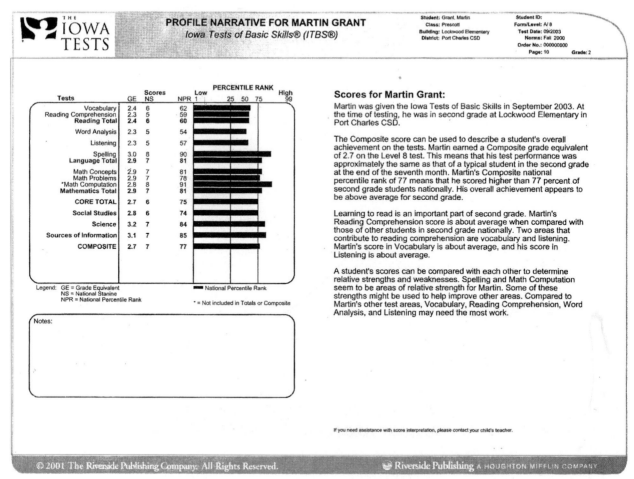

Grade and Age Equivalent Score

A **grade equivalent** (GE) or an **age equivalent** (AE) score is a description of a student's performance in terms of the grade/age levels, expressed in years and tenths of years, in the norming sample at which the average score is the same as the subject's score. Although grade- and age-equivalent scores may appear to be useful for reporting purposes (since they are easily understood by students and parents), these results can be misleading and should be used prudently. The overall grade or age equivalency may not be an accurate indicator of the student's performance and therefore is not useful for instructional planning (Linn & Gronlund, 2000; McLoughlin & Lewis, 2005; Nitko, 2001). These scores can be very misleading and lead to inaccurate generalizations. Their units are not equal; their reliability decreases as age increases; they are not compatible from test to test; they cannot be averaged; they may not indicate skill development; and they often just estimate age and grade scores (Venn, 2004).

Grade-and age-equivalent scores are most meaningful when the test students have taken is at the right level and the score is not more than a year above or below average. The Standards for Educational and Psychological Testing has been advocating that age and grade scores not be reported because their inadequate statistical properties often result in mislead interpretations (American Psychological Association, 1999). More than a decade ago, the American Psychological Association (1992) began encouraging publishers of standardized tests to stop reporting test scores as age or grade equivalencies.

Grade and/or age scores may cause interpretive problems in tests that are composed mostly of items with a limited range of difficulty. For example, a grade 2 student who earns a reading comprehension grade equivalent score of 5.5 is reading like a fifth grader in the fifth month of school; in other words, the student correctly answered a high percentage of the reading comprehension questions on a second-grade test, or the same percentage of questions that an average fifth-grade student would answer. However, the score does not mean that the student is reading at the fifth-grade level. In this case, it is more a reflection of the student's accuracy level than of the grade level of task difficulty that this student can perform. However, on an informal test (such as a reading inventory), a grade-level score does mean that the second grader is able to read fifth-grade-level material successfully.

Classroom Scenario

You are reviewing test scores for Annie, the 9-year, 4-month-old student you referred to the IEP multidisciplinary team for testing. Annie has been having significant difficulty understanding what she is reading. She was administered the Woodcock-Johnson III Tests of Achievement in the middle of grade 4. Her basic reading score, shown in Figure 2–6, indicates that she is functioning at her expected age level, and her profile indicates that she has particular strength when required to read words in isolation (letter-word identification) and apply phonic and structural analysis skills to pronounce unfamiliar words (word attack). However, considerable weaknesses are evident in her ability to read in context and comprehend what she is reading (passage comprehension). Annie's math reasoning ability is average for her age, although a significant discrepancy exists between the subtests in math. She demonstrates average calculation skills, indicating that she can solve individual math equations well, yet her ability to solve applied problems is below the math problem-solving skills of typical 9-year-old students. Testing indicates that although her academic skills (calculations and spelling) are superior, her ability to apply these skills (applied problems and writing samples) is below average. Annie's academic knowledge in the content area subjects is below average, which suggests a lack of prior knowledge needed to build a strong learning foundation. Annie's scores indicate that she is functioning within the average range in basic reading and math reasoning skills. Although these average scores suggest that she is not having academic difficulties, closer scrutiny shows that her overall scores do not tell the whole picture. Her parents note that their daughter's overall reading and math skills are average. How do you explain the score discrepancies to her parents?

Figure 2–9   Sample Terra Nova

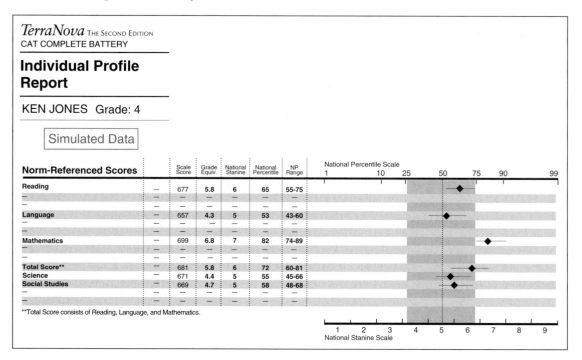

Source: CIB-5/McGraw Hill (1992) *Terra Nova* (2nd ed.) Monterey CA. Author.
Reprinted with permission of CTB/McGraw-Hill.

Critical Thinking and Reflection Activity

As you review the Terra Nova individual Profile Report results of your grade 4 students, you note that one student scored within the average-to-above-average range in all areas. Who is this student? What academic area is a particular strength for this student? (See Figure 2–9.)

SECTION 5: TECHNOLOGY— COMPUTERIZED ASSESSMENTS

As computer technology has become more commonly available in schools, teachers are using technology-based assessments to evaluate student progress. Advances in technology have provided teachers with more efficient and effective means of test development, administration, scoring, and interpretation.

Types of Assistive Technologies

There are two types of assistive technologies: technological or nontechnological. Technological devices include alternative keyboards, scanners, and speech synthesizers. Nontechnological devices include pencil grips, eyeglasses, timers, calculators, and tape recorders.

In choosing the appropriate assistive technology device to use when evaluating students, the following factors should be considered: (a) setting demands and expectations, (b) student abilities needed to address the test setting and administration demands, (c) students' functioning strengths and weaknesses, and (d) the most appropriate device among the available options. It is important to remember that the selection of assistive technology is an ongoing process because students and situations change (Rivera & Smith, 1997).

Technology-based testing allows educators to modify the presentation and response modes of items in order to tailor exams to the needs of individual students. Teachers can design, develop, administer, and score tests according to a student's individual special needs. This type of testing is especially useful for students who are linguistically diverse, because actual test questions and the interaction regarding procedures and directions can be spoken in a student's preferred language. Likely, the most commonly used form of technical assistive technology is the computer system.

Pros and Cons of Using Technology in Assessments

There are benefits and limitations to using computer technology in assessments. Among the benefits, technological devices enable assessment to be faster to administer, to be administered within a more flexible time schedule, to have more types of items available through the use of graphics and videos, and to be scored more efficiently so results that can be immediately available (Heiman, 1999).

There are also limitations in using computer technology for assessment: students are unable to use common test-taking strategies (e.g., underlining text, scratching out choices); computer screens tend to take longer to read than printed material; detecting errors on computer screens is more difficult than in printed material; a limited amount of information can be viewed on the computer; test bias may be increased (e.g., poorer areas may have limited or no computer access at home or at school); there is a clear advantage for fast typists; and tests administered on a computer might cost twice as much as printed tests (Heiman, 1999).

Assessment Computer Systems

A complete computer system can encompass item banking, item analysis, test printing, test scoring, statistical analysis, and the maintenance of student records. These computerized systems can be programmed to individual student's ability and achievement levels. Item banking is an efficient method of maintaining and retrieving test items as needed. Test questions can be coded by instructional level, instructional objectives, subject area, and so forth. Software products or teacher-made computerized assessment programs can be adapted or custom designed to meet students' needs and then matched to their IEPs. Student IEPs can be arranged and printed according to individual goals and instructional objectives and listed in a task-analysis format with items presented in order of increasing difficulty (Smith & Kortering, 1996). These programs can be tailored to add, delete, and modify test items so that questions can be adjusted (i.e., made easier or more difficult depending on how the student responds to the previous question). Test items that are too easy or too difficult can be eliminated. Tests can be set up so that those items that the student answers incorrectly on one test can be repeated or modified on subsequent tests.

This personalized test programming can be used to monitor skill mastery and long-term retrieval, thus identifying skills that need to be retaught or reviewed. Tests can be scored, statistically analyzed, and arranged in a variety of ways (e.g., designed according to percentage correct, grade equivalency) to provide reliable performance information. Students' records can be stored and retrieved as needed. This record maintenance can be especially useful for monitoring progress toward IEP goals and instructional objective mastery (Gronlund, 1998).

Technology has certain unique capabilities that provide for the creation of workable and meaningful forms of alternative assessment. Student presentations, explanations, interviews, demonstrations of thinking, and problem-solving processes can now be collected using technology (Bank Street College of Education, 1992). Computer and video recording provide expanded potential for collecting and storing student work samples. A variety of media—including text, graphics, video, and multimedia—are used by many educators and school districts to evaluate the progress of students (Greenwood & Rieth, 1994). Advances in multimedia are giving educators the technology to integrate tests, graphics, audio, and video into student assessment through the use of CD-ROM, videodiscs, sound cards, and virtual reality. With these technologies teachers have the means to monitor and evaluate students' responses to authentic situations, and students have opportunities to use and develop their critical thinking and metacognitive skills (Lawrence, 1994).

Packaged computer software programs are available in a variety of formats for informal assessment, including direct observation, entry of anecdotal information, checklists, and reports from teachers, students, and parents. Curriculum-based assessment (CBA) programs, which involve frequent collection of student performance data, can provide the teacher, student, and parent with regular feedback, reports, and graphics on student progress. Many standardized tests (e.g., the Wechsler scales and the Woodcock-Johnson III) have computerized supports that include diagnostic programs, interpretation of test results, management of test results and data, and report writing. Electronic portfolios—student folders that include a selection of work over time and the student's evaluation of the contents—are used increasingly in conjunction with authentic-based assessment to maintain and report student progress. Integrated software tools—such as word processors, databases, and spreadsheets—are used in electronic portfolio assessment. These tools allow students to express their work by scanned images; graphically with illustrations, tables, and charts; and in typed versions, audio recordings, and video clips. Some teachers include video footage of class activities, student presentations, and student-teacher conferences in electronic portfolios (Male, 2003). With the heightened emphasis and promotion of technology in the schools, the growing numbers of computers and the availability of adaptable software programs, computer-assisted and computer-adaptive testing should play an increasingly prominent role in student assessment.

SECTION 6: WRITING AND REPORTING TEST RESULTS

Writing Test Reports

Writing the test results in a comprehensive, direct style is an important component in the reporting process. Although a verbal interpretation is generally provided in eligibility and progress review conferences, a written report is required for record keeping, and it provides details and documentation that can reviewed and digested after the conference. It is important to be thorough and provide explicit examples of both strengths and areas in need of remediation, phrased in clear, behavioral terms. Reports should be written in common language, without educational or psychological jargon. When complex or professional terminology must be used, clear definitions should be provided both orally and in written form. (See Figure 2–10 for a list of positive statements that can be used to constructively reframe problem areas.)

Although psychoeducational written reports may differ in format and form, the basic content is generally very similar. (A sample format is provided in Figure 2–11.)

Reporting Test Results

An important skill for teachers is being able to interpret test results for parents and other professional staff. The goal is to inform; that is, to provide a review of the student's specific strengths and weaknesses in a comprehensive, understandable, and compassionate manner. Parents and professionals should leave the meeting feeling that they understand the child's academic status rather than feeling confused and that they were bombarded with jargon and meaningless statistics.

Reporting Assessment Results to Parents: Key Concepts

1. Be considerate of the fact that hearing assessment results can be very disturbing to parents. Be sensitive to what you say and how you say it, especially how you phrase negative information. When stressed, parents can "read" the intent underlying your words more than the words themselves.
2. Encourage both parents to attend the conference. If this is not possible, and in the case of single parents, suggest that the parent bring another family member or friend who can add support as well as additional ears.
3. Start the conference by reviewing the reason for the referral. Explain the testing process, the tests administered, how the information will be used, and how the parents will be contributing to the decision-making process.

Figure 2–10   Positive Statements for Parent Reporting

Positive Statements for Reporting to Parents	
Uncoordinated, clumsy	needs to improve fine/gross motor control; increase coordination
Steals	needs to respect other's belongings
Inattentive	needs to be more focused, improve his concentration
Rude	needs to be more respectful of others
Doesn't follow rules	needs to conform to regulations
Talks excessively	needs to improve listening skills and socialize less in class
Lazy	needs to put forth more effort
Bully	needs to interact more cooperatively with peers

Figure 2–11 Sample Assessment Report Format

ASSESSMENT REPORT

1. Identifying Data

Name

Age and Grade

2. Referral Information

A clear statement of the reason for the referral; the areas identified as the target problems.

3. Background Information

Family History: include primary language if not English, history of disability, family composition, etc.; include in narrative form general information you have obtained from the parent interview and child interview: information about family (e.g., number of children in family, history of medical, social, school adjustment problems, peer relationships, community involvements). Parents are generally the best sources for this information.

Education History: include general information about past school history attendance, group tests, report cards, disciplinary record, academic performance, classification, learning problems, referral to the prereferral team, retention, frequent moves, and any information that is relevant to the student's performance. This information is generally available in the student's cumulative or confidential files. The present and previous classroom teachers generally can provide important information.

Student Observation and Interview: include information obtained during the classroom observation and, if applicable, during observations in unstructured school settings. Student work samples/word products should be analyzed and included in the assessment interpretation. A student interview is often a critical component and can provide insights into the child's feelings and perspectives.

Test Behavior: describe observations of the student during the test administration, including the student's reaction to the testing situation: rapport development with examiner, degree of cooperation demonstrated, and degree of anxiety evidenced. Be sure to include a specific description of behavior that would support your observation; in other words, provide examples.

4. Methods of Assessment

List all assessment instruments and methods (formal and informal) used in the assessment process.

5. Test Results

Provide a summary of the data from each test, organized by domain areas, such as (a) academic, (b) social, (c) motor skills. Include test results and interpretation; standard scores and percentiles in all academic skills that were assessed. Be sure to include areas of strength along with content and skills that need to be the focus of remedial instruction.

6. Evaluation Summary

This section is a paragraph (or more) that summarizes the information from all other sections of this report. This summary should include the student's instructional levels as well as strengths and weakness in each academic subject area. Another paragraph should include important information about the student, such as learning style, emotional-social adjustment, medical issues (medication, visual/auditory acuity), communication issues, cultural issues. This statement can generally serve as the student's present level of academic achievement and functional performance statement (as required for the IEP).

7. Recommendations

This section should be written in a constructive, positively framed manner, suggesting what the child can do and what needs to be accomplished for improvement.

4. Take the time needed to be clear and answer questions. This can reduce or eliminate future family/school discord.
5. Begin the discussion by highlighting the student's strengths. This sets a more positive tone and helps parents to be better able to hear the less positive information if they feel that you recognize their child has value.
6. Be aware of your body language; lean forward; if possible, sit side-by-side rather than behind a desk, which can appear foreboding or distancing. Be aware of and sensitive to cultural differences.
7. Avoid delivering disturbing diagnostic news at IEP meetings attended by large numbers of people, or in meetings of which the parent(s) are expected to choose programs, develop goals and objectives, or plan for the future of their child.
8. Be prepared: Have examples, graphs and charts, anything that can make your presentation of assessment results clearer and more explicit. Use descriptive, nonjudgmental language, as well as specific examples or visuals to help parents understand statistical terms (e.g., standard scores, percentiles, stanines).
9. Be sure to explain terms that are not familiar to parents. Avoid education jargon.
10. Use first-person language throughout the session. Also, rather than say "learning disabled child," say "child with a learning disability." This distinction is important. Learning disabilities is one descriptor for the child but does not in any way totally define the child. Teachers and parents can and should be very sensitive to this issue.
11. Use active listening skills. Really hear what the parent is asking. This often requires attending to nonverbal communication, such as facial expressions, shrugs, and eye contact. Don't overreact or become defensive if parents respond with grief, denial, shock, anger, or guilt. Be honest, clear, and supportive.
12. Be very careful to keep all assessment results and information shared at meeting confidential. Do not discuss or compare other children.
13. Encourage parents to ask questions. End the conference with a summary of the discussion, a clear understanding of what will occur next, and scheduled dates for follow-up discussions.

SUMMARY POINTS

- Formal or standardized assessments compare a student's performance with similar age or grade-level peers and are data-driven, mathematically computed, and summarized. Informal or nonstandardized assessments describe performance and inform instruction and are content and performance driven.
- Standardized tests are administered, scored, and interpreted according to specific standards, meaning that the tests must be administered following certain criteria, ensuring that all students take the tests using exactly the same administration and scoring procedures to ensure validity and reliability.
- The primary criteria for judging the integrity of formal tests are (a) standardization (on what group was the test standardized?); (b) reliability (are test results consistent?); and (c) validity (does the test measure what it claims to measure?).

- National norm samples are generally based on national statistics, such as census data, including representational samples of students from various geographic regions nationwide; urban and rural schools of different sizes; and a balance of sexes, socioeconomic levels, and ethnic backgrounds.

- Teachers need to be familiar with how test (score) results are calculated and what the test scores mean. Commonly used scoring criteria include standard scores, percentiles, stanines, grade/age equivalencies, and standard error of measurement.

- A written report should provide details and documentation that can be reviewed and digested after the conference. In addition, it should be thorough, and provide explicit examples of both strengths and areas in need of remediation. The report should be phrased in clear, behavioral terms, and in language free of educational or psychological jargon, with definitions provided when professional terminology must be used.

Chapter Check-Ups

1. In discussing test options with the parents of a newly referred child, how would you describe the differences between formal and informal assessment and the pros and cons of each?

2. Describe to a new colleague the important considerations when administering a standardized assessment.

3. Why is test behavior an important component to consider in the testing process? What are some of the significant differences you might note during an observation of the child during the individually administered testing session and an observation during typical classroom activities?

4. How would you explain the various standardized test scoring criteria to a parent (e.g., standard scores, percentiles, stanines, grade and age equivalencies)? How would you explain a discrepancy between local and national percentiles?

5. Describe a scenario in which the use of technology would be beneficial when testing a student and a scenario in which technology might not be advantageous.

Practical Application Assessment Activities

1. Review a commercially available standardized test. Does it measure the skills and behaviors it is supposed to measure? Is it valid and reliable? Are directions for administration clear and easy to understand? Could you interpret the results for a parent or another professional?

2. Interview a teacher(s) in your community school district. Questions to be asked should include (a) what tests and assessment measures are commonly used in their schools to determine eligibility for classification, (b) what tests are used to monitor students' progress, (c) whether the same test instruments are used for all students during eligibility test and for IEP progress monitoring, (d) how these tests are used to develop individual students' IEPs, and (e) what individual and group tests are mandated by the district, county or state for all students.

3. Compare and contrast four types of derived scores: standard scores, stanines, percentile ranks, and grade or age equivalents. Then, (a) reflect on how each would be used by a classroom teacher, (b) draw an illustration of a child's test score profile to help with clarification during a parent-teacher conference, and (c) with a

partner, take turns role playing the parent and teacher in a progress reporting conference explaining these scores and providing relevant examples.

4. Work in pairs or small groups to review the section pertaining to the standardization sample of three norm-referenced test manuals. Each group will (a) compare and contrast the tests' reliability and validity, (b) determine how closely the norm sample of each test correlates with the student population of your local school district and neighboring districts; and (c) discuss the conclusions that can be drawn from this information.

Connection Between CEC, PRAXIS, and INTASC Standards and Chapter 2

The Council for Exceptional Children—Professional Standards

Council for Exceptional Children
The voice and vision of special education

Standard 1 Foundations

5. Issues in definition and identification of individuals with exceptional learning needs, including those from culturally and linguistically diverse backgrounds.

Standard 5 Learning Environments and Social Interactions

17. Establish and maintain rapport with individuals with and without exceptional learning needs.

Standard 6 Communication

3. Ways of behaving and communicating among cultures that can lead to misinterpretations and misunderstanding.
5. Use strategies to support and enhance communication skills of individuals with exceptional learning needs.
6. Use communication strategies and resources to facilitate understanding of subject matter for students whose primary language is not the dominant language.

Standard 8 Assessment

1. Basic terminology used in assessment.
2. Legal provisions and ethical principles regarding assessment of individuals.
3. Screening, pre-referral, referral, and classification procedures.
4. Use and limitations of assessment instruments.
5. National, state or provincial, and local accommodations and modifications.
6. Gather relevant background information.
7. Administer nonbiased formal and informal assessments.
8. Use technology to conduct assessments.
9. Develop or modify individualized assessment strategies.
10. Interpret information from formal and informal assessments.
11. Use assessment information in making eligibility, program, and placement decisions for individuals with exceptional learning needs, including those from culturally and/or linguistically diverse backgrounds.
12. Report assessment result to all stakeholders using effective communication skills.

13. Evaluate instruction and monitor progress of individuals with exceptional learning needs.
14. Create and maintain records.

Standard 9 Professional and Ethical Practice

4. Methods to remain current regarding research-validated practice.
5. Practice within the CEC Code of Ethics and other standards of the profession.
6. Uphold high standards of competence and integrity and exercise sound judgment in the practice of the professional.
8. Conduct professional activities in compliance with applicable laws and policies.
11. Practice within one's skill limit and obtain assistance as needed.
12. Use verbal, nonverbal, and written language effectively.
14. Access information on exceptionalities.
15. Reflect on one's practice to improve instruction and guide professional growth.
16. Engage in professional activities that benefit individuals with exceptional learning needs, their families and one's colleagues.

Standard 10 Collaboration

1. Models and strategies of consultation and collaboration.
2. Roles of individuals with exceptional learning needs, families, and school and community personnel in planning of an individualized program.
3. Concerns of families of individuals with exceptional learning needs and strategies to help address these concerns.
4. Culturally responsive factors that promote effective communication and collaboration with individuals with exceptional learning needs, families, school personnel, and community members.
5. Maintain confidential communication about individuals with exceptional learning needs.
6. Collaborate with families and others in assessment of individuals with exceptional learning needs.
7. Foster respectful and beneficial relationships between families and professionals.
8. Assist individuals with exceptional learning needs and their families in becoming active participants in the educational team.
9. Plan and conduct collaborative conferences with individuals with exceptional learning needs and their families.
13. Communicate with school personnel about the characteristics and needs of individuals.
14. Communicate effectively with families of individuals with exceptional learning needs from diverse backgrounds.

THE PRAXIS SERIES™ **PRAXIS Standards for Special Education**

Standard 1 Understanding Exceptionalities

3. Basic concepts in special education, including definitions of all major categories and specific disabilities; causation and prevention of disability; the nature of behaviors, including frequency, duration, intensity, and degrees of severity; and

classification of students with disabilities, including classifications as represented in IDEA and labeling of students.

Standard 2 Legal and Societal Issues

1. Federal laws and landmark legal cases related to special education.

Standard 3 Delivery of Services to Students with Disabilities

3. Assessment, including how to modify, construct, or select and conduct nondiscriminatory and appropriate informal and formal assessment procedures; how to interpret standardized and specialized assessment results; how to use evaluation result for various purposes, including monitoring instruction and IEP/ITP development; and how to prepare written reports and communicate findings to others.

INTASC Standards for Teacher Education

Standard 8

The teacher understands and uses formal and informal assessment strategies to evaluate and ensure the continuous intellectual, social, and physical development of the learner.

Standard 9

The teacher is a reflective practitioner who continually evaluates the effects of his/her choices and actions on others (students, parents, and other professionals in the learning community) and who actively seeks out opportunities to grow professionally.

Standard 10

The teacher fosters relationships with school colleagues, parents, and agencies in the larger community to support students' learning and well-being.

CHAPTER 3

Informal Assessment

Selecting, Scoring, Reporting

KEY TERMS AND CONCEPTS

- formal assessment
- informal assessment
- authentic assessments
- criterion-referenced assessments
- task analysis
- dynamic assessments
- curriculum-based evaluation (CBE)
- curriculum-based assessments (CBAs)
- curriculum-based measurements (CBMs)
- probe
- performance assessments
- portfolio assessments
- informal inventories
- functional/adaptive assessments
- response journals, or learning logs
- think-aloud technique
- questionnaire
- interview

- observations
- checklists
- work-sample analyses
- error analyses
- self-evaluations
- peer evaluations
- rubric
- analytical rubric
- holistic rubric
- general rubrics
- specific rubrics
- rating scale
- anchor papers
- interrater reliability
- dimension
- definitions or examples
- scale
- standards

CHAPTER OBJECTIVES

After reading this chapter, you should be able to:

- Describe the types of authentic assessments.
- Identify task analysis and dynamic assessment.
- Define a curriculum-based probe and describe its usefulness.
- Describe why and how graphs are used for charting progress.

- Compare and contrast the use of questionnaires versus interviews.
- Explain the difference between holistic and analytic rubrics.

Introduction to Informal Assessments

The purpose of classroom assessments is to inform, to provide critical information for the identification or eligibility decision-making process, and to provide key diagnostic information for programming and instructional decision making. Formal (standardized) assessments have traditionally been used to establish eligibility and qualification, as well as to determine who should be classified, who requires remedial or special education services, and how students rank or compare with their peers. Although formal tests serve a purpose and have value, as described in Chapter 2, this chapter focuses on the types, uses, and benefits of informal, or nonstandardized, assessment procedures.

INFORMAL VS. FORMAL

The use of standardized assessments has often been criticized in recent years for its failure to integrate evaluation and instruction. Teachers know that students are learning, yet the use of standardized assessments does not seem to facilitate learning or provide a good indicator of what was learned. The dissatisfaction and controversy over traditional procedures have led the reform movement in education to focus on changing assessments so that they are more fully integrated with teaching and thus provide more meaningful information about student learning and achievement. The criticisms of traditional, standardized test measures include the point that they may not be technically adequate or measure the curriculum being taught. This type of assessment is generally insensitive to small performance changes—since it is often used as pre- and post-testing—so that administration tends to be too infrequent to measure progress. A good norm-referenced, standardized test measures about 40 percent of what is taught in the classroom, yet most norm-referenced tests sample only 20 to 30 percent of what is taught (Council for Exceptional Children, 2000). Also, standardized tests emphasize discrete facts and factual knowledge; the forced selection of one correct answer rather than the option of multiple possibilities; the requirement for short, specific answers; and the requirement that students work independently and individually (U.S. Congress Office of Technology, 1992; Linn, Baker, & Dunbar, 1991).

Research has documented the effects that standardized testing can have on teaching, the curriculum, and the status of teachers. Studies have shown that teachers tend to base instruction on the content and form of tests (e.g., teaching to the test), especially when accountability issues are involved (Council for Exceptional Children, 2000; Elliott, Ysseldyke, Thurlow, & Erickson, 1998). The curriculum is often narrowed and fragmented when teachers rely on multiple-choice and true-false test formats. Too much time is spent on mastering facts and basic concepts while the application of knowledge and skills is downplayed (Witt, Elliott, Daly, Gresham, & Kramer, 1998). Frequently, much time is spent preparing students for a particular test, and other aspects of curricular importance may not get the time and attention they deserve. Others point out that standardized tests are only a proxy method of determining how well students can perform tasks. For example, writing skills are evaluated by asking questions about punctuation rather than by having students write a story, a letter, and so forth (Marlarz, D'Arcangelo, & Kiernan, 1991).

Standardized tests are typically used to measure relative standing within a group rather than an individual student's learning. Another criticism is that standardized administration and scoring procedures may impact the performance of students with

CLARIFYING TERMS:

Formal vs. Informal Assessment

Formal assessment is objective and usually involves setting a special time, using preplanned procedures (described in a test manual), using predetermined space or equipment, and recording scores.

Informal assessment is subjective and may be administered and scored under any conditions that are conducive to obtaining the information required.

exceptional learning needs and are innately unfair to students with diverse cultural backgrounds and learning styles (Puckett & Black, 2000). Research on learning supports the fact that students learn best when they are actively involved in assessing their own work rather than being passive recipients of test results (Marlarz, et al., 1991). Informal assessments—generally, the nonstandardized and unnormed evaluation procedures—provide the most useful, practical information; that is, the data that help teachers understand the student's learning process rather than just the learning product (outcome).

Features that distinguish the authentic forms of testing from the more traditional standardized assessments include production rather than recognition responses, assessment projects rather than test items, and teacher judgment rather than mechanical scoring. (See Figure 3–1.) Also, informal assessments provide more of the diagnostic information needed to develop individualized education plan (IEP) goals than do standardized or criterion-assessments, which can be demonstrated as follows:

Norm-referenced: Student scores at mid grade 4 level in math.
Criterion-referenced: Student computes whole numbers with regrouping.
Curriculum-based: Student writes correct answers to four-digit addition
                          and subtraction, with regrouping at a rate of 85 correct
                          digits per minute (King-Sears, 1998, p. 13).

The primary goal of assessments should be to enhance learning rather than simply to document learning. Too often, assessment is used solely to determine a student's grade. The informal assessment model is more practical and expedient for the teacher and more formative in nature, placing teachers' professional judgments at the center of the process (National Association for Sport & Physical Education, 1995, p. vii).

Informal assessments evaluate students' knowledge and mastery of skills that tend to change over relatively short periods of time, help teachers understand the process rather than just the product, and provide a direct linkage between evaluation and instruction. They directly measure how students perform in relation to their own abilities. According to Hallahan and Kauffman (2000), the five common features of informal assessment are that the teacher

1. Is the test administrator rather than a clinician, such as a psychologist.
2. Assesses the student directly in the classroom, with emphasis on the student's strengths (what the student knows), rather than weaknesses (what the student doesn't know), and focusing on behaviors that may affect learning and whether personal and/or environmental factors may be inhibiting classroom adjustment and/or success.
3. Observes and records the student's behavior often and on a regular basis (typically several times a week).
4. Focuses on documenting individual student growth over time (rather than comparing students with one another) and relies on this type of assessment to develop educational goals for the student to master within a designated time period.
5. Uses this type of assessment to consider the student's learning style, language proficiency, cultural and educational background, and social-emotional adjustment; to monitor the effectiveness of the instructional program in order to make curricular modifications and adjustments in teaching strategies; to ascertain program efficacy; and/or to reevaluate goals, as needed.

Figure 3–1   Differences and Similarities Between Formal and Informal Assessment

Formal Assessment	vs.	**Informal Assessment**
• standardized (e.g., multiple choice)		• non-standardized (e.g., performance, portfolio)
• given annually, one shot		• ongoing, cumulative
• based in a single setting		• based in a variety of settings
• one correct response		• open-ended, multiple possibilities
• norm-referenced		• student-centered, criterion-referenced
• test/teacher-driven		• student-driven
• "teacher proof"		• teacher-mediated
• paper/pencil		• performance
• narrow measure of skill		• real-world, integrated application that measures capacity for constructing and using knowledge
• separate from curriculum/instruction		• integral to curriculum/instruction
• drives goal selection		• supports goals
• comparisons to others		• comparisons to self and goals
• produces undesirable anxiety		• produces confidence in ability to self-assess/correct
• involves short-term memory		• involves long-term memory
• little connection to real life		• real-world applications
• not a valid predictor of performance		• measures applications in context in a real world
• not valued by students		• allows students to see usefulness of learning
• summative measure		• formative and summative measures
• passive learners		• active learners
• reduces teacher decision-making potential		• requires local control and design of teachers
• disrupts flow of classroom practices for teaching and learning		• becomes part of instruction and the learning process
• conducted in isolation		• often a collaborative effort with peer cooperation and peer evaluation for collaborative reflection
• concerned with knowing		• concerned with the process of learning
• tracks or labels		• brings about student improvement
• relies on grades for feedback		• provides continuous feedback; chronicles progress through multiple sources of evidence

Similarities Between Formal and Informal Assessment

- measure of student learning and achievement
- progress charts
- accountability measures
- can be used to adjust and improve instruction
- provide feedback on learning
- evaluate teachers and schools
- compare student performances

Source: Appalachia Educational Laboratory (1999). *On target with authentic assessment; Creating and implementing classroom models.* (AEL school excellence workshop). Charleston, WV: Author. Used with permission.

Classroom Scenario: What Would You Do?

Knowing that Joey, a beginning second-grader, is functioning at the beginning first-grade-level and has a national percentile ranking of 5 does not help you, his teacher, with instructional planning. You do not know whether he has developed phonemic awareness, whether sound-symbol recognition has emerged, whether he has mastered one-to-one correspondence, or whether he can write letters and numerals. What would you do?

SECTION 1: TYPES OF ACHIEVEMENT ASSESSMENT MEASURES

Informal (Nontraditional) Assessments

Informal tests are prepared by classroom teachers for a particular subject and under specific conditions that can be modified or adjusted to meet students' needs and teachers' purposes. There is no standardized format or procedure for administration. These evaluation measures can be objective or subjective, essay, short answer, multiple choice, demonstration, and so forth. They can be individually administered or administered in a large group. The scoring and grading procedures can be adjusted according to class norms, the test purpose, and/or the teachers' goals and objectives. Informal assessment measures directly link students' performance with the school curriculum. Although informal assessments can be challenging, students often prefer

Teacher observation of a student applying learned skills in practical situations is an example of performance assessment.

this type of assessment because it is realistic, engaging, and, most importantly, does not involve the "one-shot terrorism of the traditional test" (Reeves, 1998).

Informal assessment measures provide the means to evaluate students' ability to reason creatively and productively, to react to new situations, to review and revise their work, to evaluate their own and others' work, and to communicate in verbal and visual ways. This section discusses guidelines and terms used in administering, scoring, and interpreting informal assessment methods. (See Figures 3–2 and 3–3.)

Authentic Assessments

Authentic assessments are based on the application of knowledge and the use of meaningful, complex, relevant skills to produce products or simulate real-life activities in real-world settings rather than in artificial or contrived settings. (See Figure 3–4.) They can be administered within the context of instruction and easily incorporated into daily activities. Authentic assessments can be real or perceived, the more real-life, the more authentic. These diagnostic assessments include teacher-made tests, performance-based assessments, portfolio assessments, curriculum-based assessments, criterion-referenced tests, skill inventories, daily observations, analyses of work samples, and student interviews. (See Figure 3–5 for strategies for implementing authentic assessments.)

The contexts for authentic assessments are students' natural environment (e.g., the classroom, playground, and gymnasium). They occur during typically routine activities (e.g., cooperative group activities; activities in learning centers; large-group discussions; social interactions on the playground, in the cafeteria, and in the auditorium; and dramatic play activities), and in creative settings (e.g., in art and music classes).

Critical Thinking and Reflection Activity

Oliver Wendell Holmes once said, "One's mind, once stretched by a new idea, never regains its original dimensions." Reflect on how his statement might relate to authentic assessments.

Figure 3–2   Questions to Ask When Developing Informal Assessments

- Be very clear about WHAT is being assessed. (Is it worth learning and demonstrating?)
- Know WHY you are assessing. (What will you do with the information? Is it feedback for students, parents, your instruction, about the program?)
- Remember that an assessment is MORE than grading. Assessments should demonstrate what students know or are able to do. Assessments can "show off" learning in your program.
- SHARE the information with students, administrators, other teachers, and parents, as appropriate. (This will lend credibility to your program.)
- Start SMALL with your most cooperative group, one group, one class, one grade level, or a few students.
- Be CLEAR about the criteria, such as rubric standards or exemplary models for making judgments.
- Allow students IN on the process. Using your criteria they can evaluate themselves, their partner, or others. Allow students some choices in how they want to be assessed—including the criteria for each assessment (PE Central, 2004).

Figure 3—3   How to Develop an Assessment Task

1. **Start with an idea.**
   - From a textbook or other book
   - From a newspaper, magazine, trade journal, almanac, or catalog
   - From a conversation
   - From life
   - From a random thought
   - From a divine inspiration
2. **Test the idea.**
   - Does it meet the criteria?
   - Is it important in your locale?
   - Does it have a context your students will understand?
3. **Begin converting the idea.**
   a. Define your objectives.
      Where does it fit in the curriculum?
      What can it tell you about students?
      What will students have to know?
   b. Draft a plan.
      Describe the task.
      State purpose and objectives.
      Write directions for the students.
      Include non-directive questions that might nudge students to find needed strategies.
   c. Give the student information on evaluation criteria.
4. **Consider response formats.**
   - Written exercises or reports
   - Oral reports or performances
   - Group discussions and activities
   - Bulletin-board displays
5. **Develop teacher notes.**
   - Where the task fits into the curriculum
   - What students need to know ahead of time
   - What materials and equipment are needed
   - What problems may arise
   - What amount and kind of guidance a teacher should or should not provide and its relationship to rating.
6. **Draft an assessment approach.**
   - Decide on a holistic approach with anecdotal reports, or an analytic point system.
   - Look for assessment of processes, products, or both.
   - Consider attitudes and attributes you hope to see, such as group cooperation, persistence and resourcefulness.
   - Identify what is most important to assess, and whether "scores" should be weighted accordingly.
   - Define level of performance.
   - Be prepared to make changes or adjustments after looking at student work.
7. **Try out the task.**
   - Have one or more colleagues review and critique.
   - Administer the task in a few classrooms.
       Get feedback from students.
       Take detailed notes on what you see and what students say.
   - Decide on appropriate changes or new tasks.
8. **Revise where necessary.**
   - The task itself
   - The teacher notes
   - The assessment system

Source: Reprinted from *Mathematics Assessments: Myths, Models, Good Questions, and Practical Suggestions* by National Council of Teachers of Mathematics, 1996. All rights reserved.

Figure 3–4   Techniques for Developing Authentic Assessment Activities

1. **Group activities** encourage students to work together to develop a plan, carry it out, and communicate their findings to others.
2. **Logs and journals** provide an opportunity to brainstorm, to question, or to reflect on a problem.
3. **Non-routine problems** involve creative problem solving, critical thinking, and an innovative approach to the synthesis of ideas.
4. **Open-ended questions** probe students' ability to confront an unusual situation by applying a collection of strategies and ideas. These problems have a variety of correct responses.
5. **Student-generated questions** are formulated and written for other students and the teacher to solve.
6. **Performance tasks** consist of real-world problems that employ useful, meaningful applications for students to tackle.
7. **Portfolios** are collections of student work over time used to demonstrate overall improvement.
8. **Presentations,** single or group, explain ideas and information to others.
9. **Research projects** require students to find information not readily available in the classroom and to draw their own conclusions about implications.

Source: Appalachia Educational Laboratory (1993). *Alternative assessments in math and science: Moving toward a moving target.* Charleston, WV: Author. Used with permission.

Examples of authentic assessment tasks include open-ended questions, essays, hands-on science labs, computer simulations, and portfolio collections. This type of assessment capitalizes on the students' strengths and emerging development, focusing on purposeful learning experiences in a variety of contexts. Authentic assessments stimulate students to think, react to new situations, review and revise work, evaluate their own and others' work, and communicate results in verbal and visual ways. (See Figure 3–6.) Authentic assessments consist of tasks that require students to apply their knowledge in real-world situations, given specific performance criteria, and use a scoring rubric to evaluate the performance.

For today's students to succeed in tomorrow's workplace, they will need to be proficient in solving problems, thinking critically, working cooperatively as team members, and communicating effectively in written and oral formats. Authentic assessments measure the skills needed to become competent workers of the 21st century, requiring students to demonstrate their ability to perform a task rather than recall facts and select answers from a list of multiple-choice options. (See Figure 3–7 for points to consider when constructing authentic assessments.)

Criterion-Referenced Assessments

Criterion-referenced assessments compare students' performance to a performance standard or criterion, rather than to the performance of other students (as do norm-referenced assessments).

> **Teacher:** On the norm-referenced test, Mary, one of my second-graders, received a national score of 30 percent in reading, which indicates that she scored higher than 30 of every 100 students nationwide.

Figure 3–5   Implementing Authentic Assessments

Recommendations for Implementation

1. **Start small.** Follow someone else's example in the beginning, or do one activity in combination with a traditional test.

2. **Develop clear rubrics.** Realize that developing an effective rubric is harder than carrying out the activity. Standards and expectations must be clear. Benchmarks for levels of performance are essential. Characteristics of typical student products and performances may be used to generate performance assessment rubrics and standards for the class.

3. **Expect to use more time at first.** Developing and evaluating alternative assessments and their rubrics require additional time until you and your students become comfortable with the method.

4. **Adapt existing curriculum.** Plan assessment as you plan instruction, not as an afterthought.

5. **Have a partner.** Sharing ideas and experiences with a colleague is beneficial to teachers and to students.

6. **Make a collection.** Look for examples of alternative assessment or activities that could be modified for your students, and keep a file readily accessible.

7. **Assign a high value (grade) to the assessment.** Students need to see the experience as being important and worth their time. Make expectations clear in advance.

8. **Expect to learn by trial and error.** Be willing to take risks and learn from mistakes, just as students are expected to do. The best assessments are developed over time, with repeated use.

9. **Try peer assessment activities.** Relieve yourself of some grading responsibilities and increase student evaluation skills and accountability by involving them in administering assessments.

10. **Don't give up.** If the first tries are not as successful as you had hoped, remember, this is new to the students, too. They can help you refine the process. Once you have tried an alternative assessment, reflect and evaluate the activities. Ask yourself some questions. What worked? What needs modification? What would I do differently? Would I use this activity again? How did the students respond? Did the end results justify the time spent? Did students learn from the activity?

Source: Appalachia Educational Laboratory (1993). *Alternative assessments in math and science: Moving toward a moving target.* Charleston, WV: Author. Used with permission.

Figure 3–6   Models of Authentic Assessment

- **Performance**—solving problems, conducting experiments, teaching a skill or concept
- **Product**—visual display, written/oral report, chart/graph/concept maps created according to specific criteria
- **Portfolio**—collection of representative work over time with self-evaluation and explanation, evidence of experiences and accomplishments, and some self-selection
- **Personal communication**—individual or team interviews; conferences with teachers, administrators, community members, parents, peers; allows delving and assessment of in-depth knowledge
- **Observation and anecdotal records**—direct observation of learning process, teacher-generated data, checklist, narrative, miscue analysis, running records, strategy analysis

---

Source: Appalachia Educational Laboratory (1994). *On target with authentic assessment: Creating and implementing classroom models* (AEL School excellence workshop). Charleston, WV: Author. Used with permission.

Figure 3–7   Factors to Consider When Developing Authentic Assessments

- Does the task truly match the outcome(s) you are trying to measure?
- Does the task require the students to use critical thinking skills?
- Is the task a worthwhile use of instructional time?
- Does the assessment use engaging tasks from the "real world"?
- Is the assessment efficient, measuring several outcomes at once?
- Are the tasks fair and unbiased?
- Will the task be credible and instructionally sound?
- Is the task feasible?
- Is the task clearly defined?

Source: Adapted from Herman, Aschbacher, & Winters (1992)

Criterion-referenced testing compares students' performance with a list of behavioral objectives in highly discrete skill areas rather than to other students of the same age or in the same grade.

> **Teacher:** Mary is not performing as well as her peers in reading. I need to do a criterion-referenced test to determine exactly what skills she needs to master so that a remedial program can be developed and monitored.

Criterion-referenced testing is based on a task analytic model that is used to examine the reason for deficits in a skill or concept by tracing the missing essential task component. This type of assessment can be standardized or nonstandardized and can be purchased through publishing companies or teachers can develop their own versions. Teacher-made criterion-referenced tests are generally based on the scope and sequence of the curriculum and are directly related to instructional programming. Any missed test items can subsequently be included in the students' instructional plan (Bender, 1998). By constructing their own test, teachers can be sure that relevant objectives and test items are incorporated in the instrument. Taylor (2003) suggests the following guidelines for developing a criterion-referenced test.

How to Construct a Criterion-Referenced Test

1. Identify the skills to be measured by analyzing the scope and sequence chart of the class curriculum to determine the skill hierarchy (task analysis) or, for a classified student, refer to the IEP objectives.
2. Identify the objectives that can be taken directly from the student's IEP. If sequential objectives are not available, a task analysis of the specific skills can be performed.
3. Develop the test items and materials. Keeping in mind skill hierarchy, each behavior required for a finite, easily manageable number of behaviors (e.g., counting from one to 20) can be included. When the task is more complex and the task analysis indicates that the number of behaviors is extensive, as many items as possible should be covered in sequential order. It is important that (a) the intended learning outcomes be stated in behavioral terms, (b) each item be relevant to an important learning outcome, and (c) there be enough items to allow for adequate interpretation of skill mastery.
4. Determine the standard of performance to use for evaluation. Although speed of completion can be used as a criterion measure, typically

accuracy—the percent of items correctly answered—is the evaluation standard. Often mastery of a skill is set at 90 percent of the items passed (e.g., the student will accurately calculate nine out of 10 single-addition equations with sums to 10).

How to Administer a Criterion-Referenced Test   Before administering the test, the student should be told the (a) purpose of the test, (b) time limits (if any), (c) test conditions (e.g., "you need to show your calculations"), (d) test items (e.g., "you must answer in complete sentences"), and (e) general test regulations (e.g., "when you finish the first column, go immediately to the second and continue until you are told to stop").

How to Score and Interpret a Criterion-Referenced Test

1. To score the test, determine the number of correct and incorrect responses.
2. Compare the test results with the predetermined criterion to establish whether mastery has been reached.
3. If the student is given a sequential test containing 10 items and demonstrates mastery of the first four, the next five items should be designated as instructional objectives with the long-term goal of mastering all 10. The focus of scoring depends on the objective of the test. The goal is to gain information for instructional purposes. For example, if rate was more important than accuracy, the number of words read in a specified period of time (e.g., one minute) would be counted and scored as a percentage of correct words read per minute. IEP objectives can be developed by using the sequentially ordered items not mastered.

Task Analysis

Task analysis—generally associated with criterion-referenced testing—involves breaking down broader goals into a hierarchy or series of smaller steps. The teacher breaks down complex tasks by dividing "a target behavior into a skill sequence that comprises its essential components or substeps" (Cegelka, 1995, p. 54) to arrange for instruction in an order that facilitates their acquisition (McLoughlin & Lewis, 2005). Using task analysis, the teacher can identify particular steps or skills that need to be acquired before complete mastery of a task is accomplished.

Tasks can be analyzed in three ways: (1) temporal order—the order tasks need to be performed (e.g., add the numbers in the 10s place before those in the 100s place); (2) developmental sequence—the gradual progression of skills building on previously acquired skills (e.g., single-digit addition is taught before multidigit addition); and (3) difficulty level—the ease in which the task can be acquired (e.g., the child learns to tell time to the hour before telling time to the minute). (See Figure 3–8 for guidelines on how to construct task analysis items.)

Critical Thinking and Reflection Activity

Think about how you would develop a task analysis.

Figure 3–8   Guidelines for Task Analysis

In developing task analysis items, Guerin and Maier (1983) suggest the following guidelines:
1. Identify a specific task.
2. Determine the levels of acceptable performance.
3. Identify the required skills or behaviors needed to complete the task.
4. Record and rate the student's skills and behaviors task-related skills.
5. Determine appropriate alternative, competency, or adaptive methods of completing the task.
6. Make adaptations needed for students who require modifications.
7. Begin instruction.
8. Attend to the task, describe accomplished skills in observable, behavioral terms.

Dynamic Assessments

Dynamic assessments are an assessment method in which students are evaluated as they participate in the instructional process. This evaluation technique uses a test-teach-test model that focuses on students in the process of learning, their responsiveness to instruction, and the design of potentially effective instructional strategies (Lidz, 1997). This method is based on Vygotsky's view of the learning process (Vygotsky, 1978); specifically, that students learn higher level concepts when they receive support from their peers and adults.

Obtaining students' current functioning level is not the only objective of this model. It also provides a realistic estimate of students' abilities because it yields information about their learning and language potential (Lerner, 2003). This method is especially useful for students from culturally and linguistically diverse backgrounds, and for those who may not have had adequate opportunity because they have come from impoverished homes or received substandard schooling (Pena, Quinn, & Iglesias, 1992).

Curriculum-Based Evaluation Measures

Curriculum-based evaluation (CBE) methods are a set of standard, simple, short-duration fluency measures that monitor student growth in relevant skill domains. There are several versions of CBE measures, but the main two are curriculum-based assessments (CBAs) and curriculum-based measurements (CBMs). Some researchers and practitioners use these terms interchangeably, which causes definitions and methodologies to become convoluted. Probably the simplest way to differentiate between the two terms is knowing that CBM focuses on long-term annual goals whereas CBA focuses on short-term objectives.

Curriculum-based evaluation measures provide continuous feedback to both students and teachers (Karns, Fuchs, & Fuchs, 1995). This type of assessment is used to make instructional decisions. It links testing to teaching and to the development and evaluation of students' IEP goals (Fuchs & Deno, 1994). CBEs give students a means of monitoring their own progress by graphing and self-evaluating their performance. Since teachers base CBE on their classroom curriculum, practical application of CBE methods may vary in design from classroom to classroom and from student to student (Howell & Nolet, 2000).

Curriculum-Based Assessments

Curriculum-based assessments (CBAs) involve obtaining frequent and direct measures of a student's performance on a series of sequentially arranged objectives derived from the curriculum used in the classroom to make instructional decisions (Idol & West, 1983). CBA measures specific skills of students utilizing teacher-developed assessments.

CBA is a systematic process of developing and implementing standards through teacher evaluation of the relationship between instructional intervention and student performance (Mercer & Mercer, 2005). It is based on a mastery measurement approach to assessment. The teacher develops assessment probes to assess student mastery of specific subskills taught in the curriculum. Students are first assessed on what they know and are then reassessed after core sets of subskills have been taught (Espin, Shin, & Bush, Kruschwitz, 2001). CBAs can be used to evaluate students' learning rate. They can also be used to monitor the adequacy of instructional goals to help establish which students are acquiring specific skills but continue to need either additional instruction or practice in order to achieve a level of mastery. Besides monitoring individual student progress, CBAs are used by teachers to evaluate the effectiveness of instructional programs and the efficacy of instructional interventions (Allinder, 1996).

Curriculum-Based Measurements

Curriculum-based measurements (CBMs) are based on the use of a standardized methodology with documented reliability and validity (Fuchs & Fuchs, 2000; Fewster & MacMillan, 2002). They focus on measuring an entire school year's curriculum (e.g., defining 20 vocabulary words selected randomly from the list of words for the whole school year). With both CBA and CBM, the measures are used repeatedly; however, with CBM the measures do not change. CBM consists of a simple set of procedures for repeated measurement of student growth over time on tasks of consistent difficulty. Increases in fluency for reading, writing, spelling, and math should represent growth. The same CBM measures are used, even several times in a week, to monitor general outcome areas. Once adequate performance is reached, the probes are modified to reflect more difficult learning goals, within the same learning domain. (See Figure 3-9.) CBMs are flexible and reliable for showing where progress is and is not happening using charts and graphs, thereby allowing teachers to intervene effectively to make sure each child is getting what he or she needs to succeed. An important characteristic of CBM is the ability to develop measures that have significant technical adequacy. In other words, the measures are devised with standard development, administration, and scoring procedures in order to maintain high reliability and validity. CBMs have proven to include good screening devices (Howell & Nolet, 2000). CBMs are commonly used to place students in the curriculum, to monitor progress, to determine eligibility for special education services as part of the evaluation process, and to make placement and programming decisions (Mercer & Mercer, 2005; Venn, 2004). CBMs are also used to monitor student progress related to IEP goals and objectives, to create new intervention programs, and to assess instructional and intervention effectiveness (Hasbrouck, Woldbeck, Ihnot, & Parker, 1999; Lerner, 2003).

CBM uses direct, repeated assessments of academic behaviors (Mastropieri & Scruggs, 2004). Using CBM, student performance can be referenced in four ways: (1) individually—in comparison to how the same student has done recently on other,

FYI

ADDITIONAL REASONS FOR
USING CBMs

Curriculum-based
measurement

- Is fast and easy to
  administer.
- Promotes achievement.
- Identifies potential
  candidates for
  reintegration in general
  education.
- Determines what needs
  to be taught.
- Is useful for referral
  decisions.
- Complies with IDEA.
- Is useful for instructional
  grouping.
- Is useful for
  communicating with
  parents.

Figure 3–9   CBA vs. CBM—Differentiating Characteristics

CBA	vs.	CBM
Best for informal, flexible, student-centered assessment		Best for formal, standardized test results
Tracks daily, short-term progress		Tracks long term, annual progress
Used for instructional planning and progress monitoring		Used to aid eligibility, placement, and programming decisions
Measures specific skills using teacher-developed assessments		Uses research-validated indicators of student performance
Connects progress with classroom instruction		Compares achievement across groups of students, schools, districts, and states
Tracks student progress in learning specific skills; unique to individual students, class, program, or school		Provides information about overall progress and strengths and weaknesses in broad subject areas
Administration and scoring procedures determined by teacher		Standardized administration and scoring
Content varies depending on academic area and objective evaluated		Content varies depending on academic area and objective evaluated
Designed for continuous assessment of short-term goals		Designed for repeated measurement of annual goals

similar tasks; (2) to a goal—how the student is progressing toward a long-term goal; (3) instructionally—before or after adjustments in instruction have been made; and (4) normatively—in comparison to a local group, such as the classroom or grade level (Deno, 1985).

Curriculum-Based Probes

A **probe** is a brief, timed, easily administered quiz. Probes are an efficient way to evaluate, within a specific period of time, targeted academic behavior on material taken directly from the school curriculum. Probes measure skill acquisition, fluency, and maintenance in the basic skill areas. They can be useful for many important evaluation decisions, including screening, diagnosis, program placement, curriculum placement, instructional evaluation, and program evaluation (Shinn, Collins, & Collagner, 1998; Tindal & Marston, 1990). Curriculum-based measurement probes are given under standardized conditions, which means that the same directions are read each time a certain type of CBM is administered.

Probe results are typically considered to represent students' ability to correctly and quickly demonstrate competency in completing a taught skill, but they are not comprehensive. They test a sample of skills in order to check progress and pinpoint the kinds of errors made, but they do not cover every aspect of the learned skill. They may consist of a single skill (e.g., single-digit multiplication equations) or a mix of skills (e.g., addition, subtraction, multiplication, and division equations requiring regrouping). Generally, students are given a probe sheet of specific skills (e.g., a list of vocabulary words) to be completed (read aloud) within one minute. Teachers record accuracy by calculating the number of correct and incorrect responses, identifying any error patterns, and determining fluency based on the number of correct responses given within the designated time period (e.g., being able to read 60 percent of the words correctly in one minute). Using both fluency and accuracy rates is useful in determining whether a student's difficulty is related to the speed of production (e.g., the inability to mentally process answers or to write the responses quickly) or is related to the correctness of answers (e.g., miscalculations, indicating that the student needs additional instruction, reinforcement, review, or a different method of instruction).

The typical probe takes about five minutes of the teacher's time to administer, score, and chart results for one measurement session. Probes are administered on a regular basis, usually twice a week, to closely monitor progress in achieving instructional objectives. Accuracy rates can easily be charted and graphed to track skill development, so that instruction adaptations can be made as needed. These measures provide evidence that the interventions employed are either effective or ineffective and allow for close monitoring so that program adjustments can be made and students' annual goals and objectives can be projected and modified, as necessary.

Critical Thinking and Reflection Activity

- Identify the ways you could use a CBM probe graph in your classroom.
- What are the strengths and weaknesses of this assessment and reporting measure?
- How could you involve students in the CBM as a monitoring system?

Math, spelling, and writing probes can be administered to entire groups of students simultaneously. Students can be easily instructed on how to score and chart their own CBM probes. In addition, computer software programs can increase efficiency and streamline charting and interpretation of CBA data (Wright, 2004). Administration and record keeping can be streamlined by using computerized CBM software programs, which make scoring and interpreting CBM much faster and easier (Fuchs, Fuchs, Hamlett, Philips, & Bentz, 1994).

Charting and Graphing CBMs

CBMs are useful for instructional decision making as well as for tracking and reporting progress. Once the data are obtained, they can be graphed. A line, called the aimline, is drawn on the graph starting where current performance is noted and extending to the desired performance on the desired date (generally the annual review date). The aimline helps determine short-term objectives and whether students are progressing as they should. A trendline showing that a student's performance is repeatedly below the line (three consecutive times) indicates that steady progress toward the goal is not being made and intervention is needed (Wright, 2004).

CBM: Three Data-Point Decision-Rule   The simplest method of interpreting and graphing CBM results is the three data-point decision-rule.

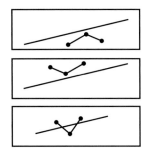

When the three most recent data points lie below the aimline at any time, this indicates that a modification needs to be made in the instructional intervention in an attempt to increase the rate of learning.

When three successive data points are plotted above the aimline, the aimline needs to be adjusted upward to reflect the increase in learning rate.

When three successive data points cluster near, both above and below the aimline, one can assume that the student is progressing at the expected rate, and no instructional modifications need to be made.

Performance Assessments

Performance assessments are based on the application of knowledge and the use of meaningful, complex, relevant skills to produce products. They are a method of measuring progress by having students demonstrate, produce, perform, create, construct, build, plan, solve, apply, illustrate, explain, convince, or persuade, as opposed to regurgitating answers on a test form. (See Figure 3–10.) Students demonstrate specific skills and competencies based on preestablished standards and rely on teacher-rater judgment for the design and interpretation of the assessment. When developing performance assessments, the criteria listed in Figures 3–11 and 3–12 should be considered.

Figure 3–10   Ways to Involve Students in Performance Assessment Development and Use

- Share the performance criteria with students at the beginning of the unit of instruction.
- Collaborate with students in keeping track of which criteria have been covered in class and which are yet to come.
- Involve students in creating prominent visual displays of important performance criteria for bulletin boards.
- Engage students in the actual development of performance exercises.
- Engage students in comparing and contrasting examples of performance, some of which reflect high-quality work and some of which do not (perhaps as part of a process of developing performance criteria).
- Involve students in the process of transforming performance criteria into checklists, rating scales, and other recording methods.
- Have students evaluate their own and each other's performance, one on one and/or in cooperative groups.
- Have students rate performance and then conduct studies of how much agreement there was among student judges; see if degree of agreement increases as students become more proficient as performers and as judges.
- Have students write about their own growth over time with respect to specified criteria.
- Have students set specific achievement goals in terms of specified criteria and then keep track of their own progress.
- Store several samples of each student's performance over time, either as a portfolio or on videotape, if appropriate, and have students compare old performance to new and discuss in terms of specific ratings.
- Have students predict their performance criterion by criterion, and then check actual evaluations to see if their predictions are accurate.

Figure 3–11   Criteria for Performance-Based Assessment

• Consequences	Does using an assessment lead to intended consequences, or does it produce unintended consequences, such as teaching to the test?
• Fairness	Does the assessment enable students from all cultural backgrounds to demonstrate their skills?
• Transfer and generalizability	Do the results generalize to other problems and situations?
• Cognitive complexity	Does the assessment adequately assess higher levels of thinking and understanding?
• Content quality	Are the tasks worth the time and effort of students and raters?
• Content coverage	Does the assessment enable adequate content coverage?
• Meaningfulness	Are the assessment tasks meaningful to students, and do they motivate them to perform their best?
• Cost and efficiency	Has attention been given to the efficiency of data collection designs and scoring procedures?

Source: North Central Regional Educational Laboratory (1991). *Criteria for valid performance-based assessments.* Naperville, Il: Author. Used with permission.

Figure 3–12   Steps to Take Before Beginning Performance Assessment Tasks

- Establish the outcome(s) to be measured.
- Devise clear instructions to be provided to students.
- Determine conditions for assessment (e.g., setting, amount of time needed, amount of intervention).
- Gather all the equipment or resource materials that may be used.
- Establish whether the student will have any choices in how to respond (e.g., oral responses).
- Determine whether the student will require accommodations or modifications.
- Develop the scoring criteria to be used.

Portfolio Assessments

Portfolio assessments refer to a purposeful, continuous, varied collection of authentic student work across a range of content areas that exhibit the student's efforts, achievements, and progress over a period of time. Portfolios are used to document and assess a student's progress. (See Figure 3–13.) They provide information about a student's communication skills, conceptual understanding, reasoning ability, work-study habits, problem-solving capability, creativity, perseverance, motivation, and attitude (Cohen & Spenciner, 1998). Perhaps the greatest overall benefits of using portfolio assessments are that students are taught by example to become independent thinkers and the development of their autonomy as learners is facilitated.

Student portfolios can include written samples of academic work, collaborative projects, lists of books read, documentation of performances, works in progress, creative art designs, journal entries, audio- and videotaped presentations, student self-reflections, and teacher anecdotal notes and behavioral observations. Portfolios are student-centered, since students participate in determining the criteria for selecting the contents and in judging their merit. Also, portfolios provide evidence of student self-reflection. Evaluating portfolio content is generally a shared responsibility, involving

Figure 3–13   Purposes of Portfolios

Portfolio assessments offer these advantages:
- Provide criteria for evaluating and monitoring individual student progress
- Provide criteria for evaluating program and curriculum effectiveness
- Provide criteria for grading
- Measure students' specific strengths and weaknesses
- Diagnose students' instructional needs
- Inform classroom instructional planning and improve instructional effectiveness
- Measure growth in second-language students
- Promote reflective practice at the school and classroom levels
- Encourage student efficacy
- Support student involvement in the assessment process by allowing students to select submissions
- Promote student development in self-assessment strategies
- Motivate students to monitor and improve their performance
- Promote focus on personal growth and improvement rather than in comparisons with peers
- Provide for clear communication of learning progress to students, parents, and others
- Allow for adjustment in individual differences
- Encourage the collection of work samples
- Provide for multidimensional assessments in authentic contexts over time
- Illustrate the range of classroom learning experiences
- Allow students to demonstrate the scope of their skill mastery
- Encourage dialogue, reflection, and collaboration among teachers, parents, and students

---

the student, the teacher, family members, administrators, and often peers (Wesson & King, 1996).

Portfolio assessments, while appropriate for all students, are a particularly appropriate evaluation technique for students from culturally and linguistically diverse backgrounds, since their progress may not be accurately measured by traditional testing strategies (Moya & O'Malley, 1994). Portfolios are also a valuable assessment tool to use with students who have disabilities, as a means of planning instruction, evaluating progress, documenting IEP achievement goals, and communicating strengths and needs (Carpenter, Ray, & Bloom, 1995).

Classroom Scenario

Jose is a second-language learner in your class. You and Jose have decided to include in his portfolio collection a series of audiotapes of language samples that he has produced over time. The intent is to measure his progress in acquiring English language skills by examining increases in fluency and vocabulary and his use of complex sentence structures.

Informal Inventories

Informal inventories are screening devices that assess selected portions of the curriculum, which are representative of the skills taught. Although this type of assessment is not comprehensive or exhaustive—since only a sampling of skills is tested—a wide range of skills and concepts can be assessed. Informal inventories are generally administered as a preteaching assessment tool. They are used to determine the student's current performance level and to identify the specific areas in the curriculum that require more extensive, diagnostic assessment. An example of an informal inventory is the informal reading inventory described in Chapter 7.

Functional/Adaptive Assessments

Functional/adaptive assessments look at how a child actually functions at home, at school, and in the community. This type of assessment shows what the student can do or needs to learn that is not being reflected in test scores. Functional assessments for some students include looking at reading, writing, and math skills. For others, evaluating whether they are able to ride the city bus, dress independently, or handle money might be considered more appropriate activities to evaluate (Alliance, 2002).

Response Journals, or Learning Logs

Response journals, or **learning logs** allow students to keep a personal record of their work, including what they learned, how they learned it, what they did not understand, why they are confused, and what help they need. Students can also use this tool to maintain a personal journal in which they can reflect on, describe, analyze, and evaluate their learning experiences, successes, and challenges, as well as to write about the conclusions they draw from these events (Stiggins, 1997). Student journal entries can include assignments they have and have not mastered, information or strategies they have found useful, questions they want to ask, ideas for future projects, steps in planning an assignment, reflections on their work, and documentation of their progress (Kulm, 1994). Students with poor writing skills may need to maintain an audio journal by recording their responses on an audiocassette.

Think-Aloud Technique

The **think-aloud technique** is a type of assessment in which students verbally explain the cognitive processes and steps they use while working on a task. This technique might include having students orally explain how they solve a math problem, outline a social studies chapter, use metacognitive skills when reading, plan for long-term assignments, and conduct science experiments. This technique helps teachers to understand how their students approach learning tasks, thus providing insight into any confusion or inaccuracies that are occurring, so that instructional objectives or interventions can be modified. To effectively employ this procedure, teachers need to be (1) astute observers of student performance, (2) knowledgeable about the scope and sequence of the curriculum, and (3) familiar with cognitive strategies (McLoughlin & Lewis, 2005). The think-aloud technique also helps students to gain insight into their own ability to organize, analyze, process information, and solve problems.

Since this may be a new experience for most students, the teacher may need to talk through the steps involved as students solve a simple problem and give them opportunities to practice this technique.

Tips for Teachers

Prompt students to think aloud by asking probing questions, such as:

"How will you solve this problem?"
"What are you doing now?"
"What is the next step?"
"How did you get that answer?"
"Can you think of another way to solve that problem?"
"How would you explain how you solved this problem to a classmate?"

Classroom Scenario

You are concerned about Susie, one of your sixth-graders. Although she seems to acquire computation skills adequately, she has difficulty applying these skills when solving word problems. Using the think-aloud technique, you ask Susie to explain how, step by step, she comes up with the answer to the problems. It is clear, through the think-aloud process, that Susie knows the math facts but confuses the order of the math processes involved (e.g., confuses the sequence of steps when multiplying and dividing).

Questionnaires

A **questionnaire** is a group of questions that allow teachers to elicit information from parents, students, or other professionals in more detail than can be elicited from a checklist or rating scale. Questionnaires can be used for face-to-face interviews, or they can be mailed to the respondent to be filled out and mailed back. The format can be open-ended, which enables respondents to share their opinions, express their concerns or feelings, or to take their time to respond thoughtfully and comprehensively. This tool is especially beneficial when respondents need to gather information, such as developmental, medical, or school history data. Other questionnaire formats include multiple-choice, true-false, and fill-in-the-blanks, and response forms, on which respondents mark the appropriate picture or icon. Questionnaires may not be appropriate for parents who find reading and/or writing difficult.

Interviews

An **interview** is an interaction, generally face to face, in which the participants verbally share information about the student. Generally, the interviewer follows a prescribed set of questions in a personal and informal atmosphere that encourages the sharing of perspectives, experiences, observations, or background information about the child. Interviews can be conducted with parents, colleagues, other professionals, and students. Interviews may be more appropriate than a questionnaire when there are literacy barriers, when the directions are complex, when questions need to be explained, when further probing is needed, or when the person being questioned needs to be reassured or encouraged to respond.

Observations

Observations are the most objective method of assessment. They are also the most pervasive and widely used method of evaluating student performance in schools. Numerous observations can be made throughout the day, but teachers need to organize and categorize observations in a systematic and meaningful way. Observations should be ongoing and can be either unstructured and spontaneous or direct and formal, involving specific coding and scoring systems.

Teachers need to be astute observers of not only how the student is doing, but also of what, when, and why the student is performing the way he or she is in the classroom. Numerous factors (e.g., medical, social, environmental, and instructional) come into play when determining why a student may be having difficulty in school. Kid watching—a concept introduced by Goodman (1978)—is a conscious effort by teachers to focus on specific behaviors of individual students or on the interactions of small groups of students to expose and reflect on their emerging capabilities, including their knowledge, skills, feelings, and dispositions.

Checklists

Checklists can be an efficient method of evaluating the level of skill mastery. Teachers can develop a checklist of skills, arranged in a consistent manner to systematically, quickly, and efficiently record whether specific skills or behaviors are or are not present (Arter & McTighe, 2001). The purpose of the checklist should determine the kind of checklist that is used.

Curriculum checklists are generally based on curricular scope and sequence charts, and specific skills are checked off as mastered, emerging, or not mastered. Behavioral checklists consist of specific problem behaviors or social skills that need to be monitored. Formats may vary. (Figure 3–14 lists guidelines for developing checklists.) Checklists can be used for an entire class or small groups, so that teachers can keep track of multiple students on one form rather than maintaining individual folders for each student being monitored. In this way, teachers can, at a glance, determine who does and does not need assistance in a specific area, a determination that is useful for instructional planning and program evaluation. In contrast, individual checklists are more useful for noting a particular student's strengths and weaknesses.

Figure 3–14   Guidelines for Developing Checklists

Among the factors to consider when developing checklists are the following:
- Determine items to be observed/evaluated.
- Determine criteria to evaluate performance.
- Ensure that criteria are specific to identify whether the performance or behavior item has occurred (e.g., checkmarks, plus/minus, mastered/unmastered).
- Determine hierarchy; arrange skills in the order they would be observed.
- Ensure that checklists are brief, specific, and to the point; they should cover all items to be observed, yet not be repetitive.
- Directly correlate items to students' performance or behavior.
- Ensure that word choice and format are consistent.
- Phrase checklist items in an objective and positive manner focusing on what the student can do (e.g., student is able to add single-digit numbers with sums to 10).

From Beaty, J. (1997). Observing development of the young child (4th ed.) Upper Saddle River, NJ: Merrill/Prentice Hall.

To be most practical, checklists should be specific and have a realistic number of attainable goals. The evaluative criteria should also be limited for ease of rating and scoring. The indicators may include evidence of completion (e.g., x = finished, 0 = not finished; yes or no), qualitative criteria (e.g., excellent, good, fair, poor), or relative level of proficiency (e.g., M = mastered, E = emerging, NS = no skill).

Work-Sample Analyses

Work-sample analyses involve reviewing students' work products by focusing on the quality and quantity of their output. These work samples—which are analyzed to determine areas of success and areas that require review or remediation—can include essays, homework assignments, lab reports, tests, and audio- and videotape recordings of a class discussion. Teachers can use error analysis (described in the following subsection) to analyze the type and frequency of correct and incorrect responses students make on everyday assignments. Also, teachers can focus on other aspects of the work product, such as whether students followed directions; answered questions completely; produced a sufficient amount of work; worked in a sequential, organized manner; used adequate motor planning; copied accurately from the board or textbook; and demonstrated adequate penmanship skills.

Error Analyses

Error analyses allow teachers to examine students' responses on work samples to identify areas of difficulty and patterns in how students approach a task. Error analyses usually focus on identifying errors related to inappropriate applications of rules and concepts, rather than careless, random errors or errors caused by lack of instruction. An important aspect of error analyses is the students' explanation of their responses (i.e., think-aloud technique), which can help the teacher pinpoint faulty conceptual or procedural knowledge for developing remedial programming.

Self-Evaluations

Self-evaluations are a method of collecting data by having students report on their feelings, activity level, or knowledge. This method can take many forms, including self-rating scales, attitude or interest inventories, portfolios, and journals or logs. It allows students to reflect on their learning, to directly apply grading standards to their work, and to contemplate on their personal strengths and areas that need remediation or reinforcement. It also helps students to project future goals and to develop strategies for achieving them. The self-evaluation process can be a powerful tool for life-long learning because it helps to promote metacognitive skills, ownership in learning, self-monitoring, and independence of thought (National Council of Teachers of Mathematics, 1991).

There are two basic requirements for making self-assessments accurate and reliable for students: (1) Students must be able to express themselves well enough verbally or nonverbally to make their desires understood; and (2) students must be reliable sources of information. As a result of these requirements, self-reports are most commonly used with older students and adults (Seaman, DePauw, Morton, & Omoto, 2003, p. 92).

Peer Evaluations

Peer evaluations help students apply criteria to samples of work in a manner that is less threatening than self-evaluation might be. They teach respect for the ideas of others and positive methods of interacting by requiring confirming statements about each other's work, as well as constructive criticism that is useful for revision. Peer evaluations promote positive learning characteristics, while increasing student motivation, responsibility, self-direction, success, and self-esteem. They also help students gain insight into the thinking and reasoning processes of their classmates.

It is important that students be involved in the development of scoring criteria for self-evaluations and peer evaluations. Doing so helps to ensure that they are committed to and invested in the evaluation procedure and that they are clearly aware of the standards being used. Involving them in this process also gives them a sense of ownership in the grading system, which helps them to understand and value the learning process. In this way, the development of scoring criteria becomes part of the learning process and reinforces student knowledge of key concepts as expectations are delineated.

Some research shows that students work better in pairs when they are allowed to choose their own partners (Meisinger, Schwanenflugel, Bradley, Kuhn, & Stahl, 2002). Allowing students to choose partners tends to result in fewer squabbles between partners and more time spent on task (Osborn, Lehr, & Hiebert, 2004).

SECTION 2: TYPES OF INFORMAL SCORING PROCEDURES

Rubrics

A **rubric** is an established guideline or planned set of criteria that describes levels of performance or of understanding for what is expected so that an assignment or a performance can be judged. Points or grades are awarded for specific levels of performance. The criteria are expressed numerically and are accompanied by specific descriptors of performance for each number. Rubrics provide a common understanding of teacher expectations for students' outcomes and validate teachers' judgment. They promote consistency and reliability of assessment. When using rubrics to evaluate students, the criteria should be provided and explained to, and modeled for, them during the initial discussion of the assignment. This information provides them with expectations about what will be assessed and standards that need to be met.

Scoring with a rubric provides benchmarks that encourage students to self-evaluate during the task completion process. Benchmarks provide examples of specific goals or outcomes within rubrics, often grade-level or course-specific with measurable, observable outcomes, progress toward achievement of a standard

Tips for Teachers

Rubrics need to be

Comprehensive—	cover all needed features to indicate performance level
Clear—	specific, unambiguous, jargon-free
Useful—	based on criteria that are directly related to instruction and standards, as well as provide needed assessment data
Valid and fair—	able to be applied and interpreted consistently by raters, be unbiased, and use criteria that are attainable

(Coalition of Essential Schools, 2001). However, when students' skill levels are below grade norms, just indicating that performance is below the grade-level benchmark does not sufficiently define the degree to which the student fails to meet the criterion. Rubrics are useful for charting students' progress toward attaining the benchmark, since they quantify students' approximation toward the ultimate goal of reaching it (Seaman, et al., 2003). Students can analyze their final scores and discover their own strengths and weaknesses by looking at the specific criteria.

Critical Thinking and Reflection Activity

Dion, a student with a traumatic brain injury, functions about two grades below average in reading skills. Thus, he does not meet the established grade-level benchmark. He is receiving remedial instructor and instructional accommodations and you anticipate that he will be making steady gains. How would you develop reading rubrics to benefit Dion?

Rubrics can provide even clearer expectations and directions than are possible using the letter-grade system. They should be developed before instruction begins and used to correlate instructional content with assessment procedures. Teachers may choose to involve students in developing the rubrics, which empowers students by allowing them to be involved in planning how they will demonstrate their learning. This not only increases their investment in the learning process, it also improves their motivation, interest, and ultimately their learning. Teachers may prefer to develop the rubrics themselves, and give students a copy of the rubrics before instruction or test administration in order to help them understand what is expected and to explain the criteria to be used for evaluating their work. Ultimately, students should be able to use the rubrics as a guide for self- and peer assessment. Teachers should carefully review the rubric and perhaps provide a model to ensure that all members of the group understand its principle features and the weight of the various dimensions.

🔍 CLARIFYING TERMS

General rubrics—can apply to many different tasks (i.e., "one fits all," adaptable)

Specific rubrics—uniquely designed for a particular task

Types of Rubrics

A rubric with two or more separate scales is called an **analytical rubric**. A scoring rubric that uses only a single scale is a global, or **holistic, rubric**. Holistic scoring is often more efficient than analytical scoring, but analytical scoring systems generally provide more detailed information for instructional planning and progress monitoring, as well as feedback for students. In addition, rubrics can be general or customized to meet the needs of the teacher or the curriculum. The scoring rubric rating scales can be quantitative (numerical), qualitative, or a combination of the two. (See Figure 3–15.)

Analytic Scoring

Analytical trait scoring is a scoring system that divides a product or performance into essential traits or dimensions so that each can be judged separately, thus providing an independent score for each criterion in the assessment scale. Descriptors can be

Figure 3–15   Quantitative vs. Qualitative Scoring

Examples of Numerical Scores Based on Qualitative Criteria

Score	Criteria
1	No attempt made
2	Attempt made, incomplete or undeveloped task performance
3	Successful attempt made, adequate performance
4	Superior effort, excellent performance

Examples of Numerical Scores Based on Quantitative Criteria

Score	Criteria
1	0 responses correct
2	1 to 3 out of 10 responses correct
3	4 to 7 out of 10 responses correct
4	8 to 10 responses correct

Examples of Quantitative Score Hierarchies

Undeveloped, developing, fully developed
Not introduced, emerging, competent, superior performance
Novice, apprentice, proficient, distinguished
No evidence, minimal evidence, partial evidence, complete evidence
Poor, fair, good, very good, excellent

either numerical or categorical. Although categorical descriptors provide more detailed, definitive information, when numerical scores are totaled and averaged they can provide useful diagnostic information as well. In analytic scoring, separate scores are given for various dimensions (referred to as traits) of students' performances or products. Points are often given for overall organization, neatness, grammar, strategy solution, and self-assessment. Analytic scoring lends itself to providing descriptive feedback on complex assignments.

It is important that each area designated be scored individually when scoring analytically, so that a poor performance in one area does not negatively affect the score in another designated area. Although time-consuming, analytic scoring may be more useful than holistic scoring when the assessment is for classroom use and the objective is to provide feedback to improve learning. Analytic scores directly and explicitly communicate to teachers, parents, and students the salient aspects of desired performance (Herman, Gearhart, & Aschbacher, 1996).

Holistic Scoring

In holistic scoring, points are awarded for the whole product or for performance based on an overall impression of a student's work. A single score or description of quality is based on clearly defined criteria, generally a scale ranging from 0 to 5 or 0 to 6. All criteria are considered simultaneously, resulting in a single score. The criteria might range from no response, to a partial response with a strategy, to a complete response with a clear explanation. Sample holistic scoring rubrics are found in the content chapters of this text (see Chapters 7 to 10). As with analytic scoring, holistic scoring should include descriptors of each achievement level. Although holistic scoring lacks the depth of information contained in analytic scoring, it tends to be easier to design and score. The purpose of a holistic rubric is (a) to judge student work products with only one trait of performance, (b) to get a quick snapshot of overall quality or achievement, and (c) to judge the "impact" of a product or performance. However, these rubrics do not provide the more detailed analyses of students' strengths and areas needing improvement that analytic rubrics do (Arter & McTighe, 2001).

Methods of rating that use holistic scoring can involve ranking students by determining overall quality of the work through the categorization of individual products. Work products are sorted into piles of excellent, good, fair, or poor work, then reread and reevaluated until the teacher has clearly ranked students' work based on the overall quality. Finally, the separate piles of excellent, good, and so forth can be converted to letter grades to fit district grading policies. Often, a breakdown is made between the final product's content (the actual message presented to the reader) and form (i.e., technical format, such as spelling, grammar, and punctuation). To help facilitate the best outcome, teachers often give students a model of excellent work or examples of products that were rated at each level (i.e., from excellent to poor) with explanations of why each work sample was rated the way it was. This provides students with clear expectations as well as examples to use when evaluating their own work and the work of others. When students understand what it takes to produce excellent papers, they are more likely to do so.

Selecting Existing Rubrics

Rather than "recreate the wheel," teachers may decide to use an existing rubric and either adopt it "as is" or adapt it by combining and modifying it to meet their specific needs. Rubrics are developed and used by schools, districts, and state departments of education nationwide. Examples of scoring rubrics can be found on educational Internet sites, in education journals, and in other professional publications. Teachers may find it helpful to review many varieties of rubrics to glean ideas and collect models. They may find it necessary to modify an existing rubric by adding descriptors to make it consistent with their district's or state's established curriculum standards (Audet & Jordan, 2003).

A rubric is the right one for the teacher's school if (1) it addresses the aspects of student work that the teacher feels are most important and (2) the teacher and his or her colleagues can generally agree on the score that should be assigned to a given piece of student work. One way to reach such consensus is for teachers to try out a few sample rubrics, use them to evaluate actual student work samples, and make the needed modifications. It is important to decide on a rubric that all teachers on the grade level, a co-teacher, or the special and general education teachers agree on. This is particularly important when the school or district is using portfolio assessment to track student achievement, since rubrics are commonly used in the evaluation progress, particularly

Critical Thinking and Reflection Activity

Examine two rubrics, reflect on which would provide you with better diagnostic information to use in planning instruction. Which would provide students and parents with the clearest feedback about students' work and how to make it better? Which would probably be more time-consuming to use?

Tips for Teachers

A practical way to gain consensus or consistency on how to rate or score students' work is to have the group members that will be using the rating scale (e.g., all grade 3 teachers) each independently rate the same piece of student work. Next, they should compare ratings, discuss the rationale behind the ratings given, and arrive at a standard for each criteria ranking. Achieving consensus or consistency generally takes negotiation and practice.

when student progress is tracked from one grade level to the next. Thus, there needs to be interrater reliability; that is, the mutually agreed on elements of quality must be used as the basis for making judgments about, and the grading of, student performance so that scoring results do not vary from teacher to teacher (Arter & McTighe, 2001).

Adapting Existing Rubrics

It is often easy to modify an existing rubric. In fact, rubrics that are based on grade and subject areas which do not match the teacher's needs can, with minor adjustments, be used. For example, a rubric for related arts subjects—such as the humanities subjects (art, music, theater)—can, with little modification, be used for a different art form. An art rubric that deals with the artistic sensory elements of line, shape, value, color, and texture might easily be modified for use as a music rubric by substituting musical sensory elements, such as rhythm, tempo, pitch, timbre, and dynamics. (See Figure 3–16 for a list of factors to consider when modifying an existing rubric.)

Another way to adapt existing rubrics or newly created rubrics is to add or average the scores from each scale on an analytic rubric to get a total score. Also, teachers can prioritize or assign more credit to one scale than to others (e.g., assign more credit for content than for grammar) by multiplying the prioritized scale by a number greater than one. If content is twice as important as all the other areas, the score on that scale is multiplied by two before the scale scores are added to get a total score.

Rating Scales

A **rating scale** identifies students' knowledge, skills, and attitudes by assigning a numerical or descriptive rating that can be used and understood by raters and those interpreting the ratings. Rating scales are used when the characteristics or dimensions

FYI

"The best rubrics are worded in a way that covers the essence of what we, as teachers, look for when we're judging quality . . ."

ARTER & McTIGHE, 2001

Figure 3–16   Strategies for Adapting Standard Rubrics

In modifying existing rubrics, you may need to:
- Change the wording of various parts of rubric, as needed.
- Modify by changing or dropping scales on an analytical rubric.
- Borrow scales from existing rubrics by mixing and matching.
- Eliminate unnecessary or inappropriate criteria.
- Adjust rubric criteria to adapt to grade level expectations.
- Section holistic rubrics into several scales.
- Add more or remove categories.
- Add a "no-response" category at the bottom of the scale.

Tips for Teachers

Below is an example of how an analytic-type rating scale might be scored as a holistic rating scale by adding the points for each trait and placing more weight (twice the number of points) on one (or more) of the traits that are deemed more important.

Writing Traits (Dimensions)	Above Average	Average	Below Average	Score
Ideas and content (x2)	(10 pts)	(6 pts)	(2 pts)	6 pts
Organization	(5 pts)	(3 pts)	(1 pt)	1 pt
Voice	(5 pts)	(3 pts)	(1 pt)	5 pts
Word Choice	(5 pts)	(3 pts)	(1 pt)	3 pts
Sentence Fluency	(5 pts)	(3 pts)	(1 pt)	5 pts
Conventions	(5 pts)	(3 pts)	(1 pt)	1 pt
Presentation	(5 pts)	(3 pts)	(1 pt)	1 pt
			Total:	22 pts
			Average:	3

of a performance or product can be identified and when these characteristics or dimensions exist to a greater or lesser degree. Teachers can use these scales to rate students' level of proficiency, and for peer evaluations and self-evaluations to be done by students. They can be used to communicate a degree of competence for specific skills or to show progress over time.

There are three types of rating scales, those that (1) describe what the student can do, (2) specify the extent that dimensions were observed, and (3) rate the quality of the performance. Rating scales place a value on the performance observed. They score the degree of performance (e.g., mastered, emerging, no skill), provide more information than dichotomous scales (yes/no, pass/fail, good/poor), are detailed, and are versatile when converting to grades. Rating scale directions may state that the learner is either to circle or to check a number on each scale that indicates the extent of the particular characteristic being rated.

The components of a primary trait-rating scale include (1) the listing of the dimensions to be rated (e.g., the student writes numbers accurately, or regroups digits in the tens' place) and (2) the scale for ranking each dimension. The scale can take several forms: (a) semantic differential scales, which use opposite (or bipolar) adjectives rated along a continuum (see Figure 3-17); (b) graphic rating scales, which rate along a graduated continuum with points separated by equal intervals (see Figure 3-18); (c) numerical scales, also referred to as Likert scales, with each behavior assigned a rating number from lowest to highest (see Figure 3-19); and (d) visual analog scales, which are continuous and are marked at any point along the scale (see Figure 3-20).

Anchor Papers

Anchor papers are representative products, papers, and performances that guide and standardize the scoring of students' work in a school or district to ensure consistency. Students can be provided with copies of anchor papers to be used as models of

🔍 CLARIFYING TERMS:

Likert Scale

A Likert, or numerical, scale is generally used to rank each behavior in, for example, the frequency of occurrence (always, often, sometimes, rarely, never) or the quality of performance, with responses tied to numerical values (from excellent performance = 5 to poor performance =1).

Figure 3–17   Semantic Differential Scale

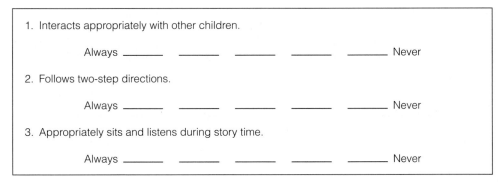

1. Interacts appropriately with other children.

   Always _____   _____   _____   _____   _____ Never

2. Follows two-step directions.

   Always _____   _____   _____   _____   _____ Never

3. Appropriately sits and listens during story time.

   Always _____   _____   _____   _____   _____ Never

Figure 3–18   Graphic Rating Scale

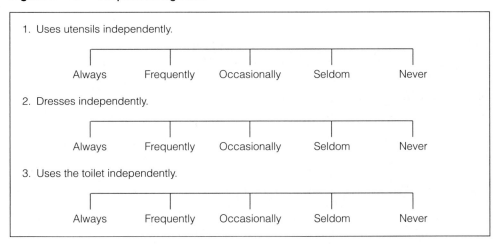

1. Uses utensils independently.

   Always   Frequently   Occasionally   Seldom   Never

2. Dresses independently.

   Always   Frequently   Occasionally   Seldom   Never

3. Uses the toilet independently.

   Always   Frequently   Occasionally   Seldom   Never

Figure 3–19   Numerical Scale

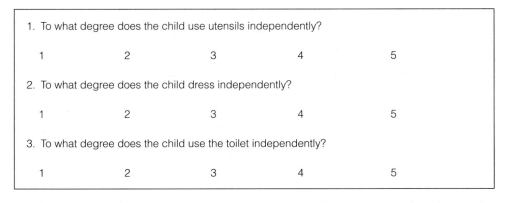

1. To what degree does the child use utensils independently?

   1   2   3   4   5

2. To what degree does the child dress independently?

   1   2   3   4   5

3. To what degree does the child use the toilet independently?

   1   2   3   4   5

Figure 3–20   Visual Analog Scale

1. Uses utensils independently.

    Always ——————————————————————————— Never

2. Dresses independently.

    Always ——————————————————————————— Never

3. Uses the toilet independently.

    Always ——————————————————————————— Never

exceptional, average, and poor papers. Parents can be given sample models and tips for helping students meet the standards.

SECTION 3: PLANNING, CONSTRUCTING, AND ADMINISTRATING SCORING PROCEDURES

How and Why to Use a Rubric

Scoring criteria can be aligned with the school district, state, or national core curriculum standards so that comparisons of groups of students can be made. The rubric should organize and clarify the scoring criteria well enough so that two teachers who apply the rubric to a student's work will generally arrive at the same score, referred to as **interrater reliability.** Teachers typically need to be trained and given opportunities to practice scoring rubrics.

One method for determining whether interrater reliability has been achieved involves having two raters independently score several examples of work produced by high-achieving, average, and low-achieving students, and note the extent to which the raters assign the same score to each piece of work. When they have finished, the ratings are compared to determine their similarity. If the ratings are dissimilar or there is no consensus, the two raters can discuss the rationale for their scores, or they may ask a third to rate the product (Cohen & Spenciner, 1998). It may be determined that the rubric criteria need to be further clarified to establish uniform scoring. As teachers become skilled at conducting rigorous, defensible analyses and gathering reliable and valid data, they will be able to use rubrics for scoring authentic instructional assessments; for IEP goal development and monitoring; and for district, state, and federal accountability issues.

 **CLARIFYING TERMS**

Interrater reliability refers to the consistency of scoring between two or more independent scorers.

Components of Rubrics

A scoring rubric has several components, each contributing to its usefulness. These components include one or more dimensions on which performance is rated, definitions and examples that illustrate the attribute(s) being measured, and a scale for rating each dimension. (See Figure 3-21.) Providing an example of student work for each rating scale level is very helpful. Ideally, there should also be examples of student work that fall into each level of the rating scale.

Figure 3–21 Development of a Rubric or Scoring Guide

- Discuss with others how performance is assessed in specific disciplines and in learning activities.
- Collect samples of students' work that reflect range of performance levels, and analyze them to delineate the important dimensions of the learning activity and the characteristics that separate excellent, good, mediocre, and poor samples.
- Compose a set of descriptors that define and provide examples of the important characteristics for each of the dimensions identified.
- Use the descriptors to create a scale for judging students' products that reflects the various levels of performance (e.g., excellent, proficient, acceptable, below expectations).
- Weigh the various rubric dimensions, if necessary.
- Examine the language and criteria used in the rubric to make sure it is understandable and credible to students, families, and other professionals, as well as feasible, fair, and unbiased.
- Disseminate and explain the rubric, and provide models and examples of each level in the rubric to students.
- Collect additional samples of students' work, and evaluate these samples using the rubric's dimensions, descriptors, and levels of performance.
- Evaluate the effectiveness and efficiency of the rubric by examining its impact on students, teachers, and other relevant parties.
- Revise elements of the rubric based on the evaluation data collected.
- Continue to field-test and revise the rubric.

Source: *Mathematics Assessment: Myths, Models, Good Questions and Practical Suggestions*, by National Council of Teachers of Mathematics, 1996. All rights reserved.

Constructing a Rubric

Many school districts are revising their traditional letter-grade designations (i.e., A, B, C, D, F) for reporting academic progress to a rubric system; that is, a numbered scale that spells out in some detail the value associated with each point on the scale. In developing the criteria for each value on the rubric scale, several factors other than the bottom-line grade should be considered. (See Figure 3–22.) Can the students express themselves clearly and comprehensively in written and/or oral form? Are they using appropriate vocabulary, sequencing information well, and including sufficient detail to adequately explain themselves? Can they personally evaluate the quality of their work product?

When developing criteria for a rubric, the teacher normally begins by writing a description about the ideal product, making sure that the criteria for the values include local and state core curriculum guidelines. When a six-level rubric structure is set up, the differentiation can be made between a satisfactory 4, 5, or 6 and the unsatisfactory 1, 2, or 3. After writing a description of the criteria for 6 (excellent work), the teacher determines the qualities that make up the remaining five values. (See Figure 3–23 for steps in constructing a rubric.)

Another way to develop a scale is to base it from 1 to 5. Scores of 1, 3, and 5 are fully defined with a list of descriptors for each. Scores of 2 and 4 can be awarded for work that falls between these benchmarks. Although scales can vary in the number of points they contain, generally scales of no more than 6 to 7 points are recommended. When using longer scales, it is difficult to differentiate between scale points (e.g., when using a 50-point scale, assigning 34 instead of 35 points can be viewed as arbitrary). Suggested criteria may be customized to match specific assignments by adapting the descriptors. It is important to think of a rubric not as a checklist of completed tasks but rather as a guide to quality (Bridges, 1995).

Figure 3–22   Criteria for Developing Rubrics

Criteria for judging each performance area may include such considerations as:

Written Report
- Depth of understanding
- Clarity
- Coherence
- Completeness
- Organization
- Sources of information cited
- Clear description of the topic/question with strong support for its importance

Visual Display
- Economy of design
- Craftsmanship
- Aesthetics
- Creativity
- Presents important, relevant information
- Can stand alone as a source of information

Oral Presentation
- Strong evidence of preparation
- Engaging delivery with eye contact and enthusiasm
- Responsiveness to questions with specific information
- Audience awareness
- Ability to summarize
- Justification of decisions/strong support
- Reflection
- Use of good examples and explanations
- Degree of progress made relative to the student's starting-point understanding of the bigger picture of the project/concept

Source: Adapted from *Mathematics Assessment: Myths, Models, Good Questions and Practical Suggestions,* by National Council of Teachers of Mathematics, 1996. All rights reserved.

Tips for Teachers

Provide examples of performances ranging from exemplary to poor using teacher models or anonymous student work samples.

Provide feedback using the vocabulary of the criteria when making suggestions on how to improve a student product (Arter & McTighe, 2001).

Critical Thinking and Reflection Activity

How could you reword the following standards used in a rubric so that they are clear to students and parents?

Reading Standard: "Construct meaning from text"
Writing Standard: "The clarity of the flow of ideas and the explicitness of the text structure or plan"

Figure 3–23   How to Construct a Rubric

Part 1: Steps for Developing a Rubric

1. List the critical components or objectives of the learning activity (e.g., comprehensiveness of content, quality of the presentation, accuracy of mechanics/grammar/spelling, variety and number of reference sources).
2. Determine the criteria to be used for the evaluation scale (e.g., 4 for excellent to 1 for poor). When more than six levels of criteria are used, scoring can become more complicated.
3. Write a description of expected performance for each criterion category (e.g., ability to focus and take a position; organization and writing skills, including coherence, depth or elaboration, clarity, word choice, and sentence variety). Criteria may also include ability to make personal, historical, or cultural connections; take risks; challenge the text; apply prior experiences; make predictions or speculate; elaborate on an emotional response; and reflect on and use complexities of language.

Part 2: Steps for Developing a Scoring Rubric

1. With colleagues, make a preliminary decision on the dimensions of the performance or product to be assessed.
2. Look at some actual examples of student work to see if important dimensions have been omitted.
3. Refine and consolidate the list of dimensions as needed.
4. Write a definition of each dimension.
5. Develop a continuum (scale) for describing the range of products/performances on each dimension.
6. Alternatively, instead of a set of rating scales, develop a holistic scale or a checklist on which to record the presence or absence of the attributes of a quality product/performance.
7. Evaluate the rubric using the criteria discussed in Part 1.
8. Pilot test the rubric or checklist on actual samples of student work.
9. Revise the rubric and try it out again.
10. Share the rubric with students and their parents.

Rubrics Scoring

The rubric scoring scale identifies the specific areas of performance and defines the levels of achievement for each performance area. (See Figure 3-24 for factors to consider when assigning point values to rubrics.) The rubric scale needs to be clearly written, free of educational jargon, and appropriate for the student's developmental level. There is no single best rubric for all purposes, and many different rubrics could be applied to the same task. (Review the suggested criteria for evaluating rubrics listed in Figure 3-25.)

SECTION 4: GRADING AND PROGRESS REPORTING TO PARENTS

Special Education Law Mandates

Before the enactment of the amendments to the Individuals with Disabilities Education Act in 1997 (IDEA-97), special education teachers were not required to document and report the progress of the students in their classes more than once a year. For many families, the annual IEP review meeting was the only time when the goals and

CLARIFYING TERMS:

Elements of a Rubric
Dimension—a trait used as the basis for rating student response
Definitions or examples—words to clarify the meaning of each trait or dimension
Scale—values that rate each dimension
Standards—specific performance levels accompanied by models or examples of each level

Figure 3—24   Assigning Point Values

Factors to consider when determining the points for a rubrics rating scale include the following:

- Point numbers may vary according to the purpose or individual need.
- Point should be very specific and well-defined.
- Longer scales with more criteria can be more challenging to differentiate between points and to reach agreement among scorers which is referred to as interrater reliability.
- Shorter scales ratings can make it difficult to differentiate between students.
- Smaller scale ranges can be used when the intent is to determine whether students' performance has exceeded, met, or failed to meet the outcome standard.
- Scales of equal length should be used when the goal is to rate several different dimensions so that they are equally weighted when results are added.

Figure 3—25   Criteria for Evaluating Rubrics

Do the criteria

- Address skills that students have acquired and that have been covered in class and sufficiently taught?
- Cover important student performance, curricular standards, and best practices in the field?
- Include dimensions or scales that are well defined and clearly specify what each scale measures?
- Clearly differentiate among scale points?
- Represent true excellence; that is, something for which students can strive?
- Allow for generalization; specifically, can the rubric criteria be applied (with minor adjustments) to more than one task?
- Address appropriate developmental level; that is, cover a range of disabilities and a range of skills at the specific grade or age level?
- Appear to be unbiased so that students' culture, race, gender, or socio-economic status would not negatively impact the score (Herman, et al., 1992; Arter & McTighe, 2001).

objectives of the IEP were reviewed, progress was reported, and new goals and objectives were developed. Although many special education teachers communicate progress to parents on a more regular basis, there was no mandate to ensure that parents were being informed as to whether their children with special needs were making satisfactory progress toward meeting annual goals.

Teachers must now make progress reports to parents of students receiving special education services at least as often as the general education teacher is required to report those students' progress (Salend & Garrick-Duhaney, 2002). Most school districts require progress reporting each marking period, which is accomplished by report cards, parent conferences, or both. This progress reporting requirement for students with disabilities not only keeps families informed, it also facilitates regular communication and collaboration between home and school, and requires that teachers maintain a regular system of assessment, there by proving a safeguard for ongoing monitoring of IEP goals and objective attainment so that modifications can be made in a timely manner.

Monitoring, Graphing, and Reporting Academic Progress

Teachers of students with special needs find that informal assessment procedures, such as CBA probes, are quick, efficient, and effective ways to evaluate students' progress toward meeting their specific goals and objectives. The results of these CBA

FYI

"Students can hit any target that they can clearly see and stands still for them."

STIGGINS, 2001

probes can easily be scored, graphed, and charted, and they can provide clear, illustrated examples of progress. The CBA probe graph is a handy means for the teacher to keep track of ongoing progress toward the projected year-end goal. By carefully charting biweekly CBA probe scores in each subject area covered in the IEP, teachers will be alerted to the need to revise teaching methods, instructional strategies, or student accommodations.

Coordinating Portfolio Criteria with Grading Standards

With the trend toward performance-based, more authentic assessment measures of achievement promoted by the Council for Exceptional Children and the professional educational organizations—such as the International Reading Association and the National Council of Teachers of Mathematics—many school districts are encouraging or mandating the use of such measurement tools as portfolio assessments. Portfolios promote self-reflection on the part of the student by focusing on three criteria—product, process, and progress—and provide direct feedback to students and parents regarding areas of strengths and weaknesses (Bradley & Calvin, 1998). Rather than rely on traditional grading systems that are inherently subjective, schools are recognizing the value of monitoring progress toward IEP goals and objectives as a process by collecting work samples and using rubrics to measure growth. Rubrics are useful for both parents and students because they delineate the exact performance expectations before assignments are begun and the criteria that will be used in grading completed work.

Although the premise of portfolio assessment is process rather than product, some school programs require numerical or letter grades for reporting purposes. (Figures 3–26 and 3–27 provide procedures for establishing a grading system that assigns specific points to criteria to be evaluated.)

It is important to remember that a major benefit of the portfolio process is student participation. When students work with teachers in the decision-making process to reach consensus on the materials to be included in portfolios and help to determine the evaluation criteria, they are empowered and more committed to mastery.

Although IDEA-2004 does not specifically identify a particular grading system to use, it does mandate that a statement be included in the IEP that indicates how often parents will be informed of their child's progress. Although grades, letter or numerical, are commonly used to provide parents with a report on the progress of their children and the skills they have or have not acquired, grades are not detailed enough to provide a thorough understanding of what a child has actually learned or accomplished. For example, the letter grade B in reading indicates that the child is performing adequately in reading, but it does not provide information to parents that the child tends to overrely on word configuration in the area of word recognition, for example, or is unable to answer implicit comprehension questions.

Narrative comments written in a positive and informative manner can address a variety of issues while still maintaining the dignity of the child. When writing comments on progress or report cards, teachers need to be aware that each child has a different rate of social and academic development. Teachers must also remember that students will likely read these comments. Negative comments can be counterproductive by reinforcing in some students their low self-esteem or their limited confidence in academic ability or ability to control their behavior.

It is also important that teachers clarify the code used to indicate when the student is not working at grade level. Often students who receive special education

Figure 3–26   Grading Systems

Letter/Number Grading	Grading is based on performance that generally ranges from A (excellent) to F (failure) or 100 (perfect score) to 0 (no credit).
Narrative Reports	Progress is written in descriptive form; students' specific strengths and weaknesses are described.
Portfolio Grading	A process of collecting work samples in which students are generally involved in the selection, with evaluation based on product, process, and progress. Rubrics are generally used for grading.
Checklists/Rating Scale	Criteria are established (e.g., IEP goals and objectives) and a graded scale is used to evaluate each skill, based on a hierarchy of rankings (e.g., mastered, emerging, not mastered).
Pass/Fail System	Grading is based on a mastery level "P" for pass or for having attained mastery level, and "F"' for failing to attain master level.
IEP Mastery Grading	Grades are based on students' progress toward meeting their specific IEP goals and objectives.
Contract Grading	Teacher and student write the contract specifying goals, tasks to be accomplished or learning objectives to be mastered, the quantity and quality of the contracted expectations, and the procedures and criteria for evaluation and grade determination.
Three-Level Grading	Grades are based on the student's mastery of skills and concepts. Performance scores are based on ability, effort, and achievement. For example, a student who has a serious learning disability and has had difficulty mastering a specific skill but has put forth exceptional effort to grasp the task may receive an A with a notation on the report card that accommodations or modifications were made.
Co-Teaching Grading	When students are taught by both a general education and a special education teacher, grading responsibilities may be shared or divided.

Figure 3–27   Converting a Rating Scale to Grades

If the student gets	The grade should be
No more than 10 percent of scores lower than a 4, with at least 40 percent 5s.	A
No more than 30 percent of scores lower than a 4, with at least 10 percent 5s.	B
No more than 10 percent of scores lower than a 3, with at least 20 percent 4 or better.	C
No more than 30 percent of scores lower than a 3, with at least 10 percent 4 or better.	D
Anything lower than a 3	F

Source: Scoring rubrics in the classroom: Using performance criteria for assessing and improving student performance, by J. Arter and J. McTighe, 2001, Thousand Oaks, CA: Corwin Press.

Tips for Teachers

Words that promote a positive view of the student:
- is thorough
- is caring
- shows commitment
- has improved tremendously
- has a good grasp of . . .

Words that convey the student needs help:
- could profit by
- requires
- finds it difficult
- has trouble with at times
- needs reinforcement in . . .

Words to avoid or use with caution:
- unable
- won't
- can't
- always

services have their grades adjusted, perhaps to indicate progress toward their goals as opposed to their standing in comparison to grade norms. For example, the general education grading system range may be 92 to 100 for an A, whereas the grade range may be adjusted to 88 to 100 for the student who is receiving special education. Another method of accommodating students with learning differences is to use the regular grading system but to designate with an asterisk that curricular modifications or instructional or testing accommodations were provided.

Progress Reporting Systems

In order to establish and maintain parental support and involvement, the teacher needs to be diplomatic and to acknowledge to parents the positive contributions their child makes to the class while providing an objective account of what the child

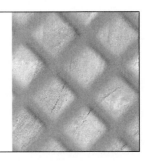

Tips for Teachers

Avoid negative wording. Always word rubric scales in positive rather than negative terms (e.g., "clueless," "totally wrong"). Write rubrics in a constructive, helpful way. Reflect on how you would comment to students when handing back papers in class: "You provided important facts but need to use more descriptive words"; "Remember to proofread"; "Focus on verb tense" (Arter & McTighe, 2001).

is doing that is inappropriate, unacceptable, or troubling. Such diplomacy requires a delicate balance between providing an objective account of the child's transgressions or work-study problems while showing concern and advocating for the child (Hallahan & Kauffman, 2000, p. 534).

When a teacher conveys only good or only bad news to parents, their level of trust can be lost and their perspective about their child can become skewed. If only positive comments are shared and later, when a serious incident arises, the parents will have had no warning of the problem and may feel that the teacher was withholding information, or overreacted if it was the first such incident (Spinelli, 1999). When teachers clearly convey their appreciation and concern for the well-being of the child rather than their feelings of frustration and anger about misbehavior or chronic academic problems, they can avoid the defensiveness that can polarize parent-teacher relationship (Kauffman, Mostert, Trent, & Hallahan, 1998).

A home-school communication system can be instituted to report compliance or noncompliance with academic, behavioral, or work-study contracts and contingency systems. This system can be set up to monitor and reinforce progress with IEP academic or behavioral goals. When teachers report progress to parents, the parents can reinforce school achievement and behavioral compliance in the home by dispensing reinforcement. Parents generally have a greater number of reinforcers than teachers have.

There are many ways to develop a home-school reporting system of communication. Rather than writing a daily report to the parents, teachers can draft a quick email response, make a brief phone call, or customize a checklist that documents progress or tracks behavior (e.g., reports on-task behavior, work completion, social interaction, or a cooperative attitude) (National Education Association, 2002). One method is a simple reporting form on which the teacher rates categories of academic, work-study, and behavioral performance on a daily, weekly, or quarterly basis. (See Figure 3–28.) This type of progress reporting can be expanded to include communication among those providing the related services, remedial specialists, paraeducators, and parents. (See Figure 3–29.) This can be an effective way to keep parents informed of new techniques for remediation introduced during that day's session and to suggest practice activities that can be monitored and reinforced both in the classroom and at home. These progress reporting forms can also have space designated for teachers, therapists, and parents to make brief comments.

Critical Thinking and Reflection Activity

How can teachers involve students in planning, developing, and grading their homework assignments?

Students are responsible for taking these progress reporting forms back and forth from school to home and should receive positive reinforcement for their compliance. Parents indicate that they have received and reviewed the progress report by their signature. The goal, as with most behavior modification systems, is to gradually decrease the frequency of reporting until this daily process is once a week, then monthly, and then quarterly as the need for such close monitoring decreases.

Figure 3–28 Sample Classroom Progress Report

STUDENT: _____

DATE: _____ REPORT PERIOD: 1 _____ 2 _____ 3 _____ 4 _____

SUBJECT AREA	Excellent Progress	Satisfactory Progress	Needs Improvement	Average Grade	Comments
Reading/Literature					
Language Arts					
Mathematics					
Science					
Social Studies					
Physical Education					
Art					
Music					
Computer					

Assignments

(Classwork/Homework)

__1. consistently well-done
__2. improvement shown
__3. fails to complete homework
__4. fails to complete class work
__5. unprepared for class
__6. needs to participate in class
__7. unsatisfactory work quality
__8. inconsistent work/effort
__9. shows lack of preparation
__10. make-up work incomplete
__11. does not follow directions
__12. shows lack of neatness
__13. incomplete
__14. carelessly completed

Comments

Assessments

(Tests, Quizzes, Projects)

__15. improvement shown
__16. unprepared for quiz/tests
__17. consistently well done
__18. unsatisfactory work
__19. low quizzes/test scores
__20. incomplete
__21. lack of neatness, legibility
__22. not turned in on time

Study Skills

(Behavior, Attitudes)

__23. shows outstanding effort
__24. asks questions to improve understanding
__25. strong organizational skills
__26. demonstrates leadership skills
__27. seeks/accepts help as needed
__28. innovative/creative thinker
__29. does not accept responsibility
__30. sincere and trying to improve
__31. does not ask questions/participate
__32. works conscientiously but subject is difficult
__33. inappropriate classroom behavior
__34. demonstrates lack of organization/study skills
__35. does not work accurately/proofread
__36. does not follow oral/written directions
__37. shows initiative
__38. works well in group
__39. shows marginal effort
__40. needs to use time wisely
__41. does not accept criticism
__42. missing assignments

Student Signature: _____ Date: _____
Teacher Signature: _____ Date: _____
Parent/Guardian Signature: _____ Date: _____

SUMMARY POINTS

- Authentic assessment is based on the application of knowledge and the use of meaningful, complex, relevant skills to produce products or simulate real-life activities in real-world settings rather than in artificial or contrived settings. These diagnostic assessments include teacher-made tests, performance-based assessments, portfolio assessments, curriculum-based assessments, criterion-referenced tests, skill inventories, daily observations, analyses of work samples, and student interviews.

Figure 3–29   Related-Service Progress Report

Student: _____		Therapy: _____		Date: _____	

Therapy skill for the week: _____

Suggestions for at-home practice: _____

This week's progress:

ATTITUDE:	Excellent	Very Good	Good	Fair	Improvement Needed
Comments:					
PARTICIPATION:	Excellent	Very Good	Good	Fair	Improvement Needed
Comments:					
BEHAVIOR:	Excellent	Very Good	Good	Fair	Improvement Needed
Comments:					
GOAL ATTAINMENT:	Excellent	Very Good	Good	Fair	Improvement Needed
Comments:					
APPLICATION:	Excellent	Very Good	Good	Fair	Improvement Needed
Comments:					

Teacher's Signature: _____   Parent's Signature:_____

- Task analysis involves breaking down broader goals into a hierarchy or series of smaller steps or into a skill sequence that comprises its essential components or substeps in an order that facilitates acquisition. Dynamic assessment is based on a test-teach-test model; specifically, the process of learning, the student's responsiveness to instruction, and the design of potentially effective instructional strategies.

- A probe is brief, timed, easily administered, efficient method of evaluating targeted academic skills, taken directly from the curriculum, within a specific period of time. Probes measure skill acquisition, fluency, and maintenance in the basic skill areas.

- Curriculum-based probe scores can be charted and graphed to determine the level of accuracy, to ascertain whether sufficient progress is being made, and to monitor gains toward projected goals and objectives. Once scores are obtained, an aimline is drawn on the graph starting where current performance is noted and continuing to the projected performance on the desired date, generally the annual review. The trendline—the line that tracks progress toward the goal—indicates whether steady progress is being made, and if not, that intervention is needed.

- A questionnaire is a group of questions that allow teachers to elicit information from parents, students, or other professionals in more detail than can be elicited from a checklist or rating scale. The format can be face-to-face interviews or mailed to the respondent, filled out, and mailed back. The latter method is especially beneficial for respondents who require time to gather information. An interview is a verbal interaction, generally face-to-face, which may be more appropriate than a questionnaire when there are literacy barriers, when the directions are complex, when questions need to be explained, when further probing is needed, or when the person being questioned needs to be reassured or encouraged to respond.

- There are two basic types of rubrics: an analytic rubric, which has two or more separate scales; and a holistic rubric, which, uses a single scale. While holistic scoring is often more efficient, analytical scoring systems generally provide more detailed information for instructional planning, progress monitoring, and providing feedback to students.

Chapter Check-Ups

1. Recognizing the similarities and differences between curriculum-based assessment (CBA) and curriculum-based measurement (CBM), describe a situation when the CBA would be most appropriate to use and a situation when a CBM would be more appropriate than a CBA.

2. A colleague asks you to explain why she should consider using curriculum-based probes as an assessment procedure for her students. What would you identify as the benefits of using probes for both general education and special education classes?

3. You are planning to contact your student's parents to obtain background information and need to determine whether to use an interview or a questionnaire to obtain this information. What factors should be considered in making this decision?

4. What criteria would you use to determine whether to use a holistic or an analytic rubric? If your grade level teacher colleagues are also using rubrics for grading purposes, what is the process called in which you all agree on the scoring considerations? What do you do to reach agreement?

5. Teachers are required to report progress to parents of students with disabilities. What federal law mandated this? How often must this progress reporting occur? What are some ways a teachers might report students' progress?

Practical Application Assessment Activities

1. Work individually, in pairs or in a small group to perform a task analysis for use in constructing a criterion-referenced test. Select a multi-step task, such as changing a tire, baking a cake, or solving a mathematical equation (e.g., involving two digit multiplication requiring regrouping, such as 37×48). Write down each sequential step in the task and then each group will share their analysis with the other groups. The focus of the concluding discussion will be on whether all groups reported the same sequence, whether the steps described were the same, what and why there were any differences and whether there is actually more than one way to successfully complete the task.

2. Obtain a sample report card from your community school district. Identify the skill criteria that a grade level teacher must address when grading each subject area. Choose several skills from each subject area and identify an authentic assessment activity for each subject area skill that could be used to determine whether the skill has been mastered, has not been mastered, or is emerging.

3. Design a rubric to be used to evaluate student work samples (e.g., a written essay, science lab report, math problem solving). Have at least three students complete these work samples and use your rubric to evaluate their work. Determine inter-

rater reliability by having a small group of your peers also rate these work samples, compare rubric results, compare and contrast rating differences. As a culminating activity, re-score the rubrics after considering the rationale of your peers. If needed, develop the rubric based on completed student work samples.

Connection Between CEC, PRAXIS, and INTASC Standards and Chapter 3

Council for Exceptional Children

The voice and vision of special education

The Council for Exceptional Children— Professional Standards

Standard 2 Development and Characteristics of Learners

1. Typical and atypical human growth and development.
2. Educational implications of characteristics of various exceptionalities.
3. Characteristics and effects of the cultural and environmental milieu of the individual with exceptional learning needs and the family.
5. Similarities and differences of individuals with and without exceptional learning needs.
6. Similarities and differences among individuals with exceptional learning needs.

Standard 3 Individual Learning Differences

1. Effects an exceptional condition(s) can have on an individual's life.
2. Impact of learners' academic and social abilities, attitudes, interests, and values on instruction and career development.

Standard 4 Instructional Strategies

1. Use strategies to facilitate integration into various settings.
5. Use procedures to increase the individual's self-awareness, self-management, self-control, self-reliance, and self-esteem.

Standard 5 Learning Environments and Social Interactions

16. Use performance data and information from all stakeholders to make or suggest modifications in learning environments.
17. Establish and maintain rapport with individuals with and without exceptional learning needs.

Standard 7 Instructional Planning

9. Use functional assessments to develop intervention plans.
10. Use task analysis.
11. Sequence, implement, and evaluate individualized learning objectives.
12. Integrate affective, social, and life skills with academic curricula.
13. Develop and select instructional content, resources, and strategies that respond to cultural, linguistic, and gender differences.

Standard 8 Assessment

1. Basic terminology used in assessment.
2. Legal provisions and ethical principles regarding assessment of individuals.
3. Screening, prereferral, referral, and classification procedures.
4. Use and limitations of assessment instruments.
5. National, state or provincial, and local accommodations and modifications.
6. Gather relevant background information.
7. Administer nonbiased formal and informal assessments.
8. Use technology to conduct assessments.
9. Develop or modify individualized assessment strategies.
10. Interpret information from formal and informal assessments.
11. Use assessment information in making eligibly, program, and placement decisions for individuals with exceptional learning needs, including those from culturally and/or linguistically diverse backgrounds.
12. Report assessment result to all stakeholders using effective communication skills.
13. Evaluate instruction and monitor progress of individuals with exceptional learning needs.
14. Create and maintain records.

Standard 9 Professional and Ethical Practice

5. Practice within the CEC Code of Ethics and other standards of the profession.
6. Uphold high standards of competence and integrity and exercise sound judgment in the practice of the professional.
7. Act ethically in advocating for appropriate services.
8. Conduct professional activities in compliance with applicable laws and policies.
9. Demonstrate commitment to developing the highest education and quality-of-life potential of individuals with exceptional learning needs.
11. Practice within one's skill limit and obtain assistance as needed.
12. Use verbal, nonverbal, and written language effectively.

Standard 10 Collaboration

5. Maintain confidential communication about individuals with exceptional learning needs.
6. Collaborate with families and others in assessment of individuals with exceptional learning needs.
9. Plan and conduct collaborative conferences with individuals with exceptional learning needs and their families.
11. Use group problem-solving skills to develop, implement, and evaluate collaborative activities.
13. Communicate with school personnel about the characteristics and needs of individuals.
14. Communicate effectively with families of individuals with exceptional learning needs from diverse backgrounds.

THE PRAXIS SERIES™

PRAXIS Standards for Special Education

Standard 1 Understanding Exceptionalities

2. Characteristics of students with disabilities, including medical/physical; educational; social; and psychological.

Standard 3 Delivery of Services to Students with Disabilities

3. Assessment, including how to modify, construct, or select and conduct nondiscriminatory and appropriate informal and formal assessment procedures; how to interpret standardized and specialized assessment results; how to use evaluation result for various purposes, including monitoring instruction and IEP/ITP development; and how to prepare written reports and communicate findings to others.

5. Curriculum and instruction, including the IEP/ITP process; instructional development and implementation (for example, instructional activities, curricular materials, resources and equipment, working with classroom personnel, tutoring and the use of technology); teaching strategies and methods (for example, direct instruction, cooperative learning, diagnostic-prescriptive method); instructional format and components (for example, individualized instruction, small- and large-group instruction, modeling, drill and practice); and areas of instruction (such as academics, study and learning skills, social, self-care, and vocational skills).

INTASC Standards for Teacher Education

Standard 6

The teacher uses knowledge of effective verbal, nonverbal, and media communication techniques to foster active inquiry, collaboration, and supportive interaction in the classroom.

Standard 8

The teacher understands and uses formal and informal assessment strategies to evaluate and ensure the continuous intellectual, social, and physical development of the learner.

Standard 9

The teacher is a reflective practitioner who continually evaluates the effects of his/her choices and actions on others (students, parents, and other professionals in the learning community) and who actively seeks out opportunities to grow professionally.

Preliminary Assessment Issues

CHAPTER 4

Accountability, Accommodations, and Alternate Assessment

KEY TERMS AND CONCEPTS

- test accommodation
- accommodations
- modifications
- accountability
- high-stakes testing
- No Child Left Behind (NCLB) Act
- content standards
- performance standards
- educational accountability

- setting accommodations
- timing accommodations
- scheduling accommodations
- presentation accommodations
- response accommodations
- modifications
- out-of-level testing
- alternate assessment

CHAPTER OBJECTIVES

After reading this chapter, you should be able to:

- Discuss the history and recently mandated changes regarding the inclusion of all students in accountability testing.
- Explain the reasons for providing accommodations to students.
- Identify the factors that determine whether special accommodations will be made.
- Describe the role of the IEP team in the documentation of accommodations.

- Identify when and what modifications can be used during standardized accountability testing.
- Identify what conditions are necessary for a student to qualify for alternate assessment.
- Define the criteria for developing alternate assessments.

Introduction to Accountability, Accommodations, and Alternate Assessments

The most recent reauthorization of the original Public Law 94-142, the Education for All Handicapped Children's Act of 1976, is Public Law 105-17, the Individuals with Disabilities Education Act Amendments of 1997 (IDEA-04). Public Law was signed into law on November 19, 2004. Since IDEA-04 was created, more than 6.2 million students with disabilities are receiving special education and related services (Digest of Education Statistics, 2002).

The enactment of IDEA-2004, with its significant refinements, demonstrates strong congressional commitment to the educational rights of students with disabilities. Although the tenets of IDEA-2004 affirm the basic principles established by Public Law 94-142, this chapter focuses on the major shifts in assessment practices. (See Figure 4-1.) It also looks at the sections of the reauthorization that deal with the assessment of students, specific accountability issues, and appropriate test accommodations and modifications for students with disabilities.

Figure 4–1   Major Shifts in Assessment Practices

Away from	Toward:
• Assessing students' knowledge of specific facts and isolated skills	• Assessing students' full knowledge base
• Comparing students' performance with other students	• Comparing students' performance with established criteria
• Designing "teacher-proof" assessment systems	• Giving support to teachers and to their informed judgement
• Making the assessment process secret, exclusive, and fixed	• Making the assessment process public, participatory, and dynamic
• Restricting students to a single way of demonstrating their knowledge	• Giving students multiple opportunities to demonstrate their full knowledge
• Developing assessment by oneself	• Developing a shared vision of what to assess and how to do it
• Using assessment to filter and select students out of the opportunities to learn	• Using assessment results to ensure that all students have the opportunity to achieve their potential
• Treating assessment as independent of curriculum or instruction	• Aligning assessment with curriculum and instruction
• Basing inferences on restricted or single sources of evidence	• Basing inferences on multiple sources of evidence
• Viewing students as the objects of assessment	• Viewing students as active participants in the assessment process
• Regarding assessment as sporadic and conclusive	• Regarding assessment as continual and recursive
• Holding only a few accountable for assessment results	• Holding all concerned with learning accountable for assessment results

Source: Regional Educational Laboratories (1998, February). *Improving classroom assessment: A toolkit for professional developers (Toolkit 98),* Portland, OR: Northwest Regional Educational Laboratory. Reprinted with permission.

SECTION 1: IDEA-2004: MANDATES FOR ASSESSMENT AND ACCOUNTABILITY

The focus of federal legislation, specifically, IDEA-2004 is based on two premises: (1) that all students, even those with disabilities, shall have access to challenging standards, and (2) that policy makers and educators should be held publicly accountable for every student's performance (P.L. 108-446). All students with disabilities must be included in the assessment procedures if they receive any instruction in the content that is being assessed, regardless of where that instruction occurs (e.g., resource center, self-contained class, inclusion program). IDEA-2004 mandates that all students participate in state and local program standards, the curricular frameworks that come from those standards, and the evaluation procedures that are used to assess their progress in that curriculum (P.L. 108-446).

Any deviation from full participation in the general assessment procedures, such as an accommodation, should be made only on an individual basis, and it must be justified as being needed for a compelling educational reason. A **test accommodation** is a change in how a test is presented or how the test taker responds, and it is not intended to give students an unfair advantage (Council for Exceptional Children (CEC), 2000).

The intent of this federal legislation mandate is to promote a strength-based way of looking at students: to expect that they can reach for and attain higher goals. The teacher's role is to determine what, if any, accommodations or modifications are needed to support students as they work toward achieving curricular standards and are evaluated using content standards. Also, teachers need to be prepared to report students' progress to the appropriate sources, including parents, school personnel, administrators, school boards, and the larger educational systems, whether local, regional, state, or federal. This reporting system is now a critical aspect because increasing emphasis is being placed on **accountability** of students' progress in meeting curricular standards and it often determines whether they are promoted or graduate.

Reasons for Reform

Reform movements—including Goals 2000, which emphasizes the development of high-level standards for all students (Phillips, 1996) and IDEA-2004, which mandates that students with disabilities be included in testing and statewide reporting—are based on the following objectives:

1. To get an accurate picture of the educational system. This is not possible if a large segment of the population is excluded (e.g., students with disabilities).
2. To obtain needed information about how students are performing, because educational reforms are increasingly driven by the results obtained from accountability systems. In order for the reforms to be productive and meet the needs of all students, reporting systems must be in compliance with legal mandates and account for all students, including those with different characteristics and levels of achievement.
3. To ensure that accurate comparisons can be made from school to school, district to district, and state to state. Serious reliability issues result when one district is testing and reporting the test results of all students, including students with disabilities, while a neighboring district is either not including all students in the testing process or is not reporting the test results of all

🔍 CLARIFYING TERMS

The following terms are often used interchangeably:

Accommodations—changes in how the test taker responds

Modifications—changes in how the test is presented

students (Erickson, Thurlow, & Thor, 1995; Erickson, Thurlow, Thor, & Seyfarth, 1996).

4. To eliminate the retention of students with disabilities or their placement in special education as a way to avoid testing them. When test results are tied to significant consequences, referred to as **high-stakes testing**, there is a tendency for schools to avoid including students who might lower overall test scores. High-stakes testing consequences might include whether a district is reconstituted or qualifies for monetary assistance to provide remedial services, whether a school gets accreditation, whether a teacher is granted tenure, and whether a student is promoted or receives a high school diploma.

5. To meet legal requirements. Section 504 of the Rehabilitation Act of 1973 and the Americans with Disabilities Act of 1990 (see Chapter 1) stipulate that (a) any individual with a disability who is otherwise qualified must be included in programs or activities that receive federal assistance, and (b) programs must make reasonable accommodations for that individual's physical or mental limitations. Improving America's Schools Act, (IASA) mandates that program accountability be based on student performance on statewide tests, which includes students with disabilities and those with limited English proficiency.

6. To promote high expectations for student learning. There has been a tendency to have low expectations for students who have disabilities. Mandating that all students be included in the testing process and that all test results be included in district reporting systems helps to ensure that educational programs follow the higher curricular standards that make up the content of the test. The **No Child Left Behind (NCLB) Act** of 2001 is a federal act that, through high-stakes testing, determines how much federal aid will be given to a state. The high-stakes tests, such as those mandated by the NCLB Act, are generated by state and federal agencies and used to determine which schools are providing adequate education to students, which schools qualify for monetary assistance to provide remedial services, and which students will receive a high school diploma.

Critical Thinking and Reflection Activity

Several teachers complain to you that making test accommodations is both time consuming and unfair to the other students. How do you respond?

There has been a drastically increased focus on higher levels of student achievement and accountability, and to more types of assessments. Individual schools, school districts, and increasingly, individual students are being held accountable for achieving both content and performance standards. In order to collect data to ensure that students are progressing, the assessment system is being expanded, with schools using various types of assessments for multiple purposes to tap into the new knowledge presented in the content standards (Salvia & Ysseldyke, 2004). New testing measures, such as performance and authentic assessments, are being used to evaluate student progress in mastery of content.

Research on educational reforms indicates that one significant consequence of the implementation of these standards is the broadening of the curriculum. Not only are more facts, concepts, and skills now required, but integrating subjects and skills so that the curriculum is multidisciplinary is also being emphasized. Subject area content is no longer taught in isolation; emphasis is now on increased writing across all domains. Also, there is a focus on the application of the content taught to ensure that students can use knowledge in practical and real-life ways. This emphasis on a multi-disciplinary, writing-intense, real-life skill curriculum has direct impact on teaching methods and subsequently on assessment methods. Instruction and assessment are now more than before hands-on, project-based, and student-directed so that students learn and demonstrate mastery by doing and applying what they learn.

A major focus of school reform is the move toward establishing and maintaining core curriculum standards now mandated at the federal level by IDEA–2004, with implementation required at the state and local district levels. There are two kinds of core standards: content standards and performance standards. **Content standards** involve the expansion and regulation of the content knowledge covered in school curriculum. In most states and districts, this involves adding new skills, competencies, and concepts to reading, written language, math, science, and social studies that teachers must teach and students must learn. **Performance standards** are levels of knowledge, competency, concepts, and skills that are driving the assessment and accountability systems in this country.

SECTION 2: ISSUES OF ACCOUNTABILITY

The need for accountability has affected the assessment process. **Educational accountability** is a systematic method of assuring that those inside and outside the educational system are moving in desired directions (Center for Policy Options, 1993). Increasingly, schools are being held accountable for how much of the public's money they spend and how they spend it. Also, there is concern that U.S. students are less capable of competing on a global basis (Erickson, Ysseldyke, Thurlow, & Elliott, 1998). As it has become increasingly clear that monitoring the process of education has not been successful, emphasis has shifted to the results of education.

In the past, the evidence that schools were working was based on process factors, such as the money spent on educational services (per-pupil expenditures), the student-teacher ratio, numbers of teachers with advanced degrees (master's degree and above), numbers of students in advanced classes, numbers of students receiving compensatory education services and in special education, the amount of parental involvement in schools, the length of the school day, the percentage of absences, and the adequacy of the school building.

Currently, a primary impact of standard-based reforms is the increased focus on the results of education, including actual student performance on district and statewide assessments, scholastic achievement test (SAT/ACT) scores, graduation and drop-out rates, numbers of students who enroll in postsecondary educational programs, and high school equivalency (GED) completion rates (Thurlow, Elliott, & Ysseldyke, 1998). The public wants to know that its tax dollars are being put to good use and that the educational system is working. The evidence of the results of education is determined primarily through assessments (rather than being based on process factors).

Accountability has become a factor at several levels. The federal government is accountable to the public for ensuring that the mandates of the NCLB Act are carried out. The state is accountable for ensuring that school districts are following IDEA–97 and NCLB mandates. Local school systems are accountable for overall student performance within their districts. Teachers are accountable for their classes' test scores. Individual students are accountable for achieving scores that are high enough so that they are promoted and ultimately receive a diploma.

According to federal mandates, public reports must be made on the numbers of students who participate in regular and alternate assessments, as was previously required for general education students. These reports must include aggregated (combined) data on the test results of all students, including those with disabilities, and disaggregated (separated) data only on the performance of students with disabilities. The exception to this requirement is when such reporting would lead to the identification of a particular student, therefore risking student confidentiality (e.g., when only one or two students take an alternate assessment).

The new regulations under the NCLB Act give states and districts more flexibility in selecting which students can be assessed using alternate achievement standards to meet adequate yearly progress goals (CEC, 2003, December 19). The regulations allow students with various disabilities to be identified as having a "significant cognitive disability." For example, students with autism, severe learning disabilities, developmental delay, emotional disturbance, or other disabilities that affect cognitive performance could now be eligible to take alternate assessments that are aligned with alternate achievement standards.

Some students with disabilities may be assessed at their achievement level or the "out-of-level-testing" used for students with special needs. While all students with disabilities will participate in assessments, the individualized education planning (IEP) team decides how an individual student will be assessed and the methods used.

Variations in Assessment Among States and Districts

Many schools administer both statewide and districtwide testing, although the type of test, the grades tested, the time of administration, and the type of assessment can vary widely. Most states require standardized, norm-referenced testing; some use criterion-referenced; and others use both types of assessments. Informal assessment measures—such as authentic/performance-based assessments, portfolios, curriculum-based assessments—are being used much more frequently. Basic skill subjects (e.g., reading, math, and written language) seem to be the primary subject areas tested, yet content area subjects (e.g., science and social studies) and other areas (e.g., oral language, study skills) may be included in the assessment process. Generally all grade levels are tested, although some states or districts test specified grade levels (e.g., grades 4, 8, and 11). The administration time is often in the spring, although some schools schedule these tests during the fall or winter.

Determining Student Participation

The IEP team, which includes the parent(s) and the student (when appropriate), determines whether accommodations, modifications, or alternate testing is needed. When the decision is made, it must be documented on the student's IEP. The IEP must include a statement identifying any accommodations or modifications needed in the administration of state- or districtwide assessments. Very few students should be excluded from the regular assessment. The most common reason for excluding students

When parents, students and teachers collaborate in the evaluation, placement and programming process, everyone benefits.

is that their instructional goals are not aligned with the purpose of the assessment (e.g., functional, self-help skills rather than traditional academic content). If the IEP team determines that the student will not participate in an assessment or in part of an assessment, a statement must be included in the student's IEP to indicate why the assessment is not appropriate and how the student will be assessed.

There is a distinction between assessment and accountability. Accountability does not mean that all students must participate in the same assessment program. What is required is that the progress of all students be monitored and accounted for. The National Center on Educational Outcomes (Elliott, Thurlow, & Ysseldyke, 1996) has developed criteria that districts and states can use to evaluate their guidelines on the participation of students with disabilities in assessment. (See Figure 4–2 for translated criteria.)

Deciding Which Students Need Accommodations

The decision regarding the need for special considerations is based on students' evaluation test results, their current level of functioning, and their unique learning characteristics; it is not based on their program placement, the category of disability, or the percent of time in the general education classroom. The intent is to use accommodations that students have been using regularly in the classroom during instruction and classroom testing. Accommodations that have not previously been used should not be introduced during district or statewide testing. A good guideline is to "test the way you teach."

Although there is a history of excluding students with disabilities from participating in state and district testing, there is little evidence that much thought has been given to preparing students to participate in testing. In determining appropriate testing modifications, a fundamental principle is to follow the type of instructional modifications used in the classroom. Modifications that are not routinely used during the instructional day and during classroom testing are not appropriate during state-mandated testing. For example, students who habitually need extended time for classroom assignments and tests will probably need extended time for state-mandated tests. Students may receive multiple test modifications if these modifications are part of the routine instruction and testing for the student.

Figure 4–2   Criteria for Evaluating Guidelines for Participation of All Students in Testing

- Decision makers start from the premise that all students, including all students with disabilities, are to participate in the accountability system and, to the extent possible, in the regular assessment.
- Decisions are made by people who know students, including their strengths and weaknesses.
- Decision makers take into account students' instructional goals, current level of functioning, and learning characteristics.
- Students' program setting, category of disability, or percentage of time in the classroom does not influence the decision.
- Students are included in any part of the test for which they receive any instruction, regardless of where the instruction occurs.
- Before a decision is made to have students participate in an alternative assessment, decision makers reconfirm that only 1% to 2% of all students in their district or state are in the alternative assessment.
- Parents are informed of participation options and about the implications of their child not being included in a particular test or in the accountability system. They are encouraged to contribute to the decision-making process.
- The decision is written in students' IEP, or on the form attached to the IEP.

Source: "Assessment guidelines that maximize the participation of students with disabilities in large-scale assessments: Characteristics and considerations" (Synthesis Report No. 25), by J. Elliott, M. Thurlow & J. Ysseldyke, 1996. National Center on Educational Outcomes. Minneapolis: University of Minnesota. Reprinted with permission.

SECTION 3: TESTING ACCOMMODATIONS AND MODIFICATIONS

Accommodations are the instructional strategies (e.g., materials, modality of presentation, grouping) or learning environment (e.g., position in class structure) that are adapted for students with a disability. Research has established that testing accommodations do help individuals with special needs (Thompson, Blount, & Thurlow, 2002). Accommodations are designed to level the playing field between students with and those without special needs. Testing accommodations should not be used to give students an unfair advantage over the students who are not receiving them. Other types of accommodations involve adjustments or supports as a means of motivating and preparing students to take tests. It is up to each state and school district to determine which students merit accommodations and which accommodations should be extended.

Classroom Scenario: What Would You Do?

Juan, a special education student included in a general education class, uses a laptop in class and at home to write. While distributing the yearly group assessment, the general education teacher told Juan that he could not use his laptop because it would provide him with an unfair advantage on the test. As Juan's special education teacher, what would you say about these instructions?

Accommodations

Accommodations are provided in relation to individual student's needs. While IDEA and its regulations do not define accommodations or modifications, there is some agreement as to what these terms mean. These supports or services are provided to help students access the curriculum and validly demonstrate their learning. "They include changes in testing materials or procedures that enable students with disabilities to participate in ways that allow abilities to be assessed rather than disabilities" (Thurlow et al., 1998, p. 28). Accommodations are implemented to allow students with disabilities to participate meaningfully in both instruction and assessment that would otherwise be denied.

The intent of accommodations is not to give these students an advantage, but rather to allow them to complete the same assignment or test as other students, with a change in the timing, formatting, setting, scheduling, response, and/or presentation without altering in any significant way what the test or assignment measures (The Alliance, 2001). Accommodations allow students to demonstrate what they know

Figure 4–3   Optional Test Accommodations

Timing Accommodations
> Allow extended timing
> Allow unlimited timing
> Allow frequent breaks during the test

Setting Accommodations
> Administer in a separate room
> Administer in a small group
> Use a study carrel or an isolated area
> Provide a distraction-free environment

Scheduling Accommodations
> Adjust the time or day of administration
> Administer the test over several shorter sessions/days
> Modify order of tests (e.g., hardest subject first; shortest test given last)

Presentation Accommodations
> Modified format: Enlarged print, test format change (e.g., multiple choice vs. essay; dictation vs. scantron; highlighted key words/directions; change in process; fewer items on page/one type of item on each page or section)
> Procedure modifications: Orally explain directions; read questions aloud; give responses orally; simplify language; allow supports (e.g., notes, outline, manipulatives); use sign language
> Assistive devices: Computer, tape recorder, video, magnification or amplification device

Response Accommodations
> Modified format: Allow circling rather than filling in bubble on scantron; allow verbal vs. written response
> Procedure modifications: Respond into a tape recorder, on a computer, in a Brailler; respond using pointing or sign language; write answers rather than make multiple-choice selections
> Assistive devices: Computer, calculator, spell-checker, tape recorder, magnification/amplification device, markers, place holders, templates, graph paper, dictionary, thesaurus, math facts sheet

without being impeded by their disability. The intent of accommodations is to offset or correct for distortions in scores that are the result of a disability (McDonnell, McLaughlin, & Morrison, 1997), not to ensure that students will not be frustrated by the assessment task or achieve a higher score on the test. (See Figure 4–3.)

Guidelines for Providing Accommodations

It should be noted that providing specific accommodations to students does not mean they will automatically do better on tests. (See Figure 4–4.) Often, the student needs to be shown or trained in how to use the device or adaptation. Also, it is not

Figure 4–4   Guiding Accommodation Principles

Do not assume that every student with disabilities needs assessment accommodations. Test accommodations should parallel instructional accommodations.

Obtain the approval of IEP team. Also, include accommodations in the IEP.

Base accommodation on student need. Do not base accommodation on disability-specific factors or determinations by educational program placement.

Be respectful of the student's cultural and ethnic background. Also, be sure that the student and the student's family understand and are comfortable with the suggested accommodation, and always communicate in the family's primary language.

Integrate assessment accommodations into classroom instruction. Never introduce an unfamiliar accommodation during an assessment.

Know whether your state and/or district has an approved list of accommodations. Although the IEP team makes accommodation decisions, it is important to follow established lists and procedures.

Plan early for accommodations. Make sure the student has enough time to learn and feel comfortable with the accommodation.

Include students in decision making. Make sure the student wants and will use the accommodation.

Understand the purpose of the assessment. Be sure the accommodations do not interfere with the intent of the test (e.g., providing a calculator on a math computation test or reading aloud to a student taking a reading skills test).

Request only accommodations that are truly needed. Too many accommodations could overload the student or multiple accommodations could interfere with each other.

Determine if selected accommodations require another accommodation. Some accommodations, such as having the test read aloud to the student, may be distracting to other students who require setting accommodations.

Provide practice opportunities for the student. Teach test-taking tips, and familiarize students with the test format and types of questions.

Remember that accommodations in test taking will not necessarily eliminate frustration for the student. The accommodations are meant to allow students to demonstrate what they know and what they can do. Accommodations will not guarantee good scores or reduced anxiety; they are intended to level the playing field.

Source: Making Assessment Accommodations: A Toolkit for Educators, (Figure 3B: Guiding Principles), by The Council for Exceptional Children, 2000, pp. 63–65. Alexandria, VA: Author. Adapted with permission.

pedagogically sound to allow students to use an accommodation for the first time during a district or statewide accountability test. They should be using these accommodations in situations before the testing session, preferably as a regular aspect of their instructional program in general education settings as well as in life settings outside the school. There are exceptions, such as when the student receives direct teacher prompts and step-by-step directions during instruction, which are not allowed during testing. A statement must be included in students' IEPs to indicate why and what accommodations are needed. These accommodations should be tracked through the IEP process to determine how students have been assessed following instruction and closely monitored to determine whether accommodations continue to be required or need to be adjusted. Accommodations fall into several categories, as described in the following subsections.

Classroom Scenario: What Would You Do?

Martha's IEP states that she should take tests in a distraction-free room and be given extended time to take the tests. On the day of one test, her teacher was absent. Since prior preparations had not been made, Martha was forced to take the test in her classroom under standard time limits. If you had been her teacher, what would you have done to avoid this situation?

Categories of Accommodations

Setting Accommodations

Setting accommodations involve changes in the location, conditions, or both in which the assessment takes place. The setting for conducting a test should always be familiar to, and comfortable for, the student. New settings tend to cause confusion, anxiety, and distractions. The test setting should be physically comfortable—not too hot or too cold, because excessive temperature can reduce students' concentration and motivation. Common reasons for needing a change in the standard setting may be that students have difficulty processing or focusing on written material; they may be easily distracted by extraneous noises or be distracting to other students taking a group test; or they may have a physical or sensory impairment requiring that they have special equipment. Students who have medical problems that prevent them from being at the testing site might need to take the test either in their home or a hospital room. (Figure 4–5 lists sample questions to be asked when evaluating the need for setting accommodations.)

Timing Accommodations

Timing accommodations involve a change in the duration of the test, most often an extension in the standard length of time allowed for test taking. Students who commonly require time accommodations have learning disabilities and may require extended time as a result of their slow work pace; difficulty in processing, retrieving, and producing answers due to perceptual problems; visual motor integration problems; or word retrieval or comprehension difficulties. Students with physical impairments

Figure 4–5   Setting Accommodations Questionnaire

Does the student need:

an aide to assist with testing in a large-group setting? _____

small-group or individual test administration? _____

a separate room that is less distracting or more conducive to thinking? _____

solitary test conditions, because student's behavior distracts other test takers? _____

solitary test conditions, because accommodations distract other test takers? _____

administration in a hospital? _____

administration in the student's home? _____

adaptive furniture for taking the test? _____

a test room with special acoustics? _____

a study carrel to work with minimal distractions? _____

a room with special lighting? _____

tests administered on an individualized or small-group basis? _____

may require more time to write, type, or dictate responses. Those with sensory impairment may need more time to use the magnifier, the tape recorder, and so forth. Pupils who are chronically ill may need extended time to allow for frequent breaks because of fatigue or medical interventions. (Figure 4-6 lists sample questions to be asked when evaluating the need for timing accommodations.)

Scheduling Accommodations

Scheduling accommodations involve changes in when tests are administered—such as the day or the time—or the order in which tests are administered. Students with short attention spans, those with medical or physical problems, and those who work very slowly or frustrate easily often require scheduling accommodations. The tests can be broken into smaller, more manageable segments, or sometimes spread out over several days. Often tests are adjusted to a specific time of the day to facilitate a time when the child is more alert, after medication is administered, or later in the week after the child has had time to settle into the learning environment. (Figure 4-7 lists sample questions to be asked when evaluating the need for scheduling accommodations.)

Figure 4–6   Timing Accommodations Questionnaire

Does the student need:

the assessment to be broken into different kinds of subtests? _____

one subtest to be given before another? _____

other accommodations that necessitate longer time to access information? _____

extended time (i.e., a specific amount of extra time) to complete the test? _____

unlimited time (i.e., as much time as needed) to complete the test? _____

frequent breaks during the test session? _____

Figure 4–7   Scheduling Accommodations Questionnaire

Does the student need:

testing to be scheduled during a specific time of day (e.g., early morning, after lunch, 30 minutes after medication is administered)? _____

subtests to be presented in a different order (e.g., longer subtest first, then shorter subtest)? ____

testing to be broken into segments administered over several days? _____

Presentation Accommodations

Presentation accommodations involve a change in the way students access test directions and items. This type of accommodation may involve changing standard procedures, altering the test format, or using some form of assistive device in the testing process. Although presentation accommodations seem to be the most frequently required by students with disabilities, they also tend to be the most controversial (e.g., when the test directions or questions are read to the student, there is often concern about the comparability of these modified presentations to tests administered by standard means).

This type of accommodation is often used by students with sensory disabilities (i.e., hearing or visual impairments), who may require an interpreter to sign the test instructions (procedural change), larger print or a Braille version of the test (format alterations), or magnification or amplification (assistive device). Students with learning or behavioral problems may need directions or questions read orally (procedural change), provisions for writing answers in the test booklet rather than on a separate scantron sheet (format change), or a spell-checker (assistive device). (Figure 4–8 lists sample questions to be asked when evaluating the need for presentation accommodations.)

Response Accommodations

Response accommodations involve a change in how students respond to the assessment. This type of accommodation includes either format alterations, procedural changes, assistive devices, or a combination of all. There tends to be some controversy about the use of response mode changes, especially regarding the "fairness" of using these accommodations. Responses should be structured to range from simple recognition and recall to those requiring higher level thinking skills, such as inference, analysis, synthesis, evaluation, and appreciation.

Students who are likely to require response accommodations have physical or sensory impairments. For example, students with a visual impairment may need to answer orally rather than in writing (format alteration), and they may need to type rather than write answers (procedural change) or use a Braille typewriter (assistive device). Students with learning disabilities may need to write their answers in detail rather than choose an answer from multiple-choice options (format alteration), have the test organized so that all of one type of problem is on one page (e.g., addition equations) and another type on another page (e.g., multiplication equations), and use a list of the multiplication facts or a calculator when solving word problems (assistive device). (Figure 4–9 lists sample questions to be asked when evaluating the need for response accommodations.)

Figure 4–8   Presentation Accommodations Questionnaire

Does the student need:

test materials that are in large print? _____

test materials to be in Braille? _____

a speech synthesizer or an electronic reader? _____

photo-enlarged test forms? _____

test directions/questions translated? _____

test items/directions presented in the student's native language? _____

key words or phrases to be color-coded, highlighted, or underlined? _____

test items that avoid or clarify double negatives in questioning? _____

visuals that help to interpret or clarify test items? _____

larger bubbles for multiple-choice questions? _____

sign language to explain directions? _____

magnification equipment? _____

directions repeated, clarified, and/or interpreted? _____

directions read aloud? _____

items ordered according to level of difficulty? _____

complete sentences on one line rather than split into two lines to maintain margins? _____

unfamiliar, abstract, or difficult-to-understand words defined? _____

verbal prompting or cues to follow directions accurately and continue working? _____

demonstration or modeling of how to complete tasks? _____

physical prompts (e.g., guiding a hand in using the computer)? _____

appropriate feedback regarding responses to test items? _____

briefer, more frequent tests? _____

alternative test measures (e.g., checklists, projects, and portfolios)? _____

test directions to be placed on each page of the test? _____

test items presented in an affixed, predictable, symmetrical sequence? _____

test papers that provide adequate space for responses? _____

test papers with sufficient space between items? _____

fewer test items on a page to avoid confusion? _____

color overlays? _____

cues (e.g., arrows, stop signs) as a guide through test sections? _____

assistance in tracking test items or turning pages? _____

Modifications

Modifications are changes in the program and curriculum that are required when the accommodations will not effectively allow the participation of the student with a disability in the general education program (e.g., usually involving an adjustment of the content of the curriculum). Modifications should be used only after all possible accommodations have been considered and determined ineffective (Seaman, DePauw, Morton, & Omoto, 2003).

Modifications either change the content of the material that is taught or adapt the specific performance standards by prioritizing, adjusting, or eliminating any that the IEP team agrees need to be modified. Any modification or move away from those standards should be done only on an individual basis for a compelling educational reason and needs to be justified. Any special arrangements or modifications that are used in

Figure 4–9   Response Mode Accommodations Questionnaire

Does the student need to:

use an assistive device (e.g., speech synthesizer, communication board)? _____

use computational aids (e.g., calculators, mathematics tables, software programs)? _____

use a word processor for narrative responses? _____

write on the test booklet and later transcribe to a sheet with fill-in-the-bubble answers? _____

mark answers in the test booklet rather than on a separate answer form? _____

use reference materials (e.g., dictionary, thesaurus)? _____

have a sample provided of an expected correct response? _____

use a template for responding? _____

point to the response? _____

respond orally? _____

respond in sign language? _____

use a Braille writer? _____

use a computer? _____

use a spell- or grammar-checker? _____

receive assistance with and interpretation of responses? _____

be reminded to review answers, complete unanswered items, and make corrections, as
needed? _____

use a scribe to record responses? _____

have spelling errors allowed without being graded down? _____

have pencils adapted in size or grip? _____

accountability testing must be in accordance with rules and procedures that protect test standardization procedures and the validity of the assessment. Modifications or special test arrangements are not intended and must never be used for score enhancement.

Whenever modification is made in the administration of state or district tests, a statement specifying exactly what the modification is must be in the student's IEP. Two examples of modifications are completing only part of a standard test, and completing an alternative assignment that is more easily achievable than the standard assignment or out-of-level testing.

Out-of-level testing is a modification that involves using a lower grade-level test (e.g., using the student's instructional level rather than his or her actual grade placement level). Out-of-level testing can be used for making instructional and planning decisions, but it is not appropriate for accountability assessments because testing at a lower grade level does not reflect the student's performance at the standard being assessed for the majority of grade-level peers.

Correlating Accommodations with Specific Learning Characteristics

Correlating students' learning styles and their accommodation needs with the development of the test structure has been found to be quite beneficial. Whenever possible, it is important that the test be formulated as a "best fit." This means that the test is designed to evaluate mastery of material using an assessment method in which students can most effectively and efficiently demonstrate their skill level. It also reduces or eliminates the barriers to fair and accurate assessment for students with disabilities, thus possibly avoiding the need for special accommodations or modifications.

For students who demonstrate strength in the area of oral communication (e.g., speaking, reciting, and debating), the test can be designed with a verbal response mode, including the use of voice recognition technology. When students demonstrate weaknesses in the areas of visual perception, the test could be developed to incorporate oral, step-by-step directions; the questions could be tape recorded; extended time could be factored into the test conditions; or the student could respond orally to the evaluator or record responses into the tape recorder. Students could be allowed to write their response in the test booklet, rather than be required to complete a separate answer sheet in which they need to fill in the bubble (scantron format). Also, students should be allowed to respond in their primary language (if other than English). The following accommodations are commonly used with specific types of student problems:

Poor comprehension
- Give directions both orally and in written form, and make sure students understand them.
- Avoid talking excessively before a test.
- Correct for content only and not for spelling or grammar.
- Provide an example of the expected correct response.
- Remind students to check tests for unanswered questions.
- When the test deals with problem-solving skills, allow students to use multiplication tables and/or calculators.
- Read test aloud for students who have difficulty reading.
- Provide a written outline for essay questions.
- Record instructions and questions for a test on an audiocassette tape.
- Allow students to tape-record responses to answers.
- Use objective rather than essay questions.

Poor Auditory Perception
- Avoid oral tests.
- Seat students in a quiet place for testing.
- Allow students to take the test in a study carrel.
- Place a "Do Not Disturb—Testing" sign on the classroom door to discourage interruptions.
- For oral tests (e.g., spelling tests), go slowly; enunciate each word distinctly.

Poor Visual Perception
- Give directions orally as well as in written form.
- Seat students away from visual distractions (e.g., window or door). Use a carrel or have their desks face the wall.
- Check students discreetly to see if they are "on track."
- Give exam orally or tape-record on audiocassette recorder.
- Use clear, easily readable, and uncluttered test forms.
- Use a test format that has ample space for students' responses; provide lined answer spaces for essay or short-answer questions.
- Avoid having other students turn in papers during the test.

- Place a "Do Not Disturb—Testing" sign on the door.
- Provide graph paper for aligning math problems.
- Provide graphic organizers to help students structure written responses.

Problems Due to Physical Challenges
- Allow oral, typed, or dictated responses.
- Allow extended or unlimited time.
- Allow the use of special equipment or materials.
- Modify environmental arrangements, furniture, and lighting.
- Reduce the length of tests.

Problems with Time Constraints
- Allow enough time for students to complete the test.
- Provide breaks during lengthy tests.
- Use untimed tests.
- Allow split-halves testing. Give half of the test one day and the remaining half the second day.
- Allow the students to complete only the odd- or even-numbered questions. Circle the appropriate questions for students who may not understand the concept of odd and even.
- Give oral or tape-recorded tests. Students with slow writing skills can answer orally to the teacher or on tape.

Test Anxiety/Embarrassment
- Before test administration, provide warm-up activities that can help to prepare while relaxing students.
- Whenever possible, structure the test to make the initial items easiest so that students can experience success and gradually increase the level of difficulty.
- Avoid rushing or pressuring students during testing.
- Confer with students privately to work out accommodations for testing.
- Teach students relaxation techniques to use before testing.
- Practice test taking with students.
- Allow students to take a retest.
- Provide positive reinforcement (e.g., encouragement) throughout the testing process.
- Grade on percentage of items completed, with partial credit for partially correct responses.
- Use a test format that students are familiar and comfortable with.
- Ensure that test modifications are not obvious and do not embarrass students.

Attention Difficulties
- Test on an individual or small-group basis.
- Test in a setting with no distractions.
- Break the test into short segments.
- Administer the test within one-half hour after students take medication.
- Extend the test time to allow for frequent breaks.
- Provide students with a template to reduce distraction from other test items.
- Bold or highlight key words or phrases.
- Organize the test so that similar types of problems and tasks are grouped together.

- To avoid impulsivity on multiple-choice tests, have students eliminate all incorrect responses rather than choose one correct answer.
- Shorten the test; adjust points per item.
- Administer parts of the test on different days.
- Seat students away from extraneous noises and confusion.
- Use study carrels, cubicles, and offices with movable partitions.

SECTION 4: ALTERNATE ASSESSMENTS

Under the NCLB Act, 95 percent of a public school's student population must participate in the school's assessment program. English language learners with limited English language skills and students with severe disabilities may be exempted from this requirement. Parents may petition to have a child excluded if they feel that a test conflicts with religious practices. Although 95 percent of students must be tested, schools may provide accommodations for certain students and still comply with the 95 percent rule.

An **alternate assessment** is a method of measuring the performance of students who are unable to participate in the standard form of assessment administered at the district or state level. According to the National Center on Educational Outcomes, a small percentage of students with disabilities—less than 15 percent (about 1 to 2 percent of the entire population)—will not be included in state- or districtwide assessments (Thompson, et al., 2002). These students will require alternate assessments, which are a substitute method of gathering information regarding students' progress in meeting content standards.

Alternate assessments are developed by the state education agency (SEA) or the local district education agency (LEA), as appropriate. They need to be aligned with the general curriculum standards set for all students and should not be assumed to be appropriate only for students with significant cognitive impairments.

The alternate assessment option has been established so that students with even the most severe disabilities can participate in the assessment process, thus ensuring accountability for all students. In order for students to qualify to receive alternate assessments, their IEPs must document that this type of assessment is required because their disability prevents them from completing a general education program, even with program adaptations. Also, students must be working on educational goals that are generally more closely aligned with independent functioning, which is verified in their IEPs. Students who are covered by Section 504 of the Rehabilitation Act should have their accommodations written into their Section 504 plan.

Measurement Procedures

An alternate assessment can be any measure of performance that is agreed on to assess students' progress. Part of the criteria for determining what makes an appropriate authentic assessment is that the results can be scored in such a way that they can be aggregated to produce an overall estimate of performance. When using an alternate assessment for students with disabilities, every score or format used to report results must match and align with the format used to report the results of the general performance assessment program, because it must be aggregated with the whole and then disaggregated for reporting to the public (Ballard et al., 1998).

Salvia and Ysseldyke (2004) have identified positive measurement approaches for an alternate assessment, including (a) observation of specific student behaviors and written documentation (e.g., anecdotal reports, video- or audiotaping); (b) recollection via interviews, checklists, or rating scales in which information is provided by teachers, parents, the student, community members, employers, and so forth; (c) record review of students' grades, school history, and IEP goals and objectives, as well as an analysis of their work samples; and (d) informal, more authentic evaluative measures, such as portfolio and curriculum-based assessments. The majority of states use portfolio or performance assessments for their alternate assessment tools (Thompson & Thurlow, 2001).

Criteria for Alternate Assessments

Students who are being instructed using a different set of curriculum content standards (e.g., life-skill curriculum rather than a traditional English, math, social studies, and science curriculum) should be given an alternate assessment. Generally, students with mild-to-moderate disabilities are able to take standard assessments with appropriate accommodations or modifications. Students with more significant cognitive disabilities—those who are not working to attain a standard high school diploma—are evaluated using alternate measures. These students generally work in a functional, survival, life-skills program that is individualized and not correlated with the more traditional academic program of studies. However, it is important to recognize that students of all ability levels generally spend at least their early primary school years in traditional curricular programs. Therefore, students with more significant disabilities often participate in modified versions of standard assessments during their early school years, before their curricular program becomes more functional and alternate assessment procedures become necessary.

Alternate assessments are curriculum-relevant in that they assess what students are learning. Also, alternate assessments must have a "common core of learning," which refers to the basic domain (or goals) that are used to aggregate evaluation data. This common core of learning can include a broad range of domains; specifically, academic (e.g., reading, math), communication, social, self-help, and vocational. These domains can be measured by a single method (e.g., performance assessment that involves demonstrating a specific skill in authentic contexts) or by multiple methods (e.g., interviews, observations, and record reviews). (See Figures 4-10, 4-11, and 4-12 for sample alternate assessment components.) Scores can be either quantitative, using a scale or checklist; or qualitative, using rubrics (e.g., performance may be rated as very good, satisfactory, or poor, or it may be rated as mastered, emerging, or not mastered).

The National Center on Educational Outcomes (Thurlow et al., 1998) has formulated seven preliminary steps to use as a guide in developing alternate assessments:

1. Establish an advisory group for the alternate assessment.
2. Define the purpose of the alternate assessment system and who qualifies to participate in it.
3. Identify the common core of learning for the alternate assessment.
4. Develop participation guidelines to determine who is eligible for the alternate assessment system.
5. Decide how to measure performance.
6. Determine how the results from the alternate assessment will be aggregated across students in the alternate assessment system.
7. Determine whether to, and how to, integrate results from the alternate assessment with results from the regular assessment (pp. 73–74).

Figure 4–10 Connection between Mathematical and Reading Standards, Objectives and Performance Task Test Skills

Academic Standards	Essence of the Standards for Students with Severe Disabilities	Skills Embedded in Authentic and Relevant Performance Tasks
MATHEMATICS STANDARDS		
Numbers, number systems, and number relationships Computation and estimation Measurement and estimation	Understands quantity, uses numbers, and performs simple calculations Measures and estimates measurements	Attends Adds 2 or 3 quantities Subtracts 2 quantities Multiplies/Divides Counts items by 1s and skip counts Matches quantity to numeral/number word Selects approximate numbers/quantities Matches identical numbers/quantities Selects numeral named Reads number Identifies value of dollars or coins Reads prices Identifies money—objects or value Orders numbers/quantities Fractions Probability and statistics Uses graphs Uses tables Evaluates length Evaluates area Evaluates volume Understands time Understands temperature Sorts/files
READING STANDARDS		
1.1 Learning to read independently 1.2 Reading critically in all content areas 1.3 Reading, analyzing, and interpreting literature 1.8 Research	Understands and responds to written, pictorial, or symbolic information Locates and uses 'literacy' information to solve problems	Attends Matches identical items Selects item named Reads Locates identical items Locates item named Selects similar items by function Selects related items Categorizes or sorts Selects by function Follows written instructions Locates item described Demonstrates or describes by function/meaning Answers who, what, where, when, why, and how questions Completes cloze passages Sequences Retells Draws conclusions by integrating information

Source: Zigmond, N., & Kappel, A. (2004). Summary of the 2004 Pennsylvania Alternate System of Assessment (PASA) Results: Reading and Mathematics (pp. 3–13) Pittsburgh, PA: University of Pittsburgh.

Figure 4–11   Alternative Test Administrator's Directions and Scorable Task Components

	Reads a Postcard: Directions at a Glance: Level A	
	Explain to the student that he/she will be reading a postcard from a friend. Show the front and back of the postcard to the student.	

	Test Administrator's Actions	**Scorable Task Components***
1.	Present 3 objects (boat, nail file, bowl) *in this order. Do not name the items.* **If the student does not scan the set of materials,** **Say: Find the materials.**	Orients toward set of objects (*Response: directs attention toward objects*)
2.	Keep the objects from the previous step in front of the student. Read the 1st, 2nd, and 3rd sentences on the postcard. Place an identical boat beneath the array *without naming it.* Point to the 2nd boat. **Say: Find the one that is the same.**	Matches identical objects—distracters are objects from same and different categories in appearance (*Response: points to boat*)
3.	Remove the objects from the previous step. Read the 4th sentence on the postcard. Present 3 sets of objects (plastic figures of people, plastic animals, pencil and notebook) *in this order, naming each as it is presented.* Present a bear and *name it.* **Say: Find the group that the bear goes with.**	Identifies category of object—distracters are objects from same and different conceptual categories (*Response: points to animals*)
4.	Remove the objects from the previous step. Read the 5th sentence on the postcard. Present 3 objects (hairbrush, fork, paintbrush) *in this order, naming each as it is presented.* **Say: Find the one you use to make pictures.**	Selects object by function—distracters are objects from same and different conceptual categories (*Response: points to paintbrush*)
5.	Remove the objects from the previous step. Present 3 objects (soap dispenser, bottle of glue, sock) *in this order. Do not name the items.* Place an identical bottle of glue beneath the array *without naming it.* Point to the 2nd bottle of glue. **Say: Find the one that is the same.**	Matches identical objects—distracters are objects from same and different categories in appearance (*Response: points to bottle of glue*)
6.	Remove the objects from the previous step. Read the 6th sentence on the postcard and the closing. Present 3 objects (flashlight, candle, box of tissues) *in this order. Do not name the items.* **Say: Find the flashlight.**	Selects object named—distracters are objects from same and different categories in appearance (*Response: points to flashlight*)
7.	Remove the objects from the previous step. Present 3 objects (hammer, drum, cup) *in this order, naming each as it is presented.* **Say: Find the one that makes music.**	Selects object by function—distracters are objects from same and different conceptual categories (*Response: points to drum*)
8.	Remove the objects from the previous step, except the drum. *Name the drum.* **Say: Show me what you do with a drum.**	Demonstrates function of object—open-ended response (*Response: hits drum*)
9.	Remove the drum from the previous step. Present 3 objects (box, spoon, book) *in this order. Do not name the items.* **Say: Find the book.**	Selects object named—distracters are objects from same and different categories in appearance (*Response: points to book*)
10.	Remove the objects from the previous step. Present 3 objects (apple, marshmallow, pencil) *in this order, naming each as it is presented.* **Say: Find what the friend ate by the campfire.**	Answers literal 'what' question by selecting object—distracters are objects from same and different conceptual categories (*Response: points to marshmallow*)

Source: Zigmond, N., Lehr, D., Lyon, S., Kappel, A. & McCall, R. (2004). *Pennsylvania Alternate System of Assessment* (PASA): *Administrator Manual.* Pittsburgh, PA: University of Pittsburgh.

Figure 4–12   Sample Tasks and Skills Assessed—One State's Alternative Reading and Math Tasks—Grades 3, 5

READING			
Grade 3	**A**	**B**	**C**
Task 2—Prepares to Plant Flowers	Orients towards set of objects Selects object named—distracters are objects from different categories in appearance Matches identical objects—distracters are objects from different categories in appearance Answers literal 'what' question by selecting object—distracters are objects from different conceptual categories Selects object by function—distracters are objects from different conceptual categories	Answers literal 'where' question by selecting picture—distracters are pictures from same conceptual category Selects picture with same beginning sound as target picture named—sounds are easier to discriminate Matches identical pictures—distracters are pictures from the same category in appearance Names item in picture—open-ended response Selects picture by function—distracters are pictures from same conceptual category Answers literal 'what' question by selecting picture—distracters are pictures from same conceptual category	Reads one word Answers literal 'where' question Matched 1–2 identical words in array of 5 words—all choices having the same beginning letter Answers literal 'what' question Selects picture demonstrating meaning of word from array of 5 Orders 3 pictures based on text

MATH			
Grade 5	**A**	**B**	**C**
Task 4—Purchases Party Supplies	Orients toward materials Selects set with most/least using fixed items—smallest difference is 3x Selects set with most/least using movable items arranged in pattern—smallest difference is 3x Matches 2 sets of items with 1–2 items each Matches item to space—one distracter is similar, one is dissimilar Selects money—one distracter is similar and one dissimilar in appearance Selects set with 1—smallest difference is 3x Matches items of same length—smallest difference is 3x	Counts one-dollar bills or pennies up to 9 Selects quantity named from array of 4 ordered sets arranged in pattern and containing 1–9 items—2 similar sets Subtracts 2 prices less than or equal to $9 or less than or equal to 9 cents by counting movable items and using subtraction to take away Draws conclusion by evaluating inequalities between 4 sets containing 1–9 items Adds 2 prices with sums less than or equal or $9 or 9 cents by counting sets of one-dollar bills or pennies Reads whole number price up to $9 or 9 cents	Reads number up to 19 Draws conclusion by evaluating inequalities among 5 numbers from 1–19 Identifies one-, five-, or ten-dollar bill Counts five-dollar bills to $15 Reads whole number price up to $19 or 19 cents Counts one-dollar bills or pennies to 19 from a larger set Adds 2 prices named and shown with sums less than or equal to $19 or less than or equal to 19 cents using a calculator, given an operation, and using action Subtracts 2 prices named and shown less than or equal to $19 or less than or equal to 19 cents using a calculator, given an operation, and using subtraction to take away

Source: Zigmond, H., & Kappel, A. (2004). Summary of the 2004 Pennsylvania Alternate System of Assessment (PASA) Results: Reading and Mathematics (pp. 3–13) Pittsburgh, PA: University of Pittsburgh.

Domains to Be Assessed

Alternate assessments must assess students' performance in the following domains:

Functional literacy   Personal and social adjustment
Communication   Domestic skills
Personal management skills   Motor skills
Leisure-recreation skills   Physical health skills
Vocational skills

Suggested Alternate Assessment Methods

- *Observations:* Noting behaviors in various settings (e.g., the classroom, the community, the vocational training programs, the work setting).
- *Interviews or checklists*: Gathering information through personal written or oral communication with teachers, family members, community members, training specialists, and employers. This communication may take the form of behavioral checklists, surveys, rating scales, written narratives, and/or interviews.
- *Record reviews*: Monitoring the prior and current records of students' school and work reports, medical/health history, standardized test scores, absentee records, and anecdotal notations.
- *Tests*: Evaluating students' progress using informal measures (e.g., performance assessments, portfolios, curriculum-based assessments).

SECTION 5: ASSESSMENT ACCOMMODATIONS AND MODIFICATIONS FOR STUDENTS WITH PHYSICAL AND SPECIAL HEALTH NEEDS

The assessment and intervention needs of students who are classified under IDEA's category of Other Health Impaired often have unique and very specific needs. Each student's situation must be considered, since this category of disability includes students who are physically disabled with orthopedic impairments, defined by the Individuals with Disabilities Education Act as:

> a severe orthopedic impairment which adversely affects a child's educational performance. The term includes impairment caused by congenital anomaly (e.g., clubfoot, absence of some member), impairment caused by disease (e.g., poliomyelitis, bone tuberculosis), and impairment from other causes (e.g., cerebral palsy, amputations, and fractures or burns which cause contractures) (Federal Register, p. 42478).

or a health impairment, defined as

> limited strength, vitality, or alertness, due to chronic or acute health problems such as a heart condition, tuberculosis, rheumatic fever, nephritis, asthma, sickle cell anemia, hemophilia, epilepsy, lead poisoning, leukemia, or diabetes, which adversely affect a child's educational performance (Federal Register, p. 42478).

Students with special health needs tend to require accommodations or modifications to address their limitations in strength, vitality, or alertness. Another important factor in determining specific accommodation need is whether the students' conditions are acute or chronic. An acute condition generally develops rather quickly and the symptoms are intense whereas a chronic condition develops slowly and progresses over time (Sirvis, Doyle, & Alcouloumre, 2001).

SUMMARY POINTS

- The reauthorization of IDEA–2004) perpetuated the mandate that students with disabilities be included in federal, state, and districtwide assessments. In the past, students who had various impairments were exempt from participating in these standardized tests or their test results were not included in school districts' accountability reporting. Excluding this segment of the school population is now prohibited under federal regulations: Students with disabilities must be included in all accountability assessments, although special accommodations or modifications in the testing may be provided.

- The accommodations provided to students during testing must have been previously used in the classroom during instruction or evaluation procedures. The range of accommodations generally considered includes an adjustment in the test setting, the amount of testing time allowed, how the test is scheduled and presented, and the manner in which students can respond.

- The decision to allow special considerations must be based on evaluation results, current educational functioning level, or the student's unique learning characteristics.

- The student's IEP team must determine whether accommodations or modifications are necessary, and if so, which are appropriate. These decisions must be clearly documented in the student's IEP.

- Modifications in testing generally consist of making adjustments in the actual content of the material (core standards) being taught or tested. Adjustments can be made in the grade level of the test material, when needed. Although out-of-level testing is useful for instructional and planning purposes, it is not appropriate for accountability purposes.

- A limited number of students (1 to 2 percent) will be unable to participate in standard district, state, or federal accountability testing even when accommodations or modifications are used. These students will be administered an alternate form of assessment. Alternate testing is designed for the relatively few students in each district who have significant cognitive disabilities; whose curriculum consists of functional, life-skill activities; and who are not expected to graduate from high school with standard diplomas.

- Alternate assessments must be curriculum-relevant (e.g., a life-skills program) and must have a common core of learning so that they can be correlated with the general education curriculum and therefore aggregated with the district's standardized test results (e.g., a reading task requiring students to correctly identify functional signs, such as exit, danger, and restroom).

Chapter Check-Ups

1. What do federal regulations mandate regarding the inclusion of student with disabilities in group testing that is used for accountability, often referred to as high stakes testing?

2. What is the difference between test accommodations and test modifications?

3. What public law mandates that students who are severely disabled, must they be included in accountability, high stakes test result reporting? Who determines and what are the criteria used to determine which students are tested in general testing with accommodations and which are administered alternate assessment?

4. How does alternate testing differ from standard accountability, or high stakes, testing?

5. List the categories of accommodations commonly used and provide a short scenario for each of the five accommodation categories, describing the type of special need that would require each accommodation category.

Practical Application Assessment Activities

1. Investigate the application of three major legislative acts, (1) IDEA, (2) Section 504, and (3) ADA. Focus on the issues of pre-referral, referral, evaluation, classification, placement, programming, and transition as they relate to each of these laws. Determine the similarities and differences of these laws and how they apply to various disabilities.

2. Prepare a list of accommodations needed for a student who has decided to attend a college program and another list of accommodations that this student would need if he decided to work in an office or factory. Also, identify the kinds of actions an institution of higher learning or an employer would be required to take to prevent discrimination.

3. Construct a resource page on IDEA-2004 that provides links to websites that provide information on the rules and regulations of IDEA. The proposed audience would be parents and general education teachers.

4. Take an opportunity to experience what an individual with physical disabilities deals with and learn how accessible (or inaccessible) the community is for someone with a physical disability. Research ADA regulations and then, using a wheelchair, maneuver through a public facility (e.g., an office building, restaurant, shopping mall, theatre) to assess whether the facility is handicap accessible according to ADA requirements. Reflect on this experience and how teachers can assess their students' ability to cope with these challenges and advocate for their basic legal rights, and what accommodations and modifications their students would need.

Connection Between CEC, PRAXIS, and INTASC Standards and Chapter 4

The Council for Exceptional Children— Professional Standards

Standard 1 Foundations

2. Laws, policies, and ethical principles regarding behavior management planning and implementation.

4. Rights and responsibilities of students, parents, teachers, and other professionals, and schools related to exceptional learning needs.

6. Issues, assurances, and due process rights related to assessment, eligibility, and placement within a continuum of services.

Standard 2 Development and Characteristics of Learners

2. Educational implications of characteristics of various exceptionalities.
3. Characteristics and effects of the cultural and environmental milieu of the individual with exceptional learning needs and the family.
5. Similarities and differences of individuals with and without exceptional learning needs.
6. Similarities and differences among individuals with exceptional learning needs.

Standard 3 Individual Learning Differences

5. Differing ways of learning of individuals with exceptional learning needs including those from culturally diverse backgrounds and strategies for addressing these differences.

Standard 4 Instructional Strategies

3. Select, adapt, and use instructional strategies and materials according to characteristics of the individual with exceptional learning needs.
4. Use strategies to facilitate maintenance and generalization of skills across learning environments.

Standard 5 Learning Environments and Social Interactions

15. Modify the learning environment to manage behaviors.
16. Use performance data and information from all stakeholders to make or suggest modifications in learning environments.

Standard 6 Communication

4. Augmentative and assistive communication strategies.
5. Use strategies to support and enhance communication skills of individuals with exceptional learning needs.

Standard 7 Instructional Planning

4. Technology for planning and managing the teaching and learning environment.
13. Develop and select instructional content, resources, and strategies that respond to cultural, linguistic, and gender differences.
14. Incorporate and implement instructional and assistive technologies into the educational program.
18. Make responsive adjustments to instruction based on continual observations.

Standard 8 Assessment

1. Basic terminology used in assessment.
2. Legal provisions and ethical principles regarding assessment of individuals.
5. National, state or provincial, and local accommodations and modifications.
8. Use technology to conduct assessments.
9. Develop or modify individualized assessment strategies.

Standard 10 Collaboration

12. Model techniques and coach others in the use of instructional methods and accommodations.
13. Communicate with school personnel about the characteristics and needs of individuals.

PRAXIS Standards for Special Education

THE PRAXIS SERIES™

Standard 1 Understanding Exceptionalities

2. Characteristics of students with disabilities, including medical/physical; educational; social; and psychological.

Standard 2 Legal and Societal Issues

1. Federal laws and landmark legal cases related to special education.

Standard 3 Delivery of Services to Students with Disabilities

1. Conceptual approaches underlying the delivery of services to students with disabilities (for example, medical, psychodynamic, behavioral, cognitive, sociological, electric).
3. Assessment, including how to modify, construct, or select and conduct nondiscriminatory and appropriate informal and formal assessment procedures; how to interpret standardized and specialized assessment results; how to use evaluation results for various purposes, including monitoring instruction and IEP/ITP development; and how to prepare written reports and communicate findings to others.
5. Curriculum and instruction, including the IEP/ITP process; instructional development and implementation; teaching strategies and methods; instructional format and components; and areas of instruction.

INTASC Standards for Teacher Education

Standard 3

The teacher understands how students differ in their approaches to learning and creates instructional opportunities that are adapted to diverse learners.

Standard 4

The teacher understands and uses a variety of instructional strategies to encourage students' development of critical thinking, problem solving, and performance skills.

Standard 8

The teacher understands and uses formal and informal assessment strategies to evaluate and ensure the continuous intellectual, social, and physical development of the learner.

CHAPTER
5

Gathering Preliminary Assessment Data

- interview process
- parental involvement
- cumulative files
- health records
- confidential files
- anecdotal records
- permanent products

- multidimensional perspective
- systematic observation
- visual efficiency
- intermittent hearing loss
- visual and auditory processing
- environmental factors
- student interview process

CHAPTER OBJECTIVES

After reading this chapter, you should be able to:

- Explain the importance of obtaining preliminary information before beginning the testing process.
- Identify the critical information obtained during a teacher interview.
- Describe the information obtained from the record review.

- Explain why the student interview is an important step in the assessment process.
- Identify ways teachers can obtain and maintain baseline information regarding student progress.

Introduction to Preliminary Assessment Data Collection

This chapter discusses the aspects of gathering baseline assessment information that are necessary to gain a broad perspective of the student being evaluated. The data collected provide the evaluator with a comprehensive understanding of the whole student. (See Figure 5-1.) During the informal assessment process, teachers gather from previous and current teachers, parents, and students information about the students' developmental and academic progress, medical history, and work habits. Interviews, checklists, and questionnaires are convenient, quick, and efficient methods of obtaining, recording, and tracking these data. Next, self-assessments guide teachers in focusing on their teaching style and the classroom environment. An interview or a questionnaire is useful in contacting the students' parents or guardians to obtain information about the home environment. Following these interviews, the students' school records are reviewed. Finally, observations and personal interviews with the students to obtain their perspectives complete the preliminary data collection process.

Figure 5–1   Informal Assessment Process

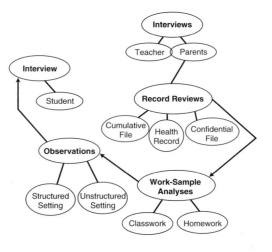

SECTION 1: TEACHER INTERVIEW

When the student is referred to the individualized education planning (IEP) evaluation team to determine whether special education and services are required, the team relies on the classroom teacher to provide critical data on how the child functions day to day. When the teacher suspects that a student is having difficulty functioning within grade and age norms—such as the second-grader who has not mastered basic reading readiness skills—the initial screening process needs to begin. The classroom teacher has the responsibility for identifying learning difficulties and can make a significant contribution in diagnosing a specific disability and with classification eligibility, placement, and program decisions.

Astute teachers have knowledge that can be invaluable in gaining perspective about how students function on a daily basis in the classroom. They not only understand child development, they are also familiar with curricular requirements, grade-level expectations, the school's scope and sequence, standards of performance and appropriate behavior, and the skills critical for success at their specific grade level. Since teachers interact with students in an authentic educational environment for extended periods of time each day, they can provide insight into their students' emotional responses to learning and the degree to which the students' learning problems or specific disability affects achievement in other subject areas. Classroom teachers are aware of the students' learning style, as well as the effects of the classroom environment and peer interaction on them. The teacher also knows the students' strengths and areas that need academic development, and their communication skills, social-emotional adjustment, and work-study skills. In addition, the teacher knows whether programmatic, curricular, environmental, or instructional modifications have been made to accommodate specific academic problems, and which have been effective.

Figure 5–2   Sample Open-Ended Teacher Academic Interview Guide

---

Teacher Interview Guide: Academic Areas

What grade-level materials are used for instruction in class? _____

Does the student function below grade norms in any subject area? _____ If so, which area?_____

What assessment measures are used to evaluate class work? _____

What is the average class level in reading?____ math?____ language?____ science?____ social studies?_____

What is the student's level in reading?____ math?____ language?____ science?____ social studies? _____

What assessment measures are used to evaluate class work (oral/written, multiple choice, short answer, essay)? _____

What are the student's academic strengths? _____ deficits?_____

Have accommodations or modifications been used?_____ If so, which have been successful?_____

Has the student been receiving any remedial services?_____ If so, in which subject(s)?_____ for how long?_____ how many times per week?_____

If the student is receiving remedial services, how much improvement has been noted?_____

What strategies have been successful? _____

Does the student seem anxious, frustrated, depressed, lethargic, or unmotivated?_____

What is the student's disposition toward learning and participating in classroom activities?

_____

Does the student function better when working independently or with a group of students? in the morning or afternoon? better in some subjects than in others?

_____

Are emotional, health, or social problems interfering with the student's school adjustment and progress? _____

Figure 5–3 Teacher Interview Checklist: Student Work-Study Behaviors

Does this student:	Mastered	Emerging	Undeveloped
remain on tasks for appropriate periods of time?			
follow oral directions?			
follow written directions?			
respond appropriately when called upon?			
listen attentively?			
recall and retain what he or she hears?			
raise a hand to be called on before speaking?			
work independently?			
work cooperatively during group activities?			
handle frustration appropriately?			
complete written work on time?			
complete homework assignments?			
become actively involved in problem solving?			
follow classroom and school rules?			
cope with minor distractions?			
adapt to varied teaching methods?			
ask for help or clarification when needed?			
follow a schedule, move from room to room?			
participate in class discussions?			
copy from the chalkboard?			
transition well from subject to subject?			
transition well from activity to activity?			
transition well from idea to idea?			
complete assignments on time?			
organize books and schoolwork?			
organize ideas into a plan of action?			
use critical thinking and make logical arguments?			
organize, plan, and carry out long-term assignments?			
copy adequately with time pressures?			
adapt to interruptions in the daily schedule?			
relate appropriately to school staff and peers?			
work cooperatively with a partner?			
behave appropriately in unstructured settings?			
take responsibilities for his or her actions?			
willingly participate in activities?			
adequately store and retrieve subject-matter information?			
grasp and apply abstract concepts?			
analyze and solve problems?			
apply and generalize new learning?			
comprehend cause-and-effect relationships?			
adjust to changes in subject content, format, or mode of response?			

In addition to the primary teachers, it is often necessary to consult with other teachers and support staff who interact with the students (e.g., teachers of other academic subjects; remedial specialists; guidance counselors; the school nurse; cafeteria and playground aides; the case manager, if the child is classified; and administrative personnel). These individuals can provide additional anecdotal information and important insights about the students from various perspectives and in settings outside the main classroom. Agency, therapeutic, or medical personnel who are or have been working with the student should also be interviewed.

Before approaching anyone for information about a student, the teacher should prepare a list of relevant and appropriate questions to ensure that the time spent in the **interview process** is productive. (Figures 5-2 and 5-3 are useful guides in preparing for discussions of students' progress with IEP evaluation team members. The questions should be individualized according to each student's particular profile.)

SECTION 2: PARENT INTERVIEW

The requirement of **parental involvement** in the assessment process has been mandated since the 1976 enactment of the Education for All Handicapped Children Act (P.L. 94–142), which requires that parents be informed of their rights and consent to the evaluation process. The reauthorization of the Individuals with Disabilities Education Act (IDEA–2004), the establishment of the National Education Goals 2000 (U.S. Department of Education, 1995), and the policies of leading professional educational organizations have placed increased emphasis on parent involvement in their children's education, particularly in the assessment process. (See Figure 5-4.)

To facilitate and maximize information gathering, teachers should make every effort to talk with the parents at a convenient time and location; to obtain an interpreter, if needed; and to encourage parents to bring a support person or advocate to the meeting (Spinelli, 1999). While interviews provide opportunities to clarify or rephrase questions and encourage elaboration of responses, a questionnaire may be more convenient for busy parents. By allowing them to complete the form at home where they can refer to record-keeping sources, this format enables them to supply detailed and accurate information. Because sharing private information is difficult for many people, parents should be assured that the information they provide will be kept confidential and shared only with school professionals on a need-to-know basis.

Critical life stages and events in the life of the child should also be considered. Being aware of the particular issues the child's family deals with helps to put proper perspective on the information and responses provided. Families of infants and children with special needs may experience high levels of stress when dealing with both normal and stressful events. The diagnosis of the child's disability, the reactions of siblings and other family members to the disability, developmental milestones (e.g., walking, talking) and social milestones (e.g., prom time, graduations), efforts to obtain services, medical crises, and transitions can be stressful and traumatic. Efforts should be made to determine additional family stresses (e.g., financial problems, illness in the family, divorce), and whether the family has a support system (e.g., extended family, clergy, community, local agencies). It is also critical that the teacher know of any cultural, ethnic, or linguistic issues, as well as the child's developmental milestones and medical history. (Figure 5-5 is a guideline for the parent interview questionnaire.)

Figure 5–4   Parents' Role in the Assessment Process

Before the evaluation, parents:

- May initiate the evaluation process by requesting that the school evaluate their child.
- Must be notified by the school of the evaluation plan meeting, invited to participate in the planning process, and give consent to begin the evaluation process before any initial or reevaluation of the child may be conducted.
- May wish to talk with the person responsible for conducting the evaluation.
- May find it useful to become informed about assessment issues in general and any specific issues relevant to their child.
- May need to advocate for a comprehensive evaluation.
- May suggest specific questions they would like to see addressed through the evaluation.
- Should inform the school of any accommodations the child will need.
- Should inform the school if they need an interpreter or other accommodations during their discussions with the school.
- May prepare their child for the evaluation process, explaining what will happen and where, thus reducing the child's anxiety.

During the evaluation, parents:

- Need to share with the school their insights into the child's background and past and present school performance.
- May wish to share with the school any prior school records, reports, tests, or evaluation information about their child.
- May need to share information about cultural differences that can illuminate the IEP multi-disciplinary team's understanding of the student.
- Need to make every effort to attend interviews the school may set up with them and provide information about their child.

After the evaluation, parents:

- Need to carefully consider the results that emerge from their child's evaluation, in light of their own observation and knowledge of the child.
- May share their insights and concerns about the evaluation results with the school and suggest areas where additional information may be needed. Schools may or may not act upon parents' suggestions, and parents have certain resources available to them under law, if they feel strongly about pursuing the matter.
- Should participate fully in the development of their child's IEP.
- Should closely monitor their child's adjustment and progress in the placement and program.

Source: "Assessing Children for the Presence of Disability," by B. B. Waterman, 1994, *NICHCY News Digest*, 4(1), p. 12. Adapted with permission from the National Information Center for Children and Youth with Disabilities (NICHCY).

Classroom Scenario: What Would You Do?

As you begin assessing two students in your class suspected of having learning disabilities, you find the parent interviews to be insightful. During the interview with Regina's parents, you learn that Regina, who is extremely quiet and withdrawn in school, is very talkative and precocious when at home and with neighborhood friends. The interview with Michael's father was also revealing. Each night and morning; Michael, who seemed to be shy and quiet but otherwise happy, had been having serious bouts of anxiety about going to school. In fact, it had been a struggle for his parents to get him to school each day. How would it help in the assessment process?

Figure 5–5 Sample Parent Interview Questionnaire

What are your child's strengths, abilities, special talents, and interests?

In what areas does your child have difficulty?

Do you think your child is progressing satisfactorily in school?

Is your child actively involved in extracurricular activities?

Does your child have any particular fears or worries?

Does your child have friends? Do these friends value education?

Do you feel your child speaks in a clear, organized, and fluent manner?

Does your child seem to have difficulty sharing ideas? asking questions?

Do you feel your child writes in an organized, legible manner?

What is your child's basic attitude about oral presentations? writing tasks?

Does your child enjoy speaking in a group or prefer one-to-one communication?

Does your child enjoy pencil-paper tasks? drawing? copying? composing? conversing?

Does your child have any difficulty with tasks that require eye-hand coordination?

Have you noticed any fine motor skill delays (e.g., inability to stay within lines when drawing; poor control of pencil, scissors, comb, or knife)?

Does your child seem to write too slowly?

Does your child have difficulty completing homework assignments?

Is there any type of assignment that is stressful or difficult for your child?

What would you like your child to do as a speaker/writer that he or she is not doing now?

Is there anything in your child's developmental, educational, or medical history that might affect skill acquisition or school performance and behavior?

Has your child had previous diagnostic testing through a school or private agency? If so, would you provide a copy of the results?

Has your child had any special school programming, such as special education, remedial reading, speech/language therapy, or counseling?

What are your goals for your child this year?

Do you have concerns about your child's school progress?

Is there information you know that would be helpful in understanding how your child learns best?

What questions do you have about helping your child become a better student?

How well is your child able to communicate wants and needs?

Is your child independent in basic hygiene and grooming skills at home?

Does your child behave appropriately at home? If not, how do you deal with misbehavior?

How does your child behave when out in the community?

How does your child deal with changes in routine at home?

Is your child able to follow basic directions at home?

Is your child able to focus on stories, puzzles, or quiet activities?

How many times has your family moved?

Was there a time when your child was unable to attend school? If so, for how long? Why?

Did your child attend school in another country? If so:

    Did your child start school speaking another language?

    Did your child learn to read before coming to the United States?

    Does your child have any difficulty reading in your native language? If so, what type of problem?

    Has your child ever been assessed for English language proficiency?

SECTION 3: RECORD REVIEW

Analysis of students' school history needs to be a priority and should be one of the initial sources of information collected early in the evaluation process. Students' **cumulative files**, also referred to as the permanent school records, include vital school background information; **health records** contain pertinent medical information; and, if the student is classified, the **confidential files** include IEP team records that can provide a critical link when evaluating present progress and planning for the future. These files may also contain permanent products (student work samples), and **anecdotal records** (data recordings of student behavior compiled by teachers and support staff who interact regularly with the child).

Recent special education and rehabilitation legislation requires that when determining what new evaluations are to be conducted, the results of previous assessments must be reviewed. Consideration must be given to minimizing the time, effort, and resources spent in conducting new and often unneeded testing (Bullis & Davis, 1999).

It is important to note that most, if not all, of this information is highly confidential. Access to these records may be difficult or impossible without prior signed consent from appropriate school personnel, and possibly, from the students' parents or guardians. Individuals who are entrusted with the information in these files must be cognizant of the professional, ethical, and legal responsibility they have to ensure that students' privacy is respected.

Cumulative Files

Cumulative files—which include a history of the child from his or her earliest experiences in school to the current academic year—are generally kept in a central location, such as the administration office or the guidance office. These files follow students who transfer from school to school, district to district, or state to state. (See Figure 5–6 for the content generally found in these files and questions to guide this record review.)

Critical Thinking and Reflection Activity

Janie's family has had to deal with many family stresses during the past few years, including her father's death and her mother's unstable job situation. The family has had to move about every six months and has recently become homeless. Janie, once a good student, is not doing well in her current school placement. In this case, what documentation in the records would be helpful in the diagnostic process?

Confidential Files

The confidential files are documents of students referred for eligibility evaluation and students classified and receiving special services. These files are generally kept in the IEP team office and are monitored for access, so that the privacy of the students and their families is secured. Data maintained in the confidential files are shared on a need-to-know basis.

FYI

CONFIDENTIAL FILE
CONTENTS

- Copy of the referral indicating specific concerns
- Documentation of pre-referral interventions
- Parental informed consent forms
- Students' IEP evaluation team assessment reports
- Classification conference report
- Initial IEP and annual review(s)

Figure 5–6 Cumulative File Contents: Focus Questions

History of Schools Attended
- Did the child attend preschool?
- Start school very young?
- Move frequently from school to school?

Retentions/Promotions
- In what grade(s) was the child retained?
- What was the reason for the retention?
- Did the child fail but was promoted after attending summer school?
- Was retention recommended but the child was not retained?
- Did performance improve during the second year in the repeated grade?

Attendance
- Were absences sequential (i.e., several days/weeks in a row)?
- Were absences due to illness, emotional problems, or family issues?
- Is there a correlation between absences and grade decrease?
- Has the student frequently been tardy?

Report Cards/Narrative Reports
- What are the child's academic strengths and weaknesses?
- Is there a history of below-average grades in a particular subject?
- Is there a pattern to low/higher performance grades?

Disciplinary Records
- Have there been disciplinary infractions? If so, how many?
- What kinds of behaviors resulted in detentions or suspensions?
- Were there any patterns (where, when, what conditions caused the problem)?
- What were the antecedents (i.e., precipitating factors)?
- What were the consequences (i.e., the outcome, such as punishments)?

Remedial Instruction Reports
- What subjects? in which grades? for how long? was progress noted?
- What kinds of interventions were provided? was improvement noted?
- What is the prognosis for remediation?
- Has the student been recommended for further services?

Group Achievement Tests
- How do local norms compare to national norms?
- How do standardized test scores compare to classroom grades?
- Does the student have poor test-taking skills (e.g., test anxiety)?

Classroom Scenario: What Would You Do?

In reviewing student records you see that Peter, a new student in your freshman English class, has always been an average or above-average student. A close inspection of his report cards shows that Peter is failing classes for the first time. Previous teachers indicated that his work-study skills have always been poor, and the narrative portions of his report cards indicate failure to complete long-term assignments, to work independently, to organize work, and to meet deadlines. These work-study skill weaknesses apparently did not significantly affect Peter's performance in the lower grades. What is happening now? What would you do next as part of your assessment?

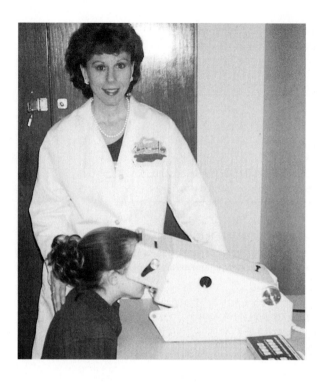

The Keystone Telebinocular Visual Survey is a screening device that the school nurse uses to assess visual efficiency.

Figure 5–7 Child Health History Survey

Did or does your child have . . .	YES	NO	UNKNOWN
• complications before, during, or following birth?			
• prenatal exposure to environmental toxins?			
• a family history of any genetic abnormalities?			
• a delay beginning to walk?			
• a delay beginning to talk?			
• general health problems?			
• any physical traumas (e.g., accidents, head injuries, abuse, poison ingestion)?			
• chronic headaches or stomach aches?			
• a history of allergies? seizures?			
• a history of frequent colds, ear infections?			
• difficulty concentrating?			
• a hereditary disorder?			
• a problem with drugs or alcohol?			
• medications to take?			
• special or unusual medical or physical needs?			
• limits on physical activities?			
• any hospitalizations? If so, for what?			
• prescriptive glasses for reading, writing?			
• prescriptive glasses for distances?			
• hearing problems? a hearing device?			

160

Health Records

Health records, which contain pertinent medical information about the student, are typically located in the school medical office. (Figure 5-7 provides a sample health history checklist to be completed by parents and is generally kept in the health file.)

SECTION 4: WORK-SAMPLE ANALYSIS

Whenever the teacher begins to be concerned about the quality or quantity of a student's work, a systematic collection of work samples, also referred to as **permanent products**, should be started. (See Figures 5-8 to 5-13 for the rationale behind collecting work samples, as well as for examples, analysis criteria, and characteristics of work-sample products.)

After determining the types of problems the student is experiencing and the student's strengths and needs based on discussions with parents and teachers, on reviews of school records, and on an analysis of the student's work, the teacher must observe the student in natural settings, particularly in settings where problems have occurred.

FYI

HEALTH RECORD CONTENTS

- School nurse's health notes
- Food or environmental allergies
- Visual or auditory acuity screening results
- Health or medical condition; need for special care and precautions
- Medications taken
- Medical exemptions from school activities

Figure 5–8   Process for Collecting Work Samples

- Collect samples in process and at culmination of activity.

- Attach a representative sample completed by an average student (useful as a comparison).

- Place in individual folder and organize sequentially.

- Label each artifact with:
  (a) student's name
  (b) date and time completed
  (c) purpose of assignment
  (d) directions given
  (e) process used to create sample
  (f) conditions under which work was completed
  (g) expected outcome

Figure 5–9   Purposes for Collecting Work Samples

- Provide database of cumulative progress
- Are a good source of intrapersonal and interpersonal comparisons for skill analysis and grading purposes
- Help in predicting rate of progress when projecting future goals/objectives
- Help in comparing daily authentic performance with standardized test scores
- Provide examples of students' work when conferring with parents, students, case manager, and administration staff
- Used for functional portion of IEP evaluation
- Involve students in collecting, selecting, reviewing, and analyzing samples, thereby helping to develop their metacognition, critical thinking, and analysis skills
- Compare actual work sample (final product) with class observation (Did student follow directions? How was accuracy and rate compared to peers? Does a pattern of errors exist?)

Figure 5–10   Work-Sample Analysis Criteria

Analyze work from:
- different class groupings (independent vs. group)
- different times of day (morning output vs. afternoon)
- different subjects (math vs. social studies)
- different type of assignment (in-class notetaking vs. homework)
- different times of the year (September vs. March vs. June)
- different grades (grades 2 to 4)
- several days to note consistency of performance and reliability of samples collected

Figure 5–11   Work-Sample Characteristics to Consider

Quality of Work	**Quantity of Work**
Poor motor planning?	Completed too quickly?
Disorganization?	Work pace too slow?
Type and number of errors?	Amount of work completed
Legible writing?	average compared to peers?
Directions followed?	Delayed response in starting?
Erasures or cross-outs?	

Figure 5–12   Sample Work-Analysis Worksheet

Name _____   Subject _____
Date _____   Time _____
Directions followed _____   Materials _____

Working Conditions
Independent _____   Partner assisted _____   Teacher assisted _____   Small group _____
Whole class _____   Learning center _____   Research _____   Homework _____
Acquisition _____   Proficiency _____   Generalization _____   Application _____

Figure 5–13   Examples of Work Samples

- In-class written assignments
- Journals entries/learning logs
- Problem-solving activities
- Dictated stories
- Audiotapes/videotapes
- Homework
- Workbook pages
- Drawings/paintings
- Completed puzzles
- Photographs of work products
- Essays
- Lecture notes
- Tests
- Block structures

SECTION 5: STUDENT OBSERVATION

Many prominent student behaviors are not evident in written records or work samples and can be identified only through direct observation in natural settings. A direct method of assessing behavior or work performance consists of ongoing observation, interaction, and analysis of one student, a small group, or a whole class. (See Figure 5–14 for a list of behaviors to observe.)

Figure 5–14   Behaviors to Observe in Children

Types of Classroom Behavior			
reading	planning	comparing	evaluating
writing	pretending	balancing	sculpturing
talking	organizing	graphing	constructing
playing	thinking	empathizing	bragging
asking	designing	interpreting	performing
researching	disassembling	projecting	classifying
computing	questioning	lifting	climbing
listening	sharing	making choices	seriating
singing	rapping	building	painting
translating	creating	listening	using
persisting	drawing	debating	problem solving
comprehending	locating	mapping	defending
role playing	interacting	explaining	helping
manipulating	running	negotiating	joking
speaking	dramatizing	simulating	inferring
labeling	estimating	reciting	enumerating
deciding	analyzing	synthesizing	formulating

For a **multidimensional perspective** on how students function, it is necessary to observe them in several authentic environments. Multiple and varied observations are needed to gain a perspective of what works, what does not work, and why. Observations should occur in different grouping situations, such as in large groups and small or cooperative groups, at learning centers, and independently. The observations should occur in the setting(s) in which the target behavior is evident, at different times of the day, and in different subject areas. Students with reading comprehension problems should be observed not only during their reading class but also during content area subjects, such as social studies and science, where they are expected to read. Important information about how students function and interact can also be obtained in remedial settings, such as a basic skills reading class or a speech and language therapy session. For the secondary-level student, observations in authentic settings may include the prevocational learning environment, vocational work-study placements, or community-based work settings. These observations are an effective way to evaluate the performance of specific and general work skills and work-related behaviors. (See Figure 5–15 for suggestions on what to look for when observing a student.)

These observations of a child provide only a sampling, or snapshot, of the child's day; in other words, the behavior recorded during the observation is simply a representative sampling of the child's behavior, observed at a specific time, and in a specific setting and situation. The child being evaluated must remain the focal point, although it is important to consider the environmental conditions and to compare this child's behavior to that of the "typical" or average student. It is important to note whether the student being observed or the other pupils in the class are acutely aware of or distracted by the presence of the observer. This awareness may make students self-conscious and affect typical classroom behaviors or reactions. When focusing on specific behavior characteristics that are frequently noted with students who have learning or social-emotional and behavioral problems, checklists can be used to structure and direct the observation.

Systematic observation can reveal how a student works through different tasks, which tasks seem most and least problematic for the student, and what the student

Figure 5–15   Factors to Consider When Using Observing for Assessment

- Student's age, sex, and type of disability
- Observation setting and structure
- Day, month, season
- Subject, period, place of observation
- Length of observation and types of activities
- Number and types of distractions during observation
- Severity (extent of the problem)
- Intensity (how much the problem interferes with the student's progress)
- Duration (length of time the problem has been evident)
- Frequency (how often the problem is occurring)
- Generality (number and types of situations in which the problem occurs)
- Consequences (effect the problem has on others)
- Conditions (factors involved and situation in which student is expected to perform)
- Intervening factors that precipitated, aggravated, or preceded an incident
- Atypical occurrences (e.g., appearance of a substitute teacher)
- Unplanned school events (e.g., an assembly)
- Disruptions in normal routine (e.g., fire drill, upcoming holidays, unexpected visitors)
- Any events significant in determining student's ability to cope with a change and transitions

does when encountering difficulties (Vallecorsa, deBettencourt, & Zigmond, 2000). Rather than evaluate isolated skills at the end of a lesson or unit of study, effective teachers assess frequently over time, looking at the full spectrum of students' learning characteristics. Skilled observers apply their knowledge of child development; psychosocial standards; and grade-level curricular, behavioral, and social norms as benchmarks when they are observing. Characteristics to note include whether students apply learning strategies in a variety of contexts, whether they make connections between new learning and personal experiences, and whether they apply new skills and concepts in meaningful and novel ways (Bridges, 1995).

Keeping a tally allows teachers to monitor students' academic progress in each subject area, as well as the students' work habits and classroom behaviors. Teachers can develop a form listing IEP objectives or curriculum core standards, which can include specific content and skills to be mastered using subject scope and sequence charts, performance tasks to be mastered (e.g., doing an experiment), group progress toward completing an assignment (e.g., brainstorming ideas, outlining a current events research project), or improvement in behavioral control (e.g., frequency of calling out in

Tips for Teachers

When observing a student, do you . . .

attend to details? maintain focus? react quickly?
have keen diagnostic listening, looking, and questioning skills?
record and summarize samples of behavior efficiently?
distinguish one behavior from another?
take in the global perspective while focusing on specific detail?
take note of environmental details (e.g., distracting location, poor lighting, noise
    adequate reinforcement, peer interaction)?

science class). While moving around the room monitoring progress, the teacher can put the checklist on a clipboard and check off behaviors observed or tasks and skills accomplished. Both individual student progress and small-group or whole-class achievement can be assessed using a checklist or tally format. The data collected can be evaluated, charted, and graphed to track progress and areas that need improvement, and the information obtained can be used for IEP goal and objective monitoring, for instructional planning purposes, and for program evaluation. It is important to remember that the target behavior must be both observable and measurable. (See Figure 5–16.)

Figure 5–16 Observation Focus Points

Behavioral Characteristics	Yes	No	N/A	Comments
Does the student . . .				
follow teacher's oral directions?				
follow written directions?				
follow routine?				
stay on task, appear attentive?				
work steadily, use time wisely?				
seem to be prepared?				
begin and complete work on time?				
accurately copy from the chalkboard?				
orally participate in class?				
interact appropriately with peers?				
interact appropriately with teachers?				
work well independently?				
write letters and numbers without reversing or transposing?				
use consistent strategies to problem solve?				
use a different strategy if the first one is unsuccessful?				
persevere in solving a difficult assignment?				
express himself or herself articulately and thoughtfully?				
respond directly to the question asked?				
take turns during conversations?				
appear to note subtle nonverbal gestures and cues?				
listen carefully to the speaker before responding?				
wear prescriptive glasses?				
work cooperatively with peers in problem solving?				
speak in a well-modulated voice, with appropriate volume, pitch, rate?				

Classroom Scenario: What Would You Do?

Jenny's general education science teacher reported that this second-grader, classified as having a specific learning disability, has recently been inattentive during science class. She does not follow directions and has not been completing independent lab reports. During the classroom observation, it was obvious that Jenny appeared to be confused; she seemed to be looking at the work of the students seated around her, and took a long time to get started on assignments. During an interview with Jenny, you learn that she has an assigned seat in the back of the room and has not been able to clearly hear the teacher's directions or instructions. When Jenny cannot hear the teacher she looks around the room to try to figure out what was assigned. This makes her late in starting and she cannot complete the work on time. When asked why she did not tell her teacher, Jenny says that she has asked for help, but her teacher was annoyed and said that if she would just pay attention, she would know what to do. What do you do?

FYI: As a result of this interview, Jenny was referred to the school nurse, who discovered that following a recent ear infection, Jenny was experiencing intermittent hearing loss.

Observations in Group Settings

Although teachers generally observe one student at a time for specific target behavior, it is often important that they observe group dynamics to see how an individual student interacts in a group situation. In these instances, teachers must be alert to peer preference, influence, dominance, indifference, or antagonism. (See Figure 5–17 for factors to consider when observing a student in a group setting. Sample forms for

Figure 5–17   Sample Group Observation Focus Questions

Group Observation Guidelines

What is the group climate like? _____

What are the seating arrangements of the groups in the room? _____

What patterns of interaction are evident? _____

Is the student a leader or a follower? _____

What role does the student take within the group? _____

Does the student participate in group activities, or is he or she on the fringe? _____

Does the student contribute to the group? _____

Does the student come to the group prepared for the group work? _____

Does the student complete all individually assigned group tasks on time and well? _____

Does the student participate in a constructive manner? _____

Is the student a good, active listener? _____

Does the student support his or her position in a strong and thoughtful manner? _____

Is the student able to compromise? _____

Is the student able to disagree in a considerate manner? _____

Does the student seem to understand the directions and general concepts? _____

Is the student able to clarify and explain questions that arise? _____

Is the student able to share responsibility for helping the group get the job done according to directions and on time? _____

Does the student require extra help? _____

Is the student accepted by group members? _____ Rejected by any members? _____

How does the student react when the teacher is not directly supervising the group? _____

Figure 5–18 Sample Form for Observing Small Group Activities

Checklist of Cooperative Group Activity

Skill	Brad	Ken	Jane	Tess	Ben	Jean	Mary	Tim
Listened to directions								
Had materials to begin								
Contributed ideas								

Figure 5–19 Sample Form for Observing Entire Class

Checklist of Class Observation

Subject: _____ Date: _____

Ratings
+ = Completed
X = In progress
O = Not started

Names of Students	Defined Vocabulary	Read Chapter Outline	Drafted Research	Answered Questions
1. _____				
2. _____				
3. _____				
4. _____				
5. _____				
6. _____				

tracking and making note of students' behavior can be found in Figure 5–18 for small-group activities and in Figure 5–19 for whole-class activities.)

Observations During the Testing Session

Another critical time to observe students is while they are being evaluated, generally while working one-to-one with the teacher-evaluator. Students' behavior, attitude, interaction, and approach to the testing experience can provide key information about the validity of the assessment results. The characteristics noted in Figure 5–20 are presented in Likert scale format, so that the degree of each behavior can be more clearly identified.

Classroom Scenario: What Would You Do?

One objective related to Evan's social-emotional goal is verbal interaction with a peer during 50 percent of a 10-minute learning center activity. An earlier teacher observation of Evan indicated that his verbal interaction with other children is increasing as he plays alongside them. During the most recent observations, however, he did not converse at all with the other children at the center. What do you do? Are Evan's verbal communication and social skills beginning to regress?

FYI: Evan's comment during a follow-up informal student interview revealed that he has been angry with several of his peers. Subsequent observations indicated that he was becoming more proficient in conversational skills, but he needs to learn to express himself appropriately when he is upset.

Figure 5–20   Observations During Testing Session

Place an X on the appropriate line for each category:

Behavior during assessment:
unusually absorbed by tasks	— — — — —	inattentive, distracted
overly confident	— — — — —	insecure, unsure of self
exceptionally cooperative	— — — — —	uncooperative
extremely polite	— — — — —	impolite
totally relaxed	— — — — —	apprehensive
very persistent	— — — — —	gives up easily
overly active	— — — — —	lethargic
accepting of ability	— — — — —	very self-critical

Work style:
fast paced	— — — — —	slow paced
deliberate actions	— — — — —	hesitant actions
processes silently	— — — — —	processes aloud
excessively organized	— — — — —	disorganized
quick, impulsive response	— — — — —	slow, unsure response

Language proficiency:
articulates well	— — — — —	articulates poorly
advanced vocabulary	— — — — —	limited vocabulary
response is direct	— — — — —	response is vague

Visual-motor ability:
good pencil grip	— — — — —	poor pencil grip
legible handwriting	— — — — —	illegible handwriting
skillful movements	— — — — —	awkward movements
careful, systematic	— — — — —	careless, haphazard
fast reaction time	— — — — —	slow reaction time

Reaction to mistakes:
very aware of errors	— — — — —	oblivious to errors
exerts increased effort	— — — — —	gives up easily
takes errors in stride	— — — — —	very agitated

Test results are:
very representative	— — — — —	poor estimate of ability

Characteristics of Visual and Auditory Acuity to Observe

Visual efficiency refers to the child's ability to clearly and comfortably see and take in information for sustained periods of time. Frequently, visual efficiency problems do not begin to surface until the upper elementary or junior high grades, when students are required to cover a significant amount of reading material (Scheiman & Rouse, 1994). Teachers should be cognizant of the following characteristics that may indicate vision efficiency problems:

- Squints, blinks, frowns, or rubs or covers one eye when doing close visual work or copying from the board
- Holds printed material too close, at an unusual angle, or far away
- Tilts or turns his or her head forward while reading and writing
- Complains of headache, nausea, or eyestrain after reading
- Tires easily or avoids doing visual work
- Has difficulty staying on lines when writing or within lines when coloring
- Inaccurately spaces letters or words when writing
- Has difficulty copying from the board
- Omits words, skips, or rereads lines
- Loses place, uses finger to track when reading
- Has difficulty judging distances
- Exhibits poor eye-hand coordination

Classroom Scenario: What Would You Do?

Julia has been unable to complete assignments and tests on time. She is beginning to become anxious when time limits are imposed. When reading orally, she is able to pronounce multisyllabic words but tends to skip over certain words, such as "a," "and," and "the." She also occasionally skips lines. What would you do?

Teachers are often the first to note that a child has a hearing impairment. Students may have varying degrees of hearing loss and not be diagnosed until they enter school. Often the student has an **intermittent hearing loss** due to the residual effects of an ear infection or other medical issues. Teachers can play an important role in the diagnosis of auditory acuity problems by noting the following behaviors:

- Lack of normal response to sound, or an inappropriate or unrelated response to sound
- Failure to respond to his or her name when called or spoken to
- Constantly requests repetition of directions and questions
- Turns up the volume of the radio, tape player, or television
- Appears confused when oral directions are given
- Watches what others do, then imitates their actions

Tips for Teachers

Students may inadvertently fail a routine school eye exam by not knowing or mispronouncing the symbols used to test them or by listening to the previous students and parroting their answers. English language learners may use "follow the leader" strategies they have developed to cope with operating in a second language. Since the eye exam is not a paper-and-pencil test, they do not always see this as cheating or understand how it prevents a proper diagnosis (*Teaching Diverse Learners*, 2004).

- Appears to be straining to push closer to the speaker
- Focuses closely on the speaker's facial expressions and lip movements
- Cups a hand behind the ear or turns the ear toward speaker
- Reacts inappropriately when given very precise directions
- Responds in an untimely, delayed manner
- Withdraws from the group, often preferring to work or play alone
- Is inattentive, daydreams
- Shows signs of frustration or fatigue during listening activities
- Prefers to work with younger, less verbal children
- Has poor articulation
- Speaks too loudly or too softly
- Speaks in dysfluent manner with unusual pauses
- Has faulty pronunciation, especially with high-frequency sounds (s, z, sh, f)
- Has an unnatural pitch of voice (monotone)
- Complains of dizziness, ringing or buzzing, or a closed feeling in the ear
- Has reoccurring ear infections, sore throats, colds, or tonsillitis
- Frequently rubs the ears; has sores in or discharges from the ear
- Has difficulty sounding out or discriminating individual sounds in words
- Reads and spells sight words better than phonetic words

Visual and Auditory Processing or Perceptual Problems

The preliminary stage of reading involves the process of seeing visual and hearing auditory patterns—specifically, clusters of letters, blends, syllables, and words—and subsequently analyzing and synthesizing these patterns into meaningful units. These processes, referred to as **visual and auditory processing**, involve the interpretation of incoming visual and auditory sensations in the form of spatial and temporal patterns to the brain, which selects, groups, organizes, and sequences them. Beginning readers must discover how to scan and be able to visually process these patterns, so that they can first analyze print to locate cues and features then distinguish between letters and words, and finally recognize, interpret, and retain what is heard.

Students with a reading disability may have adequate visual and auditory acuity yet poor processing ability, which can result in significant difficulty or inability to learn to read through the visual mode, auditory mode, or both. Visual and auditory acuity can be assessed by the school nurse, who can make a referral, if needed, to an ophthalmologist (a specialist in eye problems) or an optometrist (a nonmedical eye specialist) for visual disorders; or to an otologist or an otolaryngologist (a specialist in hearing problems) or an audiologist (a nonmedical hearing specialist) for auditory disorders. However, perceptual dysfunction may initially be identified by the classroom teacher. If serious processing deficits are suspected, a referral to the IEP evaluation team may be necessary. To begin the assessment process, the teacher needs to determine whether the student's visual and auditory perception is intact. The following list includes areas of visual perception that may affect the reading acquisition process; auditory perceptual skills are similar, but the focus there is on hearing or saying rather than on seeing or writing.

- Visual discrimination: The ability to distinguish differences (often subtle) among stimuli (e.g., letter reversals (/b/ for /d/), inversions (/p/ for /b/), and transpositions (was for saw).

    Can the student distinguish whether two similar illustrations are alike or different?

FYI

It is necessary for a teacher to ask whether the student's background might have made him or her vulnerable to potential hearing loss. For example, refugee children may have been exposed to loud noises such as gunfire or bombs. Some ELLs may have suffered from multiple or severe ear infections that went untreated due to lack of adequate medical care. Loud noises and untreated ear infections can lead to hearing loss. Basic screenings are superficial and may not pick up all the possible nuances of hearing loss. A more comprehensive check is often necessary.

Can the student distinguish between letters or words that are the same or not the same?

- Visual closure: The ability to complete the missing part or to perceive wholes.

Can the student identify letters that are incompletely formed?
Can the student identify words that have a letter or letters missing?

- Visual sequence: The ability to appropriately order visual stimuli.

Can the student read in left-to-right progression?
Can the student read from top to bottom?

- Visual figure-ground relationships: The ability to perceive one unit (letter) or groups of units (words) against a background.

Can the student locate an item in a picture with many extraneous objects?
Can the student distinguish a specific letter or word from a distracting background of print?

- Visual memory: The ability to retain and recall information that is presented visually.

Can the student view an item for a few seconds then locate this item in a series of different items?
Can the student recall a single item or a series of pictures, letters, or words?

Analysis of the Classroom Environment

Environmental factors can significantly affect students' interest, motivation, and perseverance in the classroom, and the teacher plays a major role in providing an environment conducive to learning. Teachers, too, can benefit from environmental assessments in that they allow them to conduct regular self-checks to ensure that they are providing a challenging yet supportive and accommodating environment that promotes maximum student performance.

This observation is generally followed by a student interview, when specific questions can be asked for clarification, such as, "When your lab partner mixed the chemicals, what were you doing? Why?" Often, students can give a reasonable explanation for an incident that would otherwise have seemed unreasonable to the observer.

SECTION 6: STUDENT INTERVIEW

The **student interview process** can give the evaluator insight into students' ability to communicate, and how they confront, analyze, and solve a problem. Interviews provide an opportunity to observe children's oral language skills, vocabulary development and syntax, information-processing ability, attention to task, and listening skills. When interacting on a one-to-one basis with teachers, students have the opportunity to explain, in greater detail than with other methods of assessment, what they understand, what problems they are having, and what steps they feel need to be taken to improve their learning.

Before the interview begins, teachers should prepare a list of questions that starts with broad-based queries and moves toward specific probing questions in order to elicit increasingly more elaborate and indepth responses. Questions should be asked in a nonthreatening, relaxed manner using a friendly, nonjudgmental tone. The teacher needs to actively listen and be flexible enough to ask for clarification on responses that are unclear. To get honest and detailed answers, questions should be open-ended rather than require only a yes or no response. Students should be given sufficient time to respond, since many pupils, particularly those with learning disabilities, may be slow to process orally. If students struggle to communicate their thoughts clearly, they should be encouraged to demonstrate, draw, sing, use pictures or manipulates, show an example, or act out their responses. When reluctant to verbally share, students may be more comfortable if the interview takes place when they are working on an assignment at their desks or at a learning center, or when they are involved in solitary play following the observation.

Classroom Scenario: What Would You Do?

You want to get to know a new student, José, and find out why he is not doing well in science. When you ask him what he likes about science class, he replies that he enjoys working on the experiments but not writing the lab reports. You then ask why he likes the experiments but not completing the reports. José explains that he likes working with a partner during the experiment. You need to ask some probing questions to determine why José does not like doing the reports. Does he have a problem with writing? Does he understand the reporting process? Does he feel that he does not have enough time to finish the report? After several more investigative questions, you learn that José has no friends; he does most of his home and school activities alone. He looks forward to science class because he can interact with another boy, but he resents having to return to his desk to write the lab report on his own. Therefore, his report-writing efforts are minimal, resulting in a low grade in science. Armed with this new information, what would you do?

FYI: The teacher modified the lab assignment to allow students to fill out their lab reports with their partners. José's grades have improved, his confidence level has increased, and the relationship with his lab partner has developed into a real friendship.

Interview questions should focus on confirming the observations that have been made. They should help to clarify students' interest and motivation, what they perceive as their competencies and areas of need; the strategies they have been using; the proficiency level of specific skills; attitudes toward adults, their emotional relations to play situations; and cognitive problem solving (Knoff, Stollar, Johnson, & Chenneville, 1999). (See Figure 5–21 for a sample of student interview questions.)

Critical Thinking and Reflection Activity

When children are transferred from one class to another it can be particularly traumatic for those who are educationally "at risk" and for those with learning and social-emotional disabilities. It may take these students longer than expected to adjust and be capable of participating in a new learning situation. Also, it takes time for teachers to accurately observe and document educational and behavioral concerns. If referral to the IEP team is necessary, it generally

takes several months before testing, placement, and program changes can be completed. Therefore, in cases of students who are moved frequently, the IEP team may not have the opportunity to complete the classification process, which can delay needed remedial interventions. In some cases, parents who disagree with the school's recommendation for evaluation or placement and program changes may relocate repeatedly and remain transient to avoid a confrontation and possible due process proceedings.

What effect would this have on the student? Would this scenario impact assessment results and your interpretation of those results?

Figure 5–21 Sample Student Interview Questionnaire

Student Interview Questions

Pick a written assignment and ask the student the following questions:

What part of this assignment was easiest for you? _____

What part of this assignment was most difficult for you? _____

How do you feel about your classes? _____

In what subjects are you doing well? _____

In what subjects are you having difficulty? _____

What subject is the most difficult for you? _____

Why is this subject hard for you? _____

What could be done to make this subject easier for you? _____

Are you able to stay focused in class? _____

Is there any particular subject(s) that you have difficulty concentrating on? _____

Do you usually finish assignments before, after, or with your classmates? _____

Do you usually volunteer in class? _____ If not, why not? _____

Do you complete homework assignments? _____ If not, why not? _____

Do you get along with your classmates? _____

Are you involved in any school-related clubs, such as sports activities? _____

SUMMARY POINTS

- When assessing a student, teachers need to tap into many sources of information to obtain a broad yet realistic understanding of the history of how the child has functioned in the school, home, and community, as well as how the child is currently performing in various settings.

- In gathering baseline data, the interview process allows past and present teachers and school staff to express their perspectives on the child, and the child's parents to provide a developmental history and home and familial influences on the child's learning.

- School records—specifically, the student's cumulative records, health records, and confidential files—can provide critical pieces to the diagnostic puzzle by supplying educational, health, attendance, and behavioral information that can help teachers to more thoroughly understand factors that influence how children function at school. Closely analyzing students' work and observing them in everyday activities can help to establish a pattern of strengths and weaknesses.

- The student interview process can help the teacher to establish rapport with the student, obtain insight into problems the student may be having at school, and clarify what does and does not work for the student.
- Teachers can gain key baseline diagnostic information when they listen attentively and perceptively to the student, continuously evaluate as they teach, closely monitor the interaction between curriculum requirements and the student's accomplishments, and maintain a record of the student's academic competencies, weaknesses, and progress.

Chapter Check-Ups

1. What relevant information can the student's primary teacher provide? Which additional school personnel can provide pertinent data about the student being assessed?

2. Why is it important to interview the student's parent? What background information would be particularly important to obtain from the parent of a student new to your class who has had considerable difficulty adjusting and demonstrates learning difficulties?

3. Identify the types of student records and describe what data you would expect to find in each.

4. What are the differences between visual acuity and perceptual/processing problems and auditory acuity and perceptual/processing problems? Identify the specific symptoms that are commonly noticed with acuity and perceptual/processing delays.

5. Your goal is to gain a multidimensional perspective of the student during your observation. Describe how you would accomplish this.

Practical Application Assessment Activities

1. Individually or as a group activity, interview several families of students who are receiving special education services to gain insight into what they feel about the special education system of services and to gain perspectives about their involvement during the referral, evaluation and classification process. The responses obtained from these interviews should be compared and contrasted and common experiences compiled. Families interviewed should represent diversity in culture, ethnicity, socioeconomic status, type of disability, family structure (e.g., single parents, adoptive parents, grandparents as parents), and life stage (e.g., preschool to post-secondary levels).

2. Work individually [in a small group] to (a) compose an initial contact letter to parents informing them of the need for referral, requesting permission to evaluate their child, inviting them to participate, and explaining the process and their legal rights and (b) draft a permission form for testing. Upon completion, the letters and forms will be traded with another individual [group] who will critique them to make sure that they contain all legally required information and comply with IDEA requirements, that the process is clearly explained, that the writing style is straightforward yet sensitive and can be adapted for individuals with diverse communication needs (e.g., language differences, illiteracy, blindness). As a concluding activity, the partners [group] converge to provide feedback and together make revisions.

3. Fernando's first grade teacher has expressed concern about his poor academic progress. According to the prereferral report, he is functioning at a preschool level in all basic skill subject areas. His work-study skills are underdeveloped and he has not adjusted well to the school program. What issues will you focus on when observing Fernando, interviewing his teacher and gathering background information?

4. Identify the effects of having an outside observer (i.e., someone not familiar to the children) on the behavior of the student targeted for observation. What effect does this observer have on the interactions of the other students and the typical operation of the class? What are the advantages and disadvantages of relying on the student's regular teacher to conduct and report on the observation?

Connection Between CEC, PRAXIS, and INTASC Standards and Chapter 5

The Council for Exceptional Children—Professional Standards

Council for Exceptional Children
The voice and vision of special education

Standard 1 Foundations

5. Issues in definition and identification of individuals with exceptional learning needs, including those from culturally and linguistically diverse backgrounds.

7. Family systems and the role of families in the educational process.

10. Potential impact of differences in values, languages, and customs that can exist between the home and school.

Standard 2 Development and Characteristics of Learners

1. Typical and atypical human growth and development.

2. Educational implications of characteristics of various exceptionalities.

3. Characteristics and effects of the cultural and environmental milieu of the individual with exceptional learning needs and the family.

7. Effects of various medications on individuals with exceptional learning needs.

Standard 3 Individual Learning Differences

1. Effects an exceptional condition(s) can have on an individual's life.

2. Impact of learners' academic and social abilities, attitudes, interests, and values on instruction and career development.

3. Variations in beliefs, traditions, and values across and within cultures and their effects on relationships among individuals with exceptional learning needs, their family and schooling.

Standard 5 Learning Environments and Social Interactions

1. Demands of learning environments.

4. Teacher attitudes and behaviors that influence behavior of individuals with exceptional learning needs.

Standard 8 Assessment

11. Use assessment information in making eligibility, program, and placement decisions for individuals with exceptional learning needs, including those from culturally and/or linguistically diverse backgrounds.

14. Create and maintain records.

Standard 10 Collaboration

3. Concerns of families of individuals with exceptional learning needs and strategies to help address these concerns.

5. Maintain confidential communication about individuals with exceptional learning needs.

6. Collaborate with families and others in assessment of individuals with exceptional learning needs.

8. Assist individuals with exceptional learning needs and their families in becoming active participants in the educational team.

13. Communicate with school personnel about the characteristics and needs of individuals.

14. Communicate effectively with families of individuals with exceptional learning needs from diverse backgrounds.

THE PRAXIS SERIES™

PRAXIS Standards for Special Education

Standard 1 Understanding Exceptionalities

1. Theories and principles of human development and learning, including research and theories related to human development; theories of learning; social and emotional development; language development; cognitive development; and physical development, including motor and sensory.

2. Characteristics of students with disabilities, including medical/physical; educational; social; and psychological.

Standard 2 Legal and Societal Issues

1. Federal laws and landmark legal cases related to special education.

Standard 3 Delivery of Services to Students with Disabilities

1. Conceptual approaches underlying the delivery of services to students with disabilities (for example, medical, psychodynamic, behavioral, cognitive, sociological, electric).

3. Assessment, including how to modify, construct, or select and conduct non-discriminatory and appropriate informal and formal assessment procedures; how to interpret standardized and specialized assessment results; how to use evaluation results for various purposes, including monitoring instruction and IEP/ITP development; and how to prepare written reports and communicate findings to others.

INTASC Standards for Teacher Education

Standard 8

The teacher understands and uses formal and informal assessment strategies to evaluate and ensure the continuous intellectual, social, and physical development of the learner.

Basic Skills and Content-Subject Assessment

CHAPTER 6

Oral and English Language Learner/Bilingual Assessment

KEY TERMS AND CONCEPTS

- developmental disorders
- acquired disorders
- speech disorders
- language disorders
- speech articulation
- intelligibility
- voice disorders
- fluency disorder
- dialect
- receptive language
- expressive language
- language sample
- expansion
- rapid automatized naming (RAN)
- memory or word retrieval
- semantics

- figurative language
- syntax
- pragmatics
- English as a second language (ESL)
- Culturally and linguistically diverse (CLD)
- English language learners (ELLs)
- Limited English proficiency (LED)
- Black English vernacular (BEV)
- Bilingual speaker
- language proficiency
- language dominance
- language preference
- Basic interpersonal communication skills (BICS)
- Cognitive academic language proficiency (CALP)
- environmental assessment

CHAPTER OBJECTIVES

After reading this chapter, you should be able to:

- Identify how speech and language disorders can affect communication ability.
- Compare and contrast receptive and expressive language.
- Describe the impact that rapid automatized naming (RAN) problems can have on student performance.
- Explain nondiscriminatory assessment of students with cultural and/or linguistic differences.
- Identify the second-language-acquisition phenomena that help to differentiate between a developmental delay and a cultural difference

and that may result in "false positive" identifications.
- Compare and contrast the two types of language proficiencies: basic interpersonal communication skill (BICS) and cognitive academic language proficiency (CALP).
- Identify the problems associated with many tests used to evaluate students from a minority background.
- Describe the adjustments that may be necessary to ensure that students who are culturally and linguistically diverse are evaluated in a fair and nondiscriminatory manner.

Introduction to Speech and Oral Language Assessment

Developing oral language skills is a complex process. Because oral language is not as easy to measure as other school subjects, it has not received the attention given to assessments in other academic areas. Although numerous assessment measures exist to evaluate students' academic functioning in basic skill subject areas—such as reading, math, and written language—limited assessment procedures exist for oral language (Polloway & Smith, 2000). However, in federal and state core curriculum content assessments, increasing emphasis is being put on the testing of oral communication skills.

Teachers need to understand the types of formal assessments that provide age and grade equivalencies, stanines, and percentage rankings in order to determine both how their students compare with peers and whether the students are eligible for classification. Also, teachers need to incorporate informal evaluation procedures into their repertoire of skills so that they can continually assess and monitor progress in oral language development and the status of instructional goals.

Assessing students' language skills involves observing both verbal and nonverbal behavior, including speech (articulation, voice, and fluency) and language (content; form; use; and receptive, expressive, and inner language). (See Figure 6–1.) The complexity of language acquisition and the many elements of expressive communication skills used to listen, speak, read, and write underscore the need for assessment tools and experiences that reach beyond the limits of standardized, objective assessments.

Figure 6–1   Guidelines for Observing Oral Communication

- Can student communicate as a speaker?
- Does student seem to understand what is being said?
- Does student understand nonverbal communication (e.g., foot tapping, head nodding)?
- Does student use nonverbal means to communicate (e.g., gestures, facial signals)?
- Does student appear to be fully concentrating on the speaker (e.g., attend to faces, maintain eye contact, watch lip movements)?
- Does student understand oral communication when speaker is not in full view (e.g., when back is turned, when listening to a taped discussion)?
- Does student articulate clearly?
- Is student's speech tempo appropriate for the situation?
- Does student appear to be exerting excessive energy to produce speech (e.g., head jerking, facial grimaces, erratic breathing)?
- Does student take time to think before responding?
- Is student competent in the use of words and grammar (e.g., correct use of objects, actions, events, correct tense, and word usage)?
- Does student parrot or paraphrase what has been said rather than express original thoughts?
- Is student's word usage appropriate for the context of the discussion?
- Can student communicate appropriately in different contexts (e.g. classroom, playground, library)?
- Does student communicate ideas clearly and thoroughly enough?
- Can student distinguish between relevant and irrelevant information?
- Does student's communication demonstrate a variety of possibilities and perspectives?
- Are student's responses mainly self-critical or derogatory?
- Can student assume the role or viewpoint of the speaker?
- Does student's oral language difficulty, if present, affect reading, writing, and/or speaking activities?

Tips for Teachers

Be alert for symptoms that warrant speech or language evaluation, or both.
Does the child have difficulty:

- pronouncing words through grade 3?
- speaking in a normal flow, rhythm, or both?
- using his or her voice effectively?
- speaking in an age-appropriate manner (is there evidence of immature or delayed speech patterns)?
- labeling thoughts or objects?
- putting thoughts into words?
- comprehending questions and following commands?

These tests measure only a small portion of what children have learned and understood; therefore, a variety of motivating assessment opportunities are needed to meaningfully evaluate students' language skills.

SPEECH AND LANGUAGE DISORDERS

Speech and language disorders can affect the way children talk, understand, analyze, and process information. Speech disorders affect the clarity, voice quality, and fluency of a child's spoken words. Language disorders can affect a child's ability to hold meaningful conversations, understand others, problem solve, read and comprehend, and express thoughts through spoken or written word. (See Figure 6–2.) An estimated six million children under the age of 18 have a speech or language disorder (American Speech-Language-Hearing Association, 2004). Boys make up two thirds of this population. More than one million children have received services for speech or language disorders under the Individuals with Disabilities Education Act (IDEA). This number represents a 10.5 percent increase from a decade ago (American Speech-Language-Hearing Association, 2004).

DETERMINING TYPICAL LANGUAGE DEVELOPMENT

In order to determine whether the student is experiencing speech and/or language delays, it is necessary to have a basic understanding of normal development and of expected language behaviors for each age and to recognize that children develop at different rates. Every child is unique and has his or her own rate of development. Children typically do not master skills in a given category until they reach the upper age in each age range for that category. In fact, there is a range of normal development: failing to accomplish a specific skill at the expected age level or to master all skills in a specific age range category does not mean the child has a disorder. The critical issue is whether the child is demonstrating continuous language growth (American Speech-Language-Hearing Association, 2004). (See Figure 6–3 for a chart showing the average age by which most children accomplish language-related skills.)

Linguists agree that there is a developmental progression to speech and language acquisition, and that there is a sequence of language development during the first five years (Polloway & Smith, 2000).

CLARIFYING TERMS

Developmental disorders show up as the child grows and develops.

Acquired disorders (referred to as childhood aphasia) occur as a result of a known injury (e.g., head injury, stroke) or other occurrences (American Speech-Language-Hearing Association, 2004).

Figure 6–2   General Indicators of Developmental Language Disorders

- Absence of words by age 18 months
- Absence of two-word phrases that have a message by age 2
- Inappropriate responses to questions
- Echoing of speech
- Undeveloped play skills
- Poor understanding or use of adjectives and prepositions
- Word-finding problems
- Depends on gestures to follow directions
- Requires frequent repetition of directions
- Poor social interaction with peers (does not get along with other children)
- Poor school performance
- Difficulty relating an extended narrative; explaining something or retelling a story, centering on a topic and chaining a sequence of events together in a logical order
- Narrative speech incoherent or difficult to follow
- Inability to describe the "plot" in an action picture
- Poor communication skills in school settings (e.g., interacting with the teacher, participating in class discussions, working in groups with other students)
- Difficulty role-playing different communication scenarios; discussing stories and points of view of various characters; understanding how the characters are feeling and why they are reacting a certain way; and explaining how different characters' actions affect what happens in the story
- Difficulty understanding and using vocabulary (semantics) and understanding and using grammar (syntax)
- Difficulty understanding and answering both yes-no (e.g., Is your name Bob?) and wh- questions (e.g., What do you do with a hammer?)
- Difficulty understanding extended speech, such as listening to a short story or factual passage and answering fact-based (the answers are in the passage) and inferential (the student must arrive at a conclusion based on information gathered from the reading) questions about the material
- Inability to follow directions that increase in both length and complexity
- Inability to tell an extended story (language sample) both verbally and in written form
- Inability to tell the steps needed to complete a task or tell a story, centering on a topic and chaining a sequence of events together
- Poor recall of words needed to express ideas
- Inability to express himself or herself in complete sentences, telegraphic sentences or phrases, or single words
- Speech is slurred, difficult to understand or unintelligible
- Limited social communication skills (pragmatic language)
- Inability to interpret or explain jokes, sarcastic comments, absurdities in stories or pictures (e.g., What is strange about a person using an umbrella on a sunny day?)
- Lacks proficiency in initiating conversation and conversational topics, taking turns during a discussion, and expressing thoughts clearly using a variety of words and grammatical constructions
- Inability to clarify communication when conversational partner does not understand

DISTINGUISHING BETWEEN TYPICAL AND ATYPICAL ORAL LANGUAGE DEVELOPMENT

Many factors affect the rate at which a child develops language skills. Although the order of the stages of language development is generally the same for all children, due to the extremely complex nature of language there can be significant variation in the rate at which children, especially those with disabilities, develop expressive and receptive language skills. (Figure 6–4 compares the language development patterns of a normally developing child to those of a child with a language disorder.) There may

Figure 6-3 Normal Language Development Chart

Hearing and Understanding	Talking
Birth–3 Months Startles to loud sounds Quiets or smiles when spoken to Seems to recognize voices and quiets if crying Increases or decreases sucking behavior in response to sound	**Birth–3 Months** Makes pleasure sounds (cooing, gooing) Cries differently for different needs Smiles when sees people
4 Months–6 Months Moves eyes in direction of sounds Responds to changes in tone of voice Notices toys that make sounds Pays attention to music	**4 Months–6 Months** Makes babbling sounds that are speech-like with many different sounds, including *p, b* and *m* Vocalizes excitement and displeasure Makes gurgling sounds when left alone and when playing with others
7 Months–1 Year Enjoys games such as peek-o-boo and pat-a-cake Turns and looks in direction of sounds Listens when spoken to Recognizes words for common items (e.g., "cup," "shoe," "juice") Begins to respond to requests ("Come here," "Want more?")	**7 Months–1 Year** Babbling has both long and short groups of sounds (e.g., "tata upup bibibibi") Uses speech or noncrying sounds to get and keep attention Imitates different speech sounds Has 1 or 2 words (bye-bye, dada, mama) although they may not be clear
1–2 Years Points to a few body parts when asked Follows simple commands and understands simple questions ("Roll the ball," "Kiss the baby," "Where's your shoe?") Listens to simple stories, songs, and rhymes Points to pictures in a book when named	**1– 2 Years** Says more words every month Uses some 1-2 word questions ("Where kitty?" "Go bye-bye?" "What's that?") Puts 2 words together ("more cookie," "no juice," "mommy book") Uses many different consonant sounds of the beginning of words
2–3 Years Understands differences in meaning ("go-stop," "in-on," "big-little," "up-down") Follows two requests ("Get the book and put it on the table.")	**2–3 Years** Has a word for almost everything Uses 2-3 word "sentences" to talk about and ask for things Speech is understood by familiar listeners most of the time Often asks for or directs attention to objects by naming them
3–4 Years Hears when called from another room Hears television or radio at the same loudness level as other family members Understands simple "who," "what," where," "why" questions	**3–4 Years** Talks about activities at school or friends' homes Nonfamily members usually understand child's speech Uses a lot of sentences that have 4 or more words Usually talks easily without repeating syllables or words
4–5 Years Pays attention to a short story and answers simple questions about it Hears and understands most of what is said at home and in school	**4–5 Years** Voice sounds clear like other children's Uses sentences that give lots of details (e.g., "I like to read my books.") Tells stories that stick to topic Communicates easily with other children and adults Says most sounds correctly except a few (e.g., l, j, s, r, v, z, ch, sh, th) Uses the same grammar as the rest of the family

Reprinted with permission from American Speech and Hearing Association.

Figure 6–4 Patterns of Development

Child with Normal Development			Child with a Language Disorder		
Age	Attainment	Examples	Age	Attainment	Examples
13 months	First words	here, mama, bye-bye, kitty	27 months	First words	this, mama, bye-bye, doggie
17 months	50-word vocabulary		38 months	50-word vocabulary	
18 months	First 2-word combinations	more juice here ball more TV here kitty	40 months	First 2-word combinations	this doggie more apple this mama more play
22 months	Later 2-word combinations	Andy shoe Mommy ring cup floor keys chair	48 months	Later 2-word combinations	Mimi purse Daddy coat block chair dolly table
24 months	Mean sentence length of 2.00 words. First appearance of -ing.	Andy sleeping	52 months	Mean sentence length of 2.00 words.	
30 months	Mean sentence length of 3.10 words. First appearance of -'s.	my car's gone	55 months 63 months	First appearance of -ing. Mean sentence length of 3.10 words.	Mommy eating
37 months	Mean sentence length of 4.10 words. First appearance of indirect requests	Can I have some cookies?	66 months 73 months	First appearance of -'s. Mean sentence length of 4.10 words.	The doggie's mad
40 months	Mean sentence length of 4.50 words		79 months	Mean sentence length of 4.50 words. First appearance of indirect requests.	Can I get the ball?

Source: From Leonard, L. "Language Disorders in Preschool Children" in Shames, G. H. and Wiig, E. H., *Human Communication Disorders*. Copyright © 1990 by Allyn & Bacon. Reprinted by permission.

be a slowdown in language development while children are learning other major skills—such as walking, when their concentration and energy are focused on gross motor development. Development can be affected by the amount and kind of language children are exposed to, such as when two languages are spoken at home and they are trying to learn two sets of vocabulary, process two sets of speech sounds, and understand two sets of grammatical rules. Their language skills are also affected by how people interact with and respond to them. When the child's attempts to communicate are reinforced by eye contact, acknowledged and expanded on (with comments such as, "Oh yes, and what else happened?"), this child's language skills develop faster than the skills develop for the child whose communication attempts receive little or no response.

INDICATORS OF A LANGUAGE-LEARNING DISORDER

The co-occurrence of language disorders and learning disabilities is quite high; they may be manifestations of the same underlying problem, or they may be the same problem defined differently at different times during an individual's lifetime. Difficulty in language development can result in delays in learning to listen, speak, read, or write. Problems can occur in the production, comprehension, and awareness of language at the sound, syllable, word, sentence, and discourse levels. Individuals with reading and writing problems also may experience difficulties in using language strategically to communicate, think, and learn (Schoenbrodt, Kumin, & Sloan, 1997).

Children with language disorders often do not achieve well in academics areas, particularly reading. Many have difficulty understanding and expressing language, do not perform well on tests, do not relate well to peers due to misunderstanding social cues, tend to use poor judgment, and have poor attendance due to school avoidance. (See Figure 6–5 for a list of characteristics commonly observed in students with communication problems.)

Figure 6–5 Speech-Language Skill Checklist

Does the student have:

____ a family history of delayed speech-language development or literacy problems?

____ difficulty processing sounds in words?

____ difficulty finding the words needed to express basic thoughts or ideas; more complex explanations or descriptions?

____ difficulty with the comprehension of spoken and/or written language, including, for older children, classroom handouts and textbooks?

____ delayed vocabulary development?

____ problems with the understanding and use of grammar in sentences?

____ difficulty remembering numbers and letters in sequence, questions, and directions?

____ difficulty with organization and planning, including, for older students, the drafting of school papers and longer term school projects?

____ problems expressing ideas coherently, as if the words needed are on the tip of the tongue but won't come out, and consequently, utterances are vague and difficult to understand (e.g., using unspecific vocabulary, such as "thing" or "stuff" to replace words that cannot be remembered)? Are filler words like "um" used to take up time while a word is being retrieved from memory?

____ difficulty learning new vocabulary presented orally (e.g., taught in lectures or lessons) or in print (e.g., in books)?

____ difficulty understanding questions and following directions that are heard or read?

____ difficulty recalling numbers in sequence (e.g., telephone numbers and addresses)?

____ problems understanding and retaining the details of a story's plot or a classroom lecture?

____ a pattern of slow reading and reduced comprehension of the material?

____ problems learning words to songs and rhymes?

SECTION 1: SPEECH ASSESSMENT

Types of Speech Disorders

Speech disorders are generally grouped into three categories: articulation, voice, and fluency disorders. The speech and language therapist is typically the school professional who develops and administers specialized tests to determine the type and severity of students' spoken language problem, providing the remedial program (therapy) and writing the speech and language individualized education plan (IEP). However, classroom teachers need to be familiar with the types and characteristics of spoken **language disorders** so that they can identify students who need to be referred to the speech and language therapist for screening. (See Figure 6–6 for a speech screening assessment.) Teachers may also need to work closely with the therapist to implement the classroom component of the speech IEP and to informally assess and monitor progress.

Articulation Disorders

Speech articulation is the pronunciation of individual and combined sounds assessed in single words and in conversation. Most speech sound errors fall into one of three categories: (1) omissions (e.g., "poon" for "spoon"), (2) substitutions (e.g., "wabbit" for "rabbit"), and distortions (language that sounds like the intended sounds but is not exact). Another less common type of error is the addition of sounds (e.g., "buh-lack" for "black"). The type of error affects how well the child is able to be understood, referred to as **intelligibility**. Generally, it is more difficult to understand children who omit sounds than those who distort sounds (Bankson, Bernthal, & Hodson, 2004).

Figure 6–6   Screening for Speech Disorders

Is the student's speech characterized by any of the following?

Articulation Problems
- Substitutions—replacing a letter sound with a different sound(s)
- Distortions—saying the letter sound incorrectly
- Additions—placing an extra sound(s) in words

Fluency Problems
- Repetitions—uncontrolled repeating of sounds, syllables, or words
- Prolongations—extending a portion of a word ("b-b-b-black")
- Blocks—difficulty getting sounds out at the beginning or end of a word

   Students may use "starters," which involves substituting words or phrases that they can express more fluently. They may also use circumlocution, which is a convoluted manner of talking around the feared word(s), avoiding the word(s) that they know will cause them to stutter. Children may also use hand or head gestures as they struggle to express their thoughts orally.

Voice Problems
- Intensity—excessively loud or low volume of speaking
- Frequency—pitch that is inappropriately high or low
- Hypernasality—excessive amount of air passing through the nasal cavity
- Denasality—insufficient amount of air passing through the nasal cavity (students sound like they have a cold).
- Hoarseness—strained quality of voice (deep and harsh sounding)

Voice Disorders

A **voice disorder** occurs when the pitch, loudness, or quality of the sound calls attention to itself rather than to what the speaker is saying. A voice disorder tends to hamper communication, producing a vocal output that is perceived to be markedly different from what is expected for someone of a given age, sex, and cultural background (Robinson & Crowe, 2001). It is also a problem if the speaker experiences pain or discomfort when speaking or singing. There are a variety of causes of voice problems. People can become hoarse temporarily by cheering at a baseball game, or they can sustain an injury that causes a paralysis of the vocal folds. Misusing the voice—by, for example, talking too loudly, using a pitch level that is too high or too low, breathing improperly, or smoking excessively—can result in a voice problems. The most common voice problems from vocal abuse are vocal fold nodules and polyps, although voice disorders can also occur without apparent cause.

Fluency Disorders

Normal speech is characterized by interruptions in flow. All individuals occasionally stumble or backtrack, repeat syllables or words, speak too quickly, use an inappropriate pattern of stress, pause in the wrong place in a sentence, or fill in pauses with "uh" (Hallahan & Kauffman, 2003). However, it is when these characteristics become chronic, when the speaker's intense effort to speak in a smooth, fluent manner continually results in speech flow disruptions that a diagnosis of **fluency disorder** is made. Stuttering is the most common and recognized type of fluency problem. Although only about one percent of the population is considered to be stutterers, teachers and school personnel need to be aware and sensitive to students who may

Figure 6–7 Characteristics of Normal vs. At-risk Speech Fluency

Child with Normal Dysfluency	Child at Risk of Stuttering
Often repeats whole words or phrases ("I-I-I want to want out and play.")	Repeats parts of words, either sounds or syllables ("t-t-table", "ta-ta-ta-table"); prolongs a sound ("sssun"); or breaks up words ("cow and boy")
Typically repeats parts of the word no more than times 1 or 2 times ("ta-table")	Often repeats part of the word at least 3 times ("ta-ta-ta-table) although some reports indicate that these children may repeat only 1 or 2 times
During repetitions, uses the vowel sound normally found in the word ("ta-table")	During repetitions, substitutes an "uh" vowel for the vowel in the word ("tuh-tuh-tuh-table")
Has rhythmic repetitions ("b .. b .. boy")	May use a broken rhythm during repetitions ("b, b & & b..boy")
Has 9 or fewer dysfluencies every 100 words	Has 10 or more dysfluencies every 100 words
Starts speech easily; keeps speech going even though may repeat a phrase or word later in the sentence	Opens the mouth to speak but no sound comes out or turns off the voice between sound repetitions

Based on an article in *Speech News*, Baylor College of Medicine, November 1983.

become dysfluent. Early diagnosis and intervention are critical if chronic stuttering is to be avoided. Although minor dysfluency is not uncommon as children develop verbal skills, when teachers note early symptoms of dysfluency (see Figure 6–7) they need to (1) refer the child to a speech and language pathologist and (2) be sensitive to the emotional-social impact that stuttering can cause, especially when peers begin to call attention to and tease these children. When persistent stuttering goes untreated, it often results in a lifelong disorder that affects the individual's ability to communicate, develop positive self feelings, and pursue certain educational and employment opportunities (Conture, 2001).

SECTION 2: LANGUAGE ASSESSMENT

🔍 **CLARIFYING TERMS**

A **dialect** is a variation in phonology, vocabulary, and syntax from the standard or customary use of a language.

Language problems can vary in scope and severity. Some students exhibit severe language disabilities in the classroom, including the absence of language, nonspontaneous acquisition, and severe language delay or distortion (Polloway & Smith, 2000). They require in-depth assessment and specific remedial therapy from the speech and language specialist. Although this chapter deals with mild-to-moderate language disabilities—such as oral language developmental delays that affect the student's reading, graphic, and expressive skills—it is important for teachers to be cognizant of the various types and degrees of communication problems so they can develop a remedial plan or, when necessary, refer to the professional specialist for more serious communication problems as early as possible. According to Eisenson (1990), "Children who are significantly delayed in establishing a vocabulary and learning the grammar (syntax) for the production of their oral code are also likely to be at high risk for learning to read" (p. 419).

Receptive and Expressive Language Assessment

Various factors can influence the acquisition of oral language and significantly affect the process of learning to read. Two critical areas are expressive and receptive language. **Receptive language** skills involve understanding through listening or reading; **expressive language** skills involve language used in speaking and writing. Receptive skills are more advanced than expressive abilities in most individuals, since people understand more words than they use in speech and are able to read more words than they can write (Richek, Jennings, Caldwell, and Lerner, 2002). (Figure 6–8 is a scale that rates students' receptive, inner, and expressive language skills. Figure 6–9 is a developmental checklist of receptive and expressive language skills.)

Assessing Language Samples

Teachers can compare the **language sample** of the target student with samples of two other students of the same age, sex, and linguistic background. The number of and average length of the sentences in the language sample can be calculated and compared with the samples of the peers. Students' speech and language skills are assessed not only for the students' ability to articulate but also for their ability to expand on these articulated ideas. **Expansion** includes "both the length of utterances and the nature of words used" (Polloway & Smith, 2000). When sampling students' language, such skills as verbal and communicative competence, articulation, word retrieval, vocabulary usage, syntactic structures, and fluency can be assessed. Sattler

Figure 6–8 Screening Assessment for Language Skills

	Above Average 0	Average 1	Below Average 2
I. Receptive Language			
1. Volume of voice	—	—	—
2. Understands gestures	—	—	—
3. Remembers directions	—	—	—
4. "Reads" picture stories	—	—	—
5. Response time to questions or direction	—	—	—
6. Listening vocabulary	—	—	—
7. Enjoys listening to books	—	—	—
8. Interprets anger or teasing from others	—	—	—
II. Inner Language			
9. Amount of general knowledge	—	—	—
10. Gets "point" of story or discussion	—	—	—
11. Understands directions or demonstrations	—	—	—
12. Sense of humor	—	—	—
13. Sticks to topic	—	—	—
14. Can predict what will happen next	—	—	—
15. Can summarize story	—	—	—
16. Can do simple mental arithmetic	—	—	—
III. Expressive Language			
17. Pronunciation	—	—	—
18. Speed of speech	—	—	—
19. Speaks in complete sentences	—	—	—
20. Uses words in correct order	—	—	—
21. Uses correct words in conversation	—	—	—
22. Ability to recall names for objects and people	—	—	—
23. Can repeat a story	—	—	—
24. Participates in class discussions	—	—	—

Score:

27 or less	Satisfactory performance.
28–35	Child should be watched and language abilities checked on periodically.
36 or more	Thorough evaluation needed.

Source: From *Informal Assessment in Education* by Gilbert R. Guerin and Arlee S. Maier. Copyright © 1983 by Mayfield Publishing Company. Reprinted by permission of the publisher.

(1992) suggests methods of sampling students' language. (See Figure 6-10. Guides for evaluating students' oral communication skills are provided in Figures 6-11–6-13.)

Testing Rapid Automatized Naming

Some students have language delays referred to as **rapid automatized naming (RAN)**, or word-finding, problems. Children with RAN problems cannot quickly and automatically name objects and are slow to recall the correct words (an accurate predictor of reading and learning disabilities) (Lerner, 2003). Slowness in naming is often due to **memory or word retrieval** problems, which affect the ability to access verbal information (German, 2001).

According to the Council for Exceptional Children, research indicates that many students learn to decode yet remain unable to read quickly, accurately, and fluently due to difficulty with RAN. As a result, they often become frustrated and do not want to

FYI TESTS FOR RAN

Tests for assessing word-finding difficulty include

- *Test of Word Finding* (2nd ed.), from Pro-Ed
- *Test of Adolescent/ Adult Word Finding*, from Pro-Ed

Figure 6–9 Checklist of Receptive and Expressive Language

Receptive language is the ability to understand words and sentences	**Expressive language** is the ability to use words and sentences to express thoughts and ideas
Does the student	*Does the student*
___ fail to respond when spoken to?	___ use immature speech?
___ follow conversation?	___ have unclear or mumbled speech?
___ look or act confused by verbal directions?	___ use poor grammar?
___ comprehend at a very concrete level?	___ say the same word various ways?
___ fail to keep up with the rest of class?	___ have trouble being understood?
___ have reading comprehension problems?	___ fail to follow conversation?
___ have difficulty following game rules?	___ fail to make eye contact?
___ give strange answers to questions?	___ fail to stay on topic?
___ fail to get jokes?	___ have trouble retelling stories?
___ say "huh?" frequently?	___ speak unusually slowly?
___ need a gesture or demonstration with directions?	___ have difficulty answering essay questions?
___ have trouble understanding homework assignments?	___ appear to understand more than he or she can say?
___ have difficulty understanding directions and instructions?	___ have difficulty asking and answering questions?

Figure 6–10 Methods of Obtaining Language Samples

Oral presentation: Teacher reads a short story to student, then the student repeats the story (story must be easy to comprehend).

Written presentation: Student reads a short story, then repeats the story (story must be easy to comprehend).

Visual nonsequential presentation: Student is shown a picture, then describes the picture (picture should show a familiar theme or experience).

Visual sequential presentation: Student is shown a series of pictures, then is asked to describe the sequence (pictures should have familiar theme or experience).

Self-generated concrete content: Student tells about an experience that is familiar.

Self-generated abstract content: Student talks about a given topic that is somewhat abstract.

read. Subsequently, they fall behind in vocabulary and content, they tend not to catch up with other students, and their homework and test completion suffer (CEC, 2003).

RAN assessments measure response time or rapid retrieval for various formats of visual stimuli (e.g., objects, colors, letters, numbers, or a combination of these stimuli). The purpose of these tests is to assess the student's ability to (1) sustain attention to identify and name symbols; (2) rapidly name and discriminate among symbols; (3) rapidly retrieve verbal labels; and (4) rapidly articulate words .

Assessing Language Content, Form, and Use

Another way to analyze oral language is through its content, form, and use. The content of language, also referred to as **semantics**, involves the language code—the ideas or concepts used to communicate. Semantics deal with ideas, the relationships

Figure 6–11   Sample Oral Language Checklist

Is the student able to	Mastered	Emerging	Unmastered
pronounce consonant sounds correctly?	—	—	—
pronounce consonant blends and consonant digraphs correctly?	—	—	—
pronounce the short and long vowel sounds correctly?	—	—	—
speak in one-word sentences?	—	—	—
speak in two-word sentences?	—	—	—
speak in sentences of three or more words?	—	—	—
speak in complete sentences?	—	—	—
identify familiar sounds?	—	—	—
identify similar sounds?	—	—	—
understand the language of adults?	—	—	—
understand the language of peers?	—	—	—
follow oral directions?	—	—	—
speak clearly without significant speech defects (e.g., poor articulation, stuttering)?	—	—	—
use appropriate vocabulary for maturity level?	—	—	—
use varied syntactic (grammatical) structures?	—	—	—
be understood by adults? peers?	—	—	—
understand simple forms of figurative language (metaphors, similes, proverbs)	—	—	—

Figure 6–12   Oral Language Development Scale

| Evaluation code: | 1—rarely 3—frequently | | | |
| | 2—occasionally 4—always | | | |
The student	**1**	**2**	**3**	**4**
listens attentively to a conversation.	—	—	—	—
listens attentively in a group.	—	—	—	—
listens attentively to a recitation or story.	—	—	—	—
contributes appropriately to conversations.	—	—	—	—
takes turns when conversing.	—	—	—	—
elaborates responses.	—	—	—	—
clearly articulates thoughts.	—	—	—	—
can follow oral directions.	—	—	—	—
can give sequenced oral directions.	—	—	—	—
states information in a logical manner.	—	—	—	—
is able to hold audience's attention.	—	—	—	—
provides enough oral information to be understood.	—	—	—	—

among ideas, and the words that are used to identify these ideas. Content covers vocabulary use, the ability to retrieve or recall the appropriate word, the ability to use **figurative language** (idioms, metaphors, similes, and proverbs), and the ability to use these words to communicate fluently.

Form, also referred to as **syntax**, is the structured rule system generally divided into phonology, morphology, grammar and sentence structure, and order. Phonology refers to the smallest speech sounds and the rules for combining and patterning speech sounds. It also involves the control of vocal features, such as timing, frequency, and duration of speech sounds (e.g., the intonation, pitch, and stress that affect the interpretation of what is said). Morphology is the rule structure of words and word forms, the

Figure 6–13   Oral Communication Rating Scale

Speech intensity
excessively loud   — — — — —   excessively soft

Rate of speech
extremely rapid   — — — — —   unusually slow

Ease of speech
smooth flow   — — — — —   hesitations, blocking

Pitch of voice
high pitched   — — — — —   low pitched

Quality of voice
well modulated   — — — — —   nasal, hoarse, harsh

Communication style
spontaneous   — — — — —   guarded

Reaction time
rapid   — — — — —   very slow

Manner of speech
formal   — — — — —   too relaxed, casual

Word choice
extensive   — — — — —   limited

Organization of thoughts
well organized   — — — — —   disorganized, scattered

Diction
very clear   — — — — —   unclear, poor

Fluency
smooth flow   — — — — —   repetitions, broken thoughts

Informal classroom activities can be a source of obtaining language samples.

affixes that change the meaning of base words. This deals with prefixes (e.g., dis-, pre-, bi-), suffixes (e.g., -ance, -able, -ment), and inflected endings of words (e.g., -'s, -ed, -ing).

Use, also referred to as **pragmatics**, is the function or purpose of oral communication. This aspect involves the speaker's ability to adjust his or her language to accommodate the audience and the setting (e.g., knowing that the use of loud, rough verbalization may be appropriate on the playground but not in the classroom). Often pragmatic disorders coexist with other language problems, such as vocabulary-concept development or grammar (American Speech-Language-Hearing Association, 2004). (See Figure 6–14.)

Figure 6–14   Assessment of Content, Form, and Use

	YES	NO
Assessing for Language Content: Semantics		
Does the student		
have limited vocabulary?	____	____
have difficulty relating a series of words to a meaningful association?	____	____
understand a concept but have difficulty using the correct word to express the concept?	____	____
understand simple directions?	____	____
know the name of common events, objects, and people?	____	____
use nonspecific vocabulary or phrases (e.g., "it," "that," "thing," "you know")?	____	____
use fillers in conversation (e.g., "um," "uh")?	____	____
have difficulty finding words on command (e.g., naming tasks; completing fill-in-the-blanks)?	____	____
know words but can't always say them?	____	____
pause or restart sentences in conversation?	____	____
rely on gestures, sounds, or the environment to be understood?	____	____
Assessing for Language Form: Syntax		
Does the student		
fail to order words correctly in a sentence?	____	____
have difficulty transforming passive sentences to active sentences?	____	____
use pronouns and articles to distinguish old and new information?	____	____
use words for time, (e.g., yesterday, tomorrow, last night)?	____	____
use verb tenses correctly?	____	____
put sentences together to form complex descriptions and explanations?	____	____
Assessing for Language Use: Pragmatics		
Does the student		
have difficulty taking turns in a conversation?	____	____
fail to stay on topic?	____	____
fail to ask pertinent questions?	____	____
attend to nonverbal feedback (e.g., eye contact)?	____	____
have trouble interpreting, inferring, comparing, and responding to the language of others?	____	____
have difficulty listening attentively to questions, conversation, and directions?	____	____
interrupt the speaker to insert own thoughts?	____	____
have difficulty with pitch (melody), stress (accent), juncture (pauses)?	____	____

FYI Statistics

Over the past 10 years, the Hispanic population increased by 58 percent (three to four times the growth rate of the general population). Currently, more than 14 percent of the U.S. population is Hispanic, and 16 percent of all U.S. students classified as learning disabled are Hispanic (U.S. Department of Education, 2000).

Figure 6–15 Assessing Pragmatics

	Ratings				
	Never	Seldom	Some-times	Often	Always
	1	2	3	4	5
Ritualizing					
1. Greets others appropriately					
2. Introduces him/herself appropriately					
3. Introduces people to each other appropriately					
4. Greets others appropriately when telephoning					
5. Introduces himself or herself appropriately when telephoning					
6. Asks for persons appropriately when telephoning					
7. Says farewell appropriately					
8. Asks others to repeat appropriately					
9. Gives name (first and last) on request					
10. Gives address (number, street, town) on request					
11. Gives telephone number on request					
Informing					
1. Asks others appropriately for name					
2. Asks others appropriately for address					
3. Asks others appropriately for telephone number					
4. Asks others appropriately for the location of belongings and necessities					
5. Asks others appropriately for the location of events					
6. Responds appropriately to requests for location of events					
7. Asks others appropriately for the time of events					
8. Responds appropriately to requests for the time of events					
9. Asks others appropriately for preferences or wants					
10. Responds appropriately to requests for preferences and wants					
11. Tells others realistically about abilities					
12. Tells realistically about the levels of various abilities					
13. Asks appropriately for information by telephone					
14. Asks appropriately for permission to leave message					
15. Tells appropriately who a message is for					
16. Leaves appropriate expressed messages					

In order to assess language use in context, especially during social interactions, the teacher needs to determine students' ability to communicate in socially appropriate ways. Pragmatics involve a rule system that encompasses three major communication skills: (1) using language for different purposes (e.g., greeting, informing, demanding, promising, and requesting); (2) adapting or changing language according to the needs or expectations of a listener or situation; and (3) following rules for conversation and narratives and rules for nonverbal signals in conversation (e.g., facial expressions, distance between the speaker and listener, and eye contact). These rules may vary depending on the language and culture (American Speech-Language-Hearing Association, 2004; Venn, 2004). (Figure 6–15 is an observation checklist for assessing the pragmatic performance of preadolescents and adolescents.)

SECTION 3: ASSESSMENT OF STUDENTS WITH CULTURAL OR LINGUISTIC DIVERSITY

The United States is the most demographically diverse nation—linguistically, culturally, religiously, and ethnically—in world history (Prewitt, 2002). Consequently, U.S. classrooms are becoming more diverse with increasing numbers of children from various racial and ethnic minority groups. About one in four Americans is a minority, and this proportion is growing (U.S. Department of Education, 2000). According to research from the U.S. Office of Special Education Programs, children from culturally and linguistically diverse backgrounds comprise a large percentage of public school students, particularly in large-city school districts where the percentage of minority students may be as high as 80 percent (Burnette, 2000).

English language learners (ELLs) are a significant and growing portion of the school-aged population in the United States, with estimates between 1 and 7 to 1 and 11 of all kindergarten to grade 12 students (DiCerbo, 2000; Yzquierdo, Blalock, & Torres-Velasquez, 2004). This group includes "students whose first language is not English, and encompasses both students who are just beginning to learn English and those who have already developed considerable proficiency" (LaCelle-Peterson & Rivera, 1994, p. 55). The number of ELLs who have difficulty understanding and using English increased to 3.4 million in 2000 (U.S. Census Bureau, n.d.). There are now more than 400 languages spoken by ELLs nationwide (Kindler, 2002), and the vast majority of the language minority population, 75 percent, are Spanish speakers (Artiles & Ortiz, 2002; U.S. Department of Education, 2000).

ELLs are at high risk of being misdiagnosed and overrepresented when they are referred for evaluation for possible disability and of receiving inappropriate special education services (Coutinho, Oswald, & Best, 2002; Donovan & Cross, 2002). These students may appear academically deficient or act inappropriately when, in reality, the problem is a language or cultural difference (Coutinho et al., 2002; Turnbull, Turnbull, Smith, & Leal, 2002). A disproportionate number of culturally or linguistically diverse (CLD) students are placed in special education programs, often due to their poor performance on traditional test instruments, but also due to a general lack of understanding in the school systems of the influence of linguistic, cultural, and socioeconomic differences on student learning (Heward, 2003; Ortiz & Yates, 2001; Smith, 2001).

Even when standardized tests are adapted for ELLs and are designed to be non-biased and to provide reliable results across all cultures, students' strengths and weaknesses are often misinterpreted, resulting in bilingualism being diagnosed as a disability (Hagie, Gallipo, Svien, 2003; Figueroa, 2000). CLD students are frequently suspected of having a learning disability when, in reality, their learning problems are due to their

CLARIFYING TERMS

ESL—English as a second language.

CLD—Culturally and linguistically diverse. English is not the primary language of communication.

ELL—English language learner. Does not speak, understand, or write English with the same facility as classmates.

LEP—Limited English proficient. Experiences difficulty understanding and using English.

BEV—Black English vernacular. Nonstandard dialect used by a subgroup of English speakers.

Bilingual speaker— Speaks in both the native language and a second language.

Tips for Teachers

Avoid misidentification and increase the likelihood of ruling out English proficiency as the cause of learning problems by

- assessing students in their native language and in English (assess language dominance and proficiency)
- making adaptations to existing standardized instruments and using multiple sources, tools, and strategies when assessing students.
- ensuring that assessment team members have expertise in bilingual, second language, and special education
- assessing ELLs in their homes and communities and involving parents in the assessment process (Ortiz & Yates, 2002)

FYI Misclassification Facts

Problems associated with inappropriate classification and placement include

- Being denied access to the general education curriculum
- Being placed in separate programs with more limited curriculum that may affect access to postsecondary education and employment opportunities
- Being stigmatized; a misclassification may negatively affect students' self-perception and the perceptions of them by others (U.S. Department of Education, 1997).

FYI ELL Services

English language learners who qualify for special education services do not lose their right to receive bilingual or ELL educational services (Ortiz & Yates, 2002, p. 83).

FYI Test Norming

Relatively few standardized tests have been published in languages other than English, and the majority of those tests have not been normed on second-language children living in the United States (Center for Innovations in Special Education, 1999).

difficulties in acquiring two languages simultaneously, socioeconomic factors, nutrition, health care concerns, or a combination of those factors (Ortiz, 2003; Yates & Ortiz, 1998). Often they may have little experience taking tests, become anxious or confused during the tests, or have difficulty controlling their attention and behavior during test situations (Meisels, 2001). Care must be taken to avoid confusing educational deprivation (e.g., a lack of opportunity to learn the subject matter of the tests) with an intrinsic learning problem (Amrein & Berliner, 2002; Pierce, 2002; Stiggins, 2002).

Conversely, students with CLD may not be considered for special education programs due to cultural or language differences as school personnel attempt to avoid inappropriate diagnosis and placement (Figueroa, 2000; Figueroa & Hernandez, 2002). In either situation, the child is not receiving the appropriate services (Ortiz & Yates, 2002).

IDEA Requirements for Assessing CLD Students

The Individuals with Disabilities Education Act Amendments of 1997 (IDEA-97) clearly state that students are not eligible for services if their learning problems are primarily the result of environmental, cultural, or economic disadvantages and that evaluation and placement procedures must be nondiscriminatory. Among the mandates to ensure that CLD students are evaluated fairly and in a nondiscriminatory manner and that families are informed and have their due process rights are the following:

- Tests and other evaluation materials and procedures should be administered in the native language of the child or by another mode of communication, unless it is clearly not feasible to do so.
- When determining the eligibility status of the student, assessment results must be considered by individuals knowledgeable about the child, about assessment, and about placement alternatives (U.S. Commission on Civil Rights, 1997).
- Multi-disciplinary teams (MDT) may not use a single procedure as the sole criterion for determining whether a child is disabled.
- Tests should be selected and administered so as not to be racially or culturally discriminatory and must be administered by trained and knowledgeable personnel.
- A child shall not be identified as having a disability if the determinant factor is limited English proficiency.
- Copies of notices and evaluation reports must be given to the parent in the parent's native language or through a translator.

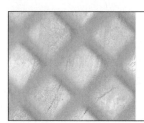

Tips for Teachers

Even when reevaluation is not required, language assessment should be updated at least annually for the ELLs whose skills may change dramatically over short periods of time (Ortiz & Yates, 2002, p. 84).

Assessment Issues: Language Disorders vs. Differences

Distinguishing between a language disorder and a learning impairment and learning difficulties due to lack of instructional opportunity for a student who is an ELL is a complex assessment process. The following questions can help to rule out a disability as the source of a student's difficulty:

- Besides the referring teacher, have others (e.g., the remedial instructor, the ELL teacher, parents) noted similar problems?
- Are the problems evident across contexts (e.g., in the general education class, in the English as a second language (ESL) class, in related arts classes, in the home)?
- Are the problems evident in the student's first language (e.g., do native speakers have difficulty understanding the student)?
- Does the student have difficulty following directions in both English and their native language?
- Does the student continue to have difficulty reading in the native language despite effective instruction?
- Is the student's progress in English language acquisition significantly slower than that of chronological age peers starting at the same level of language proficiency with comparable instruction?
- Can the difficulty be explained by cross-cultural differences (e.g., lack of eye contact as a cultural tradition, interpreted as inattention or behavioral defiance)?
- Could other factors (e.g., inconsistent school attendance or language variations) be causing the differences?
- Is there evidence of serious test anxiety, or is the student confused by the assessment process, since it may be the first time he or she has been tested in this country?
- Could procedural errors (related to administration or scoring), or a failure to provide necessary accommodations, test procedural mistakes, miscalculation or scoring error, or insufficient preparation cause the difficulty?
- Could bias in operation before, during, or after the assessment be a problem (e.g., when all ELLs are referred for special education even though the test used is not normed for ELLs, when adaptations are used inappropriately, when the evaluator's low expectations for student performance influence the administration and interpretation of results)?
- Were the prereferral interventions (e.g., clinical teaching, remedial supports, curricular or teaching modifications) unable to close the achievement gap?

Critical Thinking and Reflection Activity

In one common scenario, a child is referred for speech-language testing because she is struggling academically. In her teacher's view, she is not learning English with the expected speed and her academic skills are lagging behind those of her monolingual English-speaking classmates. Does the student have a language-learning disability or is she merely manifesting the normal process of acquiring a second language? (Roseberry-McKibbon & Brice, 2004)

🔍 CLARIFYING TERMS

Language Proficiency—refers to the student's skill level in the use of the language

Language Dominance—refers to the language in which the student shows the greatest level of skill

Language Preference—the language the student would use if allowed to choose

- Are assessment results consistent with the concerns of the student's teacher and parents? (Ortiz & Yates, 2002).

Identifying the Second-Language-Acquisition Phenomena

It is important that teachers understand the normal processes and phenomena of second-language acquisition to differentiate a developmental delay from a cultural difference and to avoid making "false positive" identifications (Pavri, 2002). Roseberry-McKibbin & Brice (2004) note the following factors to be aware of:

Interference, or transfer, from students' native language to English occurs when students make an English error due to the direct influence of their native language structure.

> **EXAMPLE:** In Spanish, "esta casa es mas grande" means "this house is bigger." The literal translation would be "this house is more bigger." A Spanish-speaking child who said "this house is more bigger" would be manifesting transfer from Spanish to English, which is a normal phenomenon, a sign of a language difference, not a language disorder.

Silent period is another common second-language-acquisition phenomenon. When students are first exposed to a second language, they may not speak much as they focus on listening and comprehension and on understanding the new language. The younger the child, the longer the silent period tends to last, with older children remaining in the silent period for a few weeks or months and preschoolers for up to a year or more.

Codeswitching is a normal phenomenon manifested by the child changing languages within phrases or sentences.

> **EXAMPLE:** A native Spanish speaker might say, "Me gustaria manejar—I'll take the car" instead of "I'd like to drive. I'll take the car." Or, a Filipino child might say, "With my teacher, I have utang ng loob [debt of gratitude] because she has been so good to me."

Language loss, also referred to as *subtractive bilingualism*, is manifested by a loss of skills and fluency in the native language if it is not reinforced or maintained as the child is learning English. This can be cognitively and linguistically very detrimental to children's learning and to their family lives (especially if the parents speak only the native language and no English). *Additive bilingualism*, the optimal phenomenon, occurs when children learn English while maintaining and reinforcing their native language and culture (Anderson, 1998; Bialystok, 2001).

Critical Thinking and Reflection Activity

Miquel has recently immigrated to the United States from Mexico. Although he is a non-English speaker and has limited proficiency in Spanish, his native language, Spanish, is considered to be his dominant language. He is assessed in Spanish. His low performance on this test results in classification and special education placement. Miquel's progress continues to be poor. What should be done?

Distinguishing Between Social and Academic Language Proficiency

There are two types of language proficiency: basic interpersonal communication skill, and cognitive academic language proficiency.

Basic interpersonal communication skill (BICS) is language proficiency in everyday communicative contexts or those aspects of language proficiency that seem to be acquired naturally and without formal schooling. It takes the average English language learner about two years to acquire BICS; that is, the context-embedded, everyday language that occurs between conversational partners (e.g., "We will have sandwiches for lunch today," and "Put the pencil in your desk") (Roseberry-McKibbin, 2004).

Cognitive academic language proficiency (CALP) is language proficiency in academic situations, or those aspects of language proficiencies that emerge and become distinctive with formal schooling. It takes about five to seven years to develop CALP; that is, the context-reduced language of academics under ideal conditions (e.g., "Compare democracy and a dictatorship," and "Explain the outcome of the battle"). However, it may take longer for a student to develop CALP due to several factors, including interrupted schooling, level of development of native language skills, or the emotional state of the child and family (CEC, 2002).

ELLs often develop conversational English (BICS) that appears fluent and adequate for everyday communication. However, they still struggle with CALP and have difficulty in certain areas (e.g., reading, writing, spelling, science, social studies, and other subject areas) where there is little context to support the language being heard or read.

Critical Thinking and Reflection Activity

Reflect on the reasons why each of the following are problematic practices when assessing students who are CLD:

1. Assessment is made by evaluators who are unaware of the students' native language or cultures.

2. Family and health information is collected in English when another language is used at home.

3. English-only tests are used with bilingual students who appear to be English proficient since they are using English pragmatically (Ortiz, cited in Byrd, 2000).

4. Only formal assessments are used.

5. Norms are based solely on U.S. populations.

6. Standardized scoring is used when the testing has been adapted.

7. The focus is on the structural aspects of language rather than on issues of semantics and use (Yzquierdo et al., 2004).

This "BICS-CALP gap" leads professionals to falsely assume that the children have language learning disabilities. School language proficiency tests are often used to assess children's level of proficiency in English. Teachers and other school personnel who work with these children see the label "fully English proficient" and assume that it is acceptable to give English standardized tests to these children, since they have been identified as being fully proficient in English. In reality, however, the children are still striving to develop CALP and thus the use of standardized tests in English is biased against them. When these standardized tests are administered, the ELLs often score very low, are labeled as having language learning disabilities, and are inappropriately placed in special education (Roseberry-McKibbin & Brice, 2004).

The ability to receive information, which includes BIC and CALP skill areas, and then to use these skills to communicate with others is what needs to be assessed. Current assessment methods minimally assess these skill areas, especially in children being considered for special education (Roseberry-McKibbin, 2004). (See Figure 6–16.)

Critical Thinking and Reflection Activity

Juanita's scores on a language assessment indicates that she is a non-English speaker while the Spanish scores rate her as a limited Spanish speaker. Which language would be considered Juanita's dominant language? In which, if any, language is she proficient?

See Figure 6–17 for examples of the age that specific language skills are generally expected. (Note the mixture of what is commonly called BICS and CALP, yet at a given age the concepts are considered to be CALP.)

Figure 6–16 BICS Acquisition Checklist

Does the student
____ demonstrate the ability to listen and comprehend and retain information sufficiently to maintain an intelligible communication?
____ have the ability to provide basic personal information (e.g., name and age) at a more advanced level that includes knowledge of birthdays of all family members, extended family members' addresses and phone numbers, etc.?
____ understand basic concepts that define space, time, numerocity, etc.?
____ have at least some minimal vocabulary skills that are growing as the age and education of the child increases?
____ recognize how verbs and verb tenses work together?
____ use verb tenses in words?
____ have the ability to discriminate similar phonemes?
____ have the abstract processing ability necessary to acquire and refine existing skills?
____ demonstrate the retelling skills necessary to carry on a given conversation with appropriate verbal give and take?
____ have question-asking skills?
____ demonstrate pragmatic skills and the social understandings of language (e.g., turn-taking, maintaining topic, body language)?

Figure 6–17   Expected Age Norms for BICS and CALP Development

0 to 6 months	Responsive to sound, nonverbal gestures, facial expression, phonemes, such as "da", "ma", babbles.
6 months to 1 year	Begins meaningful verbalization with one to two word utterances
1 to 2 years	Begins to construct short sentences, use of meaning words continues to expand, uses present tense and basic concept formation, repeats short phrases of adult speakers.
2 to 3 years	Vocabulary growth continues, including the use of past tense and action verbs (running), able to supply basic personal data (name, age, boy/girl) and academic concepts (numbers, colors, grouping), developing the basic pragmatics.
3 to 4 years	Becomes more articulate and enjoys verbal communication, vocabulary is expanding, developing phonemic awareness, can provide more personal information, academic concepts include one-to-one correspondence, growth is evident in verbal reasoning skills.
4 to 5 years	Increasing competence in phonemic awareness skills, uses irregular plurals in everyday speech and begins to use future tense, developing proficiency in question-answer skills.
5 to 6 years	Uses future tense time markers consistently; can repeat up to 10 syllable sentences; vocabulary expanded to include basic terms used in social studies, science and literature; has developed basic concept knowledge (space, time, numeration, etc.); growth in pragmatics which includes an understanding of non-verbal communication and taking turns; is able to retell simple story details in sequential order.
6 to 7 years	Significant expansion in vocabulary, uses phonemes to formulate words, incorporates conditional tense, has mastered most preliminary reading skills, more appropriate use of irregular and past tense verbs, has developed sufficient written language skill to tell a story when spelling is not a factor, pragmatics skills have expanded to include introduction and termination skills and appropriate classroom/meeting behavior.
7 to 9 years	Fundamental reading skills are mastered for word identification and comprehension, uses compound verb tenses.
9 to 11 years	Basic communication skills, including reading and writing skills are refined and used consistently, has developed spelling skills to include recognition of sight words and use of phonics skills.
11 to 13 years	Development complete for basic BICS system, traditional tests of oral language or reading at the fifth or sixth grade level is used to measure CALP system development.
13 and up	Determination of the level of CALP development often includes traditional CALP measures, particularly reading. BICS is screened using writing skills, more formal oral assessment is used for those with any written language difficulty.

Adapted from Anderson, R. (2000). *The assessment of BICS/CALP: A developmental perspective.*
http://home.earthlink.net/~psychron/homepage.htm

Figure 6–18   Categories of Language Use Survey

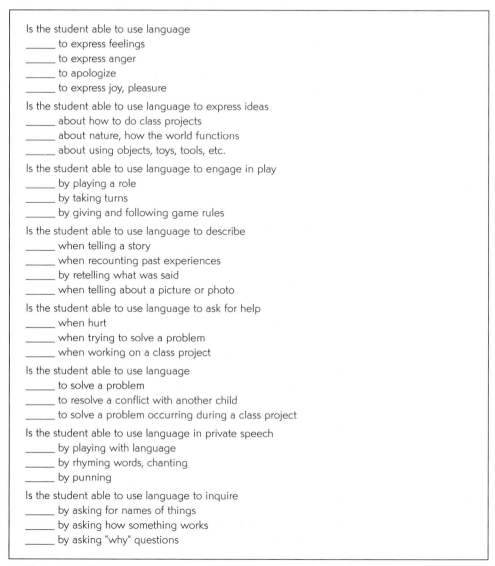

Is the student able to use language
_____ to express feelings
_____ to express anger
_____ to apologiz
_____ to express joy, pleasure

Is the student able to use language to express ideas
_____ about how to do class projects
_____ about nature, how the world functions
_____ about using objects, toys, tools, etc.

Is the student able to use language to engage in play
_____ by playing a role
_____ by taking turns
_____ by giving and following game rules

Is the student able to use language to describe
_____ when telling a story
_____ when recounting past experiences
_____ by retelling what was said
_____ when telling about a picture or photo

Is the student able to use language to ask for help
_____ when hurt
_____ when trying to solve a problem
_____ when working on a class project

Is the student able to use language
_____ to solve a problem
_____ to resolve a conflict with another child
_____ to solve a problem occurring during a class project

Is the student able to use language in private speech
_____ by playing with language
_____ by rhyming words, chanting
_____ by punning

Is the student able to use language to inquire
_____ by asking for names of things
_____ by asking how something works
_____ by asking "why" questions

Modified version of California Early Language Development Assessment Process: Categories of Language Use from the National Clearinghouse for Bilingual Education (NCBE).

Assessing Language Proficiency

According to Ortiz & Yates (2002), in most states ELLs are assessed each year using standardized language proficiency instruments. For students to be considered fluent in English, they must have a level of authenticity and automatic control of both conversational and academic language that is comparable to their peers (Parker, 1993). The important questions to ask in identifying students with fluent proficiency in English are (1) Can the student listen, speak, read, and write in English at a level comparable to English-speaking peers? and (2) Can the student achieve at the appropriate grade level in the regular instructional program (Parker, 1993)?

Assessing language use focuses on the particular situations and types of communication modes in which the student demonstrates proficiency as well as the area of

Figure 6–19   Student Oral Proficiency Rating Checklist

Comprehensive

_____Level 1   Cannot understand even simple conversation

_____Level 2   Has great difficulty following what is said. Can comprehend only "social conversation" spoken slowly and with frequent repetitions

_____Level 3   Understands most of what is said at slower-than-normal speed with repetitions

_____Level 4   Understands nearly everything at normal speed, although occasional repetition may be necessary

_____Level 5   Understands everyday conversation and normal classroom discussions without difficulty

Fluency

_____Level 1   Speech is so halting and fragmentary that conversation is virtually impossible

_____Level 2   Usually hesitant; often forced into silence by language limitations

_____Level 3   Speech in everyday communication and classroom discussion is often disrupted by the student's search for the correct manner of expression

_____Level 4   Speech in everyday communication and classroom discussion is generally fluent, with occasional lapses while the student searches for the correct manner of expression

_____Level 5   Speech in everyday conversation and in classroom discussions is fluent and effortless, approximating that of a native speaker

Vocabulary

_____Level 1   Vocabulary limitations so extreme that conversation is virtually impossible

_____Level 2   Misuse of words, very limited vocabulary, comprehension very difficult

_____Level 3   Frequently uses the wrong words; conversation somewhat limited due to inadequate vocabulary

_____Level 4   Occasionally uses inappropriate terms; must rephrase ideas due to inadequate vocabulary

_____Level 5   Use of vocabulary and idioms approximates that of a native speaker

Pronunciation

_____Level 1   Pronunciation problems are severe, speech is virtually unintelligible

_____Level 2   Very hard to understand because of pronunciation problems, usually needs to repeat to be understood

_____Level 3   Pronunciation problems necessitate listener concentration and occasionally lead to misunderstanding

_____Level 4   Always intelligible, though one is conscious of a definite accent and occasional inappropriate intonation patterns

_____Level 5   Pronunciation and intonation approximate a native speaker's

Grammar

_____Level 1   Errors in grammar and word order so severe they make speech unintelligible

_____Level 2   Grammar and word order errors make comprehension difficult. Must often rephrase or restrict what is said to basic patterns

_____Level 3   Makes frequent errors of grammar and word order, which occasionally obscures meaning

_____Level 4   Occasionally makes grammatical or word order errors, which do not obscure meaning

_____Level 5   Grammatical usage and word order approximate a native speaker's

language use that is underdeveloped or deficient. (See Figure 6–18 for a guide to assessing language use.) Ortiz and Garcia (1990) recommend effective procedures to assess conversational abilities and academic language proficiency skills (e.g., using language to predict, evaluate, and infer), which include

- Spontaneous conversation samples to assess how well a student understands and speaks the two languages with different people and in different settings and contexts
- Storytelling or dictation tasks to assess receptive academic language proficiency and the ability to understand classroom discourse and lesson content
- Storytelling tasks to assess narrative skills and the child's ability to organize information, sequence events, draw conclusions, and evaluate actions
- Cloze tests to assess a student's background and knowledge of vocabulary and grammatical structures
- Interviews with parents or family members to gain an understanding of language use in the home and community, language preference, and the level of proficiency in the native language" (pp. 24–27). (See Figure 6–19.)

SECTION 4: ENGLISH LANGUAGE LEARNER AND BILINGUAL ASSESSMENT

Traditional CLD Assessment Measures

Identifying disabilities among ELLs is a complex task (Ortiz & Graves, 2001). Recent research suggests that there has been a paradigm shift in testing procedures due to the concern about the racial and ethnic overrepresentation in special education. Standardized tests historically have underestimated the abilities of linguistically diverse students; they are reported to be suspect, at best, and determined by many researchers to be invalid and unreliable.

Numerous research studies report that the test procedures used in special education do not benefit ELLs in that the bias in these tests does not adequately distinguish between learning and/or communication disorder and lack of language proficiency (Abedi, 2000; Figueroa & Hernandez, 2002; Shakrani, 1999). There is compelling evidence that traditional assessment procedures using norm-referenced tests are inappropriate for ELLs and that reliance on standardized measures, even when adapted for ELLs, result in misdiagnosis due to multiple factors, including the lack of academic support, limited English proficiency, and cultural differences (Baca, 2002).

Additional concerns are that few standardized assessment instruments are available in languages other than English. Those that are available often have poor psychometric properties. Also, most assessment personnel have little or no training in test administration in any language but English, nor have they been trained how to understand or interpret the interaction of disabilities with linguistic, cultural, and other student characteristics (Ortiz & Yates, 2002).

Informal Authentic Assessment Measures

Based on the research on effective instructional practices (Tharp, 1997) and the relationship between second-language acquisition and academic achievement (Gandara, 1999), experts in the field strongly support assessing the instructional program

FYI FACTORS IN ASSESSING LANGUAGE DISABILITY

The likelihood of a language disability exists when the child also exhibits problems in his or her native or first language. The likelihood the problem is *not* a language disorder exists when

- the native or first-language skills are comparable to same age peers.
- the level of language proficiency is similar to peers who have been learning English for the same amount of time.
- the rate of developing English language is comparable to that of young English-speaking children.
- the child is able to communicate adequately with family members (Slentz, 1997).

before assessing the child in order to observe which ELLs are not progressing in an enriched, productive classroom (Enguidanos & Ruiz, 1997; Graves, Valles, & Rueda, 2000; Ruiz & Enguidanos, 1997; Ruiz & Figueroa, 1995). According to Figueroa (2002), "the classroom is the best place to determine what works, what does not work, and what is needed in order to 'cure' learning problems"(p. 57).

The National Research Council has emphasized the use of a more contextualized and constructivist model for assessment and has made this a cornerstone for reforming the National Assessment for Educational Progress (NAEP) (Pellegrino, Jones, & Mitchell, 1999). The combination of research and extensive policy and regulatory publications (American Educational Research Association, 1999; U.S. Department of Education, 2000) are strongly influencing the paradigm shift from a traditional assessment model to relying on observation of students in enriched, effective, instructional contexts (Figueroa, 2002), such as the classroom.

Sources of Assessment Data

Assessment information should come from a variety of procedures. The historical reliance on standardized testing for assessing students who are ELLs and bilingual students has shifted. It is now commonly recognized that assessment for CLD students should be instructionally embedded and that scripted, standardized, norm-referenced measures should be avoided. All evaluations should incorporate information about students across a variety of contexts and sources. Ethnographic information should be obtained regarding how the student communicates in the home, in the school, in the academic classroom, in unstructured school situations (e.g., the cafeteria, on the playground), with the peer group, and in the community (Brice, 2002; Goldstein, 2000). Those contributing their perceptions of the student should include the parents, the ESL and bilingual teachers, other general education teachers, compensatory education program teachers, and support staff (Westby, Burda, & Mehta, 2003).

Assessments should be conducted both in the native language and in English to provide a comprehensive view of what the student knows and can do, regardless of the language in which knowledge and skills are demonstrated. In addition, acculturation and learning styles need to be examined. Teachers need to adapt assessment techniques in response to the needs of diverse students (Venn, 2004). [See Figure 6–20 for factors to consider during the assessment process (Pierangelo & Giuliani, 1998)].

Figure 6–20 Factors to Consider When Conducting ELL-Bilingual Assessments

- Language spoken at home
- Level of language proficiency
- Extent of ESL services prior to referral
- Any experiential and/or enrichment services received
- Level of parental involvement before referral
- Amount of time and extent of services in an academic program for children who have had little or no formal schooling
- Length of residency in the United States and prior school experience in the native country and in an English language school system
- Attempts to remediate performance before referral, including any supplemental aids or support services
- Also, when evaluating students who are CLD, the screening should be conducted in both languages, as appropriate.

Figure 6–21   Student Interview Guide

Name _____ Date _____		
F = Fluent B = Broken U = Unable		
	Oral	Written
What is your name?	_____	_____
What is your address?	_____	_____
What is your telephone number?	_____	_____
What is your birthdate?	_____	_____
How old are you?	_____	_____
How many people live in your house?	_____	_____
How many brothers and sisters do you have?	_____	_____
What country are you from?	_____	_____
Why did you come to America?	_____	_____
Did you go to school before coming to America?	_____	_____
What languages do you speak?	_____	_____
What is the first language you learned to speak?	_____	_____
What language do you speak most often?	_____	_____
What language is most spoken in your home?	_____	_____
What is your favorite subject in school?	_____	_____
Why do you like that subject?	_____	_____
Read a passage from a grade appropriate book.	_____	_____

Students who cannot read will be given a picture dictionary to identify the following:
Colors _____   Family members _____
Numbers _____   Classroom items _____

This assessment process involves a review of the student's records, including standardized language proficiency test results that are typically administered periodically by the bilingual instructor or the ESL teacher to track students' growth and movement toward mastery of English.

Many measures and procedures are used in student assessments, including interviews, observations, and informal testing procedures. Student interviews might consist of a conversation sample that can be analyzed to see how effective the child is as a communication partner, and whether the student knows the rules for face-to-face conversation. (See Figure 6–21 for a sample student screening interview and factors to consider when assessing.)

Parental Contribution to the Assessment Process

In order to obtain a fully contextual account of the child's language skills, it is important to obtain extensive background about the child's previous language experience, the context of language learning, the academic learning opportunities, and the resources available to the child.

Parents can be interviewed to provide information about the cultural characteristics of the child and family, the primary language spoken by family members, and how communication skills are progressing in the home environment (Twombly, 2001; Woods & McCormick, 2002). They can also supply key details about how the child is learning and developing and describe the child's language environment. (See Figure 6–22.)

Figure 6–22   Parent-Home Language Survey

What language did/does your child . . .
    speak when beginning to talk?   English ___ Other language _____
    speak *most often* at home?   English ___ Other language _____
    speak *most often* with friends?   English ___ Other language _____
What language do you. . .
    use *most often* when speaking to your child?   English ___ Other language _____
    use *most often* when speaking to your friends?   English ___ Other language _____
What language do other family members in your
    home *usually* use when speaking to each other? English ___ Other language _____

Family Member	Native Language	Language Used at Home	Second Language Fluency
Father	_____	_____	None ___ Emerging ___ Mastery ___
Mother	_____	_____	None ___ Emerging ___ Mastery ___
Siblings	_____	_____	None ___ Emerging ___ Mastery ___
Others in home	_____	_____	None ___ Emerging ___ Mastery ___
Peers	_____	_____	None ___ Emerging ___ Mastery ___

Student's use of second language	None	Occasional	Frequent	Total
	_____	_____	_____	_____

	Speaking	Writing	Reading
Age began . . .	_____	_____	_____

Student's English
fluency
    ___ Uses basic nouns and verbs
    ___ Uses conjugated verbs, nouns, and adjectives
    ___ Speaks in full sentences uses form and structure inconsistently
    ___ Speaks fluently with good usage, form, and structure

Student's dominant language _____ Language of preference _____
Language parents prefer for school instruction _____

Student's school experience:
Native language instruction ___ Bilingual instruction ___ All English instruction ___
          ___ Bilingual aide ___ ESL Teacher ___ Regular Education
                                      Teacher

    Data obtained from parental reports can include the extent to which the significant others in the child's life, including peers, provide language assistance. This assistance might include modeling, expanding, restating, repeating, questioning, prompting, negotiating meaning, cueing, pausing, praising, and providing visual and other supports.

Observational Assessment Procedures

Careful observation of students in an optimal learning environment, over an extended period of time, allows teachers to document students' strength and weaknesses and to provide the necessary data to make clinical judgments about the presence of disabilities. When language minority students are observed at various times and in different contexts, the evaluator can more accurately assess their language competencies and progress.

Observations of students should occur in class, in unstructured settings (e.g., cafeteria, playground), and, if possible, in their homes. It is particularly important to observe students' use of language during typical classroom tasks in which they are expected to perform, such as following directions, storytelling, and participating in classroom discussions. The focus is on whether the child understands the messages the teacher is giving, comprehends the story both receptively and expressively, and actively participates in the verbal interaction.

Tips for Teachers

"Families are diverse not only in language and culture but also in other background characteristics, such as race, social class, formal education, and acculturation. How a family participates in the assessment process depends on the complex interrelationships of all these factors" (Garcia, 2002, p. 89).

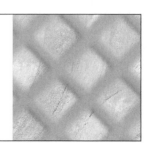

Types of Authentic Assessments

It is critical to supplement traditional standardized tests with informal, authentic measures of the student's abilities, particularly for the student with cultural and linguistic differences. Authentic assessments promote the application of knowledge and skills in situations that closely resemble real-world activities (Frisby, 2001). They are potentially more motivating than other types of assessments because they engage students in realistic uses of language and content-area concepts and promote the transfer or generalizing of learning from facts and procedures to applications in meaningful contexts (Pierce, 2002).

Curriculum-Based Assessments

Curriculum-based assessment (CBA) procedures measure what the student knows, what needs to be learned, and where in the curriculum instruction should begin. CBAs allow frequent collection of student performance data to assess instructional effectiveness (McConnell, 2000), noting progress mastery of a skill rather than comparing the student's performance with that of other students. CBAs are particularly appropriate for CLD students. First, they are not standardized so that adaptations can be made without threatening test validity, thus eliciting representative samples of children's skills under optimal conditions. Second, the tests can be operationalized to address broad general concepts that match a particular child's characteristics (Notari-Syverson, Losardo, & Young Sook, 2003).

Performance-Based Assessments

Performance-based assessment (PBA) links assessment to instruction through the use of meaningful and engaging tasks. (See Figure 6–23.) Many factors make PBAs more appropriate for students who are ELLs than traditional testing formats (Frisby, 2001). This type of assessment allows students to demonstrate a variety of language, literacy, cognitive, social, and motor skills (Losardo & Notari-Syverson, 2001). According to

Figure 6–23 Sample Performance Assessment Strategies

Role Play
Role play can be used to express skills across grade levels, across curriculum and content, individually, or in groups. An example is a teacher who assumes the role of a character who knows less than the students about the subject area. Students are motivated to convey facts or information.

Role play can be used to assess math concepts by having students assume the role of a denominator, a numerator, a proper or an improper fraction, a number line, or an equivalent fraction; science concepts by having students assume the role of the life cycle; history by assuming the role of the explorers; reading or writing by assuming the role of characters in a literature story, and so forth.

Pierce (2002), well-constructed performance tasks are more likely than traditional types of assessments to do the following:

- Provide comprehensible input to students
- Use meaningful, naturalistic context-embedded tasks through hands-on or collaborative activities
- Show what students know and can do through a variety of assessment tasks
- Support the language and cognitive need of students who are ELLs
- Allow for flexibility in meeting individual needs
- Use criterion-referenced assessment for judging student work
- Provide feedback to students on strengths and weaknesses
- Generate descriptive information that can guide instruction
- Provide information for teaching and learning that results in improved student performance

Portfolio Assessments

Portfolio assessment, in which authentic samples of student's work are collected over time, can focus on samples in both the student's native language and in English (Farr & Trumbull, 1997). Portfolios are powerful tools to facilitate communication between teachers and parents and have been used very successfully with ELL, low-income, and migrant families (Paratore, Turpie, DiBiasio, & Sullivan, 1995). Parents and caregivers can easily contribute to the collection of materials included in the portfolio with samples of work and drawings from home, and lists of books read at home (Losardo & Notari-Syverson, 2001). In addition, because portfolios are individualized for each child, they can include various products that can help parents who do not speak or read English well understand how their child is progressing in school. Portfolios are also particularly beneficial for children of migrant workers as permanent records that can be taken by families as they move from place to place (Notari-Syverson, Losardo, & Young Sook, 2003).

Dynamic Assessments

Dynamic assessment generally follows a test-teach-test paradigm where the student's initial performance is used as a baseline, intervention follows, and then the student is retested on the same task. This method of assessment involves guided support or direct participation by the evaluator who interacts with the student to determine the student's learning potential, responsiveness to instruction, and metacognitive processes (Bialystok, 2000). The data gathered, which is important for instructional planning, include not only the number of tasks mastered but also the number and types of prompts required, the amount of teacher intervention, and the support needed to elicit the response (Losardo & Notari-Syverson, 2001).

Teachers are able to ask questions if responses are unclear in order to reveal the student's thinking process, intentions, and reasoning behind the response (Lopez-Reyna & Bay, 1997). Dynamic assessment is a sensitive predictor of progress; it provides valuable information about the student's self-regulatory behaviors and compensatory processes.

Authentic Assessments

Authentic assessments—such as storytelling, closed passage, and fill-in-the-blank passages—are used to analyze whether students are developing narrative skills and whether they are increasingly mastering the linguistic structures of the language. This cross-validation of test results helps to verify test findings and reduces the chance of subtle bias in eligibility decisions by providing a comprehensive documentation of students' functioning, regarding not only their ability to function using their native language or dialect but also their proficiency in standard English. [See Figure 6–24 for suggested authentic assessment strategies. (Tannenbaum, 1996)]

Figure 6–24   Sample Nonverbal Authentic Assessment Strategies

Physical Demonstrations
Students can point to objects; use gestures or hands-on tasks; or act out vocabulary, concepts, or events. The students can respond with a thumbs up or a thumbs down or other affirming gesture when the teacher has grouped a category of items correctly (e.g., food groups, animal habitats). The teacher can use a checklist to record individual responses. Audio- or videotaping of work in process, presentations, or demonstrations is a good way to capture skill mastery or areas needing attention.

Pictorial Products
Students can produce and manipulate drawings, models, dioramas, graphs, and charts. The students label the names of the states and their products. Labeling can be used across the curriculum with diagrams, webs, and illustrations.

Illustrations
Students can draw rather than explain. Pictorial journals can be kept during units to record and illustrate comprehension (e.g., the life cycle of a plant, a butterfly).

Written Products
Students can be assessed using reading response logs, dialogue journals, narrative story writing, and so forth.

K-W-L Charts
Students can use K-W-L charts (what I know, what I want to know, what I've learned) to begin and conclude a unit of study. This strategy helps teachers to gain an awareness of background knowledge and interests and to assess the content material learned. For students with limited English proficiency, the chart can be completed in the child's first language or with illustrations.

Environmental Assessments

Environmental assessment should also be considered when evaluating the student with CLD. Is the student in a culturally responsive school climate; is the classroom conducive to learning and a supportive learning environment; and does the teacher motivate positive student behavior, provide intensive academic intervention when needed, and have high expectations for all students (Kea, Campbell-Whatley, Bratton, 2003)? Teachers need to take a cultural audit of their classroom and teaching style to determine if they are responsive to culturally different students in five areas: (1) environmental style; (2) interaction style; (3) instructional strategies for cognitive style; (4) cognitive responsiveness; and (5) assessment style (Kea, Cartledge, & Bowman, 2002). (See Figure 6–25 for a teacher self-assessment.)

Tips for Teachers

The evaluator needs to be familiar with the regional dialect of the child so a language variation is not misdiagnosed as a disability.

Criteria for Evaluators of ELLs and Bilingual Students

The professionals who evaluate and interpret the assessment results of CLD students need to be qualified; have the necessary skills and training in second-language acquisition; be fluent in the student's native language; understand relevant cultural norms; be familiar with the child's cultural experiences, values, and learning style; and have experience in assessing students with CLD (Vermont Department of Education, 2004).

The criterion for such expert evaluators is not simply being able to speak the language or be a member of the relevant linguistic or ethnic group. The expert needs to have formal training in second-language acquisition, in the development of students' English proficiency, and in understanding the role native language has on students' performance. The testing needs to be administered by a trained evaluator who specializes

Figure 6–25 Teacher Classroom Environment Self-Assessment

Teachers can do a self-analysis by asking the following questions:

- Do I send both verbal and nonverbal messages that indicate capabilities for success to my students?
- Do I provide an intellectually stimulating classroom environment?
- Are appropriate tasks selected to meet the needs of all students?
- Does my presentation style meet the information processing and learning preferences of all my students?
- Do lesson presentations involve structure, appropriate rate, and maximum engagement through questioning, as well as provide specific feedback and the use of cultural affirmations for success?
- Do I have a firm, personal commitment to use the most effective instructional procedures and research-based best practices that work with this population?
- Am I acknowledging acceptance and the infusion of culture into the curriculum?
- Am I emphasizing a strengths-based approach to sustain a culturally responsive learning community? (Kea, Cartledge, & Bowman, 2002)

in assessing diverse learners and uses instruments that limit bias in the assessment process and safeguard against discrimination. This expert must ensure that the assessment results are accurate and can be used to program for the student with limited English proficiency.

The evaluator needs to assess students' language ability in two major areas: (1) their ability to converse in everyday social interactions, and (2) their language ability in situations that are more typical of classroom contexts; that is, the academic language proficiency needed to follow teacher dialogue and the language in textbooks.

Issues to Consider When Making Test Accommodations for Students with CLD

According to Sanchez-Boyce (2000), the use of interpreters adversely affects the validity and reliability of test results. This finding resulted from the complexities of the communication patterns as two adults shifted from one language to the other (e.g. from English, to Spanish, and back to English), standardization was not consistently followed, and the decisions made were based on social constructions rather than diagnostic findings (Figueroa & Hernandez, 2000).

Even when interpreters who have native-like proficiency in the student's dominant language are used, they often do not have enough proficiency to provide on-the-spot interpretation of complex information related to the special education process (Kayser, 1995). Interpreters need to have the language proficiency necessary to interpret effectively.

Studies have also indicated that even rigorous attempts at developing dual-language versions of standardized tests (e.g., a Spanish version of a test developed originally in English) have not produced psychometrically valid and comparable results (Anderson & Olson, 1996; Olson & Goldstein, 1997; Sanchez-Boyce, 2000). These tests cannot take into account the numerous lexical and semantic (vocabulary terms) variations; the limited use of contextual clues; and the prior school experiences of students, especially those immigrating to the United States (Figueroa, 2002).

Adaptations to Test Administration and Test Accommodations for Students with CLD

Students with cultural and linguistic differences often experience difficulty in comprehending test directions; in reading, understanding, and responding to test items; and in adequately making the connection between what they have learned and what the test item is asking (Brice, 2002; Goldstein, 2000; Roseberry-McKibbin, 2002). Due to their level of language proficiency, some students with limited English proficient students need to use much greater concentration for longer periods of time when testing. These students often require both assistance from test administrators and test accommodations. The following guidelines should be considered when developing and modifying tests, and when determining appropriate test accommodations for these students (Enciso, 2001; Fassler, 2001; Langdon & Saenz, 1996; Notari-Syverson, Losardo, & Young Sook, 2003; Salend, 1998):

- Establish rapport and gain the student's trust.
- Speak the language of the student.
- Assess in both English and the student's native language.
- Have the test administered by an individual familiar to the student.

- Make sure the student has had experience with the content or the tasks assessed by the test.
- Test beyond the ceiling test item.
- Record all responses and prompts.
- Reword or expand instructions and check for understanding.
- Define key words in both English and the student's native language.
- Allow the student to use a language dictionary.
- Avoid automatic penalties for using few words or not providing details.
- Teach test-taking tips, such as when it is beneficial to guess.
- Provide opportunities for taking practice tests.
- Provide review sheets, vocabulary lists, and key terms before test administration.
- Present items and directions through graphics and pictorial representations.
- Use a translator to assist in the test administration.
- Use test items that are high in comprehension and simple in language level with predictable language formats.
- Allow extended time for test taking.
- Provide extended response time to allow for the careful processing of verbal information.
- Provide context clues.
- Allow the student to demonstrate mastery of test materials in alternative ways (e.g., cooperative learning group projects, use of manipulatives).
- Allow the student to respond in his or her native language or dialect.
- Use visual materials, real-life examples, hands-on activities, story maps, pictures, facial expressions, and gestures to elicit responses.
- Speak slowly and use simple vocabulary; ask questions that require minimal response and allow response choice.
- Have the student give oral presentations or theatrical-dramatic performances.
- Individualize use of reinforcers.
- Allow for differences in English dialects when scoring tests.
- Do not count dialectical differences as errors.
- Consider class performance, not just test performance.
- Teach the student to become "test wise."
- Have the student explain incorrect answers.

Tech Tips

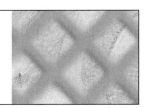

American Speech-Language-Hearing Association (ASHA) 1-800-638-8255 (Voice/TTY) or 301-897-5700; email: actioncenter@asha.org; Web site: www.asha.org.

SUMMARY POINTS

- Speech and language assessment involves the ability to talk, understand, and process information. Speech disorders affect the clarity, voice quality, and fluency of spoken words. Language disorders can affect a child's ability to hold meaningful conversations, understand others, problem solve, read and comprehend, and express thoughts through spoken and written words.

- Receptive skills involve understanding through listening or reading whereas expressive skills involve language used in speaking and writing.

- Rapid automatized naming (RAN) involves word finding. Students experiencing problems with RAN have difficulty quickly and automatically naming objects and with memory or word retrieval, which affects their ability to access verbal information.

- Nondiscriminatory testing of students who are diverse culturally, linguistically, or both requires that assessment be administered in the child's native language; that more than one procedure be used to determine a disability; that results be interpreted and eligibility determined by an individual knowledgeable about the student, assessment, and placement alternatives; that notices to parents and evaluation reports be communicated in the family's native language or through a translator; and that limited English proficiency not be the determinant factor in determining disability.

- Phenomena to consider in second-language acquisition include (a) *interference*, or *transfer*, from the student's native language to English; (b) the *silent period*, which is noted when the student is first exposed to a second language and tends to be very quiet while focusing on listening and comprehension in order to understand the new language; (c) *codeswitching*, which is manifested by the child changing languages within phrases or sentences; (d) *language loss*, which is manifested by a loss of skills and fluency in the native language if not reinforced or maintained as the child learns English; and (e) *additive bilingualism*, which is the optimal phenomenon where children learn English while maintaining and reinforcing their native language and culture.

- Basic interpersonal communication skill (BICS) is language proficiency acquired through everyday communicative contexts or is acquired naturally, without formal schooling. BICS takes an average of two years to acquire, is context-embedded, and involves everyday language occurring between conversational partners. Cognitive academic language proficiency (CALP) occurs in academic situations. CALP emerges and becomes distinctive with formal schooling, takes approximately five to seven years to develop, and is the context-reduced language of academics under ideal conditions.

- Testing students using standard psychometric methods may result in underestimating the diverse learner's potential in areas that are not tapped by traditional testing measures. When using a broad view of students' learning strengths and weaknesses, teachers can get to know their pupils as individuals, so that they can provide appropriate learning experiences and obtain more comparatively authentic assessment results.

- Adjustments may be needed to ensure that cultural and linguistically diverse students are evaluated in a fair, nondiscriminatory manner. The evaluator must have expertise in the pupil's primary language and culture and experience in evaluating this type of student. Basic test conditions must include the use of valid, reliable, and culture-free testing materials—administered in the student's primary language—which are comprehensive yet bypass the student's disability. Assessment information should cover a range of contexts, come from reliable sources, and be obtained through a variety of procedures.

Chapter Check-Ups

1. Explain the difference between speech and language disorders. Identify specific types of speech and types of language problems that students in your classroom might experience.

2. What is a word finding problem? How would you informally assess students to determine whether they have this problem and how can a word finding disorder impact the learning process?

3. Discuss the importance of proper identification of students who have disabilities and are English language learners (ELL). What do teachers need to consider when assessing students who have cultural and/or linguistic diversity to ensure that testing is fair, nondiscriminatory, valid and reliable?

4. Describe what teachers need to consider and the factors they need to be aware of when trying to assess whether a student in their class who is working on trying to acquire a second language has a specific learning disability or just typical cultural differences.

5. What is the difference between basic interpersonal communication skills (BICS) and cognitive academic language proficiency (CALP)? Describe some informal procedures that are appropriate to use for language proficiency assessment.

Practical Application Assessment Activities

1. Interview a speech and language therapist regarding (a) the most common types of speech and language problems the children in his/her caseload experience, (b) how language content, form, and use are evaluated, (c) the types of assessment tools he/she uses, (d) the types of assessment measures the classroom teacher can use, and (e) how assessment and instruction can be coordinated.

2. Working with a small group, role-play classroom scenarios in which students demonstrate the characteristics of speech and language delays. Group members take turns playing the role of the teacher and the student with the communication disorder. Each group should be assigned different types of oral language problems. After each role-play, all class members will convene to identify the language problem portrayed, what informal assessment procedures teachers might use to identify particular language problems, and discuss appropriate intervention strategies.

3. Reflect and respond to the following vignette. Sunyi is a ten-year-old student who has recently moved from Hong Kong to your school district. She is having serious academic difficulty and requires testing to determine whether she is eligible for classification and special education services. Discuss what the evaluator should consider when choosing the appropriate test(s) to use and what considerations and accommodations should be made when evaluating Sunyi.

4. Identify and discuss the important issues that school personnel need to focus on when assessing children with cultural and linguistic differences and interacting with their parents prior to and during the evaluation process. With a partner, brainstorm strategies that teachers can use to intervene and help to facilitate effective communication and ways that school personnel involved in the testing process can ensure that the most appropriate assessment practices are used.

Connection Between CEC, PRAXIS, and INTASC Standards and Chapter 6

Council for Exceptional Children
The voice and vision of special education

The Council for Exceptional Children—Professional Standards

Standard 2 Development and Characteristics of Learners

5. Similarities and differences of individuals with and without exceptional learning needs.

6. Similarities and differences among individuals with exceptional learning needs.

Standard 3 Individual Learning Differences

4. Cultural perspectives influencing the relationships among families, schools, and communities as related to instruction.

5. Differing ways of learning of individuals with exceptional learning needs, including those from culturally diverse backgrounds, and strategies for addressing these differences.

Standard 6 Communication

1. Effects of cultural and linguistic differences on growth and development.

2. Characteristics of one's own culture and use of language and the ways in which these can differ from other cultures and uses of languages.

6. Use communication strategies and resources to facilitate understanding of subject matter for students whose primary language is not the dominant language.

Standard 8 Assessment

1. Basic terminology used in assessment.

2. Legal provisions and ethical principles regarding assessment of individuals.

4. Use and limitations of assessment instruments.

5. National, state or provincial, and local accommodations and modifications.

6. Gather relevant background information.

7. Administer nonbiased formal and informal assessments.

8. Use technology to conduct assessments.

9. Develop or modify individualized assessment strategies.

10. Interpret information from formal and informal assessments.

11. Use assessment information in making eligibility, program, and placement decisions for individuals with exceptional learning needs, including those from culturally and/or linguistically diverse backgrounds.

12. Report assessment result to all stakeholders using effective communication skills.

13. Evaluate instruction and monitor progress of individuals with exceptional learning needs.

Standard 9 Professional and Ethical Practice

10. Demonstrate sensitivity of the culture, language, religion, gender, disability, socioeconomic status, and sexual orientation of individuals.

16. Engage in professional activities that benefit individuals with exceptional learning needs, their families, and one's colleagues.

Standard 10 Collaboration

4. Culturally responsive factors that promote effective communication and collaboration with individuals with exceptional learning needs, families, school personnel, and community members.

14. Communicate effectively with families of individuals with exceptional learning needs from diverse backgrounds.

PRAXIS Standards for Special Education

THE PRAXIS SERIES™

Standard 1 Understanding Exceptionalities

1. Theories and principles of human development and learning, including research and theories related to human development; theories of learning; social and emotional development; language development; cognitive development; and physical development, including motor and sensory.

3. Basic concepts in special education, including definitions of all major categories and specific disabilities; causation and prevention of disability; the nature of behaviors, including frequency, duration, intensity, and degrees of severity; and classification of students with disabilities, including classifications as represented in IDEA and labeling of students.

Standard 3 Delivery of Services to Students with Disabilities

3. Assessment, including how to modify, construct, or select and conduct nondiscriminatory and appropriate informal and formal assessment procedures; how to interpret standardized and specialized assessment results; how to use evaluation result for various purposes, including monitoring instruction and IEP/ITP development; and how to prepare written reports and communicate findings to others.

INTASC Standards for Teacher Education

Standard 3

The teacher understands how students differ in their approaches to learning and creates instructional opportunities that are adapted to diverse learners.

CCSSO
THE COUNCIL OF CHIEF STATE
SCHOOL OFFICERS

Standard 8

The teacher understands and uses formal and informal assessment strategies to evaluate and ensure the continuous intellectual, social, and physical development of the learner.

CHAPTER
7

Reading Assessment

KEY TERMS AND CONCEPTS

- Reading First Program
- emergent literacy
- oral language
- phonological awareness
- phonemic awareness
- print awareness
- knowledge of the alphabet
- phonics
- nonsense words
- structural analysis
- vocabulary development
- knowledge of word meaning
- word recognition
- functional vocabulary
- readability level
- error pattern analysis

- miscue analysis
- running records
- fluency
- automaticity
- reading fluency
- working memory
- explicit comprehension
- implicit comprehension
- critical comprehension
- cloze procedure
- maze procedure
- think-aloud approach
- retell procedure
- metacognition
- readability formula/graph

CHAPTER OBJECTIVES

After reading this chapter, you should be able to:

- Discuss the impact of students' failure to master basic reading skills.
- Identify the five essential components of reading.
- Identify the four dimensions of early literacy.
- Explain why nonsense words rather than sight words are used in phonetic analysis.
- Identify the components of vocabulary and the focus of vocabulary assessment.

- Explain reading fluency and how it is assessed.
- Describe reading comprehension, the key factors that influence comprehension, and the types of comprehension questions used in assessment.
- Discuss the types of reading assessments and the particular uses of each.
- Explain how a reading delay affects the learning process and the likely result of failing to identify a reading disability early.

Introduction to Reading Assessment

Although most students progress smoothly through the normal reading process, many do not. Those with reading disabilities can range from first-graders who have not mastered sound-symbol association to high school students who drop out of school without being able to read fluently and comprehend most reading material. The reasons for reading disability are numerous, and often many factors interact to affect the ability to master the fundamentals of reading.

Although more instructional time is spent teaching reading than any other subject, more students experience problems in reading than in any other. According to the National Reading Panel (2000), about one million children—more than 17.5 percent of the nation's students—have reading problems during the crucial first three years of schooling. In addition to these staggering statistics, studies indicate that 75 to 88 percent of students who were struggling readers in third grade continue to have reading difficulties throughout high school and their adult lives (National Institute for Child Health and Human Development, 1999; National Research Council, 1998).

It is critical to identify reading problems early so that appropriate intervention can begin. The facts speak for themselves: It takes four times as long to improve the skills of a struggling reader in the fourth grade as it does between mid-kindergarten and first grade. In other words, it takes two hours of intervention per day in the fourth grade to have the same impact as 30 minutes per day in first grade (Lyon, 1997). The National Assessment of Educational Progress (NAEP) continues to find that as many as 40 percent of the nation's fourth-graders read too poorly to understand or learn from grade-level texts; in high-poverty neighborhoods, this statistic rises to more than 60 percent (National Center for Education Statistics, 2004). According to the Council for Exceptional Children (CEC), about 80 percent of students with learning disabilities have reading problems (CEC, 2003).

These distressing results from national assessments have led to a call for action. The most recent reauthorization of the Elementary and Special Education Act, referred to as the No Child Left Behind (NCLB) Act of 2001 (P.L. 107–110), contains a **Reading First Program** designed to ensure that children learn to read no later than third grade. This program is intended to be implemented in general education and inclusive classrooms rather than in special education (Bowe, 2005). Also, the emphasis must be on early identification followed by immediate and intensive intervention (Lyon, et al., 2001).

Under the NCLB Act, students from grades 3 through 8 are assessed in reading and math each year. The purpose is to show that they are progressing satisfactorily and that teachers are following the curriculum. Beginning in the 2005–2006 school year, science tests are also included in the assessments.

The Reading First section of the NCLB Act specifies the five essential components of reading: (1) phonemic awareness, (2) phonics, (3) fluency, (4) vocabulary development, and (5) comprehension strategies. This chapter addresses each component, suggesting strategies and specific assessment procedures.

TEACHERS AS EVALUATORS

Teachers need to be skilled in both instructional and assessment strategies in order to identify students' specific strengths and areas that need reinforcement or remediation and thus be able to deal effectively with the range of skill levels in the classroom.

These teacher skills are increasingly important as more students who are at risk for learning problems (stemming from medical, nutritional, social-emotional, cultural, environmental, and/or socio-economic factors) and students who are classified as having a disability are included in general education classrooms.

A comprehensive reading evaluation for young learners generally focuses on **emergent literacy** concepts (i.e, oral language, alphabet, print, and phoneme awareness) and proceeds to assess the student's ability to *decode* (sound out) words, read words with irregular spelling patterns, read fluently, comprehend texts that differ in length and complexity, and comprehend different types of material (e.g., narrative passages, generally in the form of stories versus expository passages, also referred to as nonfiction text).

FORMAL VS. INFORMAL READING ASSESSMENTS

How does one determine the severity of a reading delay? The formal tests—which are standardized and norm-referenced, objective, and typically multiple-choice—provide broad indicators of students' performance in particular skill areas. Although these tests compare student performance among age or grade-level peers, they fail to provide needed information about how students actually function in class. In fact, norm-referenced test items generally do not closely correlate with the concepts and skills being taught through the classroom curriculum and are of little help in planning or effectively evaluating progress in remedial reading programs.

On the other hand, informal reading assessments, often nonstandardized and unnormed evaluation procedures, help teachers understand the reading process rather than just the reading product. Informal methods of evaluation—such as curriculum-based measurement, portfolio assessment, and informal reading inventories—can directly measure how students perform in relation to their own abilities.

SECTION 1: EMERGENT LITERACY ASSESSMENT

It is important to identify, often by a large-scale screening process, preschoolers and children entering kindergarten who may be at risk for reading failure. Early and intensive instruction in prereading and early reading skills can enable at-risk children to be successful (Fuchs, et al., 2001; Lovett, Lacerenza, Borden, Frijters, Steinbach, & DePalma, 2000). By the time the young learner is old enough to demonstrate problems grasping necessary reading skills, not only are interventions much less effective, but feelings of frustration and lower confidence in the learner have set in. Four dimensions that are critical to success in learning to read are (1) oral language, (2) phonological awareness, (3) print awareness, and (4) knowledge of the alphabet. Young learners must be assessed in these four areas to ascertain whether they have acquired these fundamental competencies, to monitor progress, and to plan instruction and interventions.

Oral Language

Competency in **oral language** is necessary to develop basic literacy skills, such as reading, writing, and spelling. To be good readers, students need to have an adequately developed vocabulary, use and understand complex sentence structure, and use correct grammatical form. Young readers must have fundamental oral language development, specifically receptive and expressive skills. Students need to develop competency in breaking down messages into words, in breaking down a word into a sequence of sounds, and in hearing the sounds in sequence in order to comprehend the written symbols of language.

Oral language problems must be identified and addressed early. Many preschool and kindergarten children who lack phonological awareness are first identified for speech and language therapy services. When they are dismissed from these services after reaching their targeted oral language goals, many are identified later as having a reading disability. Increasing numbers of students with mild early oral language delays present reading, writing, and spelling problems in second, third, and fourth grades when early intervention is not effective (LDA Early Childhood Committee, 2002).

An effective way to assess students' oral language development is to observe them as they interact with peers and verbalize with adults in authentic situations, both in formal (classroom) and informal (playground, during lunch) settings. The focus should be on whether the student answers questions in detail or with a one-word answer; can retell a story in sequential order; is able to complete sentences in his or her own words; asks for help when directions or concepts are misunderstood; and answers "wh" questions (i.e., why, when, what, where) directly (Richek, Caldwell, Jennings, & Lerner, 2002). (See Chapter 6 for additional oral language assessment procedures.)

Classroom Scenario: What Would You Do?

Please use the following as an example of a typical conversation between a teacher and one of her first graders.

Teacher: "What day is today?"

Student: "Yes, I brought my lunch."

Teacher: "Where is your book?"

Student: "Why not?"

CLARIFYING TERMS

Phonological awareness, the broader category, consists of identifying and manipulating parts of spoken language including words, syllables, onsets and rimes, and phonemes.

Phonemic awareness, a subcategory, is the conscious awareness that spoken language is made up of individual sounds (i.e., phonemes) (Mercer & Mercer, 2005, p. 283).

Phonemic Awareness

Phonemic awareness, also referred to as phonological awareness, is the ability to notice, think about, and work with the individual sounds in spoken words (*Put Reading First*, 2001). It includes the understanding that the sounds of spoken language work together to make words (National Reading Panel, 2000). The teacher must determine whether students understand phonemic segmentation (demonstrated by being able to identify the number of phonemes in a word) and whether they have developed phonemic awareness (demonstrated by their ability to add, move, or delete any designated phoneme and regenerate a word from the result).

Compelling and well-researched findings have established the critical relationship between phonological awareness and reading acquisition (Center for the Improvement of Early Reading Achievement, 2002; National Reading Panel, 2000). Phonological awareness also provides a basis for the development of phonics. While some children seem to develop phonological awareness intuitively, many young learners' incidental and indirect exposure to everyday language is not sufficient to develop phonemic awareness (Bartel, 2004). There is growing consensus that the most common source of reading difficulty is a core deficit related to phonological processing (Roberts & Mather, 1997; Torgesen, Wagner, & Rashotte, 1997; Zeffiro & Eden, 2000).

Classroom Scenario

Teacher: Listen to me as I clap part of the word "monkey." *(Clap, clap.)* Now you clap the sound parts that you hear in the word "monkey."

Students respond with: *Clap, clap, clap, clap.*

Researchers estimate that without direct instruction, about 25 percent of middle-class first-graders and an even higher percentage coming from less literate backgrounds will have difficulty with phonemic awareness, and are thus likely to experience difficulty learning to read and write (National Reading Panel, 2000). To ensure that students have an adequate foundation to begin early literacy instruction, their phonological development needs to be assessed.

Figure 7–1 lists phonemic awareness skills, ordered from the easiest (1) to the most difficult (7), with a description of each skill and a sample activity used to assess students' phonemic awareness or their progress after instruction and practice (Coyne, Kame'enui, & Simmons, 2001; National Panel, 2000; Polloway, Smith, & Miller, 2003). Figure 7–2 can be used as a guideline for informal observation of phonological skills in natural settings and everyday activities. An adaptation to the assessment of phonological awareness is the assessment of phonological memory. Memory can be evaluated by having students repeat strings of words, numbers, letters, and sounds of increasing length.

Print Awareness

Another readiness component that should be acquired during the initial reading instructional period is **print awareness** (also referred to as concepts about print); specifically, the awareness that print contains a message. Components of print awareness include the concepts of letter, word, picture, and sound; the understanding that letters make up words and words make up sentences; and what positional words—such as first, last, beginning, and end—mean. These concepts include how print is arranged on a page, text features (e.g., punctuation and boldface type), book-handling skills, and an overall understanding of how to approach the reading act. (These competencies can be demonstrated by assessing or observing the skills listed in Figure 7–3.)

Classroom Scenario

In your first-grade class, you are concerned because Juan still holds his storybook upside down; Tonya confuses letter sounds for letter names; and Monica writes sentences from right to left.

FYI **THE DIBELS TEST**

The Dynamic Indicators of Basic Early Literacy Skills (DIBELS) is a set of standardized, individually administered measures of early literacy development for kindergarten to grade 3. Fluency is tested for initial sounds, letter naming, phonemic segmentation, nonsense words, and oral reading. (See: www.dibels. uoregon.edu.)

Figure 7–1   Phonemic Analysis Assessment Skills and Sample Activities

Phonemic Analysis	Assessment Skill	Sample Assessment Activity
Phonemic segmentation	Can the student . . . break the word into its sounds and tap, clap out, or place a marker on the different syllables in words?	How many phonemes in *run*? *(3)*
Phoneme isolation	recognize individual sounds in words?	What is the first sound in *bike*? *(/b/)**
Phoneme blending	listen to a sequence of separately spoken sounds and combine them to form a recognized word?	What word is this? /s/e/t/ *(seat)*
Phoneme identity	recognize the common sound in different words?	What sound is the same in these words? *rake, rock, row (/r/)*
Phoneme categorization	recognize the word with the odd sound in a sequence of 3 or 4 words?	What word does not belong? *cat, cap, rat (rat)*
Rhyming	state whether or not two words rhyme or give a list of words that rhyme with a specific word?	What word sounds the same as *rake*? *(cake, take, fake)*
Phoneme deletion	recognize when a word remains after a specific phoneme is removed?	What word is "pants" without the *p*? *(ants)*

Note: Slashes (/ /) indicate that the sound should be pronounced.

Figure 7–2   Survey of Phonological Awareness Concepts

Is the student able to

- segment phonemes by tapping out the number of phonemes in words?
- segment sounds (e.g., how many sounds in the word "cake")?
- match letter sounds?
- isolate letter sounds?
- recognize words that rhyme (cake-make-bake)?
- match rhyming words (rat-sat-mat-bat)?
- recite common nursery rhymes?
- associate consonants with their initial and final sounds?
- associate consonant blends with their sounds (br, bl, st, etc.)?
- associate vowels with matching long and short sounds?
- identify consonant digraph sounds (ch, sh, ph, etc.)?
- identify same/different sounds in the initial, medial, and final position of words (big, hip, bit, etc.)?
- blend phonemes into words (e.g., "bat" for b/a/t)?
- predict unknown words and use context with letter sounds?
- identify when a phoneme is missing in a word?
- manipulate sounds (e.g., I like to "eat," "ite," "ote," "ute")?

Figure 7–3 Survey of Print Concepts

Is the student able to

- locate the title of the book?
- hold a book correctly and turn the pages?
- distinguish between the front and back of the book?
- identify where to begin reading on a page?
- indicate the direction to read words (left to right)?
- know that at the end of a line of words to continue at the beginning left of the next line of words?
- recognize that the left page is read before the right page?
- point to the top and bottom of a page and to an illustration?
- identify letters by pointing to a letter on a page?
- identify words by pointing to a word on a page?
- recognize that there are spaces between words?
- identify an uppercase letter?
- identify a lowercase letter?
- identify why some words are printed in bold?
- identify the meaning of punctuation marks?
- demonstrate awareness of print (i.e., that print contains a message)?
- recognize familiar signs and logos?
- read environmental print (STOP, Texaco, Jello)?
- use picture clues as a word identification technique?
- demonstrate awareness of inverted pages, transposed words, reversed letters?
- recognize mismatches between pictures and text, or sentences out of sequence?
- count the number of syllables in words (up to three syllables)?
- identify common suffixes (ed, es, ing, ly, s, etc.)?
- identify common prefixes (un, in, re, etc.)?
- use context and syntax to identify unknown words?
- recognize and/or write letters?
- recognize and/or write his or her name?
- demonstrate pretend writing (writing that resembles letters or numbers)?
- recognize common sight words (e.g., baby, cat, run)?
- recognize that oral language can be written down and read?

Knowledge of the Alphabet

Knowledge of the alphabet refers to the understanding that words are composed of individual letters. It is concerned with the "mapping of print to speech," or the establishment of a clear link between a letter and a sound (Kame'enui, Carnine, Dixon, Simmons, & Coyne, 2002). In numerous research studies, knowledge of the alphabet and identification of individual letters and their names have been found to be very predictive of early reading achievement (Muter, Hulme, & Taylor, 1998; National Reading Panel, 2000; Richek, et al., 2002).

Assessing letter-name knowledge involves determining whether students can match letters (associate uppercase letters with their lowercase counterparts), recognize letters (when hearing a specific letter, locate the letter in a series of letters on paper), and identify letters (when shown letters in random order, name each correctly). Children at the emergent literacy level need to be able to match and recognize (nonverbally) and identify (verbally) upper- and lowercase letters in isolation and/or in context (e.g., p/e/t). Figure 7–4 is a chart of alphabet letters. Using this chart, the teacher can have students say each letter as they read across the line and then write each letter as it is dictated orally. The letter-sound checklist in Figure 7–5 provides a format for charting specific upper- and lower-case letter identification, also referred

Figure 7—4   Alphabet Knowledge Assessment Chart

A	S	G	D	F	J	H	L	K	P	I	O	U
Y	R	T	W	E	Q	C	Z	V	X	N	B	M
a	s	g	d	f	j	h	l	k	p	l	o	u
y	r	t	w	e	q	c	z	v	x	n	b	m

Figure 7—5   Letter Identification or Letter-Sound Association Checklist

	Yes	No		Yes	No		Yes	No		Yes	No
A	___	___	N	___	___	a	___	___	n	___	___
B	___	___	O	___	___	b	___	___	o	___	___
C	___	___	P	___	___	c	___	___	p	___	___
D	___	___	Q	___	___	d	___	___	q	___	___
E	___	___	R	___	___	e	___	___	r	___	___
F	___	___	S	___	___	f	___	___	s	___	___
G	___	___	T	___	___	g	___	___	t	___	___
H	___	___	U	___	___	h	___	___	u	___	___
I	___	___	V	___	___	i	___	___	v	___	___
J	___	___	W	___	___	j	___	___	w	___	___
K	___	___	X	___	___	k	___	___	x	___	___
L	___	___	Y	___	___	l	___	___	y	___	___
M	___	___	Z	___	___	m	___	___	z	___	___

Figure 7—6   Letter-Sound Correspondence Assessment

Directions: Ask the student to give the beginning sound of each word (e.g., *cake*). The student says the initial sound of the word (i.e., /c/). Then ask the student what letter makes the sound. The student says "c." If the wrong or no response is given, repeat the directions for the student and go to the next word.

Word	Beginning Sound	Beginning Letter
cake		
dog		
yellow		
baby		

to as alphabet knowledge. This checklist can also be used to track which letter-sound associations have been established. Figure 7–6 is a sample assessment for identifying the initial letter and sound of one primer and two-syllable reading vocabulary words (Richek, et al., 2002).

SECTION 2: PHONICS ASSESSMENT

Phonetic analysis, or **phonics**, is based on the relationship between sounds (phonemes) and letters or spellings that represent sounds in writing (graphemes). Phonics (also referred to as word attack, or decoding) is the ability to pronounce words that are not within sight vocabulary. It deals with sound-symbol associations, through which students learn to retain, recall, and produce the sounds of individual letters (both vowels and consonants) and ultimately groups of letters. A precursor of phonics is phonological awareness; that is, the student's recognition that speech can be segmented into phonemic units or sounds.

Phonetic Analysis

It is critical to assess students' sound-symbol system of English in order to determine whether they have a sufficient level of mastery in sound recognition and sound blending. Because phonetic skills are taught sequentially in a hierarchical order according to complexity, when evaluating students' mastery of phonetics the teacher must consider which skills are within grade expectancy level according to the curriculum scope and sequence chart. Typically, the order of phonetic skill development is single consonants; consonant blends (consonant clusters); consonant digraphs; short and long vowels; schwa sound; vowel digraphs; vowel diphthongs; vowels with r, l, and w; word families (phonograms); homophones (homonyms); and homographs (Polloway & Smith, 2000). (Figure 7–7 is a checklist for assessing phonic skill mastery.)

A common method of assessing students' knowledge of phonics patterns is to have students read phonetically correct nonsense words. **Nonsense words**, also known as pseudowords, contain critical sound-symbol relationships. They are used to test awareness of phonetic principles and generalizations and the ability to use phonics to decode "words" that cannot be known by sight, thus eliminating the chance that the student is relying on the recall of sight vocabulary (Richek, et al., 2002). (See Figure 7–8 for an informal assessment of phonics generalizations.)

Important aspects of the assessment process dealing with phonic skill development are determining whether students know and apply phonic strategies and principles and the types of decoding errors being made (CEC, 2003). (A checklist of commonly used strategies is provided in Figure 7–9.)

Critical Thinking and Reflection Activity

Describe the differences between phonemic awareness and phonics. Can a student learn to read without developing proficiency in phonemic awareness or in phonics?

Structural Analysis

Structural analysis is a word attack approach in which words are decoded by subdividing them into meaningful parts or units and subsequently blending these parts into words (Lerner, 2003). Structural analysis consists of several subskills involving

Figure 7–7   Mastery of Phonic Skills Developmental Checklist

Directions: Check off each phonetic generalization sound and keep a tracking and monitoring system using the following skill level rating codes:

NK = no knowledge   E = emerging   M = mastered

Simple Consonants (Grade 1)
___b ___d ___f ___h ___j ___k ___l ___m ___n ___p ___r ___s
___t ___v ___w ___x ___y ___z

Consonant Digraphs (Grade 1)
___sh ___ch ___ck ___ph ___th ___qu

Beginning Consonant Blends (Grade 2)
___ st ___ gr ___ cl ___ sp ___pl ___ tr ___ br ___ dr ___ bl ___ fr ___ fl
___ pr ___ cr ___ sl ___ sw ___gl ___ str ___ z

Ending Consonant Blends (Grade 2)
___ nd ___ nk ___ nt ___ lk ___ld ___ rt ___ nk ___ rm ___ mp ___ ft
___ lt ___ ct ___ pt ___ lm

Single Long Vowels (Grades 2–3)
___ long a ___ long e ___ long i ___ long o ___ long u

Single Short Vowels (Grades 2–3)
___ short a ___ short e ___ short i ___ short o ___ short u

R-Controlled Vowels (Grade 2–3)
___ ar (car) ___ er (her) ___ ir (shirt) ___ or (for) ___ ur (fur)

Vowel Digraph Combinations (Grades 2–3)
___ ai (pail) ___ ea (each, bear) ___ oa (boat) ___ ee (bee) ___ ay (bay)
___ ea (seat, bear)

Vowel Diphthong Combinations (Grades 2–3)
___ au (auto) ___ aw (awful) ___ oo (boot, look) ___ ow (cow, low) ___ ou (out)
___ oi (oil) ___ oy (toy)

Hard and Soft C and G (Grade 3)
___ soft c (cent) ___ hard c (cake) ___ soft g (engine) ___ hard g (gate)

Silent Letters (Grades 3–4)
___ k (knife) ___ w (write) ___ l (talk) ___ t (catch) ___ g (gnat) ___ c (lack)
___ h (hour)

base or root words, prefixes, suffixes, inflections, syllabication, accent, compound words, and word origins. (Figure 7–10 is an informal test for assessing students' knowledge of structural analysis and syllabication skills.)

SECTION 3: VOCABULARY ASSESSMENT

Vocabulary development involves word identification, including affixes, multiple meanings, origins of words, content subject vocabulary, and technical vocabulary, as well as expressive, meaningful oral and silent reading. Vocabulary skills assessment

Figure 7—8   Checklist for Assessing Phonics Generalizations Using Nonsense Words

STUDENT FORM		TEACHER SCORING FORM			
		Student responses		Correct (+) Incorrect (−)	
SIMPLE SINGLE CONSONANTS (initial and final position)					
1 bim	8 hek	1	8	1	8
2 mib	9 wot	2	9	2	9
3 pud	10 tun	3	10	3	10
4 dup	11 yat	4	11	4	11
5 gop	12 ket	5	12	5	12
6 fop	13 naw	6	13	6	13
7 cuf		7		7	
MORE DIFFICULT SINGLE CONSONANTS (initial and final position)					
1 viz	5 jev	1	5	1	5
2 liv	6 qua	2	6	2	6
3 zix	7 giz	3	7	3	7
4 cij		4		4	
CONSONANT DIGRAPHS					
1 shup	4 guan	1	4	1	4
2 thop	5 dack	2	5	2	5
3 chup		3		3	
CONSONANT BLENDS					
1 sput	6 plat	1	6	1	6
2 crub	7 grut	2	7	2	7
3 flig	8 pund	3	8	3	8
4 drub	9 gert	4	9	4	9
5 strib	10 ropt	5	10	5	10
SINGLE VOWELS, LONG AND SHORT					
1 bam	6 nibe	1	6	1	6
2 bame	7 po	2	7	2	7
3 fot	8 pom	3	8	3	8
4 fote	9 lum	4	9	4	9
5 nib	10 lume	5	10	5	10
R-CONTROLLED VOWELS					
1 tar	3 por	1	3	1	3
2 det	4 spir	2	4	2	4
VOWEL COMBINATIONS					
1 foat	5 loub	1	5	1	5
2 tay	6 jeet	2	6	2	6
3 rew	7 sood	3	7	3	7
4 moil		4		4	
HARD AND SOFT C AND G					
1 cet	3 gi	1	3	1	3
2 c	4 gis	2	4	2	4
SILENT LETTERS					
1 knes	3 wrot	1	3	1	3
2 gnop	4 whes	2	4	2	4

Figure 7–9 Phonetic Strategies Checklist

Does the student
___ sound out/blend words without teacher prompting?
___ recognize familiar word parts at the beginning ___, middle ___, end ___ of words?
___ recognize consonant blends and digraphs?
___ apply short vowel sound skills?
___ apply long vowel sound skills?
___ recognize irregular vowel patterns?
___ attempt another vowel sound if something doesn't make sense?
___ recognize rule-breakers?
___ attempt another decoding strategy when the word read doesn't make sense (without teacher prompting)?

M = mastered   E = emerging   NS = no skill yet

The IEP Connection

When she is asked to read orally, Julie's reading is slow and lacks fluency due to numerous word substitutions as determined by an error analysis and a miscue analysis. She frequently asks for help in decoding words. When analyzing her errors, Julie's teacher finds that most of her word substitutions are semantic errors that distort the meaning of the passage and interfere with comprehension. Julie does not use context clues (i.e., use other words in the sentence to help her to recognize that the word was misread or to figure out the correct word).

Goal

Julie will increase her word decoding and word meaning skills from the beginning third-grade to the beginning fourth-grade level.

Specific Skills Progress Checkup

- When given a list of 20 random words containing the silent mb, p, s, and t, can the student pronounce the words and identify the silent letter(s) for 18 of the 20 words?
- When given a list of 10 random sentences each containing two homographs, can the student correctly pronounce 18 of the 20 underlined homographs?
- When reading a randomly selected passage from a second-grade text, can the student use context clues to assist in word identification 90 percent of the time?

focuses primarily on determining the knowledge of and the ability to store and retrieve the meanings and pronunciations of words. Word identification can be evaluated in isolation or in context. A common method of testing words in isolation is for sight words to be presented on flashcards, which allows the teacher to control the rate of word presentation. The goal of word recognition is automaticity, which is determined by asking whether the word is (1) recognized automatically (within one second), (2) recognized after hesitation or analysis; or (3) not identified correctly.

Figure 7–10 Informal Test for Syllabication Abilities

Directions: The student is to (1) write the following nonsense words dividing them into syllables, and then (2) pronounce these words. Teacher is to use the scoring form to record correct and incorrect responses and may write any mispronounced words in the numbered spaces allotted.

STUDENT FORM		TEACHER SCORING FORM	
Sample Nonsense Words	Nonsense Words Written in Syllables by Student	Student Pronunciation Correct (+)	Incorrect (0)
		Compound Words	
1 staybut		1.	
2 leeway		2.	
3 landom		3.	
		Structural Word Parts	
1 frogment		1.	
2 lauter		2.	
3 remanly		3.	
		Vowel Combinations	
1 lainest		1.	
2 doyter		2.	
3 spirler		3.	
		Vowel Followed by 1 Consonant	
1 witon		1.	
2 dowal		2.	
3 turmit		3.	
4 leton		4.	
		Vowel Followed by 2 Consonants	
1 pittel		1.	
2 coddat		2.	
		Combinations	
1 kepple		1.	
2 gintle		2.	

Word Meaning

Students' **knowledge of word meaning** is critical for word recognition, word attack, and reading comprehension. Understanding meaning is necessary to identify words that are not within the readers' sight vocabulary. Efficient readers learn to rely on context clues or word knowledge to assist them in decoding unfamiliar words. Reading comprehension—the main goal of the reading process—is either facilitated or impeded by competency in word meaning. For students, word knowledge is affected by their personal experiences, both real and vicarious; by the vocabulary of teachers, parents, peers, and significant others; and by the dictionary, the thesaurus, and other language sources.

The IEP Connection

Evan has just learned to recognize and define a list of technical words that he will need for his work-study program in basic electronics. As his teacher, you need to assess his ability to read and comprehend these new terms by having him apply his knowledge in an authentic activity. The performance task you assign is to follow directions to program a VCR. Evan is able to read 90 percent of the words, but he asked for assistance in pronouncing and defining three multisyllabic, technical words (conductor/programming/modulator), since he was unable to grasp the meaning of these words by using context clues. He demonstrated that he comprehended each step that he had read, but he did not perform the steps in the correct sequence. When asked to orally state what the directions said, he did not correctly order several steps. When developing his new IEP, you will need to focus on the following skills: sequencing, vocabulary knowledge, and the use of context clues.

Specific IEP Skills Progress Checkup

1. Is the student able to state the meaning of a target word as it is used in the context of the sentence?
2. Is the student able to correctly sequence 3 steps after reading a paragraph of technical directions?

Assessment in word knowledge is broad, covering more than just the ability to define a word. For a comprehensive measure of students' word knowledge, the teacher should evaluate many aspects of vocabulary development, including the ability to classify words according to their respective categories. Word knowledge assessment is also used to determine the students' ability to recognize vocabulary relationships, to demonstrate an understanding of pronoun referents, to accurately use root words and affixes to develop new words, and to use descriptive words appropriately.

When evaluating advanced students, it is important to assess their ability to know and correctly use synonyms, antonyms, homonyms, homographs, multiple meanings, abstract and colloquial terms, neologisms ("explain the probable meaning of *edzoocate*"), euphemisms ("provide a more polite word for *sweat*"), pejoratives ("explain why a word such as *amateur* might be considered negative"), and etymology ("provide the origin of the word *sandwich*"). (See Figure 7–11 for a sample word-meaning assessment.) A useful and efficient method of assessment is for students to read a passage and then define or explain specific vocabulary words within the passage.

FYI Sight

Vocabulary Hints

Assess the student's basic sight vocabulary using the words most commonly seen in print. (See Figure 8–21 in Chapter 8.)

Word Recognition

After preliminary observations and assessments of prerequisite reading skills, teachers should evaluate students' word-recognition ability. When a student seems to be functioning at the readiness, preprimer, or primer level of skill development, assessment should begin with determining whether the pupil can match, recognize, and identify letters and words in isolation and in context.

Word recognition, or word identification (often called sight vocabulary), refers to students' ability to identify a sequence of letters that form a word as a single unit.

Figure 7—11 Sample Word Meaning Assessment

Teacher's Version — Score Form	Student's Version	
Basic Vocabulary Correct Incorrect (1) angry _____ _____ (2) stove _____ _____ (3) letter _____ _____ (4) wheel _____ _____	*Read the word that means* (1) angry (2) stove (3) letter (4) wheel	*Choose from one of the following words:* lamp mail mad running ocean oven tire tear pair
Classification Correct Incorrect (1) body parts _____ _____ (2) places _____ _____ (3) jobs _____ _____ (4) furniture _____ _____	*Read the words that tell about* (1) body parts (2) places (3) jobs (4) furniture	*Choose from one of the following words:* table sofa church elbow park manager knee store teacher doctor lamp stomach
Affixes Correct Incorrect (1) <u>dis</u>agree _____ _____ (2) odor<u>less</u> _____ _____ (3) <u>re</u>try _____ _____ (4) effort<u>less</u> _____ _____	*Tell how each affix changes word meaning* (1) <u>dis</u>agree (2) odor<u>less</u> (3) retry (4) effort<u>less</u>	
Pronoun Referent Correct Incorrect (1) Jim and Mary _____ _____ (2) you and me _____ _____ (3) a boy _____ _____ (4) a mother _____ _____	*Read the word that could mean* (1) Jim and Mary (2) you and me (3) a boy (4) a mother	*Say the word that would match* her we they him me you
Vocabulary Relations Correct Incorrect (1) _____ _____ (2) _____ _____ (3) _____ _____ (4) _____ _____	*Say the underlined word in each sentence* 1. Don't <u>tear</u> your coat. 2. I <u>live</u> near you. 3. I <u>read</u> the letter yesterday. 4. The <u>wound</u> is bleeding.	

To be within students' sight vocabulary, the word must be pronounced without hesitation (in about one second) and without the use of word analysis (phonetic or structural). The scope of the sight-word list that is to be used is commonly determined by the type of curriculum—either developmental or functional. Developmental sight-word lists typically come from the vocabulary in students' basal reading series, graded word lists composed of words used in texts and listed by grade level, high-frequency words that make up the majority of written American English, and lists of phonetically irregular words.

The IEP Connection

Eric continues to have difficulty with word recognition, which affects his reading fluency and comprehension. As his teacher, you want to closely monitor his progress toward meeting the projected IEP reading goal so that you can make necessary instructional adjustments. By graphing his biweekly CBA probe results, you can track and chart his skill development. This graph can be easily converted to a reporting system that meets IDEA-2004 mandates requiring that parents receive regular progress reports.

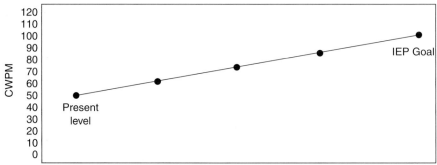

Correct words per minute (cwpm)

Present Levels of Academic Achievement and Functional Performance (9/15/05)

Eric, a student in your second-grade class, reads unrehearsed second-grade-level material with 97 percent accuracy at a rate of 50 correct words per minute.

Annual Goal

Eric will increase his ability to read unrehearsed second-grade-level material with 97 percent accuracy from a rate of 50 cwpm to a rate of 105 cwpm.

Progress Check Points

Progress Point 1: By November, when given a randomly selected, unrehearsed passage from the second-grade literacy text series, the student will read at a rate of 65 cwpm with 97 percent accuracy.

Progress Point 2: By January, when given a randomly selected, unrehearsed passage from the second-grade literacy text series, the student will read at a rate of 75 cwpm with 97 percent accuracy.

Progress Point 3: By March, when given a randomly selected, unrehearsed passage from the second-grade literacy text series, the student will read at a rate of 90 cwpm with 97 percent accuracy.

Progress Point 4: By June, when given a randomly selected, unrehearsed passage from the second-grade literacy text series, the student will read at a rate of 105 cwpm with 97 percent accuracy.

Functional sight-word lists are based on the vocabulary commonly used for students who are classified as moderately cognitively disabled and for those who have not been exposed to or have not been able to master the developmental sight words. **Functional vocabulary** lists contain words that are critical for independence in everyday life, and may include vocationally related words (e.g., part-time, salary, contract), safety words (e.g., keep out, poison, beware, danger), and environmental words (e.g., exit, entrance, bathroom, doorway).

It is important for students to be able to recognize words in various contexts. Students should be exposed to functional words in their natural context and in their typical form, rather than just on flashcards or from a list of graded vocabulary. Teachers, especially those instructing students who have learning and cognitive disabilities, need to provide authentic assessment replications or close facsimiles (e.g., employment applications, bus schedules, rental contracts). When assessing word recognition, various forms of commonly used print should be used (e.g., newspapers, signs, manuscripts and cursive writing). (See the text website www.sju.edu/cas/education/Cathleen-spinelli for the Fry word list and for a full scope and sequence of vocabulary words at various grade levels.)

Oral Reading

Word recognition can also be assessed through oral reading samples, whereby students read aloud from the textbook or other reading material. The number of words suggested for a passage ranges from 50 at the primary level to 400 at the secondary level. The passage chosen should make sense on its own and not have been read previously by the student (King-Sears, 1998). Oral reading should be fluent and relaxed,

The IEP Connection

Morgan is an 8½-year old student who has recently been placed in your third-grade class. Her last IEP was completed in the spring of last year, so her IEP present level of academic achievement and functional performance is almost 6 months old. She seems to be having difficulty reading at the instructional level identified on her IEP (mid-second-grade level), so you reevaluate her using the metalinguistic, letter identification, word attack checklists and the Fry Word Lists (see appendix).

Results indicate that Morgan is able to identify 75 percent of the first-grade-level-words, but only 50 percent of the second-grade-level words on Fry word lists. She has developed basic metalinguistic skills but has not learned to islolate, blend, or segment words. Her word attack skills are underdeveloped, she adds, omits, and substitutes sounds in the medial and final position of words. You realize that her IEP present level of performance, goals, and progress points have to be modified.

Adjusted Annual Goal
Morgan's word recognition skills will improve from a mid-first to a mid-second grade level.

Specific Skills Progress Checkup (two of many)

1. When given a list of words ending with single consonants, can the student pronounce the single sound or name another word ending with the same sound, with 90 percent accuracy?
2. When given a list of words containing single consonants in the medial position, can the student pronounce the single sound or name another word with the same sound in the medial position with 85 percent accuracy?

Figure 7–12   Silent/Oral Reading Observation Checklist

Behavioral Characteristics	Yes	No	N/A	Comments
Holds book too close	—	—	—	_____
Holds book too far	—	—	—	_____
Points to each word	—	—	—	_____
Moves finger under each line	—	—	—	_____
Runs finger down the page	—	—	—	_____
Finger points to mark place	—	—	—	_____
Loses place on page	—	—	—	_____
Skips words	—	—	—	_____
Skips lines	—	—	—	_____
Makes frequent word errors	—	—	—	_____
Does not attempt unfamiliar words	—	—	—	_____
Does not observe punctuation	—	—	—	_____
Does not read for meaning	—	—	—	_____
Does not read clearly	—	—	—	_____
Reads too slowly	—	—	—	_____
Reads too quickly	—	—	—	_____
Oral reading lacks expression	—	—	—	_____
Frequently requests assistance	—	—	—	_____
Makes lip movements	—	—	—	_____
Subvocalizes words	—	—	—	_____
Moves head while reading	—	—	—	_____
Tires easily when reading	—	—	—	_____
Makes negative comments	—	—	—	_____
Refuses to continue reading	—	—	—	_____
Other prominent behaviors	—	—	—	_____
Mispronounces words	—	—	—	_____
Does not self-correct when reading	—	—	—	_____
Does not use context clues	—	—	—	_____

with a sense of rhythm and expression. (See Figure 7-12 for a checklist of silent and oral reading characteristics.)

To determine whether the text is the appropriate **readability** (instructional) **level** for the student, his or her word recognition should be 95 percent accurate when counting miscues that change the meaning of a passage. It should be 90 percent accurate if all miscues are counted with 70 to 75 percent accuracy on comprehension questions. Oral reading research suggests that students who read with less than 90 percent word recognition accuracy are unable to obtain sufficient meaning (Mercer & Mercer, 2005). When conducting an oral reading assessment, it is important to note how students read, such as with expression, attending to punctuation, and using context clues. Guidelines for analyzing oral reading skills, including error pattern and miscue analysis, are described in the following subsections.

Reading Error Pattern Analysis

Error pattern analysis—one of the most frequently used techniques of informal reading assessment—is the study of the mistakes students make while reading orally. The incorrect responses provide information about how students are processing reading material as well as direction for remedial instruction. Figure 7-13 shows common oral reading errors, possible causes, examples, and suggested notations for marking these errors (Ekwall, 1997). For systematically analyzing the types of errors students make when sounding out and breaking down monosyllabic and multisyllabic words, see Figure 7–14, which provides examples of common word attack errors.

How to Conduct an Error Analysis

1. The teacher selects graded reading passages at the student's current reading level from textbooks, literature series, or trade books.
2. The teacher makes two copies of the selected passages: one for the student and another for the teacher to follow and mark.
3. The student reads the passage orally as the teacher records the errors.
4. The teacher analyzes and records the pattern of errors to determine how often each type of error was made and to identify the most frequently made errors.
5. The teacher should not count the same error more than once (e.g., if the student misidentifies the same word, such as "with" for *which*, several times, it is counted as only one error).
6. The teacher may record the student's oral reading in order to replay it and thereby more closely discriminate the errors.

Miscue Analysis

Another method of error pattern analysis is **miscue analysis**, which focuses on both word analysis and comprehension with emphasis on the types of errors (qualitative) rather than on how many errors (quantitative) students make. It is the study of how oral reading errors distort or change the meaning of a passage. Miscue analysis is defined by Goodman (1973, p. 5) as "an actual observed response in oral reading which does not match the expected response" (e.g., "the boy went into the horse and sat by the fire"). Goodman suggests that miscues can serve as windows on the reading process and that the relationship between miscues and expected outcomes provides a basis for investigating the way students respond to the task of reading.

In miscue analysis, the teacher is concerned about whether the word substitution is semantically incorrect (a meaning-related error) or syntactically incorrect (a grammatically related error). In a semantic error, one word is substituted for another. A semantic miscue error may significantly change the meaning of the passage (e.g., "the statue is answering the question" instead of "the student is answering the question"), but often this kind of error does not significantly change the meaning of the passage (e.g., "the pupil is answering the question" instead of "the student is answering the question"). A syntactic miscue error involves substituting one part of speech for another in a way that may affect meaning (e.g., "the boy can't go home" instead of "the boy can go home"). However, this type of miscue error may not always affect the meaning (e.g., "the boy will go home" instead of "the boy will goes home").

How to Score an Oral Reading Sample

1. Count as a major oral reading error and deduct one point for a substitution error that interferes with comprehension (e.g., "house" for *horse*).
2. Count as a minor oral reading error and deduct 1/2 point for any deviation from the printed text that does not seem to interfere significantly with comprehension (e.g., "home" for *house*).

Figure 7–13   Oral Reading Errors

Substitutions
Definition: replacing a word or series of syllables for the depicted word
Cause: may result from poor word recognition, poor word analysis, dialectic differences, or carelessness
Example: "the boy run" for *the boy ran*
Notation: cross out the incorrect word and write the substituted word above it

Omissions
Definition: leaving out a word or words
Cause: may result from poor word recognition, poor word analysis, or carelessness
Example: "the yellow house" for *the big, yellow house*
Notation: circle the omitted word(s)

Insertions
Definition: addition of a word or words
Cause: may result from poor comprehension, carelessness, or oral language that exceeds reading ability
Example: "the big, yellow house" for *the yellow house*
Notation: place a caret (^) at the point of insertion and write inserted word above the sentence

Reversals or Transpositions
Definition: confusion about the order of letters in a word or words in the sentence
Cause: may be the result of neurological or visual processing problems
Examples: reversals: "bat" for *dat*; transpositions: "rat" for *tar*; or "said Mary" for *Mary said*
Notation: draw a line through the word and write the reversed/transposed word above it

Mispronunciations
Definition: incorrect pronunciation/may not be recognizable
Cause: may be the result of poor word recognition or word analysis or articulation problems
Example: "wabbit" for *rabbit*
Notation: draw a line through the mispronounced word and write the mispronunciation above it

Self-corrections
Definition: correction of a word that was substituted, inserted, or omitted
Cause: may be the result of poor recognition/word analysis, or carelessness
Example: "she run . . . ran up the hill"
Notation: cross out the word read incorrectly, write corrected word above it.

Repetitions
Definition: saying a part of a word or a complete word more than once
Cause: may be the result of attention problems, poor word recognition, or poor word analysis
Example: "What is, what is wrong?" instead of *What is wrong?*
Notation: underline repeated material with wavy lines

Disregards punctuation
Definition: failure to pause for comma, periods, etc., or to change inflection for questions or exclamations
Cause: may be the result of not knowing the meaning of the punctuation mark or being distracted by difficulty reading
Example: "It is a dog He is a good dog." instead of *It is a dog. He is a good dog.*
Notation: circle the punctuation mark

Aid
Definition: assistance in pronouncing a word or waiting more than 10 seconds for the teacher to supply the word
Cause: may be the result of difficulty in word attack recognition skills
Example: "He is —" (teacher says: "wonderful")—"He is wonderful."
Notation: place a bracket (|}) around the word

Figure 7–14 Common Word Attack Errors

Letter omissions (e.g., "tree" for *three*)	Medial vowel substitutions (e.g., "pot" for *pat*)
Letter insertions (e.g., "chart" for *cart*)	Letter reversals (e.g., "bad" for *dad*)
Consonant substitutions:	Letter transpositions (e.g., "saw" for *was*)
• initial position (e.g., "cat" for *sat*)	Addition of endings (e.g., "wented" for *went*)
• medial position (e.g., "coat" for *colt*)	Word ending omissions (e.g., "dog" for *dogs*)
• final position (e.g., "lap" for *lab*)	Syllable omissions (e.g., "trine" for *trying*)

3. Count an inserted word as an oral reading error and deduct one-half point if it does not significantly change the meaning of the material.
4. Count a repetition as half an oral reading error and deduct one-half point if it occurs on two or more words (repeating a single word suggests that the student is using monitoring or metacognitive skills).
5. Count any word the student cannot pronounce after five seconds as an oral reading error and deduct 1 point if the word interferes with comprehension.
6. Count any word the student cannot pronounce after five seconds as an oral reading error and deduct one-half point if the word does not interfere with comprehension.
7. Do not count a self-correction as an error if it occurs within five seconds (this indicates that the student is using monitoring or metacognitive skills).
8. Do not count more than one oral reading error of the same word in any one passage.
9. Do not count a proper noun as an oral reading error.
10. Do not count oral reading errors that seem to exemplify the student's cultural or regional dialect.

How to Tally the Results of an Oral Reading Sample

1. Subtract the total number of errors from the total number of words in the passage (e.g., 31 oral reading errors from the 280 total words in the passage) to determine how many words were correctly pronounced (e.g., 249).
2. Divide the total number of words in the passage by the number of words correctly pronounced and multiply by 100 to obtain the percentage of correct words (249 ÷ 280 = 89 percent).

In this example, the results indicate about 89 percent accuracy in word identification, indicating a level of frustration. After all the oral reading errors are recorded from the material read, the teacher can determine students' reading independent, instructional, and frustration levels categorized as follows (Kuhn & Stahl, 2003):

Independent Level	Instructional Level	Frustration Level
Relatively easy text level; more than 95% accuracy	Challenging but manageable text level; 90% to 95% accuracy	Difficult text level; less than 90% accuracy

Critical Thinking and Reflection Activity

Why are the independent, instructional, and frustration levels higher for oral reading than for comprehension?

Running Records

Compiling **running records** is a system of monitoring the reading process. It involves the teacher keeping a "running record" of students' oral reading by closely monitoring and recording their errors while they read. This procedure is used to diagnose early developmental reading skills and fluency. Teachers use running records for instructional purposes to evaluate text difficulty, to match students with appropriate book levels for instruction and for independent reading, to make informed decisions for grouping students who make similar types of errors, to accelerate a student, to monitor and keep track of individual progress, and to observe particular reading strategies students use (Clay, 2000). The procedures for constructing and administrating a running record—which are similar to those for an oral reading error analysis—are listed later in this section. (See Figures 7–15 and 7–16 for scoring and charting procedures.)

When running records are used as an ongoing instructional assessment tool, students may do a *warm read* (i.e., they have already heard about or have read the book). When running records are used directly for assessing skill levels, the reading material should not be familiar to the student, referred to as a *cold read*. Although running records are used specifically to assess oral reading, reading comprehension can also be assessed by having students retell the story in a way that makes sense to them. If the child is unable to retell the story, the teacher can prompt with questions. (See retell procedures later in this chapter for more guidelines.)

Compiling running records should be ongoing, and the assessment should be done informally and in a nonthreatening, relaxed environment. As the teacher incorporates this procedure into classroom reading activities on a regular basis, students become accustomed to it. See Figure 7–15 for the basic procedures that should be followed when scoring and analyzing running records (Rug, 2001).

Tips for Teachers

Suggestions for Conducting a Running Record

1. Record the child as he or she reads.
2. Have a copy of the coding system nearby.
3. Using a printed script, write what the child says when an error occurs. After the child has finished reading, go back and fill in what the text said.
4. Set up a buddy system to practice with another teacher.
5. Practice using a videotape of children reading.

Figure 7–15   Scoring Running Records

Substitution(S): Error is written on top of line, correct word from text is written underneath (each incorrect response is counted as one error).	"want" (child) / went (text)
Multiple attempts, or repetitions (R): Student attempts to read a word several times, each attempt is recorded (counted as one error no matter how many attempts are made).	R or (ADD)
Self- correction (SC): Student corrects a word read incorrectly; the evaluator marks it SC (not counted as an error).	want | SC / went |
No response, or omission: Student provides no response or omits; the evaluator records with a dash (counted as one error).	----- / little
Insertion: Student inserts a word where one does not belong; the evaluator records with a dash (counted as one error).	many / ----
Word told (T): Student stops because he or she realizes an error has been made or because he or she does not know the word; the evaluator provides the word, records it as T (counted as one error).	where | T
Appeal for help (A): Student requests help; evaluator marks with an A and tells the student to try it (counted as one error). Only the second attempt is scored. If student gets word correct the second time, there is no error.	often | A
Repeated errors: When the student makes an error and continues to substitute the word again and again (counts as one error each time). Exception: When a proper name is substituted, it is counted as an error only the first time it is substituted.	
Words or phrases repeated: When the student accurately reads a word or phrase more than one time, no errors are counted.	

Source: L. Romeo, (1999). The literacy center companion adapted from Clay (1993).

Figure 7–16   Running Record Recording Chart

Text	Page No.	Incorrect Response	Multiple Attempts	Self-Correction	Insertion— No Response	Word Told	Appeal for Help	Error No.

How to Conduct a Running Record Assessment

1. The teacher asks the student to read a passage orally (recommended length is between 100 and 200 words).
2. The teacher records errors on a record form (such as the example in Figure 7-17).

3. If the student pauses while reading, the teacher waits a few seconds for the student to respond before saying the word. (The teacher should not wait too long, however, since the student may lose the text's meaning.)
4. The teacher should note what students say and do while reading the assigned material (e.g., substituting, omitting words).

How to Score a Running Record Assessment

1. Count each substitution, insertion, omission, word that is supplied, and appeal for help as one error.
2. Do not count repetitions, self-corrections, or appeals for help as errors unless the second attempt is incorrect.
3. When multiple attempts are made to pronounce a word, count as one error.
4. If a whole page is omitted, deduct the number of words omitted from the total word count.
5. If repeated errors are made with a proper noun, count only the first time as an error.
6. Each time a word is read incorrectly (except a proper noun), count each incorrect attempt as one error.
7. Pronunciation differences are not counted as errors.
8. To determine error rate, divide the number of errors by the number of total words.
9. To determine percent of accuracy, divide the number of words read correctly by the total number of words and multiply by 100. The percentage of accuracy data indicates the level of difficulty of the material read.
10. Scoring is determined by the percentage correct:
    - Independent reading level 95 to 100 percent
    - Instructional reading level 90 to 94 percent
    - Frustration reading level less than 90 percent (Clay, 2000)

SECTION 4: READING FLUENCY ASSESSMENT

> **⌕ CLARIFYING TERMS**
>
> **Fluency Vs. Automaticity**
> **Fluency** is accurate word identification which facilitates comprehension, whereas . . .
> **Automaticity** is the flowing, smooth processing of information that require little to no effort or attention.
> (Harris & Hodges, 1995)

Reading is a cognitive activity, and one can devote only a limited amount of attention to any one cognitive task. Reading involves at least two cognitive tasks—word recognition and comprehension—and each of these tasks compete for the reader's attention. The more the reader must attend to identifying words, the less attention is available for comprehension (Foorman & Mehta, 2002; Samuels, 2002). According to research, **reading fluency**, the ability to read a text accurately and quickly, is critical to making the bridge from word recognition to reading comprehension (Hamilton & Shinn, 2003; Richek et al., 2002). Reading rate is a good indication of fluency. Yet, it is important to remember that fluency is the development of speed after accuracy is assured.

When fluent readers read silently, they recognize words automatically (Armbruster, Lehr, & Osborn, 2001). Sight words are words that are recognized in print immediately, without any analysis. According to Samuels (1988), most good readers recognize almost all words automatically. They group words quickly in ways that help them gain meaning from what they read; they recognize words and comprehend simultaneously. Fluent readers read aloud effortlessly, with expression, and sound natural, as if they were speaking (National Reading Panel, 2000). Students who have low fluency tend to have poor comprehension (*Put Reading First*, 2000) and are likely to remain poor readers throughout their lives (National Reading Panel, 2000).

Reading Fluency

Reading fluency should be assessed regularly in the classroom. This allows for timely and effective instructional response when difficulty or delay is apparent (Snow, Burns, & Griffin, 1998). Fluency measures have been found to be valid and reliable. The ease and efficiency of these measures make them useful for ongoing assessment and for monitoring the progress of individual students, for assessing the whole class, and for comparing individual to group progress. Fluency measures are also useful in assessing how quickly and accurately the student performs a task. Since reading rate increases gradually as proficiency develops, rate can be measured over time and improvement evaluated (Crawford, 2000).

Reading fluency can be assessed using informal procedures, such as listening to students read passages orally; determining reading rate; and administering graded word lists, informal reading inventories, miscue analyses, and running records (Richek, et al., 2002). These assessment procedures require oral reading of text, and all can be used to provide an adequate index of fluency (National Reading Panel, 2000).

Informal fluency assessment can begin as early as the second semester of first grade, with teachers listening to students read and recording their reading rate and accuracy, while judging their performance. More formal assessments usually begin at the start of second grade, with teachers administering reading fluency assessments to establish baseline data for each student. This baseline data is usually the number of words read correctly in a grade-level passage in one minute. Teachers may also record the number and types of errors.

Throughout the year, teachers may use fluency assessments on a regular basis to help them evaluate student progress and to set instructional goals. Teachers can use these norms as benchmarks as they establish baseline information about the fluency of their students at the beginning of the school year. They can also refer to the norms during the school year as they work with students to increase their reading fluency. Refer to Figure 7–17 for oral and silent reading rate chart (Leslie and Caldwell, 2001, p.68).

How to Construct and Administer a Reading Fluency Assessment

1. The teacher gives the student a copy of an unpracticed selection at his or her instructional grade level to read either orally or silently.
2. The teacher follows along as the student reads, recording information about word recognition errors, rate of reading, and use of expression.
3. The teacher marks with a slash any errors the student makes.
4. The teacher determines the rate by one of two methods. *Option 1:* The student reads for exactly one minute. *Option 2:* The student reads a passage of 100 to 250 words and the teacher records the exact number of seconds the student needed to read this passage. (Option 2 is more conducive for checking comprehension as described in step 5.)
5. To check comprehension, the teacher asks the student to read the passage silently and then to answer several questions about it.

How to Score a Reading Fluency Assessment

1. Count as errors any substitutions, mispronunciations, omissions, reversals, and hesitations of more than three seconds.
2. Insertions and repetitions are not counted as errors because the extra time required for the student to add words or to repeat words increases the total reading time.

The IEP Connection

Individualized Education Plan

Antonio Angelo	1-14-97	2nd	6-1-05
Student's Name	Birthdate	Grade	Date

Present Level of Academic Achievement and Functional Performance: Reading

Given a fiction and a nonfiction reading passage from grade-level material, Antonio read 15 words with 12 errors in the fiction passage, and 33 words with 7 errors in the nonfiction passage. These results place him between the 10th and 25th percentile compared with other students in the spring of second grade in the school district.

Antonio's low reading skills affect his performance in his general education classroom, where most children read about 55 correct words per minute in the spring of second grade.

State Grade 3 Benchmark

Student will read accurately by using phonics, language structure, word meaning, and visual cues. Student will read orally with natural phrasing, expressive interpretation, flow, and pace.

Annual Goal

In one year, given a fiction and a nonfiction passage from third-grade material, Antonio will read an average of 65 correct words per minute with 5 or fewer errors. This result will place his oral reading fluency scores between the 25th and 50th percentile compared with other students in the spring of third grade in the school district.

Short-Term Objectives	Criteria	Nov. 2005	Jan. 2006	April 2006	June 2006
1. By November 2005, given a fiction and a nonfiction reading passage from third-grade material, Antonio will read . . .	37 words per minute (wpm) with 7 or fewer errors	11-10-05 40 wpm with 6 errors			
2. By the end of January 2006, given a fiction and a nonfiction reading passage from third-grade material, Antonio will read . . .	46 wpm with 6 or fewer errors		1-28-06 50 wpm with 5 errors		
3. By mid-April, given a fiction and a nonfiction passage from third-grade material, Antonio will read . . .	55 wpm with 5 or fewer errors			4–16–06 60 wpm with 5 errors	
4. By mid-June, given a fiction and a nonfiction reading passage from third-grade material, Antonio will read . . .	65 wpm with 5 or fewer errors				6–10–06 68 wpm with 5 errors

Evaluation procedures for each short-term objective		Review schedule
___ Daily work samples	___ Performance assessment	___ Weekly
___ Teacher observation	___ Clinical math interview	___ Monthly
_x_ CBA probe	___ Criterion-referenced test	_x_ Quarterly

Figure 7–17 Reading Rates Based on Instructional Grade Levels

Oral Reading		Silent Reading	
Grade Level	Words per Minute (wpm)	Grade Level	Words per Minute (wpm)
Preprimer	13–35	Second	58–122
Primer	28–68	Third	96–168
First	31–87	Fourth/Fifth	107–175
Second	52–102	Sixth	135–241
Third	85–139	Upper Middle	73–370
Fourth/Fifth	78–124	High School	65–334
Sixth	113–165		

3a. For *Option 1:* At the end of one minute, determine the student's reading fluency level by taking the total number of words read in one minute and subtracting the number of errors (only one error per word is counted). The correct words per minute (cwpm) represents the student's fluency score. For example, if a first-grade student reads 53 words in a minute and makes seven errors, the student has a fluency score of 46 cwpm. The accuracy of fluency scores can be improved by using the average of two or three fluency readings from three different passages (Bos & Vaughn, 2002).

3b. For *Option 2:* Calculate the words read per minute (wpm) by multiplying the number of words in the passage by 60. Then divide by the number of seconds it took to read the passage. This calculation yields a word-per-minute score (Richek, et al. 2002).

$$\frac{\text{Number of words} * 60}{\text{Number of seconds to read}} = \text{Words per minute}$$

4. Results can be plotted on a graph to show a student's reading fluency growth over time.

5. To determine whether the student's fluency growth is increasing at a normal rate, compare the scores with published oral reading fluency norms, such as those developed by Hasbrouck and Tindal (1992), or Good and Kaminski (2002) (Figure 7–17). According to Hook and Jones (2002) oral reading fluency mirrors spoken language fluency and the average oral speaking rate is about 140 words per minute.

When using these fluency assessment procedures, teachers should consider the following:

- Is reading choppy? Does the student stumble over or repeat words? Does the student pause excessively? Is the student reading word by word rather than in phrases?
- Is reading monotonous? Does the student read with minimal or no expression or variation in the rise and fall of his or her voice? Is the student merely pronouncing a series of words?
- Is reading too hasty? Does the student rush through text, ignoring punctuation and sentence breaks? Is the student making careless mistakes on familiar words (Wilson, 1988)?

The Impact of Reading Material and Strategies on Fluency

The kinds of texts that students are asked to read can play a role in fluency development (Hiebert & Fisher, 2002). For both beginning readers and older struggling readers, the vocabulary in the books they read affects whether and how quickly they achieve fluency (Menon & Hiebert, 2003; Torgesen, Rashotte, Alexander, Alexander, & McFee, 2002). Sight-word vocabulary consists of words that can be recognized automatically as a result how frequently they appear in text.

A repeated reading is an instructional method in which the student is required to reread a short, meaningful passage several times until a satisfactory level of fluency is reached (Samuels, 1997). In order to determine whether that satisfactory level is attained—for example, if a third-grader reads 100 correct words per minute (cwpm) with two errors—cwpm needs to be assessed, monitored, and graphed.

Figure 7–18 shows the NAEP fluency scale. Students at levels 3 and 4 are generally considered to be fluent, and those at levels 1 and 2 to be nonfluent. Two other aspects of oral reading measured in the NAEP assessment are accuracy and rate. *Accuracy* is based on the number of misread words (omitted, inserted, or substituted), and *rate* is based on the number of words read per minute.

Classroom Scenario: What Would You Do?

A fourth-grader in your class reads words correctly but his pace is extremely slow. As you devise a remedial plan, how would you set up a progress-monitoring assessment system? How would you involve the student in the implementation of the monitoring process?

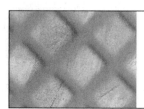

Tips for Teachers

Be careful not to overinterpret the norms, especially with regard to English language learners. Always consider exceptions to the norms.

Figure 7–18   Oral Reading Fluency Scale

Level 4	Reads primarily in larger, meaningful phrase groups. Although some regressions, repetitions, and deviations from text may be present, these do not appear to detract from the overall structure of the story. Preservation of the author's syntax is consistent. Some or most of the story is read with expressive interpretation.
Level 3	Reads primarily in three- or four-word phrase groups. Some smaller groupings may be present. However, the majority of phrasing seems appropriate and preserves the syntax of the author. Little or no expressive interpretation is present.
Level 2	Reads primarily in two-word phrases with some three- or four-word groupings. Some word-by-word reading may be present. Word groupings may seem awkward and unrelated to larger context of sentence or passage.
Level 1	Reads primarily word-by-word. Occasional two-word or three-word phrases may occur, but these are infrequent and/or they do not preserve meaningful syntax.

Source: U.S. Department of Education, National Center for Education Statistics. (1995). *Listening to Children Read Aloud* (p. 15). Washington, DC.

Reading fluency norms can serve as a stable benchmark for assessing reading fluency and can be used to set fluency goals. For example, the oral reading fluency norms (Hasbrouck & Tindal, 1992; *Put Reading First*, 2001) show that typical growth through grade 3 is a gain of about one word per week. After grade 3, the gain is slightly less but continues at the rate of about 0.5 to 0.85 words per week through grade 5. Fuchs and colleagues (1993) have suggested that students who are below the 50th percentile will need to show growth beyond this rate if the achievement gap is to be closed. See Figure 7-19 for a guide to fluency norms. Figure 7-19 for a chart of reading rates based on instructional levels and Figure 7-20 for a guide to determining placement levels and the amount of growth that should be expected (Fuchs & Deno, 1982).

Critical Thinking and Reflection Activity

Using the reading fluency chart in Figure 7–19, determine how many words per minute a second-grader in your class who is reading below the 50th percentile would have to read to keep up with grade norms.

Figure 7–19   Oral Reading Fluency Norms Chart

Grade	Fall 25% cwpm	Fall 50% cwpm	Fall 75% cwpm	Winter 25% cwpm	Winter 50% cwpm	Winter 75% cwpm	Spring 25% cwpm	Spring 50% cwpm	Spring 75% cwpm
2	23	53	82	46	78	106	65	94	124
3	65	79	107	70	93	123	87	114	142
4	72	99	125	89	112	133	92	118	143
5	77	105	125	93	118	143	100	128	151

Note: Grade 1 range is 60–80 correct words per minute (cwpm); grades 6–8 range is 150–180 cwpm; grades 9–12 range is 180–200 cwpm.

Source: "Curriculum-Based Oral Reading Fluency Norms for Students in Grade 2 through 5" by J.E. Hasbrouck & G. Tindal, 1992. Teaching Exceptional Children, 24, pp. 41-43. Copyright 1992 by the Council for Exceptional Children. Reprinted with permission.

Figure 7–20   Determining Reading Progress and Placement Levels

Grade Level	Placement Level	Correct Words Per Minute (cwpm)	Errors Per Minute	Typical Reading Growth (number of words per week)
Grade 1	Frustration	<40	>4	2.0 to 3.0
	Instructional	40–60	4 or fewer	1.5 to 2.0
Grade 2	Independent	>60	4 or fewer	1.0 to 1.5
Grade 3	Frustration	<70	>6	0.85 to 1.1
Grade 4	Instructional	70–100	6 or fewer	0.5 to 0.8
Grade 5	Independent	>100	6 or fewer	
Grade 6				

Figure 7–21 Graph of Predicted, Actual, and Expected Reading Progress

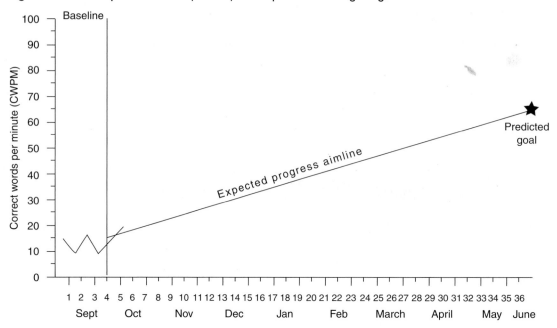

Figure 7–21 is an example of a student's baseline reading performance (the reading level at which the student was functioning when the individualized education plan (IEP) goal was developed) and the aimline to the reading IEP goal (the criterion for success) (Meyen, Vergason, & Whelan, 1996). In this case, the student will be tested two times each week and the results will be recorded on the graph. The reading passage will be taken from the curriculum specified in the student's annual IEP reading goal.

In Figure 7-22, the reading instructional program without modifications that has been in effect for the past six weeks has not been successful. This graph shows the expected rate of progress for the student's reading skill level from the time the IEP goals were initially developed to the time the next IEP goals will be developed (typically the following year). According to the graph, this student's instructional program was not only ineffective, but also detrimental, since the aimline shows the student's reading performance to have decreased. These results indicate that either the instructional program needs to be changed or the projected goal needs to be adjusted.

It is recommended that teachers collect the data twice weekly, so that at least 10 data points can be gathered, graphed, and tracked over six weeks, which allows sufficient time to monitor instructional effects and modify ineffective programming. Studies have documented that there is greater student achievement when teachers are meaningfully involved in collecting and evaluating student data (Plante & Beeson, 1999). This progress-monitoring system is both effective and efficient. According to Fuchs (1989), teachers spend an average of only 2 minutes and 15 seconds per student collecting a one-minute reading sample—which includes preparing, administering, and scoring the sample, and graphing the student's progress.

Figure 7–22 Graph of Predicted and Actual Performance Before and After Interventions

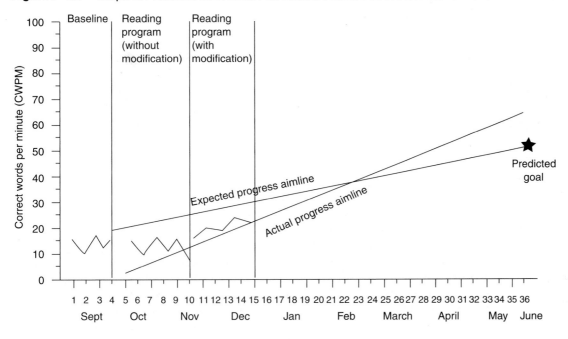

SECTION 5: READING COMPREHENSION ASSESSMENT

Text comprehension is the ability to understand, remember, and communicate what has been read. It involves making connections at the literal, interpretative, and application levels in reading text, as well as understanding literary elements, text patterns, text organizations, and author's purpose. According to Luftig (1989), the levels of reading comprehension include (a) understanding facts: recognizing and recalling facts, including the main idea; (b) reorganizing: classifying, categorizing, and summarizing; (c) inferring: interpreting and predicting; (d) evaluating: judging (e.g., reality, appropriateness); and (e) criticizing: questioning, identifying feelings, and expressing opinions. Purposeful, active readers use text comprehension strategies to make sense out of their reading. However, if students do not use comprehension strategies to improve their understanding and monitor their comprehension of text, they are unlikely to become good readers (National Reading Panel, 2002).

Components of Reading Comprehension

Several key factors that can significantly influence reading comprehension are memory, prior knowledge of the information in the reading passage, and interest in the topic being read. Memory is an important component in comprehension because students need to rely on short-term memory to retain specific details in a passage (e.g., the characters' names, relationships and roles in the story, and the details planted in the beginning of the plot which are drawn together for the conclusion).

Frequently, students with learning disabilities have distinct deficiencies in **working memory**, which is the ability to mentally operate on information in short-term memory. They do not spontaneously use the metacognitive strategies that would enhance

Tips for Teachers

Check on working memory by having the student:

* Repeat a series of digits in reverse order
* Paraphrase a series of directions
* Mentally calculate a two- to three-digit equation (if calculation is not a problem for the student)

memory (e.g., rehearsing names to themselves or categorizing information for more efficient recall). These students may have difficulty remembering as a result of poor language skills, making verbal information particularly difficult to retain and recall (Hallahan, Kauffman, & Lloyd, 1999; Silver, 2001).

Prior knowledge is another principle factor affecting comprehension. Comprehension is influenced not only by linguistic cues and semantic content, but also by students' knowledge of the topic (McLoughlin & Lewis, 2005). Students will depend less on printed material when their experiences are extensive and can be proficiently recalled (Mercer & Pullen, 2005). Unless students have a fundamental knowledge of the story components, based on previous reading or direct experience, they will be unable to easily accommodate or assimilate the new data with the old data and therefore will be unlikely to comprehend what they have read.

Interest in the reading material, which may determine whether students will even read beyond the first several pages of the story, is also a prominent factor in comprehension. Interest inventories can be administered to students so that the reading selections chosen for assessment are relevant and interesting to them.

Interest Inventory

To facilitate comprehension and to increase the validity of comprehension assessment, the teacher should provide students with materials that would be motivating to them and help to maintain their attention (CEC, 2003). An interest inventory can provide information about students' reading habits, such as their hobbies (collecting dolls, making car models); extracurricular activities (sports, clubs) and favorite recreational activities (biking, watching television). The information gained from the interest inventory can be useful in selecting reading passages to be used for assessments. For young readers, the inventory can be administered orally or in an interview format. Questionnaires, conferencing, and incomplete sentence formats can be used with older students. (See Figure 7–23 for a sample interest inventory.)

Classroom Scenario: What Would You Do?

The eighth-grader you are trying to evaluate is unwilling to read or write. He states that the test is boring and "baby stuff." What do you do?

Figure 7–23   Sample Reading Interest Inventory

Ask the student

- What is your favorite subject in school? Why?
- What subject is easy for you? Why?
- What subject is hardest for you? Why?
- What do you like best and least about school?
- What do you like to do after school? on weekends? during summer vacation?
- What are your hobbies?
- Do you play sports?
- Do you watch any sports on television?
- What are your three favorite television programs?
- What kinds of collections do you have?
- Name some special places you have been to.
- What is your favorite place?
- What do you want to be when you grow up?
- What do you know a lot about?
- What would you like to learn about?
- What book are you reading now?
- What was the last book you read?
- What kinds of stories do you like to read?
- What is the name of your favorite book?
- How much time do you spend reading?
- Do you have books in your home?
- Do you have a library card?
- Do you go to the public library to borrow books?
- Do you borrow books from the school library?
- Do you read newspapers, magazines, or comic books?

The focus of the interview questions should be to establish how students feel about reading, their reading habits, the kinds of materials they like most to read, as well as the strategies they use to retain new words, decode unfamiliar words, and figure out the meaning of unknown words. (See Figure 7-24.)

Figure 7–24   Sample Student Reading Interview

What is your favorite story? _____

Would you rather read a story or listen to a story? _____

When you have a new word to learn, how do you remember it? _____

When you are reading and come to a word that you don't know, what do you do? _____

Which subject has the hardest words: reading, science, social studies, or math? _____

Can you sound out a word that you do not know? _____

Can you break words into parts? _____

Can you memorize new vocabulary words? _____

Do you understand what words mean when reading assignments? _____

Can you retell a story in your own words? _____

Can you tell what the main idea in a story is? _____

Can you describe the characters in a story? _____

Can you figure out the problem and the solution in a story? _____

Explicit, Implicit, and Critical Comprehension

When evaluating students' ability to understand reading material, the teacher should focus on students' explicit, implicit, and critical comprehension skills.

Explicit comprehension is the ability to grasp reading matter at a literal or factual level, such as being able to identify the main idea of a story, locate significant and irrelevant details, sequence information, and read and carry out information. To determine a student's explicit comprehension skills, the teacher should ask whether the student:

- responds literally
- takes facts directly from the reading material by

  naming characters and setting

  identifying the main idea and specific details

  presenting story facts in sequence

Implicit comprehension is the ability to interpret or infer information, draw conclusions, make generalizations, predict outcomes, summarize, understand cause-and-effect and compare-and-contrast relationships, locate the implied main idea, and sense the author's mood and purpose. To determine the student's implicit comprehension skills, the teacher should ask whether the student:

- interprets
- infers from the reading material by

  summarizing

  stating the implied main idea

  predicting, concluding, and generalizing

  comparing and contrasting

  identifying cause and effect

  determining the author's mood, purpose, and intended audience

Critical comprehension, the most abstract level of the three, is the ability to "read between the lines," to be able to judge and evaluate printed text. To determine whether the student reads at a critical level, the teacher should ask whether the student:

- discriminates between fact and fiction
- evaluates the accuracy and completeness of material
- interprets figurative language
- analyzes and compares material from various sources
- senses the author's biases and agenda
- responds with a more abstract response
- demonstrates higher order thinking skills
- applies prior knowledge, summarizes, and predicts
- identifies the implied main idea
- recognizes propaganda techniques used in reading matter

Figure 7–25 is a checklist that can be used by the teacher or as a self-check by students to monitor use of comprehension strategies. The following performance levels are recommended for students when evaluating comprehension (Mercer & Mercer, 2005):

independent level = < 90 percent

instructional level = 75 to 89 percent

frustration level = > 75 percent

Figure 7–25 Comprehension Strategy Checklist

Comprehension Strategies	Always	Occasionally	Rarely	Never
Uses prior knowledge				
Determines purpose				
Asks self what is important about topic				
Makes predictions				
Identifies main idea				
Uses context clues				
Analyzes characters				
Adjusts reading rate				
Compares and contrasts				
Monitors understanding				
Makes generalizations				
Makes inferences				
Recognizes cause and effect				
Recalls supporting details				
Recalls sequence of ideas				
Differentiates fact and fiction				
Draws a conclusion				
Understands figurative language				
Visualizes and images				
Uses story maps				
Summarizes				

Cloze Procedure

The **cloze procedure** is used to assess word-prediction abilities, to measure comprehension, and to determine how students use context clues to identify words. It is also an efficient way of determining whether textbooks are written at the grade level appropriate to students' reading ability. In this method, students read a passage and must supply the missing word or a semantically acceptable substitute, which requires them to analyze the context and its structure. This assessment procedure measures students' ability to read and interpret written passages, to understand the context of reading material, to use word-prediction abilities for comprehension, and to use cues to identify words. It also measures their knowledge of linguistic structures. This procedure can be administered individually or in groups; and because it focuses on comprehension rather than fluency, it is untimed. (See Figure 7–26.)

How to Construct Cloze Procedure Materials

1. The teacher selects a passage from the beginning of a story, chapter, or text of 250–300 words (100–200 words for grades 1 and 2).
2. The teacher types the passage, using complete paragraphs and leaving the first and last sentences intact.
3. Beginning with the second sentence, the teacher deletes every fifth word and replaces it with a blank.
4. The blanks should be uniform in length (10–15 spaces) to avoid spacing clues for missing words.
5. The teacher makes two copies: one for the teacher and one for the student.

Figure 7–26   Sample Cloze Procedure

<table>
<tr><td>

Cloze Procedure Passage

The Miracle

I lived with my grandpa on the corner of Oak and Second Streets. We lived together in _____ large, brown cardboard box _____ we ate as many _____ of food as we _____ find. It was a _____ December and the ground _____ covered with snow. We _____ running out of food _____ were low on blankets. _____ had started coughing a _____. We needed a miracle _____ we would both die _____ starvation or frostbite. One _____ I was lying awake _____ the hard, cold cement _____ not to think of _____ very hungry I was. _____ face was flushed and _____ was frail and as _____ as a stick. I _____ I had to think _____ a way to help _____. That frigid night I _____ soundly until six in _____ morning when the bright _____ warmed my face. As _____ opened my eyes I _____ a huge table of _____ foods. It was a _____ come true. Grandpa's face _____ up as he watched _____ enjoying a hot cinnamon _____ while he drank a _____ cup of coffee and _____ a piece of freshly _____ bread. I drifted off _____ sleep dreaming happy thoughts. _____ woke suddenly to see _____ shadowy white figure in _____ distance standing beside my _____ as he slept. Grandpa _____ up and smiled at _____ figure. The white figure _____ into the sky with _____ grasping her outstretched hands. _____ is gone now but _____ has not forgotten me. He has _____ the angel back to _____ over me. Now, I have everything I need, except Grandpa.

</td><td>

Cloze Procedure Passage Answers

The Miracle

I lived with my grandpa on the corner of Oak and Second Streets. We lived together in __a__ large, brown cardboard box __and__. we ate as many __scraps__ of food as we __could__ find. It was a __cold__ December and the ground __was__ covered with snow. We __were__ running out of food __and__ were low on blankets. __Grandpa__ had started coughing a __lot__. We needed a miracle __or__ we would both die __of__ starvation or frostbite. One __night__ I was lying awake __on__ the hard, cold cement __trying__ not to think of __how__ very hungry I was. __Grandpa's__ face was flushed and __he__ was frail and as __thin__ as a stick. I __knew__ I had to think __of__ a way to help __him__. That frigid night I __slept__ soundly until six in __the__ morning when the bright __sunshine__ warmed my face. As __I__ opened my eyes I __saw__ a huge table of __delicious__ foods. It was a __dream__ come true. Grandpa's face __lit__ up as he watched __me__ enjoying a hot cinnamon __bun__ while he drank a __steaming__ cup of coffee and __ate__ a piece of freshly __baked__ bread. I drifted off __to__ sleep dreaming happy thoughts. __I__ woke suddenly to see __a__ shadowy white figure in __the__ distance standing beside my __Grandpa__ as he slept. Grandpa __sat__ up and smiled at __the__ figure. The white figure __flew__ into the sky with __Grandpa__ grasping her outstretched hands. __Grandpa__ is gone now but __he__ has not forgotten me. He has __sent__ the angel back to __watch__ over me. Now, I have everything I need, except Grandpa.

</td></tr>
</table>

Written by: Julie Spinelli (1995).

How to Administer the Cloze Procedure

The teacher provides a model so that the procedure can be demonstrated, or provides the student with a practice passage with easy sentences to ensure that he or she understands and can follow the directions (e.g., "Old MacDonald had a _____"). The teacher tells the student to:

1. Read the whole passage.
2. Reread the passage and fill in the missing words.

3. Try to use the exact words you think the author would have used.
4. Write one word on each line (or tell the word to the teacher).
5. Skip and go to the next blank if you are having difficulty with one, and go back
    and try to fill in the remaining blanks when you get to the end of the passage.

How to Score the Cloze Method of Assessment

- Do not count misspellings as incorrect if the word is recognizable.
- Do not impose a time limit.
- Exact replacement words are recommended for ease of scoring, but synonyms
  that do not change the meaning may be accepted.

Scoring Criteria

- Independent reading level = 57 to 100 percent
- Instructional reading level = 44 to 56 percent
- Frustration reading level = less than 43 percent (Ekwall, 1997)

Maze Procedure

The **maze procedure** is an assessment technique, similar to the cloze procedure, that assesses reading comprehension and knowledge of linguistic structures. Rather than leave
blank spaces for students' responses as in the cloze method, the maze method provides
students with choices, presented in a vertical or a horizontal format. This technique gives
students three words to choose from—only one of which is correct. This procedure is a
more valid indicator of reading comprehension for a child who has word retrieval problems, because it provides optional choices rather than requiring the child to produce his
or her own word. Students whose primary language is other than English also profit from
these language cues. The following sentences are examples of the maze procedure:

	foot	it	buy
Jim did not have foam so he went shopping in the grocery store to bake food.			
	food	on	bite

Jane went back to _____ because she was tired.
(school, work, sleep)

Scoring Criteria

The criteria for determining reading levels when using the maze procedure are based
on the percentage of correct responses (Ekwall, 1997):

- Independent reading level = more than 85 percent
- Instructional reading level = 50 to 84 percent
- Frustration reading level = 49 percent or less

Critical Thinking and Reflection Activity

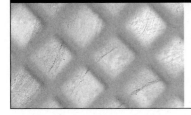

You have been using a maze procedure with a student who has word-retrieval problems. As her skills
improve you want to gradually begin using a cloze
procedure. What would you do to slowly decrease
the supports used in the maze approach?

Think-Aloud Procedure

The **think-aloud procedure** is a method of attaining insight into the reader's approach to text processing. Verbalizations made before, during, and after reading a selection are used to assess students' thinking processes and their use of metacognitive strategies. Readers are asked to stop at specific points while reading to "think aloud" about the processes and strategies being used. The teacher tells students the title of the selected passage, asking them to reflect on the topic and tell how they feel about it. Students are then asked to read the passage but to stop after each sentence and to think out loud about what they have read. When students have completed reading the passage, the teacher should ask about its content, structure, and difficulty level. It may be helpful to record students as they read and respond to the passage for later analysis. (See Figure 7–27 for sample questions.)

Retell Procedure

In the **retell procedure**, students are required to demonstrate their understanding of reading material by retelling or paraphrasing the passage. This comprehension procedure can be administered in either oral or written form; both methods engage students in holistic comprehension and organization of thought, instead of just isolated pieces of information. Students are asked to read a selection and retell the passage as if relating it to someone who has never heard it before. Using this method of assessment, the teacher can obtain qualitative, quantitative, and organization measures for determining whether students understand the story structure and can accurately recall details from the story in a logical, proper sequence (Lipson & Wixson, 1997). For example, when reading a narrative passage, students should be able to retell the story in a structured manner and identify the setting, characters, goal, problem, main events, and story resolution. The teacher should use prompts—such as asking "What comes next?" or "Then what happened?"—only when necessary. After reading expository text, students should be able to recall the main idea followed by the supporting details.

The retell procedure must involve more than merely repeating the story verbatim (Anderson & Roit, 1998). Students should be asked to explain the passage in their own words, which helps to assess their comprehension rather than just their ability to recall facts. This type of assessment may not be a reliable indicator for students whose first language is not English or for those who have an expressive language disorder (Carlisle, 1999).

Figure 7–28 is a retell rating scale developed by Tindal and Marston (1990). It provides a guide for determining relative competency. (See also the retell checklist in Figure 7–29.) Although no established standard has been established, scores of 3 and above have been found to be easily produced by primary-level students reading primary passages (Howell & Nolet, 2000). According to Johns and Lenski (1997, p. 284), the following are retelling expectations for expository passages:

Independent level will generally reflect

- The text structure
- Organization of how the material was presented
- Main ideas and details in the text

Figure 7–27   Sample Think-Aloud Questions

- How does the student use existing information?
- Can the student relate existing information with new information?
- Can the student integrate new information with prior knowledge?
- How does the student deal with new words and concepts?
- Is the student using any metacognitive strategies to facilitate comprehension?
- Can the student predict or anticipate upcoming events in a story?

Figure 7–28   Retell Rating Scale

Rating	Interpretation
5	Generalizations are made beyond the text; includes central thesis and major points, supporting details, and relevant supplemental information; exhibits coherence, completeness, and comprehensibility
4	Includes central thesis, major points, supporting details, and relevant supplemental information; exhibits coherence, completeness, and comprehensibility
3	Relates major ideas, includes supporting details and relevant supplemental information; exhibits adequate coherence, completeness, and comprehensibility
2	Relates a few major ideas, supporting details and relevant supplemental information; exhibits some coherence, completeness, and comprehensibility
1	Relates no major ideas, and details only irrelevant supplemental information; low degree of coherence, completeness, and comprehensibility

Pass: rating of 4 or 5
No pass: rating of 3, 2, 1

Figure 7–29   Retell Skill Checklist

Can the student
_____ tell story events in sequential order?
_____ include some important details?
_____ refer to story characters by name?
_____ define personal traits of the characters?
_____ describe story problems and solutions?
_____ respond with literal interpretation?
_____ include only important and exclude unimportant information?
_____ respond with interpretation reflecting higher level thinking?
_____ provide adequate responses to teacher questions and prompts?
_____ retell the entire story with only 2 or 3 questions or prompts?
S= satisfactory   I = improving   NI = needs improvement

Instructional level will generally reflect

- Less content than at the independent level
- Some minor misrepresentations and inaccuracies
- Organization that differs from the actual text

Frustration level will generally be

- Haphazard
- Incomplete
- Characterized by bits of information not related logically or sequentially

Metacognition

Metacognition involves the awareness of one's own thinking processes, the strategies used, and the ability to regulate these processes or strategies to ensure successful learning; that is, to be aware of "what to do (what strategies to use) when you don't know what to do" (Anderson, 2002). Research studies have shown that metacognition is especially important for comprehension (Mastropieri & Scruggs, 1997; Mastropieri, Scruggs, Bakken, & Wheldon, 1996; Morocco, 2001).

Reading is a metacognitive act of self-determination (Manzo & Manzo, 1995) in which the reader develops "in-the-head" strategies (Clay, 2000). This internal awareness, referred to as metacognition, allows the reader to consciously or unconsciously monitor comprehension during reading to assure that reading material makes sense. These thinking strategies help students set purposes for reading, activate background (prior) knowledge, attend to the main idea, draw inferences, and monitor comprehension (Deshler, Ellis, & Lenz, 1996; Mastropieri & Scruggs, 1997). Readers can either continue to read or select and apply strategies to solve problems encountered while reading (Irvin, Buchl, & Klemp, 2003).

Students who have difficulty reading and comprehending often do not understand or do not adequately utilize metacognitive strategies, including memory processing for words and comprehension monitoring (Mercer & Pullen, 2005). Studies indicate that many students with learning disabilities do not effectively use elaborate encoding strategies—such as rehearsals, categorization, and association—when attempting to retain or recall words or to comprehend while reading (Deshler, et al., 1996; Fuchs, Fuchs, Mathes, Lipocy, & Eaton, 2000; Miller & Felton, 2001). According to Bos and Vaughn (2002), poor readers do not automatically monitor comprehension or engage in strategic behavior to restore meaning when there is a comprehension breakdown.

Classroom Scenario: What Would You Do?

You suspect that the sixth-grader you are evaluating is not using metacognitive strategies. You have decided to use the self-assessment tests in Figure 7–31 and 7–32. However, you question her ability to read accurately and comprehend what she is reading. How can you increase the likelihood that her responses will be reliable and valid?

Metacognition combines thinking and reflective processes; an understanding of when, where, and how to apply and assess the success of these strategies (Anderson, 2002; Mastropieri & Scruggs, 1997). The teacher needs to determine whether students are employing metacognitive strategies, and if so, how fully and effectively they are using the five primary components: (1) preparing and planning for learning, (2) selecting and using learning strategies, (3) monitoring strategy use, (4) orchestrating various strategies, and (5) evaluating strategy use and learning (Anderson, 2002). Samuels (1983) identified specific questions asked by skilled readers, such as:

- Why am I reading this?
- Do I want to read this for superficial overview or for detail?
- Do I know when there is a breakdown in comprehension?
- When there is a breakdown in understanding what can I do to get back on the track again?

- What are the major and minor points of this text?
- Can I summarize or synthesize the major points made in this text?

Elementary and middle-school teachers can assess students' knowledge of strategic reading processes by using the metacomprehension strategy index in Figure 7–30. It is important for students to learn to self-monitor their metacognitive skills. (Figure 7–31 is a skill analysis that students can use to identify their use of metacognitive strategies, and Figure 7–32 is a self-checklist to help students learn to self-monitor.)

SECTION 6: GENERAL READING ASSESSMENT MEASURES

This section addresses various evaluative methods for assessing all five reading components. Some are best used individually and others can be used with small or large groups. The evaluative procedures can be used appropriately with regular and special education students. They can also be adapted or modified to accommodate an individual's abilities and disabilities and used on a regular basis for diagnostic-prescriptive purposes. The sooner the teacher identifies students' reading problems, the faster remediation procedures can be implemented.

Portfolio Assessment

An authentic method of assessment involving the collection and evaluation of students' work that is regularly performed in a natural or authentic context is portfolio assessment. Portfolio assessment is based on the continuous process of gathering genuine evidence of students' efforts, progress, and achievements in one or more areas. Portfolio assessment is a holistic evaluation that focuses on the process of learning as well as on the product of learning—rather than emphasizing outcomes, as with standardized testing procedures (Venn, 2004).

Portfolios provide a vehicle to ensure students and teachers that there are links with the important literacy experiences that students have, in and out of school, as well as assessment links that are productive rather than judgmental. The goal of portfolio assessment is to be responsive to what students are doing: to represent the range of things they are involved in, the processes they enlist, the effort they put forth, and the improvement and the range of abilities they have demonstrated (Stiggins, 2001). Since this is a flexible technique, it can be used to facilitate communication for those working with special education students. When students are mainstreamed, special education and regular education teachers can use portfolios for record keeping and as a process for sharing information—including students' progress—with school staff, parents or guardians, and the students themselves.

Tips for Teachers

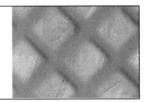

Portfolio pieces are useful for demonstrating explicit examples of student progress, especially for parent conferences and IEP annual review meetings.

Figure 7–30   Metacomprehension Strategy Index

Part I: Choose the one statement that tells a good thing to do to help you understand a story better *before* you read it.

1. Before I begin reading, it's a good time to:
    A. See how many pages are in the story.
    B. Look up all of the big words in the dictionary.
    C. Make some guesses about what I think will happen in the story.
    D. Think about what has happened so far in the story.

2. Before I begin reading, it's a good idea to:
    A. Look at the pictures to see what the story is about.
    B. Decide how long it will take me to read the story.
    C. Sound out the words I don't know.
    D. Check to see if the story is making sense.

3. Before I begin reading, it's a good idea to:
    A. Ask someone to read the story to me.
    B. Read the title to see what the story is about.
    C. Check to see if most of the words have long or short vowels in them.
    D. Check to see if the pictures are in order and make sense.

4. Before I begin reading, it's a good idea to:
    A. Check to see that no pages are missing.
    B. Make a list of the words I'm not sure about.
    C. Use the title and pictures to help me make guesses about what will happen in the story.
    D. Read the last sentence so I will know how the story ends.

5. Before I begin reading, it's a good idea to:
    A. Decide on why I am going to read the story.
    B. Use the difficult words to help me make guesses about what will happen in the story.
    C. Reread some parts to see if I can figure out what is happening if things aren't making sense.
    D. Ask for help with the difficult words.

6. Before I begin reading, it's a good idea to:
    A. Retell all of the main points that have happened so far.
    B. Ask myself questions that I would like to have answered in the story.
    C. Think about the meanings of the words that have more than one meaning.
    D. Look through the story to find all of the words with three or more syllables.

7. Before I begin reading, it's a good idea to:
    A. Check to see if I have read this story before.
    B. Use my questions and guesses as a reason for reading the story.
    C. Make sure I can pronounce all of the words before I start.
    D. Think of a better title for the story.

8. Before I begin reading, it's a good idea to:
    A. Think of what I already know about the pictures.
    B. See how many pages are in the story.
    C. Chose the best part of the story to read again.
    D. Read the story aloud to someone.

9. Before I begin reading, it's a good idea to:
    A. Practice reading the story aloud.
    B. Retell all of the main points to make sure I can remember the story.
    C. Think of what the people in the story might be like.
    D. Decide if I have enough time to read the story.

10. Before I begin reading, it's a good idea to:
    A. Check to see if I am understanding the story so far.
    B. Check to see if the words have more than one meaning.
    C. Think about where the story might be taking place.
    D. List all of the important details.

Part II: Choose the statement that tells a good thing to do to help you understand better *while* reading.

11. While I'm reading, it's a good idea to:
    A. Read the story very slowly so that I will not miss any important parts.
    B. Read the title to see what the story is about.
    C. Check to see if the pictures have anything missing.
    D. Check if the story is making sense by seeing if I can tell what's happened so far.

12. While I'm reading, it's a good idea to:
    A. Stop to retell main points to see if I am understanding what has happened so far.
    B. Read the story quickly so that I can find out what happened.
    C. Read only the beginning and the end of the story to find out what it is about.
    D. Skip the parts that are too difficult for me.

13. While I'm reading, it's a good idea to:
    A. Look all of the big words up in the dictionary.
    B. Put the book away and find another one if things aren't making sense.
    C. Keep thinking about the title and pictures to help me decide what is going to happen next.
    D. Keep track of how many pages I have left to read.

14. While I'm reading, it's a good idea to:
    A. Keep track of how long it is taking me to read the story.
    B. Check to see if I can answer any of the questions I asked before I started reading.
    C. Read the title to see what the story is going to be about.
    D. Add the missing details to the pictures.

15. While I'm reading, it's a good idea to:
    A. Have someone read the story aloud to me.
    B. Keep track of how many pages I have read.
    C. List the story's main character.
    D. Check to see if my guesses are right or wrong.

16. While I'm reading, it's a good idea to:
    A. Check to see that the characters are real.
    B. Make a lot of guesses about what is going to happen next.
    C. Not look at the pictures because they might confuse me.
    D. Read the story aloud to someone.

17. While I'm reading, it's a good idea to:
    A. Try to answer the questions I asked myself.
    B. Try not to confuse what I already know with what I'm reading about.
    C. Read the story silently.
    D. Check to see if I am saying the new vocabulary words correctly.

18. While I'm reading, it's a good idea to:
    A. Try to see if my guesses are going to be right or wrong.
    B. Reread to be sure I haven't missed any of the words.
    C. Decide on why I am reading the story.
    D. List what happened first, second, third, and so on.

19. While I'm reading, it's a good idea to:
    A. See if I can recognize the new vocabulary words.
    B. Be careful not to skip any parts of the story.
    C. Check to see how many of the words I already know.
    D. Keep thinking of what I already know about the things and ideas in the story to help me decide what is going to happen.

Figure 7–30 (*Continued*)

20. While I'm reading, it's a good idea to:
    A. Reread parts or read ahead to see if I can figure what's happening if things don't make sense.
    B. Take my time reading so that I can be sure I understand what is happening.
    C. Change the ending so that it makes sense.
    D. Check to see if there are enough pictures to help make the story ideas clear.

Part III: In each set of four, choose the one statement that tells a good thing to do to help you understand a story better *after* you have read it.

21. After I've read a story it's a good idea to:
    A. Count how many pages I read with no mistake.
    B. Check to see if there were enough pictures to go with the story to make it interesting.
    C. Check to see if I met my purpose for reading the story.
    D. Underline the causes and effects.

22. After I've read a story it's a good idea to:
    A. Underline the main idea.
    B. Retell the main points of the whole story so I can check to see if I understand it.
    C. Read the story again to be sure I said all of the words right.
    D. Practice reading the story aloud.

23. After I've read a story it's a good idea to:
    A. Read the title and look over the story to see what it is about.
    B. Check to see if I skipped any of the vocabulary words.
    C. Think about what made me make good or bad predictions.
    D. Make a guess about what will happen next in the story.

24. After I've read a story it's a good idea to:
    A. Look up all of the big words in the dictionary.
    B. Read the best parts aloud.
    C. Have someone read the story aloud to me.
    D. Think about how the story was like things I already knew about before I started reading.

25. After I've read a story it's a good idea to:
    A. Think about how I would have acted if I were the main character in the story.
    B. Practice reading the story silently for practice of good reading.
    C. Look over the story title and pictures to see what will happen.
    D. Make a list of the things I understood the most.

Answer key:

Section I (before reading)		Section II (during reading)		Section III (after reading)
1. C	6. B	11. D	16. B	21. C
2. A	7. B	12. A	17. A	22. B
3. B	8. A	13. C	18. A	23. C
4. C	9. C	14. B	19. D	24. D
5. A	10. C	15. D	20. A	25. A

Schmitt indicated the test item numbers that assess students' awareness regarding the following metacomprehension categories:

Predicting and verifying	1, 4, 13, 15, 16, 18, 23
Previewing	2, 3
Purpose setting	5, 7, 21
Self-questioning	6, 14, 17
Drawing from background knowledge	8, 9, 10, 19, 24, 25
Summarizing/fix-up strategies	11, 12, 20, 22

Source: "A Questionnaire to Measure Children's Awareness of Strategic Reading Processes," by M. C. Schmitt, 1990. *The Reading Teacher, 43*(7), pp. 454–461. Reprinted with permission from the International Reading Association.

Figure 7—31   Student Metacognitive Skill Self-Analysis

Before beginning to read, do you

- identify the purpose for reading?
- think about what you already know about the topic?
- ask yourself what you need to know about the topic?
- think about or discuss experiences related to the topic?
- ask yourself what you expect to learn from this reading?
- think about the strategies you might use to help you understand the material?
- look over and think about the illustrations?
- read the headings and topic sentences and use these to predict what you will be reading?

While you are reading, do you

- stop and ask yourself if you understand what you have just read?
- adjust your reading rate (slow down) if the material gets confusing or difficult?
- pay attention to signal words in the text (e.g., *therefore, such as, finally*)?
- highlight or underline any parts that are important or may be unclear?
- write words, questions, or comments in the margin so that you can reread or check them later?
- make predictions about what might happen next?
- make an outline or a semantic map to help you organize and remember characters, plot, and so forth?

After you have finished reading, do you

- ask yourself if you learned what you wanted to know?
- go back to reread specific sections that were confusing or unclear?
- think about what the author was trying to convey?
- determine if your predictions were correct, and if not, how they differed?
- summarize what you have read?
- ask yourself how you feel about what you read, whether you agree or disagree, and why?
- think about how you might use this information in the future?
- decide whether you need to read more about this topic?

Figure 7—32   Self-Assessment—Metacognitive Strategies

Skill	Self-Assessment Question	Response		
		Always	Sometimes	Never
Know	Do I have prior knowledge?	_____	_____	_____
Regulate	Do I understand what is taking place?	_____	_____	_____
Check	Do I comprehend what I am reading?	_____	_____	_____
Repair	Do I know how to correct problems?	_____	_____	_____
Plan	Do I ask myself prereading questions?	_____	_____	_____
Strategize	Do I set a purpose, know how and what to read?	_____	_____	_____
Monitor	Do I ask myself how I am performing?	_____	_____	_____
Evaluate	Do I know how well I have done?	_____	_____	_____
	Do I understand what I have read?	_____	_____	_____

Source: Wiener, R.B. (1994). *Literacy Portfolios: Using Assessment to Guide Instruction.* Upper Saddle River, NJ: Merrill/Prentice Hall, p. 26.

Content of Student Portfolios

Portfolios can include a vast range of materials, but for them to have a clear purpose for the assessment, the content must be predetermined and unambiguous. According to Nolet (1992), determining what goes into a portfolio depends on (a) who the intended audience will be; (b) what the audience will want to know about the student's learning; (c) whether the portfolio will focus on displaying aspects of student's progress or just corroborate evidence that test scores have already documented; (d) what types of evidence will demonstrate how the student has progressed toward learning goals; (e) whether the portfolio should contain the student's best work, a progressive record of growth, or both; and (f) whether the portfolio should include only finished pieces or items in progress, such as sketches and revisions.

According to Vavrus (1990), the teacher should make decisions on five critical points before developing a portfolio assessment:

1. What should the portfolio look like? The physical structure (the actual arrangement of the entries) and the conceptual structure (setting the learning goals) should be predetermined.
2. What goes into the portfolio? (See Figure 7–33 for purposes of and product ideas for portfolios.)

Figure 7–33 Portfolio Assessment Purposes and Products

Purposes for Portfolio Assessment

To provide an alternative to traditional forms of assessment (e.g., standardized testing)
To assess students' multidimensional growth over time
To provide evidence of the range of learning abilities
To highlight students' strengths and identify areas in need of improvement
To promote students' involvement, purpose, motivation, commitment, and accomplishment
To involve students in the planning and evaluation process
To allow students to reflect on their performance and analyze progress toward goals
To collect authentic evidence of progress to share with parents and IEP members
To individualize and connect assessment evaluation and instruction
To evaluate the effectiveness of curriculum and instructional programs
To compile evidence of progress in particular skills that is tracked from grade to grade
To promote opportunities for dialogue and collaboration among educators
To showcase work products in process as well as final pieces

Products to Include in Reading Portfolios

Projects, surveys, reports, and units from reading
Favorite poems, songs, stories, comments
Literacy extensions—scripts for dramas, visual arts, webs, charts, time lines, and so on
Students' record of books read with summaries and personal reactions
Audio tape of selected reading passages
Reports of individual reading conferences
Teacher's observations
Transcripts of story retelling
Logs of vocabulary words
Responses to pre- and postreading questions
Journal entries

3. How and when will the entries be selected? This depends on whether typical work samples or just exemplary work will be included and on whether the entries should be included on an ongoing basis or at the end of a unit, semester, or school year.
4. How will the portfolio be evaluated? It must be decided whether the work will be evaluated by a letter grade, narrative, rubrics, and so forth.
5. How will the portfolio be passed on? Should it be passed on from grade to grade? A portfolio should be a continuous process of assessment.

Coordinating Portfolio Criteria and Grading Standards

Although the premise of portfolio assessment is based on process rather than product, some school programs require numerical or letter grades for reporting purposes. The following list is an example of a grading system that assigns specific points to evaluation criteria:

Portfolio Grading Criteria	Possible Points
Content accurate	15
Subject knowledge evident	15
Required information included	15
Careful analysis, reflection, and attempts at improvement evident	15
Presentation well organized, sequential, clearly labeled	10
Graphs, illustrations, etc. creative (as required)	10
Vocabulary and word usage appropriate	10
Sentence structure, spelling, and mechanics accurate	<u>10</u>
Total Points Possible	100

The points system can easily be modified to fit specific criteria designated by core standards, curricular expectations, or district grade-level mastery expectations. The correspondence of letter grade to point range should be adjusted according to the school's grading system. An example of a match between portfolio criteria and progress reporting is as follows:

Point Range	Grade
95 to 100	A+
90 to 94	A
85 to 89	B+
80 to 84	B
75 to 79	C+
70 to 74	C
69 or less	F

Resubmitted work may be reevaluated and additional point credit considered. Bonus points may be awarded for doing extra work or for submitting work before the assigned due date.

Critical Thinking and Reflection Activity

Based on one of your class portfolio work samples, develop grading criteria points and a grading system.

A major benefit of the portfolio process is students' participation. When students work with teachers in the decision-making process to reach consensus as to what materials should be included in the portfolio and help to determine the evaluation criteria, they feel empowered and are more committed to mastery.

Informal Reading Inventory

An informal reading inventory (IRI) may be prepared commercially or by the teacher or clinician. An IRI typically consists of graded classroom word lists and reading passages with comprehension questions for each passage (Mercer & Mercer, 2005). Graded word lists are used to determine which passages should be administered, to assess sight vocabulary for isolated words, and to provide information about how students decode unknown words. Graded passages provide information about students' understanding of words in context, attention to meaning, and strategies for coping with unfamiliar words. To ensure that students do not focus solely on fluency at the expense of comprehension the student is expected to summarize the text or answer questions about it (National Reading Panel, 2000). Comprehension questions sample students' understanding at various levels; students can read the passages orally or silently, or the teacher can read the passage to students, depending on the goal of the assessment.

Performance levels—independent, instructional, frustration, and listening—are determined according to the number of words read accurately and the percentage of comprehension questions answered correctly. Most reading inventories use Betts' criteria for evaluating word recognition and comprehension:

Independent Level
- Level at which reading is fluent, understandable, and requires no assistance
- Level chosen for pleasure reading
- Represented by scores that exceed one standard deviation above the mean
- Comprehension rate of 90 percent or higher for oral reading; substantially higher rate for silent reading
- Correct word recognition (in context) rate of 98 percent
- Freedom from tension
- Fluent reading

Instructional Level
- Level at which the material is challenging but neither too difficult nor too easy
- Critical score—the level at which instruction should begin
- Represented by scores that fall within one standard deviation (plus or minus) of the mean
- Comprehension range for oral reading of 70 to 89 percent; substantially higher rate for silent reading

- Correct word recognition range of 90 to 97 percent
- Ability to anticipate meaning with freedom from tension

Frustration Level
- Level at which the material is too difficult to read or understand
- Represented by scores that fall more than one standard deviation below the mean
- Comprehension below 70 percent
- Correct word recognition of less than 90 percent
- Slow, halting reading and signs of tension

Listening Comprehension Level
- Level at which material read to student is understood
- Typically exceeds frustration level (Betts, 1946, pp. 445–452).

How to Construct an Informal Reading Inventory

1. To develop a graded word list, the teacher randomly selects 20 to 25 words from the glossary list for each grade level of the basal reading series.
2. The teacher selects a passage for each grade level, ranging from about 50-word passages at the preprimer level to passages ranging from 150 to 250 words for secondary-level passages.
3. The teacher selects five passages (two below the student's grade level, one at grade level, and two above grade level).
4. The teacher makes two copies of each passage, one for the teacher to record errors as the student reads the passages orally, and one for the student.

How to Administer an Informal Reading Inventory

1. The student begins by reading a list of vocabulary words in isolation that is at least one grade below the student's estimated reading level and continues until the words become too difficult to read. The teacher marks the errors as the student reads from the word list and determines the word recognition independent level.
2. The student begins to read the passages at the highest independent level and continues reading passages at each subsequent grade level until the material becomes too difficult to decode, comprehend, or both.
3. The teacher records the percentage of words read accurately in each passage. To determine the student's independent, instructional, and frustration levels, the teacher divides the number of words read accurately by the number of words in the passage.
4. The teacher constructs five questions for each passage that require the student to recall facts, make inferences, and define vocabulary to determine the student's independent, instructional, and frustration levels. Additional questions may need to be asked when appropriate to probe for the student's level of understanding.
5. The teacher should be alert for signs of frustration.
6. The student reads the passages at the next highest level when the independent or instructional level is determined, or the next lowest level

passage if the student has scored at the frustration level. Once the frustration level has been reached, the testing stops.

7. The student's listening comprehension level is determined by having the student read aloud a passage that is one grade level below the student's present grade placement. This process continues until the student reaches his or her highest instructional level.

8. The teacher can modify this process as needed to assess word attack skills, oral reading performance, and comprehension ability.

Scoring Criteria for Determining Independent, Instructional, and Frustration Levels

- Word identification in isolation (word lists): Number of words correctly identified divided by the total number of words
- Word identification in context (oral reading of passages): Number of words in a passage minus number of miscues divided by total number of words in passage
- Comprehension (questions): Number of questions correctly answered divided by total number of questions
- Reading rate (words per minute): WPM = Number of words in passage divided by number of seconds to read the passage (Leslie & Caldwell, 2001, p. 58).

Commercially Prepared Informal Reading Inventories

There are numerous commercially prepared informal reading inventories. Among the more commonly used are the *Critical Reading Inventory* (Applegate, Quinn, & Applegate, 2004); *Analytical Reading Inventory* (7th ed.) (Woods & Moe, 2003); the *Informal Reading Inventory* (Burns & Roe, 2002); the *Basic Reading Inventory* (8th ed.) (Johns, 2001); the *Standardized Reading Inventory-2* (Newcomer, 1999); the *Classroom Reading Inventory* (9th ed.) (Silvaroli & Wheelock, 2000); the *Stieglitz Informal Reading Inventory: Assessing Reading Behaviors from Emergent to Advanced* (Stieglitz, 2002); and the *Qualitative Reading Inventory-3* (Leslie & Caldwell, 2001).

Published IRIs may focus on reading skills that are different from those emphasized by the reading series or other instructional material currently being used in the classroom. When administering a commercially published IRI, it is important to carefully read the directions for scoring, and interpretation before administration because each inventory has specific criteria and procedures that need to be followed in order to obtain valid and reliable results.

Tips for Teachers

Before using an IRI, carefully read the administration manuals because significant variations in administration of IRIs affect results. Some, for example, require that a passage be read both orally and silently before questioning; others require questioning after oral reading and questioning after a different passage at the same grade level has been read silently.

When the student's instructional reading level obtained on an IRI is, for example, the fourth grade, books at that grade level are typically appropriate for the student's reading instruction. However, this student may not be able to read a fourth-grade social studies textbook. Therefore, when using selections from textbooks for teacher-generated IRI samples, teachers must realize that the readability of texts may vary from subject to subject. The grade levels for content-area texts refer to subject matter, not to reading level, and these texts often require that the student have reading ability above grade level. To select instructional materials and texts that appropriately match the student's reading ability, a readability measure, such as a readability graph, can be used. Computer software is also available to determine the readability of printed material.

Readability Graph

A **readability formula**, or **readability graph** can be used to determine the reading level of students' text, reading material, or trade books. One commonly used readability graph was developed by Fry (1977), and it can be used with reading matter from first grade through college levels, with extended versions for preprimer and primer materials and projecting to the graduate level. (See Figure 7–34.) Once the teacher identifies appropriate material by a readability analysis, the comprehension ability of students can be ascertained by using such techniques as the cloze procedure or an oral reading sample.

Critical Thinking and Reflection Activity

Do you know the reading levels for the newspapers, journals, and textbooks you read daily? Practice checking readability using the Fry readability graph in Figure 7–34.

Curriculum-Based Measurement

Curriculum-based measurement (CBM), a form of the broader curriculum-based assessment model, consists of a specific set of standardized procedures that are used to assess students' achievement in their academic curriculum (Mastropieri & Scruggs, 2004). With the reading CBM, the teacher's purpose is to establish district or classroom performance standards and generally to monitor progress toward individual long-range goals; however, CBMs can also be used to monitor progress toward short-range goals. The following steps are used to construct, administer, and score a reading CBM (Mercer & Mercer, 2005).

How to Construct a Reading CBM/Fluency Measure

1. The teacher can construct a reading CBM from a reading sample used in the grade-level curriculum (e.g., from a basal series, textbook, a trade book, or the literature series). Three passages should be selected: one from the

Figure 7–34   Fry Readability Graph

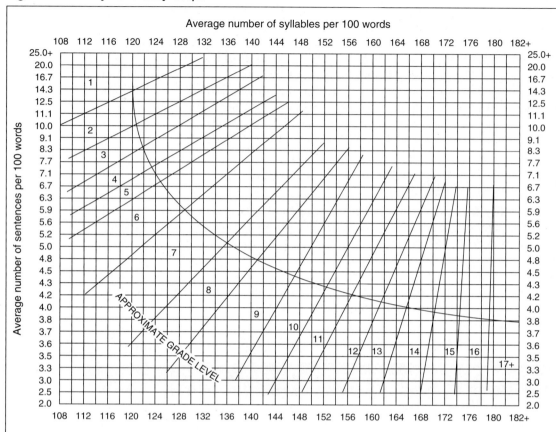

Fry's Readability Formula

1. Randomly select three text samples of exactly 100 words; start at the beginning of a sentence. Count proper nouns, numerals, and initializations as words.
2. Count the number of sentences in each 100-word sample, estimating the length of the last sentence to the nearest one-tenth.
3. Count the total number of syllables in each 100-word sample. Count one syllable for each numeral or initial or symbol; for example, 1990 is one word and four syllables, LD is one word and two syllables, and "&" is one word and one syllable.
4. Average the number of sentences and number of syllables across the three samples.
5. Enter the average sentence length and average number of syllables on the graph. Put a dot where the two lines intersect. The area on which the dot is plotted will give an approximate estimate of readability.
6. If there is a great deal of variability in the syllable or sentence count across the three samples, more samples can be added.

Source: "Fry's Readability Graph: Clarifications, Validity, and Extension to Level 17," "Journal of Reading", 21(3), 247–252, by E. Fry, 1977. Reprinted with permission.

beginning, one from the middle, and one from the end of the book. The passages should be 50 to 100 words for first- through third-grade-level students (150 to 200 words for fourth grade and beyond). The selections should not contain illustrations, have minimal or no dialogue, consist of text and not play or poetry material, not contain unusual or foreign words, and

It is important that students be directed to books that are appropriate for their reading level. A readability graph can be used to determine readability levels.

make sense on their own without a supporting paragraph. The reading material should not have been read previously by the student and is generally the next page to be read in the student's text, novel, etc.

2. The teacher places an asterisk or other identifying mark at the beginning of the designated passage and another mark signaling the end of the passage. When counting words, numeral groups (e.g., 4506) and hyphenated words (mother-in-law) are considered single word units.

3. The teacher makes a copy for the student to read and a copy for the teacher to use for marking the word recognition errors and the responses to the comprehension questions. The teacher develops a set of comprehension questions (5 to 8) for each passage. The questions should cover the following skills: (a) vocabulary meaning, (b) fact and detail, (c) inference, (d) sequence, and (e) main idea.

How to Administer a Reading CBM Fluency Measure

1. To determine oral reading fluency rate as well as accuracy, the teacher uses a stopwatch or a clock with a second hand to record the number of seconds it takes the student to read each 50/100 (150/200) word passage.

Tips for Teachers

Consider using a transparency on your copy of the reading passage so that it can be reused. When typing passages, leave a wide right-hand margin to place corresponding running word counts and to make error notations.

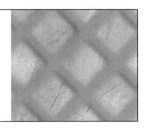

2. The teacher makes a notation when the student starts reading and another notation at the exact second that the 100th (200th) word has been read. The student should be allowed to continue reading to the end of the sentence or paragraph.

3. The teacher tells the student to read the passage, and to try to read every word. While reading, if the student stops or struggles with a word for 3 seconds (3-second rule), the teacher provides the word and the word is marked as incorrect. Errors are recorded by marking a slash (/) through the incorrectly read word.

4. To determine the accuracy rate (the number of words correctly identified), word recognition errors are recorded on the teacher's copy of the reading passage. (See Figure 7–14 for a detailed list of common word recognition errors.) The teacher can write the type of error above the printed word for later analysis of the specific types of errors made, which is used in designing remediation.

5. For an oral reading measure, both the student's reading rate and accuracy rate can be recorded and scored. For a silent reading measure, only a fluency rate score can be obtained.

How to Score a Reading CBM Fluency Measure

1. When the student finishes reading each passage, the teacher records the number of seconds it took the student to read each 100(200) word passage (e.g., 2 minutes, 5 seconds is converted to 125 seconds).

2. To determine accuracy, score as follows:

Counted as errors:	*Counted as correct:*
Substitutions	Self-corrected words within 3 seconds
Mispronunciations	Repetitions within 3 seconds
Omissions	Dialectical speech
Transpositions	Inserted words are ignored
Words read by evaluator after 3 seconds	

3. *Option 1:* To determine the number of correct words read per minute (cwpm), the teacher multiplies the accuracy rate (e.g., 100 words read with 35 word recognition errors equals an accuracy rate of 65 percent) by 60 (the number of seconds in a minute). The teacher then divides this number by the total number of seconds the student took to read each 100-word passage.

$$\frac{\text{Accuracy rate} * 60}{\text{Total number of seconds}} = \text{Correct words per minute (cwpm)}$$

Option 2: The student reads for exactly one minute, at which time the teacher says "stop". The last word read should be marked with a bracket (]).

4. Compute the average number of correct words read per minute for all passages by dividing the total number of correct words read per minute by the number of passages (*Put Reading First*, 2001).

5. *Put Reading First* (2001) has suggested a cwpm rate for fluency standards for grades 1 through 3 as follows:

End of grade 1: 60 cwpm
End of grade 2: 90–110 cwpm
End of grade 3: 114 cwpm

CBM fluency measures need to be administered to students individually. Although these measures are used to monitor and plot individual student progress, comparisons can be made among students to determine how a particular student is functioning in relation to his or her age group or grade-level peers. It is important to compare the test results of average students and not those who are well above or well below the average range (Idol & West, 1993). (Sample reading passages for a CBM, which measures the student's progress toward short-term objectives, are provided in Figures 7–35 and 7–36. A sample form for recording progress on a CBM is shown in Figure 7–37.)

To increase efficiency even more, the teacher can use CBM computer software programs to collect, graph, and analyze student performance data and to evaluate progress toward annual IEP goals and objectives. The *Monitoring Basic Skills Progress MBSP*, 2nd ed. (Fuchs, Hamlett, & Fuchs, 1997) is a software program that allows the student to take a series of fluency measures that are scored by the computer. It automatically displays the number of correct words, results are presented in graph form to demonstrate progress, and the performance results are analyzed to provide suggested teaching strategies, such as to raise the aimline (goal) or change the teaching approach. It also provides feedback to the student and saves the student's scores and responses and graph the scores (Fuchs et al., 1997).

Figure 7–35 Example of Elementary School Reading Passage

Passage

The children hurried to put on their boots, coats and mittens because they knew it was almost time to leave. Their mother called to everyone to jump into the car already crowded with suitcases and presents. Before they left, the family walked to their neighbor's house who would be taking care of their pet, Muffy, while they were away. Muffy barked loudly as they all said goodbye. Now they were off to their grandparents' house. The children knew they had a long trip ahead but they were excited and anxious to see their cousins who would also be there to celebrate grandmother's birthday. There would be cake, and ice cream, gifts, and lots of fun.

Comprehension Questions

(TE) 1. Who were the children going to visit? (their grandparents)
(TE) 2. Whose birthday were they going to celebrate? (grandmother's)
(TI) 3. During what season did the story occur? (winter)
(TI) 4. Would they be staying overnight? How do you know? (yes, they took suitcases)
(SI) 5. Why were the children excited? (they were going to a party; they would see their cousins and grandparents).
(SI) 6. Who was Muffy? Why do you think she did not go with them? (their dog; because it was a long trip; maybe their grandparents didn't like dogs, there was no room in the car for the dog).

Figure 7–36   Sample Secondary School Literature

England in Literature   Grade 10

Passage Macbeth Scene 7

—Outside a banqueting hall in MACBETH's castle. (Played on the Platform.) Hautboys and torches. Enter a SEWER, and divers SERVANTS with dishes and service, and pass over the stage. Then enter MACBETH.

MACBETH. If it were done when 'tis done, then 'twere well
It were done quickly; if the assassination
Could trammel up the consequence, and catch
With his surcease success; that but this blow
Might be the be-all and the end-all here,
But here, upon this bank and shoal of time.
We'ld jump the life to come. But in these cases
We still have judgment here that we but teach
Bloody instructions, which, being taught, return
To plague the inventor; this even-handed justice
Commands the ingredients of our poisoned chalice
To our own lips. He's here in double trust;
First, as I am his kinsman and his subject,
Strong both against the dead; then, as his host
Who should against his murderer shut the door
Not bear the knife myself. Beside, this Duncan
Hath born his faculties so meek, hath been
So clear in his great office, that his virtues
Will plead like angels, trumpet-tongued, against
The deep damnation of his taking off.

Comprehension Questions

(TE) 1. What plan was Macbeth discussing? (The assassination of Duncan)
(TE) 2. What was the setting of this scene? (Macbeth's castle; outside a banquet hall)
(TI) 3. Did Macbeth feel that he should be the one to carry out the assassination? (No, because Macbeth was Duncan's subject)
(TI) 4. What was Duncan's role in the story? (He was the king)
(SI) 5. What was Macbeth plotting? (To have Duncan murdered)
(SI) 6. How did Macbeth feel about having Duncan killed? (He should not be involved in the murder; that someone else should kill Duncan)

Source: Macbeth by William Shakespeare.

Performance-Based Assessment

Performance assessment of reading abilities measures specific skill components and evaluates demonstrations of reading abilities. During performance assessment students read a passage or story for a purpose, use one or more cognitive skills as they construct meaning from the text, and write about or perform a task about what they read, usually in response to a prompt or task (Farr & Tone, 1998). (Figure 7–38 is a list of suggested reading performance activities.) Performance assessment can also be used in program planning and program evaluation. (See Figure 7–39.) Rubrics—such as the sample in Figure 7–40—can be used to rate reading performance assessment activities.

Figure 7–37 CBM Progress-Rating Recording Form

Date of administration					
Passage read/grade level					
Percent of word-recognition errors					
Number of substitution errors					
Number of omission errors					
Number of addition errors					
Other types of word-recognition errors					
Percent of correct answers to comprehension questions					
Explicit comprehension errors					
Implicit comprehension errors					
Critical comprehension errors					
Number of seconds to read passage					
$\dfrac{\% \text{ correct words} \times 60}{\text{time in seconds}}$					
Correct words per minute (cwpm)					

Figure 7–38 Suggested Reading Performance Activities

Write and act out plays	Write dialogue for narrative story
Present original writing	Compare a film to a novel
Perform a production through mime	Follow directions to program a VCR
Play editor after reading articles	Read and critique children's stories
Read and act out a puppet show	Dramatize characters in a story
Do a role-playing production	Illustrate a story

Figure 7–39 Performance Scoring Chart

90–100	exceptional performance	= competency
80–89	mastery level	= competency
70–79	minor types/number of errors	= adequate
60–69	many types/number of errors	= adequate
40–59	fails to complete	= inadequate
20–39	inability to begin task	= inadequate
0–19	no attempt	

Figure 7–40   Reading Rubrics Chart

	Inadequate Ability (1)	Limited Ability (2)	Partial Ability (3)	Adequate Ability (4)	Strong Ability (5)	Superior Ability (6)
Readiness for Reading	• Recognizes no letter of the alphabet • Unfamiliar with "book parts" concept	• Recognizes most of the alphabet • Recognizes some book-part concepts (cover, title)	• Has beginning and ending sounds/ symbol correspondence • Recognizes some high-frequency words	• Tracks left to right and top to bottom on a page with one-to-one correspondence • Reads signs, labels, high-interest words	• Can analyze and identify sounds and words in correct sequence	• Can decode simple words • Uses independent strategies for reading simple text
Readiness for Writing	• Scribbles and pretends to write • Uses letters or letter-like signs to represent writing	• Uses letters to represent words • Writes from left to right • Writes name	• Can write some sight words • Copies words needed for meaningful writing	• Can invent spelling of words using phonetic clues	• Can write one meaningful sentence	• Can compose two or more related sentences
Student Reads Critically	• Gains no meaning from printed page • Cannot recall details	• With teacher guidance, gains some meaning from printed page and recalls some detail	• With teacher guidance, gains meaning from printed page, recalls some details, makes some predictions	• With teacher guidance, makes predictions, draws conclusions	• Draws conclusions independently	• Makes judgments independently
Student Responds to Reading Material	• Student's response shows lack of prior knowledge	• Student's response shows minimal prior knowledge • Can understand common vocabulary	• Teacher can assess prior knowledge • Can understand common vocabulary	• Student identifies facts • Can understand grade-appropriate vocabulary	• Draws some conclusions based on fact • Can understand advanced vocabulary	• Draws conclusions without teacher assistance • Uses rich vocabulary
Student Uses Word Recognition Skills	• Uses erratic recognition of initial consonants	• Uses initial consonants • Uses minimal context clues	• Uses initial and final sounds • Uses some vowels with consonants • Uses some context clues	• Uses medial sounds • Decodes word by word • Uses available context clues	• Decodes with automaticity • Decodes words in any context • Decodes base words and ending	• Uses independent strategies to decode new words

Scoring

Grade	Items	Critical Score (below average)
1	1–2	6/12 or below
2–5	3–5	9/18 or below

Source: Mount Laurel School District, Mt. Laurel, N.J. Reprinted with permission.

SUMMARY POINTS

- Research suggests that when students do not attain basic literacy skills during the primary school grades, they often continue to be poor readers into adulthood. Having difficulty with the reading process not only affects academic achievement, but can also affect the students' self-image, self-confidence, emotional and social adjustment, and employability.

- The five essential components of reading are (1) phonemic awareness, (2) phonics, (3) fluency, (4) vocabulary development, and (5) comprehension strategies.

- The four dimensions of early literacy are oral language, phonemic awareness, print awareness, and knowledge of the alphabet.

- Phonics—also referred to as decoding or word attack—is the ability to identify and blend individual letter sounds into words. Nonsense words, or pseudowords, are used to assess phonemic analysis rather than known sight words, which are recalled by memory.

- The components of vocabulary are word meaning, word recognition, and oral reading. Vocabulary assessment involves assessing the ability to store and retrieve the meaning and pronunciation of words.

- Reading fluency—the ability to read text both accurately and quickly—is necessary to become a competent reader. Assessment focuses on the number of words read and the number of words read correctly within a specific time period.

- Reading comprehension—the ability to understand, retain, recall, and communicate what is read—is the basis of the reading process. The key factors that influence how a student comprehends include memory, prior knowledge, and interest. Working memory is also an important component in comprehension. An important aspect of the assessment process is to determine students' explicit, implicit, and critical comprehension skills.

- The types of reading assessments include portfolio assessments, reading inventories, CBMs, and performance assessments. Portfolio assessment involves the collection and evaluation of students' work. Informal reading inventories, which consist of graded reading passages, help to determine students' independent, instructional, and frustration levels in word recognition and comprehension. Curriculum-based measurements provide a means to frequently measure students' curricular progress and are easily administered, scored, and graphed. Performance assessments provide an opportunity to evaluate reading skill development using authentic tasks. Students are asked to create an answer or product that demonstrates their knowledge or skills.

- Reading disabilities are reported to be the main cause of failure in school. If the specific reading problem is not identified, appropriate remedial techniques are not employed, and continual monitoring is not initiated, these deficient skills will not be ameliorated and long-term effects will likely evolve.

Chapter Check-Ups

1. Identify the components of emergent literacy. Describe why it is important to assess students' competency in each of these skills.

2. What is the difference between phonetic analysis and structural analysis? How would you assess each of these?

3. Identify the skills that need to be assessed when evaluating word meaning vs. oral reading skills. Explain the importance of each of these important aspects of the reading process. What is the instructional level, or percent of accuracy for oral reading? Why is the readability level higher for oral reading than the instructional level for reading comprehension?

4. Explain miscue analysis. Describe the differences between semantic and syntactic errors.

5. Why is reading fluency a critical aspect of the reading process? What is a fluent vs. a non-fluent reader? Describe fluency assessment techniques.

Practical Application Assessment Activities

1. Practice using a readability graph. Gather a variety of available reading materials (e.g., local and regional newspapers, educational journals, popular magazines, novels, textbooks, written directions for assembling). Use the Fry readability graph in the textbook (Figure 7–34) to estimate the reading level of each of these artifacts. Discuss the relevance of the vast range of readability levels of common reading material and share your experiences using the graph.

2. Locate a school that uses a portfolio assessment system. Interview school personnel to determine how the material is collected and used, plus what role, if any, the child plays in the selection and assemblage process. Ask these professionals what they view as the strengths and weaknesses of using portfolios as an assessment system. Share finding with the class and discuss issues, such as, (a) what would be involved in getting a whole school committed to using portfolio assessment, (b) what potential technical problems might surface and how they can be resolved, and (c) what ways accountability or high stakes factor into such a system.

3. Administer the Metacomprehension Strategy Index (see Figure 7–30) to two students, one with below average reading comprehension skills and the other with average reading comprehension skills. Compare and discuss the results.

4. Construct a cloze procedure using a book chapter, a newspaper or journal article. Administer, score and analyze results. Next, construct a maze procedure using the same reading material but a different section of words. Administer the maze to the same student that you administered the cloze procedure, score and analyze the results. Compare and contrast the results of these two procedures, taking note of the different instructional levels.

Connection Between CEC, PRAXIS and INTASC Standards and Chapter 7

Council for Exceptional Children
The voice and vision of special education

The Council for Exceptional Children—Professional Standards

Standard 3 Individual Learning Differences

1. Effects an exceptional condition(s) can have on an individual's life.
2. Impact of learners' academic and social abilities, attitudes, interests, and values on instruction and career development.

Standard 5 Learning Environments and Social Interactions

1. Demands of learning environments.
13. Identify supports needed for integration into various programs placements.

16. Use performance data and information from all stakeholders to make or suggest modifications in learning environments.

Standard 7 Instructional Planning

3. National, state or provincial, and local curricula standards.
6. Identify and prioritize areas of the general curriculum and accommodations for individuals with exceptional learning needs.
7. Develop and implement comprehensive, longitudinal individualized programs in collaboration with team members.
8. Involve the individual and family in setting instructional goals and monitoring progress.
9. Use functional assessments to develop intervention plans.
10. Use task analysis.
11. Sequence, implement, evaluate individualized learning objectives.

Standard 8 Assessment

1. Basic terminology used in assessment.
4. Use and limitations of assessment instruments.
5. National, state/provincial, and local accommodations and modifications.
6. Gather relevant background information.
7. Administer nonbiased formal and informal assessments.
8. Use technology to conduct assessments.
9. Develop or modify individualized assessment strategies.
10. Interpret information from formal and informal assessments.
11. Use assessment information in making eligibility, program, placement decisions for individuals with exceptional learning needs, including those from culturally and/or linguistically diverse backgrounds.
13. Evaluate instruction and monitor progress of individuals with exceptional learning needs.
14. Create and maintain records.

PRAXIS Standards for Special Education   THE PRAXIS SERIES™

Standard 1 Understanding Exceptionalities

1. Theories and principles of human development and learning, including research and theories related to human development; theories of learning; social and emotional development; language development; cognitive development; and physical development, including motor and sensory.
2. Characteristics of students with disabilities, including medical/physical; educational; social; and psychological.
3. Basic concepts in special education, including definitions of all major categories and specific disabilities; causation and prevention of disability; the nature of behaviors, including frequency, duration, intensity, and degrees of severity; and classification of students with disabilities, including classifications as represented in IDEA and labeling of students.

Standard 2 Legal and Societal Issues

1. Federal laws and landmark legal cases related to special education.
2. Issues related to school, family, and/or community, such as teacher advocacy for students and families, including advocating for educational change and developing students' self-advocacy; family participation and support systems; public attitudes toward individuals with disabilities; and cultural and community influences.

Standard 3 Delivery of Services to Students with Disabilities

3. Assessment, including how to modify, construct, or select and conduct non-discriminatory and appropriate informal and formal assessment procedures; how to interpret standardized and specialized assessment results; how to use evaluation result for various purposes, including monitoring instruction and IEP/ITP development; and how to prepare written reports and communicate findings to others.
4. Placement and program issues (including continuum of services; mainstreaming; integration; inclusion; least restrictive environment; non-categorical, categorical, and cross-categorical programs; related services; early intervention; community-based training; transition of students into and within special education placements; postschool transition; and access to assistive technology).
5. Curriculum and instruction, including the IEP/ITP process; instructional development and implementation (for example, instructional activities, curricular materials, resources and equipment, working with classroom personnel, tutoring and the use of technology); teaching strategies and methods (for example, direct instruction, cooperative learning, diagnostic-prescriptive method); instructional format and components (for example, individualized instruction, small- and large-group instruction, modeling, drill and practice); and areas of instruction (such as academics, study and learning skills, social, self-care, and vocational skills).

INTASC Standards for Teacher Education

Standard 7

The teacher plans instruction based upon knowledge of subject matter, students, the community, and curriculum goals.

Standard 8

The teacher understands and uses formal and informal assessment strategies to evaluate and ensure the continuous intellectual, social, and physical development of the learner.

Reading Assessment Chart			
Methods of Assessment	**Purpose**	**Advantages**	**Disadvantages**
Cloze/Maze Procedure	• To assess word prediction skills and the use of context clues • To determine comprehension of text • To determine reading instructional levels	• Clarity of approach • Ease of scoring • Maze procedure is an adaptation for the cloze procedure • Maze procedure provides students who have language problems with word options to choose from • Assesses knowledge of language • Assesses comprehension of text at sentence level • Determines ability to use cues to identify words • Valid and reliable measure of determining reading levels for grade 3 and above	• Cloze procedure generally not valid for students with word retrieval or language processing problems • Does not assess literal comprehension • Not valid or reliable for determining reading levels below grade 3
Criterion-Referenced	• To measure student knowledge on relatively small and discrete units	• Useful for determining what to teach and for developing IEP goals and objectives • Numerous items per area • Describes student performance on specific learning tasks	• Generally limited range of items • Identifies what to teach, not how to teach skill • Measures product (final response) rather than process (determining how response was reached)
Curriculum-Based Assessment (Probes)	• To observe and record students' performance within a time sample to assess acquisition, fluency, and maintenance of specific skills • To provide individualized, direct, and repeated measures of proficiency and progress in the curriculum	• Directly links testing, teaching, and evaluation • Less time-consuming than formal tests • Easy to develop and evaluate progress toward meeting IEP objectives • Used to monitor progress • Allows teachers to measure progress as a regular part of instruction rather than as a separate activity • Informs the teaching and learning process	• Reliability and validity of results depend on method of administration (may lack the precision needed to measure the complexities associated with the reading process) • Measures isolated skills rather than evaluating reading as an interactive process
Error Pattern Analysis	• To identify oral reading mistakes and error patterns • To determine how students are processing what they read	• Identifies response patterns in work samples • Used to design instructional goals, objectives, and programs	• Does not identify random errors or those due to lack of training • Can be analyzed beyond the point of instructional utility • Can be too time-consuming for students with minor problems
Informal Reading Inventory	• To diagnose independent, instructional, and frustration reading levels	• Assesses reading levels and specific strengths and weaknesses in reading strategies, knowledge, and skills	• Accuracy depends on teacher's administration, the student's interest in the topic, and the organization of the passage

Methods of Assessment	Purpose	Advantages	Disadvantages
	• To diagnose word recognition and oral, silent, and listening comprehension		
Interest Inventory	• To ascertain the student's hobbies, talents, extra-curricular and other activities, favorite books and topics	• Provides information about the student's reading preferences, which helps to stimulate reading activities	• Interest level may not correlate with the student's independent or instructional reading level
Metacognitive Strategy Analysis	• To assess the student's ability to identify his or her thinking process • To use and regulate compensatory strategies	• The student learns to self-analyze reading comprehension strategies	• Designed only for middle and upper grades
Miscue Analysis	• To analyze oral reading to determine how errors distort or change the meaning of a passage • Measures syntactic/semantic acceptability, meaning change, graphic and sound similarity, and ability to self-correct	• Good alternative for evaluating mature readers because the focus is more on passage comprehension than on word-for-word accuracy	• Time consuming • Students' dialect will affect the interpretation given to graphic, syntactic, and semantic miscues
Peer Conferencing	• To provide valuable feedback, support, and perspective	• Peers learn along with the student they are helping • Helps maintain enthusiasm for writing • Critique helps writer to understand audience	• Peers may not be skilled in critiquing or be objective
Performance Assessment	• To evaluate the student's ability to create an authentic product that demonstrates knowledge and skills • To assess generalization and application skills using meaningful, relevant learning activities	• Assesses cognitive processing and reasoning skills • Demonstrates ability to plan and solve problems • Allows the student with disabilities to demonstrate skills that are not evident on pencil-paper tests • Puts the student in realistic situations in which he or she demonstrates the ability to integrate knowledge and skills to perform a target activity • Reflects important curriculum targets • Assesses the ability to create a product, collaborate, and use resources and higher-order thinking skills	• Time-consuming to create, observe, and score • Less valid because it tends to yield a smaller work/behavior sample • Not as efficient in assessing facts, definitions, names of people, places • Limited psychometric evidence for making diagnosis and placement decisions • Teachers need to develop technical knowledge in how to develop, administer, score, and use results to guide instruction • Limited ability to assess discrete, basic skills

Methods of Assessment	Purpose	Advantages	Disadvantages
			• Limited usefulness in providing diagnostic data for developing skill-oriented remedial programs
Portfolio Assessment	• To create a continuous and purposeful collection of authentic work products that provide a record of the student's progress evidenced by products completed over time	• Student-centered • Actively involves the student with the learning process • Documents progress over time • Encourages discussion and attention to issues, such as purpose, audience, and contents • Promotes sense of ownership of work • Promotes critical self-reflection and decision making • Illustrates the processes and procedures that student follows • Particularly useful method for assessing the student with various cultural and linguistic differences • Items included can be decided by the student and teacher	• Concerns about inter-rater reliability, stability of performance across time, and establishment of acceptable standards • Training required to design, implement, manage, and assess portfolios • Time-consuming • Requires a significant amount of individualized attention
Running Record	• To diagnose and track word identification errors, noting emergent reading skills	• Used for evaluation of text difficulty • Used for grouping or accelerating children • Used to monitor progress • Used to observe the types of reading errors made	• May be too time-consuming for students with minor problems
Story Retelling-Paraphrasing	• Used to sample reading comprehension; the student may paraphrase or restate exactly what was said	• Can be administered informally so the student is less anxious, therefore a more accurate measure of comprehension can be obtained	• Retelling word-for-word indicates skill in remembering, not understanding • Paraphrasing requires a well-developed vocabulary, which is difficult for students with language impairments in vocabulary or processing
Think-Aloud Procedure	• To assess thinking processes and use of metacognitive strategies	• Useful for assessing how the student constructs meaning, determines what is important, relates information across sentences and paragraphs, and deals with difficulties in making sense of the text	• Student may be uncomfortable or be inexperienced with this procedure and need a model, coaching, and practice before results are useful

CHAPTER
8

Written Language Assessment

KEY TERMS AND CONCEPTS

- ideas and content
- organization
- voice
- word choice
- sentence fluency
- conventions
- presentation
- personal reflection journal
- subject content journal
- writing process
- story starters
- writing probes
- dysgraphia
- phonetic misspellings
- performance spelling
- orthographic memory
- handwriting legibility
- anchors
- benchmarks
- anchor paper scoring method

CHAPTER OBJECTIVES

After reading this chapter, you should be able to:

- Identify the three main components of written language
- Name the six traits of writing and the newest trait
- Explain the skills assessed in the writing process
- Identify components to consider when analyzing a writing sample
- Describe the types of common spelling errors
- Identify the handwriting errors that often result in illegibility
- Explain the anchor paper scoring method

Introduction to Written Language

Written language—the ability to communicate effectively in writing—is the most complex language task, since it requires the linking of language, thought, and motor skills. Because the three components of written language are interwoven, when students have difficulty in one aspect of writing (such as spelling or handwriting), the other aspect—written expression, or the ability to express ideas in a readable manner—is affected, thus limiting their ability to communicate effectively (Lerner, 2003). Inability to write legibly or encode can also affect the way individuals are perceived by others, their level of confidence, and their willingness to attempt writing tasks. Writing requires the simultaneous coordination of several modalities and more synchronization than any other school task. Poor written expression skills can have a negative impact on individuals' ability to cope and succeed, not only in school but also in employment situations (Troia, Graham, & Harris, 1998; Vogel, 1998). Therefore, teachers need to be knowledgeable about the various components that affect students' written language competencies; they also need to develop the assessment skills required to diagnose the specific problem, initiate intervention, and monitor progress.

Written expression is one of the highest forms of communication. It requires complex thought processes because it is based on multiple skills, including talking, listening, reading, penmanship, and spelling. It demonstrates how an individual organizes ideas to convey a message. Students generally do not begin to develop competency in written language until they have had extensive experience in reading, spelling, handwriting, and expressing their thoughts verbally.

Writing is a multidimensional process that is closely related to oral language development. The original six traits of writing are now referred to as the Six Traits + One, with the addition of presentation to the original traits: (1) ideas and content, (2) organization, (3) voice, (4) word choice, (5) sentence fluency, and (6) conventions. Spelling and handwriting are also aspects of the ability to express oneself in written form, broadly included in the convention component. Each of these traits has some interrelationship with the development of comprehensive, intelligible writing.

Ideas and content refer to idea generation, coherence of all parts of the composition to the topic or theme, and awareness of the audience. **Organization** is the internal structure of the writing, its logical sequence; in other words, the structure or the way that words are combined to form phrases, clauses, and sentences. **Voice** refers to the personal style of the author, providing the sense of a real person speaking. **Word choice** refers to the originality or maturity of the vocabulary as well as the variety of words and sentences used in a writing task. **Sentence fluency** refers to the quantity of verbal output, the number of words written in relation to age, and includes sentence length and complexity, and how the writing flows, often with a rhythm or cadence. **Conventions** involve the more technical aspects of writing (such as punctuation, capitalization, abbreviations, and numbers) and the mechanical correctness, including spelling and grammar. The new seventh trait is **presentation**, which refers to the legibility and readability of the final product, such as a handwritten or typed outcome that is spaced adequately using the appropriate font, illustrations, title, paging, and/or bullets.

SECTION 1: WRITTEN LANGUAGE ASSESSMENT PROCEDURES

When evaluating students' written products, teachers should obtain samples from varied sources. Before beginning specific test measures, teachers should assess daily classroom procedures, products, and intrinsic factors that affect students' overall abilities, output, and attitude. It is important to consider students' writing interests; whether the classroom environment is conducive to facilitating, stimulating, and accommodating young writers; and how they perform on daily work products, student journal entries, and self-assessment measures. Observing students while they are writing can provide insights and information that cannot be so clearly ascertained in the testing process.

Interest Inventory

Teachers can learn much from students by asking them about their interests and writing habits and discussing their attitude toward activities involving language. When students have an interest in a particular topic or direct knowledge of and experience in a situation, they tend to be more willing and able to write fluent, descriptive, and readable pieces. An interest inventory can provide information about their favorite stories, hobbies, talents, favorite sports and recreational activities, pets, playthings, and special holidays and vacations. This information can spur story starters, structure cooperative grouping, and direct research topics. Students' interests can be assessed through inventories, questionnaires, and interviews. (See Figure 8–1 and 8–2.)

Figure 8–1   Sample Questions for Student Writing Interest Inventory

- What do you like to write about? _____
- What kind of writing do you do in school? _____
- What kind of writing do you do at home? _____
- What kind of writing would you like to learn to do better? _____
- What is your favorite story? _____
- What is your favorite animal? _____
- Which holiday is your favorite? Why? _____
- What are your favorite toys and special items? _____
- What are your hobbies and special interests? _____
- What kinds of collections do you have? _____
- What do you like to do after school? on weekends? during summer vacation? _____
- What is your favorite holiday? _____
- Name some special places you have visited. _____
- What is your favorite place? _____
- What was the last book you read? _____
- What kinds of stories do you like to read? _____
- What is the name of your favorite book? _____
- Do you write in a journal? _____
- Do you like to write letters to friends? _____
- Do you have a pen pal? If not, would you like to have one? _____

Figure 8–2   Sample Student Interview Questions

- Are you a good storyteller? _____
- Are you a good story writer? _____
- How did you learn to write? _____
- What do you think a good writer does to write well? _____
- What do you like about your writing? _____
- What would you like to improve about your writing? _____
- What do you enjoy talking about? _____
- What do you like to write about? _____
- Would you rather tell a story or write a story? _____
- What kinds of writing do you prefer to do (e.g., stories, letters, reports)? _____
- When asked to write a story, what do you do first? _____
- How do you decide what to write? _____
- How does your teacher decide which pieces of writing are good ones? _____
- Do you revise or edit what you write? If so, can you describe how you do this? _____
- Can you copy from a textbook? _____
- Can you retell a story in your own words? _____
- Are you able to tell what the main idea in a story is? _____
- Can you describe the characters in a story? _____
- Can you figure out the problem and the solution in a story? _____
- Do you understand what words mean when reading assignments? _____
- Are you able to memorize new vocabulary words? _____
- When you are writing and don't know how to spell a word, what do you do? _____
- Which subject has the hardest words to spell: reading, science, social studies, or _____
  mathematics? _____
- Can you break words into parts? _____
- When you have a new spelling word to learn, how do you remember it? _____
- What do you think a good writer needs to write well? _____

Analyzing the Classroom Writing Environment

Environmental factors can significantly affect students' interest, motivation, and perseverance in written performance activities, and the teacher plays a major role in providing an environment that is conducive to learning. The environmental checklist in Figure 8–3 is useful for teachers who do regular self-checks to ensure that they are providing a challenging yet supportive and accommodating environment to promote maximum writing performance.

Work-Sample Analysis

Assessing students' written products is an important aspect of the preliminary evaluation process. Written language is well suited to work-sample analysis because a permanent product is produced (Pierangelo & Giuliani, 1998). Work-sample analysis involves reviewing students' classwork and homework, such as creative writing papers, end-of-the-unit exercises, and informal classroom tests (e.g., weekly spelling tests). It is prudent to analyze work samples from different subject areas (e.g., science and math, as well as language arts) and various types of written assignments (e.g., in-class writing, homework, and note taking). It is also beneficial to compare the student's functioning from earlier in the school year (or the previous year, if possible) with the student's current functioning in order to note progress or regression. Teachers should determine if error patterns are consistent throughout the school day and across the school curriculum. When analyzing work samples from school subjects other than

Figure 8–3   Questions for Assessing the Classroom Writing Environment

In this classroom, does the teacher:
- facilitate and encourage speaking and writing opportunities?
- model and share the students' interest in writing?
- provide an environment that promotes easy interaction, conferencing, and independence?
- allow sufficient time in the daily schedule to promote oral and written communication?
- ensure that time is allotted for sharing ideas and writing drafts?
- assign daily writing that focuses on a variety of purposes and audiences?
- ensure that the classroom environment is conducive to writing (e.g., easy access to materials and supplies for writing)?
- provide a structured writing environment where opinion, creative thought, and sharing of ideas are valued?
- enable all students to make choices about what they write?
- encourage divergent, creative thinking when assigning writing and speaking tasks?
- engage students in a wide variety of writing activities (e.g., topics, styles, audience)?
- encourage students to use writing and dialoguing as a natural response to reading?
- promote and teach the stages of the writing process (prewriting, drafting, sharing, revising, editing, publishing)?
- conference on a regular basis with students about their writing?
- respond to written and oral presentations with positive, constructive comments?
- promote peer conferencing and self-assessment for the revision and editing process?
- display and publish students' writing?
- collect portfolio entries that are authentic and selected with students' input?
- use assessment information from writing samples to guide instructional decisions?
- record students' responses and participation during writing activities?
- share information about the class speaking and writing activities with parents or guardians?
- encourage parents to read and discuss literature with their children?
- celebrate literacy and learning on a daily basis?

written language, it is important to keep in mind the specific requirements and specifications common to that particular subject area. A science report may require technical vocabulary, abbreviations, formulas, and numbers. Social studies papers generally require a standard structure, specific vocabulary, and the use of cause and effect, persuasion, and opinion. An arithmetic paper typically requires precise, organized alignment of numbers, as well as clear vocabulary and statements to explain results (Choate, Enright, Miller, Poteet, & Rakes, 1995). (Focus questions to use as a guide when evaluating students' written products are provided in Figure 8–4.)

Student Writing Journals

Keeping a notebook or journal allows students to record their work as well as their attitudes and feelings about their writing and the writing of others. A journal can contain sample pieces that students have written as well as spontaneous types of entries. Journals are useful for monitoring daily progress, for providing rehearsal opportunities to practice new skills, for providing regular supportive and corrective feedback, for program planning, and for program evaluation. There are two types of journals: personal reflection journals and subject content journals. In **personal reflection journals**, students reflect on events and experiences in their lives. In **subject content journals**, they keep notes on the most important things they learned from a subject content area.

Figure 8–4   Work Sample Analysis Questionnaire

- Does the student write in manuscript or cursive form consistently? _____
- Is the handwriting legible? _____
- Is there evidence of handwriting problems with letter and number formation or spacing? _____
- Is the print properly aligned within line boundaries? _____
- Are the letters and numbers proportionate to each other? _____
- Is the letter or number slant appropriate? _____
- Is line quality precise, consistent? _____
- Is there evidence of excessive erasures? _____
- Does student write in left-to-right progression? _____
- Are any letters or numbers reversed, transposed, or inverted? _____
- Can the student spell phonetically regular words? _____
- Can the student spell phonetically irregular words? _____
- Does the student substitute, omit, or add sounds in words? _____
- Does the student confuse common synonyms (*house* for *home*) _____
- Does the student confuse common homonyms (*blue* for *blew*)? _____
- Does the student confuse vowel sounds (*sit* for *sat*)? _____

Tips for Teachers:

Journal writing samples can include

- Monologues
- Personal essays
- Teacher or peer dialogue
- Short stories
- Vignettes
- Ideas for future writing projects
- Interdisciplinary writing
- Plays
- Anecdotes

Student Self- and Peer Assessment

Self-assessment allows students to analyze their own writing and reflect on their own learning. Checklists that students and their peers can use to proofread their work products are provided in Figures 8-5 to 8-7 for the primary and intermediate levels.

Observation of Writing Tasks

Handwriting and spelling problems may manifest several ways, therefore observation is important in the assessment process. The teacher needs to determine whether the young child has acquired the preliminary or prerequisite skills to begin the **writing process**. (Figure 8-8 is a checklist for observing writing habits.)

Figure 8–5 Self-Assessment Checklist for Written Products—Primary Level

	Yes	Some-times	No
• I check my posture when I write.	____	____	____
• I hold my pencil appropriately.	____	____	____
• I write lowercase letters correctly.	____	____	____
• I write uppercase letters correctly.	____	____	____
• I write numbers correctly.	____	____	____
• I try to write neatly.	____	____	____
• My letters and numbers are consistent in size.	____	____	____
• I cross and dot letters properly.	____	____	____
• I leave the right amount of space between letters and words.	____	____	____
• I write letters and numbers that touch the lines correctly.	____	____	____
• I use my sounds to write.	____	____	____
• I use spelling rules when writing words.	____	____	____
• I plan before beginning to write.	____	____	____
• I use titles to tell my main idea.	____	____	____
• My writing has a beginning, middle, and end.	____	____	____
• I use different types of writing (personal stories, letters, reports).	____	____	____
• I use many descriptive words in my writing.	____	____	____
• I use capital letters for names, addresses, and dates.	____	____	____
• I use capital letters to begin sentences.	____	____	____
• I use periods (.) correctly.	____	____	____
• I use question marks (?) correctly.	____	____	____
• I use exclamation marks (!) correctly.	____	____	____
• I use quotation marks (" ") in my writing.	____	____	____
• I share my writing with others.	____	____	____
• I read and reread my work before handing it in.	____	____	____
• I correct my work before handing it in.	____	____	____

Figure 8–6 Student Editing Checklist

Have I checked and corrected for	Checked	Corrected	Need Help
• Capital letters	____	____	____
• Periods	____	____	____
• Commas	____	____	____
• Question marks	____	____	____
• Exclamation points	____	____	____
• Quotation marks	____	____	____
• Sentence fragments	____	____	____
• Run-on sentences	____	____	____
• Subject-verb agreement	____	____	____
• Pronoun agreement	____	____	____

Figure 8–6 *(Continued)*

	Checked	Corrected	Need Help
• Correct pronoun form	———	———	———
• Noun plurals	———	———	———
• Noun possessives	———	———	———
• Verb tense	———	———	———
• Irregular verbs	———	———	———
• Comparison of adjectives and adverbs	———	———	———
• Use of double negatives	———	———	———
• Paragraphing	———	———	———
• Hyphens	———	———	———
• Spelling	———	———	———
• Word usage	———	———	———

Figure 8–7 Peer and Self-Assessment Checklist

	Self-Evaluation		Peer Evaluation		
	Yes	No	Yes	No	Teacher's Comments
Content					
1. Is each word group a sentence?					
2. Is each sentence worded clearly?					
3. Are descriptive words used?					
4. Is the main idea clear?					
5. Are more sentences needed to tell about the main idea?					
Organization					
1. Does the composition have a clear beginning, middle, and end?					
2. Are the ideas grouped into paragraphs?					
3. Are the sentences in a paragraph put in logical order?					
Mechanics					
1. Are capital letters used correctly?					
2. Are punctuation marks used correctly?					
3. Are words spelled correctly?					
4. Are tenses (present, past, or future) used appropriately throughout the composition?					
5. Is the handwriting neat and readable?					
6. Can this composition be improved? If so, how?					

Teacher: _____

Student: _____

Peer: _____

Figure 8–8 Checklist for Observing Writing Habits

As the student writes, teachers should consider the following:

- What hand is used for writing, cutting, pasting, and so forth? _____
- Does the student consistently use the same hand for handwriting activities? _____
- How does the student hold the pencil? _____
- Does the student switch hands while writing? _____
- Does the student hold the pencil in the triangle formed by the thumb and the first two fingers, with the thumb resting lightly on its outer edge? _____
- Is the student's pencil grip moderate, not too tight or too loose? _____
- Is the right- (left-) handed student's pencil grasp about 1 inch above the writing point, with the pencil end pointed toward the right (left) shoulder? _____
- Are the student's desk and chair the appropriate size? _____
- Does the student sit correctly when writing, with the lower back touching the back chair? _____
- Is the student's head too close or too far away from the paper? _____
- Do both of the student's feet rest flat on the floor? _____
- Is the student's desk height slightly above the elbows; do both forearms rest on top? _____
- Is the student's paper positioned properly on the writing surface? _____
- Does the student slightly slant the paper when writing? _____
- Does the student rotate paper or book or both? _____
- Does the student hold the paper steady with the nonwriting hand? _____
- Is the student writing from left to right? _____
- Is the student's work organized well, demonstrating planning? _____
- Does the student have difficulty copying from text to paper? _____
- Does the student have difficulty copying from the chalkboard to paper? _____
- Does the student have difficulty organizing writing neatly on paper? _____
- Does the student stay within line boundaries? _____
- Does the student consistently use manuscript form? _____
- Does the student consistently use cursive form? _____
- Is the written product written legibly? _____
- Does the student recognize errors and correct them? _____
- Does the student frequently erase, scribble out, or tear the written product? _____
- Does the student show signs of fatigue, frustration, or nervousness when writing? _____
- Is the student negative about writing and appear bored or distracted? _____
- Does the student require monitoring or encouragement to drawing and writing to tasks? _____
- Does the student take excessive time to complete drawing and writing tasks? _____
- Does the student work too quickly, resulting in poor quality? _____
- Does the student show signs of fatigue when drawing or writing? _____

Through observation and direct assessment, the teacher can determine whether mastery has been attained in the basic skill areas. Because different tasks make different demands on the writer, observations should be made when the student is (a) copying from books, (b) copying from written material on the chalkboard, (c) composing a written piece, and for older students, (d) taking notes. Areas of focus should include posture, handedness, grip of the writing instrument, and the quality and speed of writing.

SECTION 2: WRITTEN EXPRESSION ASSESSMENT

When assessing students' written expression, teachers should emphasize that while students are to do their best, they should not be overly concerned with handwriting or spelling. Because the goal is to determine how the student writes independently, the teacher should not help them with spelling, mechanics, and so forth. Written expression assessment should focus on the components of writing: content, organization, structure, word choice, usage, and mechanics.

Assessing the Writing Process

Teachers who plan to teach written language in the schools need to understand the developmental writing process: the preplanning before beginning to write, writing drafts, revising and editing written work, proofreading, and sharing the final product. (See Figure 8–9.) They must also be able to analyze written work samples. (See Figure 8–10.) Finally, they must know how to develop specific instructional plans to help students succeed in writing. To construct instructional programs that increase writing competence and determine appropriate interventions, it is critical to identify and prioritize the areas of need, identify strengths, and determine students' present performance levels. (Figure 8–11 provides a helpful tool for monitoring writing progress.)

Written Expression Error Analysis

Error analysis focuses on identifying response patterns in students' work samples. To analyze performance, teachers can select from various writing samples, including journal writing, essays, in-class and homework assignments, and spelling tests. After collecting

Figure 8–9   Assessing Steps in the Writing Process

Step 1—Prewriting, Planning

Can the student generate or select a topic and brainstorm ideas? Can the writer select a purpose, audience, and suitable topic? Can the writer use various strategies to explore ideas and plan for writing (e.g., brainstorming, clustering, note taking, webbing, researching, using graphic organizers)?

Step 2—Writing, Drafting

Can the student complete the first draft without focusing on mechanics or spelling? Is the writer's prewriting, planning, and organization transformed into complete sentences and paragraphs in this rough-draft stage (without extensively focusing on errors at this point in the process)?

Step 3—Revising, Editing

Can the student read the draft aloud to a peer who suggests clarification or expansion? Can the writer review the work for possible changes and revisions? Is the focus on the content of the piece, clarifying that the purpose of the writing is met and the intended meaning is conveyed? Are peer sharing and conferencing included as part of this step?

Step 4—Proofreading

Can the student reread the draft and revise and edit based on suggestions for change? Can the writer revise the draft by inspecting it for mechanical errors, attending to the English conventions that are consistent with the developmental level?

Step 5—Publishing, Sharing

Can the student publish and distribute the final draft? Does the writer share the work via oral presentation, a written publication (e.g., illustrating, typing, and binding the narrative story or expository notes), or reading it to a peer or a younger class?

Figure 8–10   Guide to Writing Process Assessment

Writing Content

Does the student

- choose a topic?
- use beginning, middle, and ending sentences and paragraphs?
- use topic sentences?
- develop a good conclusion?
- write in complete sentences?
- write about personal experiences and observations?
- use age- and grade-appropriate vocabulary levels when writing?
- use sufficient detail and description?
- use a range of sentence types (declarative, interrogatory, exclamatory)?
- try different types of writing?
- write in an organized, appropriately sequenced manner?
- use technical supports (e.g., encyclopedia, dictionary, thesaurus)?

Writing Mechanics

Does the student

- form uppercase and lowercase letters and numerals legibly?
- trace full name? copy name? write name without model?
- write in appropriate uppercase and lowercase letters?
- rely on pictures to convey meaning? use pictures to support print?
- label personal illustrations?
- use capitalization at age- and grade-appropriate levels?
- use punctuation at age- and grade-appropriate levels?
- space letters and words adequately?
- use invented spelling?
- use age- and grade-appropriate spelling strategies?

Writing Process

Does the student

- brainstorm, discuss ideas before beginning to write?
- develop semantic webs, charts, or graphs before writing?
- determine the purpose and audience before writing?
- discuss ideas with peers? teachers?
- take and give suggestions for improvement?
- carefully make revisions to work?
- produce a legible final product with minimal errors?
- share the final product with others via oral reading or publishing the work?

several samples of students' written products, the teacher counts the number of words used appropriately, the number of words spelled correctly, the number of sentences, the types of sentences (simple, compound, complex), the length of sentences, and so forth. Error analysis—a systematic approach for determining mistakes in written products—can be used by both the teacher and the student. This analysis has three purposes: (1) to identify the types and patterns of errors; (2) to establish the cause of the errors; and (3) to provide appropriate instruction to ameliorate the error pattern (Cohen & Spenciner, 1998). A checklist can be developed by the teacher alone or in collaboration with the student to identify isolated errors and error patterns, track progress in correcting the errors, and assist in preparing appropriate instruction.

How to Do an Error Analysis

1. The student writes a sample passage.
2. The teacher analyzes and records the pattern of errors to determine how often each type of error is made and to identify the most frequently made errors.

Figure 8–11   Written Language Proofreading Checklist

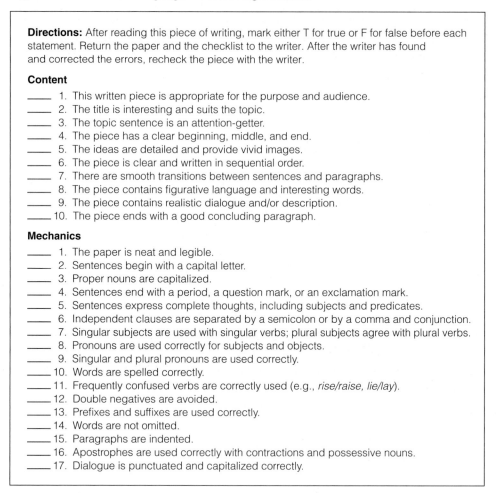

Directions: After reading this piece of writing, mark either T for true or F for false before each statement. Return the paper and the checklist to the writer. After the writer has found and corrected the errors, recheck the piece with the writer.

Content

_____ 1. This written piece is appropriate for the purpose and audience.
_____ 2. The title is interesting and suits the topic.
_____ 3. The topic sentence is an attention-getter.
_____ 4. The piece has a clear beginning, middle, and end.
_____ 5. The ideas are detailed and provide vivid images.
_____ 6. The piece is clear and written in sequential order.
_____ 7. There are smooth transitions between sentences and paragraphs.
_____ 8. The piece contains figurative language and interesting words.
_____ 9. The piece contains realistic dialogue and/or description.
_____ 10. The piece ends with a good concluding paragraph.

Mechanics

_____ 1. The paper is neat and legible.
_____ 2. Sentences begin with a capital letter.
_____ 3. Proper nouns are capitalized.
_____ 4. Sentences end with a period, a question mark, or an exclamation mark.
_____ 5. Sentences express complete thoughts, including subjects and predicates.
_____ 6. Independent clauses are separated by a semicolon or by a comma and conjunction.
_____ 7. Singular subjects are used with singular verbs; plural subjects agree with plural verbs.
_____ 8. Pronouns are used correctly for subjects and objects.
_____ 9. Singular and plural pronouns are used correctly.
_____ 10. Words are spelled correctly.
_____ 11. Frequently confused verbs are correctly used (e.g., _rise/raise, lie/lay_).
_____ 12. Double negatives are avoided.
_____ 13. Prefixes and suffixes are used correctly.
_____ 14. Words are not omitted.
_____ 15. Paragraphs are indented.
_____ 16. Apostrophes are used correctly with contractions and possessive nouns.
_____ 17. Dialogue is punctuated and capitalized correctly.

3. The same error should not be counted more than once (e.g., if the student misspells a word or omits a comma several times, this should be noted but counted as only one error).

Portfolio Assessment of Written Expression

Portfolio assessment involves the systematic collection of students' work to document their learning experiences and achievements. Portfolios can benefit students, teachers, and parents. Students can use portfolios to focus on how they have grown as writers. By becoming participants in the assessment process, they learn to set goals and evaluate learning in progress, where their strengths lie, and the areas where they need improvement. Teachers can use portfolios to assess students' growth over a period of time so that they can plan remedial assistance, if necessary. Portfolio assessment also helps them to understand how students develop as writers and provides them with information that encourages sensitive and relevant instructional modifications. Parents can benefit from viewing their children's portfolios because they can

The Grading Connection

Connecting Skills to Points to Grades		Accumulated Points				
1. Prewriting	6	12	18	24	30
2. Writing, Drafting	5	10	15	20	25
3. Revising, Editing	4	8	12	16	20
4. Proofreading	3	6	9	12	15
5. Publishing, Sharing	2	4	6	8	10
Total Scores	**20**	**40**	**60**	**80**	**100**

Conversion Table

95–100	=	A	57–62	=	C
90–94	=	A–	50–56	=	C–
83–89	=	B+	43–49	=	D+
77–82	=	B	37–42	=	D
70–76	=	B–	30–36	=	D–
63–69	=	C+	below 30	=	F

see growth in their writing skills and areas that need improvement in a more meaningful manner than is provided by standard letter or number grades.

Teachers often provide students with suggestions for authentic writing activities that can be included in their portfolios. (See Figure 8–12.) Many types of writing assignments can be used effectively for portfolio assessment, including the following (Meyen, Vergason, & Whelan, 1996):

- Selected prewriting activities
- Scrapbook of representative writing samples
- Illustrations or diagrams for a written piece
- Log or journal of writing ideas, vocabulary, semantic maps, and compositions
- Conference notes and observation narratives
- Student-selected best performance
- Self-evaluation checklists and teacher checklists

Written Expression Curriculum-Based Measurement

Written language ability can be assessed through repeated three-minute writing samples using stimulus **story starters** or topic sentences. Timed writing samples (probes) are general assessments of writing skills rather than diagnostic assessments of specific writing deficits. This type of evaluation allows the teacher to base instructional decisions on direct, repeated measurement.

Writing probes can also be useful in identifying serious language problems followed by more in-depth evaluation, if needed. The administration of a writing probe begins with the teacher reading a story starter to the student. (Figure 8–13 is a sample writing prompt. Ideally the prompt is developed by the teacher based on the student's individual interests. The student has one minute to plan and three minutes to write the story. The number of words written correctly or the number of correct word sequences (cws) can be used as the criterion for monitoring progress. (Figure 8–14 is an example of a three-minute timed writing sample based on a writing prompt that measures basic capitalization skills.) The following procedures are used to administer

Figure 8–12   Writing Motivators

Ask students to create and write:

Advertisements	Crossword puzzles	Invitations	Pamphlets
Advice columns	Definitions	Itineraries	Parenting tips
Almanacs	Descriptions	Jeopardy questions	Passports
Analogies	Diagrams	Job applications	Persuasive articles
Announcements	Diaries	Jokes	Picture captions
Applications	Dictionaries	Jump-rope journals	Plays
Apologies	Directions	Labels	Pledges
Autobiographies	Editorials	Laws	Poems
Awards	Epitaphs	Letters	Postcards
Beauty suggestions	Essays	Lists	Posters
Bibliographies	Eyewitness accounts	Lyrics	Proposals
Billboards	Expense reports	Magazines	Proverbs
Biographies	Fables	Mail order catalogs	Puns
Birth certificates	Fairy tales	Maps	Puppet shows
Book jackets	Fictional stories	Meeting minutes	Purchase receipts
Book reviews	Fortune-cookie messages	Memoirs	Puzzles
Books	Games	Metaphors	Questionnaires
Bulletins	Ghost stories	Menus	Quizzes
Bumper stickers	Gossip columns	Monologues	Quotations
Buyer's guides	Graduation announcements	Movie reviews	Rebuttals
Calendars	Greeting cards	Mysteries	Recipes
Catalogs	Grocery lists	Myths	Recommendations
Chain letters	Headlines	Narratives	Recreational ideas
Character sketches	Histories	Newscasts	Regulations
Charts	Horoscopes	Newspapers	Remedies
Checklists	How-to-articles	News releases	Resumes
Comic strips	Idioms	Notices	Reviews
Commercials	Indexes	Nursery rhymes	Riddles
Community newsletters	Inquiries	Obituaries	Rules
Conversations	Interviews	Opinions	Safety tips

and score curriculum-based measurement (CBM) written expression measures, determine long-range goals, and graph data.

How to Administer a CBM Writing Probe

1. To establish a baseline (present level of performance), the teacher provides each student with a lined sheet of paper and the same story starter or topic sentence on any three days of the week.
2. For one minute, the students brainstorm ideas to base their writing.

Figure 8–13   Sample CBM Writing Prompt

Today, a playful kangaroo hopped into our classroom and . . .

_____

_____

_____

Figure 8–14 Sample Written Expression Probe

Directions: Circle the words that should *not* be capitalized, and draw a line under the words that *should be* capitalized.

It was drew's birthday - august 12, 2001. it was sunday, and there was no School. drew and his sister julie went to the Store to buy items for the party. they bought candy, ice cream, chocolate layer cake with fluffy vanilla icing, soda, chips, and pretzels. on the way back home, They decided to walk to fifty-second street and stopped at mrs. smith's craft Store to buy balloons and ribbons to decorate the playroom, kitchen and porch.

Directions: Put in all of the commas, periods, and apostrophes that should be in the story.

It was Drew's birthday August 12 2001 it was Sunday and there was no school Drew and his sister, Julie, went to the store to buy items for the party They bought candy ice cream chocolate layer cake with fluffy vanilla icing soda chips and pretzels On the way back home they decided to walk to Fifty second Street and stopped at Mrs Smiths craft store to buy balloons and ribbons to decorate the playroom kitchen and porch

---

3. Next, the teacher tells the students to write for three minutes. If a student stops before the three minutes are up, the teacher strongly encourages him or her to continue writing.

4. At the end of the three minutes, the teacher tells the students to stop writing and immediately collects their papers.

Options for Scoring the CBM Writing Probe

CBM writing probe samples can be scored several ways. Option 1 is to count the number of words written and Option 2 is to count the number of letters written the focus is to score fluency but not accuracy.

1. Count the number of words written—whether correct or incorrect—and only include the story starter if it is repeated.

2. To get correct words per minute, the total number of words from step 1 is divided by 3.

3. If the student stopped writing before the three minutes were up, count the number of words written, divide by the number of seconds it took to write them, and multiply by 60 to get the total number of correct words per minute (wpm).

4. The following cutoff levels correlate with instructional grade levels (Alper & Mills, 2001):

Grade		WPM		Grade		WPM
1	=	15		4	=	41
2	=	28		5	=	49
3	=	37		6	=	53

Option 3 involves counting only the words spelled correctly. Words are counted separately, not within the context of a sentence. Each word is considered in isolation and if it represents a correctly spelled word in English, it is included in the tally.

Option 4 involves counting the number of words written in correct sequence. This option considers units in writing and their relation to one another, and scores for the correct word sequence (cws) as follows.

Figure 8–15   Example of Correct Word Sequence Scoring

Example:	^The^playful,^ fluffy^ pup^ is^ happy^ to^ see^ his^ master.^	= 11
	the plaful, flufie pup^ is hapy to^ see^ his master v v v v v v v v	= 3

Grade	Mean for Total Number of Words Read in 3 Minutes	Mean Number of CWS
3	26	27
4	48	41
5	50	48
6	54	59

(Tindal & Marston, 1990)

How to Score a CBM Writing CWS Probe

1. Count the number of correct word sequences (i.e., two adjacent, correctly spelled words that are grammatically acceptable within the context of the phrase).
   a. Words in the story starter or topic sentence are not counted. Misspellings, punctuation, content, and organization are disregarded.
   b. Words beginning and words ending a sentence correctly are credited with one correct word sequence. (When punctuation or capitalization are missing or wrong, however, it is not correct.)
   c. An inverted caret (v) is inserted for incorrect sequences (invert before and after misspelled words).
   d. Carets are inserted at the beginning and at the end of sentences (noting capitalization, punctuation, and spelling).
   e. The number of cws is divided by the total number of sequences to get the proportion of cws. (See Figure 8-15 for an example of CWS Scoring and grade norms.)
2. Continue this procedure for two more days, giving two new story starters or topic sentences during the week. (See Figure 8–16 for a chart of the expected number of words on a writing sample per grade.)

Figure 8–16   Writing Fluency Grade Norms

Unlimited Time			3-Minute Limit		
Grade		Words	Grade		Words
1	=	15	1	=	15
2	=	30	2	=	28
3	=	50	3	=	37
4	=	70	4	=	41
5	=	110	5	=	49
6	=	115	6	=	53
(Choate, Enright, Miller, Poteet, & Rakes, 1995)			(Deno, Fuchs, Wesson, Tindal, Marston, & Kuehnle, 1981)		

3. Find the median score from the three baseline scores (i.e., the middle number when ranked from lowest to highest).

4. To compute the long-range goal, count the number of weeks left in the school year or semester; multiply the number of weeks by 2.0 (rate of growth); and add the median score obtained from the baseline week (e.g., 21 weeks × 2.0 = 42; 42 + 14 [baseline median] = 56 [goal]).

5. Next, plot the goal data point on the graph on the line for the last week, and draw the aimline connecting the baseline median data point to the goal data point. This line represents the students' projected performance for the school year.

6. Beginning with the first week after the baseline, measure the students' performance two times each week. On two different days in a given week, the students are given a different story starter or topic sentence. Following a brief discussion of the story starter or topic, tell the students to begin writing for three minutes.

7. At the end of three minutes, students are told to stop writing. To score, count the number of words or letter sequences representing words written after the given story starter or topic sentence.

8. Next, plot each score on the graph in the space corresponding with the day and week, and then connect the data points.

9. Continue this procedure throughout the year, analyzing student error patterns.

The purpose of the scoring chart is to provide information for planning instructional lessons and for making decisions regarding teaching strategies. Graphs also can be made to monitor progress in specific skills, such as capitalization, punctuation, and subject-verb agreement. Figure 8–17 provides a sample graph of a student's progress on a CBM indicating baseline level, aimline toward anticipated level of achievement,

Figure 8–17 Graph of a Written Expression CBM

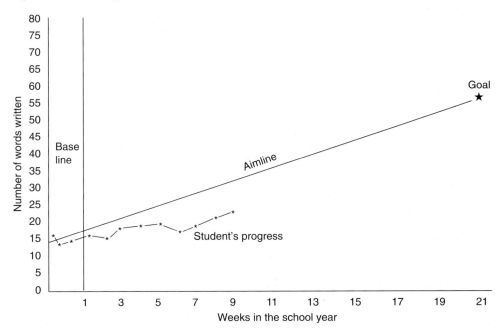

Tips for Teachers

Use the following general guidelines to create norms for your own class.
    Expected growth:
    12 total words per year
    10 cws per year

(Crawford, 2000; Howell & Nolet, 2000)

and progress toward meeting individualized education plan (IEP) goals (Mercer & Mercer, 2005).

Performance-Based Assessment

Performance assessment of writing abilities measures specific skill components and evaluates demonstrations of writing abilities. Having students demonstrate their developmental level—their degree of competency in specific tasks that are authentic or meaningful to their life experiences—helps the teacher assess students' skill proficiency, develop meaningful instructional tasks and remedial interventions, and monitor progress.

Evaluation and instruction can be closely integrated when the teacher uses performance assessment. Activities can be individualized, geared toward specific instructional levels, and modified to accommodate individual strengths and weaknesses. The teaching-testing-(re)teaching cycle flows smoothly, test anxiety can be eliminated, and students see a direct connection between what, why, how, and how much they are learning when performance assessment is used. When developing performance assessment activities for the classroom, the teacher must (1) clarify what performance will be evaluated, (2) prepare performance activities, and (3) devise a system for scoring and recording the assessment results (Stiggins, 1997). (Figure 8–18 suggests writing activities that incorporate basic writing skills for assessment and for devising practical instruction-remedial procedures.)

Diagnostic Inventory

A comprehensive inventory assesses the students' written language skills in specific areas. Figure 8–19 is the language section of the Basic School Skills Inventory used to identify students who may need special services; it can also be used to monitor progress.

SECTION 3: SPELLING ASSESSMENT

Four factors are involved in evaluating spelling. First, teachers must be knowledgeable about typical language development, language disabilities, and how disabilities can affect the development of written language. Second, they must evaluate spelling on the basis of authentic writing experiences rather than on tests of words in isolation. Third, they must evaluate spelling analytically rather than as correct or incorrect. Finally, teachers must analyze spelling by discovering the strategies that were used in

Figure 8—18 Examples of Performance Assessment Activities

Writing friendly letters, business letters, thank-you letters, inquiry letters, letters to the editor	Requires using salutations and closings; addressing an envelope with the correct postal abbreviations; and capitalization of titles and places; and punctuating, indenting, writing legibility, spelling, and so forth
Writing a story of a field trip, a family party, a special school event, a news happening, an article for the school paper	Requires using the writing process: preplanning, writing, revising, rewriting, editing, publishing; using indentation, topic and closing sentences, main idea, sequencing, summarizing, and so forth
Writing poems, a school play, a speech, a puppet show	Requires using direct quotes and punctuation: underlining titles, using exclamation points and colons, and capitalizing titles, the first line of verses, first word in a direct quote, and so forth
Writing descriptions, lists of items, recipes, directions, party invitation	Requires writing numbers, using tense and plurals, sequential organization, punctuation (e.g., using semicolons and commas for lists) and capitalizing proper nouns (e.g., holidays and street names)
Writing a resume, completing a job application, writing an advertisement	Requires knowing how to read and fill in a form, make an outline, write abbreviations, when to use hyphens and contractions, and so forth

Figure 8—19 Basic School Skills Inventory-Diagnostic Writing Skills

1. *Writes from left to right.* Ask the child to write something for you on a piece of paper. Letters or words may be illegible, poorly formed, misspelled, or otherwise inadequate and still be given full credit if, in the execution of his or her written efforts, the child consistently proceeds from left to right.

2. *Writes first name without a model.* The letters do not have to be properly formed nor does spelling have to be exactly correct. The result must, however, be clearly recognizable as being the child's actual name.

3. *Copies a short word from written example.* Place a card containing a common short word (about three or four letters) on the child's desk and instruct the child to copy the word on to another piece of paper. To receive full credit, the child must produce recognizable letters in the proper order.

4. *Copies a short word from the chalkboard.* Write a common short word (about three or four letters) on the chalkboard. The size and style of the print should be what you typically use. The child should sit in his or her usual location in the classroom to copy the word. To receive full credit, the child must produce recognizable letters in the proper order.

5. *Writes single letters when asked (e.g., b, h, m, t, a, e).* Ask the child to write each of the following letters as you say them: b, h, m, t, a, e. All of the letters do not have to be perfectly formed and either lowercase or capital letters may be written, but all six letters must be clearly legible for the child to receive full credit.

6. *Writes last name without a model.* To receive credit for this item, the child should make a solid attempt at writing his or her last name. The name may be misspelled, and some of the letters may be reversed or poorly formed. The child receives full credit for producing a clearly recognizable version of his or her last name.

Figure 8–19 **(Continued)**

7. *Stays on the line when writing.* Ask the child to write something for you on a piece of lined paper. In scoring the item, focus attention on the child's skill at organizing and spacing the letters squarely on the line. Full credit may be awarded regardless of the legibility or quality of the letters themselves.

8. *Copies sentences from the chalkboard to paper.* Write the following sentence, using the size and type of print you typically use, on the chalkboard: *The dog is brown.* The child must copy the sentence as it appears on the board. Spelling, capitalization, punctuation, and word order must be correct. The child should receive full credit even though the letters may be poorly formed and spaced, as long as the sentence has been properly copied otherwise.

9. *Writes short words dictated by the teacher.* Select three simple words (about three or four letters) that are definitely in the child's vocabulary. Ask the child to write each word after it is dictated. You may repeat words or use the words in context if necessary. To receive full credit for the item, the child must produce a clearly recognizable version of each of the three words. However, the words do not have to be correctly spelled, nor do the letters have to be perfectly formed or spaced.

10. *Writes sentence dictated by the teacher.* Create a simple sentence containing no more than four words that are in the child's vocabulary. Ask the child to write the sentence after you say it in a natural, coversational manner. Do not pause between words to enable the child to write each word after it is presented. You may repeat the sentence once if the child does not appear to understand or remember it. To receive full credit, the child must write each of the words in the correct sequence from left to right. Spelling, capitalization, punctuation, and penmanship should not be considered in scoring the item.

11. *Spells simple words correctly.* Ask the child to write each of the following words: cat, in, make. Say each word to the child, use the word in a simple sentence, and then repeat the word (e.g., "in . . . The boy is in the house . . . in"). Although the quality of formation of letters is not important, the child must produce clearly recognizable letters in the correct sequences for all three words to receive full credit for the item.

12. *Writes a complete sentence, using correct grammar and sentence structure, consisting of at least four words.* Ask the child to write a brief story. To receive full credit, the child must write at least one complete sentence in which at least four words are used with correct grammar and sentence structure. Spelling, penmanship, capitalization, and punctuation do not have to be correct. However, the child's response must clearly include at least four words used properly as a complete unit containing a subject-predicate relationship (e.g., "The boy is tall.").

13. *Shares information with others through self-initiated writing.* To receive credit for this item, the child must demonstrate self-initiated and self-directed writing. Examples of self-initiated writing include notes and letters written to the teacher, other students, or relatives.

14. *Writes a story containing three or more related sentences.* To receive full credit for this item, the child must write three or more related sentences. Although the sentences do not have to be grammatically or syntactically perfect, they must be related to some extent in theme or topic. Credit should be awarded even if the relationship among the sentences is minimal (e.g., "Tom is my brother. He is big. He likes ice cream." In this story, all three sentences relate to the topic of Tom). Spelling, capitalization, punctuation, and handwriting quality do not affect the scoring on this item.

15. *Capitalizes first letter in sentence and puts period at the end.* Ask the child to write the following two sentences as you dictate them: *I have a ball. The ball is red.* The sentences may be repeated, and pauses between words are allowed, to enable the child to write each word as it is said. The child receives full credit if he or she capitalizes the first letter in each sentence and places a period at the end of both sentences. Scoring of the item is not affected by the child's spelling or quality of handwriting.

16. ***Takes notes when listening to teacher.*** Full credit is awarded if a child exhibits the ability to take notes or write down information when listening to the teacher. Spelling, grammar, or penmanship do not affect scoring for this item. The primary focus in scoring pertains to thoroughness and accuracy of content, in accordance with the teacher's expectations for the child's age. Although the child must write the notes independently, the behavior can be self-initiated or performed at the suggestion of the teacher.

17. ***Organizes writing into simple paragraphs.*** Ask the child to write a brief essay (about one page) on a topic. The writing assignment only needs to be of sufficient length and complexity to create an opportunity to organize the sentences into paragraphs. Regardless of other aspects of the child's writing (handwriting, spelling, grammar, etc.), full credit is awarded if the sentences are grouped topically or in some reasonable manner within two or more paragraphs.

18. ***Writes logical, cohesive story containing several paragraphs.*** Ask the child to write a story containing at least three paragraphs. Handwriting, spelling, and grammar do not affect scoring. However the story should contain a clear theme or plot that is logically and cohesively developed through three or more topical paragraphs.

19. ***Expresses high level of abstract thoughts in writing.*** Give a writing assignment on a topic or theme that requires some degree of abstract, conceptual thinking (e.g., "Why Friends Are Important" or "What Freedom Means to Me"). The child receives full credit, regardless of handwriting, spelling, grammar, and so forth, if he or she is able to communicate higher level, abstract ideas or concepts effectively through writing.

20. ***Edits own writing.*** For purposes of this item, the editing behavior can be either self-initiated or requested by the teacher. In either case, the teacher should not instruct the child regarding where or how to edit the paper. To receive full credit, the child must independently read and make at least two corrections or other editorial changes to the paper he or she writes. These revisions should, in the teacher's estimation, result in some degree of improvement or further development in the child's paper.

Source: Basic School Inventory (3rd ed.), by D. D. Hammill, J. E. Leigh, N. A. Pearson, & T. Maddox, pp. 13–16. Copyright 1998 by Pro-Ed. Inc. Reprinted with permission.

the context of writing (Lerner, 2003). A variety of spelling assessment techniques are identified in this section.

Spelling Error Analysis

Spelling errors and error patterns can be assessed on various writing samples, including narrative stories, reports, letters, descriptions, journals, and poems. By carefully analyzing the students spelling, the teacher can focus on consistent patterns of errors and plan appropriate instruction. Error analysis spelling charts can provide a profile of the types of student errors and the frequency of specific errors. Spelling errors may consist of letter additions, omissions, substitutions, reversals, and transpositions. The following is a list of common spelling errors.

Spelling Errors and Examples

Spelling error	Example
Addition of a vowel	*sait* for *sat*
Addition of a consonant	*allways* for *always*
Omission of a silent letter	*hym* for *hymn*
Omission of a sounded letter	*han* for *hand*

CLARIFYING TERMS

Students who are not proficient in transferring information from the visual system to the motor system, and who have poorly developed visual kinesthetic memory and/or motor skills, are often diagnosed as having **dysgraphia**, a disturbance in visual motor integration.

Ommission of a double letter	*winer* for *winner*
Substitution for a phonetic vowel	*stey* for *stay*
Substitution for a phonetic consonant	*ceam* for *seam*
Substitution of a complete phonetic syllable	*cuff* for *cough*
Substitution of a complete phonetic word	*break* for *brake*
Substitution of a nonphonetic vowel	*went* for *want*
Substitution of a nonphonetic consonant	*storn* for *storm*
Substitution of vowels in unaccented syllables	*cottin* for *cotton*
Substitution of r-controlled vowels	*dert* for *dirt*
Reversal of consonants	*dig* for *big*
Reversal of whole words	*owt* for *two*
Reversal of vowels	*saet* for *seat*
Reversal or consonant order	*rbown* for *brown*
Reversals of consonant or vowel directionality	*praty* for *party*
Transposition of letters	*angle* for *angel*
Reflections of child's mispronounciations	*pin* for *pen*
Reflections of dialectical speech patterns	*Cuber* for *Cuba*
Inaccurate recall of spelling rules	*giveing* for *giving*

Errors can also be categorized as phonetic or nonphonetic. **Phonetic misspellings** occur when students attempt to use phonic rules to spell a word but apply the rules incorrectly, or the word does not adhere to those rules. Nonphonetic spellings do not appear to be based on the application of phonics rules (McLoughlin & Lewis, 2005). Studies indicate that most spelling errors occur in vowels in midsyllables of words; 67 percent of the errors result from substitution or omission of letters; and 20 percent result from addition, insertion, or transposition of letters (Mercer & Mercer, 2005). To conduct error analysis in spelling, it is important to know what spelling errors are the most common (Polloway & Patton, 2000).

Spelling Demons

Certain words are commonly misspelled by the general population. Shanker and Ekwall (2003) report that the 100 most frequently misspelled words comprise 60 percent of all the words used in early writing. They note that only eight words: *the, of, and, a, to, is, in,* and *you* represent 18 percent of all the words used in writing. The 100 commonly misspelled words, known as spelling "demons," are as follows (Kuska, Webster, & Elford, 1994) (teachers may want to assess their students' ability to spell these words by testing them with words appropriate to their grade level):

ache	boy's	easier	guessed
afraid	buried	eighth	happened
against	busily	either	happily
all right	carrying	enemy	here's
although	certain	families	holiday
angry	choose	fasten	hungry
answered	Christmas	fault	husband
asks	climbed	February	it's
beautiful	clothes	forgotten	its
because	course	friendly	kitchen
beginning	double	good-bye	knives

language	passed	quietly	squirrel
lettuce	peaceful	rapidly	stepped
listening	perfectly	receive	straight
lose	piano	rotten	studying
marriage	picnic	safety	success
meant	picture	said	taught
minute	piece	sandwich	their
neighbor	pitcher	scratch	there's
neither	pleasant	sense	through
nickel	potato	separate	valentine
niece	practice	shining	whose
ninety	prettiest	silence	worst
ninth	pumpkin	since	writing
onion	purpose	soldier	yours

Source: From *Spelling in Language Arts* 6th edition by A. Kuska, © 1976. Reprinted with permission of Nelson Thomson Learning, a division of Thomson Learning.

Dictated Spelling Tests

The dictated spelling test is a commonly used procedure for assessing spelling skills and assessing proficiency on spelling grade-level word lists. Words can be selected from any graded word list, and students' performance indicates their spelling grade level. The instructional level is determined when the student achieves 75 to 90 percent accuracy. Students' ability to spell words that are frequently used can be assessed, as well as words that are commonly misspelled.

Each time readers see a word in print, it triggers in their memory information about the word's spelling, pronunciation, and meaning (Ehri, 1995). A mere 107 words make up almost half of the total words in written text (Zeno, Ivens, Millard, & Duvvuri, 1995). When using this spelling list for assessment, the teacher can evaluate and monitor students' mastery of at least 50 percent of all the words they need to know for written work. (See Figure 8–20.)

Informal Spelling Inventory

An informal spelling inventory (ISI) can be used to determine the approximate grade-level proficiency for spelling words in isolation. Teachers can construct their own ISI based on their spelling curriculum, using words taken from the basal spelling series, from spelling texts, from graded textbooks in basal and content area subjects, literature series, and trade books. Each ISI graded word list generally consists of 20 words for grades 2 through 8, with fewer words, generally about 15, for grade 1. To ensure random selection of these words, the teacher divides the total number of words at each level by 20. For example, from a grade-level word list of 300 spelling words, dividing by 20 equals 15; therefore, every 15th word should be included in the ISI. For students in grade 4 and below, testing should begin with first-grade-level words. For students in grades 5 and above, assessment should start with words at the third-grade level. The list of words is dictated to the student; the teacher says the word, uses it in a sentence, and repeats the word. Some students prefer that the word be given without being used in a sentence (Mercer & Mercer, 2005, p. 344). Generally a seven- to 10-second interval between words is sufficient. The test is completed when the student reaches a ceiling level, with six consecutive words spelled incorrectly.

FYI

One half of written text consists of content words, or words that give meaning to the text. Although the same sight words may be used repeatedly, key content words, frequently multisyllabic, may appear only once. Often students have to stop and use decoding strategies to figure out unfamiliar words, and the one-time appearance of many key words in a selection can disrupt fluency. Even with several readings, reading selections that contain a large number of one-use multisyllabic content words can hinder the development of fluency for some students (Hiebert, 2003).

Figure 8–20   The 107 Most Frequently Used Words in Written English

A	Did	In	No	Than	We
About	Do	Into	Not	That	Were
After	Down	Is	Now	The	What
All	Each	It	Of	Their	When
Also	Even	Its	On	Them	Where
An	First	Just	One	Then	Which
And	For	Know	Only	There	Who
Are	From	Like	Or	These	Will
As	Get	Little	Other	They	With
At	Had	Made	Our	This	Would
Back	Has	Make	Out	Through	You
Be	Have	Many	Over	Time	Your
Because	He	May	People	To	
Been	Her	More	Said	Two	
But	Him	Most	See	Up	
By	His	Much	She	Very	
Called	How	Must	So	Was	
Can	I	My	Some	Water	
Could	If	New	Such	Way	

The criteria indicating adequate mastery is the highest level at which students respond correctly to 90 to 100 percent of the items, and the instructional level is the highest level at which students score 75 to 89 percent correct (Mercer & Mercer, 2005, p. 344). An error analysis technique can be used with the ISI to provide additional diagnostic information.

Another strategy is to design an inventory that covers the specific spelling skills in the students' curriculum. Mercer and Mercer (2005) have developed an assessment protocol that measures specific aspects of spelling. This inventory (see Figure 8–21), consists of a dictated spelling test and objectives. It is designed for a typical second- and third-grade spelling curriculum (e.g., the first five items address short vowel sounds). Teachers can also use it as a model for developing an inventory that directly correlates with the curriculum level they are teaching. An inventory can help to determine which specific skills need further evaluation.

Cloze Procedure

A cloze procedure is a visual means of testing spelling. When using the cloze method of assessment, students are given sentences with missing words or words with missing letters. They may be required to complete a sentence by writing the correct response in the blank; for example: "The opposite of boy is _____" (girl). In addition, students may be asked to complete a word or supply missing letters: "I eat when I am _____" (hungry), or "Ducks swim in _____" (water).

Figure 8—21   Diagnostic Spelling Inventory

Spelling Word	Spelling Objectives	Spelling Words Used in Sentences
1. man	short vowels and	The *man* is big.
2. pit	selected consonants	The *pit* in the fruit was hard.
3. dug		We *dug* a hole.
4. web		She saw the spider's *web*.
5. dot		Don't forget to *dot* the i.
6. mask	words beginning and/or	On Halloween the child wore a *mask*.
7. drum	ending with consonant blends	He beat the *drum* in the parade.
8. line	consonant-vowel-	Get in *line* for lunch.
9. cake	consonant—silent *e*	We had a birthday *cake*.
10. coat	two vowels together	Put on your winter *coat*.
11. rain		Take an umbrella in the *rain*.
12. ice	variant consonant sounds	*Ice* is frozen water.
13. large	for *c* and *g*	This is a *large* room.
14. mouth	words containing vowel	Open your *mouth* to brush your teeth.
15. town	diphthongs	We went to *town* to shop.
16. boy		The *boy* and girl went to school.
17. bikes	plurals	The children got new *bikes* for their birthday.
18. glasses		Get some *glasses* for the drinks.
19. happy	short *i* sounds of *y*	John is very *happy* now.
20. monkey		We saw a *monkey* at the zoo.
21. war	words with *r*-controlled	Bombs were used in the *war*.
22. dirt	vowels	The pigs were in the *dirt*.
23. foot	two sounds of *oo*	Put the shoe on your *foot*.
24. moon		Three men walked on the *moon*.
25. light	words with silent	Turn on the *light* so we can see.
26. knife	letters	Get a fork and *knife*.
27. pill	final consonant doubled	The doctor gave me a *pill*.
28. bat	consonant-vowel-consonant	The baseball player got a new *bat*.
29. batter	pattern in which final consonant is doubled before adding ending	The *batter* hit a home run.
30. didn't	contractions	They *didn't* want to come.
31. isn't		It *isn't* raining today.
32. take	final *e* is dropped before	Please *take* off your coat.
33. taking	adding suffix	He is *taking* me to the show.
34. any	nonphonetic spellings	I did not have *any* lunch.
35. could		Maybe you *could* go on a trip.
36. ate	homonyms	Mary *ate* breakfast at home.
37. eight		There are *eight* children in the family.
38. blue		The sky is *blue*.
39. blew		The wind *blew* away the hat.
40. baseball	compound words	They played *baseball* outside.

Source: Teaching Students with Learning Problems (6th ed.) by C. D. Mercer and A. R. Mercer. © 2001. p. 376. Reprinted by permission of Pearson Education Inc. Upper Saddle River, NJ 07458.

The student's knowledge and application of spelling skills can be informally assessed through the cloze procedure.

How to Administer the Cloze Procedure for Spelling

1. The teacher gives the student explicit instructions.
2. The student is to read the sentence orally (or silently if testing a group of students).
3. The student is directed to write the missing spelling word in the blank.
4. The teacher provides a model to demonstrate the procedure and to allow the student to practice with easy words.
5. There should be no time limit.
6. The teacher may need to provide the beginning letter or a few letters (e.g., middle, final) until the student becomes more proficient.

Spelling Curriculum-Based Measurement Assessment

Curriculum-based measurement is a procedure for administering and scoring spelling proficiency using vocabulary words from students' grade curricular material (e.g., spelling word lists, vocabulary from literature, science, and social studies). Students' scores can be charted and graphed to determine the efficacy of instructional procedures and to plot their progress toward achieving their individualized education plan (IEP) goals.

Spelling can be efficiently and effectively assessed through the use of probes. Students work on the probe sheet for one minute, then the teacher records the rate of correct and incorrect responses and notes any error patterns. The probe task can be spelling the correct word from a picture, spelling a contraction from two words, spelling a word from dictation, or seeing a partial word and filling in the missing letters. Each probe can be administered several times to provide a more reliable index of students' performance. (See Figure 8–22 for a sample spelling word probe.) The following are administration and scoring directions for CBM procedures for spelling assessment (Mercer & Mercer, 2005, p. 347).

Figure 8–22   Sample CBM Spelling Word Probe

Directions: Write homonyms for the spelling words listed below.

here	_____	read	_____
see	_____	eye	_____
bye	_____	sun	_____
there	_____	way	_____
blew	_____	knot	_____
too	_____	hare	_____
knight	_____	break	_____
weak	_____	board	_____

Time: 1 minute

Number of correct words written: _____

Number of incorrect words written: _____

How to Administer a CBM Spelling Word Probe Measure

1. The teacher randomly selects 15 to 20 words from the grade-level spelling curriculum material.
2. The teacher presents each student with lined, numbered paper.
3. The teacher provides directions and administers the spelling test by pronouncing each word on the list then in isolation, then in a sentence or phrase, and again in isolation. The words are dictated at a pace of one every seven to 10 seconds, or sooner if all students finish. The test is terminated after two minutes.

How to Score a CBM Spelling Word Probe Measure

The teacher can (1) count the words written and subtract the number of words spelled incorrectly to determine the total number of words correctly spelled; or (2) count the words spelled correctly and base the scoring criteria on the speed and accuracy of the number of words per minute (wpm). (See Figure 8–23 for an example of a graph illustrating a student's progress on a CBM.)

Another type of CBM probe is the measurement of correct letter sequence (cls), which is a pair of letters (or spaces) correctly sequenced within words. This measure gives credit for even partial competencies. In this probe, spelling words are deemed to consist of smaller units, referred to as letter sequences. Using a letter sequence per minute (lspm) probe, students are given credit for each letter in a word that is placed in the proper order. This method of scoring is very sensitive to even small, short-term student gains in spelling skills (Wright, 2004). Directions for constructing, administrating, and scoring a CBM spelling word probe measure are as follows.

How to Construct and Administer a CBM Spelling Probe: Letter Sequence Per Minute

1. The teacher chooses three sets of six words from the spelling curriculum.
2. For a two-minute probe, the teacher dictates one word every 10 seconds.
3. Three probes are given.

The IEP Connection

A correct word sequence (CWS) is two words next to each other with correct spelling, grammar, and punctuation. When two words are correctly written and make sense, a correct word sequence is marked with caret (^).

Examples:

^Drew^got^a^new^bike^for^his^birthday^.   CWS = 9

drew got^a shine knew bic for^his birthday   CWS = 3

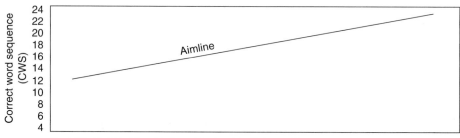

Present Levels of Academic Achievement and Fuctional Performance (9/15/05)

Tiesha, a student in your third-grade class (when given 30 seconds minute to plan and 3 minutes to write) writes 24 total words with 13 correct word sequences (cws) that make grammatical sense, compared to the third-grade norm of 26 total words and 27 cws that make grammatical sense.

Progress Points 1: By November (given 30 seconds to plan and 3 minutes to write.), Tiesha will compose a story that has 16 correct word sequences.

Progress Points 2: By January (given 30 seconds to plan and 3 minutes to write), Tiesha will compose a story that has 18 correct word sequences.

Progress Points 3: By March (given 30 seconds to plan and 3 minutes to write), Tiesha will compose a story that has 20 correct word sequences.

Progress Points 4: By June (given 30 seconds to plan and 3 minutes to write), Tiesha will compose a story that has 23 correct word sequences.

How to Score a Correct Letter Sequence Probe

1. Mark with a caret (^) the space before a correct first letter in the word and the space after the last letter of the word only if correct.
2. Count the inverted carets (^) to determine the number of earned lspm.
3. For each correct letter-pair, or sequence, written in the correct order, one point is given (marked with a caret [^]). Example: the word "cat" has four letter sequences.

    a. ^ c = is the first letter sequence (space-letter).
    b. c^a = is the second letter sequence.
    c. a^t = is the third letter sequence.
    d. t ^ = is the fourth letter sequence (letter-space).

4. Begin instruction based on students' error patterns.

Figure 8–23 Spelling CBM Graph

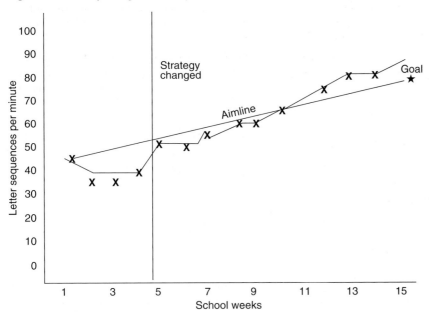

5. The total possible number of letter sequences, within a word, plus the before-and-after-word spaces, equals the number of letters in the word (King-Sears, 1998). (See Figure 8–24.)
6. The total number of correct letters is divided by 2 to get the lspm (Alper & Mills, 2001; King-Sears, 1998).

The following are guidelines for lspm instructional ranges and projected goal ranges (Alper & Mills, 2001).

	Grades 1–2	Grades 3–6
Mastery	more than 60 lspm	more than 80 lspm
Upper instructional (move on to next grade level)	40–59 lspm	60–79 lspm
Instructional	20–39 lspm	40–59 lspm
Frustration	less than 20 lspm	less than 40 lspm

Performance Spelling Assessment

Performance spelling is a method of increasing students' use of spelling words to communicate and to advance their writing skills. In this individualized approach to spelling, each student takes part in selecting the words to be used, in developing

Figure 8–24 Example of Correct Letter Sequence Scoring

Example	Student Spelling	Scoring
cat	^c^ a^ t^	cls = 4
cat	k c^ a^ t^	cls = 3
cat	k a ^ t ^	cls = 2

their own sentences, and in scoring and monitoring their progress. Using this system, students choose five target words and their teacher selects another five words, for a total of 10 words per week. The words selected should be those that students use in everyday conversation, have seen in their readings, and are a part of their school subjects. Students have a week to study and prepare for the test, which consists of students writing each of the 10 target words in a sentence. Students are familiar with the scoring criteria and should be encouraged to plot their own weekly progress. (The scoring criteria and standards for performance spelling can be found in Figure 8–25.)

As the year progresses, students should be made to write a paragraph using their five selected target words and another paragraph using the teacher's five target words. Each category and then the overall score can be characterized by the following performance standards:

Exemplary = 90–100 percent
Satisfactory = 50–89 percent
Inadequate = 0–49 percent

Figure 8–25 Performance Spelling Scoring Criteria and Standards

Accuracy	(0–1)	0 = incorrect spelling 1 = correct spelling
	Exemplary 90–100%, Satisfactory 70–89%, Inadequate 0–69%	
Usage	(0–2)	0 = not used or used incorrectly 1 = acceptable basic use 2 = elaborate use (enriched vocabulary and language use, adjectives, etc.) Examples: ate (0) He had ate books. (1) My dog ate his food. (2) She ate the delicious meal her father prepared.
	Exemplary 90–100%, Satisfactory 50–89%, Inadequate 0–49%	
Punctuation	(0–3)	0 = no beginning capital letter or ending mark 1 = either beginning OR ending 2 = both beginning and ending 3 = both, plus additional punctuation (quotation marks, commas, etc.)
	Exemplary 90–100%, Satisfactory 67–89%, Inadequate 0–66%	
Legibility	(0–2)	0 = generally, illegible (majority) 1 = acceptable 2 = cursive, no trace overs
	Exemplary 90–100%, Satisfactory 50–89%, Inadequate 0–49%	

Source: Assessment of At-Risk and Special Needs Children (2nd ed.), by J. C. Witt, S. N. Elliott, E. J. Daly III, R. M. Gresham, & J. J. Kramer (1998). Boston: McGraw Hill, p. 171. Reprinted with permission of the McGraw-Hill Companies.

Phonemic Awareness Spelling Assessment

To determine whether young children have phonemic awareness, the teacher asks them to spell words that they do not already know. Because they have not learned to spell these words, they must rely on invented spelling, the inner capacity to forge connections between letters and sounds. Analyzing students' invented productions can be an effective strategy for determining their word knowledge. A technique for assessing phonemic awareness and information on administering, scoring, and interpreting the results are as follows:

Phonemic Awareness Word List

bite	(three phonemes: BIT = 3 points; BT = 2 points; B = 1 point)
seat	(three phonemes: SET or CET = 3 points; ST, CT = 2 points)
dear	(three phonemes: DER = 3 points; DIR or DR = 2 points)
bones	(four phonemes: BONS or BONZ = 4 points; BOS or BOZ = 3 points)
mint	(four phonemes: MENT or MINT = 4 points; MET or MIT = 3 points; MT = 2 points)
rolled	(four phonemes: ROLD = 4 points; ROL or ROD = 3 points)
race	(three phonemes: RAS, RAC or RAFC = 3 points; RC or RS = 2 points)
roar	(three phonemes: ROR or ROER = 3 points; RR = 2 points)
beast	(four phonemes: BEST = 4 points; BES or BST = 3 points; BS or BT = 2 points)
groan	(four phonemes: GRON = 4 points; GRN = 3 points; GN = 2 points)
TOTAL	Thirty-five points

Source: From J. W. Gillet and C. Temple, *Understanding Reading Problems: Assessment and Instruction* 5e, © 2000 by Allyn & Bacon. Reprinted by permission.

How to Administer the Phonemic Awareness Assessment

1. The teacher calls out each word on the word list at least twice, or as many times as the student requests.
2. The teacher tells the students to spell each word as best they can, writing each sound they hear in the words.
3. The teacher tells the students to write a dash (—) if they are unable to spell a particular sound in a word.

How to Score the Phonemic Awareness Assessment

1. After all 10 words are dictated (or fewer if modifications are needed), count the number of reasonable letters written for each word.
2. Compare the number of letters written to the phonemes in the word.
3. Each word is scored according to the points designated at the right of each word, and then the total number of points received is compared with the total number of possible points.

The IEP Connection

Evan, a student in your fourth-grade class, has difficulty spelling words correctly. His poor encoding ability is affecting not only his spelling grades but also his grades in content subjects, especially on in-class written assignments and homework. You have completed a diagnostic spelling inventory, followed by an error analysis. You are administrating CBM probes to note progress on the special skill areas that have been designated to be in need of remediation. The IEP progress reporting criteria are based on weekly spelling tests.

Individualized Education Plan

Evan Morgan	1-31-96	4th	3-15-05
Student's Name	Birthdate	Grade	Date

Present Level of Academic Achievement and Functional Performance: Spelling

Evan is averaging 30 percent accuracy in weekly spelling tests, and his ability to correctly apply spelling words that he has acquired is inconsistent. On the spelling test when 17 (fourth) grade-level words were dictated, Evan wrote six words correctly and 19 of 40 correct letter sequences, which places him at about the 10th percentile compared with his grade-level peers according to spring norms. Evan's difficulties with spelling make it problematic for him to communicate in writing on grade-level assignments.

State Grade 4 Benchmark

Student will correctly spell grade-level words.

Annual Goal

In one year, when 20 (fourth-grade level) spelling words are dictated, Evan will write nine words correct and 31 correct letter sequences, which would place him at the 25th percentile compared to fourth graders on district spring semester norms.

Progress skill check-up for parent reporting	Criteria	June 2005	Nov. 2005	Jan. 2006	Mar. 2006
1. When dictated 17 grade-level 4 spelling words, Evan will write . . .	6 words correct, 22 correct letter sequences (CLS)				
2. When dictated 17 grade-level 4 spelling words, Evan will write . . .	7 words correct, 25 CLS				
3. When dictated 17 grade-level 4 spelling words, Evan will write . . .	8 words correct, 28 CLS				
4. When dictated 17 grade-level 4 spelling words, Evan will write . . .	9 words correct, 31 CLS				

Evaluation procedures for each short-term objective

____ Daily work samples   ____ Performance assessment

____ Teacher observation   ____ Clinical math interview

_x_ CBA probe   ____ Criterion-referenced test

Review schedule

____ Weekly

____ Monthly

_x_ Quarterly

Scoring Criteria/Interpretation for the Phonemic Awareness Assessment

1. Students who consistently write three or four letters have some ability to segment phonemes.
2. Students who write nothing or string together letters indiscriminately have not learned to segment phonemes.
3. Students who write only one or two reasonable letters per word are beginning to segment phonemes (Gillet & Temple, 2000, p. 235).

Inventory of Word Knowledge

The Schlagal Qualitative Inventory of Word Knowledge is a comprehensive spelling test that includes specific patterns students should master in grades 1 to 6. (See Figure 8–26.)

How to Administer and Score the Qualitative Inventory of Word Knowledge

1. The beginning test should be one grade below the student's instructional reading level.
2. Testing continues at each level until the student scores below 40 percent.
3. The highest level at which the student scores 50 percent or above is the student's spelling instructional level. Typically, the spelling level is slightly lower than the student's reading level.
4. The teacher compares the student's spelling with the correct spelling of the words. Identifying error patterns can help to determine instructional needs.

Spelling Word Test: Flow List

Taking the standard spelling test can be stressful and unproductive for students. Often a more practical and useful spelling word assessment procedure is to administer fewer words and closely monitor progress toward mastery. The teacher selects several key words and assesses them three days in a row. If the word is spelled correctly three days in a row, proficiency is assumed. To check maintenance, or long-term mastery, the teacher dictates the word again one week later. Once mastery is achieved, the teacher adds more words to the ongoing spelling mastery list. (See Figure 8–27.)

SECTION 4: HANDWRITING ASSESSMENT

Before initiating formal handwriting instruction, teachers need to determine whether students have developed certain prerequisite skills: muscular control, eye-hand coordination, and visual discrimination. Readiness skills can be assessed in several ways—cutting, tracing, coloring, and copying shapes (Salend, 1997). Muscular coordination

Figure 8—26   Schlagal Qualitative Inventory of Word Knowledge

Level 1	Level 2	Level 3	Level 4	Level 5	Level 6
1. girl	1. traded	1. send	1. force	1. lunar	1. satisfied
2. want	2. cool	2. gift	2. nature	2. population	2. abundance
3. plane	3. beaches	3. rule	3. slammed	3. bushel	3. mental
4. drop	4. center	4. trust	4. curl	4. joint	4. violence
5. when	5. short	5. soap	5. preparing	5. compare	5. impolite
6. trap	6. trapped	6. batter	6. pebble	6. explosion	6. musician
7. wish	7. thick	7. knee	7. cellar	7. delivered	7. hostility
8. cut	8. plant	8. mind	8. market	8. normal	8. illustrate
9. bike	9. dress	9. scream	9. popped	9. justice	9. acknowledge
10. trip	10. carry	10. sight	10. harvest	10. dismiss	10. prosperity
11. flat	11. stuff	11. chain	11. doctor	11. decide	11. accustom
12. ship	12. try	12. count	12. stocked	12. suffering	12. patriotic
13. drive	13. crop	13. knock	13. gunner	13. stunned	13. impossible
14. fill	14. year	14. caught	14. badge	14. lately	14. correspond
15. sister	15. chore	15. noise	15. cattle	15. peace	15. admission
16. bump	16. angry	16. careful	16. gazed	16. amusing	16. wreckage
17. plate	17. chase	17. stepping	17. cabbage	17. reduction	17. commotion
18. mud	18. queen	18. chasing	18. plastic	18. preserve	18. sensible
19. chop	19. wise	19. straw	19. maple	19. settlement	19. dredge
20. bed	20. drown	20. nerve	20. stared	20. measure	20. conceive
	21. cloud	21. thirsty	21. gravel	21. protective	21. profitable
	22. grabbed	22. baseball	22. traffic	22. regular	22. replying
	23. train	23. circus	23. honey	23. offered	23. admitted
	24. shopping	24. handle	24. cable	24. division	24. introduction
	25. float	25. sudden	25. scurry	25. needle	25. operating
			26. camel	26. expressive	26. decision
			27. silent	27. complete	27. combination
			28. cozy	28. honorable	28. declaration
			29. graceful	29. baggage	29. connect
			30. checked	30. television	30. patient

Source: *Reading Psychology : An International Journal* (1989) vol. 10(3), p. 230, R.C. Schlagal "Constancy and Change in Spelling Development," published by Taylor and Francis, Washington, D.C.

can be assessed through manipulative experiences, such as cutting with scissors, pasting, folding, tracing, coloring, finger painting, and picking up small items using a pincer grasp. Eye-hand coordination can be assessed by having pupils draw simple shapes (e.g., circles) and by copying geometric forms (e.g., vertical and horizontal lines, and crosses). Visual discrimination can be assessed by determining whether students can distinguish differences in various shapes, sizes, and details that are a precursor to their awareness of letters and numbers and their formation. Having pupils use the chalkboard to form basic lines and shapes is useful for determining whether they have sufficient muscle balance and coordination in their shoulders, arms, hands, and fingers. (See Figure 8–28.)

Figure 8–27   Spelling Flow List

	M	T	W	Th	F	M	T	W	Th	F	M	T	W	Th	F
1. write	C	C	C					C							
2. bright	C	C	C					C							
3. light	C	C	C					C			Review				
4. kite	✓	C	C	C					C						
5. run	C	C	C					C							
6. runner	✓	✓	C	C	C					✓	C	C	C		
7. running				C		C	C	C				C			
8. day				✓	C	✓	C	C	C				C		
9. today								C	C	C	✓	C	✓	C	C
10. yesterday								C	C	C	C	✓	C	C	C
11. jacket							C	✓	C	C	C				
12. racket						✓	C	✓	C	C	C				
13. money						C	C	C						C	C
14. funny						C	C	C						C	C
15. heavy															
16. stories															
17. ladies															
18. flies															
19. leaves															
20. trees															

Handwriting Sample Assessment

Teachers can assess **handwriting legibility** (the clarity and readability of handwriting) and fluency (the rate of written production) by observing students as they write and by analyzing their writing samples. (See Figure 8–29 for checklist of handwriting skills.) Mann, Suiter, and McClung (1992) recommend obtaining three writing samples to analyze: students' usual, best, and fastest handwriting. The teacher should have students copy the same sentence for each sample. An ideal sentence to use that contains all the alphabet letters is:

The quick brown fox jumps over the lazy brown dog.

For the usual sample, the writing should be done under typical, nonfatiguing conditions. When getting the best sample, students should be told to take their time and put forth their best effort. For the fastest sample, the students write the sentence as many times as possible within a specified period of time (e.g., two or three minutes). When evaluating the three samples, the teacher can assess legibility and fluency. Teachers can also analyze the writing samples for error patterns.

Writing fluency can be a serious problem for many students. Some find writing to be laborious, and their production can be very deliberate and therefore extremely

⌕ CLARIFYING TERMS

Orthographic memory is "the ability to represent the unique array of letters that defines a printed word, as well as general attributes of the writing system, such as sequential dependencies, structural redundancies, and letter position frequencies" (Vellutino, Scanlon, & Tanzman, 1994, p. 279).

Figure 8–28   Checklist for Handwriting Readiness Skills

Behavioral Characteristics	Yes	No	N/A	Comments
Moves hand up and down	—	—	—	_____
Moves hand left to right	—	—	—	_____
Moves hand backward and forward	—	—	—	_____
Connects dots on paper	—	—	—	_____
Traces dotted lines	—	—	—	_____
Traces geometric shapes	—	—	—	_____
Draws horizontal line from left to right	—	—	—	_____
Draws vertical line from top to bottom	—	—	—	_____
Draws vertical line from bottom to top	—	—	—	_____
Draws a forward circle	—	—	—	_____
Draws a backward circle	—	—	—	_____
Draws a curved line	—	—	—	_____
Draws slanted lines vertically	—	—	—	_____
Copies simple designs and shapes	—	—	—	_____
Names letters	—	—	—	_____
Identifies likenesses and differences in letters	—	—	—	_____

Figure 8–29   Checklist of Handwriting Skills

	Yes	No
General Observations		
• Adequate grasp of writing instrument	_____	_____
• Proper slant of paper	_____	_____
• Appropriate posture when writing	_____	_____
• Even pencil pressure	_____	_____
• Handwriting size adjusted for a given paper	_____	_____
• Neat writing in final copy	_____	_____
• Handwriting evaluated by student according to established criteria	_____	_____
Letter Formation, Alignment, Line Quality		
• Closed letters are closed	_____	_____
• Looped letters are looped	_____	_____
• Straight letters are not looped	_____	_____
• Dotted letters (j/i) are dotted directly above	_____	_____
• Crossed letters (x/t) are crossed accurately	_____	_____
• _M_s and _N_s have the correct number of humps	_____	_____
• _Y_s and _U_s are clearly differentiated	_____	_____
• Connecting strokes of _v_ and _y_ are clearly not _rv_ and _ry_	_____	_____
• Uppercase letters are accurately formed	_____	_____
• Numbers are correctly formed	_____	_____
• Letters are not reversed	_____	_____
• Lowercase letters begin on line (unless they follow _b, o, v,_ or _w_)	_____	_____
• Lowercase letters (except _b, o, v,_ and _w_) end on the line	_____	_____
• Letters are aligned correctly (not formed within line boundaries)	_____	_____
• Letter line quality is not too heavy or too light	_____	_____

slow. Some students who are proficient in letter formation, alignment, and spacing can produce very legible writing, but their speed is also slow, which can seriously affect their efficiency when doing written assignments in class and at home. Other students may be quite fluent but sacrifice legibility for speed. Thus, when under pressure to write within timed situations or when taking dictation or notes, their penmanship can be illegible. Both speed and fluency are critical issues for successful written products.

Tasks as basic as copying from the chalkboard or from a text can be very frustrating and difficult for some students, perhaps because of their inattention or difficulty in forming letters individually rather than as a connected series. Also, difficulty in copying may be the result of poor visual memory, which requires copying letters in words one by one rather than as whole words or even whole sentences may result otherwise from a lack of automatized skill in letter formation, which requires students to look several times at a single letter that is being copied to see how it is formed (Graham, Harris, & Fink, 2000).

Curriculum-Based Measurement: Handwriting Probes

Probes are fast, efficient assessment measures used to assess a specific handwriting skill and determine instructional targets. Students are given a handwriting probe sheet and asked to write a line of, for example, the same letter, either uppercase or lowercase; numbers; or their first or last name. They are timed for one minute. Accuracy and speed are recorded and tracked. Probes can be administered on a daily or regular basis in order to chart and monitor progress in mastering letter formation, spacing, alignment, fluency, and so forth. (See Figure 8–30 for a sample handwriting probe sheet.)

Handwriting Error Analysis

There are a variety of common handwriting problems, including slow writing pace, misdirection of letters and numbers, excessive or insufficient slant, poor spacing, messiness, misalignment, illegible letters, and excessive or insufficient amount of pencil pressure (Mercer & Mercer, 2005).

Types of Errors

In a classic study of 2,381 pupils, which analyzed types of errors, Newland (1932) identified the most common cursive writing illegibilities made by the elementary students. It was noted that almost half of the illegibilities in cursive writing were associ-

Figure 8–30 Handwriting Probe for Lower Case Letters

Name _____ Date _____

Time _____ Rate (letters per minute) _____ Correct _____ Incorrect _____

ated with the letters a, e, r, and t. Tompkins (2002) identified the most troublesome cursive letter as the lowercase r, with the other most misformed letters as k, p, and z. According to Horton (1970), 12 percent of all errors are due to the incorrect formation of the letter r. Therefore, it is apparent that most handwriting errors result from the incorrect formation of only a few letters. Incorrect size is the most common type of error, and it is seen more often in the descender letters p, q, y, g, and j. The most frequently reversed letters are N, d, q, and y. Incorrect relationship of parts occurs most frequently in k, R, M, and m. Partial omissions occur most frequently in m, U, and I. Additions often occur in q, C, k, m, and y. The most frequently misshapen letters are j, G, and J. Number malformations are also common, with the most errors associated with writing 5 like 3, 6 like 0, 7 like 9, and 9 like 4 (Mercer & Mercer, 2005, p. 367).

Error Analysis Procedure

A writing error analysis can be used to evaluate the types of illegibilities students make. (See Figure 8–31 for a method of tracking a group of students' progress.) Procedures for administering an error analysis are as follows.

How to Administer an Error Analysis

Option 1
1. The teacher dictates a series of letters for the student to write (either the complete alphabet or just the letters that are most commonly formed incorrectly: a, b, e, h, m, n, r, and t.
2. The student writes rows of letters in print form.
3. The student writes rows of letters in cursive form.

Option 2
1. The student produces a handwriting sample, either spontaneous or elicited.
2. The teacher circles the letters identified as the most frequently malformed letters and then carefully evaluates them for accuracy.

Criteria for rating accuracy are provided in Figure 8–32, which specifies the letters identified in the literature as being common handwriting demons that cause or contribute to most of the illegibilities in cursive writing.

Figure 8–31   Letter Formation Error Analysis Tracking Chart

Type of Error	Students Making Errors*
Incorrect letter formation (a)	Mary, Bob, Jack
Reversed /b/ for /d/	Peter, Mary, Janie
Inadequate spacing	Joey, Mary, Pat S
* Use of students' names is for instructional grouping.	

Figure 8–32 Analysis of Handwriting Errors

Directions: Score 2 for developed skill, score 1 for emerging skill, 0 for no attempt.

I. Letter formation
    A. Capitals (score each letter 1 or 2)

A ____	G ____	M ____	S ____	Y ____
B ____	H ____	N ____	T ____	Z ____
C ____	I ____	O ____	U ____	
D ____	J ____	P ____	V ____	
E ____	K ____	Q ____	W ____	
F ____	L ____	R ____	X ____	Total ____

    B. Lowercase (score by groups) Score (1 or 2)
       1. Round letters
         a. Counterclockwise: *a, c, d, g, o, q*   ____
         b. Clockwise: *k, p*   ____
       2. Looped letters
         a. Above line: *b, d, e, f, h, k, l*   ____
         b. Below line: *f, g, j, p, q, y*   ____
       3. Retraced letters: *u, t, i, w, y*   ____
       4. Humped letters: *h, m, n, v, x, z*   ____
       5. Others: *r, s*   ____   Total ____

    C. Numerals (score each number 1 or 2)

1 ____	4 ____	7 ____	10–20 ____	
2 ____	5 ____	8 ____	21–99 ____	
3 ____	6 ____	9 ____	100–1,000 ____	Total ____

II. Spatial relationships   Score (1 or 2)
    A. Alignment (letters on line)   ____
    B. Uniform slant   ____
    C. Size of letters
       1. To each other   ____
       2. To available space   ____
    D. Space between letters   ____
    E. Space between words   ____
    F. Anticipation of end of the line (hyphenates, moves to next line) ____   Total ____

III. Rate of writing (letters per minute)   Score (1 or 2)
    Grade 1:20   4:45   7 and above: 75
             2:30   5:55
             3:35   6:65   Total ____

Scoring	Underdeveloped skill	Developing skill	Developed skill
I. Letter formation			
A. Capitals	26	39	40+
B. Lowercase	7	10	11+
C. Numerals	12	18	19+
II. Spatial relationships	7	10	11+
III. Rate of writing	1	2	6+

Source: Informal Assessment in Education by Gilbert R. Gueron and Arlene S. Maier. Copyright © 1983 by Mayfield Publishing Company. Reprinted by permission of the publisher.

Zaner-Bloser Evaluation Scale

A holistic method of assessing manuscript writing in grades 1 and 2 and cursive writing in grades 2 to 6 is the Zaner-Bloser Evaluation Scale (1996). This untimed evaluation measure is a rather gross assessment of students' penmanship that rates performance based on samples provided for comparison. (See Figure 8–33.) This scale allows the teacher to determine whether a particular student's handwriting is significantly below average, within the average range, or above average when compared with grade norms. Areas assessed include letter formation, slant, alignment, proportion, spacing, and line quality. To get the most information from this scale, the teacher needs to carefully analyze student errors (using examples of common errors noted earlier) in order to formulate a remedial program. Instructions for administration and scoring are as follows.

How to Administer and Score Penmanship Using the Zaner-Bloser Evaluation Scale

1. The teacher writes a sample sentence on the chalkboard.
2. The student is given several opportunities to practice writing the sentence.
3. The student is given a sheet of paper to copy the sample sentence.
4. The student is allowed two minutes to complete the task.
5. The student's written sentence is compared with a series of five specimen sentences appropriate to the student's grade placement.
6. The quality of the student's sentence is rated as excellent, good, average, fair, or poor.
7. Handwriting proficiency rates are as follows:

Grade	Line per minute	Grade	Line per minute
1	25	4	45
2	30	5	60
3	38	6	67

Figure 8–33   Zaner-Bloser Evaluation Scale

Evaluation Guide

How to evaluate handwriting with this guide:

1. The teacher writes the sentence from the Evaluation Guide on the chalkboard.

2. Students practice writing the sentence on paper ruled with writing lines like those on the Evaluation Guide.

3. Students should use their best handwriting to write the sentence again.

4. Compare the students' writing with the examples on the Evaluation Guide, using the *keys to legibility*. The evaluation should be done as follows:

   EXCELLENT—All keys are acceptable.

   GOOD—At least three keys are acceptable.

   AVERAGE—Only two keys are acceptable.

   POOR—Only one or none of the keys is acceptable.

5. Repeat the evaluation procedure at least once each grading period.

I like to write about playing with my friends.

I like to write about playing with my friends.

I like to write about play ing with my friends.

I like to write about playing with my friends.

Figure 8–33 *(Continued)*

Excellent
All keys acceptable

Careful self-evaluation is necessary for improvement in handwriting. Practice is next.

Good
Spacing not acceptable

Careful   self- evaluation is necessary for improvement in handwriting. Practice is next.

Average
Slant and spacing not acceptable

Careful self-evaluation is necessary   for improvement in   handwriting. Practice is   next.

Poor
No key acceptable

Careful   self   evaluation is   necessary   for improvement   in handwriting.   Practice is   next.

Source: "Zaner-Bloser Evaluation Scale," (1996) Columbus, OH: Zaner-Bloser Educational Publishers. Used with permission from Zaner-Bloser, Inc.

The IEP Connection

As the first-grade inclusion teacher, you have several students who are classified and have fine motor integration and/or visual processing or motor planning problems. You track individual student progress by graphing each student's ability to accurately form manuscript letters. Charting errors and graphing are effective methods of monitoring progress toward each student's IEP goal.

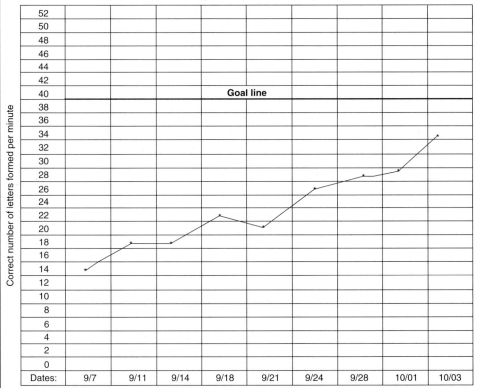

Graph of Letter Formation

Criteria: The student will correctly write dictated letters at a rate of 38 letters per minute (lpm).

SECTION 5: WRITTEN LANGUAGE SCORING-RATING METHODS

Holistic Scoring

Holistic language scoring is a quick and efficient method of assessing written products. In this type of assessment, one score is assigned to a piece of work—after examining it as a whole—that provides an overall impression of the student's ability (Arter & McTighe, 2001). Holistic scoring for written products is based on the assumption that all elements of writing—such as ideas/content, organization, voice, word choice, sentence fluency, conventions, and presentations—are critical to the effectiveness of the written product. These scores are based on comparing students' writings with the

Tips for Teachers

Too often, in analyzing the writing of students, we tend to look at what they cannot yet do: Punctuation is arbitrary, words are omitted, spelling is phonetic, it's too short, it doesn't say a lot, it's hard to read. In our eagerness to have them succeed, we anxiously list and record all the things they cannot yet do—sometimes overlooking the many strengths that show themselves a little differently at the primary level. The Six Trait Writing Assessment Model helps users see early writing with new eyes: Instead of looking for what a student can't yet do, we look for and build on what they can do (Spandel, 1996).

Figure 8–34   Holistic Scoring Scale—Written Products

Numerical Rating	Strong Command of Written Language	
6	• Opening and closing • Relates to single focus • Organized, logical progression • Variety of cohesive devices • Risks resulting in vivid responses	• Few, if any, errors in usage, sentence construction, and mechanics • Language adapted to audience and purpose • Strong voice

	Generally Strong Command of Written Language	
5	• Opening and closing • Relates to topic with single focus • Organized, logical progression • Appropriate and varied details • Strongly connected ideas	• Compositional risks • Papers may be flawed though complete and unified • Few errors in usage, mechanics, and sentence construction

	Command of Written Language	
4	• Opening and closing • Responses related to topic • Single, organized focus • Transition from idea to idea • Loosely connected ideas	• May have bare, unelaborated details • Some errors in usage with no consistent pattern • Few errors in sentence construction • Some errors in mechanics

	Partial Command of Written Language	
3	• May or may not have opening or closing • Has single focus • May drift or shift from focus • May be sparse in details	• Organizational flaws and lapses • Lack of transition • Patterns of errors in usage • Errors in sentence construction • Pattern of mechanical errors

	Limited Command of Written Language	
2	• May or may not have opening or closing • Some attempt at organization • May drift from primary focus	• Little elaboration of details • Severe usage problem • Numerous sentence construction errors • Numerous serious mechanical errors

	Very Poor Command of Written Language	
1	• Does not have opening or closing • Lacks coherence • Uncertain focus • Disorganized	• Numerous errors in usage • Grammatically incorrect sentences • Severe mechanical errors that detract from meaning

writings of their peers rather than against a predetermined scale. The comparisons can be made by comparing the piece to other pieces (called **anchors**, or **benchmarks**) or to papers in a set of compositions (Lipson & Wixson, 1997).

A holistic scoring rubric requires teachers or other raters to give a single overall score to students' performance. The first step in this scoring process is for the teacher or group of teachers to collect samples of students' written products (e.g., compositions or research papers). The next step is to read the papers and choose one or two model papers that are considered high quality. These anchor papers are models of exemplary products, papers, and performances used to guide and standardize the scoring of all students' work products and to "anchor" the scoring of student's work in a school or district, thereby ensuring consistency. The **anchor paper scoring method** does not focus on quantifying specific error types; rather it provides qualitative indices across specific dimensions of students' work, as well as serving as an overall qualitative index.

Students' papers are reviewed by the teacher, who determines an example of a paper deemed to be of above average quality, another which is average, and another which is below average. These three examples are the anchor papers. Next, the teacher evaluates all of the student papers and compares them holistically with the anchor papers in order to categorize them according to the high-, medium-, or poor-quality or a numerical rating (Lipson & Wixson, 1997). (See Figures 8–34 and 8–35.)

Another type of holistic scoring occurs when teachers read a complete set of all their students' papers at one time. They then place the papers in three piles, which are rated as good, poor, and somewhere in between. Next, they read the papers a second time to validate their first impression. Papers can be moved from one stack to another, and subsequently receive a holistic score of 1, 2, or 3.

Holistic scoring of written products can be a useful screening process. It is commonly used both in classroom assessments and in large-scale assessments, such as statewide assessments of writing. This type of scoring takes less time to apply than analytic schemes. Also, it may be favored where large numbers of portfolios need to be scored and where small differences in time per portfolio can translate into sizable financial savings, particularly with district- or state-level portfolio assessment systems (Herman, Gearhart, & Aschbacher, 1996). A distinct disadvantage of holistic scoring is that it does not provide detailed ratings on the specific areas of writing as analytic scoring does.

Analytic Scoring

Analytic language scoring produces a detailed analysis of oral presentation or written text. Analytic rubrics designate separate ratings for each aspect of performance. The teacher uses a scale or rubric to assign points to various components of the oral or written product, which are then totaled to obtain a grade or score. After analyzing the

Tips for Teachers

Provide students with copies of anchor papers to be used as models of exceptional, average, and poor papers. Parents can be given sample models and tips for helping students meet standards.

Figure 8–35 Fourth- to Fifth Grade-Level Writing Rubrics

	Topic	Organization	Style/Voice	Conventions
6	• Addresses topic thoroughly and coherently, understandable • Presents and explains topic in interesting, engaging manner • Writes a strong topic sentence, many detail sentences, and an interesting, strong closure or summary sentence	• Writes a 5-paragraph essay that is well developed, chronological, and has transitional sentences • Writes well-developed ideas with at least four details per paragraph • Includes introductory and concluding paragraphs that support each other	• Demonstrates exceptional control and variation of sentence structure • Uses thoughtful, precise, and appropriate language • Uses varied word choice • Uses a variety of literary techniques • Demonstrates exceptional sense of audience	• Spells almost all irregular words correctly • Demonstrates an exceptional command of spelling strategies • Consistently uses varied punctuation ("/'/'s/,/;) • Demonstrates exceptional knowledge of pronouns, adjectives, conjunctions, irregular verbs, and adverbial forms
5	• Addresses topic thoroughly and coherently, understandably • Writes a good topic sentence, interesting detail sentences, and good closing sentence	• Groups ideas into at least three paragraphs • Writes well-articulated ideas with at least two or three details per paragraph • Includes introductory and concluding paragraphs	• Uses varied sentences, structured consistently (complete, complex sentences) • Uses varied and thoughtful vocabulary that enriches description	• Spells most irregular words correctly • Demonstrates exceptional command of basic grammar • Uses pronouns, adjectives, conjunctions, irregular verbs, and adverbial forms correctly • Demonstrates exceptional control of punctuation (!/./?/,/"/') and capitalization • Demonstrates exceptional knowledge of nouns, pronouns, and adjectives
4	• Addresses topic thoroughly and coherently • Topic and closing sentence • More than three detail sentences	• May organize ideas into at least two paragraphs • Supporting sentences • Uses some transition words • Writes chronologically • Uses more details and facts	• Uses some complex vocabulary • Uses specific, descriptive language (adverbs, adjectives) • Begins to use a variety of literary techniques (metaphors, simile, onomatopoeia, personification) • Uses dialogue with increasing skill	• Spells some irregular words correctly and all high-frequency words correctly • Demonstrates a strong command of varied spelling strategies (roots, suffixes, prefixes) • Uses varied punctuation • Uses pronouns, adjectives, conjunctions, irregular, and adverbial forms correctly • Uses correct plurals for irregular nouns • Uses correct comparisons (good, better, best)

	Topic	Organization	Style/Voice	Conventions
3	• Addresses topic in a coherent manner • Includes well-developed, specific examples • Writes a topic sentence, at least three detail sentences, and closing sentence	• Develops central idea, incident, or problem with supporting details and in depth • Moves beyond simple sequence	• Demonstrates exceptional command of simple sentence structure • Uses varied sentence structure (complete, complex sentences) • Writes to avoid confusing the reader	• Spells most irregular words in understandable way and all high-frequency words correctly • Uses a variety of strategies to spell all words • Uses basic grammar correctly and consistently • Experiments with varied punctuation (!/./?/,/"/') • Demonstrates exceptional control of punctuation and capitalization
2	• Starts a paragraph with a topic sentence • Three or more sentences provide specific examples • May or may not have closing sentence	• May or may not write a full paragraph to develop central idea, incident, or problem • Demonstrates a sense of chronology • Begins to move beyond simple sequence	• Begins to use varied sentence structure • Begins to use adverbs, continues to use adjectives • Uses varied word choice • Incorporates sense of audience through specific vocabulary, description • Uses descriptive and expressive voice	• Spells almost all high-frequency words correctly • Uses phonics rules and other strategies to spell irregular words conventionally • Uses ' " and , • Uses basic grammar correctly • Uses nouns, pronouns, and adjectives correctly • Begins to use irregular verbs and adverbial forms correctly
1	• Begins to combine three sentences to develop one topic in a paragraph	• Develops central idea with several details that are mostly relevant to the topic • Writes in a simple sentence	• Begins to use varied sentence structure, without scaffolding • Uses specific, descriptive language like adjectives • Begins to incorporate sense of audience through specific vocabulary, description • Begins to use descriptive and expressive voice • Begins to include dialogue	• Spells most high-frequency words correctly • Uses phonics rules and other strategies to spell irregular words conventionally (syllable words with blends, orthographic patterns, contractions, compounds, and homophones) • Begins to use ' " and , (greetings, closure, dates, and series) • Begins to use basic grammar without scaffolding • Begins to use nouns, pronouns, and adjectives correctly

Source: Table 1: 4th/5th Grade Writing Rubrics—Working Draft by M. L. Langerock. *Teaching Exceptional Children* (2000, Nov/Dec) p. 29. Reprinted with permission.

written product, the teacher can tailor instruction to the particular aspects that are causing a student difficulty.

Major areas typically evaluated are ideas, content, context, structure, fluency, mechanics, and presentation. The teacher may decide to assess the performance of students in specific areas (e.g., organization, mechanics, and fluency). The teacher rates the students' oral presentation or writing samples by using a point system for each major area (see Figure 8-36) or on a scale from 1 to 5 in each major area, so that students can receive separate scores for each skill area (see Figure 8-37). Analytic scoring chart for the six traits of writing is provided in Figure 8-38.

Figure 8–36　Analytic Scoring Scale—Written Language

Content (20 pts)　　　　　　　　　　　　　　　　Points earned: _____

Topic is narrowed.
Main idea is clear.
Main idea or theme is developed.
Details are tailored to the main idea.
Ideas are complete.
Reasons and examples are convincing.
Conclusion is clearly stated.
Evidence of writing is mature.

Structure/Organization (20 pts)　　　　　　　　Points earned: _____

Ideas are sequenced (beginning, middle, end).
Writing follows assigned structure (expository form).
Sentences are varied (simple, compound, and complex).
Sentences are complete, fully developed.
Statements are logically supported.

Usage (20 pts)　　　　　　　　　　　　　　　　Points earned: _____

Paragraphs contain topic sentences.
Correct style has been used.
Sentences are complete thoughts.
Transitions and conjunctions are used to connect ideas.
Conventional word endings are accurate.
Singular and plural possessives are correct.
Verb tense is appropriate.
Subject-verb agreement is correct.
Personal pronouns are used appropriately.
Homophones are used correctly.
Comparisons are made.

Mechanics (20 pts)　　　　　　　　　　　　　　Points earned: _____

Contractions are correctly used.
Spelling is accurate.
Punctuation is correct.
Capitalization is correct.
Numbers are used accurately.

Word Choice (20 pts)　　　　　　　　　　　　　Points earned: _____

Word choices are appropriate and varied.
Words are chosen to express purpose of writing.
Words are used that are descriptive.
Fluency is adequate to express ideas.

Total points possible: 100　　　　　　　　　　**Total points earned: _____**

Figure 8–37   Sample Analytic Scoring Criteria Chart

Characteristics	1	2	3	4	5
Idea	• Lacks coherency • Rambling • Ideas not well developed • Lacks foundation, poor establishment of reader's background knowledge	• Literal translation of topic • Seems to have copied multiple sentences from another source • Nothing seems to happen • Ideas presented in list-like format (may be in a single sentence)	• Imaginative • Ideas begin to emerge • Main idea is carried through • Ideas stated generally with little elaboration (e.g., one idea per sentence) • Seems to have copied directly from another source (limited)	• Well-developed, cohesive ideas • Creative spark • Consistent point of view • Some idea elaboration, but inconsistent, "other source" ideas paraphrased	• Well-developed, cohesive ideas • "Other source" ideas paraphrased • Obviously creative/researched • Ideas presented in own words • Ideas elaborated upon extensively • Consistent point of view
Style	• Limited vocabulary, general lack of adjectives • Short, choppy sentences	• Generally lacks attempts to go beyond common words	• Attempts to use expanded vocabulary • Some use of adjectives • Stronger verb selection	• Use of adjectives and adverbs • Use of transitional words and phrases to help flow of writing • Use of signal words (e.g., first, second in comparison) to help reader comprehend message	• Extensive use of adjectives and adverbs • Use of transitional words and phrases to help flow of writing • Use of signal words (e.g., first, second in comparison) to help reader comprehend message • Effective paragraph transitions
Organization	• Lacks indention paragraphing • Lacks sequence • Lacks main ideas and supporting details	• Has multiple paragraphs • Generally indents • Lacks progression of ideas	• Lacks thesis statement • Inconsistent use of explicit main idea statements • Some main ideas inconsistent with overall implied thesis • Some supporting statements	• Thesis statement in first paragraph • Main ideas usually stated clearly • Topic sentences follow thesis statement • Supporting details follow topic sentences	• Thesis paragraph • Main ideas stated clearly • Topic sentences follow thesis statement • Supporting details follow topic sentences

Figure 8–37 (*Continued*)

Characteristics	1	2	3	4	5
Mechanics	• Misuse of capitals • Lacks capitalization of proper nouns • Frequent capitals in middle of words, lack of punctuation	• Capitals at beginning of sentences • Inconsistent capitalization and end punctuation	• Capitals at beginning of sentences • Occasional capital in middle of words or beginning of words in middle of sentences • End marks used	• Uses a variety of mechanics well • Uses end marks other than periods • Uses commas in series	• Few errors in mechanics • Generally proper use of commas for sophisticated sentences
Usage	• Incorrect tense • Shift tense within compositions • Frequent word omission	• Subject-verb agreement evidence but inconsistent	• Satisfactory subject-verb agreement (generally consistent) • Tense inconsistent	• Good subject-verb agreement (generally consistent) • Tense generally consistent • Possessives used	• Few grammatical errors
Sentence Structure	• Extensive sentence fragments and run-ons	• Some awareness of sentence structure • Some sentence fragments • Little variance in sentence patterns	• Some variance in sentence patterns • Most sentences declarative • Limited use of phrases • No dependent clauses	• Varied sentence patterns • No sentence fragments or run-ons • Varies use of phrases and dependent clauses	• No sentence errors • Use of compound-complex sentences • Frequent use of sophisticated sentence structure
Hand-writing	• Many words unreadable • Poor spacing • Messy	• Not neat • Poor spacing • Inconsistencies in letter size, formation, and alignment • Shows disregard for margins • Some words unreadable	• No scratch-outs • Occasional spacing problem • Some erasure marks • Inconsistent margin	• Generally neat • Sticks to margins • Spacing okay • Neat hand-writing	• Very clean paper • Very good handwriting • Very attractive work
Spelling	• Many words unintelligible • Most words misspelled • Lacks sound-symbol corres-pondence • Omits vowels	• Misspells common words • Phonetic approach to spelling most words	• Misspells common words occasionally • Attempts to spell difficult words are phonetic	• Misspells few words • Generally successful attempts at spelling difficult words	• No words misspelled

Figure 8–38 Six Trait Analytic Scoring: Primary Continuum for Beginning Writers

Writing Criteria for Ideas and Content

The Exploring Writer
_____Uses pictures to express ideas.
_____Uses scribbles to express ideas.
_____Creates shapes that imitate print or cursive text.
_____Dictates story, message, or label for picture.
_____Writes random "letters."
_____Reader needs help to interpret pictures or "text."

The Emerging Writer
_____Creates pictures and text that reader can interpret with inferences and good guesses.
_____Combines pictures with imitative text, letters, or "just readable" words.
_____Uses labels to expand meaning.
_____Pictures carry more meaning than text.

The Developing Writer
_____Creates easily recognizable pictures and text.
_____Creates stand-alone text that expresses a clear message.
_____Attends to detail in pictures and/or text (more than a quick scribble or sketch).
_____Text carries as much meaning as pictures (or slightly more).

The Fluent/Experienced Writer
_____Creates pictures and/or stand-alone text that makes a point or tells a simple story.
_____Elaborates on message or story.
_____Incorporates the kinds of significant, less-than-obvious details that give both text and pictures interest, depth, and meaning.
_____Presents ideas that catch a reader's attention.
_____Shows knowledge of topic.
_____Text carries most or all of the meaning (though pictures may be used to enhance meaning).

Writing Criteria for Organization

The Exploring Writer
_____Places letters, shapes, scribbles, or pictures randomly on the page.
_____May fill one corner of the page or the whole page.

The Emerging Writer
_____Shows a growing sense of balance in placement of scribbles, text, or pictures.
_____Shows clear sense of coordination between text and pictures (e.g., a reader can readily see that they go together).
_____Begins to "center" work on the page.

The Developing Writer
_____Shows a beginning sense of sequencing or patterning (e.g., chronological order, main point and support) in written text.
_____Shows skill with story boarding (creating pictures in sequence to make a point or tell a story).
_____Writes multiple sentences in an order that supports a main point or story.
_____Shows a sense of beginning: This is a story of . . . One day . . . My favorite food . . .

Figure 8–38 *(Continued)*

_____Uses conventions, such as title, indentation, numbers (1, 2 or first, second), and "The End" to help structure written text.
_____Presents work in a visually balanced way on the page.

The Fluent/Experienced Writer
_____Uses definite beginning and concluding statements (other than simply "The End") in text.
_____Uses transitional words and phrases (next, then, so, but, while, after that, because, etc.) to connect ideas.
_____Shows skill in sequencing a simple story chronologically.
_____In informational writing, shows skill in grouping "like" bits of information together sticking with one main topic moving from one support point to another (e.g., from where sea turtles live to what sea turtles eat).
_____Skillfully uses conventions such as title, indentation, or statement of purpose to structure text.
_____Creates a "complete" text. Doesn't just stop at the end of the page.
_____Presents work in a visually appealing way on the page.

Writing Criteria for Voice

The Exploring Writer
_____Copies words or letter shapes from environmental print.
_____Creates shapes or scribbles that represent words, even though a reader cannot yet translate them without help.
_____Writes in letter strings (all "letters" may not be recognizable).

The Emerging Writer
_____Writes recognizable words.
_____Uses labeling to enhance or "dress up" pictures.
_____Chooses words or labels or short phrases that clearly go with picture text.
_____Uses various parts of speech, such as naming words (nouns), describing words (adjectives), and action words (verbs).

The Developing Writer
_____Enjoys combining pictures with more extended text.
_____Uses expressive or descriptive phrases and short sentences, not just one- or two-word labels.
_____"Stretches" to use new words, even if she or he cannot spell them yet (e.g., The lage harabel ants are planing to get the jucsy red appel from the bird.).
_____Creates text that conveys a clear general meaning (e.g., My dog runs fast.).

The Fluent/Experienced Writer
_____Chooses words that make meaning clear and also create a particular mood or build a picture in the reader's mind (e.g., Dad and the ball collided.).
_____Uses individual phrasing that enhances personal voice (e.g., My dog's ears were flourishing with thick fur.).
_____Experiments with language in a variety of ways: imitating, inventing new words, rhyming, and/or looking for a particular "just right" word.
_____Relies only minimally on general words (e.g., nice, great, fun, wonderful, special).
_____Uses a variety of words, with little redundancy.

Writing Criteria for Sentence Fluency

The Exploring Writer

_____May use scribbles or imitative letter strings: **LIEKPTLSSINKT.**

_____Does not yet write in sentences or word strings.

The Emerging Writer

_____Writes in word strings or simple sentence patterns (some sentences may not be complete).

_____Writes one sentence or an "almost" sentence (e.g., **I LIK TO PLAY WITH MY BLOKS. ME BIK AN THE SUN.**).

_____May use repetitive sentence patterns (e.g., I am a ball. I like be a ball. I lik Jim.).

The Developing Writer

_____Writes in sentences; often includes more than one sentence in given text.

_____May imitate sentence patterns he or she has heard.

_____Begins sentences in different ways.

_____Creates text that another person can readily read aloud (e.g., I have a toy. The toy I have is my favrit toy and this toy is my bear.).

The Fluent/Experienced Writer

_____Written text begins to imitate oral fluency.

_____Shows variety in sentence lengths and beginnings.

_____Writes as many sentences as he or she needs to complete the text.

_____Creates text that is easy for another to read aloud with expression.

_____Experiments with sentence fluency through some of the following:

    _____varied beginnings

    _____longer sentences

    _____more complex sentences

    _____use of dialogue

    _____poetry

    _____rhythmic patterns

_____Creates text with a natural, "easy flow" kind of sound (e.g., My name is Watcher because I am an eye tooth. Just today I was cleaned. It sort of hurts but I've gotten to like it.).

Writing Criteria for Conventions

The Exploring Writer

_____Experiments with print by

    _____ creating scribbles to represent text

    _____ creating scribbles that represent individual letters

_____May write with letter strings, usually prephonetic (e.g., **SAMSAAUATT**).

_____Can put own name (or a version thereof) on paper.

_____May create some recognizable letters or numbers (e.g., **NAT02**).

The Emerging Writer

_____Imitates many features of environmental print:

    _____ shapes that resemble letters

    _____ letters or letter shapes that face the right direction

    _____ left-to-right orientation on the page, up-to-down orientation on the page

    _____ blending of text with illustrations

Figure 8–38 *(Continued)*

_____Distinguishes between upper and lower case letters; begins to associate capitals with "important" words (may not always place capitals correctly).

_____Experiments with punctuation, especially periods, which may be randomly placed (e.g., I Luv. My Dog.).

_____Writes own name on personal work.

_____Uses beginning (prephonetic) spelling with a few sounds—mostly consonants, few vowels (e.g., **I lik t d nts** [I like to draw knights]).

_____Continues to write with letter strings and short word strings, expanding to multiple words and simple sentences (e.g., I rn fast.).

_____Often uses labels, titles, or both.

The Developing Writer

_____Incorporates more conventions from environmental print into own text:

   _____ spacing between words

   _____ spacing between lines

   _____ appropriate directional placement of letters—E, not Ǝ

   _____ consistent left-right and up-down orientation

   _____ use of a title

   _____ margins

_____Uses both upper and lower case letters, (some of which may be randomly placed); often capitalizes "I," own name, names of others, and words of significance (e.g., I luv my Dog).

_____Experiments with other forms of punctuation: question marks, ellipses, commas, quotation marks, etc.

_____Expands to basic phonetic spelling with more consonant sounds and more vowels (e.g., I lik tu dru nits [I like to draw knights.]).

_____Writes own name and other significant words. Guesses at many words.

_____Uses inventive spelling well enough to create readable text (e.g., My dinosaur cam bak. He ets fish. He is my frnd.).

_____Usually places periods at the ends of sentences (e.g., I luv my dog.).

The Fluent/Experienced Writer

_____Consistently incorporates conventions of spacing and directional placement of letters into own text.

_____Regularly uses both upper and lower case letters, and usually places them correctly (e.g., caps on names, caps at beginnings of sentences, capitalizing pronoun "I"). May also capitalize words that are simply important to him or her (e.g., My Dog is my Frend.).

_____Usually places periods and question marks correctly.

_____Continues to experiment with other punctuation: dashes, commas, quotation marks, ellipses, colons, semicolons, parentheses, and such. Places punctuation correctly, or makes a good guess.

_____Uses readable spelling for most words. Conventionally correct spelling of simple, familiar words (e.g., **I like to draw nites** [I like to draw knights.]), good guesses on difficult words (e.g., The bright yellow sun reflects off the trueds [tremendous] airplane.).

_____Writes more than one paragraph if needed.

_____Uses title if needed.

_____Uses margins.

SUMMARY POINTS

- The three main components of written language are language, thought, and motor skills.
- The six traits of writing are now referred to as the Six Traits + One, with the addition of presentation, to the original traits: (1) ideas and content, (2) organization, (3) voice, (4) word choice, (5) sentence fluency, and (6) conventions.
- Assessment of the writing process includes observing and analyzing the following skills: (a) preplanning before beginning to write, (b) writing drafts, (c) revising and editing work, (d) proofreading, and (e) sharing the final product.
- A writing sample analysis generally includes counting the number and types of words written; the words spelled correctly; and the number, types, and length of sentences.
- Spelling error analyses generally identify the most common types of spelling errors, which include letter additions, substitutions, omissions, reversals, and transpositions.
- The types of handwriting errors that often result in illegibility include poor letter formation, slant, alignment, proportion, spacing, and line quality.
- The anchor paper scoring method is a rating system in which students' papers are compared, ranked according to levels of proficiency, and used as "anchors" or benchmarks (i.e., qualitative indicators) to categorize papers for grading or level of proficiency.

Chapter Check-Ups

1. Describe the connection between oral language development, written language development and reading skill development.
2. Compare and contrast a written language work sample and a specific, timed writing sample.
3. Discuss how the teacher can most effectively use the information from studies which identify the most common types of spelling errors, the most frequently misspelled words, and the most typical handwriting errors.
4. What significance does the instructional, social, and physical environment have on the acquisition and application of written language?
5. Provide a scenario in which the teacher would assess students' correct word sequence or correct letter sequence rather than requiring a longer writing sample. Likewise, describe a scenario in which a longer writing sample would be more appropriate.

Practical Application Assessment Activities

1. Practice analyzing a spontaneous writing sample. Collect two samples of writing from an elementary student. Use the sample assessment formats in the textbook to informally analyze the writing samples. Look for similarities and differences in the samples based on the purpose and audience of the writing task (ideation).

2. Complete an error analysis based on a sample page of children's spelling. Identify the type of encoding errors made, determine whether a pattern of errors exists, and provide specific examples.

3. Construct a curriculum based assessment (CBA) using several pages from an elementary level spelling text or workbook. After the administration of the CBA, construct a graph to be used to monitor weekly progress.

4. Obtain handwriting fluency samples from two students and use the Analysis of Handwriting Errors (Figure 8–32) or the Zaner Bloser Evaluation Scale (Figure 8–33) to rate and compare their performances.

Connection Between CEC, PRAXIS, and INTASC Standards and Chapter 8

Council for Exceptional Children
The voice and vision of special education

The Council for Exceptional Children—Professional Standards
Standard 3 Individual Learning Differences

1. Effects an exceptional condition(s) can have on an individual's life.

2. Impact of learners' academic and social abilities, attitudes, interests, and values on instruction and career development.

Standard 5 Learning Environments and Social Interactions

1. Demands of learning environments.

13. Identify supports needed for integration into various programs placements.

16. Use performance data and information from all stakeholders to make or suggest modifications in learning environments.

Standard 7 Instructional Planning

3. National, state or provincial, and local curricula standards.

6. Identify and prioritize areas of the general curriculum and accommodations for individuals with exceptional learning needs.

7. Develop and implement comprehensive, longitudinal individualized programs in collaboration with team members.

8. Involve the individual and family in setting instructional goals and monitoring progress.

9. Use functional assessments to develop intervention plans.

10. Use task analysis.

11. Sequence, implement, and evaluate individualized learning objectives.

Standard 8 Assessment

1. Basic terminology used in assessment.

4. Use and limitations of assessment instruments.

5. National, state/provincial, local accommodations and modifications.

6. Gather relevant background information.

7. Administer nonbiased formal and informal assessments.

8. Use technology to conduct assessments.

9. Develop or modify individualized assessment strategies.

10. Interpret information from formal and informal assessments.

11. Use assessment information in making eligibility, program, placement decisions for individuals with exceptional learning needs, including those from culturally and/or linguistically diverse backgrounds.

13. Evaluate instruction and monitor progress of individuals with exceptional learning needs.

14. Create and maintain records.

PRAXIS Standards for Special Education

THE PRAXIS SERIES™

Standard 1 Understanding Exceptionalities

1. Theories and principles of human development and learning, including research and theories related to human development; theories of learning; social and emotional development; language development; cognitive development; and physical development, including motor and sensory.

2. Characteristics of students with disabilities, including medical/physical, educational, social, and psychological.

3. Basic concepts in special education, including definitions of all major categories and specific disabilities; causation and prevention of disability; the nature of behaviors, including frequency, duration, intensity, and degrees of severity; and classification of students with disabilities, including classifications as represented in IDEA and labeling of students.

Standard 2 Legal and Societal Issues

1. Federal laws and landmark legal cases related to special education.

2. Issues related to school, family, and/or community, such as teacher advocacy for students and families, including advocating for educational change and developing students' self-advocacy; family participation and support systems; public attitudes toward individuals with disabilities; and cultural and community influences.

Standard 3 Delivery of Services to Students with Disabilities

3. Assessment, including how to modify, construct, or select and conduct non-discriminatory and appropriate informal and formal assessment procedures; how to interpret standardized and specialized assessment results; how to use evaluation result for various purposes, including monitoring instruction and IEP/ITP development; and how to prepare written reports and communicate findings to others.

4. Placement and program issues (including continuum of services; mainstreaming; integration; inclusion; least restrictive environment; noncategorical, categorical, and cross-categorical programs; related services; early intervention; community-based training; transition of students into and within special education placements; postschool transition; and access to assistive technology).

5. Curriculum and instruction, including the IEP/ITP process; instructional development and implementation (for example, instructional activities, curricular materials, resources and equipment, working with classroom personnel, tutoring and the use of technology); teaching strategies and methods (for example, direct instruction, cooperative learning, diagnostic-prescriptive method); instructional

format and components (for example, individualized instruction, small- and large-group instruction, modeling, drill and practice); and areas of instruction (such as academics, study and learning skills, social, self-care, and vocational skills).

INTASC Standards for Teacher Education
Standard 7

The teacher plans instruction based upon knowledge of subject matter, students, the community, and curriculum goals.

Standard 8

The teacher understands and uses formal and informal assessment strategies to evaluate and ensure the continuous intellectual, social, and physical development of the learner.

Written Language Assessment Chart			
Methods of Assessment	**Purpose**	**Advantages**	**Disadvantages**
Curriculum-Based Assessment (Probes)	• To provide individualized, direct, and repeated measures of proficiency and progress in the language curriculum	• Enhances instructional decision making due to frequent administration • Good screening procedure • Used for determining placement in curriculum • Used to monitor progress • Assists in special program placement • Effective communicative tool with parents • Used to assess fluency, writing maturity and complexity, vocabulary diversity, structure, or the mechanical aspects of the writing process, and organization	• Viewed as being simplistic and does not consider the learning process itself • CBA probes have been considered insufficient for program decision making for students with cognitive delays
Error Pattern Analysis	• To assess the student's responses to tasks • To assess the way the task is approached • To identify specific skill mistakes and patterns of errors	• Useful for identifying the use of rules and concepts • Used to design instructional goals, objectives, and programs	• Can be time-consuming • Poor handwriting can affect ability to determine whether spelling errors or letter formation problems are evident
Journal Writing	• To determine how students feel about the lesson, which skills/concepts are unclear, and what instructional methods were effective or ineffective	• Allows students to assemble some of their own assessment information • Enables teachers to conduct assessment at the most convenient time • Encourages students to connect science to their daily lives • Encourages candid teacher-to-student communication	• Difficult for students with written language or fine motor problems (may need to modify, e.g., have student dictate into tape recorder)
Language Samples	• To analyze the student's communication by recorded transcription of oral language • To analyze patterns of language to determine linguistic constructions	• Determines deviant or absent linguistic constructions • Used to plan specific remedial interventions • Assesses how child uses language in natural context • Used to assess voice, pronunciation, fluency, syntax, morphology, and semantics	• Oral sample needs to be either audio taped or the recorder must have skill in accurate transcribing • Evaluator must be trained or have skill in analyzing speech skills and patterns

Written Language Assessment Chart			
Methods of Assessment	**Purpose**	**Advantages**	**Disadvantages**
Performance-Based Assessment	• An alternative assessment that requires the student to *do* (e.g., produce, create, construct, show, explain, demonstrate)	• Allows students to apply their learning in a flexible, authentic way rather than rely on rote responses • Assesses higher order thinking skills • Assesses ability to apply knowledge • Informs teaching	• More costly than traditional pencil-paper tests • Time intense: administration, scoring, and interpretation of results • Caution regarding limited evidence of reliability and validity
Portfolio Assessment	• To collect written and/or oral language work samples that exhibit the student's efforts, progress, and achievement in one or more areas completed over time	• Allows teachers, students and parents to reflect on student progress and to adjust instruction accordingly • Can be used for formative and summative evaluation • Effectively used to identify minority children who are gifted and not identified in more traditional measures (e.g., IQ tests)	• Time consuming and labor intense • Interrater reliability should be established • Students with disabilities may require extra attention when selecting and evaluating work samples
Self-Assessment	• To assess student's ability to self-analyze learning • To determine what the student has learned, the quality of that learning, what the student needs to learn; and to promote personal goal setting	• Helps the student to focus on strengths and weaknesses • Helps the student to determine what steps to take to deal with weaknesses • Promotes motivated, self-regulated learners	• Student may not be able to identify their errors • Student may not have the skills to evaluate work without direct guidance
Writing Process Assessment	• To determine the student's ability to communicate through writing, using planning, transcribing, reviewing, and revising	• Used to assess the student's sentence structure; knowledge of mechanics, vocabulary, word relationships, kinds of sentences, verb tense, and parallel structure; use of transition words and sequence of events; use of voice, tone and mood, creativity and imagination; and ability to pre-plan, proofread, and edit	• Requires time, careful analysis, and structure • Student needs training in self-analysis, peer editing, and conferencing

Written Language Assessment Chart (*Continued*)			
Methods of Assessment	**Purpose**	**Advantages**	**Disadvantages**
Curriculum-Based Assessment (spelling-handwriting probes)	• To provide individualized, direct, and repeated measures of proficiency and progress in the spelling and handwriting curriculum	• Used for ongoing assessment of progress • Determines strengths and weaknesses • Measures accuracy and fluency • Used to monitor progress • Informs the teaching and learning process • Less time-consuming than formal tests	• Validity based on the curriculum • Small samples of skill, which may not be generalizable
Error Pattern Analysis	• To diagnose the type of mistakes and the pattern of mistakes	• Useful for identifying the use of rules and concepts • Used to design instructional goals, objectives, and programs	• Poor handwriting may be the result of the student's attempt to compensate for poor spelling or language skills rather than actual handwriting deficits • Apparent spelling errors may be due to poor letter formation rather than poor spelling skills • Mistakes may be made due to visual (e.g., not being able to see the board when copying) or visual motor problems, not actual spelling or handwriting errors
Spelling Cloze Technique	• To assess knowledge of linguistic structures • To assess instructional levels	• Fast and accurate device for determining whether material is appropriate • Used for grouping and placement • Can be used diagnostically to determine what students know; whether they use context clues or can read critically	• Not a valid measure to use with students who have language processing or memory problems (e.g., word retrieval)
Performance Spelling Assessment	• To assess the student's use of spelling words to communicate and to advance their writing skills	• Approach is individualized to each student • Encourages parent involvement in helping to select and study words • Uses a scoring and progress-monitoring system that can be used by students • Authentic and curriculum-based • Results used to plan instructional program	• Most performance-based assessments are language-based, thus may be problematic for students with language diversity

Mathematical Assessment

KEY TERMS AND CONCEPTS

- learned helplessness
- math probes
- mathematical error analysis
- oral math interview

- math inventory
- specific performance criteria
- mathematics-based life skills

CHAPTER OBJECTIVES

After reading this chapter, you should be able to:

- Describe the impact educational reforms have on math assessment
- Discuss math assessment standard reforms promoted by the NCTM
- Discuss how an evaluator can determine students' math dispositions
- Identify and describe factors that affect the math learning process

- Identify how information-processing problems affect math mastery
- Describe the types of errors that can be determined by using a math error analysis
- Identify the types of informal math assessments
- Discuss the importance of assessing mathematical life skills

Introduction to Mathematical Assessment

Mathematics is a multidimensional, cumulative process in which skills and concepts become increasingly complex and abstract. Skills learned during the earliest school years provide the foundation for mathematical conceptual development as well as the structure for subsequent higher level skill mastery. For example, the concept of fractional parts that is introduced at the readiness level when the teacher cuts an apple in half is continued throughout elementary and secondary grades as students learn to compute all basic operational functions with fractions and apply these concepts in advanced algebraic and geometric formats. Failure to understand the basic concepts of the math curriculum can seriously affect students' ability to succeed at subsequent levels of instruction. The developmental sequence of skills is evident when the curriculum focus at various grade levels is examined.

A math scope and sequence chart can be used to determine the skills covered in students' curriculum (scope) and the order (sequence) that these skills should be taught, thereby enabling the teacher to regularly evaluate students' progress in mastery of these skills. (See Figure 9–1 for a sample scope and sequence chart.)

Assessment should support the learning of mathematics skills and concepts and provide useful information to both teachers and students (National Council of Teachers of Mathematics, 2000). Traditional mathematical assessment has primarily focused on evaluating students' basic fact and computation skill development.

Educational reforms supported by research and promoted by the National Council of Teachers of Mathematics (NCTM) have called for a shift in emphasis. This professional education organization is promoting the use of assessment procedures that "(a) are criterion-referenced (tied directly to the instructional objectives and how well each student is doing in regard to them), (b) provide feedback (that is, specific information on what was done correctly, what is incorrect, and how to improve), and (c) are formative rather than summative because it is part of monitoring students' progress during instruction" (Gentile & Lalley, 2003, p. 39).

The NCTM has recommended assessing domains that seemed unfamiliar to many teachers: "dispositions toward mathematics," ability to "translate from one mode of representation to another," and ability to "express mathematical ideas by speaking, writing, demonstrating, and depicting them visually." The NCTM has endorsed revisions in the assessment and instructional processes that are more relevant and practical for students with special needs. The revised standards focus on promoting the active involvement of students in their learning, cooperative learning experiences in which students work with peers to develop meaningful solutions to mathematical problems, and increased emphasis on having students evaluate their own mathematical performance.

Evaluation procedures that teachers can use to measure these goals include observing students while solving problems, listening to their discussions of problem-solving processes, analyzing students' work samples (including tests, homework, journals, and essays), and using more authentic testing procedures. Figure 9–2 provides an overview of the impact of these assessment reforms. It highlights how these reforms reflect a move toward more authentic curricula and assessments that emphasize a performance-based approach and promote a positive attitude toward math, while also developing fluency and preparing students for real-life math experiences.

CLARIFYING TERMS

Dyscalculia is a severe disability in learning mathematical concepts and computation associated with central nervous system dysfunction (*Rourke & Conway, 1997*).

Figure 9–1   Math Scope and Sequence Chart

	Number and Operations	Geometry	Measurement	Data Analysis	Algebra
Kinder-garten	• Meaning, reading, and writing numbers (0–20) • Counting to 30 • Comparing/ordering (0–10) • Identifying ordinals (tenth) • Meaning of addition (part + part = whole)	• Location words • Recognize and name two-dimensional shapes • Recognize and name three-dimensional shapes • Describe attributes of shapes	• Measuring (length with units, comparing/estimating length, capacity, weight, temperature, and time) • Time (calendar, hour) • Money (penny)	• Classifying and sorting (comparing and contrasting attributes)	• Patterns (identify, reproduce, extend, create, and describe using shapes, objects, and numbers)
Grade 1	• Strategies • Meaning of addition and subtraction • Place value (ones, tens) • Two-digit addition/subtraction with and without regrouping • Addition and subtraction facts (to 12) • Fact families	• Solid shapes and faces (two and three dimensions)	• Measurement (process, linear) 1 minute • Time (hour, half hour, elapsed time) • Money (identifying, counting and comparing mixed coins, equivalents)	• Creating and reading graphs (bar and pictograph)	• Patterns (growing by +, −) • Properties of addition • Open number sentences
Grade 2	• Addition and subtraction facts (to 18) • Two- and three-digit addition and subtraction with regrouping • Place value (one thousands) • Concept of fractions • Estimation	• Properties of shapes • Congruency • Symmetry	• Measurement (weight, liquid, capacity, temperature) • Time (1, 5, and 15 minutes, elapsed, estimated) • Money (all coins and bills, relationships, compare and estimate)	• Types of graphs (circle) • Making comparisons • Using and interpreting data	• Patterns • Open sentences • Function machines
Grade 3	• Estimation and mental math • Money (making change +, −) • Multiplication (meaning, vocabulary, facts to 12, arrays, one-digit multiplier) • Division (meaning, vocabulary, one-digit divisor with remainders) • Logical reasoning	• Properties of two-dimensional shapes • Congruency (transformations) • Symmetry	• Concept of perimeter and area • Concept of $\frac{1}{2}$, $\frac{1}{4}$ • Measuring concrete units • Comparing units of measurement • Concept of temperature	• Choosing and constructing graphs and tables (line, pictograph, bar) • Timelines and graphs • Probability (likely or unlikely, fair or unfair)	• Plotting ordered pairs • Logical reasoning • Flowcharts • Properties of multiplication

Figure 9–1 *(Continued)*

	Number and Operations	Geometry	Measurement	Data Analysis	Algebra
Grade 4	• Decimals (+, −, $) • Meaning, strategy, algorithms (+, −, ×, /) • Fractions (concrete concepts) • Place value (millions to hundredths) • Estimation and mental math	• Comparing properties two- and three-dimensional figures (lines, angles, faces, vertices, sides)	• Measuring concrete objects • Linear measurement (1/8, 1/16) • Choosing approximate units for measurement • Finding perimeter, area, and volume	• Making and analyzing graphs • Probability • Tree diagrams • Mean, median, mode, range	• Input and output • Number sentences (with and without variables)
Grade 5	• All operations of decimals and fractions • Relationships among fractions, decimals, and percentages • Percent/ratio concept • Place value with decimals • Estimation and mental math • Number theory • Developing algorithms for fraction operation	• Measuring angles • Surface area and volume	• Recognizing and using appropriate measuring tools • Constructing of formulas for triangles and rectangles • Elapsed time	• Connecting decimals, fractions, and percentages with data analysis • Probability as decimals, fractions, percentages	• Properties of operations • Tables, rules, equations, graphs • Variables, use of formulas • Concrete materials, tables, graphs, verbal rules, algebraic notation
Grade 6	• Exponents • Variables and expressions • Estimation and mental math • Order of operations • Equations and number sense • Concept and proportion	• Plane geometry • Solid geometry • Perspective	• Perimeter and area • Surface area and volume • Irregular figures • Metric conversions	• Collecting data to generalize geometric relationships and formulas	• Informal expressions • Equations
Grade 7	• Scientific notation • Proportion-percentage connections • Equations and inverse operations • Absolute value • Estimation and mental math	• Similar figures • Dilations • Scale drawings • Indirect measurement	• Scale drawings • Indirect measurement • Metric proportionality • Standard measurement with proportions	• Central tendency analysis • Census, sampling • Graph constructions • Predictions, probability	• Proportional equations • Percentage equations • Real-life graphs (cause and effect) • Coordinate graphs • Impact area and volume
Grade 8	• Inequalities • Rational and irrational numbers • Squares and square roots • Estimation and mental math	• Pythagorean theorem • Transformations • Congruency • Symmetry	• Indirect measurement with variables	• Scatterplots and line fitting • Collecting and analyzing data to graph linear equations, functions • Predictions	• Nonterminating decimals • Nonlinear vs. linear equations • Functions • Inequalities • Polynomials

Source: Mount Laurel, NJ Board of Education Curriculum. Reprinted with permission.

Figure 9–2 Major Shifts in Mathematical Assessment Practices

Toward	Away from
Assessing students' full mathematical power	Assessing only students' knowledge of specific facts and isolated skills
Comparing students' performance with established criteria	Comparing students' performance with that of other students
Giving support to teachers and credence to their informed judgment	Designing "teacher-proof" assessment systems
Making the assessment process public, participatory, and dynamic	Making the assessment process secret, exclusive, and fixed
Providing students multiple opportunities to demonstrate their full mathematical power	Restricting students to a single way for demonstrating mathematical knowledge
Developing a shared vision of what to assess and how to do it	Developing assessment by oneself
Using assessment results to ensure that all students have the opportunity to achieve potential	Using assessment to filter and eliminate students from opportunities to learn their mathematics
Aligning assessment with curriculum and instruction	Treating assessment as independent of curriculum or instruction
Basing inferences on multiple sources of evidence	Basing inferences on restricted or single sources of evidence
Viewing students as active participants in the assessment process	Viewing students as the objects of assessment
Regarding assessment as continual and recursive	Regarding assessment as sporadic and conclusive
Holding all concerned with mathematics learning accountable for assessment results	Holding only a few accountable for assessment results

SECTION 1: MATHEMATICAL PROCEDURES

Besides mathematics tests, various assessment procedures are available to provide a comprehensive view of the whole child. These procedures include interviews involving the teacher and student, analyses of math work samples and measures in which the students themselves or their classmates rate their math performance, observations of the child while he or she is working on math-related tasks, and self- and peer assessment. Issues that affect mathematic skill and concept mastery are described in this section.

Interviews: Teachers, Parents, and Students

The teacher and the parents can provide information about the student's conceptual and strategic knowledge. They have a unique perspective on the student's math history, current strengths and weaknesses, how the student handles class work and homework, and the methods of instruction and/or interventions that have been beneficial. (See Figure 9–3.)

Student interviews are valuable in ascertaining students' insights and dispositions toward math: how they view their competency in math, and what areas of math they

Figure 9–3   Sample Parent-Teacher Interview Focus Questions

Does the student:

- appear confident when using mathematics for solving problems? _____
- plan before acting, revising plans when necessary? _____
- persevere in solving mathematical problems without being easily distracted? _____
- become actively involved in the problem? _____
- use calculators, computers, or other needed tools effectively? _____
- explain organizational and mathematical ideas? _____
- support arguments with evidence? _____
- demonstrate curiosity when performing mathematics activities? _____
- ask probing mathematical questions? _____
- demonstrate flexibility in solving mathematics problems? _____
- appear to see the value in applying mathematics to life activities? _____
- complete the task? _____
- review the process and the results? _____

like and do not like. In structured interviews, students can be asked strategy questions to determine how they approach word problems. In fact, the interviewing process can give teachers insight into how students communicate their mathematical knowledge, and how they confront, analyze, and solve word problems. (See Figure 9–4.)

Student interviews can be structured in several ways. One way is to ask students how they would perform a specific mathematical task, such as how to determine the amount of fencing needed to enclose the ball field. A second way is to allow students with reading or oral language problems, or those whose native language is not English, to communicate math problem-solving skills nonverbally through pantomime or by using manipulatives. A third option is to encourage students who demonstrate a high level of cognitive ability to verbally explain how they make judgments, justify, and evaluate their solutions to problems. (Figure 9–5 provides questions that can form the basis for a math interview.)

Figure 9–4   Interview Questions to Assess Problem-Solving Skills

Problem: _____

__ Self-Assessment   __ Peer Assessment   __ Teacher Assessment

Yes	Not Yet	Questions
1. ___	___	Can you explain the problem?
2. ___	___	Can you estimate a reasonable answer?
3. ___	___	Can you list steps to solve the problem?
4. ___	___	Can you think of another problem like it?
5. ___	___	Can you give an alternative solution?

Problem: _____

Operation to Use: _____

First Step: _____

Figure 9–5 Sample Student Math interview Questions

- Do you enjoy mathematics? _____
- How do you feel in math class? _____
- What was the best thing you learned today or this week in math class? _____
- What type of math activities do you most like? _____
- What math activities do you do particularly well? _____
- What types of math activities do you like least? _____
- What math activities are the hardest for you? _____
- What would you like more help with in math? _____
- Describe one particular problem that you found difficult. _____
- What do you do when you don't know how to solve a math problem? _____
- What errors do you make most often in math? _____
- Why do you think you make math errors? _____
- Tell about one new problem that you can now solve. _____
- How do you use math outside of school? _____
- Do you feel you learn best in math when you have to discover the answer by trial and error? _____ when tasks are demonstrated? _____ when you have a model? _____ when you can use manipulatives (e.g., sticks, a number line)? _____
- Do you learn best when you work with a whole class? _____ in small groups? _____ by yourself? _____
- How could math class be improved? _____

Analysis of Math Work Samples

A comprehensive math assessment involves careful analysis of students' work products, such as class assignments, board work, math worksheets, workbook pages, math textbook problems (copied and calculated), performance activities (both in process and the final activity), homework, and video or audiotape productions. (Figure 9–6 is a checklist for analyzing math work samples.)

Observation During Math Activities

Students should be observed while they are working on math tasks, during math instructional lessons, while involved in a cooperative activity in a small group (e.g., a performance task), and during large-group math instruction. (Focus questions that can serve as a guide when observing students who are solving word problems are provided in Figure 9–7.)

Tips for Teachers

Observation is important in understanding how students process information, focus, and communicate. How do they respond to new tasks or situations? How do they interpret math questions or directions? Can they transition from one idea or skill to another? Can they work without constant reinforcement or redirection?

Figure 9–6   Work-Sample Checklist: Math Performance Skills

Is the student able to:	Yes	No
• copy equations accurately from the chalkboard or textbook?	____	____
• complete a sufficient amount of math work within designated time limits?	____	____
• align numbers correctly when copying computation problems?	____	____
• maintain place on a math worksheet without skipping digits or equations?	____	____
• write numbers without reversing, transposing, or inverting?	____	____
• attend to the operational sign when working on a mixed-problem worksheet?	____	____
• solve basic computation without using fingers or manipulatives?	____	____
• align columns of numbers accurately?	____	____
• compute columns of numbers without losing his or her place?	____	____
• calculate equations in the right column?	____	____
• correctly sequence steps when computing equations with multiple digits?	____	____
• consistently use regrouping procedures (e.g., "borrowing" in 10s place)?	____	____
• tell time, recalling the months of the year, or days of the week?	____	____
• write multidigit equations from dictation?	____	____
• choose and use the correct operation when solving word problems?	____	____
• distinguish and ignore irrelevant information in story problems?	____	____
• read multidigit numbers without ordering or spacing problems?	____	____
• remember number words and digits?	____	____
• accurately space and place numbers when calculating multidigit equations?	____	____
• correctly use decimals in addition? subtraction? multiplication? division?	____	____
• reach "unreasonable" answers?	____	____
• recall number facts automatically (i.e., perform simple calculations)?	____	____
• check calculations, not settling for the first answer?	____	____
• work at an adequate pace when computing equations? when solving word problems?	____	____
• solve multistep problems?	____	____
• understand the language of math?	____	____

Student Self-Assessment

In the self-assessment process, students describe aloud or in written form during an instructional activity their perceptions of their math skills, motivation, and confidence level. (See Figures 9–8 and 9–9.) This process can give teachers information about what students are thinking, what they are doing, and how they feel they are doing while engaged in math tasks.

Students can list the steps they are following and tell if they are in correct sequence for calculating equations or solving problems. They can report on how they feel when required to solve math problems, as well as whether they can determine which operation to use, distinguish between relevant and irrelevant information in word problems, and accurately solve problems. To help students to think about what they learned or practiced during a particular activity, teachers may need to provide verbal prompts, such as

- Tell me what you did when you were first given a word problem to solve.
- Tell (or show) me how you did it.

Figure 9–7 Observation Questionaire

- Does the student seem interested in working on math tasks? _____
- Can the student maintain attention when working on math-related tasks? _____
- Does the student ask for oral directions to be repeated or clarified? _____
- Does the student understand and follow written directions? _____
- Can the student work independently? _____
- How often does the student need teacher or peer assistance? _____
- Does the student work cooperatively with peers in problem solving? _____
- Does the student copy at an adequate pace? _____ too quickly? _____ too slowly? _____
- Does the student appear to read the problem carefully? _____
- Does the student attend to details? _____
- Can the student copy and write numbers without reversing, inverting, or transposing? _____
- Does the student line up answers in the correct column (place value)? _____
- Does the student use the correct arithmetic processes (add instead of subtract)? _____
- Can the student shift from one arithmetic process to another? _____
- Does the student draw pictures to illustrate a problem? _____
- How does the student initially attack math problems? _____
- Can the student calculate without using concrete counting aids (fingers, markers)? _____
- Does the student use math manipulatives often? _____ accurately? _____
- Does the student use an appropriate strategy or attempt to use the last strategy taught? ____
- Does the student use a different strategy if the first one was unsuccessful? _____
- Is the student organized and using consistent strategies to solve math problems? _____
- What math strategies does the student use most often? _____
- Does the student make careless mistakes? _____ If so, what kind and why? _____
- Does the student persevere in solving a difficult math problem? _____
- Does the student use all the working space on the paper? _____
- Does the student give the same answer to different problems (perseverate)? _____

- Why did you decide to . . . ?
- What were you thinking about when you . . . ?
- What did you learn when you were working on the word problem?
- What problems did you have while working on it? How did you solve the problem?

Figure 9–8 Student Self-Report

While doing this assignment, I felt (check one)

___ confident that I knew how to solve all of the problems. I feel that I can teach others how to solve similar problems.

___ like I knew how to solve some problems, but there were many that I did not feel sure about. Please explain _____

_____

___ like I thought I could solve the problems when I started, but then I got confused and couldn't remember how to solve them. Please explain _____

_____

___ lost from the start. I never understood what the teacher was doing during instruction. Please explain _____

_____

Figure 9–9   Student Self-Assessment

Things We Do in Math Class	I Like	I Don't Like
Count objects		
Group objects		
Draw shapes		
Play math games		
Use a calculator		
Solve number problems		
Solve story problems		
Measure		
Tell time		
Make change		

- What would you do differently if you could work on the problem again?
- Did you choose the correct strategy to solve the problem?
- Did you organize and make a good plan before attempting to solve the problem?
- Did you use the appropriate operation to calculate the problem?

Students benefit when they begin to take more responsibility for their learning. To promote self-monitoring, teachers can provide them with self-evaluation questions that they should eventually begin to ask themselves. (See Figure 9–10.)

Peer Assessment

Peer assessment is a method of evaluation that allows students to compare their work with that of others and to gain insight into the reasoning and problem-solving abilities of their peers. This process promotes collaborative learning, analysis skills, and

Figure 9–10   Sample Self-Evaluation Questions

Before beginning a computation or word problem, briefly *focus* on:
- What am I about to do? Can I picture myself, or feel myself doing it well?
- What standards/criteria do I want to use to evaluate my performance?
- What do I want to remember from previous performances that will help me do better this time?

During the task, use *standards* or *criteria:*
- What are the standards I am using to judge whether I am doing this task well?
- How am I solving this equation/problem?
- Do I need to do anything differently?

After the task is complete, *think about learning and making connections:*
- What did I do?
- How did I do it?
- How well did I do it?
- How does this equation/problem relate to others I have done? What does it remind me of?
- What big ideas can I get from this?

Source: Appalachia Educational Laboratories (1994). On target with authentic assessment: Creating and implementing classroom models (AEL School Excellence Workshop). Charleston, WV. Reprinted with permission.

Figure 9–11   Peer Assessment—Math Word Problem Solving

When solving the problems, did the student:	Yes	No
• carefully read the problem?		
• restate the problem?		
• determine what is called for in the problem?		
• develop a plan?		
• underline the relevant information?		
• cross out irrelevant information?		
• visualize and draw the problem?		
• organize multiple steps into a correct sequence?		
• select the correct operation?		
• estimate the answer?		
• solve the problem?		
• check the answer?		

reflective skills. By applying criteria to the work of others, students learn to monitor the mathematical process in a way that is less threatening than self-assessment. In addition, peer assessment fosters respect for the work of others, and provides opportunities for positive interaction as students learn to give constructive criticism. (See Figure 9–11 for a sample peer assessment.)

SECTION 2: ASSESSMENT OF COMMON MATHEMATICAL PROBLEM AREAS

Mathematical Language Assessment

Students with learning problems often have difficulty comprehending, organizing, and appropriately using the language terms associated with mathematics, despite having adequate auditory skills (Lerner, 2003). An important step in the assessment process is to determine students' understanding of and ability to use mathematical terms, both in written and oral form, such as the following (Bryant, Bryant, & Hammill, 2000):

Does the Student

- understand mathematical relationships (greater than/less than)?
- understand the multiple meanings of math words, or instead
  a. confuse the noun form of a word ("color the circle red") with the same word used as a verb ("circle the group of four")?
  b. confuse synonyms that describe the same operation (addition, plus, more than)?
  c. confuse the meaning of group, place value, and minus?
- have the ability to differentiate between the symbolic aspects of math (e.g., understand operational signs and symbols)?
- have difficulty solving word problems, especially those with longer sentences and complex vocabulary?

- have trouble verbalizing what he or she is doing while analyzing, planning, calculating, and carrying out steps to solve word or computation problems?
- have difficulty comprehending the words that describe the many relationships in mathematics?

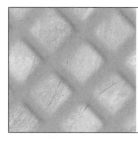

Tips for Teachers

Be alert for students who have adequate math ability but do poorly in class or on tests. Consider linguistic factors—not just computation skills—when students are experiencing difficulty. Math terms can be confusing, not only to students who have cultural and/or linguistic differences, but also for students with communication or learning disabilities.

Cultural and Language Differences

Students from culturally and linguistically diverse backgrounds who have learning difficulty often experience particular problems with the language of mathematics, especially with regard to semantics, linguistics, and symbols. The linguistic and symbolic features of mathematics can be difficult for these students to discern due to cultural factors (Scott & Raborn, 1996).

Does the Student

- understand words that are culturally unfamiliar (e.g., odd and even)?
- recognize the differences in structural relationships between words and syntax that can be confusing (e.g., the order of words in sentences) and algorithmic formats (e.g., reading from left to right, up and down)?

Math skill can be reinforced and attainment of specific skills can be assessed informally through fun activities, such as teacher-made board games.

Cognitive Factors

Students who have learning problems may have difficulty with cognitive processing or intellectual functioning. Information on these factors can often be obtained from baseline assessments, such as teacher-parent interviews, record reviews, work-sample analyses, classroom observations, and student interviews. Students who have cognitive disabilities demonstrate difficulty in the following areas:

Does the Student

- grasp new skills or concepts at a level comparable to age?
- learn new information at a rate comparable to age peers?
- retain information?
- comprehend and solve problems?
- analyze and synthesize information?
- grasp new learning without ongoing repetition?
- understand relationships, and cause and effect?
- evaluate and make judgments?
- attend to salient aspects of a situation?
- draw inferences, make conclusions, and hypothesize?
- reason abstractly and deal with complex issues?

Attitudes Toward Math and Emotional Factors

Many affective factors influence mathematical performance. Attitude seems to play an important role in academic performance. When students have a positive perception of their ability and a good attitude toward mathematics, they are more likely to approach math instruction in a positive manner and make a commitment to learning (Montague, 1997). Students who are anxious or depressed can have difficulty concentrating on math problems or during instruction, or in remembering number facts and rules, which may make them feel confused or overwhelmed. When students repeatedly try to solve problems but have little or no understanding of the math skills or concepts involved, they tend to become overdependent on the teacher for help. This pattern, referred to as **learned helplessness**, results in students becoming passive learners in math. Students who have experience these intense negative feelings about mathematics often display classic symptoms, which may be ascertained by asking the following questions related to their experience:

Does the Student

- perform poorly on math tests?
- display a serious dislike and avoidance of math activities?
- appear apathetic?
- have low self-confidence?
- give up easily or make excuses?
- lack of motivation?
- demonstrate classroom behavior problems?
- erase excessively?
- become inattentive or fidgety during math class?
- try to avoid doing any math tasks?
- fail to complete math assignments?
- submit assignments that are incomplete or done carelessly?

- complete work at an extremely slow pace or in a compulsive manner?
- show reluctance to even attempt a new task?
- tend to make self-deprecating comments about his or her poor ability?
- make excuses to avoid doing the math assignments?
- become physically ill when forced to take tests or quizzes?
- demonstrate symptoms of anxiety or phobia (e.g., rapid heart rate, increased breathing pace, stomach upset, onset of tension headaches, dizziness)?

CLARIFYING TERMS

Students who do not succeed in math—experiencing repeated failures or low grades—often develop a poor attitude and math anxiety. This serious phobic reaction is referred to as **mathophobia**.

Classroom Scenario: What Would You Do?

Maritsa has a long history of poor performance in math. When you approach her to do a math assessment, she resists. What would you do?

Ineffective Instruction

Because mathematics is a subject in which one skill builds upon another, students who do not have a solid foundation of core concepts and skills struggle to understand the new skills introduced into the curriculum. Often, students who fail at math have not had good or sufficient instruction.

When math instruction does not include good examples, lacks opportunities for students to use newly acquired math knowledge in meaningful ways, and does not represent math as being a valued and necessary part of daily life, students are deprived of the solid skill development and motivation they need to become competent in math. Asking the following questions can help determine whether a student's math incompetency is due to ineffective instruction (Ginsburg, 1997):

Does the Child have a Teacher who

- did not clearly demonstrate new skills?
- failed to ensure that each skill was acquired and proficiency established?
- neglected to allot sufficient time for practice and review?
- did not provide opportunities for application and generalization of each new skill with clear connections to real-life situations?
- inadvertently passed on negative feelings about math to students?
- failed to make math activities interesting and fun?
- did not prioritize math in the daily schedule?
- failed to make math instruction engaging by incorporating intriguing activities and topics into lessons?
- isolated math instruction rather than find opportunities to integrate math into other subject areas?

Classroom Scenario: What Would You Do?

Antonio, the new child in your fourth grade class, is a hard worker and a bright child, but he has not been doing well on tests. Your record review indicates that his family has moved in and out of state nine times since he was in kindergarten. What information will help you properly assess him?

Poor Abstract or Symbolic Thinking

Many students succeed in their math assignments only when the problems are illustrated or demonstrated, or when manipulatives are provided. Some students may be able to reach a level of proficiency on tasks that require rote manipulation of numbers, but when the level of conceptualization moves from concrete to abstract, they often have difficulty comprehending these higher level relationships and generalizations. To ascertain whether the student has poor abstract or symbolic thinking, the following questions should be asked:

Does the Student

- retain and recall fundamental facts?
- apply this knowledge to basic equations?
- understand basic math concepts?
- think abstractly symbolically?

Poor Reading Skills

Inadequate reading ability is frequently the reason that students have difficulty with the written portion of math assessments, specifically word problems. When students misread or cannot read the mathematical information, it is not clear whether their math problems are due to reading difficulties or to their inability to calculate and process mathematically. To help ascertain the cause of the students' difficulty, the teacher can ask the following questions:

Does the Student

- have the ability to correctly read mathematical word problems? the directions?
- identify the main idea or what the question is asking?
- determine the extraneous information?
- determine the order of operations, and sequence accurately?

Failure to Use Common Sense in Mathematics

Often students with learning problems have difficulty applying and generalizing what they learn. In many cases, they need to develop not only basic math skills, but also confidence in their ability to apply the logical and reasoning skills they use in non-academic situations to academic situations, specifically to mathematical problem solving. The following questions can help to ascertain whether a student has difficulty generalizing what he or she has learned.

Does the Student

- know how to calculate an equation or solve a word problem, but make a simple error and fail to note it?
- multiply instead of divide, and when the solution is a large number, fail to recognize that he or she used the wrong mathematical process?
- fail to use reasoning skills to analyze whether the sum, difference, or product could possibly be a reasonable answer to the problem he or she is trying to solve?
- have difficulty making realistic estimations of the solution to a problem?

> ## Classroom Scenario: What Would You Do?
>
> Carlita: rushes through word problems without giving them careful thought. For example, when asked how many candies she would need to buy in order to give her six friends three candies each, she responded, "Three." You know she can add and multiply. What do you do when assessing her?

Information Processing Problems

Students with learning disabilities often experience difficulty processing information, which determines what and how information is understood. Poor performance in mathematical operations, applications, reasoning, and communication may be due to attention deficits, or problems with auditory-processing or working memory. They may also be caused by deficits in visual-spatial, motor, cognitive and metacognitive problem solving, or general information processing (Wilson & Swanson, 2001). Students' mathematical competence may be complicated by problems with spatial relations, visual discrimination, sequencing and orientation confusion regarding procedures and mathematical rules, visual motor integration, or difficulty making transitions with a tendency to perseverate. Examples of mathematical processing problems include the following.

Attention Deficits

Does the Student

- have difficulty sustaining attention to critical instruction or directions?
- have difficulty maintaining focus on details?
- skip steps in algorithms or in the process of solving a problem?
- forget to subtract from the regrouped number when solving subtraction equations?
- neglect to add the carried number when solving addition or multiplication equations?

Auditory Processing Difficulties

Does the Student

- have difficulty during oral math drills?
- have difficulty counting in sequence?

Memory Problems

Does the Student

- have difficulty recalling and retaining numerals, strategies, sequences, facts, rules, or procedures?
- have difficulty retaining addition and subtraction facts, and the multiplication tables?
- have difficulty recalling the steps involved in or the order of mathematical processes?
- have difficulty with skills, such as telling time, or solving multistep word problems?

Difficulty in Mentally Shifting Between Mathematical Processes

Does the Student

- accurately solve equations involving one mathematical process (e.g., addition) but have difficulty making the transition to another process (e.g., subtraction)?

Mathematical Judgment and Reasoning Problems

Does the Student

- tend to be unaware when the solution to a math problem or an equation is unreasonable?
- have difficulty determining which process to use when trying to solve a word problem, resulting in an answer that is not feasible?
  Problem: Mary has 12 apples and wants to give her four friends an equal number of apples. How many apples does each friend get?
  Student response: 48 apples

Spatial Disorganization

Does the Student

- reverse numbers (backward 3 (Ɛ) for 3)?
- invert numbers (6 for 9)?
- transpose numbers (72 for 27)?
- align numbers inaccurately in columns?
- subtract the top from the bottom number in a computation problem?

Poor Number Formation

Does the student

- distort the shape or direction of numbers?
- copy or write numbers that are too large or small, or are poorly produced?

Inattention to Visual Detail

Does the Student

- misinterpret or misread mathematical signs?
- neglect to use decimals or dollar signs?

Motor Disabilities

Does the Student

- have difficulty writing numbers legibly or accurately?
- write at a slow rate?
- have difficulty forming numbers small enough to fit into required spaces, such as filling numbers in boxes on a form?

Tips for Teachers

Assessment should be comprehensive. Be sure to include a range of math skills. Students may not be proficient at computation but they may be able to solve applied problems. The child who has not mastered math facts may have good mathematical reasoning skills.

The IEP Connection

Based on the second-grade scope and sequence curriculum, you administer a criterion-referenced test to determine Julie's numerical operations skill as compared to second-grade norms. Results will be used to develop her individual education plan (IEP) goals for the annual review. You indicate on her IEP that Julie will require accommodations in order to be able to regroup subtraction equations.

Second-Grade Level Skills: Numerical Operations

Expected Second-Grade Addition and Subtraction Skills. Add and subtract basic facts with sums or differences to 18, with and without regrouping.

Julie's Addition and Subtraction Skill Assessment Results:

1. Julie has mastered the ability to add basic facts with sums to 18 without regrouping; her ability to add basic facts with sums to 18 with regrouping is beginning to emerge.
2. Julie has mastered the ability to subtract basic facts with sums to 10 without regrouping, but she is unable to subtract digits requiring regrouping.

IEP Progress Skill Check Points (matching assessment results):

1. Using manipulatives and given 20 two-digit equations with sums to 18 requiring regrouping, Julie will be able to correctly add 80% of the equations.
2. Using a number line and given 20 two-digit equations with differences to 18 not requiring regrouping, Julie will be able to correctly subtract 80% of the equations.
3. Using a number line and manipulatives and given 20 two-digit equations with differences to 18 requiring regrouping, Julie will be able to correctly subtract 80% of the equations.

SECTION 3: MATHEMATICAL ASSESSMENT MEASURES

Mathematics Curriculum-Based Measurement

Curriculum-based measurement (CBM) is an effective and efficient means to assess and monitor students' progress in the mathematics curriculum. A math CBM can test a single math skill or skills in several areas.

Math probes, used in association with curriculum-based measures, are quick and efficient ways to measure and monitor students' progress in their math curriculum.

Curriculum-Based Math Probes

Probes are timed samples that assess skill accuracy and fluency. Accuracy, which is used to identify whether students have acquired a skill, is generally the area that is stressed in evaluation. Fluency is based on how quickly students perform or recall a math fact, process, or procedure. When students are fluent in completing a skill, they are more likely to remember it, become more automatic in performing it, and are better able to master more advanced skills. They are also more likely to be successful with higher level skills. When students can complete math tasks quickly, they are more likely to perform at a level comparable to their grade peers, which enables them to be more successful in inclusive class settings. (See Figure 9–12 for a primary-level missing-number probe and Figures 9–13 and 9–14 for elementary- and secondary–level multiple-skill math calculation probes.)

Figure 9–12 Sample Primary-Level CBM Math Probe: Missing Numbers

Directions: Fill in the missing number in the space provided for each of the following number sequences.

				score:
1 ___ 3	2 ___ 4	1 2 ___	2 3 ___	___ / 4 of 4
5 6 ___ 7	7 ___ 9	___ 6 7	4 ___ 5	___ / 4 of 8
___ 8 9	___ 4 5	___ 9 10	6 7 ___	___ / 4 of 12

Figure 9–13 Sample Elementary-Level Math Calculation CBM

Directions: Perform the calculations required for each of the following problems and write your answer in the space provided.

Addition: | | | **Subtraction:**

| 1. 4
 + 3 | 2. 3
 + 5 | 3. 6
 + 2 | 4. 5
 − 4 | 5. 9
 − 7 | 6. 7
 − 3 |

Missing addend:

7. 6 + __ = 8   8. 3 + __ = 9   9. 9 + __ = 19

Two-digit addition:

| 10. 76
 + 12 | 11. 54
 + 45 | 12. 32
 + 67 | 13. 46
 + 47 | 14. 38
 + 43 | 15. 65
 + 38 |

Two-digit subtract:

| 16. 14
 − 6 | 17. 18
 − 9 | 18. 12
 − 7 | 19. 47
 − 23 | 20. 56
 − 42 | 21. 74
 − 63 |

Write the numbers:

22. 4 tens, 3 ones   23. 5 hundreds, 7 tens, 3 ones   24. 8 thousands, 7 ones

_____   _____   _____

Tell what place 5 holds:

25. 256 _____   26. 583 _____   27. 495 _____

Compare the numbers using > or <:

28. 64 _____ 46   29. 12 _____ 2 × 4   30. 26 − 7 _____ 24

Figure 9–14   Sample Secondary-Level CBM Math Probe: Order of Operations

---

Directions: Fill in the missing number in the space provided for each of the following calculations.

$7 + 2 - \_\_\_ = 3$	$6 \times 47 \times \_\_\_ = 282$	$98 - 49 + \_\_\_ = 77$	$9 + 4 \times \_\_\_ = 13$
$81 \div \_\_\_ + 37 = 46$	$64 \div \_\_\_ \times 33 = 528$	$45 \div \_\_\_ + 26 = 31$	$40 \div 5 + \_\_\_ = 12$
$\_\_\_ \times 26 + 47 = 255$	$7 \times 19 + 21 \times \_\_\_ = 196$	$\_\_\_ \div 9 \times 25 = 125$	$76 \times 43 - \_\_\_ = 3{,}265$

When constructing math probes, at least four items per target skill should be included in order to provide an adequate sampling of the skills covered in the curriculum and for error analysis. This helps to determine whether the mistake was a random error or whether a pattern of error exists. To ensure reliability, each probe should be administered at least three times. Generally, a calculation rate of 40 to 60 correct digits per minute is considered appropriate for students in grades 3 and above (Crawford, 2000; Starkin & Starkin, 1973). Students should master a minimum of one operation each year. Some students may have difficulty writing 100 digits in one minute. When writing numbers is difficult, the response mode should be changed. For example, the student can respond orally as the teacher records the response or checks the answer sheet (Crawford, 2000).

How to Conduct a Curriculum-Based Math Probe

1. Students are given a sheet of math equations. For a single-skill probe, only one type of equation (e.g., single-digit addition or single-digit subtraction) is on the probe sheet. For a multiple-skill probe, several types of equations (e.g., a mixture of several addition and subtraction equations not requiring regrouping, several requiring regrouping, several single-digit multiplication equations, and several single-digit division equations) are on the probe sheet.
2. Students are told to start with the first equation on the left on the top row (and shown where to begin), to work across and then to go to the next row, and to continue without skipping any equations or rows.
3. Students are told to complete the page as quickly and carefully as possible.
4. Students who have difficulty with an equation are told to write their best answer and to then move on.
5. Students are told not to erase.
6. The teacher monitors the students to make sure that they are following directions and that they are working in sequential order rather than randomly skipping around to solve the easier problems.
7. Students are told to stop at one minute.

How to Score a Curriculum-Based Math Probe

1. Count the number of correctly written digits, even if the equations are not completed (do not count digits written for regrouping purposes).
2. Place value is important; the number must be in the correct column to be marked correct.
3. Do not give points to numbers marked at the top of a number column used as reminders to regroup or carry (e.g., in the example in step 9, the 2 carried in 10s' place in the multiplication equation is not counted).

4. Do not mark reversed or rotated numbers as incorrect.
5. Do not give points for remainders of zero.
6. Give full credit (the total number of correct digits) even if the calculation work is not shown.
7. If the calculation work is shown but the answer is incorrect, give 1 point for each correct digit in the answer.
8. Count digits above and below the line.
9. Each correct digit is counted (rather than scoring 1 point for all the digits in a correct answer) because digit count scores are more sensitive to changes in student performance (Tindal & Marston, 1990). On complicated equations, point values need to be assigned, with points assigned to each correctly performed step in the equation. For example, a correct digit (CD) is a digit in the equation that is in the proper place-value location:

$$
\begin{array}{llll}
 & & (2) & \\
\quad 4 & \quad 56 & \quad 47 & \quad 12r35\ (4\ CD) \\
+\ 5 & -\ 23 & *\ \ 3 & 42\overline{)539} \\
\hline
9\ (1\ CD) & 33\ (2\ CD) & 141\ (\ 3\ CD) & \underline{42x} \\
 & & & 119\ (3\ CD) \\
 & & & \underline{84}\ (2\ CD) \\
 & & & 35\ (2\ CD)\ =\ (11\ CD)
\end{array}
$$

10. To determine correct digits per minute (cdpm), divide the number of digits correct on a two-minute probe by 2. If the student completes the probe in less than two minutes, calculate the cdpm by dividing the number of correct digits by the number of seconds and multiplying by 60.
11. The following cutoff levels can be used to determine whether the student is functioning at an independent, instructional, or frustration level (Alper & Mills, 2001):

	Grades 1–3	**Grades 4+**
Mastery	20+ cdpm	40+ cdpm
Instructional	10–19 cdpm	20–39 cdpm
Frustration	20 cdpm	40+ cdpm

Suggested scoring guides for basic addition, subtraction, multiplication, and division equations are provided in Figures 9–15 and 9–16. However, rate can vary depending on the student's age and motor skill competence (ability to form numbers), as well as the difficulty level of the task. Researched math calculation norm probes are listed in Figure 9–17.

Graphing Math Probe Results

Graphing students' scores is a method of monitoring their progress. A chart is developed for a specific period of time (e.g., eight weeks, a marking period). Students' individualized education plan (IEP) goals and objectives can be used as a projected level of mastery. This mastery level is plotted on the graph as a mastery or an aimline for each skill that is being monitored. When the graphed scores are below the aimline three or more times, intervention should be revised. Likewise, when steady progress

Figure 9–15   Mathematics CBM Mastery Checklist

Concepts	Problem Numbers	Day 1	Day 2	Day 3	Total Score	Mastery 8/9
Addition facts (0–9)	1, 2, 3	__ /3	__ /3	__ /3	__ /9	__
Addition facts (10–19)	4, 5, 6	__ /3	__ /3	__ /3	__ /9	__
Subtraction facts (0–9)	7, 8, 9	__ /3	__ /3	__ /3	__ /9	__
Subtraction facts (10–19)	10, 11, 12	__ /3	__ /3	__ /3	__ /9	__
Missing addends (0–9)	13, 14, 15	__ /3	__ /3	__ /3	__ /9	__
Missing addends (10–19)	16, 17, 18	__ /3	__ /3	__ /3	__ /9	__
Add 2 digits (no regrouping)	19, 20, 21	__ /3	__ /3	__ /3	__ /9	__
Add 2 digits (regrouping)	22, 23, 24	__ /3	__ /3	__ /3	__ /9	__
Add 3 digits (1 regrouping)	25, 26, 27	__ /3	__ /3	__ /3	__ /9	__
Add 3 digits (2 regroupings)	28, 29, 30	__ /3	__ /3	__ /3	__ /9	__
Subtraction facts (2 digit − 1 digit)	31, 32, 33	__ /3	__ /3	__ /3	__ /9	__
Subtract 2 digits (no regrouping)	34, 35, 36	__ /3	__ /3	__ /3	__ /9	__
Write digits	37, 38, 39	__ /3	__ /3	__ /3	__ /9	__
Place value	40, 41, 42	__ /3	__ /3	__ /3	__ /9	__
Compare numbers	43, 44, 45	__ /3	__ /3	__ /3	__ /9	__

Time: 1 minute

Materials: Student—response sheet, pencils
                    Teacher—timer

Figure 9–16   Grade-Level Computation Scoring Guide

Objective	Grade Level	Time	No. Completed	No. Errors
Addition facts (0–9)	2–3	1 minute	20–30 digits	2 or fewer
Subtraction facts (difference to 5)	2–3	1 minute	20–30 digits	2 or fewer
Addition and subtraction facts	3–4	1 minute	40–60 digits	2 or fewer
Addition: 2 column with regrouping	4–5	1 minute	40–60 digits	2 or fewer
Subtraction: 2 column with regrouping	4–6	1 minute	40–60 digits	2 or fewer
Multiplication facts	5–6	1 minute	40–60 digits	2 or fewer
Division facts	6	1 minute	40–60 digits	2 or fewer

is charted with recordings consistently above the aimline, the goal line should be adjusted upward. (Figure 9–18 is an example of a CBA math probe with the target set for 50 correct digits per minute.)

Mathematical Error Analysis

A common way to grade math papers is to look at the answer and mark it correct or incorrect, calculate the percentage or rate of correct responses, and place the score or letter grade at the top of the paper. When a teacher uses this method of evaluation,

Figure 9–17 CBM Norms for Math Computation Fluency

Grades 1 through 3		
Instructional Level	**Digits Correct Per Minute**	**Digits Incorrect Per Minute**
Frustration	0–9	8 or more
Instructional	10–19	3–7
Mastery	20 or more	2 or fewer
Grades 4 and above		
Instructional Level	**Digits Correct Per Minute**	**Digits Incorrect Per Minute**
Frustration	0–19	8 or more
Instructional	20–39	3–7
Mastery	40 or more	2 or fewer

Based on research from *Data-based program modification: A manual*, by S. L. Deno & P. K. Mirkin, 1977, Reston, VA: Council for Exceptional Children.

Figure 9–18 Sample Math CBM Probe Graph

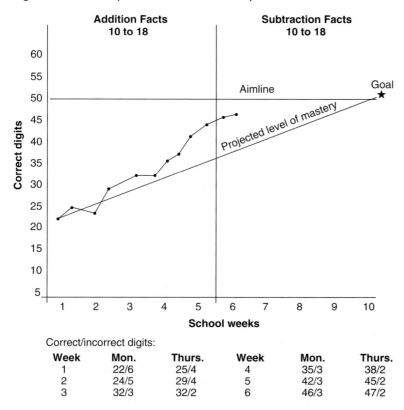

Correct/incorrect digits:

Week	Mon.	Thurs.	Week	Mon.	Thurs.
1	22/6	25/4	4	35/3	38/2
2	24/5	29/4	5	42/3	45/2
3	32/3	32/2	6	46/3	47/2

Figure 9–19 Sample Miscue Analysis for Math Word Problems

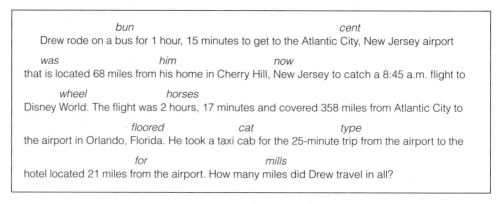

important diagnostic information can be omitted. It is necessary to analyze the process used in order to discover the reason the error was made.

Mathematical error analysis enables the teacher to (a) identify the types of content, operations, applications, problem-solving, and consumer skill errors being made; (b) figure out why the student is making these errors, and (c) determine if a pattern of errors is apparent, which ultimately provides critical instructional data that can be used to remediate the problem(s) (Ashlock, 2002). (See Figure 9–19 for a sample miscue analysis, and Figure 9–20 for a math skills assessment scale.)

After completing the mathematical error analysis, a summary and graph of the types of errors can be developed for instructional planning purposes and to monitor progress (e.g., IEP math progress skill points). Errors may not fall into a specific pattern, and some errors may not indicate a serious or consistent problem.

Figure 9–20 Math Skills Assessment Scale

Nov	Mar	Jan		
☐	☐	☐	**Effort**	
☐	☐	☐	**Class participation**	
☐	☐	☐	**Beginning**	Solves problems and completes assignments with support; shows some understanding of math concepts; requires support to produce accurate work in learning to use math facts
☐	☐	☐	**Developing**	Completes required assignments; solves problems with assistance; needs assistance learning math concepts; needs support to produce accurate assignments; beginning to use math facts
☐	☐	☐	**Capable**	Completes required assignments; solves problems with occasional assistance; understands math concepts; visually accurate on assignments; recalls and uses math facts
☐	☐	☐	**Strong**	Does some enrichment/extra credit math work; solves problems independently; applies previously learned math concepts; accurately completes assignments; confidently recalls and uses math facts
☐	☐	☐	**Exceptional**	Uses higher order thinking strategies extensively to solve problems independently; independently applies previously learned math concepts; demonstrates high level of accuracy on assignments; confidently recalls and uses all math facts

Steps in Error Analysis

STEP 1: Get a sample or an informal inventory of the student's math work by collecting examples of the types of equations and math problems used in the student's current math curriculum and using at least three to four items from each type. Recent class work, math workbook pages, homework, and worksheets can also be used to initially analyze the skills that have been mastered, those that are emerging, and those that have not yet been acquired.

STEP 2: Grade the math inventory or work sample. Identify types of errors that were made, focusing on the particular pattern of mistakes.

STEP 3: If the reason for the errors is not obvious, use a task analysis to break down the particular equation or problem into small steps of components (see the discussion of task analysis later in this chapter). This will help to isolate the point in the mathematical process in which the problem is occurring.

STEP 4: Do an oral math interview with the student (see the discussion of oral math interviews later in this chapter). This allows the student to verbally describe the thought process he or she used while working to solve the equation or word problem. This is an excellent way to determine how students tackle a problem, if they are using the correct mathematical operation, if they are correctly sequencing the steps, at which step in the process they become confused, if they are using good reasoning skills, and so forth.

STEP 5: When analyzing word problems, check to determine the magnitude of the discrepancy between the incorrect and correct responses. Often, small discrepancies for large numbers indicate carelessness in the computational aspect of the task. Also, the magnitude of the response may indicate the selection of the wrong operation (e.g., the teacher expects the answer to be a small number because the requested operation is division but student gives a large answer, which suggests he or she may have incorrectly used the multiplication process). Check whether the response could have resulted from calculating the wrong numerical data in the problem (e.g., when extraneous information is present).

STEP 6: Conduct a reading miscue analysis to identify whether the student is using correct strategies for solving story problems. This analysis is used to identify reading behaviors that can interfere with problem solving, such as substituting incorrect words or omitting key words. Students first read the passage silently, and then orally. Errors due to decoding or comprehension breakdowns are noted. Miscue errors often affect the semantic or syntactic integrity of the passage (e.g., vocabulary or grammar errors). Thus, word problem inaccuracies may result from reading problems rather than from students' inability to compute accurately or their inability to accurately use computation in applied situations (See Figure 9–19 for a sample miscue analysis and the steps involved in checking for understanding.)

STEP 7: Determine whether the errors are systemic or sporadic. This is an important step in analyzing both written equation calculations and word problems. Systemic errors result from the consistent use of an incorrect number fact, operation, or algorithm. This type of error generally means that the student does not understand a rule or fact and consistently misapplies it. Sporadic errors are inconsistent and random with no particular pattern. This type of error usually indicates that the student is guessing because he or she has not learned or cannot remember the facts or rules to apply.

STEP 8:   Analyze and categorize the errors by type. This step is needed to determine the pattern of errors that occur consistently over several problems and frequently over time. Common types of mistakes include random errors (especially for students with achievement problems), incorrect algorithms (the most common for all other students), inaccurate number facts, and incorrect operations. More than one type of error may be noted for many math problems.

STEP 9:   Rate the developmental level of performance. (See Figure 9–20.)

STEP 10: Graph the errors so that a record of progress can be maintained.

Recognizing Mathematical Errors

Teachers should be familiar with the following types of errors students tend to make when solving equations and applied problems.

Basic fact error.   Was the operation performed correctly but a simple calculation error made due to inaccurate recall of number facts? For example, the student doesn't know the multiplication facts:

$$6 \times 7 = 49$$

Regrouping.   Was there confusion about place value, either carrying or borrowing numerals incorrectly or failing to regroup when appropriate? For example, the student wrotes the entire sum of each column without regrouping:

$$\begin{array}{r} 28 \\ + \ 8 \\ \hline 216 \end{array}$$

Incorrect operation.   Was the wrong operation or process used during one or more of the computation steps, creating a different algorithm that resulted in an incorrect answer? For example, the student used the addition process to solve a multiplication equation:

$$\begin{array}{r} 34 \\ \times \ 2 \\ \hline 36 \end{array}$$

Incorrect algorithm.   Were the procedures used to solve the problem inappropriate? Was a step skipped, were steps out of sequence, or was the operation performed inappropriately? For example, the student attempted to solve the equation by subtracting the smaller number from the larger number:

$$\begin{array}{r} 43 \\ - \ 29 \\ \hline 26 \end{array}$$

Directional.   Although the computation is accurate, were the steps performed in the wrong direction or order? For example, the student used a left-to-right progression when calculating:

The IEP Connection

As Emily's teacher, you used CBA probes to determine Emily's present level of math performance and to monitor her progress throughout the year on a biweekly basis. By graphing her progress, you are able to determine whether she has met her projected IEP goals and can better predict goals for the coming year as you prepare for her end-of-year annual review. The following is a draft of her IEP, which specifies grade-level state core standard benchmarks, expected progress, and dates when indicators of progress will be recorded throughout the next school year.

Individualized Education Plan

Emily Rose	9-26-99	1st	4-27-05
Student's Name	Birthdate	Grade	Date

Present Level of Academic Achievement and Functional Performance: Math

Emily can add and subtract single-digit equations with sums to 10 with 80 percent accuracy, but when sums increase to 12 her accuracy decreases to 70 percent even with the use of manipulatives. She has acquired the ability to compute two-digit addition and subtraction without regrouping but has not developed proficiency in this skill with only 60 percent accuracy. She is able to use place value in the ones and tens place but needs to use graph paper for correct alignment of numbers. She is able to count by fives and tens consistently, and her ability to count by twos is emerging.

State Grade 2 Benchmark

Maintain addition and subtraction facts to 12.
Master addition and subtraction facts from 13 to 18.

Annual Goal

In one year, when given math probes, Emily will add and subtract equations to 12 with 80 percent accuracy without relying on manipulatives. She will add two-digit equations with regrouping to 18 with 80 percent accuracy and subtract two-digit equations with 70 percent accuracy using a number line. She will count by twos and threes.

$$\begin{array}{r} 3 \\ 57 \\ + 85 \\ \hline 115 \end{array}$$

Omission. Is a step in the process missing or has part of the answer been left out? For example, the student failed to multiply in the 10s place.

$$\begin{array}{r} 423 \\ \times 241 \\ \hline 423 \\ 846 \\ \hline 85023 \end{array}$$

The IEP Connection (Continued)

Progress Skill Checkup Points	Criteria	June 2005	Nov. 2005	Jan. 2006	Mar. 2006
1. Given a math probe, Emily will accurately solve problems involving addition and subtraction to 12 not requiring regrouping with . . .	80% accuracy (8 out of 10 problems)	6-2005			
2. Given a math probe, Emily will accurately solve problems involving two-digit addition to 18 requiring regrouping with . . .	80% accuracy (8 out of 10 problems)		11-2005		
3. Given a math probe, Emily will accurately solve problems involving two-digit subtraction to 18 requiring regrouping with . . .	70% accuracy (7 out of 10 problems)			1-2006	
4. Emily will accurately count by . . .	twos and threes				3-2006

Evaluation procedures for each Progress Points   **Review schedule**

✓ Daily work samples   ✓ Performance assessment   ✓ Weekly
✓ Teacher observation   — Clinical math interview   — Monthly
✓ CBA probe   — Criterion-reference test   — Quarterly

Placement.   Is the computation correct but the answer inaccurate because the numbers were written in the wrong column? For example, the student misaligned numbers in the multiplication process:

$$
\begin{array}{r}
72 \\
\times\ 31 \\
\hline
72 \\
216 \\
\hline
288
\end{array}
$$

Attention to sign.   Was the operational sign ignored, causing the wrong mathematical operation to be performed? Did the student fail to attend to, understands, or perceive the correct shape of the computation sign, such as failing to note the difference between the addition sign ($+$), the subtraction sign ($-$) and the multiplication sign ($\times$)? For example, the student confused the process, using the subtraction process on an addition equation:

$$
\begin{array}{r}
765 \\
+\ 24 \\
\hline
741
\end{array}
$$

Random error. Is the response incorrect and apparently a guess? Do the errors demonstrate a lack of basic understanding of the processes or skills being assessed? For example, the student made careless errors:

$$
\begin{array}{r}
25 \\
+\ 43 \\
\hline
100
\end{array}
$$

Common Calculation Errors Made by Elementary Students

Addition

Errors in combinations
Counting
Added carried number last
Forgot to add carried number
Repeated work after partly done
Wrote number to be carried
Irregular procedure in column
Carried wrong number
Grouped two or more numbers
Split numbers into parts
Used wrong fundamental
  operation
Lost place in column
Depended on visualization
Disregarded column position
Errors in reading numbers

Dropped back one or more tens
Derived unknown combination from
  familiar one
Disregarded one column
Error in writing answer
Skipped one or more decades
Carried when there was nothing
  to carry
Omitted one or more digits
Used scratch paper
Added in pairs, giving last sum as
  answer
Added same number twice
Added same digit in two columns
Wrote carried number in
  answer

Subtraction

Errors in combinations
Did not allow for having
  borrowed
Counting mistakes
Errors due to zero in minuend
Subtracted minuend from
  subtrahend
Failed to borrow; gave zero as
  answer
Added instead of subtracted
Error in reading
Skipped one or more decimals
Omitted a column
Used trial-and-error addition
Deducted from minuend when
  borrowing was not necessary
Ignored a digit

Split numbers
Deducted twice from minuend after
  borrowing
Error due to minuend, subtrahend digits
  being same
Increased minuend digit after
  borrowing
Used minuend or subtrahend as
  remainder
Confused process of division with
  multiplication
Derived unknown from known
  combination
Used same digit in two-column
  multiplication
Based subtraction on multiplication
  combination

Multiplication

Errors in combinations
Error in adding the carried number
Wrote rows of zeros
Carried a wrong number
Errors in addition
Forgot to carry
Based unknown combination on known one
Error in single-zero combinations, zero as multiplier
Errors due to zero in multiplier
Used wrong process—added
Error in single-zero combinations, zero as multiplicand
Errors due to zero in multiplicand
Error in position of partial products
Counted to get multiplication combinations
Reversed digits in product

Confused products when multiplier has two or more digits
Repeated part of table
Multiplied by adding
Did not multiply a digit in multiplicand
Used multiplicand as multiplier
Wrote tables
Errors in reading
Counted to carry
Omitted digit in writing product
Errors in carrying into zero
Multiplied by same digit twice
Omitted digit in multiplier
Split multiplier
Wrote wrong digit of product
Illegible figures
Forgot to add partial products

Division

Errors in division combinations
Errors in subtraction
Errors in multiplication
Used remainder larger than divisor
Found quotient by trial multiplication
Neglected to use remainder within problem
Used dividend or divisor as quotient
Counted to get quotient
Repeated part of multiplication table
Used short division form for long division
Wrote remainders within problem
Omitted zero resulting from zero in dividend
Omitted final remainder
Used long-division form for short division
Said example backward

Used remainder without new dividend figure
Errors in reading
Derived unknown combinations from known one
Split dividend
Grouped too many digits in dividend
Omitted zero resulting from another digit
Reversed dividend and divisor
Found quotient by adding
Used too large a product
Used digits of divisor separately
Wrote remainders at end of problem
Misinterpreted table
Used digit in dividend twice
Used second digit or divisor to find quotient
Began dividing at units digit of dividend

The IEP Connection

As the special education teacher co-teaching with the general education teacher in a fourth-grade class, you have developed a system to track progress toward meeting IEP goals and report progress to parents. Your students' math computation instructional levels range from third to fourth grade. You monitor and document progress with the following:

Math Facts	Progress Skill Checkup Points	Check Dates		
		N	M	J
Grade 3	Student will be able to:			
2d# + 2d# + 2d# w/reg.	add three 2-digit numbers, regrouping ones and tens	☐	☐	☐
3d# − 3d#	subtract 3-digit number from 3-digit number	☐	☐	☐
3d# × 1d# w/reg.	multiply 3-digit by 1-digit number, regrouping 1s, 10s, 100s	☐	☐	☐
Grade 4	Student will be able to:			
3d# × 2d#, w/0 reg.	multiply 3-digit number by 2-digit numbers, no regrouping	☐	☐	☐
4d#/2d#, w/0 rem.	divide 4-digit number by 2-digit number, no remainder	☐	☐	☐

Oral Math Interview

The **oral math interview** is an effective method for gaining insight into how students approach a task, process information, use mathematical strategies, as well as the analysis skills they use to arrive at a final product as they explain the steps they would go through in tackling a specific math task (Vallecorsa, deBettencourt, & Zigmond, 2001). This method of informal assessment allows the teacher to hear and identify specific problems and error patterns, and to better understand students' thought processes while they "think aloud" the solution to math problems. The oral interview is also a means of assessing students' math language skills (see Figure 9–21), and their social-emotional reaction to math by determining whether they have a negative attitude toward math tasks or feel anxious when working with math equations or word problems. Also, the interview can be useful when planning instruction for teaching the correct algorithm and developing an understanding of math processes.

Tips for Teachers

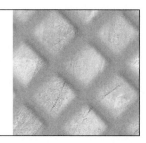

At least until competency is reached, a "think aloud" should be conducted individually to avoid embarrassing the student. For example, asking a student to go to the chalkboard and explain the problem in front of the class, even if peers are doing this, can be very upsetting to a child who is struggling with math. (See the section on attitudes toward math.)

Figure 9–21   Math Language Checklist

The student can identify:	Mastered	Emerging	Unmastered
Relationship words			
• Temporal: before, after, first, last, early, late			
• Positional: top, bottom, under, over, on, in, off, over, under			
• Comparative: greater than, less than, bigger, shorter, longer			
• Spatial: long, narrow, near, far, tall, short, thin, fat, wide, narrow			
• Sequential: next, between, after, in front of, behind, before			
Number words			
• Counting: numbers starting with 1, 2, 3, 4, 5, . . .			
• Whole: numbers including zero—0, 1, 2, 3, 4, 5, . . .			
• Cardinal: the total of a set (e.g., //// = 4)			
• Ordinal: identify a position—first, second, third, . . .			
Time words			
• General time: morning, early, night, noon, tomorrow, day, yesterday			
• Clock words: watch, hour hand, seconds, long hand, minutes, alarm clock			
• Calendar words: date, birthday, vacation, holiday, days of the week, month, yesterday, names of the seasons			
Shape words			
• Round, corners, flat, triangle, cylinder, sides, box			
Symbols of math			
• Ideas: numbers (1, 2, 3), elements (X, Y)			
• Relations: $=, \neq, <, >$			
• Operations: $+, -, \times, \div$			
• Punctuation			
decimal point: $4.50			
comma: 4,500			
parentheses: $7 + (9 - 4) = 12$			
brackets: $5 \times [2 + (3 + 2)] = 35$			
braces ($C = \{2, 4, 6\}$)			

The interview process involves both talking to and observing students. Generally, the interview is completed one on one between the teacher and the individual student. The teacher may need to guide students through the process as they compute an equation or solve a word problem by asking leading questions and giving prompts, particularly if this is a new procedure for them.

Steps in Error Analysis

Step 1:   Identify the area of difficulty by (a) observing the student in class; (b) analyzing math worksheets, workbooks, homework assignments, and so forth; and (c) noting errors on standardized or informal classroom tests (Bartel, 2004).

Step 2:   Analyze the types of problems (see the discussion of error analysis earlier in this chapter) and choose one of the simplest or easiest type of errors to begin with. Use a task analysis approach, making sure to choose the first type of problem according to its hierarchy in a task analysis. For example, if the student is making errors on addition, multiplication, and division equations, choose the addition equation first and then move to the multiplication before the division equation.

Step 3:   Plan to begin the process slowly and on a small scale. The first interview session should be short, and following sessions increased in length and complexity as the student becomes more experienced in this process. Have a tape recorder available to record the interview, so that you can analyze it later. Make sure the student is aware that the session is being taped.

Step 4:   Explain the purpose of the interview, making sure the student is comfortable and rapport is established.

Step 5:   Provide the student with the problem to be solved.

Step 6:   Ask the student to solve the problem on paper or on a chalkboard while orally explaining what he or she is doing (keep in mind that this is a diagnostic exercise, not an instructional lesson).

Step 7:   If the student begins to write the problem without orally explaining the process or steps involved, ask, "Why did you do that?"

Step 8:   Allow the student to solve the problem without making comments, providing clues, asking leading questions, or answering questions. If the student asks a question or seeks guidance, reply that it is important that he or she tries to solve the problem without help.

Step 9:   Reinforce the student's responses by nodding, smiling, and generally affirming the feedback you are getting. If the student's response is unclear, repeat the last statement and pause as if waiting for the student to continue, or ask the student to describe what was done in another way.

Step 10: If the student's response lacks sufficient detail, ask leading questions, such as, "Can you tell me why you put that number 3 there?"

Step 11: Continue until all problems are presented and orally explained by the student. Stop and reschedule for another time if the student appears to become tired, distracted, or discouraged.

Step 12: Formulate a summary of the student's strengths and weaknesses in each skill area.

Task Analysis

Task analysis is used to determine a hierarchical sequence of skills. Each mathematical operation or process can be broken down into the discrete components or steps involved in arriving at a solution. Once the task is broken down into these discrete

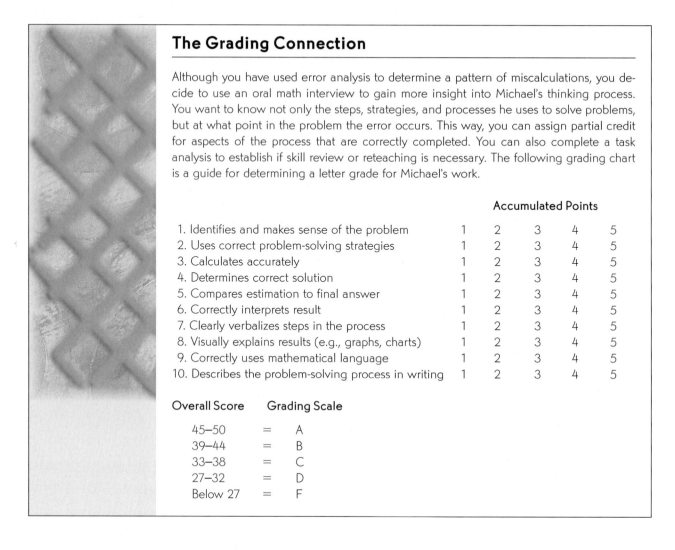

The Grading Connection

Although you have used error analysis to determine a pattern of miscalculations, you decide to use an oral math interview to gain more insight into Michael's thinking process. You want to know not only the steps, strategies, and processes he uses to solve problems, but at what point in the problem the error occurs. This way, you can assign partial credit for aspects of the process that are correctly completed. You can also complete a task analysis to establish if skill review or reteaching is necessary. The following grading chart is a guide for determining a letter grade for Michael's work.

Accumulated Points

1. Identifies and makes sense of the problem	1	2	3	4	5
2. Uses correct problem-solving strategies	1	2	3	4	5
3. Calculates accurately	1	2	3	4	5
4. Determines correct solution	1	2	3	4	5
5. Compares estimation to final answer	1	2	3	4	5
6. Correctly interprets result	1	2	3	4	5
7. Clearly verbalizes steps in the process	1	2	3	4	5
8. Visually explains results (e.g., graphs, charts)	1	2	3	4	5
9. Correctly uses mathematical language	1	2	3	4	5
10. Describes the problem-solving process in writing	1	2	3	4	5

Overall Score   Grading Scale

45–50	=	A
39–44	=	B
33–38	=	C
27–32	=	D
Below 27	=	F

steps and analyzed, checklists can be developed that correspond to each step, and students' progress toward mastery can be closely monitored. (See Figure 9–22 for a sample task analysis checklist of a multidigit addition equation requiring regrouping.) The grade-level scope and sequence chart is useful for determining the order of skills to be presented in the curriculum. (See Figure 9-1)

Critical Thinking and Reflection Activity

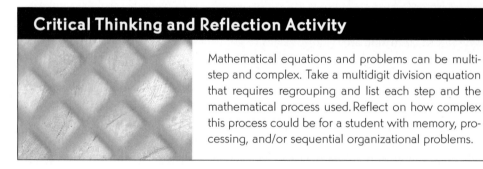

Mathematical equations and problems can be multistep and complex. Take a multidigit division equation that requires regrouping and list each step and the mathematical process used. Reflect on how complex this process could be for a student with memory, processing, and/or sequential organizational problems.

Figure 9–22   Task Analysis Checklist

Task: Solve this addition equation: 571
                                        + 299

	Mastered	Emerging	Not Mastered
Prerequisite Skills			
Follows written and oral directions			
Matches numerals			
Visually discriminates numbers			
Identifies numerals			
Writes numerals			
Identifies the addition sign			
States the concept of adding numbers			
States the concept of place value			
Demonstrates the ability to regroup numbers			

	Mastered	Emerging	Not Mastered
Computation Skills			
Identifies the equation as addition			
Adds in right-to-left direction			
Recognizes the starting point			
Adds 1 and 9			
Writes a 0 under the 9, in the ones column			
Writes the 1 above the tens column			
Moves to the tens place			
Adds 7 and 9 and 1 carried into the tens column			
Writes the 7 under the 9, in the tens column			
Moves to the hundreds place			
Adds the 5 and 2 and the carried 1			
Writes the 8 under the 2 in the hundreds column			

The IEP Connection

Joan, who has recently been placed in your sixth-grade inclusion class, has a significant learning disability in mathematics. To closely monitor her progress, you develop a skills checklist compiled from your school district's math scope and sequence curriculum chart (see Figure 9–1 and text website www.sju.edu/cas/education/cathleen-spinelli for grade level scope and sequence charts). The basic math computation and problem-solving checklist (see Figure 9–23) helps you keep track of the skills Joan has mastered and those that she needs to develop. IEP progress skill points can easily be developed using the checklist as a guide.

Example

Using the checklist as a guide, you check off that Joan inconsistently carries ones and tens when adding.

IEP Progress Skill Checkup Points. The student will add two 2-digit numbers, regrouping ones and tens.

Checklists

Checklists can be a very effective means of monitoring IEP goals and objectives when appropriate, in that they maintain a record of the date when each skill was introduced and the status of skill development and instruction (i.e., skill mastered, emerging, needs to be retaught). Checklists can serve as both an assessment and a recording system. Instructional and intervention plans can be developed based on the responses recorded on the checklists. Figure 9–23 is a checklist of basic mathematical computation skills that can be used as a guide when analyzing work samples, interviewing, or observing students in class.

Math Inventory

A **math inventory** provides a means of listing skills and concepts that students have mastered, those that are emerging, and those that need to be developed. Inventories are similar to checklists, although checklists generally suggest the direction that

Figure 9–23   Basic Math Computation and Problem-Solving Checklist

Does the student	Yes	Inconsistent	No
• correctly carry 1s and 10s when adding?			
• remember to carry 10s and 100s when adding?			
• remember to regroup when subtracting 10s and 100s?			
• regroup accurately when adding?			
• regroup accurately when subtracting?			
• perform the correct operation (e.g., adds, subtracts)?			
• know basic addition number facts?			
• know basic subtraction number facts?			
• carry correctly when multiplying?			
• regroup accurately when dividing?			
• use place value correctly when dividing?			
• calculate and record answers in right-to-left order?			
• align numbers in correct columns?			
• know multiplication number facts?			
• cancel fractions correctly?			
• reduce fractions to lowest common denominators?			
• remember to report the remainder?			
• convert mixed numbers to fractions?			
• read and comprehend word problems?			
• comprehend and focus on the context of word problems?			
• comprehend the question to be answered?			
• comprehend the language and vocabulary of the problem?			
• differentiate between relevant and irrelevant information?			
• develop a plan before proceeding with a word problem?			
• use the correct mathematical operation?			
• identify the number and sequence of steps in word problems?			
• perform all mathematical operations (e.g., +, −, ×, ÷)?			
• check calculations and whether question was answered?			

Figure 9–24   Sample Math Attitude and Disposition Inventory

Student seems to exhibit	Consistently	Inconsistently	Not Evident
• confidence in working with math equations and word problems			
• flexibility in arriving at strategies and solutions			
• perseverance by making several attempts at problem solving			
• curiosity in investigating various ways to tackle a problem			
• reflection in thinking of all possible methods and aspects of a problem			
• skill in applying math strategies to real-life situations			
• appreciation of the importance of mathematics in everyday activities			

growth, development, and learning should be following, whereas inventories highlight growth, development, and learning as it occurs. Engle (1990) makes the analogy that a checklist is to a prescription as an inventory is to a description. An example of a math inventory is provided in Figure 9–24.

Mathematical Journal Writing

Journal writing gives students the opportunity to reflect on their work, to write what they have learned about mathematics, and to record any concepts that are unclear or require further review or instruction. Students' journals may include a list of questions or comments to share with teachers or peers in upcoming math periods. Teachers find math journals to be helpful in assessing whether students are using the math principles, processes, and procedures they have been taught. Therefore, journals can provide useful information for both program planning and evaluation.

Math journals promote the development of students' self-evaluation skills. They can be used to maintain a personal record of students' progress in mastering mathematical knowledge, either by recording personal reflections about their learning or by keeping a score of their narrative or letter grades. Students make journal entries that can be used as a guide or reference, such as recording the strategies and approaches they find useful. They also use journals to make notes, write examples, and create illustrations and other metacognitive cues to assist them in recalling strategies and procedures as they approach more complex equations or word problems. (See Figure 9–25 for a sample of math journal topics.)

Tips of Teachers

Assistive technology devices, such as calculators and word processors, may be needed to address individual students' needs when using journal entries as an assessment method.

Figure 9–25   Sample Student Math Journal Topics

Your math journal is for you to explore your thoughts on mathematics in writing. Suggestions for topics include the following:

Discuss a math problem you completed in class successfully.
• What did you do to solve the problem?
• What was easy?
• What challenges did you encounter?
• What did you learn?

Discuss a problem you completed in class unsuccessfully.
• Where did you get stuck?
• What were you able to complete in the problem?
• How might you be able to solve this problem?

Explain to a classmate what you learned today.
• What are you having trouble with in the unit?
• What do you think about _____?
• Describe what it was like working in a group on a problem.

Think about and describe how you might solve a problem in a totally different way.
Write about:
• Important issues in mathematics
• The most interesting thing I learned in class today
• What I understand best about the math lesson today
• What I need more help with
• Two examples of problems I solved
• Ways to use math skills in real life.

Modified from a website created by Greg Collins (2002): http://www.edu.yorku.ca:8080/_greg_collins/mjournal.htm

FYI JOURNAL FORMAT
SUGGESTIONS

• Present a problem and partial solution, have students complete the solution.
• Present a problem with all the facts and conditions, have students write an appropriate question, solve the problem, and write their perceptions about the adequacy of the solution.
• Have students explain how they would solve a given problem, using only words, then solve the problem and construct a similar problem.
• After solving a problem, have students write a new problem with a different context but using the original problem structure.

(*King-Sears, 1998*, p. 108)

Journals can be personal reflections, or they can be dialogues in which the teacher and student share thoughts and issues about topics presented during class or during independent work periods, such as homework sessions. Besides assessing written communication, journals can also be used to evaluate higher order thinking skills for math problem solving.

Performance-Based Assessment

Performance-based assessment is used to evaluate students' ability to develop a product or demonstrate a skill indicating proficiency. This method of assessment is effective for monitoring instructional skill mastery and for evaluating whether students can apply and generalize what they have learned. Performance assessment tasks require that pupils apply knowledge in real-life situations. These assessment results are used for program planning and evaluation. The tasks are assigned specific performance criteria within a scoring rubric that is used to rate students' performance. (Sample performance indicators are provided in Figure 9–26.) The following are the types of questions to ask when using performance assessment:

• Are students able to make a workable plan for useful data collecting?
• Do they have a hypothesis?
• Do they effectively use statistical ideas, such as matrix sampling or surveys?
• Have they used outside resources, such as the library, computers, telephone?
• Can they justify their choice of techniques?
• Have they organized their information in a reasonable manner?
• Do they compare their results with their hypothesis?

Figure 9–26 Sample Performance Indicators

Not Understanding	Developing	Understanding and Applying
	Understanding the Problem or Situation	
• Does not attempt the problem • Misunderstands the problem • Routinely requires explanation of the problem	• Copies the problem • Identifies key words • May misinterpret or misunderstand part of the problem • May have a sense of the answer	• Can restate or explain the problem coherently • Understands chief conditions • Eliminates unnecessary information • Identifies needed information • Has a sense of the answer
	Understanding the Concept (e.g., multiplication, symmetry)	
• Does not routinely model the concept correctly • Cannot explain the concept • Does not attempt problems • Does not make connections	• Demonstrates partial or satisfactory understanding • Can demonstrate and explain using a variety of modes (e.g., oral, written, models) • Is starting to make how and why connections • Relates concepts to prior knowledge and experiences • Creates related problems • Accomplishes tasks, though with minor flaws	• Correctly applies rules and algorithms for how to manipulate symbols • Connects both how and why • Can apply the concept in new or problem situations • Can see and explain connections • Accomplishes tasks, can create related problems, and goes beyond what is required
	Measuring (length, mass, capacity)	
• Does not make direct comparisons between objects • Cannot order objects according to measure • Does not distinguish differences in measurement problems	• Can compare and order using nonstandard units • Can estimate and measure using nonstandard units • Can estimate and measure using standard units • Can solve some related problems	• Can estimate and measure using standard units • Can select appropriate measure units for task • Can use fractional increments to measure • Can solve related problems
	Estimating	
• Makes unrealistic guesses • Does not use strategies to refine estimates • Cannot model or explain the specified strategy • Cannot apply strategy even with prompts	• Refines guesses or estimates by partitioning or comparing • Can model, explain, and apply a strategy when asked • Has some strategies; others are not yet in place • Uses estimation when appropriate	• Makes realistic guesses or estimates • Refines estimates to suggest a more exact estimate • Uses estimates when appropriate • Recognizes and readily uses a variety of strategies
	Verifying Results	
• Does not review calculations, procedures • Does not recognize whether answer is reasonable	• Reviews calculations procedures • Can ascertain reasonableness if questioned	• Checks reasonableness of results • Recognizes unreasonableness

Figure 9–26   (Continued)

Not Understanding	Developing	Understanding and Applying
Collecting, Organizing, and Displaying Data		
• Makes no attempt • Cannot proceed without direction and assistance • Makes major mistakes in collecting or displaying data	• Can collect and display data, given a method to record • Has minor flaws in collecting or displaying data • Can correct errors when they are pointed out	• Can collect and display data in organized manner • Accurately and appropriately labels diagrams, graphs, etc.
Summarizing and Interpreting Results		
• Makes no attempt to summarize or describe data • May answer simple questions • Cannot communicate results in rudimentary form	• Summarizes and describes data appropriately • Can generate and answer questions related to data • Can communicate results in rudimentary form	• Draws valid conclusions and interpretations • Makes generalizations • Communicates results clearly and logically

- Can they communicate their ideas and results to the class orally and with visual aids?
- Has every member of the group contributed?
- Do they go beyond the immediate problem and ask new questions?

Math Portfolio

Math portfolios are used to document and assess mathematical ability by collecting a representative sampling of students' work over a period of time, which is generally chosen by students and their teachers. Portfolios provide information about students' conceptual understanding of mathematical processes, problem solving, reasoning, communication skills, disposition and attitude toward mathematics, creativity, and work habits. The portfolio process is particularly beneficial in helping students see that the study of math is more than just discrete rules and procedures (Kulm, 1994). Items in students' math portfolios should demonstrate progress toward meeting IEP goals, including

- Written math reports
- Learning log entries regarding problem-solving strategies
- Checklists of student progress in math
- Art illustrations related to math
- Photographs of student involved in math activities
- Printout of computer math work
- Write-up of structured observation during math period
- Math quizzes and assignments
- Group and individual math projects
- Student interest survey
- Journal entry, including self-assessments
- Photographs of students' math projects
- Artifacts from projects, such as designing new shapes
- Performance task using their concept of geometry
- Experiments that involve calculating probability
- Audiotape of students discussing how to finance a car or a home

- Videotapes of students collaborating on math projects
- Reports on math investigations
- Homework assignment samples
- Teacher conference notes
- Descriptions, diagrams, and graphs of math grades

Specific performance criteria are determined to evaluate the quality of the portfolio work products. The evaluation includes noting the progress students made through their choice of appropriate mathematical procedures and strategies, as well as in decision making, problem solving, observing, making connections, evaluating alternatives, drawing conclusions, applying, generalizing, and extending math skills and concepts to real-life situations. The teacher might ask the following questions when evaluating a portfolio dealing with math calculations:

- Were the answers to the problems correct?
- What computation skills were used?
- Were unnecessary steps added or steps missed when solving problems?
- Was there evidence of organizational, sequencing, or placement errors?
- Did reading errors contribute to incorrect solutions? If so, what were they?
- Were the mathematical strategies used appropriate for each problem?
- What visual aids (e.g., pictures, graphs, tallies) were used?

Life Consumer Skills

Mathematics-based life skills are incorporated to varying degrees into kindergarten through grade 12 curricula. All students need to acquire basic financial, consumer, and employment survival skills if they are to become successful, competent adults. The categories of skills that need to be covered and assessed to determine whether a level of competence is occurring include employment or further education, home and family, leisure pursuits, physical and emotional health, community participation, and personal responsibility and interpersonal relationships. Figure 9–27 is a checklist of secondary-level math consumer skills, and Figure 9–28 is an assessment checklist of independent community living and home-care math skills (Sabornie & deBettencourt, 2004, pp. 202–205).

Figure 9–27   Checklist of Secondary-Level Math Consumer Skills

Can the student	Mastered Skill	Developing Skill	Not Skilled
• order items from a catalog (involving taxes and shipping costs)?	_____	_____	_____
• shop comparatively, using newspaper ads (e.g., comparing rents, cost of grocery items)?	_____	_____	_____
• use credit for purchases (involving costs of credit)?	_____	_____	_____
• compare costs of similar items at different stores (e.g., grocery, clothing, department, hardware)?	_____	_____	_____
• buy groceries in bulk to save money?	_____	_____	_____
• compute sales tax?	_____	_____	_____
• apply for consumer loans?	_____	_____	_____
• budget for and estimate expenses for food, rent, recreation, utilities, phone, transportation, clothing?	_____	_____	_____
• pay bills using cash, check, and/or bank debits?	_____	_____	_____
• check sales slips and exchange items at stores?	_____	_____	_____
• buy by installment and on sale?	_____	_____	_____

Figure 9–28   Checklist of Secondary-Level Life Math Skills

Community Living/Home Care Math Skills

	Proficient	Emergent	Lacks skill
Can the student determine the			
• benefits of renting vs. buying a house?	_____	_____	_____
• costs of furnishing a residence?	_____	_____	_____
• closing costs and mortgage lending?	_____	_____	_____
• property and real estate taxes?	_____	_____	_____
• costs of water, electricity, cable?	_____	_____	_____
• cost of telephone services?	_____	_____	_____
• average monthly expenses?	_____	_____	_____
• benefits of leasing vs. purchasing?	_____	_____	_____
• costs of furniture and appliances?	_____	_____	_____
• cost of purchasing homeowner' or rental insurance?	_____	_____	_____
• cost of home maintenance and home improvement?	_____	_____	_____
• cost of buying appliances and tools?	_____	_____	_____
• measurements for purchasing wallpaper, carpeting, windows?	_____	_____	_____
• tip in a restaurant, a hair salon, etc.,?	_____	_____	_____

Health Care Math Skills

	Proficient	Emergent	Lacks skill
Can the student determine	_____	_____	_____
• the costs and need for health and disability insurance?	_____	_____	_____
• the differences between costs and benefits of various health plans?	_____	_____	_____
• the cost of buying prescriptions?	_____	_____	_____
• the cost of insurance deductibles and co-pays?	_____	_____	_____
• how to use a thermometer?	_____	_____	_____
• how to measure and dispense the correct dose of prescriptions?	_____	_____	_____
• how to count calories, cholesterol, fat?	_____	_____	_____
• how to determine blood pressure and pulse rate?	_____	_____	_____

Transportation Math Skills

	Proficient	Emergent	Lacks skill
Can the student determine			
• the miles per gallon of gasoline?	_____	_____	_____
• the cost comparison of used vs. new cars?	_____	_____	_____
• the cost of buying, leasing, down payments, and financing a car?	_____	_____	_____
• how to use bus, train, and plane schedules?	_____	_____	_____
• how to calculate a taxi fare?	_____	_____	_____
• how to use and purchase a bus pass?	_____	_____	_____
• the distance in miles between two points?	_____	_____	_____
• how to read local, state, and national maps?	_____	_____	_____

Classroom Scenario: What Would You Do?

You suspect that many of your secondary students lack certain basic consumer skills. As you develop their transition assessment, what do you do?

SECTION 4: MATHEMATICAL SCORING-RATING PROCEDURES

Mathematical Holistic and Analytic Scoring

Holistic scoring results in a single overall score that is assigned to a student performance or product. In holistic scoring, points are awarded for the whole product, with a single score or description of quality based on clearly defined criteria (generally a scale ranging from 0 to 5). The criteria might range from no response, to a partial response with a strategy, to a complete response with a clear explanation. (See Figure 9–29 for a sample holistic scoring math rubric.)

In analytic scoring, separate scores are given for various dimensions (referred to as traits) of students' performances or products. Points are often given for such math-related traits as organization, communication, accuracy, strategy solution, and problem solving. Analytic scoring lends itself to providing descriptive feedback on complex assignments. (See Figure 9–30 for a sample of math analytic scoring.)

Mathematical Rubrics

A rubric is an established guideline or a set of criteria by which a complex performance can be judged. Points or grades are awarded for specific levels of performance. (See Figures 9-31 and 9-32 for sample mathematical rubrics.)

Mathematical Rating Scales

A mathematics rating scale is used to evaluate students' knowledge, skills, and attitude by assigning a numerical or descriptive rating that can be used and understood by raters and those interpreting the ratings. Rating scales are used when the characteristics or dimensions of a performance or product may be identified and when these characteristics or dimensions exist to a greater or lesser degree. Rating scales can be used by teachers to rate students' level of proficiency and also for peer evaluations and self-evaluations. They can be used to communicate a degree of competence for specific skills or to show progress over time. The components of a primary trait rating scale include (1) the listing of the dimensions to be rated (e.g., the student writes numbers accurately, regroups digits in the 10s place); and (2) the scale (referred to as a Likert scale) for rating each dimension (e.g., always, sometimes, never; excellent, good, fair, poor; mastered, emerging, not acquired). The directions may state that the learner is either to circle or to check a number on each scale that indicates the extent of the particular characteristic being rated. See Figure 9–33 for a sample rating scale listing strategic math skills (Northern Examining Association, 1990).

Figure 9–29   Sample Holistic Scoring Scale for Mathematics

---

4   **Exemplary Response**

4.1 Complete with clear, coherent, unambiguous, insightful explanation
4.2 Shows understanding of underlying math concepts, procedures, and structures
4.3 Examines and satisfies all essential conditions of the problem
4.4 Presents strong supporting arguments with examples as appropriate
4.5 Process is efficient and shows evidence of reflection and checking of work
4.6 Appropriately applies mathematics to the situation

3   **Competent Response**

3.1 Gives a fairly complete response with reasonably clear explanations
3.2 Shows understanding of underlying math concepts, procedures, and structures
3.3 Examines and satisfies most essential conditions of the problem
3.4 Presents adequate supporting arguments with examples as appropriate
3.5 Solution and work show some evidence of reflection and checking of work
3.6 Appropriately applies mathematics to the solution

2   **Minimal Response**

2.1 Gives response, but explanations may be unclear or lack detail
2.2 Exhibits minor flaws in underlying math concepts, procedures, and structures
2.3 Examines and satisfies some essential conditions of the problem
2.4 Draws some accurate conclusions, but reasoning may be faulty or incomplete
2.5 Shows little evidence of reflection and checking of work
2.6 Some attempt to apply mathematics to the situation

1   **Inadequate Response**

1.1 Response is incomplete and explanation is insufficient or not understandable
1.2 Exhibits major flaws in underlying math concepts, procedures, and structures
1.3 Fails to address essential conditions of the problem
1.4 Uses faulty reasoning and draws incorrect conclusions
1.5 Shows no evidence of reflection and checking of work
1.6 Fails to apply mathematics to the situation

0   **No Attempt**

0.1 Provides irrelevant or no response
0.2 Copies part of the problem but does not attempt a solution
0.3 Illegible response

Source: Connecting Performance Assessment to Instruction (p. 24), by L. S. Fuchs, 1994, Reston, VA: Council for Exceptional Children. Copyright 1994 by CEC. Reprinted with permission.

Figure 9–30   Sample Analytic Scoring Scale

Comprehending the Problem

2   Has full grasp of the problem and all the components
1   Misinterprets a portion of the problem and some of the components
0   Completely misinterprets the problem

Deciding on and Using a Strategy

2   Chooses a strategy and plan that leads to a correct solution.
1   Chooses a partially appropriate strategy based on the portion of the problem that was correctly interpreted.
0   No attempt to solve the problem or an inappropriate plan

Solving the Problem

2   Correct solution
1   Computation error, copying error, or partial answer for a problem with more than one solution
0   No solution or incorrect solution due to incorrect strategy

---

Figure 9–31   Rubric for Mathematical Reasoning

Focus: Students communicate their mathematical reasoning in writing.

Outcome: Student will accurately represent number relationships with graphs, tables, or a written explanation that may include examples, strategies, or solutions.

Indicators:
Student solves problem correctly.
Student understands basic number relationships/concepts.
Student shows all the math needed to solve the problem correctly.
Number relationships are represented through (specify):

Graph   Table   Writing   Visual Graphic   Other

Graphics:
4   Graphic shows all the reasoning, and/or process leads to a conclusion. Graphic is clear, neatly drawn, and easy to understand.
3   Graphic does not completely show whole process. Graphic is clear, neatly drawn, and easy to understand.
2   Reader can guess how graphic works, but graphic is unclear
1   Graphic makes no sense or is not related to task.
0   Blank—did not do task.

Written Explanation:
4   Writing includes all the reasoning and leads to a conclusion. It is easy to understand, student uses mathematical vocabulary correctly.
3   Explanation partially explains the student's reasoning. It may or may not lead to a conclusion. Any vocabulary is used correctly, except there is a lack of clarity over a word or phrase.
2   Reader can only infer what student means from the writing. There is no conclusion. Student lists steps and does not explain (the reasoning).
1   Writing makes no sense or is not related to task.
0   No explanation was given.

Follows Task Directions:
4. Perfect   3. Well done   2. Satisfactory   1. Attempted   0. No attempt

Explanation has:
___ one strategy   ___ multiple strategies   ___ multiple solutions

Source: "Pathways to Planning: Improving Student Achievement in Inclusive Classrooms," by A. Shure, C. Cobb Moroco, L. Lyman DiGisi, & L. Yenkin, 1999. *Teaching Exceptional Children.* September/October pp. 48–54. Reprinted with permission.

Figure 9–32 Math Journal Rubric

Criteria	Level 1 (D range)	Level 2 (C range)	Level 3 (B range)	Level 4 (A range)
Communication: Evaluates how well you use mathematical language and symbols in your journal	Much improvement needed. Your journals show limited math terminology and symbols. You do not always communicate clearly and precisely.	Improvement needed. Your journals use some appropriate mathematical terminology and symbols. You do not always communicate clearly and precisely.	Good! Your journals use appropriate mathematical terminology and symbols. You communicate clearly and precisely. Good work!	Excellent! Your journals always use appropriate mathematical terminology and symbols. You communicate clearly, precisely, and confidently. Well done!
Application of mathematical procedures: Evaluates how well you use mathematical procedures learned in class in your journal entries	Much improvement needed. Your journals show few appropriate procedures for solving problems, and you rarely justify the choices you make. You make several serious errors and/or omissions in your journals.	Improvement needed. Your journals show some appropriate procedures for solving problems, and sometimes you justify the choices you make. You make errors and/or omissions in your journals.	Good! Your journals show appropriate procedures for solving problems, and you can justify the choices you make. You make a few minor errors and/or omissions.	Excellent! Your journals show the most appropriate procedures for solving problems, and you can justify the choices you make. You make practically no minor errors and/or omissions.
Understanding of concepts: Evaluates how accurate and appropriate your explanations are for your work	Much improvement needed. Your journals show only a few appropriate explanations and that you can apply only a few of the concepts in a few contexts with assistance. Your journals show only a few required concepts.	Improvement needed. Your journals show some appropriate explanations and that you can apply some of the concepts in a few different contexts with assistance. Your journals demonstrate some of the required concepts.	Good! Your journals show both appropriate and detailed explanations and that you can apply the concepts in different contexts independently. Your journals show most of the required concepts.	Excellent! Your journals show both appropriate and complete explanations and that you can apply the concepts in various contexts independently. Your journals show all of the required concepts.
Problem solving: Evaluates the strategies you use to solve problems	Much improvement needed. You solve problems with a limited range of appropriate strategies. You worked with assistance in class. You rarely use accurate problem solving strategies.	Improvement needed. You solve problems with some appropriate strategies. You required limited assistance with some of your problems and your problem solving is somewhat accurate, but could improve.	Good! You solve problems by choosing the most appropriate strategies. You show that you have worked independently in class. Your problem solving shows good accuracy.	Excellent! You solve problems by modifying known strategies or creating new strategies. You show that you have worked independently in class. Your problem solving strategy is highly accurate.

Figure 9–33   Sample Math Rating Scale

---

1. Understands and responds to a task
Student can determine the appropriate mathematical process to use, analyze the problem and break it into manageable steps, identify realistic goals, and choose appropriate equipment.

1	2	3	4	5
Never	Occasionally	50% of the time	Most of the time	Always

2. Reasons and makes deductions
Student can adequately assess a problem, determine the strategies needed to solve the problem, identify extraneous information, determine critical information, and estimate a reasonable answer.

1	2	3	4	5
Never	Occasionally	50% of the time	Most of the time	Always

3. Works on a task
Student can figure out the materials and equipment needed to complete a mathematical task, collect and organize these supplies, perform calculation and problem solving with an appropriate degree of accuracy, devise alternatives, work cooperatively with a group, complete a task when working independently, verify results, and hand in his or her best work within designated time limits.

1	2	3	4	5
Never	Occasionally	50% of the time	Most of the time	Always

4. Uses equipment
Student accurately uses calculators, computer programs, measuring devices, geometric apparatus, rulers, timepieces, protractors, stylus, and so forth.

1	2	3	4	5
Never	Occasionally	50% of the time	Most of the time	Always

5. Estimates and makes mental calculations
Student can make realistic and sensible approximations and estimations when calculating physical quantities.

1	2	3	4	5
Never	Occasionally	50% of the time	Most of the time	Always

6. Communicates mathematically
Student can clearly present oral and written reports of completed work, explaining thought processes involved in planning, the series of processes used, steps involved in calculation, and the final result.

1	2	3	4	5
Never	Occasionally	50% of the time	Most of the time	Always

SUMMARY POINTS

- Educational reforms, supported by the NCTM, have promoted shifting the emphasis of assessment procedures to methods that are criterion-referenced, provide feedback, and are formative rather than summative.
- The NCTM recommends assessing dispositions toward math; the ability to translate from one mode of representation to another; and the ability to express math ideas by speaking, writing, demonstrating, and depicting visually.
- Interviews can provide insight into students' disposition toward math, such as their attitude, perception of competency, and experiences that have influenced their self-confidence and self-concept toward their math ability.
- Factors that may affect the math learning process include oral language problems, cultural and language differences, cognitive factors, poor attitude or dispositions, ineffective instruction, poor abstract or symbolic thinking, reading disorders, lack of common sense, and information-processing problems.
- Information-processing factors that may affect students' performance in acquiring basic math concepts, and in math operations, application, reasoning, and communication include overall attention, auditory processing, memory, the ability to mentally shift between mathematical processes, judgment and reasoning, spatial organization, number formation, attention to visual detail, and motor functioning.
- Using a mathematical error analysis, the evaluator can determine types of errors and error patterns, including basic fact errors, regrouping errors, incorrect operations, incorrect algorithms, directional errors, omission errors, placement errors, inattention-to-sign errors, and random errors.
- The types of informal mathematical assessments include curriculum-based measurement, error analysis, oral math interview, task analysis, checklists, math inventory, journal writing, performance-based measurement, portfolio, and measurements of life consumer skills.
- Mathematic life skills need to be assessed to determine the level of competence in basic financial, consumer, and employment survival skills.

Chapter Check-Ups

1. How would you explain to a parent the importance of assessing the student's mathematical language skills?
2. Describe what a teacher would focus on when trying to determine whether a student's mathematical problems are due to ineffective teaching/lack of sufficient instruction or to information processing problems.
3. Discuss the differences between an oral mathematical interview and a mathematical think aloud.
4. What is learned helplessness? How would you identify learned helplessness in a student?
5. What are the main benefits of doing a mathematic error analysis rather than just marking an equation or word problem incorrect?

Practical Application Assessment Activities

1. Construct a curriculum based assessment (CBA) based on several pages from an elementary or secondary level mathematics text or workbook. After the

administration of the CBA, do an error analysis of the final product. Provide a summary of your findings.

2. Choose a partner and take turns administering an oral math interview to each other. Prior to starting the interview, each team member should write a short scenario of a student experiencing problems with specific math skills (the role they will play as the partner being tested). After completing the oral interviews, the interviewers will write a short summary of their diagnosis and both partners will compare diagnostic results.

3. Identify three informal assessment testing procedures or strategies that can be used with a fourth grader who has difficulty solving mathematical word problems. Discuss factors that may complicate skill acquisition, particularly factors that affect students with disabilities.

Connection Between CEC, PRAXIS, and INTASC Standards and Chapter 9

The Council for Exceptional Children—Professional Standards

Council for Exceptional Children
The voice and vision of special education

Standard 3 Individual Learning Differences

1. Effects an exceptional condition(s) can have on an individual's life.
2. Impact of learners' academic and social abilities, attitudes, interests, and values on instruction and career development.

Standard 5 Learning Environments and Social Interactions

1. Demands of learning environments.
13. Identify supports needed for integration into various program placements.
16. Use performance data and information from all stakeholders to make or suggest modifications in learning environments.

Standard 7 Instructional Planning

3. National, state or provincial, and local curricula standards.
6. Identify and prioritize areas of the general curriculum and accommodations for individuals with exceptional learning needs.
7. Develop and implement comprehensive, longitudinal individualized programs in collaboration with team members.
8. Involve the individual and family in setting instructional goals and monitoring progress.
9. Use functional assessments to develop intervention plans.
10. Use task analysis.
11. Sequence, implement, and evaluate individualized learning objectives.

Standard 8 Assessment

1. Basic terminology used in assessment.
4. Use and limitations of assessment instruments.
5. National, state/provincial, local accommodations and modifications.

6. Gather relevant background information.

7. Administer nonbiased formal and informal assessments.

8. Use technology to conduct assessments.

9. Develop or modify individualized assessment strategies.

10. Interpret information from formal and informal assessments.

11. Use assessment information in making eligibility, program, placement decisions for individuals with exceptional learning needs, including those from culturally and/or linguistically diverse backgrounds.

13. Evaluate instruction and monitor progress of individuals with exceptional learning needs.

14. Create and maintain records.

THE PRAXIS SERIES™ **PRAXIS Standards for Special Education**

Standard 1 Understanding Exceptionalities

1. Theories and principles of human development and learning, including research and theories related to human development; theories of learning; social and emotional development; language development; cognitive development; and physical development, including motor and sensory.

2. Characteristics of students with disabilities, including medical/physical; educational; social; and psychological.

3. Basic concepts in special education, including definitions of all major categories and specific disabilities; causation and prevention of disability; the nature of behaviors, including frequency, duration, intensity, and degrees of severity; and classification of students with disabilities, including classifications as represented in IDEA and labeling of students.

Standard 2 Legal and Societal Issues

1. Federal laws and landmark legal cases related to special education.

2. Issues related to school, family, and/or community, such as teacher advocacy for students and families, including advocating for educational change and developing students' self-advocacy; family participation and support systems; public attitudes toward individuals with disabilities; and cultural and community influences.

Standard 3 Delivery of Services to Students with Disabilities

3. Assessment, including how to modify, construct, or select and conduct non-discriminatory and appropriate informal and formal assessment procedures; how to interpret standardized and specialized assessment results; how to use evaluation result for various purposes, including monitoring instruction and IEP/ITP development; and how to prepare written reports and communicate findings to others.

4. Placement and program issues (including continuum of services; mainstreaming; integration; inclusion; least restrictive environment; noncategorical, categorical, and cross-categorical programs; related services; early intervention; community-based training; transition of students into and within special education placements; postschool transition; and access to assistive technology).

5. Curriculum and instruction, including the IEP/ITP process; instructional development and implementation (for example, instructional activities, curricular materials, resources and equipment, working with classroom personnel, tutoring and the use of technology); teaching strategies and methods (for example, direct instruction, cooperative learning, diagnostic-prescriptive method); instructional format and components (for example, individualized instruction, small- and large-group instruction, modeling, drill and practice); and areas of instruction (such as academics, study and learning skills, social, self-care, and vocational skills).

INTASC Standards for Teacher Education

Standard 7

The teacher plans instruction based upon knowledge of subject matter, students, the community, and curriculum goals.

Standard 8

The teacher understands and uses formal and informal assessment strategies to evaluate and ensure the continuous intellectual, social, and physical development of the learner.

Mathematics Assessment Chart			
Methods of Assessment	**Purpose**	**Advantages**	**Disadvantages**
Curriculum-Based Assessment (Probes)	• To provide individualized, direct, and repeated measures of proficiency and progress in the math curriculum	• Links testing, teaching, and evaluation • Easy to develop and evaluate progress toward meeting IEP objectives	• Reliability and validity of results are based on administration and the curriculum • Measures accuracy and fluency but does not identify understanding of mathematical processes and broad concepts
Math Error Analysis	• To examine calculation and words to identify specific skills errors and patterns of errors	• Identifies use of math rules and concepts	• Does not identify random errors or those due to lack of training
Math Journal Writing	• To determine how students feel about the lesson/math, what skills/concepts are unclear, what instructional methods were effective or ineffective	• Students learn to use words to explain mathematical processes and how they arrived at their answers; useful for communicating math experiences	• Difficult for students with written language or fine motor problems (may need to modify, e.g., have student dictate into tape recorder)
Math Oral Interview	• To determine the planning and mathematical processes used as students describe their thoughts as they compute math problems	• Helps students to analyze mathematical processes • Provides teachers with information about how students process math and helps to identify students' problem areas	• Difficult for students who are anxious, frustrated, lack confidence in math and for those who have problems with expressive or receptive language
Math Peer Assessment	• To provide valuable feedback, support, and perspective	• Peers learn along with the student they are helping • Provides students with a purpose for their work • Helps maintain enthusiasm for writing • Critique helps writer to understand audience • Is consistent with collaborative/cooperative learning	• Peers may not be skilled in constructively critiquing others • Peers need to be objective in their analysis
Math Performance-Based Assessment	• To assess generalization and application skills using meaningful, relevant learning activities	• Demonstrates ability to plan and problem solve • Determines ability to apply skills to contextualized problems and real-life situations	• Time-consuming to create and score • Reliability depends on skill of administrator • Considered to be a cost-inefficient assessment

Mathematics Assessment Chart (Continued)			
Methods of Assessment	**Purpose**	**Advantages**	**Disadvantages**
		• Closely integrates assessment and instruction • Moves beyond the "one and only one answer" mentality	
Math Portfolio Assessment	• To create a continuous and purposeful collection of authentic work products	• Student-centered • Particularly useful method for assessing students with various cultural and linguistic differences	• Time consuming • Requires commitment on the part of student and teacher • Long term process • Requires grade conversion on system
Math Self-Assessment	• To determine students' perception of their strengths and weaknesses • To assess students' ability to self-evaluate, rate, rank and self-correct.	• Develops self reflection, promotes self-reliance • Helps student to focus on evaluation criteria that need to be addressed when writing • Encourages goal setting • Increases self-esteem	• Student may not attend to or neglect to report analysis • They may not have the skills to evaluate their work without direct guidance
Math Skill Task Analysis	• To break down math tasks into the smallest steps needed to complete the task	• Identifies the exact steps in the problem the student has or has not mastered	• Requires detailed analysis • Measures specific, isolated skills rather than evaluating understanding of broad, integrated math concepts

Content Area and Related Arts Assessment

KEY TERMS AND CONCEPTS

- textbook-oriented instruction
- activities-oriented instruction
- inquiry-oriented instruction
- taxonomy
- mental models
- concept mapping
- text considerateness

- narrative text
- expository text
- adaptive physical education
- sensory integration
- related arts standards
- computer literacy skills
- motor skills screening test

CHAPTER OBJECTIVES

After reading this chapter, you should be able to:

- Describe why it is important to assess students' learning style to determine the most appropriate instructional approach
- Identify and explain a theoretical model that a teacher would use when asking content questions that address the various levels of knowledge and skills in a diverse class
- Explain the benefits of performance assessment in content and related arts subject areas

- Discuss why and how a teacher would use mental models as a diagnostic tool
- Describe what assessment data can be obtained by using a concept map
- Explain why it is important to assess students with special needs in physical education class
- Identify factors to consider when assessing students' ability to succeed or progress in related arts subjects

Introduction to Content Area Subjects: Science and Social Studies

Content area subjects generally consist of science and social studies—disciplines that have major life-skill implications involving the physical and social aspects of the world in which people live (Polloway & Patton, 2000). (Figure 10–1 depicts content area components.) Historically, these subjects have had a low priority in the academic curriculum of most students with learning difficulties (Patton, Polloway, & Cronin, 1994). However, as more students with disabilities are included in general education programs, science and social studies have taken on a more significant role in the school curriculum. Most states now require competencies in these subjects to be part of basic high school graduation criteria.

Content area subjects are often the first subjects for which students in self-contained special education classes are mainstreamed. Evaluations in science and social studies are important for determining students' background knowledge, current educational level, and need for modifications and adaptations, as well as for monitoring their progress.

To be successful in developing the basic skills in content area subjects, students must use study skills to master the skills and concepts that they can generalize and

Figure 10–1   Components of Content Area Subjects

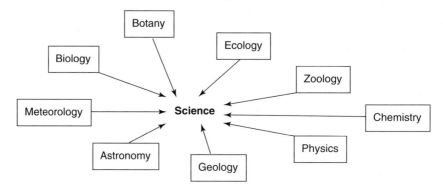

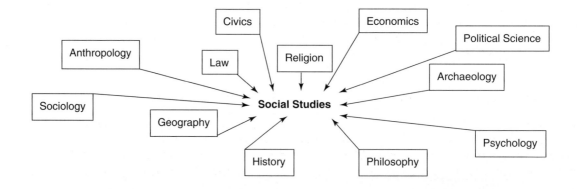

apply to newly acquired knowledge. By employing study skills, students are able to organize, store, locate, process, and transfer information. This ability helps to advance their knowledge in all disciplines. Mastering study skills empowers students to become independent learners. (See Chapter 11.)

SECTION 1: THE PROCESS OF CONTENT AREA ASSESSMENT

A major purpose of educational assessment is to direct teaching practice. Assessment in the content areas, like all subjects, needs to be developmentally appropriate, systematic, and language and culturally sensitive. Content area assessment should be a fluid, ongoing process that is instructionally embedded; that is, intrinsically linked to program goals and has an impact on instructional practice. Also, content area assessment should be contextual, realistic rather than contrived or staged, developmentally appropriate, and linguistically multifaceted (Krajcik, Czerniak, & Berger, 1999). Assessment should improve curriculum and instruction by determining students' background knowledge, by identifying what students need to know, by monitoring how well they are acquiring new skills and concepts, by ascertaining how fluent and proficient they are in applying what they have learned, and by noting whether they can generalize mastered skills to new situations.

Teacher's daily observations and interactions with students are the most important sources for understanding what and how students learn. Comprehensive assessment requires that teachers know not only the content they are teaching, but also a great deal about their students' backgrounds, experiences, and goals. In fact, assessment in content area subjects is intended to do more than just determine students' science and social studies grades and measure achievement; according to Krajcik and colleagues (1999, p. 209), assessment should help teachers

- Measure students' understanding, skills, and motivation in situations that closely match real life.
- Plan and revise instruction.
- Continuously monitor student progress.
- Measure academic progress fairly and accurately by using a variety of sources and techniques.
- Assist students in becoming self-reflective, self-regulated learners who monitor their own learning (learning is something that students and teachers do together, not something the teacher does to the student).
- Assess the progress of individual students rather than using group norms or comparing one student with another.

Evaluating Instruction in Relation to Student Needs

Evaluation of students must include indications not only of whether the answer is right or wrong but also of the quality and depth of subject area knowledge. When authentic assessment measures are used, the focus is on students' strengths, and the goal is to determine what they know and how they can use what they know (Hallahan

& Kauffman, 2003). With authentic evaluation measures, there is a direct correlation between the instructional approach and the methods used to determine academic progress in the content areas.

In **textbook-oriented instruction**, teachers focus their assessment on students' background knowledge; vocabulary development; critical thinking; reading comprehension; ability to interpret illustrations, graphs, and charts; and retention of material; as well as on their ability to generalize from text references to real-life situations. Teachers must also determine the readability of textbooks and how they need to be adapted to meet individual student's needs. In **activities-oriented instruction**, teachers evaluate students' ability to work independently and in groups, to complete special projects, to do experiments, to debate, and to write and speak persuasively for a variety of audiences. In **inquiry-oriented instruction**, teachers assess students' abilities to plan, research, solve problems, invent, discover, infer, compare, project, evaluate, and construct new knowledge.

Assessment procedures should be structured to promote flexibility, individuality, creative expression, and interdisciplinary learning (Owens & Sanders, 1998). In many traditional classrooms, multiple-choice questions dominate testing formats even though teachers have used a variety of teaching strategies. Often, students must produce an exact response, a replica of statements in their textbooks, or a copy of what teachers have in their minds. Creative ways of demonstrating conceptual understanding or skill mastery are not encouraged, and students are forced to imitate rather than innovate. The evaluation process should require the use of higher order thinking skills, consist of an open-ended format, reflect real-life situations, and incorporate a variety of formats so that a range of content area skills and attitudes can be assessed (Farris & Cooper, 1997). Assessment should be aligned with curriculum and teaching activities; involve creativity, problem solving, hands-on performance, and process; and occur during as well as following instruction (Hanson, 1997). Students and teachers should be actively involved in the assessment decision process. The main goal of authentic assessment is to determine whether children can extend and apply their learning to related situations and contexts. Because authentic assessment is a continuous process embedded in learning (rather than an end in itself) and is closely correlated with the instructional activities in the classroom, a high degree of validity is ensured (Farris & Cooper, 1997).

Serious learning problems can result in missing information. By using a **taxonomy**, or classification of skills, as a guide, teachers can design questions to elicit specific levels of knowledge or thinking skill. This information can help to diagnose any weakness or misunderstanding and provide prescriptive profiles for future grouping or instruction. Although numerous educational theorists have developed cognitive taxonomies, Bloom's model (1956) is considered to be a classic. (See Figure 10–2.)

Vocabulary skills are the most critical to success in the content area subjects, yet are difficult to master because many terms have multiple meanings and varied contextual usage. Further, the vast number of new vocabulary words that students must learn makes mastery essential for comprehension (Williams & Hounshell, 1998). Numerous technical and nontechnical words are introduced in each lesson. Technical vocabulary words (e.g., in science: fungi, migrate, capillary; in social studies: globe, citizen, volcano) need to be pronounced, explained with several examples, and connected to familiar experiences in order to be mastered by most students. The nontechnical content area subject vocabulary (e.g., in science: light, pupil, spring; in

Figure 10–2   Bloom's Cognitive Taxonomy of Educational Objectives

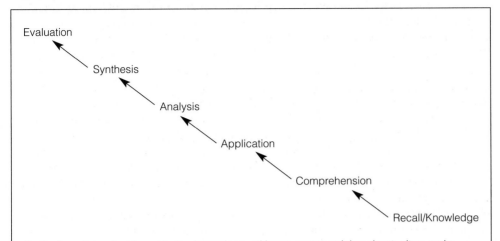

Evaluation—lists, decides, rejects, determines, critiques, states opinion about, cites, ranks, judges, compares
> Example: Compare the size of each state to its population.

Synthesis—revises, combines, reorganizes, generates, brainstorms, generalizes, predicts, organizes solutions, organizes concepts, diagrams, adds to, investigates, creates, presents
> Example: Using the graph, predict which state will have the largest population by the next decade.

Analysis—outlines, uncovers, categorizes, examines, deduces, inspects, searches, tests for, compares, contrasts, relates events or causes
> Example: Compare and contrast the size and population of the East Coast vs. the West Coast states.

Application—explains sequence or process, relates, utilizes, solves problems, operates, manipulates, puts to use, makes use of, explains how, classifies, demonstrates
> Example: Explain how a per-capita number is determined.

Comprehension—tells meaning, changes, converts, restates, infers, defines, outlines, proposes, calculates, projects, interprets, gives examples
> Example: Determine the state with the largest and smallest population.

Recall/knowledge—names, arranges, labels, groups, picks, quotes, says, shows, spells, writes, recites, identifies, matches, lists, locates, repeats, describes
> Example: Name each state in the country.

social studies: trade, reservations, depression) can be very confusing due to the unfamiliar ways that the words are used.

Students may also have difficulty understanding information presented in visual formats (e.g., maps, charts, graphs, timelines, pictures, and tables). Content area subject activities, such as experiments, may be new experiences for students. Often it is assumed that students can use the discovery method to figure out how to proceed. However, students with disabilities generally require direct instruction—or a guided discovery approach with specific instruction and direction—so that they can be successful in acquiring and understanding content area knowledge. They also need to have adequate work and study skills in order to be included and successful in science and social studies classes. Teachers need to evaluate and monitor the development of study skills to ensure that these students are able to cope with the demands in general education science and social study classes. When students have adequate work-study skills in metacognition, listening, memory, time management, organization, note taking, test taking, and basic research, they have the prerequisites to be successful in the content area subjects.

SECTION 2: CONTENT AREA SUBJECT ASSESSMENT PROCEDURES

Observation and Interview in the Content Area

Teachers need to be keen, sensitive observers of their students in content area subject classes. They must recognize and appreciate individual differences, such as personal learning characteristics, as they identify academic needs and areas of proficiency. An optimal time for student observation and interview is generally after the teacher-parent interview has been completed, when class expectations and the student's perceived strengths and weaknesses have been discussed.

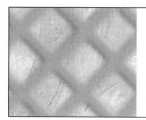

Tips for Teachers

When assessing students' science skills, be sure to carefully consider safety factors. Are safety glasses used? Is lab work closely supervised? Does the student have the necessary motor, visual, attention, and listening skills to use tools or operate equipment?

Figures 10–3 through 10–5 are sample forms that can be used to record skill mastery or the behavior of individual students, small groups of students, and an entire class of students, as well as to record how the student being evaluated compares with classmates.

Student Self-Assessment Reflection

Because self-assessment and monitoring progress are the ultimate goals for most students, it is critical that they understand the standards and criteria involved and have frequent opportunities to evaluate their own work. Self-analysis helps students to be attuned to evaluation criteria, provides information about behaviors that cannot be directly observed, and promotes self-monitoring, a skill needed for independent learning (Friend & Bursuck, 2002).

Self-evaluation skills need to be taught and nurtured. It takes time and practice for students to develop the ability to recognize the elements that make a piece of work a quality production. Acquiring this skill enables students to judge the quality of various aspects of their work, recognize and reflect on the strengths and weaknesses of the overall product, and ultimately refine their work.

The teacher can help students develop their self-assessment skills by encouraging them to talk and write about their reactions on what they have learned; by describing in oral and written form their attitudes about the project; and by explaining

Figure 10–3 Sample Form for Observing Individual Student's Skills

Checklist of Scientific Inquiry Skills

Check as follows:

M = Mastered skill   E = Emerging skill   NS = No skill

_____ *Observation*—uses senses to find out about subjects and events

_____ *Measurement*—makes quantitative observations

_____ *Classification*—groups things according to similarities or differences

_____ *Communication*—uses written and spoken words, drawings, diagrams, or tallies to transmit information and ideas to others

_____ *Data collection, organization, and graphing*—makes quantitative data sensible, primarily through graphic techniques

_____ *Inference*—explains an observation or set of observations

_____ *Prediction*—makes forecasts of future events or conditions, based on observations or inferences

_____ *Data interpretation*—finds patterns among sets of data that lead to the construction of inferences, predictions, or hypotheses

_____ *Formulation of hypothesis*—make an educated guess based on evidence that can be tested

_____ *Experimentation*—investigates, manipulates, and tests to achieve or verify a result

Figure 10–4 Sample Form for Observing Small-Group Activities

Checklist of Cooperative Group Activity

Skill	Brad	Ken	Jane	Tess	Ben	Jean	Mary	Tim
Listened to directions								
Had materials to begin								
Contributed ideas								

the problem-solving process they used, why the process did or did not work, and what they would do differently next time.

As students become more skilled in the process, they can keep learning logs of their daily progress, reporting and describing what they do, and noting their thoughts about and reasons for various decisions and choices they have made. Once students can discuss and write about their learning experiences, they become increasingly confident in their ability to self-evaluate and more willing to share and discuss their work, ponder other strategies to use to improve their work, and make judgments and decisions about their personal likes and dislikes. They also begin to distinguish

Figure 10–5   Sample Form for Observing Whole Class

	Defined Vocabulary	Read Chapter Outline	Drafted Research	Answered Questions
Subject: _____		Date: _____		

Ratings
+ = Completed
X = In progress
O = Not started

Names of Students

1. _____
2. _____
3. _____
4. _____
5. _____
6. _____

Figure 10–6   Sample Research Project Self-Evaluation Form

Name: _____   Subject: _____
Date: _____   Project: _____

1. I contributed to this group research project.

   0   1   2   3   4   5   6   7   8   9   10
   Not at all   A little bit   A whole lot

2. My participation in the project was:

   0   1   2   3   4   5   6   7   8   9   10
   Not as good as   Good but not   My very best
   it should have been   my best   effort

3. My major contribution consisted of:

   Researching in the library _____ Researching on the Web _____
   Reading and summarizing _____ Writing the paper _____
   Presenting findings to the class _____

4. Some things I learned about the topic: _____
   _____

5. Some things I learned about doing research: _____
   _____

6. Some things I learned about making oral presentations: _____
   _____

7. Some things I learned that will make my research better next time: _____
   _____

among the criteria that make one product of higher quality than another, and become more comfortable discussing, hearing, and learning about the perspectives of others. They also become more proficient in using their self-evaluation skills to constructively critique the works of their peers. (Figure 10–6 is a sample self-evaluation for a research project.)

Peer Assessment

Most students can learn a good deal from their peers and seem to enjoy doing so. The content area subjects are conducive to this form of assessment by having peers work cooperatively on planning, researching, discussing ideas and achievements, and ultimately presenting, performing, or producing a final product. Collaborative group work helps students to share tools, techniques, and ideas to develop their understanding of the world around them and to communicate solutions to real-life problems. Authentic assessment lends itself to cooperative learning or other forms of group work. (See Figures 10–7 and 10–8 for sample self- and peer assessment forms.)

Learning Logs and Journals

Learning logs and journals have been used primarily for written language assessment. These forms of assessment are also ideal for content area subjects because they provide excellent opportunities for evaluation. Learning logs are direct, factual,

Figure 10–7　Sample Peer Assessment Form for Content Area Oral Report

Rater's name: _____

Presenter's name: _____ Date: _____

Subject: _____Topic: _____

Rate the presenter:	Excellent	Good	Fair	Poor
1. Followed assignment directions				
2. Included all required components				
3. Appeared to be organized				
2. Spoke in a loud and clear voice				
3. Established eye contact with audience				
4. Stood straight				
5. Avoided "umms" and "ahhs"				
6. Kept to the topic				
7. Involved the audience				
8. Maintained the audience's attention				
9. Allowed time for questions				
10. Finished within the allotted time limits				

List three things the presenter did well:

1. _____

2. _____

3. _____

Figure 10–8 Sample Self- and Peer Rating Scale

Research Report Assessment

Rate each category from 1 to 5 (from poor [1] to terrific [5]). Use the "Comments" area to write your reasons.

Self-Assessment	Skill	Peer Assessment
1 2 3 4 5	Organized thoughts in writing	1 2 3 4 5
1 2 3 4 5	Completed report from outline	1 2 3 4 5
1 2 3 4 5	Included only necessary information	1 2 3 4 5
1 2 3 4 5	Used proper sentence structure	1 2 3 4 5
1 2 3 4 5	Used proper punctuation	1 2 3 4 5
1 2 3 4 5	Used proper grammar and spelling	1 2 3 4 5
1 2 3 4 5	Stated clear introductory statement	1 2 3 4 5
1 2 3 4 5	Included clear concluding statement	1 2 3 4 5

Comments

_____

_____

Figure 10–9 Examples of a Journal Starter and a Journal Entry

---

Select one of the following stem statements to use in your journal entry:

Suggested Journal Starters:

In class today, I learned about . . .   I am confused about . . .
The most interesting fact was . . .   History is important because . . .
It is hard to believe that . . .   I was bothered by today's lesson because . . .
I can relate to this lesson because . . .   A different way to think about the issue is . . .
If I had a time machine, I would . . .   If I were a famous scientist, I would . . .

Journal Entry:

It is hard to believe that *so many teenager boys and young man all from this whole country had to fight against each other and killed each other in the Civil War. So many people died. Over on problems that now seems so horrable. Sometimes family, even brothers had to fight against the other and even though they loved each other they had to fight because there side said so. If I lived then I don't think I could have ever hurt anyone else especially my brother. I'm glad that war is over and that we do not have any more people made to be slaves in this country any more.*

From *The Mindful School: How to Assess Authentic Learning*, Third Edition, by Kay Burke. © 1999, 1994, 1993 SkyLight Training and Publishing Inc. Reprinted by permission of SkyLight Professional Development. www.skylightedu.com

Figure 10–10   Methods of Scoring Content Area Learning Logs and Journals

Scoring methods may be letter or numerical grades or point values that can be converted to grades. Examples of various types of scoring are as follows

* Ratings based on a holistic approach.

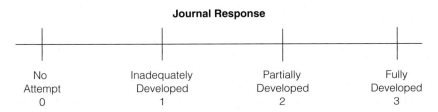

Journal Response

| No
Attempt
0 | Inadequately
Developed
1 | Partially
Developed
2 | Fully
Developed
3 |

* Specific criteria related to content area subjects using an individual class lesson or unit content; districts' scope and sequence curriculum guides; or district, state, or national core curriculum standards are used as criteria for evaluation of content.

Little **Evidence of Correct** **Sentence Structure**	**Some** **Evidence of Correct** **Sentence Structure**	**Strong** **Evidence of Correct** **Sentence Structure**

Many fragments
Several run-ons
Few complete
   sentences
	Several fragments
	One run-on
	Many complete,
	   grammatically correct
	   sentences
		No fragments
		No run-ons
		Complete and
		   well written
		   sentences

* Specific numbers of points designated for meeting preestablished criteria.

10	points for learning logs or journal completed and handed in on due date and time
15	points for creativity and original ideas
15	points for making personal connections
15	points for evidence of higher order thinking
20	points for adequate sentence structure, grammar, and spelling
<u>25</u>	points for personal reflection
100	total points

* Specific criteria and indicators rated using a Likert scale that measures growth on a continuum.

Sample Criteria and Indicators

Descriptive words	Number of entries
Length of response	Use of concrete images
Dialogue	Connections to other subjects
Creativity	Originality

Journal Entries

Descriptive words:

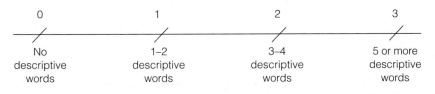

0	1	2	3
No descriptive words	1–2 descriptive words	3–4 descriptive words	5 or more descriptive words

generally short, objective entries used for documentation. Examples of learning log entries are observations of science experiments, reactions to a history presentation, questions about the day's lesson, summaries of related readings, answers to the homework assignment, steps for solving specific problems, and enumeration of the processes involved in researching a topic.

Journal entries are generally detailed, thoughtful, longer, and more subjective than learning log entries. They are written in narrative form and often consist of personal reflections, comments on the reaction to an experience, or dialogues between teachers and students. An example of a journal starter that helped a student complete a journal entry is provided in Figure 10–9. Figure 10–10 presents scoring methods for learning logs and journal entries.

SECTION 3: CONTENT AREA SUBJECT ASSESSMENT MEASURES

Performance-Based Assessment

Performance-based assessment emphasizes a hands-on approach to testing, measuring whether a student can use knowledge in a meaningful way in everyday life activities. A major focus is to actively involve students in the decision-making process. Performance-based assessment also promotes students' ability to work independently and become productive team members who collaborate and integrate ideas as the teacher assesses their ability to do so and to apply the many skills and concepts learned. Performance-based assessment is authentic because it promotes active student involvement in simulated, real-life experiences. It is considered a valid measure of progress because activities are based on curricular goals and instructional practices.

When teachers use activity- or project-based instructional procedures, there is a direct correlation between the teaching method and the evaluation procedure. A fundamental aspect of performance assessment is that it measures both specific academic skills and students' understanding of the process involved and their ability to apply their new learning in practical applications that ultimately reinforce learning. Authentic assessment is developmentally appropriate, promotes the use of higher order thinking skills, and evaluates both cognitive skills (e.g., asking questions, designing investigations, gathering information, drawing conclusions) and affective outcomes (e.g., responsibility, precision, objectivity).

In a traditional standardized test, students might be asked to select the correct definition of the word "atmosphere." While they may be able to choose the correct multiple-choice answer or even repeat a memorized definition, they may have no understanding of what atmosphere actually is. Performance assessment provides an effective and authentic means of evaluating their grasp of the concept by having them actually apply new knowledge to demonstrate understanding (e.g., by reporting atmospheric pressure using a barometer). Also, this type of informal assessment can provide the teacher with pragmatic, real-life examples of how students apply and generalize new skills and concepts. Results can be documented and provide concrete evidence of students' progress when reporting to administrators and parents. (See Figure 10–11 for examples of content area performance assessment projects.)

The IEP Connection

As Sandy's teacher, you are concerned about her ability to generalize and apply the skills she has acquired. She tends to be a rote learner, so you decide to assess her ability to perform authentic tasks using a performance assessment: drafting a neighborhood map.

Sandy was able to illustrate and label streets and landmarks with minimal teacher cues, but she was unable to identify specific landmarks when asked to point to the streets where the school, church, and grocery store are located. She was also confused by directional positions (i.e., east, west) when asked, "Which direction is the school from the front of your house?"

Sandy's task score was 70 (adequate), although problem areas need to be addressed in the IEP.

Progress Check Points

1. Given a map of the neighborhood, the student will locate eight out of 10 specific landmarks.
2. Given a street map, the student will identify directional positions (north, south, east, and west) with 80 percent accuracy.

Figure 10–11 Examples of Content Area Performance Assessment Projects

- Participating in science experiments, projects, and fairs
- Participating in social studies role playing
- Debating historical and current event issues
- Interviewing or writing to scientists and historians
- Holding discussions with guest lecturers
- Doing computer simulation exercises
- Conducting mock trials
- Cleaning up a polluted stream
- Writing for student newspapers and literary magazines
- Creating and maintaining greenhouses, aquariums, and terrariums
- Displaying art exhibits, murals, or poster about a science fair or social studies play
- Interviewing a nutritionist or dietitian
- Making a model of the United Nations
- Reporting community current events on local television or radio broadcasts
- Participating in historic battle simulations
- Reporting on field trips to museums, aquariums, police or fire departments
- Participating in community service activities
- Comparing pulse, heart rate, and breathing rate of team after physical challenge course
- Creating and labeling a map of the neighborhood
- Writing an editiorial
- Creating a scientific invention
- Creating a mobile, diorama, or display about a social studies theme
- Designing a Scientists Come Alive production
- Creating an imaginary planet

Content Area Subject Curriculum-Based Measures

Curriculum-based measurement (CBM) is a method of direct and frequent assessment of students' progress in course content. Probes—brief measurements of skill—are used in the CBM process during instructional time. Probes are designed to be frequently administered and easily and quickly scored (King-Sears, Burgess, & Lawson, 1999). CBM probes contain items that can be observed and counted (e.g., writing the correct definition of scientific terms, orally describing the battles of the Revolutionary War, matching chemistry terms to symbols). The premise of the CBM is to select and measure critical skills that serve as indicators, or benchmarks, of students' progress toward an annual goal(Carpenter & King-Sears, 1998). (Figure 10–12 provides suggestions for content area CBM probes. Figure 10–13 is a CBM probe graph used to monitor IEP goals and progress check points.)

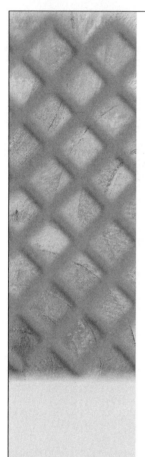

The IEP Connection

Juan, a 12-year-old boy with learning disabilities, is in your seventh-grade science class. He is unable to attain a passing grade on the biweekly science vocabulary test. You decide to modify his test administration by giving him fewer words to master at a time and a CBA probe format so that his progress can be tracked.

Progress Check Points:

Given five vocabulary words from the chapter on the solar system, Juan will be able to write the correct definitions with 100 percent accuracy within three minutes.

Directions:

Define each of the following vocabulary words:
1. galaxy _____
2. meteor _____
3. comet _____
4. asteroid belt _____
5. atmosphere _____

Science Vocabulary Graph

Dates

Number of correctly defined words											
5											
4											
3											
2											
1											

Direction

1. Graph scores daily (student or teacher).
2. Target: Mastery is 10 days.
3. List interventions and dates used:
   a.
   b.

Figure 10–12 Examples of CBA Content Area Probes

Geography
- Identify each state's location on a map by writing the correct state abbreviation.
- Match the terrain of an area to the corresponding industry and products.
- Compare and contrast regions so that two similarities and two differences are provided.

Science
- Given science terms to define, write the correct definitions.
- Identify steps in the scientific process and describe how to apply each step to a given hypothesis.
- Describe the human body systems so that each system's function and relationship to other systems are stated.

Source: "Applying Curriculum-Based Assessment in Inclusive Settings," by M. E. King-Sears, M. Burgess, & T. L. Lawson, September/October 1999 *Teaching Exceptional Children*, pp. 30–38, Reprinted with permission.

Figure 10–13 Sample Social Studies Probe Graph

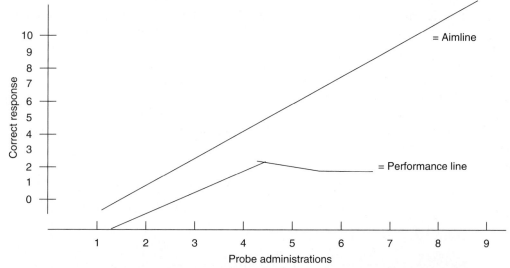

Objective: Given a probe containing 10 questions from a unit on the branches of government, the student will choose the correct answer to the question with 100 percent accuracy within three minutes. (Performance plateau days 4 to 7, intervention needed.)

Drawing Mental Models

Drawing **mental models** (e.g., sketching mental "pictures" of scientific concepts) is a dynamic instructional method, as well as a diagnostic tool for probing the depth of students' understanding of a subject. By examining students' drawings, teachers can determine what concepts students understand, what knowledge gaps and misconceptions they have, and whether they are fully knowledgeable about a concept's multiple features and how those features fit together (Glynn, 1997).

Concept Map Assessment

Concept mapping is a strategy used to probe the knowledge structures of learners, as well as a vehicle to represent and assess changes in students' understanding about science (Horton, et al., 1993). Concept mapping is initially used to identify students' preinstructional understanding of concepts (Dorough, Rye, & Rubba, 1995). It can be used as an alternative to student interviewing for evaluating students' prior knowledge, and it can be the focus of a class discussion about the relationships among ideas that surface while investigating and researching for concept data. Concept mapping can also be used to probe students about their interpretations of research findings.

Further, this technique can be an effective tool for planning and evaluating instruction. By presenting students with a list of concepts that will be the focus of an upcoming lesson and asking them to construct a map using their prior knowledge of the concept, teachers can determine how extensive students' backgrounds are and where gaps in learning have occurred. The ability to work cooperatively in groups, communicate and share ideas with others, and solve problems, as well as other affective attributes, can be evaluated as students work together to construct a detailed and accurate map (Dorough & Rye, 1997). Concept mapping can also be used to promote self-evaluation and peer evaluation as students use preestablished rubric criteria to determine how accurate and comprehensive their contribution is. Students can consult with classmates for feedback, and they can collaborate on their concept maps to illustrate the relationships among their findings. Teachers find concept mapping to be a useful postinstructional assessment tool as well.

Because concept mapping is often a new procedure for students, teachers may need to provide a model. The teacher can draw a model concept map on the chalkboard, on an LCD pad, or on an overhead projector using transparencies while verbally describing the step-by-step process. Students can gradually be introduced to more complex and detailed maps. Concept-mapping software can be used to help students and teachers monitor the learning process and to present results (Pisha & Coyne, 2001).

Concept mapping is often a new procedure to students. Teachers can use examples and verbal instructions for them to follow along.

Figure 10–14   How to Construct a Concept Map

- **Select the concepts.** List the concepts that are most important to understanding the central topic.

- **Cluster the concepts.** Group the concepts that seem most similar in nature and/or rank the concepts from "most general" to "most specific."

- **Position the central topic and begin linking concepts.** Write the central topic at the top of a blank sheet of paper. Write each of the remaining terms on very small self-adhesive notes to save erasing while rearranging the concepts and making meaning of the map. Start with a more inclusive concept to link to the central topic.

- **Finish mapping all concepts.** Continue to construct the map by relating additional concepts from the list to concepts already on the map. Work from more inclusive terms to more specific terms until the concepts are mapped. As the map is developed, make horizontal rather than vertical branches when linking long strings of concepts.

Source: "Mapping for Understanding," D. K. Dorough, & J. A. Rye, January 1997, *The Science Teacher*, pp. 37–41. Reprinted with permission.

Figure 10–15   Concept Map Made by an Eighth-Grade Student

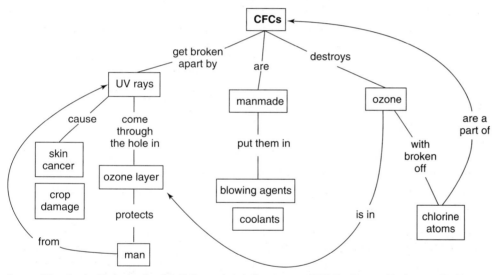

Source: "Mapping for Understanding," D. K. Dorough, J. A. Rye, January 1997, *The Science Teacher*, pp. 37–41. Reprinted with permission.

(Figure 10-14 lists the process that can be used to develop a concept map. Figure 10-15 is an example of a student's concept map.)

Concept maps are generally evaluated and scored using rubrics. The scoring is based on the complexity of the conceptual relationships illustrated. The National Science Education Standards (National Research Council, 1996) recommends using scoring rubrics when the performance standards are defined, appropriately refined for the target student population, and used to differentiate student performance. The rubrics can be constructed either to indicate pass or fail or to indicate multiple levels of achievement (Arter & McTighe, 2001). Students might be awarded one point for every hierarchical level in a concept map, quantifying the complexity of their thinking.

Figure 10–16 How to Score a Concept Map

Number of relevant concepts: Used when students are expected to provide the majority of relevant concepts to be mapped. Teachers provide only the overarching topic concept and possibly a few seed concepts to get students started. The number of relevant concepts are simply counted or the concepts can be weighted according to their degree of inclusiveness.

Number of valid propositions: Especially important to examine in the assessment of concept maps. The teacher should check each proposal for validity, that is, is the relationship scientifically correct? is it inappropriate (does it illustrate a misconception or alternative conception)? Propositions can be weighted equally or differently, according to the degree of importance ascribed to the relationship by the teacher.

Branching: This parameter acknowledges the progressive differentiation of concepts. A branch is established when a concept at one level in the concept hierarchy is appropriately linked to two or more concepts at the next level. Again, the rubric can be designed so that instances of branching can be weighted equally or differently.

Number of appropriate cross-links: This parameter allows for assessing maps on the degree of integrative, meaningful connections between concepts in different vertical segments of the concept hierarchy.

Number of examples of specific concepts: Students can include examples of specific concepts in their maps to facilitate the anchoring of concepts in their conceptual understanding or to assess whether or not they can identify types of objects, events, and so on that the concept label represents.

Bonus points: Depending on the goal of the lesson, students may earn extra points for creativity. Also, credit can be given for individual contributions and group interaction when working in cooperative groups. Additional points may be allotted when students demonstrate that they can generalize concepts and/or apply these concepts in real-world applications.

Source: "Mapping for Understanding," D. K. Dorough, & J. A. Rye, January 1997, *The Science Teacher*, pp. 37–41. Reprinted with permission.

A point can be given each time a concept is branched into a new category. Award points can be designated for cross-links and when branches or cross-links are incorporated into the map at higher hierarchical levels (Krajcik, et al., 1999). (Figure 10–16 lists the criteria for developing a concept map scoring rubric.)

Content Area Oral Interview

Oral interviews are effective procedures for evaluating the finished authentic product and for gaining insight into how students do their work. By having students "talk through" their work—describing what they are doing and why they are doing it at this time and in this way—the teacher can evaluate the outcome and, more importantly, analyze the process students go through and the reasoning behind what they are doing. Students need to be able to communicate how they solved the problem, which decisions they made along the way, and what connections they made with other learning during the problem-solving process (Yell, 1999). Figure 10–17 lists sample questions that can be used to guide the oral interview process (Krajcik, et al., 1999).

Content Area Subject Portfolio Assessment

Portfolios are collections of carefully selected work products that exhibit students' efforts, progress, and achievement. The content area portfolio is a cumulative record that includes various documents and artifacts of students' work, experiences, and

Figure 10–17 Sample Oral Interview Questions

- Describe your project.
- What are the project requirements?
- Why did you select this project?
- What is the design of your investigation?
- What did you do to prepare for your investigation?
- What steps are required to complete your project?
- What material or equipment did you use?
- What have you accomplished so far?
- What decisions did you make along the way?
- What connections were made along the way with prior learning?
- What do you expect to occur?
- What did you observe?
- Are you having any problem(s)?
- What do you think has caused the problem(s)?
- How did you solve the problem(s)?
- What kinds of results have you obtained?
- Where did you record your findings?
- What do you think would happen if . . . ?
- What are your conclusions so far?
- What do you intend to do next?
- Describe the most important thing you learned or accomplished in your research.
- What do you like best about your project?
- If you could do anything differently, what would it be?
- What skills and knowledge from other subjects did you use to complete this project?
- What skills, concepts, or insights have you learned from completing this project?

accomplishments in the areas of science, geography, history, and so forth. Work in portfolios may be final drafts, completed products, or works in progress. (Figure 10-18 shows the wide range of artifacts that may be included in student portfolios.)

Portfolios do not have to be graded, but they should document growth over time and demonstrate the process of improvement—not just the increase in quality of the product but also the quality of thinking that students exhibit. An important aspect of portfolio assessment is that students participate in selecting portfolio content, have input in the criteria selected for judging merit, and have an opportunity for self-reflection and analysis. (Figure 10-19 presents criteria for assessing portfolios.)

Checklist for Content Area Subjects

The checklist—a systematic means of recording the knowledge, skills, behavior, and/or attitude of individual students or whole classes—is a particularly handy assessment procedure for identifying and monitoring in an inclusive class setting. For example, a teacher might decide to use a class roster to quickly tally the frequency that a student calls out inappropriately during a social studies lesson. Another example is to maintain a checklist of important science concepts or assignments and rapidly check off the names of all the students in the class who have successfully mastered the concept or completed the task and those who need further instruction or reinforcement (e.g., each step in the science laboratory experiment). This strategy is also an excellent source of record keeping. The checklist can be used as evidence that a content area subject skill has been mastered or that progress has not been made (see Figure 10-20). This method allows the teacher to closely monitor students' progress toward meeting individualized education plan (IEP) goal progress points with ecorded documentation of dates and levels of mastery. Checklists are also useful when teachers

Figure 10–18   Suggested Items for Science and Social Studies Portfolios

- Notes from science or history fair project
- History journal entries, including self-evaluation
- Design of travel brochure, packet, or itinerary of trip
- Research assigned related to a specific topic
- Report on a historical or contemporary character or event
- Concept web illustrating a topic search
- Construction of a relief map
- Photograph of a geographic relief map
- Videotape of a famous battle representation
- Timelines of historic or current events
- Artistic construction illustrating a social studies topic
- Audiotape of a dramatic historic speech or debate
- Diagrams, charts, and graphs of a scientific experiment
- Crucial questions related to a political event
- Letter to the editor related to a community planning controversy
- Journal entries about working on an environmental project
- Written interview of a political candidate
- Photograph collection of community current events
- Laser disc presentation of a research project
- Selected science or social studies homework assignments
- Laboratory reports
- Summaries of performance-based assessments
- Videotapes of the student completing laboratory experiments
- Teacher observations and anecdotal records
- Conference records (student-teacher-parent)
- Current events with student's commentary and analysis
- Field trip reports
- Interest inventories
- Scientific investigations
- Proposals for experiments or research
- Project reports, summaries, or videos
- Computer disks of research material
- File notes on the student's contribution to group work

are developing lesson plans and completing report cards, and when they are discussing progress with parents, administrators, case managers, and students.

SECTION 4: TEXTBOOK EVALUATION

Much emphasis in science and social studies lessons—for both in-class and homework assignments—is placed on textbook use. As students proceed through the grades, the expectation for independent textbook study increases (Deshler, Ellis, & Lenz, 1996). Many science and social studies textbooks are not written with **text considerateness**, meaning that they are not designed with the needs of the diverse learner in mind. Content area textbooks are often written at a readability level that is advanced, and authors tend not to use writing styles that students are familiar with (i.e., **narrative text** writing style that relies on character, plot, conflict, and resolution).

The writing style of most content area texts is expository. **Expository text** formats tend to be written at a higher readability level than that of the grade level for which they are being used, and they are heavily weighted with concepts and theories

Figure 10–19   Criteria for Grading a Portfolio

Portfolio Assessment

- Circle three criteria that could be used to assess a content area subject portfolio:

Accuracy	Evidence of understanding	Organization
Completeness	Form (Mechanics)	Reflectiveness
Creativity	Growth	Visual appeal

- Develop three subpoints that could explain each criterion more fully:

Example: Evidence of understanding
Knowledge of content
Ability to problem solve
Application of ideas

- Create a checklist to evaluate a portfolio.

Portfolio Checklist

Criteria and Subpoints	Does Not Meet Expectations 1	Meets Expectations 2	Exceeds Expectations 3	Total Score
☐				
*				
*				
*				
☐				
*				
*				
*				
☐				

From *The Mindful School: How to Assess Authentic Learning,* Third Edition, by Kay Burke. © 1999, 1994, 1993 SkyLight Training and Publishing Inc. Reprinted by permission of SkyLight Professional Development. www.skylightedu.com

(Paxton, 1999). The organization and writing format of these texts are often unfamiliar to students, and are based on patterns of problem and solution, cause and effect, classification, definition, and example. The language used tends to be complex and detailed; technical terms are often not clearly defined; and too many concepts are introduced for students with disabilities to comprehend, retain, or recall (Lederer, 2000).

Teachers or curriculum committee members selecting the appropriate text for exceptional learners need to carefully consider whether the traditional format and objective test question format can be sufficiently adapted or modified to meet the needs of all learners. The following outline lists issues that must be considered when evaluating a content area text for use with students who have special learning needs (Mastropieri & Scruggs, 2004; Pisha & Coyne, 2001).

Figure 10–20   Science Process Skills Checklist

Rate student's progress toward meeting his or her science IEP objectives using the rubrics rating scores listed below

Nov	Mar	June	
☐	☐	☐	**Observing** Using one or more of the five senses to gather information; may include use of instruments (e.g., hand lens)
☐	☐	☐	**Classifying** Grouping or ordering objects or events according to an established scheme, based on observations
☐	☐	☐	**Inferring** Developing ideas based on observations; requires evaluation and judgment based on past experiences
☐	☐	☐	**Predicting** Forming an idea of an expected result; based on inferences
☐	☐	☐	**Measuring** Comparing objects to arbitrary units that may or may not be standardized
☐	☐	☐	**Communicating** Giving or exchanging information verbally or in writing
☐	☐	☐	**Defining Operationally** Stating specific information about an object or a phenomenon based on experience with it
☐	☐	☐	**Hypothesizing** Stating a problem to be solved as a question that can be tested by an experiment
☐	☐	☐	**Making Models** Developing a physical or mental representation to explain an idea, object, or event
☐	☐	☐	**Estimating** Approximating or calculating quantity or value, based on judgment
☐	☐	☐	**Controlling Variables** Manipulating one factor that may affect the outcome of an event while other factors are held constant
☐	☐	☐	**Collecting Data** Gathering information about observations and measurements in a systematic way
☐	☐	☐	**Making a Graph** Converting numerical quantities into a diagram that shows the relationships among the quantities
☐	☐	☐	**Interpreting Data** Explaining the information presented in a table and/or using it to answer questions
☐	☐	☐	**Reading a Graph** Explaining the information presented in a graph and/or using it to answer questions
☐	☐	☐	**Reading a Diagram** Explaining the information presented in a diagram (including maps)

Readability

- Is the reading level appropriate? (See Figure 7–34 in Chapter 7 for a readability graph and formula.)
- Is the vocabulary and language understandable, not too advanced or too "sophisticated"?
- Are the complex terms or vocabulary defined with examples?
- Are new concepts clearly explained with sufficient examples or visual aids?
- Are there sufficient illustrations, color, and so forth to maintain interest and motivation?

Content Coverage

- Is the content appropriate and current?
- Is the material in each lesson too detailed? too limited?
- Does the content cover the scope and sequence of district, state, and national guidelines?
- Is the material presented in a manner that promotes critical analysis and higher order thinking?
- Are chapter objectives listed?
- Is there a summary statement at the end of each section or chapter?
- Are application problems and critical thinking supplemental activities included?
- Is there a section that includes practice and reinforcement activities?
- Does the text address diversity issues, provide information about cultural perspectives, and address cross-cultural differences?

Text Structure

- Is the topic clearly introduced?
- Is the content presented in an organized form?
- Does the content follow a logical, sequential order of presentation?
- Are there sufficient transitions to help students adjust to a change in topic?
- Is there a relationship between and among concepts?
- Are there heading and subheadings that highlight key concepts?
- Are main ideas, key terms, and difficult vocabulary highlighted or underlined?
- Is the format easy to follow, with consistent layout in each chapter?
- Is the format presented without excessive material on each page?
- Are there sufficient visuals, illustrating important facts and figures?
- Is the font size appropriate for readability?
- Is the format well organized with illustrations and graphic organizers closely connected to textual material?
- Are graphic relationships provided between chapters and within the entire unit?
- Is an illustrated layout or organizer of the content displayed?
- Are there transition words that illustrate time and order (before, next, later), enumeration (first, next), compare and contrast (similarly, in contrast), cause and effect (therefore, because, resulted in), sequence (first, second), and classification (type of, group of)?

Evaluation Procedures

- Are evaluation methods appropriate for the text format?
- Is there a match between course objectives and assessment focus?
- Is there an assortment of informal assessment procedures (curriculum-based, performance-based, portfolio-based)?
- Are directions for the evaluation procedures explicit and easy to follow?
- Is there a match between the order of questions and the order of concepts presented in the text?
- Are study guides or strategies incorporated into the chapters?
- Is the format of the questions appropriate (multiple-choice, true-false, fill-in-the-blank, essay, "open-ended")?

- Are the evaluation measures adaptable to address the varying cognitive thinking processes of individual students (e.g., using Bloom's taxonomy)?
- Are end of section, chapter, or unit questions provided for self-assessment?

SECTION 5: RELATED ARTS: THE ASSESSMENT PROCESS

Although the primary focus of assessment is the basic skills and content area subjects, students do spend a portion of their school day in the related arts subjects, often referred to as the "specials." Physical education, the performing arts, and computer instruction seem to be the most common "special" subjects covered in the school curriculum. Interestingly, while these subjects are frequently in most students' daily schedule (even that of students who do not attend general education for any academic subject), they are rarely the focus of assessment. If students are to adjust to and be successful in these classes, it is important to know if they have the skills to meet at least the basic requirements and to have some assessment system in place to monitor progress. This section provides skills checklists and other assessment strategies in these special subjects.

Physical Education: The Related Arts Subject

Federal law mandates that physical education be provided to students with disabilities, defining physical education as the development of:

- physical and motor skills;
- fundamental motor skills and patterns (e.g., throwing, catching, walking, running); and
- skills in aquatics, dance, and individual and group games and sports (including intramural and lifetime sports).

The inclusion of all students in physical education encompasses assessment, according to IDEA–2004, and includes determining the physical education grade that students receive on their report card. Therefore, if the school's regular curriculum includes physical fitness, motor, or content knowledge assessments, students with disabilities must be included in these general assessments or be among the very minimal number of students who are provided alternative assessments.

Adaptive Physical Education: The Special Service

Many students are physically capable of participating in physical education class, however, some—due to medical conditions, chronic health impairment, physical disability, or serious coordination or processing problems—may require significant adaptations to the standard physical education curriculum. These students require **adaptive physical education** (APE); that is, developmentally appropriate physical education that adapts (modifies) the curriculum, task, and/or environment so that all students can fully participate in physical education (Seaman, DePauw, Morton, & Omoto, 2003). The APE program is designed specifically to adapt or modify a physical activity so that it is appropriate for students with and without disabilities. (See Figure 10–21 for suggestions on how to modify sports and activities so that all students can

Figure 10–21   Disability Awareness-Physical Activity Best Practices

Equipment
Larger/lighter bat
Use of velcro
Larger goal/target
Mark positions on playing field
Lower goal/target
Scoops for catching
Variety of balls (size, weight, color, texture)

Boundary/Playing Field
Decrease distance
Use well-defined boundaries
Simplify patterns
Adapt playing area (smaller, obstacles removed)

Time
Vary the tempo
Slow the activity pace
Lengthen the time
Shorten the time
Provide frequent rest periods

Basketball
Variety of balls (size, weight, texture, color)
Allow traveling
Allow two-hand dribble
Disregard three-second lane violation
Use larger/lower goal
Slow the pace, especially when first learning
Allow students in wheelchairs to hold ball on their lap
    while pushing wheelchair
Use beeper ball or radio under basket for students with
    visual impairment

Soccer
Allow walking instead of running
Have well-defined boundaries
Reduce playing area
Play six-a-side soccer
Allow students in wheelchairs to hold ball on their lap
    while pushing wheelchair
Use a deflated ball, nerf ball, beeper ball, brightly colored ball
Use a target that makes noise when hit

Volleyball
Use larger, lighter, softer, or bright colored balls
Allow players to catch ball instead of volleying
Allow student to self toss and set ball
Lower the net
Reduce the playing court
Stand closer to net on serve
Allow ball to bounce first
Hold ball and have student hit it

Rules Prompts, Cues
Demonstrate/model activity
Allow partner assists
Disregard time limits

Allow oral prompts
More space between students
Eliminate outs/strike-outs
Allow ball to remain stationary
Allow batter to sit in chair
Place student with disability near teacher

Actions
Change locomotor patterns
Modify grasps
Modify body positions
Reduce number of actions
Use different body parts

Bowling
Simplify/reduce the number of steps
Use two hands instead of one
Remain in stationary position
Use a ramp
Use a partner
Give continuous verbal cues

Golf
Use a club with a larger head
Use shorter/lighter club
Use colored/larger balls
Practice without a ball
Use tee for all shots
Shorten distance to hole

Softball
Use velcro balls and mitts
Use larger or smaller bats
Use a batting tee
Reduce the base distances
Use Incrediballs
Shorten the pitching distance
Allow students in wheelchairs to hold ball on
    their lap while pushing wheelchair
Use beeper balls
Provide a peer to assist
Players without disabilities play regular depth defense
Students without disabilities count to 10 before
    tagging out a student with a disability

Tennis
Use larger, lighter balls
Use shorter, lighter racquets
Use larger head racquets
Slow down the ball
Lower the net or do not use a net
Use brightly colored balls
Hit ball off tee
Allow a drop serve
Stand closer to net on serve
Do not use service court
Use a peer for assistance

Used by permission of PE Central (pecentral.org), the premier web site for physical educators.

be successful.) The goal is for the instructional program to consist of activities in which all students can have a positive experience.

The APE teacher is a direct service provider, not a related service provider. This is because adapted physical education is a federally mandated component of special education services [USCA. § 1402(25)], (unlike physical therapy and occupational therapy, which are deemed related services). Therefore, physical education must be provided to students with a disability as part of their special education program. Another form of service that some students with disabilities require is **sensory integration**; that is, the relationship between neurological processes and motor behavior—specifically, it is the interference with the awareness of the body and body movements (Seaman, et al., 2003). Sensory integration is assessed by occupational therapists. The sensory integration therapies, which must be identified in the IEP, are provided to the child with disabilities only if he or she needs them in order to benefit from instruction (PE Central, 2004). While a few emerging, or below average skill responses on a checklist such as Figure 10-25 may be representative of typical behavior of children based on age and experience, a cluster of underdevelop skills may indicate that a referral to a physical therapist is appropriate (Dole, 2004).

The IEP Connection

Present level of performance: Antonio is able to walk, run, hop, gallop, and balance at an age-appropriate level. He has not mastered the long and vertical jump. He can do a six-inch standing jump but cannot do a long running jump and he loses his balance when trying to jump vertically.

Long term goal: Antonio will improve the distance of his long running and standing vertical jumps by using appropriate arm and leg actions when jumping.

Progress Skill Check-up Point: When performing the running long jump Antonio will, with minimal prompting, use an appropriate arm swing pattern by moving his arms high and to the rear at the start of the running jump and swinging them forward with force during takeoff, during four out of five trials.

Arts Education

Other content areas have borrowed heavily from the assessment techniques used in the arts, such as the portfolio review in the visual arts and performance assessment historically used for dance, music, and theatre (Consortium of National Arts Education Associations (CNAEA), 1994).

The **related arts standards** are comprehensive, rigorous, and help to combat the uninformed idea that the arts are an "academically soft" area of study. The standards are based on knowledge and skills that cannot always be measured on a numerical scale but rather sometimes only by informed critical judgment. As in any curricular area, assessment in the arts—specifically, music and art education—should be valid and reliable as well as sensitive to students' learning context (CNAEA, 1994).

Because the standards are consensus statements about what a student should "know and be able to do" and what an educational program in the related, performance arts should contain, they can provide a basis for student assessment and for evaluating programs at national, state, and local levels (CNAEA, 1994).

Computer and Library Research Education

Increasing numbers of states and school districts require students to meet computer proficiency requirements in order to receive a high school diploma. The goal of a computer skills requirement is to foster skill development so that students have sufficient computer skills for use in school, at home, and in the workplace. These skills often have particular benefit for students with disabilities. Computers or word processing devices are commonly listed as technological accommodations for students with learning, physical, communication, and cognitive disabilities, and for those with traumatic brain injuries. **Computer literacy skills** curricula generally focus on three major goals:

1. To demonstrate knowledge and skills in using computer technology
2. To understand the important issues of a technology-based society and to exhibit ethical behavior in the use of computer technology
3. To use a variety of computer technologies to access, analyze, interpret, synthesize, apply, and communicate information.

Students need to become problem solvers, information seekers and users, and effective communicators. Today's students need to be prepared for a technology-filled twenty-first century. Therefore, a meaningful, unified computer literacy curriculum must be more than "laundry lists" of isolated skills, such as knowing the parts of the computer, writing drafts and final products with a word processor, and searching for information using a CD-ROM database. While these skills are important for students to learn, learning isolated skills does not provide an adequate model for students to transfer and apply the skills from situation to situation. These curricula address the "how" of computer use, but rarely the "when" or "why." Students may learn isolated skills and tools, but they will lack an understanding of how those skills fit together to solve problems and complete tasks.

There is a definite overlap among many skills involving computer literacy, information problem-solving, and library research. In most state and district curriculum standards, basic computer literacy skills must be authentically demonstrated as a competency before graduation. Internet-related skills are increasingly becoming a work-study requirement.

When assessing skills, the focus should be on whether students are able to use computers flexibly, creatively, and purposefully; whether they can recognize what they need to accomplish and determine whether a computer will help them to do so; and then be able to use the computer to help them accomplish their task. (See Figure 10–22.) Individual computer skills take on a new meaning when they are integrated within this type of information problem-solving process, and students develop true "computer literacy."

SECTION 6: RELATED ARTS ASSESSMENT PROCEDURES

Cognitive Assessment of Performance Skills

With complex skills or when students are introduced to new skills, learning often occurs slowly, therefore performance of the whole skill is not a good indicator of learning and improvement. In these instances it is often more useful to use qualitative types of assessment where the focus is on evaluating changes in the quality of skill development as it is performed rather than the outcome. Doing a task analysis—breaking

Figure 10–22   Basic Computer Skills Mastery Checklist

Prerequisite Computer Skills

Has the student demonstrated adequate	No Skill	Emerging Skill	Mastered Skill
• eye-hand coordination skills?	_____	_____	_____
• processing skills?	_____	_____	_____
• speed and accuracy?	_____	_____	_____
• left-right orientation?	_____	_____	_____
• tracking skills?	_____	_____	_____
• spatial orientation?	_____	_____	_____
• sequencing skills?	_____	_____	_____
• ability to follow oral directions?	_____	_____	_____
• ability to follow written directions?	_____	_____	_____

Basic Computer Skills

Is the student able to	No Skill	Emerging Skill	Mastered Skill
• turn the computer on and off?	_____	_____	_____
• locate programs and files?	_____	_____	_____
• open files?	_____	_____	_____
• begin and end programs?	_____	_____	_____
• save files?	_____	_____	_____
• delete files?	_____	_____	_____
• install software?	_____	_____	_____
• create shortcuts?	_____	_____	_____
• deal with a computer freeze?	_____	_____	_____
• send and respond to email messages?	_____	_____	_____
• make and use address lists?	_____	_____	_____
• access downloadable files?	_____	_____	_____
• access and create html pages?	_____	_____	_____
• join a listserv?	_____	_____	_____
• use a printer?	_____	_____	_____
• make an Internet connection?	_____	_____	_____
• surf the web?	_____	_____	_____
• use a scanner?	_____	_____	_____
• use a digital camera?	_____	_____	_____

Computer Programming Skills

Is the student able to use	No Skill	Emerging Skill	Mastered Skill
• word processing software?	_____	_____	_____
• desktop publishing software?	_____	_____	_____
• computerized presentation programs?	_____	_____	_____
• Internet programs?	_____	_____	_____
• spreadsheet programs?	_____	_____	_____
• database programs?	_____	_____	_____
• charts and poster creations?	_____	_____	_____
• illustrations programs?	_____	_____	_____
• drawing programs?	_____	_____	_____
• painting programs?	_____	_____	_____

down a broad task into specific skills and measuring the quality of the progress toward the final product—can provide a measure of learning and a means of assessing teaching effectiveness.

There are many ways to assess a student's knowledge of the key parts of a skill. In addition to demonstrating them to a teacher or peer, a student can communicate knowledge about them cognitively. Such assessments provide inclusion for students who, while understanding the hows and whys of concepts or skills in physical education, computer, art, music, or library referencing, as yet, may be unable to demonstrate proficiency in performing them.

Performance Assessment

Performance assessment involves having students create a demonstration of their knowledge, rather than respond to, or recognize, information provided by the teacher as in traditional testing formats. Inherent in this process is one of the benefits of these assessment techniques: They are instructional while at the same time indicating an understanding of content. Because of the varied manner in which students can demonstrate skill mastery, students who lack literacy skills or are hindered linguistically can select a mode of communication that will enable them to communicate most effectively. (See Figure 10–23.)

Self- and Peer Assessment Activities

As stressed throughout this text, assessment should be a continuous process, yet it can be time-consuming for teachers. When teachers create a self- or peer assessment system, not only does this reduce teachers direct involvement, but students become part of the process, take some of responsibility for it, become aware of what they have learned, and informed about future expectations. Getting students involved and responsible for tracking their learning and the learning of their classmates empowers and motivates them, increases their self-evaluation skills, and promotes peer cooperation. (See Figure 10–24.)

Portfolio Assessment

The portfolio has become an increasingly popular form of assessment in related arts subjects as a means to evaluate students' progress, challenges, and creativity, and the effectiveness of accommodations (Seaman, et al., 2003). Products effective for use in

Figure 10–23   Examples of Physical or Adaptive Education Performance Assessments

- Write an article for the school newspaper that provides instruction about a motor skill. Include clarifying information, such as outside sources and illustrations or photos.
- Create a form, checklist, or rubric to assess the qualitative performance of a peer. Critical components should be included and weighted. Explain the use of the evaluation and provide support for the weightings in a short (one-page) instruction sheet to accompany the evaluation form.
- Create a three-minute instructional videotape about a skill or a concept.
- Write and illustrate a brochure about a skill or a concept.
- Write a letter or videotape a message to parents about what you learned in a particular unit.
- Create a mnemonic device to remember critical components of a skill.
- Teach a skill or a concept to a younger, or less skilled or experienced student.
- Demonstrate a skill or a concept using visual aids to highlight information.
- Write a song, rap, poem, story, advertisement, play about a physical activity.
- Create a game that teaches a skill, concept, or strategy.

Source: Jefferies, Jefferies, & Mustain, 1997.

Figure 10–24   Partner Physical Activity Checklist

Skill Challenges

How many times can you jump rope in one minute?

Can you jump rope for 45 seconds without a miss?

How many baskets can you make in one minute?

How many free throws can you make in 10 tries?

How many sit-ups can you do in one minute?

How many push-ups can you do in 30 seconds?

How many times out of 10 tries can you throw a tennis ball 25 feet and hit the target?

How long does it take you to complete one mile?

Can you hula hoop around your waist 30 seconds?

How many times in a row can you and a partner catch a tennis ball from a distance of 25 feet?

How long can you hold a handstand?

How many "ups" can you do with a tennis racket in one minute?

How many "downs" can you do with a tennis racket in one minute?

How many times in a row can you and a partner correctly volley trainer volleyball?

How many times can you kick a soccer ball against a wall with your right foot in one minute?

How many times can you kick a soccer ball against a wall with your left foot in one minute?

How far can you punt a ball?

How far can you throw a ball?

How far can you kick a ball off a tee?

How fast can you run 50 yards?

Can you walk the length of a balance beam and back without falling off?

How many times in a row can you and a partner volley with a pickel ball racket and wiffleball?

Used by permission of PE Central (pecentral.org), the premier web site for physical educators.

assessing the frequency, duration, and context of physical, performance, and creative activity for students with disabilities include the following (Seaman, et al., 2003):

- log of daily or weekly activity progress
- fitness skill test results
- written, taped, or illustrated report on favorite activities, creations, or accomplishments
- awards (e.g., certificates, ribbons, or medals from Special Olympics, musical performances, art display entries, or extracurricular activities or competitions)
- drawings or photographs of participation in games, competitions, presentations, or performances, or of special equipment
- records of participation (e.g., bowling score sheets; used ski lift tickets; receipts from skating rink, concerts, theater, movies)
- newsworthy reporting (e.g., daily writing on upcoming performances; reporting on school club activities, local athletic activities, favorite sports column newspaper articles, cartoons).

Related Arts Journals or Activity Logs

An activity log or a journal reports on the frequency and context of an activity. Keeping a record of regular exercise or physical activity is a useful means for students to track the amount of exercise they are getting and how they feel as their physical activity increases (e.g., how they slept, how their appetite was affected, their energy level). Students can reflect on how the increased activity affected their mood, feelings of accomplishment, and so forth. They may also record changes in body composition, strength, flexibility, and aerobic capacity. This helps the teacher to manage data collection for assessment while increasing student involvement in goal setting, practicing, and taking responsibility for their own activity program (Seaman, et al., 2003, p. 137).

Observations and Interviews in Related Arts Activities

As part of a comprehensive evaluation, the teacher should observe students in their related arts class activities. Even in a large physical education class, teacher observation can be an effective assessment strategy. A well-structured checklist can help teachers document skill acquisition, proficiency, and maintenance on an ongoing basis (Jefferies, Jefferies, & Mustain, 1997).

Consideration should be given not only to students' ability to participate but also to the environment and program requirements. This helps when determining the need for modifications, accommodations, adaptations, or further assessment by a physical therapist. The following list of program considerations focuses primarily on a physical education class observation. With minor modifications, it can be a guide for observation in other related arts subjects as well (Seaman, et al., 2003).

Formation: Is there sufficient space and clear boundaries? How are students placed or positioned within the space? Do students have difficulty with spatial orientation, left-right orientation, or organization that affects successful participation?

Equipment: What equipment is used? Is it the appropriate size and adaptable to meet varying needs? Is there concern that the equipment used could be dangerous or inappropriate considering student's disability?

Number of players: How many students are participating? Are the activities large or small group? Are teams members assigned or are students paired with peers?

Rules: Are the rules clear? Do they change frequently? Do students having difficulty remembering or following commands or the order of directions? Are transitions between activities smooth?

Objectives: Is the skill level developmentally appropriate? Is the focus of the lesson affective, cognitive, social, or motor?

Environment: How do students deal with the social environment, the facilities, sensory environment?

Language: Are students following instructions? Are the requirements or steps clear and sequential? Are the concepts complex and require problem solving? Are students required to give direction or follow directions? Is communication facilitated between students? Is consideration given to language and cultural diversity?

Motor Skills Screening Tests

A **motor skills screening test** is usually completed if the teacher or parent has concerns about the students' gross motor skills, coordination, processing ability, or ability to perform successfully in a physical education program without intervention. The

Figure 10–25   Sample Adapted Physical Education Screening Checklist

	Satisfactory	Emerging Competency	Poor Skill; Below peers
• Motor coordination (not clumsy, awkward)	_____	_____	_____
• Agility (steady, balanced gait)	_____	_____	_____
• Movements smooth and fluid	_____	_____	_____
• Stands on one foot (at least 2 seconds)	_____	_____	_____
• Jumps in place (on 2 feet, 5 consecutive times)	_____	_____	_____
• Hops on two feet	_____	_____	_____
• Throws 15 feet	_____	_____	_____
• Bounces and catches to self	_____	_____	_____
• Hits a ball off a batting "T"	_____	_____	_____
• Jumps rope turned by others (5 consecutive jumps)	_____	_____	_____
• Turns own jump rope (5 consecutive jumps)	_____	_____	_____
• Skips	_____	_____	_____
• Kicks a stationary ball	_____	_____	_____
• Follows oral directions	_____	_____	_____
• Performs tasks at a typical pace	_____	_____	_____
• Stays focused and waits turn	_____	_____	_____
• Interacts cooperatively with peers	_____	_____	_____
• Understands basic directional prepositions (e.g., up, under, left)	_____	_____	_____
• Eye-hand coordination	_____	_____	_____
• Eye-foot coordination	_____	_____	_____
• Physical endurance	_____	_____	_____

screening process generally involves observing students' motor skills while working with them in class or by observing them at play or in an athletic activity. There are specific screening instruments that can be administered by regular physical education teachers. The purpose is to determine if the child requires further, more extensive, testing in the motor area and if unique motor needs exist. (Figure 10–25 is a sample informal screening assessment, which is generally completed by observing the student participating in physical activities and often in a group setting.)

These screenings generally are pass/fail or yes/no teacher-made checklists (e.g., student catches using his hands: yes/no; student moves to the ball to catch it: yes/no). A motor skills screening test typically looks at balance, manipulative ball skills (throwing, kicking, catching, striking), fundamental locomotor skills (run, jump, hop, etc.), and playground skills (PE Central, 2004). (See Figure 10–26.) If the screening test determines that the child is lagging behind in age-appropriate skills, then referral is made for further testing, generally by the physical or occupational therapist. (See Chapter 1 for a description of professional roles.)

SECTION 7: CONTENT AREA AND RELATED ARTS SCORING AND GRADING MEASURES

Rating, scoring, and graphing progress are not only beneficial for monitoring the individual student's progress and comparing how the student ranks according to class norms, but they are also ideal methods for providing clear data for reporting to

Figure 10–26 Sample Locomotor Skills Assessment and Rubric Scoring System

Directions: Use the following checklist to help determine students' locomotor abilities. This can be done with a number of students or privately with one student. Have the student/students do each of the following tasks either at a station or in front of you privately. Use the following rubric to mark the progress next to the locomotor skill listed. Use the comments section to write notes that you may want to share with the students' parents or include in teacher record-keeping.

Rubric:
DG = Doing Great—uses a mature pattern (or very close to one)
GT = Getting There—needs more practice on this skill
NW = Needs Work—more practice and teaching needed to work towards mature level

Skill/Task	Rubric Score/Comments	Things to Work on
1. Hop five times.		
2. Jump five times.		
3. Hop on your left foot three times.		
4. Hop on your right foot three times.		
5. Leap.		
6. Run and leap.		
7. Skip until told to stop.		
8. Gallop.		
9. Gallop with your right leg in front.		
10. Gallop with your left leg in front.		
11. Run forward.		
12. Slide.		
13. Slide to the left.		
14. Slide to the right.		

Used by permission of PE Central (pec@pecentral.org), the premier website of physical educators.

parents. Students and parents can identify the criteria, determine where the student stands according to curriculum standards and grade expectations, and identify the direction for developing goals for improvement. Figures 10-27 to 10-33 are sample rubrics and scoring charts.

Figure 10–27   How to Construct a Science or Social Studies Rubric

Step 1 List the critical components or objectives of the learning activity (e.g., comprehensiveness of content; quality of the presentation; accuracy of mechanics, grammar, and spelling; variety and number of reference sources).

Step 2 Determine the criteria to be used for the evaluation scale (e.g., 4 for excellent to 1 for poor). When more than six levels of criteria are used, scoring can become more complicated.

Step 3 Write a description of expected performance for each criterion category. This could include students' ability to focus and take a position; their organization; writing skills, including coherence; depth or elaboration; clarity; word choice; and sentence variety. Additional criteria may be students' ability to make personal, historical, or cultural connections; take risks; challenge the text; apply prior experiences; make predictions or speculation; elaborate on an emotional response; reflect on and use complexities of language.

Sample Rubrics Scoring Criteria

Score 4 Fully accomplishes the purpose of the task. Shows full grasp and use of the central ideas using a combination of skills.

Score 3 Substantially accomplishes the purpose of the task. Shows essential grasp of the central idea. In general, the work communicates the student's thinking.

Score 2 Partially accomplishes the purpose of the task. Shows partial but limited grasp of the idea. Recorded work may be incomplete, misdirected, or not clearly presented.

Score 1 Little or no progress toward accomplishing the task. Shows little or no grasp of the central idea. Work is hard to understand.

Figure 10–28 Sample Presentation Rubric—Evaluating Oral Presentations

	1	2	3	4
Subject Knowledge	Lacks a grasp of the information: unable to answer questions about the subject	Is uncomfortable with information and can answer only rudimentary questions	Is at ease with expected answers to all questions, but fails to elaborate	Demonstrates full knowledge (more than required) by answering all class questions with explanations and elaborations
Elocution	Mumbles, mispronounces terms, speaking volume too low to be heard in back of classroom	Voice is low; incorrectly pronounces terms; audience has difficulty hearing presentation	Voice is clear; pronounces most words correctly; most audience members can hear	Uses a clear voice and correct, precise pronunciation of terms so that audience can hear presentation
Organization	Audience cannot understand presentation because there is no sequence of information	Jumps around in topic; audience has difficulty following presentation	Presents information in logical sequence that audience can follow	Presents information in logical, interesting sequence that audience can follow
Eye Contact	Reads all of report with no eye contact	Occasionally uses eye contact, but still reads most of report	Maintains eye contact most of the time but often returns to notes	Maintains eye contact with audience, seldom returning to notes
Mechanics	Presentation has five or more spelling errors and/or grammatical errors	Presentation has three or four misspellings and/or grammatical errors	Presentation has no more than two misspellings and/or grammatical errors	Presentation has no misspellings or grammatical errors

Figure 10–29   Sample Science/Social Studies Oral Presentation Holistic Scoring Chart

	+	*	−
Planning was evident; presentation was well prepared and organized			
Content included all required components			
Illustration(s) were visually appealing and easy to interpret			
Oral presentation displayed depth of understanding			
Oral presentation was well executed in a clear, audible, and comprehensive manner			
Prepared handout demonstrated insight and thought			
Presentation was at least 8 minutes but not more than the 10-minute limit			

Scoring

+ = High-quality work
* = Met requirements
− = Did not do this adequately

Figure 10–30   Sample Science/Social Studies Written Report Holistic Scoring Scale

	Superior Performance	Acceptable Performance	Novice Performance	Unacceptable Performance
Thoroughness	Excellent detail; includes all essential facts	Good detail; includes some essential facts	Limited detail; includes few essential facts	No attempt at thoroughness
Accuracy	Information completely accurate	Information partially accurate	Information inaccurate	No attempt at accuracy
Visual Effects	Very effective; numerous visual presentations (e.g., illustrations, charts, graphs, diagrams)	Moderately effective; several visual presentations	Lacks effectiveness; visual presentations described in text form	No attempt at visual effects
Organization	Highly organized; excellent structure and format	Somewhat organized; adequate structure and format	Unorganized; poor structure and format	No attempt at organization
Mechanics	Excellent sentence structure and use of capitalization, punctuation, and grammar	Good sentence structure and use of capitalization, punctuation, and grammar	Poor sentence structure and use of capitalization, punctuation, and grammar	No attempt at the correct use of mechanics
References	All sources cited and referenced accurately	Some sources cited and referenced accurately	Few sources cited or referenced accurately	No attempt to cite or reference sources

Figure 10–31   Rubrics Scale for Concept Processing Checklist

1 = Beginning
> Shows little or no interest; understands some concepts; limits participation; needs support to produce assignments

2 = Developing
> Shows interest occasionally; understands most concepts; participates infrequently; sometimes meets requirements on assignments

3 = Capable
> Shows interest; understands concepts; participates independently and in a group; meets requirements

4 = Strong
> Shows interest and enthusiasm; demonstrates understanding of concepts; participates very independently and in a group; high-quality work on most assignments; sometimes extends self beyond requirements; sometimes uses additional resources

5 = Exceptional
> Shows interest and enthusiasm; understands concepts and demonstrates learning; participates extremely well independently and in a group; high-quality work on all assignments; consistently extends self beyond requirements; uses a variety and wealth of resources

Source: Regional Educational Laboratories (1998 February) *Improving classroom assessment: A toolkit for professional developers (Toolkit 98).* Portland, OR, Northwest Regional Educational Laboratory. Reprinted with permission.

Figure 10–32   Sample Research Report Rubric

- The research clearly addressed the topic assigned.
  1   2   3   4   5
- Research outline accurately identified primary and secondary facts.
  1   2   3   4   5
- The information researched addressed many aspects of the problem.
  1   2   3   4   5
- The information researched addressed alternatives for solution.
  1   2   3   4   5
- The information researched addressed the best solution.
  1   2   3   4   5
- The research reference search involved multiple sources.
  1   2   3   4   5
- Research information was correctly referenced.
  1   2   3   4   5
- Written product was carefully proofread for spelling, grammar, and content organization errors.
  1   2   3   4   5
- The end product had some visual aspect (e.g., illustrations, graphic organizers, charts, maps).
  1   2   3   4   5
- The student demonstrated understanding of topic during follow-up discussion.
  1   2   3   4   5

Total Points Possible: 50 points

Total Points Earned:_____

Figure 10—33   Sample Presentation Project Rubric

Attributes	Well Accomplished	Meets Expectation	Below Expectation
Organization of written product	Very well-organized, all directions followed; very complete and factual; correctly formatted	Organized; complete and factual; directions and basic format followed	Unorganized; directions and format not accurately followed
Research and reference sources	Very comprehensive; reflects a deep understanding of assigned content; contains abundant and detailed facts; numerous and clear evidence of reliable resources; accuracy referencing with correct format	Adequate content coverage; reflects a basic understanding of assigned content; contains required amount of factual information; references accurate but some formatting errors	Insufficient content coverage; does not demonstrate a clear understanding of assigned content; lack of factual information; incorrect or inadequate references
Group presentation	Very well-organized; clear, logical sequence; evidence of detailed planning; use of two or more high quality visual aids	Fairly well-organized; sequence mostly logical; some evidence of planning; use of one high quality visual aid	Poorly organized; sequence not logical; little evidence of planning; low quality or no visual aids
Communication skills	Very well articulated; volume sufficient for all to hear; excellent eye contact; very sensitive to audience response	Adequate articulation; volume adequate; makes occasional eye contact with audience; somewhat attentive to the audience response	Poor articulation; volume too low to be consistently heard; poor eye contact with audience; lack of focus to audience response
Group involvement	All members very actively involved in research, planning, organization, and presentation	All members contributed in some way to the research, planning, organization, and presentation process	Inconsistent effort by group members
Quality of summary statement	Summary very clear and well-supported by three or more factual statements	Summary is clear and supported by one or two factual statements	Decision is unclear and/or is unsupported or is supported mostly by opinions

SUMMARY POINTS

- It is important to assess students' learning style to determine the most appropriate instructional approach. For the *textbook-oriented approach*, assess background knowledge, vocabulary development, critical thinking, reading comprehension, interpretive skills, retention of material, ability to generalize, and textbook readability. For the *activities-oriented approach*, teachers need to evaluate students' ability to work independently as well as in groups, to complete special projects, to do experiments, to debate, and to write and speak persuasively for a variety of audiences. For the *inquiry-oriented approach*, teachers need to assess students' abilities to plan, research, solve problems, invent, discover, infer, compare, project, evaluate, and construct new knowledge.

- A taxonomy—or classification of skills—is a useful guide for teachers who are developing questions that elicit information for various levels of knowledge or thinking skills. Bloom's model is an example of a commonly used cognitive taxonomy.

- A fundamental benefit of performance assessment in the content area and related arts subjects is that it can measure students' mastery of academic knowledge and skills, as well as their understanding of the process involved and ability to apply and generalize new learning in practical applications in authentic situations.

- An assessment procedure that probes the depth of students' understanding involves drawing mental models. By having students sketch mental "pictures" of concepts, teachers can determine what concepts they understand, what knowledge gaps or misconceptions they may have, and whether they can recognize and integrate a concept's multiple features.
- Concept mapping is a strategy used to probe knowledge structures of learners, to identify their preinstructional understanding of concepts, and to assess changes in their conceptual knowledge.
- All students with disabilities who are included in physical education need to have their progress reported to their parents, and their progress in achieving their IEP goals monitored. It also must be determined whether they need accommodations or modifications and whether they need adapted physical education.
- When assessing students' ability to succeed in related arts subjects, consideration should be given not only to students' individual skill levels, but also to environment and program requirements. A determination must be made regarding the need for modifications, accommodations, adaptations, or further assessment by specialists, such as physical therapists.

Chapter Check-Ups

1. Explain why it is important to determine the instructional approach used in the content area subject in classroom before placing a student with special needs.
2. Describe how the teacher can use a taxonomy to design assessment questions and procedures to accommodate diverse learning styles and a range of instructional levels.
3. Discuss the benefits of using performance assessment for evaluating and monitoring progress in content area and related arts subjects.
4. Explain what is meant by text considerateness and describe the criterion that should be considered in evaluating a text to be used by a diverse population of students.
5. Why is it important to assess in the related arts subjects? Provide a specific reason for assessing student's level of skill in each related arts subject.

Practical Application Assessment Activities

1. Obtain a grade level content area scope and sequence chart from a local school district. Compare the curriculum skills expected to be taught in the school to the content area test items on a commonly used standardized test (attempt to use the test used by the school). Identify the test items that represent the curriculum covered in the class and those items that are not covered in the curriculum. Reflect on your findings; make a report providing conclusions and recommendations.
2. Decide on a content area subject project for a primary/middle/secondary level student in an inclusive class. Construct a performance assessment and design a rubric for scoring. Develop a list of accommodations, including grading modifications that could be used for students with disabilities.
3. As you plan on developing a portfolio assessment for science or social studies, describe how you would (a) involve the child in the selection of potential items to be included, (b) determine the method(s) of evaluation, and (c) report progress.

Connection Between CEC, PRAXIS, and INTASC Standards and Chapter 10

The voice and vision of special education

The Council for Exceptional Children—Professional Standards

Standard 3 Individual Learning Differences

1. Effects an exceptional condition(s) can have on an individual's life.
2. Impact of learners' academic and social abilities, attitudes, interests, and values on instruction and career development.

Standard 5 Learning Environments and Social Interactions

1. Demands of learning environments.
13. Identify supports needed for integration into various programs placements.
16. Use performance data and information from all stakeholders to make or suggest modifications in learning environments.

Standard 7 Instructional Planning

3. National, state or provincial, and local curricula standards.
6. Identify and prioritize areas of the general curriculum and accommodations for individuals with exceptional learning needs.
7. Develop and implement comprehensive, longitudinal individualized programs in collaboration with team members.
8. Involve the individual and family in setting instructional goals and monitoring progress.
9. Use functional assessments to develop intervention plans.
10. Use task analysis.
11. Sequence, implement, and evaluate individualized learning objectives.

Standard 8 Assessment

1. Basic terminology used in assessment.
4. Use and limitations of assessment instruments.
5. National, state/provincial, local accommodations and modifications.
6. Gather relevant background information.
7. Administer nonbiased formal and informal assessments.
8. Use technology to conduct assessments.
9. Develop or modify individualized assessment strategies.
10. Interpret information from formal and informal assessments.
11. Use assessment information in making eligibility, program, placement decisions for individuals with exceptional learning needs, including those from culturally and/or linguistically diverse backgrounds.
13. Evaluate instruction and monitor progress of individuals with exceptional learning needs.
14. Create and maintain records.

THE PRAXIS SERIES™   ### PRAXIS Standards for Special Education

Standard 1 Understanding Exceptionalities

1. Theories and principles of human development and learning, including research and theories related to human development; theories of learning; social and

emotional development; language development; cognitive development; and physical development, including motor and sensory.

2. Characteristics of students with disabilities, including medical/physical; educational; social; and psychological.

3. Basic concepts in special education, including definitions of all major categories and specific disabilities; causation and prevention of disability; the nature of behaviors, including frequency, duration, intensity, and degrees of severity; and classification of students with disabilities, including classifications as represented in IDEA and labeling of students.

Standard 2 Legal and Societal Issues

1. Federal laws and landmark legal cases related to special education.

2. Issues related to school, family, and/or community, such as teacher advocacy for students and families, including advocating for educational change and developing students self-advocacy; family participation and support systems; public attitudes toward individuals with disabilities; and cultural and community influences.

Standard 3 Delivery of Services to Students with Disabilities

3. Assessment, including how to modify, construct, or select and conduct nondiscriminatory and appropriate informal and formal assessment procedures; how to interpret standardized and specialized assessment results; how to use evaluation result for various purposes, including monitoring instruction and IEP/ITP development; and how to prepare written reports and communicate findings to others.

4. Placement and program issues (including continuum of services; mainstreaming; integration; inclusion; least restrictive environment; noncategorical, categorical, and cross-categorical programs; related services; early intervention; community-based training; transition of students into and within special education placements; postschool transition; and access to assistive technology).

5. Curriculum and instruction, including the IEP/ITP process; instructional development and implementation (for example, instructional activities, curricular materials, resources and equipment, working with classroom personnel, tutoring and the use of technology); teaching strategies and methods (for example, direct instruction, cooperative learning, diagnostic-prescriptive method); instructional format and components (for example, individualized instruction, small- and large-group instruction, modeling, drill and practice); and areas of instruction (such as academics, study and learning skills, social, self-care, and vocational skills).

INTASC Standards for Teacher Education

Standard 7

The teacher plans instruction based upon knowledge of subject matter, students, the community, and curriculum goals.

Standard 8

The teacher understands and uses formal and informal assessment strategies to evaluate and ensure the continuous intellectual, social, and physical development of the learner.

Content Area Subject Assessment Chart			
Methods of Assessment	**Purpose**	**Advantages**	**Disadvantages**
Concept Map Assessment	• Diagrams constructed to represent understanding of a particular topic or idea • Graphic means of assessing students' conceptual strategies	• Empower learners by making them aware of their own thinking • Help learners develop meaningful understanding by structuring information into long-term memory • Method of organizing key terms • Probes preinstructional understanding • Promotes cooperative learning • Used as advanced organizers • Used to evaluate post-instructional knowledge	• Needs to be introduced with clear instruction and models • May be a difficult cognitive activity because it requires students to construct a map and understand links among new concepts • Students with memory or languages processing problems may have difficulty coming up with or understanding concepts • Students who have sequencing problems may have difficulty with determining hierarchy or subconcepts
Content Area Oral Interview	• Method of understanding students' thought processes and comprehension as they explain the process, concept, problem, and so forth	• Allows students with writing problems to respond orally • Teacher can gain insight into how students process information and the methods they use to arrive at an answer • Teacher can encourage students to elaborate, can ask clarifying questions	• Students may be unfamiliar with this method and need a lot of modeling and practice • Teachers may need to take notes or taperecord comments, which may intimidate and cause students to stop talking • Can be too time-consuming
Contract	• Negotiated agreement to accomplish designated specific tasks between teacher and students	• Promotes self-responsibility • Forces students to think about their responsibilities, to plan, to monitor progress toward completion, to predetermine evaluation criteria, to deal with consequences of their actions • Method of measuring self-monitoring skills • Way of assessing work-study skills	• Students with learning disabilities may not be able to work independently • Contract may not have sufficient contingencies to deal with problems that occur
Peer Assessment	• Assessment of a student's work by another student	• Students learn to give and take constructive criticism • Learn to listen and respond to the feedback of others • Learn to work cooperatively	• This is not an effective method when students do not have good interpersonal skills or are unable to collaborate

Methods of Assessment	Purpose	Advantages	Disadvantages
Performance-Based Assessment	• Assessment procedures that reflect real-life activities based on content area subject matter	• Determines ability to apply learned content area subject skills to contextualized problems and real-life situations • Method of directly examining students' knowledge, skills, and dispositions • Assesses application and generalization of concepts • Way of measuring problem-solving skills	• Time-consuming; teachers must devise activities using materials and procedures that parallel those used during the instruction process • Interpretation is subjective • Students with special needs often lack the preskills necessary for problem-solving • Students who are impulsive may have difficulty thinking and working through the problem • Students with learning disabilities often need additional structure and direction because they tend not to do well with discovery methods
Portfolio	• Collection of students' work to document patterns of growth over time	• Measures the process, not just the product • Students can contribute by selecting and collecting work to be assessed • Allows for multiple sources of information • Encourages student reflections, self-monitoring, and goal setting	• Is labor intense • Needs interrater reliability if using a rubric scoring method • Students with disabilities may need assistance in determining how to select and evaluate their work samples
Self-Assessment Reflections	• Students write about what they understand after reading a chapter or completing a unit of study	• Means for students to make connections or interpretations • Develops students' ability to self-assess	• Students may have difficulty with insight • Students may need modeling and directed guidance to evaluate their own work
Curriculum-Based Assessment (Probe)	• Ongoing assessment directly linked to curriculum	• Short and frequent assessment of skills that allows teacher to modify instruction and assess progress toward meeting IEP goals and objectives • Avoids assessing students on tasks, skills, and knowledge they have not been taught • Sensitive to short-term improvement in student achievement, so day-to-day instructional decisions can be made	• The validity of the CBA is based on the validity of the curriculum • Reliability depends on the method of administration • Measures isolated skills rather than evaluating understanding of broad, integrated concepts

Methods of Assessment	Purpose	Advantages	Disadvantages
Drawing Mental Model	• Pictorial representation of the mental images that students have of a concept	• Method of evaluating if and what students understand or misunderstand • Determines misconceptions or gaps in learning • Provides a way for visual learners to demonstrate their knowledge in a comfortable way • Drawings can be used to express attitudes or feelings through pictures, colors, and texture • Effective method for primary students when they cannot read or write well • Language-delayed students may be able to express themselves more clearly through drawings than through words	• May be an inappropriate technique for students with visual or spatial difficulties
Learning Log and Journal	• Method of assessing what students understand or are confused about by their written statements of observations, questions, inferences, and predictions	• Combines content area subjects with language arts by enabling students to write about their learning experience in an open-ended manner • Kept on a daily basis • Involves students in the assessment process • Helps students to connect science to their daily lives • Encourages student-teacher interactions	• Is labor intense—teacher needs to be a frequent reader and commenter • May be intimidating or frustrating process for students with writing or language processing problems

PART 4

Special Focus Assessment

Study Skills Assessment and Test-Taking Skills

KEY TERMS AND CONCEPTS

- study skills
- executive functioning skills
- metacognitive reflection
- note taking
- research skills

- personal contracts
- test preparation
- test wise
- test anxiety

CHAPTER OBJECTIVES

After reading this chapter, you should be able to:

- Identify the main components of work-study skills
- Describe why it is important to assess study skills development
- Identify the factors to consider when assessing students' ability to retain information
- Identify the work-study skills that need to be assessed when determining students' ability to succeed with school-related tasks

- Describe the factors that affect students' test performance
- Explain how test anxiety can affect performance during the test process
- Describe motivational support and test-preparation strategies that can be used with students who have anxiety or test-taking difficulties

Introduction to Study and Test-Taking Skill Assessment

Study skills are support skills used to organize, store, locate, integrate, process, evaluate, and transfer oral and written information in the process of learning. Although study skills are useful for students in the primary grades, they are particularly important for academic success at the upper elementary, middle, and secondary levels when the curriculum becomes more complex and abstract. Good study skills help to advance students' knowledge in all disciplines; mastering study skills empowers them to become independent learners.

Although critical for success, these skills, in general, are not, explicitly taught or included in standard school curriculum. Many students learn by experience, often by trial and error, how to prepare for tests, organize their school work time and materials, take notes, and plan for long-term assignments. They adapt their work-study habits to meet their learning style and instructional needs. However, most students with special needs require individualized study techniques—often to compensate for their particular learning or cognitive processing disability—and require direct instruction. Assessment is necessary to determine the level and types of skills they use to complete assignments, to retain newly acquired curricular information, and to prepare for tests.

Research indicates that students with mild disabilities often have documented deficiencies in study skills (Polloway & Patton, 2000; Deshler, Ellis, & Lenz, 1996). As students with special needs are increasingly included in regular education classes, they are expected to work more independently, have more curricular demands placed on them, and have increased responsibility for their learning. Yet, research indicates that students with mild disabilities often have documented deficiencies in study skills (Polloway & Patton, 2000; Deshler, et al., 1996). Students who do not have basic work-study skills and the ability to work independently are likely to be unsuccessful. Therefore, it is important to identify these students' strengths and areas of need as soon as possible in order to initiate a plan to develop their work-study skills and closely monitor progress as they work in an inclusive class setting (Friend & Bursuck, 2002). Study skills assessment focuses on the use of specific abilities and provides insight into how students interact with the learning task (McLoughlin & Lewis, 2005).

SECTION 1: WORK-STUDY SKILL ASSESSMENT STRATEGIES

Executive functioning skills are basically work-study skills that include the ability to (1) plan, organize, and attend to details; (2) keep track of assignments and school materials; (3) listen and attend to details; and (4) to provide solutions to problems, using reasoning and problem-solving skills. The skills described in this section—involving listening, memory, organization, metacognitive reflection, note taking, and research—must be the focus of assessment when evaluating a student's ability to succeed at school-related tasks.

Listening Skills: Attention

Many students who have difficulty with study and work skills often are inattentive and easily distracted, so that irrelevant thoughts, ambient noise, and/or excessive visual stimulation "get in the way" of paying attention to incoming information. Attention can be difficult to measure directly because it is so closely tied to a task. Students may appear to have difficulty focusing on a task, but it may be that the task they are attending to is having a direct bearing on the amount of time and degree to which they are able to concentrate on it.

A task that is of little interest to students may not hold the interest and attention of even the most focused student. Likewise, a student who generally has a limited ability to attend to a task in most situations may become extremely focused on an activity that is motivating or is perceived by the student to be interesting. Thus, attention can be task-specific, which is why valid and reliable assessment must be done in authentic situations, in a variety of settings and conditions, using various evaluative measures (McLoughlin & Lewis, 2005). Teachers and parents should be interviewed regarding their observations of students' ability to attend to task. (See Figure 11–1.) Figure 11–2 is a sample checklist for assessing listening in the academic classroom.

Retention and Recall: Memory Skills

Expository content instruction is comprehensive and generally requires that students acquire and retain a massive and often diverse amount of information, including technical vocabulary related to the subject area. Retention and recall of this material can

Figure 11–1   Listening Skills Observation and Interview Focus Questions

- Can the student filter out distractions? _____
- Can the student comprehend verbal interaction? _____
- Can the student apply meaning to verbal messages? _____
- Does the student understand the importance of listening skills? _____
- Does the student have difficulty focusing on directions, conversations, and so forth? _____
- Does the student have difficulty focusing when a particular modality is used (e.g., visual, auditory, kinesthetics-tactile)? _____
- Can the student shift attention from one task to another? _____
- Does the student's capacity to focus on relevant tasks diminish at an unusually rapid rate? ___
- Is the duration of the student's attention to task unusually brief? _____
- Does the student have difficulty focusing on specific kinds of tasks? situations? _____
- Does increasing reinforcement contingencies fail to make an appreciable change in eliciting, maintaining, or increasing the focus or duration of attention to task? _____
- Does making the task easier by reducing irrelevant cues and increasing relevant cues fail to make an appreciable difference in the student's ability to attend to task? _____
- Does altering conditions that precede, occur during, or immediately follow inattentive behavior fail to result in any appreciable change in the ability to attend to task? _____

Figure 11–2   Assessment of Listening Skills in the Classroom

Does the student	Often	Sometimes	Rarely	Never
• identify the main idea of a class discussion?				
• make inferences or draw logical conclusions from discussions?				
• identify and discuss pertinent detail from a listening situation?				
• recognize when the details of two discussions are similar?				
• concisely summarize information heard, presenting important information in the correct sequence?				
• understand and use language concepts such as categorization, time, and quantity?				
• understand the underlying message in a lesson well enough to apply it to a new situation?				
• figure out solutions and predict outcomes from information heard?				
• understand information heard the first time it is presented?				
• understand the importance of good listening skills?				

be critical to success for students with disabilities, especially when they are in inclusive settings. When students can adequately store and retrieve what they have learned, they are better able to associate prior knowledge to new learning and are thus more effective in remembering the interrelationships between science and social studies terms and concepts. Teachers can assess students' memory skills and the methods they are using in order to monitor students' progress and to provide any supportive strategies they may require.

Factors that can affect students' ability to focus on and retain information include (a) the type of information to be recalled (familiar and meaningful information is easier to remember); (b) the amount of time that has expired since the original presentation of the information (longer intervals require more time to recall what was said); (c) the type of memory task (recognition memory requires only that learners indicate that they had previously been exposed to the material, whereas recall memory requires that the student remember a specific series of information in a fixed order); and (d) how the recalled information needs to be organized (free recall when information is not retrieved in any particular order versus serial recall when information needs to be retrieved in a certain order (such as reciting the alphabet in order or rote-counting numbers, 1,2,3,...) (McLoughlin & Lewis, 2005). (See Figure 11–3 for a sample memory skill survey.)

Figure 11–3   Memory Skill Survey

Does the student
- Chunk information into smaller bits for retention?
- Put recently acquired data into categories or clusters for more efficient storage and retrieval?
- Use mnemonics by linking new information to previously learned information?
- Recite facts orally or put them to music to help retention?
- Orally rehearse essential facts with frequent and spaced reviews rather than attempt to read ahead and "overlearn" before a lesson or test?
- Mentally visualize a concept, an event, a rule, or an item?
- Use narrative chaining by devising a story as a technique to retain information?
- Use the key word technique by associating a new vocabulary word with a similar sounding word?

Figure 11–4   Time Management/Organizational Skills Survey

Does the student
- Follow written and oral directions?
- Arrive to class on time?
- Know the purpose of and what is expected for each assignment?
- Keep a daily log of assignments and projects?
- Keep track of materials and assignments?
- Have all books and materials required for class work and homework?
- Plan and organize daily activities and responsibilities effectively?
- Complete class assignments well and on time?
- Complete homework assignments well and on time?
- Plan and organize weekly and monthly schedules?
- Understand the importance of effective time management?
- Reorganize priorities when necessary?
- Accept responsibility for managing time?
- Meet scheduled deadlines?
- Allow sufficient time to complete tasks?
- Adjust time allotment to complete tasks?

Time Management and Organizational Skills

Some students seem to have adequate work and study skills, but their school achievement is poor because they have difficulty with time management; specifically, organizing and planning their work. Because these students have not learned to manage their time efficiently, they are unable to complete school or homework assignments in a timely manner. They tend to lose track of possessions and have trouble completing tasks efficiently and thoroughly. Their chronic lateness or failure to hand in an assignment or a project can significantly affect their grades, their ability to function independently, and ultimately their success in school. Planning and organizing for writing letters and papers are also affected, resulting in a lack of focus or an unorganized sequence of ideas. (In assessing students' particular long- and short-term planning skill difficulties, the questions in Figure 11–4 can serve as a guide.)

Metacognitive Reflection

It is critical that students become aware of their own thinking processes. According to Fusco and Fountain (1992), **metacognitive reflection** involves the monitoring and control of attitudes, such as students' beliefs about themselves, the value of persistence, the nature of work, and their personal responsibility in accomplishing a goal (p. 240). To be effective learners, students need to reflect on how they learn best, which strategies do and do not work, how they attempt to solve problems, what steps they use in problem solving, and so forth. (Refer to Figure 7–34.) They need to be able to adjust their reading pace to match the type and purpose of what they are reading. They need to know when and how to read at a study rate (e.g., reading and comprehending new material while identifying main ideas, key points, and deciphering vocabulary); a normal reading rate (e.g., typical reading pace for reading novels, chapters assigned from texts); a rapid rate (e.g., reading relatively easy material, such as magazines and newspaper articles); and a reference rate (e.g., reading for an overview or to rapidly locate information, skimming or scanning).

Note Taking

Note taking is a complex task, one that is especially difficult for students with learning problems. This skill requires that students record the most significant aspects and details of an oral presentation or a written text for review and study at a later time.

The IEP Connection

This year, as an eighth grader, Michael has expressed an interest in helping to develop his IEP. Together, as you consider his strengths and weaknesses in the subject area, you identify specific skills and discuss how to convert them into IEP progress skill check-up points using (a) descriptive verbs that are able to be measured and observed, (b) the conditions—specifically, the context in which the skill will be observed, and (c) the criteria for the level of proficiency expected. The following lists can be used as guidelines when writing the IEP.

Examples of verbs that can be observed and measured

write	label	solve
read	demonstrate	identify
spell	participate	compare
name	construct	analyze
list	summarize	differentiate

Examples of verbs that cannot be observed or measured

understand	believe	instill
know	comprehend	foster
appreciate	grasp	enjoy

Conditions under which the behavior is expected to occur

Given a paragraph to read orally . . .
Given a list of 10th grade-level vocabulary words . . .
Given a two-step math problem involving measurement . . .
With the use of a calculator . . .

Criteria level for acceptance performance

Ratio-based mastery level; 7 out of every 10 attempts . . .
Time-based mastery level; 5 answers within a 15-minute period . . .
Percent-based mastery level: 80% of the time . . .

Figure 11–5   Note-Taking Skills Survey Questions

Does the student
- Take brief, clear, and legible notes?
- Write notes in his or her own words?
- Record essential information?
- Use headings and subheadings appropriately?
- Recognize when information is missing?
- Maintain notes in an organized manner?
- Apply note-keeping skills during lectures and discussions?
- Use an outline technique to plan writing?

They need to be able to classify, organize, and document key information as they are reading or listening to a discussion. This requires coordination and competency with a complex set of simultaneous tasks. (See Figure 11-5 for note-taking skill survey questions.)

Many students with learning problems have difficulty with the specific prerequisites needed for effective note taking. These skills include being able to differentiate more important from less important information, identifying the main idea, listening to or reading material carefully, and summarizing key points. Other factors that may affect students' note-taking skills are problems with motor planning, organizing, proofreading, writing legibly, basic spelling skills, maintaining attention, actively listening, sequencing, short- and long-term memory, and recognizing that they do not understand something.

Teachers assess whether students have these prerequisite skills by observation or interview when deciding whether to design goals to ameliorate any deficiencies or to help to develop needed prerequisite skills. It may be necessary for the teacher to focus on providing students with the accommodations needed to compensate for their deficiencies (Suritsky & Hughes, 1997), such as providing taped lectures or teacher-made study guides. Because the major component of note taking is identifying the main idea in text, a method of assessing this skill is to make a copy of a section in their textbook and have students underline or highlight aspects of the section that seem to be most important. Another method is to require students to read a section of the content area textbook and take notes on the reading as if preparing for a test (Leslie & Caldwell, 2001).

Research Skills

In this age of massive information processing, all students need to develop **research skills**, which includes the ability to search for data by using encyclopedias, dictionaries, thesauruses, journals, texts, newspapers, the Internet, and library references. To determine whether students can effectively access these resources, preliminary skills need to be assessed, including the ability to alphabetize; recognize the correct spelling of a word; know basic parts of speech; understand definitions; identify synonyms and antonyms; correctly interpret charts, graphs, and maps; find information using directories, glossaries, indexes, and online resources; and know what type of reference source is appropriate to meet various needs. (See Figure 11-6 for questions on student research skills, and Figure 11-7 for a study skills inventory.)

Figure 11—6   Research Skills Survey Questions

Does the student
- Recognize the importance of reference materials?
- Identify which type of reference material is needed for various projects?
- Locate needed reference books and materials in the library?
- Use the cataloguing system (card or computerized) effectively?
- Use guide words to locate information?
- Use materials appropriately to complete assignments?
- Locate and use the services of the media specialist?
- Use a thesaurus to improve word choice in original writings?
- Use a dictionary to verify correct multiple meanings?
- Use an encyclopedia to select information on a specific topic?

Figure 11—7   Study Skills Inventory

Completed by: _____ Student: _____ Date: _____

Place the appropriate number (1, 2, or 3) in the box next to each study skill subskill (1 = Mastered—regular, appropriate use of skill; 2 = Partially Mastered—needs some improvement; 3 = Not Mastered—infrequent use of skill).

Reading Rate
- ☐ Skimming
- ☐ Scanning
- ☐ Rapid reading
- ☐ Normal rate
- ☐ Study or careful reading
- ☐ Understands importance of reading rates

Listening
- ☐ Attends to listening activities
- ☐ Applies meaning to verbal messages
- ☐ Filters out auditory distractions
- ☐ Comprehends verbal messages
- ☐ Understands importance of listening skills

Note Taking/Outlining
- ☐ Uses heading/subheadings appropriately
- ☐ Takes brief and clear notes
- ☐ Records essential information
- ☐ Applies skill during writing activities
- ☐ Uses skill during lectures
- ☐ Develops organized outlines
- ☐ Follows consistent note-taking format
- ☐ Understands importance of note taking
- ☐ Understands importance of outlining

Report Writing
- ☐ Organizes thoughts in writing
- ☐ Completes written reports from outline
- ☐ Includes only necessary information
- ☐ Uses proper sentence structure
- ☐ Uses proper punctuation
- ☐ Uses proper grammar and spelling

- ☐ Proofreads written assignments
- ☐ States clear introductory statement
- ☐ Includes clear concluding statements
- ☐ Understands importance of writing reports

Oral Presentations
- ☐ Freely participates in oral presentations
- ☐ Oral presentations are well organized
- ☐ Uses gestures appropriately
- ☐ Speaks clearly
- ☐ Uses proper language when reporting orally
- ☐ Understands importance of oral reporting

Graphic Aids
- ☐ Attends to relevant elements in visual material
- ☐ Uses visuals appropriately in presentations
- ☐ Develops own graphic material
- ☐ Is not confused or distracted by visual material in presentations
- ☐ Understands importance of visual material

Test Taking
- ☐ Studies for tests in an organized way
- ☐ Spends appropriate amount of time studying different topics covered on a test
- ☐ Organizes narrative responses appropriately
- ☐ Reads and understands directions before answering questions
- ☐ Proofreads responses and checks for errors
- ☐ Identifies and uses clue words in questions
- ☐ Properly records answers
- ☐ Saves difficult items until last
- ☐ Eliminates obviously wrong answers
- ☐ Corrects previous test-taking errors
- ☐ Avoids cramming for tests

Figure 11–7 (Continued)

☐ Systematically reviews completed tests to determine test-taking or test-studying errors
☐ Understands importance of test-taking skills

Library Usage
☐ Uses cataloging system (card or computerized) effectively
☐ Able to locate library materials
☐ Understands organizational layout of library
☐ Understands and uses services of media specialist
☐ Understands overall functions and purposes of a library
☐ Understands importance of library usage skills

Reference Materials
☐ Able to identify components of different reference materials
☐ Uses guide words appropriately
☐ Consults references materials when necessary
☐ Uses materials appropriately to complete assignments
☐ Able to identify different types of reference materials and sources
☐ Understands importance of reference materials

Time Management
☐ Completes tasks on time
☐ Plans and organizes daily activities and responsibilities effectively
☐ Plans and organizes weekly and monthly schedules
☐ Reorganizes priorities when necessary
☐ Meets scheduled deadlines
☐ Accurately perceives the amount of time required to complete tasks
☐ Adjusts time allotment to complete tasks
☐ Accepts responsibility for managing own time
☐ Understands importance of effective time management

Self-Management
☐ Monitors own behavior
☐ Changes own behavior as necessary
☐ Thinks before acting
☐ Responsible for own behavior
☐ Identifies behaviors that interfere with own learning
☐ Understands importance of self-management

Summary of Study Skill Proficiency

Summarize in the chart below the number of Mastered (1), Partially Mastered (2), and Not Mastered (3) study skills subskills. The number next to each study skill represents the total number of subskills for each area.

Study Skill				Study Skill			
Reading Rate—6				Test Taking—13			
Listening—5				Library Usage—6			
Note taking/Outlining—9				Reference Materials—6			
Report Writing—10				Time Management—9			
Oral Presentations—6				Self-Management—6			
Graphic Aids—5							

Summary Comments:

Source: Teaching Students with Learning Problems to Use Study Skills: A Teacher's Guide, by J. Hoover & J. Patton, 1995, Austin, TX: Pro-Ed. Copyright 1995 by Pro-Ed, Inc. Reprinted with permission.

Contract System

Personal contracts between students and teachers can be an effective method for having students commit to a project and for teachers to monitor progress. Contracts are also effective in developing students' self-monitoring skills. Contracts provide a method of evaluating concept knowledge in the content areas and a means of measuring study skills (e.g., organization, time management, note taking, and research skills). (Figure 11–8 is an example of a content area assignment contract, and Figure 11–9 is an example of an individual research contract.)

Figure 11–8   Sample Content Area Assignment Contract

Assignment	Time Completed	Comments
• Read and outline Chapter 2.	_____	_____
• Highlight new vocabulary words.	_____	_____
• Make a list of the chief products produced in your state.	_____	
• Write a letter to your pen pal explaining the climate and cultural highlights of your state.	_____	_____
• In your journal, compare and contrast the seasonal differences between your state and a distant state of your choice.	_____	_____

_____	_____	_____	_____
Signed	Date	Witness	Date

Figure 11–9   Sample of an Individual Research Project Contract

I agree to complete this project and to meet all deadlines agreed to below:

Research topic: _____	Date project is due: _____
Outline completed by: _____	I will have an outline (plan) by: _____
I will start working on _____	By (date) I will have completed _____
By (date) I will have _____ completed.	By (date) I will have completed _____
I will have a progress report ready by: _____	My project will be completed by _____

_____	_____	_____	_____
Signed	Date	Witness	Date

SECTION 2: FACTORS INFLUENCING TEST-TAKING PERFORMANCE

FYI

Certain factors—such as attentiveness, motivation, anxiety, and understanding of the test directions—can affect students' test scores (Alliance, 2001).

There are numerous factors that influence how well a student performs on a test. Besides the obvious—which is the mastery of the material covered—other critical factors include motivation and interest, self-confidence, anxiety, attention to detail, the ability to follow directions, and time factors—all of which can affect the outcome of a test (Alliance, 2001). An unfortunate reality is that many students with disabilities who have not had prior experience with test taking and have not developed test-taking strategies or have a history of poor test results have developed test anxiety. These issues are described and assessment strategies are suggested in the following sections.

Test Preparation

Test preparation for standardized tests involves familiarizing students with the specific regulations and requirements that are necessary to maintain standardized procedures. Students may need to practice reading questions in test booklets and answering the questions on separate answer sheets. They need to be aware of the type of response required—circling the correct number on a multiple-choice format, connecting the correct words on a matching format, or filling in the bubble on a scantron sheet. Students must also be able to complete the test within time limits. They need to understand that norm-referenced tests may contain test items that are too difficult for them to answer. They need to be taught how to recognize clue words, answer easy questions first, read carefully, and check answers.

When time limits are a factor, teachers should discuss how to schedule time, making it clear to students that they should not spend too much time on items that are too difficult and move on to subsequent items. Often when students are faced with a series of items that they are unable to answer, they are likely to become frustrated or so anxious that they are unable to continue to do their best. If available, samples of previous tests should be reviewed so that the student can become familiar with the test formats.

Test-taking preparation skills should also be taught. Teachers can improve students' test-taking skills by providing opportunities for them to practice working under standardized testing conditions in simulated situations. Students who enter a test situation armed with test-taking strategies, referred to as **test wiseness**, are less anxious because they have developed methods to manage their time and efforts in the testing process. They tend to have more confidence in their ability to do well and are therefore more motivated to do their best, which can increase the reliability of the results because students will be able to demonstrate their true functioning level. Examples of test-taking strategies include reading all optional items, eliminating answers that are obviously incorrect, and knowing the meaning of certain phrases, such as "find the one that is different" and "which one comes next in the following sequence."

Observing and Interviewing Students Regarding Test-Taking Skills

When observing students during a study session, teachers can note numerous work-study characteristics, including whether they are focusing on the task, how long they appear to be concentrating on the subject, whether they are using a specific study strategy, how well they have prepared for the study session (e.g., having the appropriate materials); whether they use a visual, oral/auditory, or multisensory approach; whether they appear to have an organized system or study plan; and whether they are able to follow this plan. It is also helpful to take into account the environment in which the students are studying. (See Figure 11–10.) Are there minimal distractions in the test preparation and test-taking environment? Is the test area quiet and well lit? Is the student studying with peers?

Open-ended questions, such as the following, can be asked during or after the observation:

- How do you keep track of your assignments?
- How do you prepare for tests?
- What did you do to get ready for studying?
- How do you keep your study materials organized?
- If you find that you do not understand something while studying, what do you do?
- What time of day do you feel is best for you to study?
- Where do you study?
- What conditions tend to cause you to become distracted?

Figure 11–10   Sample Teacher Interview Questions: General Study Skills

Does student:	Always	Occasionally	Never
• finish assigned work?			
• consistently do his or her best work?			
• seem to understand assignments?			
• come to class prepared with materials?			
• budget sufficient time for studying?			
• proofread completed assignments?			
• appear to be attentive in class?			
• take notes adequately?			
• begin assigned work on time?			
• use textbooks appropriately?			
• prefer to work alone?			
• prefer to work in a small group?			
• prefer to work in a large group?			
• ask for help when needed?			
• organize study time well?			
• have the ability to outline study materials?			
• demonstrate the ability to organize?			
• self-monitor his or her progress?			
• use study strategies to recall facts, rules, and so forth?			
• use the Survey, Question, Read, Recite, and Review (SQ3R) study method?			
• follow written directions?			
• follow oral directions?			
• monitor daily time schedule?			
• use homework assignment book?			
• rank personal "things to do" list?			

- When you feel confused while studying, what do you do?
- How do you organize your study sessions?
- Describe how you learn best (when you read, write, listen, draw pictures, or discuss).
- How do you plan your time when you have to complete a big project?
- How do you keep track of your progress in a class?

Test Anxiety

Test anxiety is the feeling of uneasiness or apprehension felt before, during, or after a test due to worrying or fear of failure. Everyone experiences anxiety from time to time, and low levels of anxiety can motivate students to study and perform well. However, high levels of anxiety can be detrimental both test taking and the learning process. Often anxiety can cause students to "blank out" or have difficulty paying attention and affect their ability to think clearly and do their best work (Evans, 2003).

Test anxiety can result in psychological distress, academic underachievement, academic failure, and insecurity.

The three major components of test anxiety are cognitive, affective, and behavioral. Students whose test anxiety has a more cognitive perspective tend to be worriers who lack self-confidence. They tend to be preoccupied by negative thoughts, doubt their academic ability and intellectual competence, are likely to overemphasize their potential negative results, and feel helpless in test situations (Zeidner, 1998).

The affective perspective of test anxiety causes many students to experience physiological reactions, such as increased heart rate, increased perspiration, cold hands, dry mouth, muscle spasms, feeling nauseated, and frequent urination. In addition to these physiological reactions, emotions (such as worry), fear of failure, and panic are often experienced (Zeidner, 1998). When students are unable to control their emotions, they feel more stressed and tend to have more difficulty concentrating (Harris & Coy, 2003).

The behavioral perspective often manifests with procrastination and ineffective study and test-taking skills. Also, test-anxious students often have a more difficult time interpreting information and organizing it into larger patterns of meaning. Students' test-taking skills can also be physically affected during test administration if students feel tired because of poor diet or sleep habits, or general health problems.

Many students who have learning problems are not good test takers, and a series of poor test grades tends to result in the problem being complicated by test anxiety (Hughes, 1997). Test anxiety afflicts one student out of every five. This intense apprehension results from anticipation of taking a test. This fear can cause test scores to be lower than they should be; immediately following the test, highly anxious test takers may report a rush of recall. Fleege and colleagues (1992) found that stress during testing was observed in students as early as kindergarten. Although students who experience anxiety often have mastered the material being tested, their nervousness, lowered self-esteem, and feelings of being unable to control outside events interfere with their ability to concentrate and perform in test situations (Swanson & Howell, 1996). Eliminating time pressure can minimize anxiety and improve test performance. Reviewing the directions and providing a review of the material to be covered before the administration of a test can also reduce anxiety.

Additional strategies that teachers and school personnel can use to provide a more test-friendly environment and to help students effectively manage test anxiety include.

- Ensuring that students have the test accommodations written on their individualized education plan (IEP)
- Providing discussions or support sessions to devise ways that individual students can manage their test anxiety
- Practicing various forms of relaxation techniques
- Giving practice tests
- Teaching test-taking strategies (e.g., understanding time limits, pacing, and different types of test formats, such as multiple choice, essay, fill-in-the-blank)
- Designing some classroom tests using standardized test format and administration guidelines
- Teaching students about test ceilings (i.e., that some tests penalize for incorrect answers, so on these tests it is better to leave blanks than to guess)
- Sending a note to parents about the upcoming test dates and times so they can make sure the child gets sufficient rest and a nutritious breakfast before the test

Attitude and Motivational Factors

One major factor in test-taking performance is students' motivation to take and do their best on tests. This factor becomes critical when students perceive the test to be unfair. Many students fail to see the relevance of testing to their lives or how standardized tests are connected to their world and their classrooms. They need to feel that the test is a mechanism for them to demonstrate what they have learned, that it is not designed to trick them. Research indicates that students who are successful taking tests:

- understand the purpose for testing
- comprehend how the results will be used
- recognize the importance of the test
- understand the relevance of the test to instruction
- expect to do well on standardized tests
- are confident in their test taking abilities

Students need to feel self-determined and empowered; they need to be made aware of the process. They should be given adequate notice before tests are administered. Tests should be announced in advance and information provided as to the general type, content, and approximate length of any test that is scheduled. Students need sufficient time to prepare and be in optimal condition to take the test (e.g., be well nourished, have adequate sleep, feel relaxed, be mentally alert). Parents should be notified about upcoming tests, especially standardized tests, and reminded of the importance of making sure their child is at his or her best.

Often students may need extrinsic motivators to help them to begin and complete a test while putting forth their best effort. Some may require only verbal encouragement (e.g., "I can see you are working hard"). Others may need to work toward a specific goal or tangible reward (e.g., extra outdoor playtime, stickers). (See Figure 11–11 for a self-determination and self-advocacy checklist.)

Appropriate Accommodations

To ensure that teachers can accurately assess students' individual accommodation needs and accurately match the accommodation to the diagnosed need, specific educational training is needed. Research suggests that teachers are not taking full advantage of the range of accommodations available for students with disabilities. (See Chapter 4.) Teachers may tend to use test modifications that can be used with all students, those that maintain academic integrity yet do not require extra planning, individualization, time, or resources. A national survey of teachers by Jayanthi and colleagues (1996) found that the test accommodations perceived as being most helpful included (a) giving individual help with directions during tests, (b) reading test questions to students, and (c) simplifying the wording of test items.

SECTION 3: TEST-TAKING SKILLS TECHNIQUES

Helping Students to Become "Test Wise"

Teachers need to determine how "**test wise**" students are so that a plan can be developed for maximizing their performance on evaluation measures. Students need to understand the mechanics of test-taking, such as the need to carefully follow instructions, to check their work, and so forth. They need to use appropriate test-taking

Figure 11–11   Self-Determination/Self-Advocacy Checklist

How well do you know yourself? How well do you know what you like or prefer for yourself? How well do you know what you value as important in your life and how those values affect your decisions? How well can you tell others about yourself—your strengths and weaknesses?

How well can you tell others how they can be supportive and helpful to you when you need help? How well can you look at your life and make changes when you see things you want to change?

The checklist below will help you know yourself better in these areas. Answer as honestly as you can. If you don't know, you may say that you don't know by checking DK.

Descriptions of Me	School		Home/Community		
	Yes	No	Yes	No	DK
I can describe my strengths.	☐	☐	☐	☐	☐
I can describe my weaknesses.	☐	☐	☐	☐	☐
I can explain my disability label.	☐	☐	☐	☐	☐
I can explain what I need from special services.	☐	☐	☐	☐	☐
I can explain how I learn best.	☐	☐	☐	☐	☐
I can explain what does not help in learning.	☐	☐	☐	☐	☐
I know my interests.	☐	☐	☐	☐	☐
I know my values.	☐	☐	☐	☐	☐
I can ask for help without getting upset.	☐	☐	☐	☐	☐
I can state what I want to learn.	☐	☐	☐	☐	☐
I can state what I want to do when I graduate.	☐	☐	☐	☐	☐
I can state my rights as a person with a disability.	☐	☐	☐	☐	☐
I speak confidently and with eye contact when talking with others.	☐	☐	☐	☐	☐
I can tell teachers or work supervisors what I need to be able to do my work.	☐	☐	☐	☐	☐
I know how to look for support or help.	☐	☐	☐	☐	☐
I know how to set goals for myself.	☐	☐	☐	☐	☐
I know how to get information to make decisions.	☐	☐	☐	☐	☐
I can solve problems that come up in my life.	☐	☐	☐	☐	☐
I can develop a plan of action for goals.	☐	☐	☐	☐	☐
I can begin my work on time.	☐	☐	☐	☐	☐
I can stay on a work schedule or time plan.	☐	☐	☐	☐	☐
I can work independently.	☐	☐	☐	☐	☐
I can manage my time to stay on task until done.	☐	☐	☐	☐	☐
I can compare my work to a standard and evaluate its quality.	☐	☐	☐	☐	☐
I can tell when my plan of action is working or not.	☐	☐	☐	☐	☐
I can change goals or my plan of action.	☐	☐	☐	☐	☐

Source: Transition Planning Inventory, by G. Clark and J.R. Patton, 1998, Austin, TX: Pro-Ed. Copyright 1998 by Pro-Ed, Inc. Reprinted with permission.

strategies, including ways to address test items and make educated guesses. In addition, they need to practice their test-taking skills to refine their abilities and to become more comfortable in testing situations. Research (Alliance, 2001) also suggests that students who are test wise are more successful in testing situations because they:

- Are able to follow instructions and directions
- Are familiar with item formats
- Know how to avoid common mistakes
- Know how to use their time effectively and efficiently

Computerized test formats may be the best option for some students

Figure 11–12   Checklist of Test Preparation Study Skills

	Yes	No	Comment
Test Preparation *Does the student use the following strategies*: • Set up a quiet, comfortable area conducive to study? • Gather and organize all study materials before beginning to study? • Find out exactly what will be covered on the test? • Find out what kind of test it will be (essay, multiple choice, matching, etc.)? • Prioritize information and determine hierarchy of content to be studied? • Develop a study plan, deciding objectives for each projected study session? • Look up hard vocabulary to understand meanings? • Skim chapter headings to recall the overall ideas in each chapter? • Reread chapter summaries? • Review all visual illustrations when studying? • Space studying over an extended period of time rather than cram for tests? • Systematically review previous tests to determine test-taking/studying errors? **Test Taking** • Apply memory strategies (e.g., mnemonics, keywords)? • Maintain a positive attitude when taking tests? • Understand directions before answering questions? • Identify and carefully use clue words? • Use test-taking strategies (e.g., eliminate wrong answers)? • Answer easy questions first, difficult last? • Write answers neatly and legibly? • Carefully record answers? • Proofread answers and check for errors?			

Figure 11—13   Test-Taking Skills and Abilities Checklist

Does the student:

_____ 1. Read all directions before beginning the test.

_____ 2. Follow directions carefully.

_____ 3. Budget time well.

_____ 4. Check work carefully.

_____ 5. Read the entire item and all answers.

_____ 6. Answer easier questions first and persist to the end.

_____ 7. Make educated guesses.

_____ 8. Use test item formats for practice.

_____ 9. Review all the practice items available.

_____10. Practice using an answer sheet.

- Can maximize their scores by informed and educated guessing
- Have been exposed to a variety of testing situations
- Can apply test-taking strategies to solve different kinds of problems

Students need to be able to demonstrate their proficiency in content on teacher-made as well as standardized tests. Often students have sufficient grasp of the content but insufficient test-taking skills. To be successful at taking multiple-choice, true-and-false, fill-in-the-blank, and short-answer tests, students need to be able to effectively process information in an organized format, retrieve the information needed for the test, read and understand test questions, monitor test time, and make educated guesses. Figure 11-12 is a sample test preparation and test-taking checklist; Figure 11-13 is a test-taking skills and abilities checklist.)

SUMMARY POINTS

- The main components of work-study skills include the ability to plan, organize, and attend to details; keep track of assignments and school materials; listen and attend to details; and provide solutions to problems using reasoning and problem-solving skills.

- Study skills acquisition should be assessed in order to identify strengths and areas of need, to develop a work-study skills program of study, to provide insight into how students interact with learning tasks, and to closely monitor progress.

- When assessing students' ability to retain information, the factors to consider include the type of information to be recalled; the time that has expired since the original presentation of the information; the type of memory task required (e.g., recognition or recall); and the way that recalled information needs to be organized (e.g., free or serial recall).

- The skills to focus on when evaluating a student's ability to succeed at school-related tasks involve listening, memory, organization, metacognitive reflection, note taking, and research.

- Factors that influence students' test performance include mastery and retention of the curricular content, motivation, interest, self-confidence, anxiety, attention to detail, the ability to follow directions, and time limitations.

- Test anxiety can cause students to "blank out"; that is, to have difficulty maintaining attention, thinking clearly, and doing their best work. It can cause psychological distress, academic underachievement, academic failure, and feelings of insecurity.
- Students with disabilities may need to have support in dealing with test anxiety or lack of motivation. They may require direct instruction on how to use test-taking strategies to facilitate their participation in standardized accountability testing.

Chapter Check-Ups

1. Discuss why it is important to assess students' study skills. What types of problems tend to more prevalent with students who have learning difficulties.
2. Define executive functioning skills. Describe each of these skills and identify an assessment strategy that could be used to assess each executive functioning skill.
3. Why is note taking considered to be such a complex task?
4. Describe the factors that impact students' performance on tests and what strategies can be used to ameliorate problems that student experience preparing for and taking tests.
5. What does it mean to be "test wise" and how would a teacher assess students' test-taking skills?

Practical Application Assessment Activities

1. In a small group, discuss your experiences with assessment. What types of test formats worked best for you and what formats did you find more difficult? Determine which format type is likely to be best for various types of learning problems.
2. Reflect on the issue of test anxiety. Have you experienced test anxiety? What test anxiety-reducing strategies and/or study techniques have you used? How have your experiences influenced what you believe should be done for children with special needs? In a small group, share experiences and brainstorm strategies to help students with various disabilities prepare for test taking and develop a list of techniques for alleviating test anxiety.
3. Visit a local elementary and middle school classroom. Prior to your observation, construct a checklist to be used when observing the learning, physical and social environment of these classes. Focus on the aspects of the environment that support the students' work-study skills. Identify changes in the environment that would better facilitate students' learning.

Connection Between CEC, PRAXIS, and INTASC Standards and Chapter 11

Council for Exceptional Children
The voice and vision of special education

The Council for Exceptional Children—Professional Standards

Standard 2 Development and Characteristics of Learners

5. Similarities and differences of individuals with and without exceptional learning needs.
6. Similarities and differences among individuals with exceptional learning needs.

Standard 3 Individual Learning Differences

5. Differing ways of learning of individuals with exceptional learning needs including those from culturally diverse backgrounds and strategies for addressing these differences.

Standard 4 Instructional Strategies

1. Use strategies to facilitate integration into various settings.
3. Select, adapt, and use instructional strategies and materials according to characteristics of the individual with exceptional learning needs.

Standard 5 Learning Environments and Social Interactions

16. Use performance data and information from all stakeholders to make or suggest modifications in learning environments.
19. Create an environment that encourages self-advocacy and increased independence.

Standard 7 Instructional Planning

11. Sequence, implement, and evaluate individualized learning objectives.
12. Integrate affective, social, and life skills with academic curricula.
13. Develop and select instructional content, resources, and strategies that respond to cultural, linguistic, and gender differences.
14. Incorporate and implement instructional and assistive technologies into the educational program.
18. Make responsive adjustments to instruction based on continual observations.

Standard 8 Assessment

5. National, state or provincial, and local accommodations and modifications.
6. Gather relevant background information.
7. Administer nonbiased formal and informal assessments.
8. Use technology to conduct assessments.
9. Develop or modify individualized assessment strategies.
10. Interpret information from formal and informal assessments.
11. Use assessment information in making eligibility, program, and placement decisions for individuals with exceptional learning needs, including those from culturally and/or linguistically diverse backgrounds.
12. Report assessment result to all stakeholders using effective communication skills.
13. Evaluate instruction and monitor progress of individuals with exceptional learning needs.
14. Create and maintain records.

Standard 9 Professional and Ethical Practice

14. Access information on exceptionalities.
15. Reflect on one's practice to improve instruction and guide professional growth.
16. Engage in professional activities that benefit individuals with exceptional learning needs, their families and one's colleagues.

Standard 10 Collaboration

6. Collaborate with families and others in assessment of individuals with exceptional learning needs.

THE PRAXIS SERIES™

PRAXIS Standards for Special Education

Standard 1 Understanding Exceptionalities

2. Characteristics of students with disabilities, including medical/physical; educational; social; and psychological.

3. Basic concepts in special education, including definitions of all major categories and specific disabilities; causation and prevention of disability; the nature of behaviors, including frequency, duration, intensity, and degrees of severity; and classification of students with disabilities, including classifications as represented in IDEA and labeling of students.

Standard 2 Legal and Societal Issues

2. Issues related to school, family, and/or community, such as teacher advocacy for students and families, including advocating for educational change and developing students' self-advocacy; family participation and support systems; public attitudes toward individuals with disabilities; and cultural and community influences.

Standard 3 Delivery of Services to Students with Disabilities

3. Assessment, including how to modify, construct, or select and conduct nondiscriminatory and appropriate informal and formal assessment procedures; how to interpret standardized and specialized assessment results; how to use evaluation result for various purposes, including monitoring instruction and IEP/ITP development; and how to prepare written reports and communicate findings to others.

5. Curriculum and instruction, including the IEP/ITP process; instructional development and implementation (for example, instructional activities, curricular materials, resources and equipment, working with classroom personnel, tutoring and the use of technology); teaching strategies and methods (for example, direct instruction, cooperative learning, diagnostic-prescriptive method); instructional format and components (for example, individualized instruction, small- and large-group instruction, modeling, drill and practice); and areas of instruction (such as academics, study and learning skills, social, self-care, and vocational skills).

INTASC Standards for Teacher Education

Standard 1

The teacher understands the central concepts, tools of inquiry, and structures of the discipline(s) he or she teaches and can create learning experiences that make these aspects of subject matter meaningful for students.

Standard 3

The teacher understands how students differ in their approaches to learning and creates instructional opportunities that are adapted to diverse learners.

CCSSO
THE COUNCIL OF CHIEF STATE
SCHOOL OFFICERS

Standard 4

The teacher understands and uses a variety of instructional strategies to encourage students' development of critical thinking, problem solving, and performance skills.

Standard 5

The teacher uses an understanding of individual and group motivation and behavior to create a learning environment that encourages positive social interaction, active engagement in learning, and self-motivation.

Standard 6

The teacher uses knowledge of effective verbal, nonverbal, and media communication techniques to foster active inquiry, collaboration, and supportive interaction in the classroom.

Standard 8

The teacher understands and uses formal and informal assessment strategies to evaluate and ensure the continuous intellectual, social, and physical development of the learner.

CHAPTER 12

Emotional, Social, and Character Education

KEY TERMS AND CONCEPTS

- emotional and behavioral disorder
- direct analysis of behavior
- event recording
- duration recording
- latency recording
- interval recording
- time sampling

- running record
- anecdotal records
- functional behavioral assessment
- character education assessment
- social skills assessment
- sociograms

CHAPTER OBJECTIVES

After reading this chapter, you should be able to:

- Describe the purpose of a functional behavioral assessment.
- Compare and contrast event recording, latency recording, and duration recording.

- Name the three types of interval recordings and when they are used.
- Describe a character education assessment.
- Explain a sociogram and its purpose.

Introduction to Emotional, Social, and Character Assessment

Assessing students' emotional and social behavior and character involves various types of evaluation procedures, including observation, interviews, self-reports, environmental assessments, behavior rating scales, functional behavioral assessments, and sociograms. The focus of such assessments should be on determining (1) the degree to which students believe personal behaviors make a difference in their life, (2) their tolerance for frustration, (3) their general activity level, (4) how they view themselves, (5) how they respond emotionally to situations, and (5) how much conflict they are experiencing (Pierangelo & Giuliani, 1998, pp. 181).

Consideration should be given to beginning the assessment process when a general pattern exists in which the student exhibits one or more of the following behaviors (Pierangelo & Giuliani, 1998):

- an inability to learn on a consistent basis that cannot be explained by intellectual capability, hearing or visual status, or physical health anomalies
- an inability or unwillingness to develop or maintain satisfactory interpersonal relationships with peers, teachers, parents, or other adults
- extreme overreaction to minimally stressful situations over a prolonged period of time
- a general pervasive mood of sadness or depression
- a tendency toward somatic complaints, pains, or excessive fears associated with home, school, or social situations
- lack of knowledge and skill acquisition in academic and social behaviors not attributed to intellectual capability, hearing and vision status, and physical health anomalies
- observable periods of diminished verbal and motor activity, such as moods of depression or unhappiness

SECTION 1: EMOTIONAL AND BEHAVIORAL DISORDERS

An **emotional and behavioral disorder** (EBD) in the school setting is a condition in which certain responses of students are so different from generally accepted, age-appropriate, ethnic, or cultural norms that they adversely affect the students' performance in such areas as self-care, social relationships, personal adjustments, academic progress, class behavior, and work adjustment. This is the number one cited reason that students are referred for mental health services. EBD can negatively interfere with a student's academic, vocational, and social skills. Since students with EBD are usually underserved, they must be serviced in a collaborative fashion. It is important to identify students with EBD as early as possible so that interventions can begin and possibly lessen the negative effects on the academic and social aspects of their education. (See Figure 12–1.)

Currently EBDs afflict about 1.3 to 4.0 million students in preschool to high school. Unfortunately, this disorder among students is increasing at an alarming rate, making it increasingly difficult to educate all students, since students who display persistent patterns of emotional and behavior problems can cause significant disruptions

Figure 12–1   Social-Emotional Behaviors That Signal the Need for Evaluation

- High levels of tension and anxiety exhibited in behavior
- Aggressive behavior
- Lack of motivation or indications of low energy levels
- Patterns of denial
- Oppositional behavior
- Despondency
- Inconsistent academic performance, ranging from very low to very high
- History of inappropriate judgment
- Lack of impulse control
- Extreme and consistent attention-seeking behavior
- Patterns of provocative behavior
(Pierangelo & Giuliani, p. 24)

that affect other students as well. For those who have EBDs, these behaviors generally continue throughout their life. The indicators of EBDs in students include the following:

1. Acting and reacting aggressively toward others
2. Physically abusing others
3. Purposefully destroying the property of others
4. Bullying, threatening, or intimidating others
5. Readily blaming others for their own misdeeds
6. Showing little or no empathy for the feelings or well-being of others

To be identified as having an EBD, students must display the behavior in at least two different settings, and school must be one of them. In addition to obtaining data about the student's behavioral or emotional functioning from multiple sources, it is imperative that the assessment identify both the strengths and the weaknesses of the student, and take into consideration the program the student is participating in, and the people with whom he or she interacts. It should also be determined whether or not the student's problems could be due primarily to transient development or environmental variables, cultural or linguistic differences, or the influences of other handicapping conditions. The referral for special services should not be based on an effort to resolve conflict or as a disciplinary action. There are three main steps in the assessment process:

1. Gather relevant information about the student in both the social and instructional environment
2. Assimilate the data to create an overall picture of the concerns
3. Develop short- and long-term goals and strategies for intervention

SECTION 2: BEHAVIORAL ANALYSIS PROCEDURES

Direct analysis of behavior focuses on the actions surrounding misbehavior, ineffective behavior, and inappropriate behavior. It is the assessment method of choice when behavior is clearly disruptive or dysfunctional.

Indirect assessment—which provides data on attitudes and feelings that are not easily identified during observation—is the method to use when motivational and other personal information is needed to shed light on the problem. A comprehensive analysis of behavior includes (Guerin & Maier, 1983, pp. 304–305):

- The nature of misbehavior and the circumstances under which it occurs
- The student's appropriate behavior and when it occurs

- The onset, circumstances, and duration of the problem
- The age level or circumstances under which the behavior might be appropriate
- Patterns of good behavior and misbehavior
- The quality of a student's interpersonal relations in various school and out-of-school situations
- The student's skill level during periods of appropriate versus inappropriate behavior
- Coping styles and how they are supported or reinforced in the school setting
- The student's willingness to participate in change
- Assessment of motivation, feelings, attitudes, beliefs, and abilities
- The student's role in the class and at school during different activities
- Home and peer support for misbehavior

Behaviors that may need to be assessed generally fall into one of the following three categories (Guerin & Maier, 1983, p. 305):

Social Interactions	Academic/Skill	Feelings/Affect
Cooperation	Responsibility	Interests
Friendliness	Completion	Moods
Acceptance	Coherence	Patience
Courtesy	Relevance	Frustrations
Helpfulness	Clarity	Emotions
Respectfulness	Attentiveness	Persistence
Talkativeness	Understanding	Angers
	Memory	Fears
	Language	Affections

Classroom Scenario: What Would You Do?

You, Mary's science teacher, observe that at times, Mary is actively involved in classroom discussions and can answer questions well. At other times, she does not contribute positively to the verbal interaction in class; she is restless, even disruptive, during some science lessons. Recently, you had to send her to the principal's office several times during one week because of her distracting behavior. During a personal interview with Mary, you find out that she enjoys science and is very interested in this subject, but that she has difficulty understanding what she is reading in her science text. With some direct questioning, you determine that Mary's background information and listening comprehension skills are well developed in science, but her limited reading vocabulary is greatly affecting her ability to understand what she reads. Mary is a proud child who takes pride in "showing off" her knowledge in science. She indicates that she is embarrassed when the class discussion is based on the previous night's reading assignment, and she is upset when she cannot be a leader in the discussion because she could not fluently read it. Mary is coping with her embarrassment by using an avoidance technique. She has decided that it is better to act out and be sent to the principal's office than to be called on in class and humiliated by her inability to answer the questions. What would you do?

SECTION 3: GENERAL AND DIRECT OBSERVATIONS AND INTERVIEW PROCEDURES

General Observations

In order to obtain a comprehensive view of the student, the observations should occur in various settings, at various times, and under a variety of circumstances. This includes structured and unstructured settings (e.g., the classroom, gym, playground, cafeteria, school bus); at different times of the day (e.g., before and after lunch); in different classes (e.g., reading, art, math, music); and various situations (e.g., working independently, in small and large groups). (See Figure 12-2 for a behavioral skills checklist.)

Figure 12–2   Behavioral Skills Checklist

Behaviorial Skill	Always	Most of the Time	Rarely	Never
On Time and Prepared				
• Arrives to class on time				
• Brings necessary materials				
• Completes homework				
Respects Peers				
• Respects property of others				
• Listens to peers				
• Responds appropriately to peers				
• Respects opinions of others				
• Refrains from abusive language				
Respects Teacher and Staff				
• Follows directions				
• Listens to teacher and staff				
• Accepts responsibility for actions				
Demonstrates Appropriate Character Traits				
• Demonstrates positive character traits (e.g., kindness, trustworthy, honesty)				
• Demonstrates productive character traits (e.g., patience, thoroughness, hard work)				
• Demonstrates concern for others				
Demonstrates a Level of Concern for Learning				
• Remains on task				
• Allows others to remain on task				

SECTION 4: TYPES OF DIRECT OBSERVATIONS

Event Recording

Event recording is a method of direct observation in which the observer counts the number of times a target behavior occurs. This type of observation is also known as frequency recording. When the event recording is directly related to time, it is known as rate recording (e.g., 12 times per minute, 4 times per hour). Event recording can be used when the behavior has a definite beginning and end, also referred to as a discrete behavior (Alberto & Troutman, 1998).

Teachers often apply event recording to everyday class activities. When the number of correct multiplication facts the second-grader recites, the number of misspelled words in a middle-school child's written passage, or the number of times the high-schooler leaves his desk during a 45-minute reading period is recorded, event recording is being used. Event recording can be relatively easy to do. Recordings can be done by making slash marks on a notepad, by using a handheld counter, or by simply moving a rubber band from one finger to the next to count incidents of specific target behavior (Sabornie & deBettencourt, 1997).

> To record the frequency of Nancy's inappropriate calling out in your class, you use an event recording technique. You find that Nancy called out 9 times during your 45-minute science class on Monday, 10 times on Tuesday, 7 times on Wednesday, 12 times on Thursday, and 11 times on Friday. You graph the frequency for reporting purposes. (See Figure 12–4, page 475.)

Figure 12–3   Psycho-Social-Emotional Adjustment Checklist

The student . . .	Often	Occasionally	Rarely/Never
• is impulsive.	_____	_____	_____
• gives excuses for inappropriate behavior.	_____	_____	_____
• constantly blames others for problems.	_____	_____	_____
• panics easily.	_____	_____	_____
• is highly distractible.	_____	_____	_____
• lies continually.	_____	_____	_____
• is fearful with adults.	_____	_____	_____
• is fearful of new situations.	_____	_____	_____
• is verbally hesitant.	_____	_____	_____
• is hyperactive.	_____	_____	_____
• has a short attention span.	_____	_____	_____
• is overactive.	_____	_____	_____
• is physical with others.	_____	_____	_____
• is intrusive.	_____	_____	_____
• is unable to focus on task.	_____	_____	_____
• procrastinates.	_____	_____	_____
• is very disorganized.	_____	_____	_____
• is inflexible.	_____	_____	_____
• is irresponsible.	_____	_____	_____
• uses poor judgment.	_____	_____	_____
• is in denial.	_____	_____	_____
• is unwilling to reason.	_____	_____	_____
• demonstrates social withdrawal.	_____	_____	_____
• is constantly self-critical.	_____	_____	_____
• bullies other children.	_____	_____	_____
• needs constant reassurance.	_____	_____	_____

Figure 12-4 Sample of Event Recording Chart

Name: Nancy			Date: 9/10-9/15
Target Behavior: Any inappropriate verbalizations			
Day	**Observation Period**	**Frequency**	**Total for Period**
Monday	1:00 PM to 1:45 PM	⊥⊦⊦⊤ ‖‖	9
Tuesday	12:45 PM to 1:30 PM	⊥⊦⊦⊤ ⊥⊦⊦⊤	10
Wednesday	12:48 PM to 1:33 PM	⊥⊦⊦⊤ ‖	7
Thursday	1:15 PM to 2:00 PM	⊥⊦⊦⊤ ⊥⊦⊦⊤ ‖	12
Friday	1:02 PM to 1:47 PM	⊥⊦⊦⊤ ⊥⊦⊦⊤ ‖	11
TOTAL			49

Duration Recording

Duration recording is a type of direct measurement used to record how long a specific behavior lasts. In some situations, the duration of a certain behavior may be more significant than how often it occurs. For meaningful duration recording, the behavior must have a clear beginning and end.

> Ted turned his head to look out the classroom window two times during his study hall period. The first time, he stared out the window for 15 minutes and the second time for 18 minutes. It is more significant to report that he was off task for more than half of the 45-minute period than it is to report that he looked away from his work only twice during the period.

There are two methods of duration recording. The teacher can either total or average the segments of time that the behavior occurred during a specific period of time. To obtain the total, the teacher adds each recorded period of time that the behavior occurred. To obtain an average, the total number of minutes that the behavior occurred is divided by the number of times that the behavior was observed during the identified period.

> During the first hour of the school day, you observe that Jesse sucked his thumb for 10-minute, 7-minute, 3-minute, 8-minute, and 12-minute segments. You calculate that during one hour of school, Jesse had a total of 40 minutes of thumb sucking with an average of 8 minutes each time he sucked his thumb. (See Figure 12-5.)

Latency Recording

Latency recording is similar to duration recording in that time is a critical factor, although the focus is not on how long the behavior occurred but rather on how long it took before the student actually engaged in the targeted behavior. This type of assessment is particularly useful for students who are often off task, unfocused, uncooperative, unable to process directions well, or slow to initiate or follow through on an assignment. Results can be calculated in average time or total latency, whichever most clearly defines the issue.

> As Marcy's teacher, you are concerned about her slow response time. You begin to record the time from the end of the verbal directions until the time that Marcy begins the assignment. You will need this information to clarify your concerns to her parents. (See Figure 12-6.)

Figure 12–5   Sample Duration Recording Chart

Name: Jesse		Date: 11/3
Target Behavior: Thumb sucking		
Behavior Began	**Behavior Ended**	**Duration**
8:30 AM	8:40 AM	10 minutes
8:45 AM	8:52 AM	7 minutes
8:55 AM	8:58 AM	3 minutes
9:00 AM	9:08 AM	8 minutes
9:18 AM	9:30 AM	12 minutes
TOTAL		40 minutes
AVERAGE DURATION	8 minutes	

Figure 12–6   Sample Graph of Latency Recording

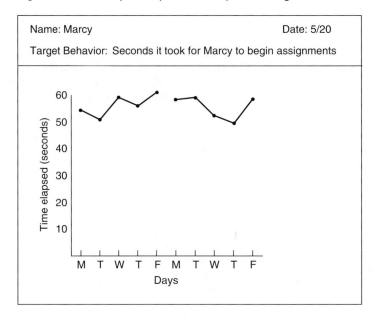

Interval Recording

Interval recording is another direct method of observing specific target behaviors. The teacher chooses a specific amount of time for the observation—for example, 20 minutes—and divides this time period into smaller, equal time segments—for example, 10-second intervals. During each 10-second interval, the teacher carefully watches the student and records whether the target behavior is observed. If so, the teacher marks the prepared rating sheet with a plus sign (+) or some other code to indicate that the behavior was observed. If during that interval the behavior was not observed, a minus sign (−) or a zero (0) is entered on the rating sheet. Three types of interval recordings can be made: (1) a partial interval recording is when the behavior

Figure 12–7   Sample Interval Recording Graph

Name: Jesse				Date: 10/2	
Target Behavior: On task					
+ 5 min.	− 10 min.	− 15 min.	+ 20 min.	+ 25 min.	− 30 min.
− 35 min.	− 40 min.	− 45 min.	+ 50 min.	− 55 min.	− 60 min.

occurs at any time during the interval (e.g., for 2 seconds during the 10-second interval); (2) percentage interval recording is when the observer records the percent of time that the behavior occurred during the interval (e.g., 20% of the 10-second interval); and (3) total interval is when the behavior occurs throughout the complete interval (e.g., 2 out of 10 seconds would be recorded as a minus [−], but 10 seconds out of the 10-second interval would be recorded as a plus [+]).

Time sampling is another type of interval recording method. Using this method, an observation period of 20 minutes can be divided into 10 equal two-minute intervals. During class, at the end of each two-minute interval, the teacher checks to see if the targeted behavior is occurring at that exact time. If so, a plus (+) is noted on the recording sheet. If the behavior occurred during the first minute of the interval but stopped before the end of the two-minute interval (the exact time at which the teacher is scheduled to look for the behavior), a minus (−) is recorded. A stopwatch or beeper system is often used to keep track of time when using all types of interval recording, including time sampling.

> You suspect that Jesse, an active second-grader in your class, is off task more than he is on task, and you want to verify and document your suspicions. Because you have no aide in the classroom and have to teach while doing the recording, you choose to use the time sampling method of interval recording. You decide to record when Jesse is on task at set intervals and set your wrist alarm watch to beep every five minutes for a one-hour period. Using a small notepad, you discreetly record your observations at the end of each interval as you walk around checking students' work. (See Figure 12–7.)

Anecdotal Records

Anecdotal records are running records of notable behavior. They are narrative and dated reports used to measure student progress, to record behaviors, and to analyze patterns of behavior over time. (See Figure 12–8.) These records are written by the teacher based on direct observation and in as much detail as possible to describe the behavior and the incident in which it occurred, including context and setting. These reports should be completed as soon as possible following the incident in

Figure 12–8   Sample Form for Recording Behaviors

Student's name: _____

Date: _____ Time: _____

Location: _____

Activity: _____

Antecedent: _____

Behavior(s) observed: _____

Significance of behavior: _____

Have these or similar behaviors been observed before? _____

under similar _____ different _____ circumstances?

order to reduce the risk of erroneous recordings caused by inaccurate recall and the tendency to generalize negative judgments about more than one behavior. Each entry can be brief but should contain the date, time, description of the setting, the context of the situation, the antecedent, a summary of the noted behavior or activity, including what was said or done by the child or children involved (e.g., the student being observed while responding to a comment made by another student). The teacher's interpretation of the observed behavior may be included, although the interpretation or the possible explanation for it should be clearly identified by placing it in brackets or marked in some way to avoid confusing the interpretation of the behavior with the observation of it (e.g., Dan did not contribute to his peer group discussion [maybe because he was teased by two members of the group yesterday]). Anecdotal records may need to be interpreted cautiously because of the reliability issues relating to teachers' reporting their interpretation experience and skill.

> You are concerned about Jackie's distracting and inappropriate classroom behavior. Because her behavior is unpredictable, you decide to keep a running record of her behavior patterns. This record will be used to document the kinds of behaviors, the precipitating factors, and the conditions and circumstances in which these behaviorial problems surface. (See Figure 12-9.)

Figure 12–9   Sample Behavior Record

Name: Jackie		Date: 11/8
Period: Independent work period after lunch		

12:30 PM	Students enter room and go right to their desks.
12:35 PM	Jackie is the last to enter the room.
12:35 PM	Jackie goes toward her desk, but after sitting for a few seconds leaves her desk and goes to the sink to get drink.
12:37 PM	Teacher tells students to finish their morning seatwork. Jackie splashes two children with the sink water.
12:39 PM	Jackie is told to return to her seat but continues splashing another student.
12:40 PM	Jackie hits the student who asked her to stop splashing the water.

A series of recordings, or running records, helps the teacher to note whether certain behaviors are chronic or incidental, whether a pattern exists, or whether the behaviors are increasing or decreasing. Records might be kept on a daily, weekly, or monthly basis; successful as well as unsuccessful efforts should be noted. It is important to observe and record students in a variety of situations, such as (a) working in discussion or writing conference groups, (b) participating in independent writing activities, (c) interacting in cooperative groups, (d) using strategies in writing, (e) applying strategies when studying informational text, and (f) encountering an unknown word or confusing passage (Gunning, 1998). Teachers may jot down notes during class as they walk around the room monitoring progress in activities, such as a laboratory assignment. Some teachers, particularly those teaching young children who require much hands-on involvement, may find it difficult to take notes during class time. They find it more manageable to develop understandable abbreviations for students, actions, and contexts by setting up a key and color-coded system for different dated entries (e.g., 1 = yes, 2 = no, O = often, S = sometimes, R = rarely). In this way, they can rely on a tally sheet or checklist to note, for example, how often the student contributed to the group discussion about the week's current events topic. (See Figure 12–10).

Figure 12–10   Sample Anecdotal Record

Actions, Activities, Behaviors Observed	Date: 10/2
Target Student: Betsy	

Time:	
11:00 AM	T tell ss to open bk, & hmwrk nbk, turn to pg 57, do prblms 1–20.
11:01	B looks around rm, then stares out wdo.
11:02	B looks over at other ss.
11:03	T asks for volunteers to read hmwrk answ.
11:04	B's glance returns to wdo.
11:05	T tells B to take out hmwrk nbk and explain 1st prblm.
11:06–11:08	B looking in dsk for hmwrk.
11:09	T asks if she has hmwrk.
11:10	B says she forgot to do it.
11:11	T calls on J.
11:11–11:16	J explains 1st math prblm, writes answ on chlkbd.
	R looks at his nbk.
11:17	B reverts to staring out wdo.
11:18	T reminds B to check hmwrk.
11:19	B looks at nbk.
11:20	R is asked to explain prblm #2.
11:21–11:25	B picks up pcl and doodles on bk cover.

Key:

B = Betsy	wdo = window	dsk = desk
T = Teacher	pcl = pencil	prblm = problem
R = Roger	bk = book	chlkbd = chalkboard
J = Jill	nbk = notebook	rm = room
ss = student	hmwrk = homework	answ = answer

Once the recordings are made, the notes or tallies can be saved and later translated into narrative reports; or teachers may prefer to transpose their mental notes onto paper during lunch or after school hours. Notations can be jotted down in notebooks, in individual student folders, on index cards, on sticky notepaper, or on a hand-held or palmtop computer. Additional ways to keep track of progress are self-evaluation questionnaires, charts, journal entries, and daily folders.

Besides providing information about students' academic skills, anecdotal records may be used to track students' strategy use, work habits, interaction with classmates and teachers, interests, and attitudes toward particular activities and assigned tasks (Gunning, 1998). These records should be reviewed periodically and summarized, and any developmental trends or patterns noted (Rhodes & Nathenson-Mejia, 1992). Thus, anecdotal records can be invaluable when teachers are considering the student's present level of educational performance, when writing progress reports to parents, and when reviewing the student's day-to-day progress as they project the next year's individualized education plan (IEP) goals, and when appropriate, objectives.

Interviews

Interviewing students is critical in learning about their self-perceptions of loneliness and social satisfaction. Two ways to obtain this information are through informal interviews and self-report inventories (Pavri, 2001). Interviews should involve multiple sources. Peers can provide information through informal questioning, peer ratings, peer nominations, and social ratings. Parents and other significant adults in the student's life can provide information about the student's social behavior and adjustment in different situations and settings (e.g., home, school, extracurricular settings). See Figure 12–3 for a psycho-social-emotional adjustment checklist. Questions that can be used in the interview process include the following:

- How long have behavioral problems been evident?
- Is there a relationship between behavior and developmental or situational stressors?
- Have previous attempts been made to resolve these problems? If so, please describe.

SECTION 5: FUNCTIONAL BEHAVIORAL ASSESSMENT

Functional behavioral assessment (FBA) involves direct observation to analyze students' behavior in relation to social and physical aspects of the environment (Janney & Snell, 2000). The purpose of FBAs is to establish what behavioral supports are needed for students who exhibit a range of challenging behaviors, such as physical and verbal outbursts, property destruction, and disruptive behavior (e.g., temper tantrums, yelling). When a student's behavior does not respond to standard interventions, an FBA can provide additional information to assist the IEP team in planning more effective interventions. Information on the student is gathered from various settings: the school, the playground, on transportation, in the community, and at home (Alpner, Ryndak, & Schloss, 2001). (See Figure 12–11 for a guide to conducting an FBA.)

Functional assessments are mandated by the Individuals with Disabilities Education Act for use by IEP teams addressing behavioral concerns. Many states also have laws or regulations stipulating the need for a functional assessment before permitting significant behavioral interventions to occur. The observations may lead to a

Figure 12–11 How to Conduct a Functional Assessment

When conducting a functional assessment:

1. Verify the seriousness of the problem.
2. Define the problem behavior in concrete terms (e.g., tantrums, hitting others, throwing objects).
3. Collect data on possible causes of the behavior.
4. Analyze the data.
5. Formulate and test a hypothesis (e.g., allow a time out, do a role play).
   (Seaman, De Pauw, Morton, & Omoto, 2003, p. 92).

determination that behavior strategies are not necessary. Instead, the behaviors may have a medical cause. Allergies, infections, menstrual cycle effects, toothaches, chronic constipation, and other medical conditions may bring on challenging behaviors. Medication also can influence behavior. (See Figure 12-12.)

Figure 12–12 Functional Performance and Participation Checklist

• Does the child have difficulties in mobility either access to or within the environment (e.g., hallways, classroom, gym, cafeteria, transportation, bathroom, field trips)?	Y	N
• Does the child seem to be excessively fatigued (e.g., compared with other children)? If so, does this affect the child's attention or participation?	Y	N
• Does the child display a lack of willingness or interest in participating in social/play activities (e.g., prefers to be or play alone at recess, tries to avoid of cooperative activities)?	Y	N
• Does the child have difficulty sitting calmly and attentively in class (e.g., cannot stay seated, displays excess or seemingly unnecessary movement, is restless and fidgety)?	Y	N
• Does the child need more supervision and adult assistance than peers to perform routine class activities (e.g., motor-planning issues, carrying out directions, working independently, completing tasks in sequence)?	Y	N
• Does the child have difficulty keeping up with peers in daily routine activities (e.g., tires easily, appears sleepy or disinterested, daydreams)?	Y	N
• Does the child's decreased attention or inability to focus lead to behaviors of greatly increased or decreased physical activity (e.g., hyperactivity; repetitive movements; slumping in seat; leaning on walls, furniture, or other people or objects)?	Y	N
• Does the child display significant clumsiness or awkwardness that is significantly greater than peers (e.g., lacks coordination and smoothness of movement)?	Y	N
• Does the child act inappropriately or disrespectfully to adults or to peers (e.g., is critical, unkind, abusive, physically or verbally aggressive)?	Y	N
• Do the difficulties seem to be getting worse (over the last six months), or do they worsen under situations of stress or excitement (e.g., loud or complex environments, new situations, specific times of the day)?	Y	N
Additional comments and explanations for all "yes" answers:		

A functional behavioral assessment should:

1. Clearly describe the problem behavior(s).
2. Identify the events, times, and situations that predict when the challenging behaviors will and will not occur across the range of daily routines, including
   - what was happening in the environment before the behavior occurred,
   - what the actual behavior was, and
   - what the student achieved as a result of the behavior.
3. Identify the consequences that maintain the challenging behaviors (e.g., what the student is "getting out of" the behavior, such as attention, avoidance).
4. Develop one or more statements or hypotheses describing specific behaviors and include the types of situations in which the behaviors occurs, and the reinforcers that maintain the behaviors in these situations.
5. Collect directly observed examples that support these statements. (Alliance, 2001)

Categories of Functional Assessment

Information gathering.   Gathering information involves talking to the parents, former and current teachers, the student, and individuals who know the student well. The information may be obtained through formal interviews, questionnaires, or rating scales to identify which events in an environment are linked to the specific problem behavior. The questioning should cover

- What challenging behaviors cause the concern
- What events or physical conditions exist before the behavior occurs that increase the behavior's predictability
- What result appears to motivate or maintain the challenging behavior
- What appropriate behaviors could produce the same result
- What can be learned from previous behavioral support efforts about strategies that are ineffective, partially effective, or effective for only a short time

Direct observation.   The observations can be done by teachers, support staff, and/or family members. The observer should be able to observe the student in natural settings and over an extended period of time in order to observe incidents of the target behavior, yet not be disruptive to the student's normal routine. The observer records when a problem behavior occurs and the following (O'Neil, et al. 1997):

- Identifiy what happened just before the behavior occurred
- Record what happened after the behavior occurred
- Note—after 10 to 15 instances of observing the behavior—his or her perceptions regarding the function of the behavior and whether a pattern exists

SECTION 6: CHARACTER EDUCATION ASSESSMENT

Public awareness of **character education assessment** has increased in recent years and is now a focus in many school districts. The intent of character education is for schools to emphasize universally shared values. The six pillars of character education are respect, responsibility, trustworthiness, fairness, caring, and citizenship. (See **Figure 12-13**.)

Figure 12–13 Character Education: School Profile

School as a Caring Community Profile—2

Directions: The first 25 items relate to perceptions of students; the final 17 items relate to perceptions of adults. Younger children may be asked to answer only items 1 through 34. The SCCP identifies areas of strength and areas for improvement. Areas of relatively low ratings, and areas where there are significant discrepancies between ratings by different groups, can then become the focus of efforts to strengthen the experience of the school as a caring community.

Circle one:
    (1) Student—Please write the number of the grade you are in: ___
    (2) Administrator   (3) Teacher   (4) Professional Support Staff
    (5) Other staff   (6) Parent   (7) Other _____

Please circle the appropriate number that describes how often you observe the following behaviors in your school.

(1) Almost Never	**(2) Sometimes**	**(3) As often as not**	**(4) Frequently**	**(5) Almost Always**

1. Students treat classmates with respect.	1	2	3	4	5
2. Students exclude those who are different (e.g., belong to a different race, religion, or culture).	1	2	3	4	5
3. Students try to comfort peers who have experienced sadness.	1	2	3	4	5
4. Students respect the personal property of others.	1	2	3	4	5
5. Students help each other, even if they are not friends.	1	2	3	4	5
6. When students do something hurtful, they try to make up for it (e.g., they apologize).	1	2	3	4	5
7. Students show respect for school property (e.g., desks, walls, bathrooms, buses, buildings, and grounds).	1	2	3	4	5
8. Students encourage other students to follow school rules.	1	2	3	4	5
9. Students behave respectfully toward all school staff (including secretaries, custodians, aides, and bus drivers).	1	2	3	4	5
10. Students work well together.	1	2	3	4	5
11. Students help to improve the school.	1	2	3	4	5
12. Students are respectful toward their teachers.	1	2	3	4	5
13. Students help new students feel accepted.	1	2	3	4	5
14. Students try to have a positive influence on the behavior of other students.	1	2	3	4	5
15. Students refrain from picking on other students.	1	2	3	4	5
16. Students are willing to forgive each other.	1	2	3	4	5
17. Students show good sportsmanship.	1	2	3	4	5
18. Students are patient with each other.	1	2	3	4	5
19. Students resolve conflicts without fighting, insults, or threats.	1	2	3	4	5
20. Students are respectful toward their schoolmates.	1	2	3	4	5
21. Students listen to each other in class discussion.	1	2	3	4	5
22. When students see another student being picked on, they try to stop it.	1	2	3	4	5
23. Students refrain from put-downs (negative, hurtful comments).	1	2	3	4	5
24. Students share what they have with others.	1	2	3	4	5
25. Students are involved in helping to solve school problems.	1	2	3	4	5
26. Students can talk to their teachers about problems that are bothering them.	1	2	3	4	5
27. Parents show that they care about their child's education and school behavior.	1	2	3	4	5
28. Students are respectful toward their parents in the school environment.	1	2	3	4	5
29. Teachers go out of their way to help students who need extra help.	1	2	3	4	5
30. Teachers treat parents with respect.	1	2	3	4	5

Figure 12-13   *(Continued)*

(1) Almost Never	(2) Sometimes	(3) As often as not	(4) Frequently	(5) Almost Always				

	1	2	3	4	5
31. In this school, adults try to ensure that students are safe.	1	2	3	4	5
32. Teachers are fair in their treatment of students.	1	2	3	4	5
33. In this school, parents treat other parents with respect.	1	2	3	4	5
34. Parents show respect for teachers.	1	2	3	4	5
35. In their interactions with students, teachers act in ways that demonstrate the character qualities the school is trying to teach.	1	2	3	4	5
36. In their interactions with students, all school staff (the principal, other administrators, counselors, coaches, aides, custodians, and others) act in ways that demonstrate the character qualities the school is try to teach.	1	2	3	4	5
37. In their interactions with children, parents display character qualities the school is trying to teach.	1	2	3	4	5
38. Faculty and staff treat each other with respect (are caring, supportive, etc.).	1	2	3	4	5
39. Faculty and staff are involved in helping to make school decisions.	1	2	3	4	5
40. This school shows appreciation for the efforts of faculty and staff.	1	2	3	4	5
41. This school treats parents with respect.	1	2	3	4	5
42. Parents are actively involved in this school.	1	2	3	4	5

Scale Description

Sub-scale 1A—Perceptions of Student Respect (9 items)

    1, 4, 7, 9, 12, 15, 17, 20, 23

Sub-scale 1B—Perceptions of Student Friendships and Belonging (9 items)

    2, 3, 5, 10, 13, 16, 18, 21, 24

Sub-scale 1C—Perceptions of Students' Shaping of the Environment (7 items)

    6, 8, 11, 14, 19, 22, 25

Sub-scale 11A—Perceptions of Support and Care By and For Faculty/Staff (10 items)

    26, 29, 31, 32, 34, 35, 36, 38, 39, 40

Sub-scale 11B—Perceptions of Support and Care By and For Parents (7 items)

    27, 28, 30, 33, 37, 41, 42

The SCCP-2 was developed by T. Lickona and M. Davidson at the Center for the 4th and 5th Rs, SUNY Cortland, PO Box 2000, Cortland, NY 13045. May be duplicated without permission of the authors (last revised January, 2003).

Figure 12-14 is a character assessment instrument. This rating tool assesses character behaviors considered to be common of learners in the kindergarten through grade 12 classroom setting. This instrument, developed by Helen R. Stiff-Williams, enables teachers and counselors to identify poor and/or unacceptable behaviors so that they can design remediation experiences that promote improvement and curtail unacceptable behaviors. Figure 12-15, also developed by Stiff-Williams, is a 12-step action plan teachers can use as a guideline when promoting character development in their students.

Figure 12–14   Character Education: Student Personal Development Assessment Instrument

Criteria	N/O	UnSat	Poor	Sat	Good	Excel
Personal Behaviors						
Brings books and other learning tools to class						
Completes homework assignments						
Is punctual; reports to school in a timely manner						
Meets responsibility as a classroom citizen						
Respects institution and property						
Safeguards his/her possessions						
Makes appropriate decisions						
Demonstrates honesty						
Respects self						
Appreciates learning opportunities						
Demonstrates integrity						
Thinks and makes independent decisions						
Volunteers to complete tasks						
Listens to receive information						
Values work						
Manages time well						
Stays on task						
Interactions with Others						
Works collaboratively with others						
Respects others' expressions						
Responds properly to authority figures						
Participates in class interactions						
Meets responsibilities with a work group						
Acts appropriately in informal settings						
Responds appropriately with different age groups						
Respects (is tolerant of) the diversity of others						
Appropriately resolves conflict with others						
Offers ideas to advance the work of the group						
Total						

KEY
N/O—"Not observed" – no evidence available
UnSat—"Unsatisfactory" – needs to demonstrate substantial improvement
Poor—"Poor" – needs to demonstrate much improvement
Sat—"Satisfactory" – acceptable behavior; could demonstrate some
Good—"Good" – generally meets and/or exceeds general expectations
Excel—"Excellent" – consistently meets and/or exceeds expectations

Source: Developed by Dr. Helen Stiff-Williams, Regent University, Virginia Beach, VA. Permission granted by author. All rights retained. Online posting of this document expressly prohibited. For further information on this assessment instrument, contact Dr. Stiff-Williams at Regent University.

Figure 12–15   Character Development Action Plan

Character Development in K-12 Schools
12-Step Action Plan for the Personal Development of Students

1. If age-appropriate, invite students to complete a self-assessment at the beginning of the school year or a selected time in the school year.
2. Assess student performance and determine if changes in behaviors are evident after a period of intervention. Continue to identify areas for improvement to be addressed for succeeding periods of instruction and assessment.
3. Collect and maintain a file of data to support the ratings on the personal assessment form. These data might include copies of notes that recognize successful achievements, disciplinary referrals, records of personal conferences with students about problems, pictures, artifacts, academic products that reflect poor quality work or improved to excellent work, etc.
4. Meet with each student individually to review his/her progress at the end of each marking period. If the number of students that you teach is very large, then identify only those students who need to be targeted for improvement in their character development.
5. Use the character assessment instrument (See Figure 12–14) to derive summative assessments to be recorded on the report card or quarterly academic report of progress.
6. Derive a summative rating at the end of the school year. Use the final rating for comparison with the student's self-assessment and the teacher's preliminary assessment completed during the first marking period. Highlight areas of improvement and personal growth.
7. Provide the summary report to the student and the student's parents.

Developed by Helen Stiff-Williams, all rights retained. Permission granted for use. ©Stiff-Williams, at Regent University, June 2001.

SECTION 7: SOCIAL SKILLS ASSESSMENT

Social skills assessment should occur in the social environments in which the student functions. Social skills are acceptable learned behaviors that enable people to interact with others in ways that elicit positive responses, and are characterized by such behaviors as sharing, helping, initiating communications, requesting help from others, and giving compliments universally (Elliott, Malecki, & Demaray, 2001). Assessment of social skills generally includes student observations, interviews, teacher rating scales, behavioral role playing, and sociograms.

Social Skills Development

Social development begins at birth and progresses rapidly during the preschool years (McClellan & Katz, 2001). During the past two decades, a convincing body of evidence has accumulated to indicate that unless children achieve minimal social competence by about age 6, they have a high probability of being at risk for long-term problems with social and emotional adaptation, academic-cognitive development, citizenship, and effective functioning as adults (Cho, Hudley, & Back, 2003; Kinsey, 2000; Ladd, 2000; McClellan & Kinsey, 1999). The manner in which children act toward and are treated by their classmates, whether cooperative/aggressive, helpful/demanding, etc., seems to have a substantial impact on the relationships they develop (Ladd, 2000). Learning and school performance in children can be negatively affected by psychosocial problems ranging from hostility, aggression, and uncooperative behavior to fearful, anxious, and withdrawn behavior (Cowen, et al., 1996). Adolescents' school achievement is often directly related to their emotional adjustment, which includes whether they experience depression, anxiety, peer rejection, and/or isolation (Anderson, 2002; Kim & Yeh, 2002). Higher levels of emotional distress have been directly correlated to lower school achievement (Cho, Hudley, & Back, 2003). (See Figure 12-16 for a social skills rating checklist.)

Figure 12–16   School and Community Social Skills Rating Checklist

Directions: Check each item that describes the student.

Classroom-Related Behaviors

The student adequately and appropriately:

☐   1. attends to teacher during instruction.

☐   2. maintains correct sitting posture.

☐   3. gains the teacher's attention.

☐   4. answers questions asked by teachers.

☐   5. asks teacher for assistance or information.

☐   6. shares materials with classmates.

☐   7. keeps own desk in order.

☐   8. enters class without disruption.

☐   9. follows classroom rules.

☐   10. cooperates with work partners.

☐   11. ignores distractions.

☐   12. stays on task during seatwork.

☐   13. completes work on time.

☐   14. participates politely in classroom discussion.

☐   15. makes relevant remarks during classroom discussion.

☐   16. follows verbal directions.

☐   17. follows written directions.

☐   18. speaks politely about schoolwork.

☐   19. participates in classroom introductions.

☐   20. completes homework on time.

☐   21. uses free time in class productively.

School-Building-Related Behaviors

The student adequately and appropriately:

☐   22. follows procedures for boarding school bus.

☐   23. follows bus riding rules.

☐   24. walks through hallways and passes to class.

☐   25. waits in lines.

☐   26. uses rest room facilities.

☐   27. uses drinking fountain.

☐   28. follows lunchroom rules.

☐   29. uses table manners.

Figure 12–16 (*Continued*)

☐   30. responds to school authority.

☐   31. deals with accusations at school.

Personal Skills

    The student adequately and appropriately:

☐   32. says "please" and "thank you."

☐   33. speaks in tone of voice for the situation.

☐   34. takes turns in games and activities.

☐   35. tells the truth.

☐   36. accepts consequences for wrongdoing.

☐   37. maintains grooming.

☐   38. avoids inappropriate physical contact.

☐   39. exhibits hygienic behavior.

☐   40. expresses enthusiasm.

☐   41. makes positive statements about self.

☐   42. expresses anger in nonaggressive ways.

☐   43. accepts praise.

☐   44. stays out of fights.

☐   45. deals with embarrassment.

☐   46. chooses clothing for social events.

☐   47. deals with failure.

☐   48. deals with being left out.

Interaction Initiative Skills

    The student adequately and appropriately:

☐   49. greets peers.

☐   50. borrows from peers.

☐   51. asks other children to play.

☐   52. expresses sympathy.

☐   53. asks peers for help.

☐   54. makes invitations.

☐   55. introduces self.

☐   56. makes introductions.

☐   57. initiates conversations.

☐   58. joins activities with peers.

☐   59. congratulates peers and adults.

☐   60. makes apologies.

☐   61. excuses self from groups and conversations.

☐   62. expresses feelings.

☐   63. expresses affection.

☐   64. stands up for a friend.

☐   65. asks for dates.

☐   66. gives compliments.

☐   67. makes complaints.

Figure 12–16 *(Continued)*

Interaction Response Skills

The student adequately and appropriately:

☐ 68. smiles when encountering acquaintances.

☐ 69. listens when another child speaks.

☐ 70. participates in group activities.

☐ 71. helps peers when asked.

☐ 72. accepts ideas different from own.

☐ 73. meets with adults.

☐ 74. maintains conversations.

☐ 75. responds to teasing and name calling.

☐ 76. responds to constructive criticism.

☐ 77. recognizes feeling of others.

☐ 78. respects the space of others.

☐ 79. responds to peer pressure.

☐ 80. deals with an angry person.

☐ 81. makes refusals.

☐ 82. answers complaints.

Community-Related Skills

The student adequately and appropriately:

☐ 83. asks for directions in public.

☐ 84. gives directions.

☐ 85. exhibits sportsmanship as a game participant.

☐ 86. exhibits polite behavior and sportsmanship as a spectator.

☐ 87. disposes of wastepaper and debris in public.

☐ 88. respects the rights of others in public.

☐ 89. respects private property.

☐ 90. exhibits good audience behaviors.

☐ 91. responds to public authority.

☐ 92. asserts self to gain service.

☐ 93. deals with public officials over the phone.

Work-Related Social Skills

The student adequately and appropriately:

☐ 94. sets goals for work.

☐ 95. negotiates on the job.

☐ 96. responds to unwarranted criticism.

☐ 97. asks for feedback on the job.

☐ 98. minds own business on the job.

☐ 99. chooses a time for small talk.

☐ 100. refrains from excessive complaining.

The teacher can do much to assess and facilitate social skills development.

It seems that the quality is more important than the quantity of students' friendships. Even children who are rejected by most classmates but who have one close friend feel positively about school over time (Ladd, 2000). Therefore, it is important to assess and monitor students' social-emotional and behavioral development. (See Figure 12–17 for a social attributes checklist that teachers are encouraged to use to monitor social skills development several times a year.)

Children with disabilities tend to experience higher incidences of social problems, isolation, and subsequent feelings of loneliness. An important reason for identifying social skills problems is the growing awareness that early social deficits of children and youth may lead to significant social problems later in life (Crowley, & Merrell, 2003). These students often have difficulty reading and processing social cues and developing social relationships, resulting in less peer acceptance (Haaer & Vaughn, 1995). Many students who often have difficulty expressing themselves and behaving appropriately in social situations tend to be rejected by their peers. Another reason students with disabilities have social adjustment problems is that they do not always have equal opportunities for full participation in educational and extracurricular activities at school (Pavri, 2001). (See Figure 12–18 for an interpersonal relationship checklist.)

Classroom Scenario: What Would You Do?

Jasmine is very interested in joining the computer-users after school club. However, she is introverted, self-conscious, and her social skills are undeveloped. When she goes to the club meetings, she gets to the door and turns away. As her teacher, you are in the process of assessing her social skills. You want to come up with a way to help her go through the door, begin to interact with club members, and feel accepted in the group so that she will return for subsequent meetings. What do you do?

Figure 12–17   Social Attributes Checklist for Individual Students

Attributes	Yes	No	N/A
The child			
• is usually in a positive mood.	____	____	____
• is not excessively dependent on adults.	____	____	____
• usually comes to the program willingly.	____	____	____
• usually copes with rebuffs adequately.	____	____	____
• shows the capacity to empathize.	____	____	____
• has positive relationships with one or two peers.	____	____	____
• displays the capacity for humor.	____	____	____
• does not seem to be acutely lonely.	____	____	____
Social Skills Attributes			
The child			
• approaches others positively.	____	____	____
• expresses wishes and preferences clearly.	____	____	____
• gives reasons for actions and positions.	____	____	____
• asserts own rights and needs appropriately.	____	____	____
• is not easily intimidated by bullies.	____	____	____
• expresses frustrations and anger effectively.	____	____	____
• gains access to ongoing groups at play and work.	____	____	____
• enters ongoing discussion on the subject.	____	____	____
• takes turns fairly easily.	____	____	____
• shows interest in others; exchanges information with and requests information from others.	____	____	____
• does not draw inappropriate attention to self.	____	____	____
• accepts and enjoys peers and adults of ethnic groups other than his/her own.	____	____	____
• interacts nonverbally with other children with smiles, waves, nods, etc.	____	____	____
Peer Relationship Attributes			
The child			
• is usually accepted versus neglected or rejected by other children.	____	____	____
• is sometimes invited by other children to join them in play, friendship, and work.	____	____	____
• is named by other children as someone they are friends with or like to play with.	____	____	____

Source: Assessing Young Children's Social Competence, *ERIC Digest*, by D. E. McClellan & L. G. Katz (2001).

Sociograms

Sociometric techniques, such as sociograms, are the most commonly used method of social skills assessment (Bukowski, Sippola, Hoza, & Newcomb, 2000). **Sociograms** are used to assess students' social status by graphically tracking the manner and frequency of students' social interactions. Specifically, sociograms track the number and types of overtures a student makes toward other students during a specified time period. This information can be used as a measure of students' current social interaction patterns. It is necessary to track interactions over an extended period of time in order to determine whether a pattern exists. Using the sociogram is a three-step process involving: (1) peer nomination, (2) sociogram development, and (3) data analysis. The peer nomination involves asking all students in the class to identify their peer preferences. For example, students are asked who they would pick to work with on a school project. Next, they are told to make another choice in case the first person is not available. (See Figure 12–19 for a sample sociogram.)

Figure 12–18   Interpersonal Relationship Checklist

Directions: For each question, consider how you would respond in each of the four settings. Place a check in the box after you have considered that situation.

	At Home	At School	In the Community	On the Job

Conflict

1. When a problem comes up, what do you usually do?

2. What is the best thing to do when a problem comes up?

3. When a problem comes up, what do you fear most?

4. How do you to cope with being afraid?

5. Who would be a good person (or what would be a good place) to go to for more help when you are afraid?

6. How do you handle the stress of problems?

7. How is this working for you?

8. When a problem comes up, do you feel sad, upset, or angry?

9. What do you do when you feel sad?

10. What do you do when you feel angry?

11. What problems are you having now?

12. How are you handling these problems?

13. Is there someone you trust who is a good person to go to when you have a problem?

Friends

14. Who are your friends or people who you like a lot?

15. How did you go about making these friends?

16. Do you get along well with your friends and people you like?

17. What do you like most about these people?

18. What do you think they like most about you?

Resolution

19. What would you like to change about your social situation or interpersonal relationships?

20. Do you think you can change these areas?

21. Do you know how to change these areas?

22. How motivated are you to change these areas by making changes yourself?

23. Who can you ask or where can you go for help?

The sociogram is developed by representing the peer-nominations pictorially; data analysis consists of inspecting the sociogram to determine which students are class leaders, members of cliques, loners, or outcasts (Watkins & Schloss, 2001). The following is an example of the procedure for developing and analyzing sociograms.

Figure 12–19 Sample Sociogram

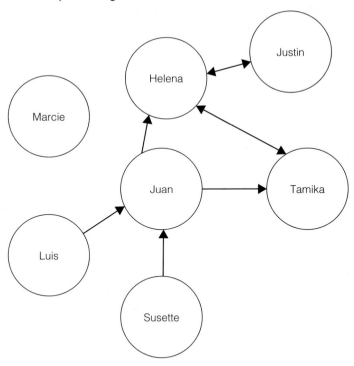

How to Use a Sociogram

1. At the same time of day for a period of two weeks, the teacher spends a few minutes observing the students in class and checking the level of social development for each student. (See Figure 12–20.)

Figure 12–20 Class Social Skills Observation Checklist

Student Name	Unoccupied	Solitary	Onlooker	Parallel	Associative	Cooperative
1.						
2.						
3.						
4.						
5.						
6.						
7.						
8.						
9.						
10.						
Total number of recordings						
Percentage						

TECH TIPS

http://teach-nology.com/
web_tools/rubrics-rubrics maker

2. After the two-week period, the teacher totals the checks for each student by adding down the column under each category, and then adding all the totals from left to right to get a grand total.
3. The teacher divides the total number in each social category by the grand total to get a percentage for that social level.
4. The percentages can then be plotted on an individual social graph for each student. (See Figures 12–21 and 12–22.) This information is useful for determining how each child is functioning socially and whether his or her developmental levels are age-appropriate (Guerin & Maier, 1983, pp. 41–42).

Figure 12–21   Sample Individual Social Graph

Percent of time	Unoccupied					Solitary					Onlooker					Parallel					Associative					Cooperative				
100																														
90																														
80																														
70																														
60																														
50																														
40																														
30																														
20																														
10																														
0																														
Observe	1	2	3	4	5	1	2	3	4	5	1	2	3	4	5	1	2	3	4	5	1	2	3	4	5	1	2	3	4	5
%																														

Source: *School for Young Children: Developmentally Appropriate Practices*, by C. H. Wolfgang & M. E. Wolfgang, 1999. Needham Heights, MA: Allyn & Bacon, p 24. Reprinted with permission.

Figure 12–22   Sample Group Social Graph

Sociogram Matrix for Project Choices

	Bob	**Tina**	**Josh**	**Theresa**	**Jose**	**Maria**	**Tim**	**Andre**	**Gina**
Bob			1		2				
Tina				2				1	
Josh		1		2					
Theresa		1							
Jose									2
Maria			1					1	2
Tim	2		2					2	
Andre							2		
Gina			1				2	1	1

	Bob	Tina	Josh	Theresa	Jose	Maria	Tim	Andre	Gina
1st choice	0	2	3	0	0	0	0	3	1
2nd choice	1	0	1	2	1	0	2	1	2
Frequency Chosen	1	2	4	2	1	0	2	4	3
Rating	5th	2nd	1st	4th	5th	6th	4th	1st	3rd

Source: Modified version of Guerin, G. R. & Maier, A. S. *Informal Assessment in Education* (1983). pp. 41–42.

Rating Scales

Rating scales allow teachers to ask questions in a standardized way. They are accompanied by the same stimulus materials, and they provide a standardized set of response options. Rating scales usually need to be supplemented with direct observations or follow-up interviews to enhance their specificity and utility. These follow-ups help to accurately identify target behaviors for remediation (Elliott, Malecki, & Demaray, 2001).

SUMMARY POINTS

- Functional behavioral analysis is a method of assessment used to establish the behavioral supports needed by students who exhibit a range of challenging behaviors, such as physical and verbal outbursts, property destruction, and disruptive behavior. When a student's behavior does not respond to standard interventions, a functional behavioral assessment can provide additional information to assist the IEP team in planning more effective interventions.

- *Event recording* is a method of direct observation of targeted behavior, which is counted each time it occurs. *Duration recording* is a type of direct measurement used to record how long a specific behavior lasts rather than how frequently it occurs. *Latency recording* is a measure of how long it takes for the targeted behavior to occur. These types of behavior recordings should have a definite beginning and end.

FYI

BEHAVIOR CHECKLISTS AND RATING SCALES

Achenbach Rating Scales (1) Teacher's form, (2) Parent's form, and (3) Children's form. Achenbach System of Empirically Based Assessment (ASEBA) (802-264-6432)

Attention Deficit Disorders Evaluation Scale – Revised. Hawthorne Educational Services (800-542-1673)

Conners Behavior Checklist Parent and Teacher Rating Scales. Multi-Health Systems Incorporated (800-456-3003)

- Three types of interval recordings are (1) *partial interval recording*, used when the observer records the targeted behavior that occurs at any time during the interval; (2) *percentage interval recording*, used when the observer records the period of time that the behavior occurred during the interval; and (3) *total interval recording*, used when the observer records behavior that occurs throughout the entire interval.

- Character education assessment enables teachers and counselors to identify poor and/or unacceptable behaviors in order to design remediation experiences that promote improvement and curtail unacceptable behaviors.

- Sociograms are used to assess a student's social status; it is a method of graphically tracking the manner and frequency of their social interactions.

Chapter Check-Ups

1. Explain the differences between event, duration and latency recording. Provide an appropriate example for each of these types of direct observation.

2. Compare and contrast the three methods of interval recording and the time sampling method of interval recording.

3. Describe when and why a functional behavior assessment (FBA) would be used. Identify the components of a complete FBA.

4. What are the components of character education? Why would a teacher administer a character education assessment?

5. Explain (a) why social competence is an important aspect of child development, (b) why students with learning difficulties often have social adjustment problems, and (c) the methods that can be used to evaluate and monitor social skill development.

Practical Application Assessment Activities

1. Both you and a partner observe a child for the same forty-minute period. Prior to initiating the observation, decide on the type of direct observation recording system you will use. Following the observation, each partner will individually summarize their observations, identify critical factors, make inferences and recommendations for future instructional planning or modifications. Observations should be shared and carefully compared. What points were observed by both partners, what points were missed by one partner, what points were noticed but not recorded and why were these particular incidents not recorded? Were your inferences objective? How similar were your recommendations?

2. Interview a teacher about a student who is experiencing social adjustment problems in the classroom. Based on the results of the interview, identify the target behaviors to be assessed and determine how you would gather baseline information. Decide what information you would need to gather and construct a checklist that covers all areas.

3. You are about to observe a student who has been demonstrating problems with out-of-seat behavior. Describe an example of this type of behavior. Decide whether you should use event, duration, or latency recording and provide a rationale for your decision.

Connection Between CEC, PRAXIS, and INTASC Standards and Chapter 12

The Council for Exceptional Children—Professional Standards

Standard 1 Foundations

2. Laws, policies, and ethical principles regarding behavior management planning and implementation.

Standard 3 Individual Learning Differences

2. Impact of learners' academic and social abilities, attitudes, interests, and values on instruction and career development.

Standard 4 Instructional Strategies

2. Teach individuals to use self-assessment, problem solving, and other cognitive strategies to meet their needs.
5. Use procedures to increase the individual's self-awareness, self-management, self-control, self-reliance, and self-esteem.

Standard 5 Learning Environments and Social Interactions

2. Basic classroom management theories and strategies for individuals with exceptional learning needs.
4. Teacher attitudes and behaviors that influence behavior of individuals with exceptional learning needs.
5. Social skills needed for educational and other environments.
12. Identify realistic expectations for personal and social behavior in various settings.
15. Modify the learning environment to manage behaviors.

Standard 7 Instructional Planning

9. Use functional assessments to develop intervention plans.
10. Use task analysis.

Standard 8 Assessment

4. Use and limitations of assessment instruments.
5. National, state or province, and local accommodations and modifications.
6. Gather relevant background information.
7. Administer nonbiased formal and informal assessments.
9. Develop or modify individualized assessment strategies.
10. Interpret information from formal and informal assessments.
11. Use assessment information in making eligibility program, and placement decisions for individuals with exceptional learning needs, including those from culturally and/or linguistically diverse backgrounds.
12. Report assessment result to all stakeholders using effective communication skills.
13. Evaluate instruction and monitor progress of individuals with exceptional learning needs.
14. Create and maintain records.

Standard 10 Collaboration

6. Collaborate with families and others in assessment of individuals with exceptional learning needs.

PRAXIS Standards for Special Education

Standard 1 Understanding Exceptionalities

2. Characteristics of students with disabilities, including medical/physical; educational; social; and psychological.

3. Basic concepts in special education, including definitions of all major categories and specific disabilities; causation and prevention of disability; the nature of behaviors, including frequency, duration, intensity, and degrees of severity; and classification of students with disabilities, including classifications as represented in IDEA and labeling of students.

Standard 2 Legal and Societal Issues

2. Issues related to school, family, and/or community, such as teacher advocacy for students and families, including advocating for educational change and developing students' self-advocacy; family participation and support systems; public attitudes toward individuals with disabilities; and cultural and community influences.

Standard 3 Delivery of Services to Students with Disabilities

3. Assessment, including how to modify, construct, or select and conduct non-discriminatory and appropriate informal and formal assessment procedures; how to interpret standardized and specialized assessment results; how to use evaluation result for various purposes, including monitoring instruction and IEP/ITP development; and how to prepare written reports and communicate findings to others.

6. Management of the learning environment, including behavior management (for example, behavior analysis-identification and definition of antecedents, target behavior, and consequent events, data-gathering procedures, selecting and using behavioral interventions); classroom organization/management (for example, providing the appropriate physical-social environment for learning-expectations, rules, consequences, consistency, attitudes, lighting, seating, access, and strategies for positive interactions, transitions between lessons and activities); grouping of students; and effective and efficient documentation (such as parent/teacher contacts and legal records).

INTASC Standards for Teacher Education

Standard 5

The teacher uses an understanding of individual and group motivation and behavior to create a learning environment that encourages positive social interaction, active engagement in learning, and self-motivation.

Standard 6

The teacher uses knowledge of effective verbal, nonverbal, and media communication techniques to foster active inquiry, collaboration, and supportive interaction in the classroom.

Standard 8

The teacher understands and uses formal and informal assessment strategies to evaluate and ensure the continuous intellectual, social, and physical development of the learner.

CHAPTER 13

Transition Assessment: Across the Ages

KEY TERMS AND CONCEPTS

- educational transition
- transition plan
- individualized family service plan
- family assessment
- developmental assessment
- splinter skill
- critical period
- competitive employment
- extended employment
- transition assessment

- kidwatching
- play-based assessment
- arena assessment
- person-centered planning
- person-center assessment
- situational assessment
- career assessment
- self-determination assessment
- curriculum-based vocational assessment

CHAPTER OBJECTIVES

After reading this chapter, you should be able to:

- Define an educational transition
- List the main components of the planning process
- Identify the three factors that influence the transition experience
- Explain the family assessment aspect of the individual family service plan (IFSP)

- Explain the age requirements for developing the transition plan of the IEP
- Describe the differences between play-based assessment and arena assessment
- Describe a person-centered assessment
- Explain the process of situational assessment

Introduction to Transition Assessment from Early Childhood to Postsecondary School

Transition is a normal aspect of human experience, occurring as individuals move through life. Although all transitions can be stressful, many are expected, developmentally appropriate, and eagerly anticipated (e.g., promotions, graduations, marriage, birth of a baby). Others are unexpected, unplanned for, and can be life altering (e.g., illnesses, accidents, loss of job, divorce). An **educational transition** is a passage from one academic setting, grade, program, or experience to another.

CRITICAL TRANSITION POINTS

Early childhood is a time of transition that can be very stressful for children and their families. The first major educationally-related transition can occur when the infant or toddler who has been receiving early childhood intervention services moves to a preschool education program. The second is when the young child makes the transition from the preschool education program to a school-aged program. Additional times of transition occur as the child moves from elementary to middle school and from middle school to high school. Transitions occur for some students as they move from self-contained to inclusion classes and transition back to school after hospitalization or rehabilitation. Although significant and stressful changes can occur during these times, the primary periods of transition—and those that are the main focus of this chapter—occur during early childhood; the preadolescent, pubescent period; and late adolescence to young adulthood.

TRANSITION PLANNING

The key factors in a successful transition are planning and cooperation involving three main components: (1) assessment, (2) planning, and (3) follow-through. Assessment is the first stage in the transition process. At this stage, it is necessary to both determine the demands and requirements of the new environment and assess the students' capabilities, interests, and ability to deal with the demands of the new situation. In the planning stage, it is necessary to use the assessment results to develop a

Figure 13–1   School-Related Transitions for Students and Their Family

- Home to early intervention services
- Early intervention to preschool disabilities class
- Preschool disabilities class to transition class or kindergarten
- Kindergarten or part-day program to full-day elementary grades
- Elementary school to middle school or junior high school
- Middle school to high school
- Class to class in middle school and high school
- High school to postsecondary educational program or employment
- Special education to general education classes
- District-to-district transfers
- Movement from school to school within a district
- Promotions from grade level to grade level
- Academic classes to classes in related arts subjects (e.g., art, physical education, music)
- School-day program to after-school activity
- School year classes to extended school year programs

plan that helps to make the transition to the next setting as smooth and successful as possible. The plan may include curricular changes, psychosocial and physical adaptations, as well as preparation of the people, equipment, and environment in the new situation for the inclusion of the student.

Follow-through is the final component in the transition process. In this stage, the planning, usually detailed in the goals and objectives in a student's individualized education plan (IEP), is carried out. In other words, the follow-through is the actual implementation of the plan. It may occur in the classroom, as the student learns the skills necessary to succeed in a kindergarten class (e.g., learning to sit cooperatively and quietly for specific periods of time). It may be part of a postsecondary program (e.g., long-term planning, developing a course schedule), or used to help students function in the job sector (e.g., how to complete W-2 forms, write a resume). It may occur in an authentic or a simulated setting in the primary grades (e.g., the young child rides the school bus), the secondary school setting (e.g., where the student must negotiate a wheelchair from class to class), or in an office-like setting (e.g., where the student performs some of the tasks required on the job). The follow-through may require preparing the new site to facilitate a smooth transition as the student with disabilities learns to cope or adapt to the new educational setting (e.g., preparing books on tape) or employment setting (e.g., adapting office equipment).

Research indicates that three factors influence students' transition experience: (1) their skills and prior school-related experiences, (2) their home lives, and (3) the classroom characteristics. According to Maxwell & Elder (1999):

- Children who are socially adjusted have better transitions (e.g., parents have initiated social opportunities for their children).

- Children who have been rejected have difficulty with transitions.

- Children with more school experience (e.g., preschool) have fewer transition adjustments.

- Children whose parents expect them to do well do better than children whose parents who have lower expectations.

- Developmentally appropriate classrooms and practices promote easier and smoother transitions for children.

SECTION 1: TRANSITION LEGISLATION

The U.S. Congress has acknowledged the special challenges of certain transitions by requiring that formal transition planning occur for families with toddlers who are leaving Part H services for preschool, as well as for young adults with disabilities completing public education and entering the workforce or postsecondary education. Transition planning is intended to increase the individual's options in order to promote satisfactory relocation, provide for continuity in instruction and experience, and prepare the student for successful entry into a new program (Moon & Inge, 2000; Sitlington, Clark, & Kolstoe, 2000). Although numerous pieces of legislation address transition issues, this chapter focuses on the Individuals with Disabilities Education Act (IDEA) and its amendments.

Early Childhood Transition Legislation

The term "transition" began to be commonly used in the mid-1980s, when the Education of the Handicapped Act Amendments of 1986 (P.L. 99-457) mandated that a **transition plan** be developed by age 3 for all children who were classified and attending an early childhood program (Part H of the Act). The purpose for this plan is to facilitate

Figure 13-2 Comparison of the Required Components of IFSPs and IEPs

Individualized Family Service Plan (IFSP)	*Individualized Education Plan (IEP)*
• A statement of the child's present levels of development in cognitive, communication, social/emotional, and adaptive (self-help) skill development, based on objective criteria	• A statement of the child's present levels of educational performance, including academic achievement, prevocational/vocational skills, social adaptation, psychomotor, and self-help skills
• A statement of the family's resources, priorities, and concerns related to enhancing the child's development (family assessment)	• A statement of annual goals and objectives or benchmarks that meet the student's needs resulting from his or her disability to enable the student to be involved and progress in general education
• A statement of specific early intervention services necessary to meet the unique needs of the child and family (i.e., frequency, intensity, and method of delivering services)	• A statement of specific educational services, the special education program, related services, and any special instructional media, materials, or accommodations needed
• A statement of the natural environments in which early intervention services will be provided	• An explanation of the extent, if any, to which the student shall not participate with nondisabled students in general education and districtwide or statewide assessment
• The projected dates for initiation of and anticipated duration of services	• The projected date for the initiation of and the expected duration of services
• Name of the family service coordinator who will be responsible for implementing the plan and coordinating with other agencies and persons	• A list of the individuals who are responsible for implementing the IEP and a description of the evaluation measures used to determine progress
• A statement of expected outcomes, criteria, procedures, and timelines to document progress (usually 6-month intervals with 12-month intervals for reevaluation)	• Date scheduled for the periodic review of progress toward meeting goals and objectives (at least annually)
• Procedures to support the transition of toddlers to preschool or other agencies for appropriate placements (IDEA, Part B)	• A description of the plan, including strategies and procedures used to prepare students for postsecondary education or job placement
• An explanation of the plan to parents, who must give written consent before the implementation of services	• A statement of how parent will be informed of student's progress toward meeting goals/objectives at least as often as their nondisabled peers

Source: Adapted from the Education of the Handicapped Act Amendments 1986 §677[d]: Individuals with Disabilities Education Act Amendments, 1991, §14[c].

communication and coordination among the agencies providing special services for infants and toddlers (ages 0 to 3 years) and those providing special services for young children (ages 3 to 5) as specified in Parts C (formerly Part H) and Part B of the Act.

In 1991, Public Law 102–119 reauthorized and amended Part H (infants/toddlers) and Part B (preschoolers). This law focuses on eliminating some of the confusion about when children were deemed to make the transition from early intervention to preschool programs, resulting in a "seamless system." Regulations promoted by P.L. 102–119 incorporated the use of an **individualized family service plan** (IFSP) rather than an individualized education plan (IEP) for this population of young children.

Although the basic components of the IFSP and the IEP are similar (see Figure 13–2), the IFSP includes specific requirements for parental participation in the assessment and plan development phases and additional regulations for assessing the child and the family. The focus of the **family assessment** is to determine the child's needs and the way that the child's disability affects family functioning and parent-child interactions, as well as to determine the specific strengths and needs of the family that ultimately affect the child. (See Figure 13–3 for a sample IFSP.)

Figure 13–3 Sample Preschool Transition Plan

A. Pupil's Preferences and Interests _____

_____

B. Anticipated Outcomes
- Regular preschool program
- Special preschool program
- Regular kindergarten program
- Regular kindergarten program and related services
- Other _____

C. Transitional Services and Activities

Instruction

- Provide opportunities for preschoolers to participate in regular preschool programs.
- Continue to practice and review developmentally appropriate activities.
- Teach classmates about the specific impact of a child's particular disability when appropriate.
- Other _____

Services

- Case manager will explain transition at annual review of preschooler.
- Case manager will facilitate exchange of information among preschool special needs staff and regular education staff.
- Other _____

Community Experiences

- Parents will be involved in all aspects of the transition process.
- Parents will continue to practice developmentally appropriate activities according to their child's individual needs.
- Other _____

Secondary-Level Transition Legislation

Several key components of the Individuals with Disabilities Education Act Amendments of 2004 (IDEA-97) (P.L. 105-17) deal directly with transition and specifically with assessment for transition planning. These include access to the general curriculum, clear measurement of student progress, student participation in statewide accountability testing (standard or alternative), the role of families and students as partners in the transition process, the inclusion of the regular educator as part of the IEP and individualized transition plan (ITP) team, and the transfer of rights to students who reach the age of majority. The transition plan may be an attachment to the student's IEP, accompanied by individual transition goals and activities designed to meet those goals; or it may be a separate document, the ITP. The contents of the transition plan are provided in Figure 13-4. Figure 13-5 is a sample secondary-level transition plan (Blalock & Patton, 1996).

In response to concern about the dropout rate and testimony regarding the importance of beginning early to plan a programmatic or placement change, the age requirement for the initiation of services was revised. IDEA-2004 mandated that the first IEP in effect when the student is 16 and updated annually thereafter must contain appropriate measurable postsecondary goals based upon age appropriate transition assessments related to training, education, employment, and, where appropriate, independent living skills. This IEP must include the transition services (including courses of study) needed to assist the child in reaching those goals. Also, beginning no later than one year before the child reaches the age of majority under State law, a statement must be included informing the student of their rights under this law which will be transferred to them when they reach the age of majority (Sec. 614) (d) (A) (VIII).

Comprehensive Data Collection

As in all aspects of assessment, it is important to gain a comprehensive perspective of the student rather than relying on group or individually administered evaluation procedures. Comprehensive assessment involves not only evaluating individual students'

Figure 13—4 Contents of the Transition Plan

The individualized transition plan (ITP) must address the following areas:

1. **Present levels of educational performance** Students' current functioning levels in all basic skill areas, including cognition, academics, social-emotional adjustment, and physical status

2. **Interests and aptitude** Students' preferences, goals, dreams, and areas in which students demonstrate or feel that they have talent or potential skill

3. **Postschool goals** Students' postsecondary goals for community living, employment, postsecondary education, and/or training as identified by the transition team, which includes students, their parents, teachers, counselors, and/or vocational specialists

4. **Transition activities** Students' specific transitional activities in areas such as vocational and career education, work experience, and community-based instruction

5. **Designated responsible persons** Person or agency responsible for the continuation of the transition after students' high school years

6. **Review** Students' transition plan to be reviewed and revised as necessary

Figure 13–5   Sample Secondary-Level Transition Plan

A. **Student Preferences and Interests** _____

B. **Student Strengths and Capabilities** _____

C. **Postsecondary Programmatic Goals** _____
   _____ Postsecondary education
   _____ Vocational training
   _____ Competitive employment
   _____ Military service
   _____ Other: _____

D. **Recommended Referral**
   _____ For vocational assessment
   _____ For aptitude and interest testing
   _____ To state department of rehabilitation services
   _____ To county vocational center
   _____ To community-based training
   _____ To job placement services
   _____ To job coaching services
   _____ To state department for the visually impaired
   _____ To county services for mental health
   _____ To county association for citizens with mental retardation

E. **Transitional Services and Activities**
   Instruction
   _____ Secondary options and plans reviewed with guidance counselor and other
            appropriate school personnel on an annual basis
   _____ Student to attend information meeting with counselors from secondary school
            program and vocational school program
   _____ Assistance with career planning and/or employment activities by involvement in
            life-skills classes and career exploration
   _____ Secondary school program that supports core curriculum standards with
            appropriate special education services
   _____ Other: _____

   Services
   _____ Guidance counselor to arrange for visits to postsecondary options
   _____ Social worker to contact parents to discuss high school choice and application
            process to postsecondary work or school setting
   _____ Other: _____

   Community Experiences
   Sample secondary-level transition plan
   _____ Student and parent to tour college, vocational training, or work setting
   _____ Other: _____

Figure 13–5 *(Continued)*

F. Notice of Rights upon Reaching Age of Majority (to be completed at IEP meeting or immediately preceding student's 18th birthday)

_____ I have been informed of my rights pertaining to special education upon reaching 18 years of age. I have received a copy of "Procedural Safeguards and Parent Rights Pertaining to Special Education."

Date of Review: _____

_____ Parent/guardian has signed permission for release of information.

---

skills, but also assessing the environment in which they learn (Sitlington, Neubert, Begun, Lombard, & Leconte, 1996). When gathering data related to successful transition, students' chronological age, developmental level, and the severity of their disability determine the primary focus of the process. When assessing preschoolers, the focus of data collection is through the parents or guardians. When preparing for transition from elementary to secondary and from secondary to postsecondary placements, students are generally able to contribute a major amount of information. In all areas of transition, both the present teacher and the personnel at the proposed settings can contribute to assessing how the student will be able to adapt and how the students' current goals and objectives will need to be developed or adjusted to accommodate the new environment.

SECTION 2: TRANSITION FROM PRESCHOOL TO THE PRIMARY GRADES

Early Childhood Assessment

The assessment of young children is a highly individualized process. "Normal" development is the pattern of skill acquisition that the average child follows in growth and development. Child development specialists have found there is a remarkably similar pattern of normal, or typical, development throughout the years of childhood. This pattern provides a standard, or the criteria, of behavior for measuring the developmental progress of individual children. While there is a range of normal behavior, there is also a broad spectrum of individual skills and behavior within the normal range. Teachers must be aware that each child has a unique range of skills, with individual strengths and weaknesses. Therefore, when observing a group of children of the same age, teachers should be aware that the children's physical characteristics, social behavior, and cognitive and language skills can vary tremendously and still fall within the normal range (Catron & Allen, 1999).

It is important to understand that assessment in and of itself is of limited value. The linkage between assessment and curriculum planning is the critical component. The value of good assessment is that it provides teachers with an awareness of a student's developmental needs so that they can develop personalized IFSP goals and objectives correlated with core content curriculum standards, plan and implement program activities, and use assessment to evaluate and subsequently modify IFSPs or develop IEP goals and objectives.

Doors open for students as they transition in and out of school programs from kindergarten through the secondary levels.

Early childhood special education assessment procedures have historically relied on standardized, norm-based, or criterion-based procedures. The emphasis now is on ecologically-based, functional assessments. (See Figure 13–6.) Traditional testing procedures are being replaced by more authentic measures. Performance or authentic assessment is appropriate for early childhood special education because it (a) is a

Figure 13–6   Skills Checklist for Preschool to Elementary School Transition

Does the child
____ separate easily from parents?
____ demonstrate age-appropriate social skills?
____ have a positive self-concept as a learner?
____ spend an age-appropriate time on task or task completion?
____ have adequate motor skills?
____ have the knowledge and skills necessary to play with others?
____ have a work ethic for school and home?
____ work well independently?
____ work cooperatively in a small or large group?
____ attend to and complete a task?
____ listen to a story in a group?
____ follow two to three step oral directions?
____ take turns and share?
____ care for personal toileting needs?
____ independently put on and take off outdoor clothes?
____ care for his or her own belongings?
____ follow classroom rules?
____ respect the property of others?

Figure 13–6   (Continued)

____	work within time and space constraints of the class setting?
____	demonstrate gross motor skill competencies (e.g., walking, running, climbing)?
____	demonstrate fine motor skill competencies (e.g., use pencil, crayon, scissors)?
____	print own name?
____	recognize name in writing?
____	name colors, shapes, and sizes?
____	demonstrate comprehension of concepts (e.g., same/different)?
____	sort objects into groups with similar characteristics?
____	express self fluently using a variety of words?
____	understand conversations and stories?
____	recognize when objects/sounds are alike or different?
____	identify the name and sounds of letters?
____	identify the name and quantity of numerals?
____	count more than 10 objects?
____	know his or her address and phone number?
____	retell a simple story in his or her own words?
____	understand that reading is from right to left?

Florida Center for Parent Involvement, 1999; Peth-Pierce, 2000.

Figure 13–7   Recommended Assessment Practices: Early Childhood Special Education

Assessment should

- Be useful for early intervention and education.
- Clearly identify developmental or behavioral objectives for change.
- Help to select and guide treatment activities.
- Contribute to evaluating intervention or program efficacy.
- Be judged as valuable and acceptable.
- Identify goals and objectives that are judged as worthwhile and important.
- Use materials and methods that are judged as acceptable.
- Result in decisions based on a wide base of information.
- Involve evaluation batteries that contain several types of scales (e.g., norm-based, curriculum-based, judgment-based, and eco-based).
- Include observation and interviews in order to provide the most valid appraisal of the child's status, needs, and progress.
- Include data and reports from parents and other significant individuals who may be able to supplement or challenge other findings.
- Be done on multiple occasions, especially with young children.

Source: From Division for Early Childhood, 1993, *DEC Recommended Practices: Indicators of Quality in Programs for Infants and Young Children with Special Needs and Their Families* (pp. 12–15). Copyright 1993 by The Council for Exceptional Children. Reprinted with permission.

flexible process, (b) provides qualitative data, (c) provides relevant and useful information, (d) occurs in the natural environment, and (e) is collected over time (Davis, Kilgo, & Gamel-McCormick, 1998). (See Figure 13-7 for best-practice test recommendations.)

Components of Early Childhood Assessment

The major focus of evaluation when preschool age children make the transition from preschool to primary-level educational programs involve the following domains (Lerner, 2004; Nuttall, Romero, & Kalesnik, 1999).

Cognitive ability. The cognitive ability domain involves how children collect, store, categorize, integrate, and use knowledge about their worlds, including short- and long-term memory; and the abilities to sequence, to detect differences among objects or events, and to predict occurrences. Subsets of cognitive ability include attention, memory, comprehension, reasoning, concept formation, and problem solving. Basic tasks that assess cognitive development include classifying objects according to size, shape, and color; determining similarities and differences; repeating phrases or sets of numbers; and naming letters and numbers. It is important to evaluate cognitive development in relation to the child's aptitude and the child's achievement in order to determine both school readiness and whether the child has a specific learning disability.

Communication skills. The communication skills domain involves how the child communicates with others about wants, desires, feelings, ideas, and preferences, including vocalizations, gestures, formal and informal sign language, as well as behavior that nonverbally communicates needs. Also included is the use of augmentative devices (e.g., ranging from a piece of paper with pictures to a portable computer that produces digital speech). Language is divided into receptive and expressive abilities. Receptive language involves the ability to understand what is said, whereas expressive language involves the ability to speak or make wants known through either verbal (i.e., speaking) or nonverbal means (i.e., sign language, gestures, facial expressions, writing, or typing). Informal receptive language assessment tasks include observing motor reaction to verbal interaction (e.g., nodding, pointing). Expressive language assessment focuses on analyzing the child's speech for syntax and grammar, sentence length and complexity, word use, and grammatical features. Articulation, voice quality, and rate are generally evaluated by the speech and language therapist. Speech and language assessment plays a predominant role in early childhood assessment because the ability to communicate effectively, especially with language, is vital to thinking and establishing social relations.

Social-emotional development. The social-emotional development domain involves how children identify and communicate feelings, including their capacity to act on emotions while respecting the rights of others. It also concerns the way children interact with adults and/or peers in one-to-one, small-group, and large-group interactions, including whether children initiate interactions, respond to being approached by others, and respond in group situations. The following factors are the focus of social-emotional developmental assessments: the ability to relate to others, to follow rules, to comprehend right and wrong, and to separate from parents without anxiety. Of all developmental domains, social-emotional development has the widest range of individual differences. It is therefore the most difficult area for which to determine "normal" patterns.

Physical functioning. The physical functioning domain encompasses children's vision, hearing, touch, taste, and smell, as well as their ability to move around in the environment (gross motor skills) and to use their hands (fine motor skills). Visual and auditory acuity are generally evaluated annually by the school nurse. Physical co-ordination skills assessment covers gross motor skills (including the ability to run, jump, hop, skip, balance, and slide); body manipulation skills (e.g., stretching, curling, rolling, bending, and balancing); and object manipulation skills (e.g., throwing, catching, striking, kicking, and bouncing a ball). Often the development of gross motor skills in preschoolers can be uneven. Fine motor skills involve primarily eye-hand co-ordination and include such tasks as coloring, drawing, cutting, and manipulating small objects. Physical skills are another prominent focus because of their critical role in play and exploration.

Adaptive skills.   The adaptive skills domain involves how children are able to in-dependently take care of their personal needs, including eating, grooming, toileting, and dressing. Children's ability to adapt, their attitude of independence toward adults, and their control over the environment are also factors in assessing adaptive skills.

Developmental Assessment

Developmental assessment is used to note the patterns of individual development and to determine the extent and nature of any deviation from normal development. Children's developmental process depends, in part, on the maturation of their nervous system. Although each child's development is different, there is a predictable sequence and pattern of normal development. Lower level skills need to be acquired before higher level skills can develop. It is important to assess whether children have devel-oped prerequisite skills before introducing more advanced skills (e.g., the ability to scribble develops before the ability to draw geometric shapes). Developmental skill do-mains do not develop in isolation, and when a problem exists in one area, other areas are affected. Developmental differences in skill domains influence not only the ideal time for a child to learn a particular skill, but also when the child's skills best match the instructional expectations or demands of the formal educational system.

Developmental assessment focuses on students' physical and psychological matu-ration, as well as on identifying their individual strengths and weaknesses within and across learning areas, and detecting gaps in development or splinter skills. A gap in de-velopment refers to a delay or slowdown in the development of higher skills or sets of skills. A **splinter skill** refers to a skill learned in isolation from other related skills, such as learning to write the letters of the alphabet without understanding the meaning of the letters. Problems with basic fine motor coordination may affect the development of higher level eye-hand integration skills, such as cutting, pasting, tracing, and copying. It may be difficult or unlikely for children to master a particular skill if they have not reached the **critical period** (also referred to as the teachable moment or the optimal time for mastery learning) during which time children are physically, psychologically, and emotionally ready to learn a particular skill. When teachers attempt to introduce a new skill before the critical moment, it can be difficult, if not impossible, for the child to learn it. Likewise, when a skill is introduced after the critical period, acquisition may also be difficult (Venn, 2004). Children with mild-to-moderate disabilities often skip stages of development, which may lead to gaps in development or splinter skills, and children with more severe disabilities often demonstrate abnormal patterns of develop-ment, but this generally depends on the severity of the disability (Venn, 2004).

According to the National Association for the Education of Young Children (NAEYC), developmentally appropriate assessments of young children's progress and achievement should (a) be ongoing, strategic, and purposeful; (b) reflect progress toward important learning and developmental goals; (c) be appropriate for the age and experiences of young children; (d) tailored to a specific purpose and used only for the purpose for which they have been demonstrated to produce reliable, valid information; (e) be based on multiple assessment procedures and never be made on the basis of a single developmental assessment screening device; and (f) be considerate of individual variation in learners and allow for differences in style and rates of learning (Bredekamp & Copple, 1997).

SECTION 3: TRANSITION DURING THE MIDDLE YEARS: ELEMENTARY TO MIDDLE TO HIGH SCHOOL

The transition from one school setting to another can be extremely stressful for students with disabilities and their families (Rous & Hallam, 1998). Assessment and advanced planning are important if a smooth transition is to occur (LaParo, Pianta, & Cox, 2000).

Puberty seems to be one of the major transitions in the life of youngsters with disabilities. Primary issues of concern during preadolescence and adolescence include independence, peer relationships, physical growth, and sexual maturation. Although many of the issues are similar from elementary to middle and from middle to high school, significant differences exist.

Transition from Elementary to Middle School

The middle school years are more about change than any other period in a student's school life. For the first time, students are expected to be responsible for being prepared to learn. Their classes are larger, their class settings change throughout the day, and they have several teachers to report and relate to. Often several elementary schools funnel into one middle school, which brings together a more diverse set of economic, educational, and cultural perspectives than occurs in elementary school.

Key issues of concern when planning for this transition include what changes will be needed in the IEP, and who will be responsible for implementing the plan and needed educational supports. Many issues can affect the student's smooth transition and ultimate adjustment to middle school. During the elementary years, the child's experience tends to be in a nurturing, self-contained environment where students are responsible to one teacher who knows them personally, assigns all their homework, and plans all their tests. In middle school, which tends to be structured departmentally, the child has to adjust to multiple teachers, homework and tests from many classes, a rigid class schedule, and other matters (e.g., using lockers). The expected level of independence, responsibility, time management, and so forth generally requires careful planning and a support system for students with disabilities.

Transition from Middle to High School

The main focus of transition assessment at all critical points, and particularly when students move from middle school to high school, is to facilitate curriculum and instruction decisions, to determine the needed support services, and to abide by the legislation dealing with transition. At this point in their educational program, students must become increasingly self-sufficient; that is, independent and able to self-advocate. They no longer follow a fully structured curricular scope and sequence; instead their class program and schedule are directed by their aptitudes and interests—college preparation, job preparation, and so forth.

When transition assessment and subsequent planning are not conducted, students can be affected in critical areas. The needed services or accommodations that they had received throughout their school career may be interrupted or discontinued. For example, students who had been provided with or allowed to use a computer, or who had required and received extended time on reading and writing tasks, may have these options denied. Or, they may receive less assistance with their efforts to cope and adjust to the new environment, for which they may need specific training, opportunities for role-playing simulations, or time to plan and negotiate any environmental, social, or academic roadblocks they may encounter. Also, the administration and staff in the students' new environment may need to be informed about the physical, emotional-social, or academic needs of these students in order to provide the support and comfort level to make the transition acceptable.

Each transition requires adjustments for students and their families. Students with special needs have more difficulty dealing with these transitions than students who do not have disabilities. Issues that must be addressed during these times include determining (a) whether the student is, or continues to be, eligible for services; (b) what services the student is eligible for; (c) where these services will occur; (d) how they will be provided; and (e) who will provide them. The planning process is a critical component in making transitions successful.

SECTION 4: TRANSITION FROM SPECIAL EDUCATION TO GENERAL EDUCATION AND FROM HOSPITAL/HOME TO SCHOOL

The Transition from Special to Regular Education

With least restrictive environment foremost in educational planning, the IEP team should always be focused on assessing the student's capability of being successful in the most inclusive environment possible. Besides the obvious academic competencies of the student, a successful transition requires that the student have the necessary work-study skills and emotional maturity. See Figure 13–8 for examples of skills and dispositions that should be considered when assessing transition readiness and facilitating adjustment for the move from a self-contained or resource center special education class to inclusion in a regular education class.

Figure 13–8   Examples of Skills Needed to Transition to a Less Restrictive Classroom Environment

IS THE STUDENT ABLE TO
- Sit and focus for extended periods of time?
- Follow class routine?
- Access school lockers?
- Maneuver through the cafeteria line?
- Follow departmentalized school schedules?
- Cooperate in group activities?
- Follow basic directions?

The Transition from Hospital/Rehabilitation/ Home to School

Students with physical, medical, or emotional disabilities often need skill and environmental assessment as they return to school after being hospitalized, on homebound instruction, or in a rehabilitation facility. Often the physical and emotional energy normally spent in learning and completing course assignments is now used to cope with their medical or emotional condition (National Institutes of Health, 2002). Thus, it is important to consult and coordinate with the medical and therapeutic specialists who have worked with the students as part of their assessment process (Spinelli, 2003). Often the situation that resulted in their leaving the school program affected their academic facility, emotional adjustment, ability to function in the school program each day, and coping mechanisms (Spinelli, 2004). Freqently these students require special accommodations, such as a shortened school day, a modified curriculum or an adjustment to required assignments, the use of assistive technologies, appropriate positioning so that they can participate in activities, and communicative devices (Downing & Demchak, 2002). (See Figure 13-9 for a list of academic and social-emotional factors to consider in the assessment and planning process.)

Figure 13–9   Academic and Psychosocial Factors to Consider in Transitions

Cognitive-Academic Issues

- Neurological damage
- Short and long-term memory impairment
- Disorganization
- Information processing/problem-solving deficits
- Poor retention of new learning
- Delayed speed of mental processing
- Spatial orientation problems
- Poor sequencing
- Motor planning dysfunction
- Sustained attention and vigilance problems
- Visual-spatial-motor coordination impairment
- Body image disorientation

Psychosocial Issues

- Social isolation
- Peer rejection
- Tendency to withdrawal
- Embarrassment
- Feelings of being overwhelmed/stressed
- Anxiety, insecurity
- Depression
- Fear/phobia
- Frustration/guilt
- Low self-esteem/self-concept

Source: "Dealing with Cancer in the Classroom: The Teacher's Role and Responsibilities," by C. G. Spinelli, 2004, *Teaching Exceptional Children, 36*(4), 14–21.

Classroom Scenario

Juan is preparing to transition back into school after a horrific car accident in which his parents were killed and he received serious injury to his legs and head trauma. He will need to be assessed to determine his ability to cope emotionally, ability to physically maneuver around the school, and the need for accommodations as a result of neurological damage.

Drew has been trying to keep up with his school work, although his efforts have been hampered because of many surgeries and extensive rounds of chemotherapy to battle his cancer. Assessment will help to determine the curricular, work assignment, and accommodations (e.g., a shortened day due to fatigue) he will require.

SECTION 5: SECONDARY TO POSTSECONDARY TRANSITION

From Assessment to Transition Planning

Following the assessment process, the IEP team writes a transition plan designed to address the strategies and services needed in the student's educational program (Huefner, 2000). This plan structures the program to prepare students to leave school with the skills necessary to transition to a postsecondary academic or vocational-training program, the armed forces, or competitive or extended employment. Since the range of abilities and disabilities varies among students with special needs, their post-high-school plans must be individualized. A student with mild learning disabilities may plan to attend college or decide on **competitive employment**, working independently in the community. For this student, the transition assessment plan might include evaluating independent work-study skills, planning and time management skills, and self-advocacy skills. A student who is more severely disabled may be placed in **extended employment** (previously referred to as sheltered workshops) following secondary school. For this student, the transition assessment plan could include evaluating vocational interests, aptitude, as well as ability and functional self-help and life skills.

Components of Secondary Transitions

Transition services must be based on the student's needs, taking into account his or her preferences and interests. The services should include instruction, community experiences, the development of employment and other postschool adult-living objectives, and, if needed, training in daily living skills and access to functional vocational evaluations.

The following major domains are the focus of evaluation when adolescents transition from secondary-level programs to postsecondary educational or employment settings (Clark, 1998).

Cognitive ability.   The cognitive ability domain involves the ability of students to verbally and nonverbally solve problems. Cognitive processing skills include visual perception, linguistic processes, attention and/or memory, learning, analyzing, synthesizing, and reasoning.

Social-emotional adjustment. The social-emotional adjustment domain involves how students cope, adapt, share, relate, interact, cooperate, collaborate, respect the property and privacy of others, and demonstrate socially appropriate or inappropriate behavior. This domain also includes students' sensitivity to others' feelings, preferences, and multicultural diversity, and how they deal with frustration, anger, hardship, and change. Students who have a history of learning problems are often at risk for depression and anxiety. Many disorders (e.g., pervasive developmental delays, emotional disturbance, and schizophrenia), by their nature, tend to have a significant impact on social-emotional adjustment. Further, addictive disorders—such as drug, alcohol, or eating problems—can be detected through evaluation procedures. It is critical to determine whether students have social-emotional problems that may affect their postsecondary choices and functioning in these settings.

Communication skills. The communication skills domain encompasses speech and language skills, including expressive skills (the ability to verbally and nonverbally articulate clearly and effectively) and receptive skills (the ability to understand information presented in either verbal or written form). The ability to adequately express oneself verbally and the ability to comprehend verbal interactions are generally critical components of a successful transition. Oral communication includes specific speech skills, such as articulation (production of sounds in words), fluency (flow of connected speech, including stuttering and cluttering), voice quality (pitch, volume), and rate of speaking (too slow or too fast). Oral communication also deals with language skills, such as semantics (vocabulary, figurative language, and word retrieval), syntax (order of words in sentences), and pragmatics (use of language in social context for effective communication, including eye contact, the appropriate use of slang or jargon, topic maintenance, response to common expressions, and social conversation). Written communication involves written language skills, such as spelling, punctuation, and grammar. Good communication skills are a prerequisite for success in most postsecondary settings. The teacher must determine what the problem areas are, what strategies the student needs to use to compensate or remediate the problem, and an appropriate method of evaluating and monitoring progress.

Academic functioning. The academic functioning domain, which concerns the basic academic levels of students, is a crucial component of the assessment process. It is necessary to know students' basic skill levels in reading, written language, and mathematics when making postsecondary placement decisions and when determining goals and objectives for transition planning. The teacher needs to ascertain whether students require accommodations or modifications in the postsecondary educational program.

Physical stamina. The physical stamina domain involves basic health and physical conditioning, including strength, mobility, endurance, stamina, and range of motion. This domain also covers fine and gross motor skills, such as manual and finger dexterity, small- and large-muscle motor coordination, agility, and flexibility.

Adaptive behavior. The adaptive behavior domain involves a wide variety of skills and human activities. The adaptive and daily living skills of the adolescent and young adult involve functioning skills, including independent life skills, job-related skills, and community living skills. Basic tasks include personal hygiene skills (e.g., basic grooming, including shaving, use of deodorant), advanced dressing skills (e.g., choosing appropriate clothing for weather, utility, professionalism); food shopping and preparation (e.g., planning, storing, cooking, cleanup); simple home maintenance (e.g., changing a light bulb, unclogging a drain); transportation (e.g., automotive care, determining bus routes); financial independence (e.g., check writing and balancing, resume writing, application forms); and community involvement (e.g., attaining legal assistance and health care).

Reasonable Accommodations for Postsecondary Settings

A critical aspect of transition assessment is determining students' self-awareness and self-advocacy skills. Students need to be able to explain their disability, their specific strengths and areas of need, and the accommodations that enable them to function optimally not only to cope but to thrive in postsecondary settings. This requires that they self-advocate by clearly articulating what they need in order to function and to seek out these needed services and/or accommodations, and by having the self-motivation and interest to do what it takes to succeed. All public and many private organizations, companies, educational facilities, and so forth receiving federal financial assistance are subject to the regulations of Section 504 of the Rehabilitation Act of 1973 (P.L. 93–112), which states:

> No otherwise qualified handicapped individual . . . shall, solely by reason of his/her handicap, be excluded from participation in, be denied the benefits of, or be subject to discrimination under any program or activity receiving federal financial assistance.

This legislation requires that all individuals receive reasonable accommodations. Postsecondary students, whether in academic programs or employed, are eligible for these supports after they provide their institutions with evidence of documented need (Rothstein, 1998).

There are no definitive parameters for what qualifies as reasonable accommodations in the world of work. The "reasonable" standard seems to include any modification or adaptation in working conditions or the work environment that enable the worker to function and fulfill the job description requirements without placing unreasonable hardship on the employer or coworkers. Examples of such accommodations include adjustments in work requirements (e.g., modified hours, frequent breaks), special equipment (e.g., amplification on telephones, modified desks to accommodate wheelchairs, laptop computers), work environments (e.g., private room, lowered bathroom sinks, office change from a higher to a lower floor, special air filtration).

Common types of accommodations that are considered reasonable by most colleges and postsecondary educational settings are listed in Figure 13–10. Most require current documentation that the student is eligible for special services under Section 504. This includes recent aptitude and achievement test results, generally as recent as one year. Once it is verified that the student qualifies for accommodations, support services are coordinated through the campus disabilities office, which provides services to students with disabilities in dealing with admissions, course advising, testing procedures, advocacy, and counseling. Other scheduling options need to be considered for students with disabilities making the transition into a postsecondary program. These scheduling accommodations might include limiting the number of courses per day, scheduling fewer credit hours each semester, allowing additional

Figure 13–10   Examples of Test and Instructional Modifications for Postsecondary Educational Facilities

- Modify test-taking procedures to adjust for specific disabilities (e.g., enlarged print for visually impaired; computers for physically disabled, administer orally).
- Modify test protocols to accommodate individual needs (e.g., essays rather than multiple choice, substitute a project for a test).
- Modify test administration procedures (e.g., allow unlimited or extended time; break test sessions into shorter blocks; administer tests individually in a quiet room).
- Adapt instructional method.
- Substitute an alternative course for a required course (e.g., foreign language).
- Provide audiotapes of textbooks.
- Allow note takers to help students with lectures.
- Allow taperecording of lectures.
- Provide students with outline for structuring note taking.
- Provide study guides.
- Allow work to be previewed for suggestions before final submission.
- Offer counseling services to the students.
- Provide basic skills instruction in reading, mathematics, and language.
- Photocopy class notes.
- Provide instructional tutors.
- Provide laptop computers with spelling and grammar checks.
- Provide support programs (e.g., college survival, study skills, time management).

time to complete the program, permitting a part-time rather than a full-time program of study, and providing programming breaks between rigorous courses.

SECTION 6: THE SECONDARY-LEVEL ASSESSMENT PROCESS

Assessment is the cornerstone of effective transition planning. According to Sitlington, Neubert, & Leconte (1997, p. 7), **transition assessment** is the ongoing process of collecting data on the individual's strengths, needs, preferences, and interests as they relate to the demands of current and future working, educational, living, personal, and social environments. Assessment data serve as the common thread in the transition process and form the basis for defining goals and services to be included in the IEP. (Figure 13–11 lists affective attributes that contribute to success in both educational and workplace environments.)

The focus of transition assessment depends mainly on the individual and the specific situation. But in general, transition assessment includes the following purposes:

1. To identify students' career goals and interests, preferences, independence, strengths, hobbies, interpersonal relationships, self-advocacy, and abilities in relation to postsecondary goals, including employment opportunities, postsecondary education and training opportunities, independent living situations, community involvement, and personal/social goals.
2. To make an ecological assessment of the new setting in order to determine the psychological, physical, social, emotional, and cognitive demands and requirements of the postsecondary setting.

FYI   **ASSESSMENT DOMAINS**

- Community participation
- Communication
- Daily living
- Employment
- Financial/income management
- Health
- Independent living (includes living arrangements)
- Leisure/recreation
- Postsecondary education/training
- Relationships/social skills
- Self-determination
- Transportation/mobility
- Vocational training

Figure 13–11   Affective Attributes Inventory

Is the student:	Always	Often	Sometimes	Never	N/A
• ambitious to investigate?					
• able to compromise with others?					
• able to cooperate with others?					
• curious about the world?					
• dependable?					
• using higher order thinking?					
• enthusiastic to continue?					
• excited about science?					
• fascinated with findings?					
• flexible with ideas?					
• honest in artifacts?					
• independent?					
• objective?					
• open-minded?					
• patient with others?					
• persistent with a task?					
• precise?					
• questioning what is not clear?					
• respectful of evidence?					
• responsible to projects?					
• satisfied with artifacts?					
• self-confident?					
• self-disciplined?					
• self-reliant?					
• sensitive to others?					
• skeptical about results?					
• thorough?					
• tolerant of change?					
• willing to change?					

Source: Adapted from *Teaching Children Science: A Project-Based Approach,* by J. Krajcik, C. Czerniak, & C. Berger, © 1999, Boston: McGraw Hill. Reproduced with permission of the McGraw-Hill Companies.

3. To assess students' current and desired skill levels; to determine their ability to deal with the impending demands of postsecondary education, employment, or community participation and independent living.

4. To determine the particular curricular, social-emotional, and physical skills that need to be addressed in the transition plan, as well as students' self-determination skills.

5. To determine the appropriate placements within educational, vocational, and community settings that facilitate the attainment of these postsecondary goals.

6. To determine the accommodations, supports, and services individuals with disabilities will need to attain and maintain their postsecondary goals related to employment, postsecondary education and training programs, independent living, community involvement, and social/personal roles and relationships (Sitlington, et al., 1996).

7. To determine a system for evaluating the success of the transition program (Dunn, 1996).

The areas covered in this basic assessment process include students' cognitive and academic abilities, social and interpersonal skills, emotional maturity, general health and physical stamina, career interests and aptitudes, awareness of occupational options, career planning skills, and community experience. Also included are the acquisition of daily living skills; ability to work independently; ability to recognize personal and educational needs; ability to self-advocate and recognize the need for accommodations, compensatory strategies, and job or training modifications; personal or social support network; level of community involvement; personally preferred leisure activities; access to transportation options; and status of family and living arrangements (deFur & Patton, 1999; Sitlington, et al., 1996). Additionally, secondary students must pass a competency test or another measure of skill acquisition to be granted a diploma. To ensure that students adequately meet these criteria, decisions must be made regarding whether they require testing accommodations, modifications, or alternative assessments. Because these issues are critical and may affect diploma status, school exit, and long-term transition goals, they must be a part of long-term transition planning (deFur & Patton, 1999).

The following guidelines for selecting methods to use in the transition assessment process have been suggested by Sitlington, et al. (1997, p. 75):

1. Assessment methods must be tailored to the type of information needed and the decisions to be made regarding transition planning and various postsecondary outcomes.
2. Specific methods selected must be appropriate for the learning characteristics of the individual, including cultural and linguistic differences.
3. Assessment methods must incorporate assistive technology or accommodations that will allow an individual to demonstrate his or her abilities and potential.
4. Assessment methods must occur in environments that resemble actual vocational training, employment, independent living, or community environments.
5. Assessment methods must produce outcomes that contribute to ongoing development, planning, and implementation of "next steps" in the individual's transition process.
6. Assessment methods must be carried out and include a sequence of activities that sample an individual's behavior and skills over time.
7. Assessment data must be verified by more than one method and by more than one person.
8. Assessment data must be synthesized and interpreted to individuals with disabilities, their families, and transition team members.
9. Assessment data and the results of the assessment process must be documented in a format that can be used to facilitate transition planning.

SECTION 7: ASSESSMENTS AT CRITICAL TRANSITION POINTS: PRESCHOOL TO ELEMENTARY SCHOOL

Early Childhood Standardized Tests

Standardized tests have been used by most school districts when assessing preschoolers and kindergartners in order to determine school readiness, eligibility for transitional programming, retention in kindergarten, and eligibility for classification.

However, according to most early childhood educators—including the National Association for the Education of Young Children (NAEYC), the foremost organization for the education of young children—standardized tests are considered developmentally inappropriate for young children.

Another drawback is that standardized tests do not recognize the true capabilities of the young child. The standardized test is a structured instrument that is designed to determine what a child does or does not know in relation to a defined set of criteria. This "snapshot" is not representative of the child interacting in a natural, authentic context, such as the classroom. Not understanding the importance or significance of the test, preschool youngsters may make random guesses. They may fail to comprehend or accurately follow directions; be unfamiliar with the language of the test due to social, cultural, or linguistic differences; or be unable to track or follow numbered questions in the correct sequence (Gullo, 1997). The inconsistency of day-to-day performance may have a significant effect on test reliability at this age. Because developmental spurts and lags are common in young children, one day's scores may be a poor indicator of the child's growth, development, and potential, as well as educational classification, placement, and programmatic needs (Seefeldt & Barbour, 1998). Therefore, informal assessments are commonly used.

Preschool to Elementary School Informal Assessment Procedures

There are a variety of efficient and effective methods of collecting data when observing children during work-play activities. These include checklists, anecdotal records, and tape recordings. The observer can use checklists to identify the child's level of mastery on tasks directly related to the IEP goals and objectives. Many teachers make anecdotal notes as they walk around the classroom observing children in play or work-task activities. Video and audio recordings of social and work-study interactions are also an effective way to record children's behavior. The environment could be in the classroom, on the playground, or in the home or community.

Observational Assessment

Systematic observation of children is an effective way to evaluate their growth and achievement. It is also a method of evaluating programs and teaching effectiveness. This type of assessment is authentic and unobtrusive. Children are observed in their natural environment as they go about their typical activities rather than as they work on contrived tasks. Observations that are collected and analyzed over time provide a good deal of information about the child (Brown, Odom, & Holcombe, 1996). Additional factors to consider when observing the child are the specific antecedents and consequences that occur immediately before and after the observed behaviors (e.g., attention-getting behavior initiated by a peer and the teacher's verbal reprimand).

A very effective method of assessing young children is through a process referred to by Goodman (1978) as kidwatching. **Kidwatching** consists of informal observations of children in a variety of settings and activities. To gain a broad perspective of their skills, temperament, adjustment, and so forth, the teacher observes them as they function in varied settings and situations. This might include observing them working independently, in pairs, in small and large groups in the classroom, interacting in other school-related settings (e.g., the playground, gym, cafeteria, auditorium, on field trips,

Figure 13–12 Suggested Observation Opportunities

Specific Behaviors

Is the child able to:

- separate from the parent or teacher without difficulty?
- shift from one task to another?
- maintain focus and attention to task?
- follow basic one- and two-step directions?
- work for at least one-half hour at a project?
- work at a steady, adequate pace?
- retell a story using pictures?

Specific Situations

Observe the child's ability to:

- deal with frustration
- solve problems
- communicate verbally and nonverbally (e.g., facial expressions, gestures, drawing, writing)
- interact with students who have cultural, ethnic, and/or linguistic differences
- interact socially with peers and adults
- demonstrate emotional control
- demonstrate pre-academic skills (e.g., rote counting; identifying shapes, colors, and so on)
- demonstrate self-help skills (e.g., washing hands, buttoning coat, blowing nose)
- demonstrate motor skills (e.g., cutting, pasting, running, jumping)

Observe children while they are:

- involved in daily class routines
- participating in group share time
- interacting during center time and recess

Observe to determine the child's:

- ability to work on specific activities
- process for completing activities
- learning style
- interest levels
- skill levels
- coping techniques
- strategies for decision making and problem solving
- interactions with other children

---

on bus rides), and during various times of the day (e.g., morning or afternoon). Rather than plan one specific time period to observe, the teacher should engage in ongoing observational assessment or kidwatching. (Figure 13–12 suggests situations, settings, and behaviors to focus on when observing young children.)

Play-Based Assessment

One of the more authentic methods of assessment is **play-based assessment**; it is useful in understanding the abilities and needs of all children, especially those with disabilities. During play-based assessment, the teacher can observe cognitive, physical, emotional, adaptive, and fine motor development, as well as broad patterns of thinking, problem solving, and informal communication, rather than assessing isolated skills out of context (Myers, McBride, & Peterson, 1996). By being cognizant of developmental levels and observant of the child's interaction with others, the teacher can

Figure 13–13   Developmental Levels of Social Play

Children's Developmental Play Stages

Unoccupied behavior   Not playing, focuses fleeting attention on anything that appears to be of momentary interest.

Solitary play   Plays alone, plays with toys not used by neighboring peers, no evidence of communication with others (approximately age 0 to 24 months).

Onlooker behavior   Watches others play, may talk to peers, ask questions, make suggestions but does not overtly enter into play activity (approximately 1 to 2 years).

Parallel play   Plays beside rather than with other children, may play with the same types of toys but does not interact or communicate with peers while playing (approximately 2 to 3 years).

Associative play   Plays with other children, converses, borrows and loans toys, follows and is followed while playing but there is no division of labor or any organization of the activity (approximately 3 to 4 years).

Cooperative or organized supplementary play   Plays in an organized group for the purpose of making some material product, to attain some cooperative goal, to dramatize the activity of adults or to play a formal game with rules (approximately 4 to 5 years).

Source: School for Children: Developmentally Appropriate Practices (2nd ed.), by C. H. Wolfgang & M. E. Wolfgang, 1999, Needham Heights, MA: Allyn & Bacon, p. 23. Reprinted with permission.

also determine the child's level of social development. (Figure 13–13 lists developmental levels of social play.)

Play-based assessment involves observing children in a play environment where there are toys, dolls, and other interesting material and equipment that entice the child to explore and initiate his or her own play actions and interactions. Play-based assessment is, by its nature, both reliable and valid. In the preschool classroom, playtime is generally a regular aspect of the program; therefore, reliability is increased because teachers have multiple opportunities to observe the child playing with familiar materials and playmates. Also, the validity of this type of assessment is enhanced by its real or authentic context. (See Figure 13–14.) For example, assessing the child's fine motor and gross motor planning skills is more authentic when the child is putting together puzzles, setting the table for a tea party, or building a fort out of blocks rather than assessing the child when he or she is taking paper-and-pencil tests.

Arena Assessment

Arena assessment is a method used primarily with preschool-aged children. It is a procedure whereby the teacher is not the only observer and recorder; family members and other early childhood specialists (e.g., the speech and language pathologist, psychologist, occupational or physical therapist) are also involved in the process. One member of the group (often the parent) acts as the facilitator, who interacts with the child (e.g., handing the child toys), while the other members record their observations. When the assessment has been completed, the group members discuss their observations and develop an intervention plan. When several perspectives and the expertise of parents, teachers, and specialists are involved, a more integrated and holistic view of the child can be obtained.

Figure 13—14 Checklist of Levels of Play in Learning Contexts

Learning Contexts	Solitary Play	Peer Play	Small Group	Child with Adult	Group with Adult
Reading and Writing Activities					
Math Activities					
Science Activities					
Social Studies Activities					
Art and Music Activities					
Fine and Gross Motor Activities					
Outdoor Activities					

Types of Play
Functional (sensorimotor) play Repeated actions for pleasure, such as pouring sand or riding a tricycle (FP).
Constructive play Play with intent to build something that represents an object in real or imaginary world (CP).
Dramatic play Play involving make-believe objects, roles, and situations represented by gesture and/or language (DP).
Games with rules Play with rules that are set forth or negotiated before play begins (GP).

Dates	Observations and Comments

Source: From *Play at the Center of the Curriculum* by J. Van Hoorn et al., © 1993. Adapted by permission of Pearson Education, Inc., Upper Saddle River, NJ.

Self-Evaluation

Students as young as age 4 can describe how they feel about being in their school program, what they like best, what makes them uncomfortable, and what could be changed to improve their program (Barclay & Benelli, 1996). When young children are encouraged to think and talk about their learning, it helps the teacher gain insight into how they process and interpret information and which activities or experiences are most beneficial. It also helps students learn to monitor and reflect on their own learning. They learn to recognize their strengths and weaknesses, contribute to decisions about their programs, and begin the process of becoming self-advocates.

Figure 13–15   Sample Child Interview Questions

- What do you most like to do in school? What do you least like to do in school?
- What are your favorite things to do when you are at home?
- What things do you do in school that are hard for you to do? What things are easy for you to do?
- What kinds of things do you like to do with your friends? with your family?
- What things are scary to you? What do you worry about?
- What would you like to be learning next year?

Figure 13–16   Sample Student Self-Assessment Questions

- What did you learn today? _____
- Why was it important to know? _____
- Did you know anything about it before it was discussed in class today? _____
- What is the hardest thing you have to do in school? _____
- Why do you think that is hard for you to do? _____
- What do you want to learn next? _____
- What is the best way for you to learn to do that? _____
- What does your teacher do to help you learn? _____
- What do you do when you want to remember something? _____

(See Figures 13–15 and 13–16 for sample questions that teachers can use for student interviews and to promote student self-assessment.)

Portfolios

Preschool and primary-level teachers have used portfolios for years to collect students' class work and art projects so that students can take them home to share with parents on a daily or weekly basis. Many teachers keep work samples from the beginning of the school year, so they can compare students' more primitive, early work to their end-of-the-year samples in order to demonstrate growth or lack thereof as the school year progresses. This practice of collecting and showcasing work products has been refined and expanded and is now known as portfolio assessment.

Portfolios are the most valid and the best indicators of children's true strengths and weaknesses when they contain work samples that demonstrate competence in skill areas needed for success in future academic tasks. Children should be encouraged to contribute to decisions about the items that will be included in their portfolios. Teachers should guide them in their selection by helping them choose work products that were particularly challenging to do, illustrate a special accomplishment, or have special merit or meaning. (See Figure 13–17.)

Curriculum-Based Assessment

The benefits of curriculum-based measurement (CBM) have been discussed in detail in Chapter 3, but there is an additional benefit to using this form of assessment with primary-level students. During the early school years, curriculum-based evaluation methods can help to identify skill gaps. When assessment reveals such gaps, the

Figure 13–17 Portfolio Work Samples

- Photographs of children working (e.g., block construction)
- Collection of drawings, paintings, scribbling
- Samples of manuscript printing
- Creative writing or journal entries that use invented or conventional spelling
- List of books read to or by children
- Special report or project
- Anecdotal report on behavior
- Notes from student interviews (e.g., favorite books, pets, things to do)
- Samples of artwork using various media
- Samples demonstrating cutting and/or pasting activities
- Sample of written numbers and/or letters
- Audiotape of student telling or reading a story or reciting a poem
- Videotapes of classroom and playground activities
- Stories that are dictated, written, or illustrated by the student

teacher can modify students' instructional program to ensure that the missed skill is reintroduced, reinforced, and reevaluated several times until mastery is accomplished and before the child progresses to the next grade. Curriculum-based evaluation can provide a direct link between assessment and the development of curriculum-related intervention goals and objectives. (See Figure 13–18 for IEP/IFSP goal and objective indicators.)

Figure 13–18 Indicators of High-Quality IEP/IFSP Goals and Objectives for Infants and Young Children

Functionality

1. Will the skill increase the child's ability to interact with people/objects within the daily environment?
2. Will the skill have to be performed by someone else if the child cannot do it?

Generality

3. Does the skill represent a general concept or class of responses?
4. Can the skill be adapted or modified for a variety of disabling conditions?
5. Can the skill be generalized across a variety of settings, materials, and/or people?

Instructional Context

6. Can the skill be taught in a way that reflects the manner the skill will be used in the daily environment?
7. Can the skill be elicited easily by the teacher/parent within classroom/home activities?

Measurability

8. Can the skill be seen and/or heard?
9. Can the skill be directly counted (e.g., by frequency, duration, measures of distance, such as how far a child is able to ride a tricycle, throw a ball, or propel a wheelchair)?
10. Does the skill contain or lend itself to determination of performance criteria?

Hierarchical Relation Between Long-Range Goals and Short-Term Goals

11. Is the short-term objective a developmental subskill or step thought to be critical to the achievement of the long-range goal?

Source: "Putting Real-Life Skills into IEP/IFSPs for Infants and Young Children," by A. R. Notari-Syverson, & S. L. Shuster, 1995, *Teaching Exceptional Children, 27(2),* 29–32. Reprinted with permission.

Classroom Scenario

Morgan, a verbally precocious preschooler, has poor motor development due to a neurological impairment that occurred during birth. She is being closely monitored in eye-hand coordination by her special education teacher. Her ability to trace and cut across a straight and then a crooked line are being assessed through a series of probes. The probes are administered twice each week and graphed on a chart so that the teacher can track Morgan's progress toward meeting her goal of developing her fine motor skills by demonstrating the ability to control a pencil and scissors sufficiently to complete these tasks.

Specific Skill Checklists

Checklists can be individually designed to monitor a student's progress toward completing IFSP and IEP goals and objectives. They can also be used when assessing small or large groups of students to note progress toward mastery of specific curriculum core standards and attainment of skills using the program's scope and sequence. Teachers use checklists as an efficient and effective means of determining whether students have exhibited required skills, the level of skill development (e.g., no skill, emerging, mastery), how often the skill is implemented, and whether the skill is used across settings and situations. (See Figures 13–19 through 13–21.)

Figure 13–19   IEP Goals and Objectives: Emergent Literacy Checklist

	Observation Dates			
Goal: Prerequisite Skills	**Nov.**	**Jan.**	**March**	**May**
Objectives				
• Has adequate visual acuity				
• Has adequate auditory acuity				
• Has adequate eye-hand coordination				
Goal: Metalinguistic Skills				
Objectives				
• Recognizes the difference between letter sound and symbol				
• Recognizes the difference between letters, words, and sentences				
• Differentiates between letter shapes				
• Discriminates between commonly reversed letters (e.g., *d* and *b*)				
• Makes connection between pictures or objects and words				
• Recognizes left-right sequence				
• Recognizes up-down direction				
• Recognizes that print has different meaning (e.g., questions, statements)				

Figure 13–20   Checklist of Young Students' Social Decision-Making
and Problem-Solving Strengths Across Situations

In what situations is this student able to use the following:

Self-Control Skills   **Situations**

- Listen carefully and accurately   _____
- Remember and follow directions   _____
- Concentrate and follow through on tasks   _____
- Calm him/herself down   _____
- Carry on a conversation without upsetting or provoking others   _____

Social Awareness and Group Participation Skills

- Accept praise or approval   _____
- Choose praiseworthy and caring friends   _____
- Know when help is needed   _____
- Ask for help when needed   _____
- Work as part of a problem-solving team   _____

Social Decision-Making and Problem-Solving Skills

- Recognize signs of feelings in self   _____
- Recognize signs of feelings in others   _____
- Describe accurately a range of feelings   _____
- Put problems into words clearly   _____
- Think of different types of solutions   _____
- Think of several ways to solve a problem or reach a goal   _____

*Enter the number of those situations in which particular skills appear to be demonstrated,
using the following codes:

    1 = with peers in classroom
    2 = with peers in other situations in school
    3 = with teachers
    4 = with other adults in school
    5 = with parent(s)
    6 = with siblings or other relatives
    7 = with peers outside school
    8 = when under academic stress or pressure
    9 = when under social or peer-related stress or pressure
   10 = when under family-related stress or pressure

Source: Problem-Solving/Decision-Making for Social and Academic Success, 1990, Washington, DC: National
Education Association. Reprinted with permission.

When developing checklists, skills and behaviors should be listed in order of
developmental level, based on generally accepted age-expectancy accomplishment
levels. Checklist objectives should be phrased in positive terms—identified as the
skill children are expected to accomplish rather than what they are not supposed to
be doing (e.g., "Phyllis will be able to contribute appropriately to the show-and-tell
group discussion," rather than "Phyllis will not yell out during show and tell"). By
writing the expected performance or behavior in objective terms, they can be easily
incorporated into IEP goals and objectives.

Figure 13–21 Preschool to Kindergarten Transition Checklist

	Mastered	Emerging	Not Mastered
Social Behaviors and Classroom Conduct			
• Understands role as part of a group			
• Respects others and their property			
• Interacts and defends self without aggression			
• Plays cooperatively; shares toys and materials			
• Expressions emotions and affection appropriately			
• Takes turns; participates appropriately in games			
• Is willing to try something new			
• Follows class rules and routines			
• Lines up and waits appropriately			
• Imitates peer actions			
• Sits appropriately			
• Plays independently			
Communication Behaviors			
• Follows two- to three-part directions			
• Initiates and maintains peer interactions			
• Modifies behavior when given verbal feedback			
• Asks peers and teachers for information or assistance			
• Recalls and follows directions previously given			
• Follows group instruction			
• Relates ideas and experience			
• Communicates own needs and wants			
Task-Related Behaviors			
• Finds materials needed for task			
• Does not disrupt peers during activities			
• Complies quickly with teacher instructions			
• Generalizes skills across tasks and situations			
• Follows task directions in small or large group			
• Replaces materials and cleans up work space			
• Monitors own behavior; knows when task is done			
• Begins and completes work at appropriate time without extra teacher attention			
• Make choices			
• Stays in own space			
• Follows routine in transition			
• Uses a variety of materials			
• Seeks attention appropriately			
• Attends to teacher in a large group			
Self-Help Behaviors			
• Recognizes when a problem exists			
• Locates and cares for personal belongings			
• Avoids dangers and responds to warning words			
• Takes outer clothing off and puts it on in a reasonable amount of time			
• Tries strategies to solve problems			
• Feeds self independently			
• Cares for own toileting needs			

Source: "Steps in Preparing for Transition: Preschool to Kindergarten," by L. K. Chandler, *Teaching Exceptional Children, 25,* 1993, p 48. Copyright © 1993 by The Council for Exceptional Children. Reprinted with permission.

Videotape, Audiotape, and Photographic Recordings

Technological advancements allow teachers to easily record children's performance for later analysis and for presenting explicit documentation of performance to parents through video and audiotaping. Many classrooms have this type of technology as part of their standard equipment, or teachers can easily obtain them when planned activities would be ideal for permanent recording. The teacher can use these audio- and videotapes to note progress or a need for improvement in many domains, especially social and motor development. Audiotaping can be most useful in analyzing and monitoring progress in speech and language development. Tape recorders can be strategically placed around the classroom to capture conversations among students as well as verbal interactions in group activities and between the teacher and student. Teachers can tape the child reciting or telling a story and listen to the tape repeatedly in order to gain insight into the child's thought processes, to carefully listen to the child's speech patterns and use of language, and to clarify misarticulated words.

Videotaping is one of the most accurate ways to observe and record interaction. In addition to the video moving picture, sounds and spoken words are included. It is important that the video camera not become a classroom distraction, however. By putting the video camera on a tripod and using it regularly to record classroom events and accomplishments, students can become accustomed to being captured on video.

Another benefit of taping students is self-evaluation. Children enjoy viewing and listening to themselves and can be guided in noting behaviors that should be enhanced or eliminated. Photographs can be a quick and easy way to record the result of a project and children's reaction or participation in an assignment. Periodic photo taking can be used to provide visible evidence of progress in mastering a skill. By dating and recording the specifics of the activity, the teacher can compile a record of sequential development and include it in a portfolio assessment collection.

SECTION 8: ASSESSMENTS AT THE CRITICAL TRANSITION POINTS: MIDDLE TO SECONDARY SCHOOL YEARS

Assessment involves evaluating students' skills as well as the postsecondary setting demands and determining whether any discrepancies exist between those skills and those demands.

Person-Centered Planning

As students progress through their high school years and as the focus shifts to transition planning, students need to develop insight into who they are, who they want to be, where they want to go, and what they want to do with their lives. Most young adults struggle to balance making decisions, taking responsibility for those decisions, and learning to exert more control over their lives. **Person-centered planning** is a vehicle to this end (Sax & Thoma, 2002, p 14).

Person-centered assessment may incorporate standardized test results, ecological assessment information, and the input of students, parents, family members, and service providers. Person-centered planning and the IEP transition planning process have the same purposes: to build connections and linkages to the community, to support an individual's career preferences and interests, and to help the person achieve satisfactory adult lifestyle outcomes (Menchetti & Piland, 2001).

Person-centered approaches focus on the unique and specific wants and needs of an individual. The tools and strategies associated with person-centered approaches encourage support personnel and family members to think about people first and systems second (Everson & Reid, 1999). The focus planning process is to ensure equal participation, positive and clear communication, and active involvement of the student. Those participating must be willing to focus on the student and be prepared to hear things that may not always match their preconceived ideas (Sax & Thoma, 2002, p. 15).

Situational Assessment

Situational assessment is the use of systematic observation to evaluate work- and job-related performance and functional skills under actual conditions in authentic environments (Venn, 2004). Special educators and vocational training specialists use situational assessments to measure and evaluate in various settings—including school, home, community, and often on the job site or in simulated environments (Bigge & Stump, 1999; Wehman, 2001). This form of assessment may involve quantitative measures (baseline, results after intervention, how long and how often a behavior occurs) or qualitative measures, such as adult demands, peer expectations, and conditions in the environment (Flexer & Luft, 2005). It is important to make a "situational match"; that is, to match students' abilities to the demands of the postsecondary setting. This is accomplished by observing the environment and performing a work-site analysis to determine the requirements of the setting and match them to the individual student. This situational match can be a critical factor in the success of the student and requires correlating students' aptitudes and abilities to the performance situation and demands.

A situational inventory may be completed to analyze the specific task behaviors and program or work-site skills that are necessary for students to be successful in a given situation, whether it is an educational program or a job setting. The teacher may begin the assessment process by using on-the-job assessment. By entering and assessing the postsecondary environment, a list of needed skills can be compiled and broken down into components (as in a task analysis described in detail in Chapter 3). Next, the student with disabilities is observed in a situation requiring these work-site skills. Skills analysis may require event recording, duration recording, and so forth. (See Chapter 12.) Next, a determination is made about whether the student is able to perform the required task. The final assessment focuses on programmatic planning and evaluation. The required job skills that have not been mastered, or those that are emerging, need to be identified and incorporated into ITP goals and objectives for instructional planning. Evaluation of skill development can also be monitored by checking skills as they are mastered.

Situational assessments can be used in schools to create "simulations" of community environments as a type of training assessment. Examples of behaviors used in situational assessments include the following (Flexer & Luft, 2005):

- Getting along with coworkers
- Accepting criticism
- Following directions
- Heeding punctuality and attendance requirements
- Greeting known neighbors in apartment building and stores
- Crossing streets safely
- Waiting for change when paying for items

Figure 13—22 Sample Transition Student Interview Questions

- Are you having or have you had a particular academic problem in school?
- What academic subjects are your best? Your hardest?
- Have you ever had a part-time job?
- What are your vocational interests? Career aspirations?
- What job would you like when you finish your high school, college, or training program?
- Do you like to work alone or with others?
- Would you like a job in which you work from your desk or use physical skills?
- Do you think your disability will interfere with your ability to succeed in the postsecondary setting you choose? If so, why?
- Who would you contact for any assistance you need in the postsecondary setting?
- What kind of special help do you think you would require?
- What types of obstacles do you think you might encounter? How would you deal with them?

The Interview Process

Interviewing secondary-level students can provide much of the relevant information needed when planning for transitions. Interview questions should focus on clarifying behaviors noted during observations; procuring information about students' academic and work history; and providing teachers with students' personal preferences, goals, and aspirations in order to develop personalized transition plans that address their strengths and needs. Interviews are also a good way to ascertain whether students understand their disability, are aware of their special needs, know how to access the assistance they need, and have the inclination and ability to self-advocate. This information is important because if students are unable to advocate for themselves in post-high-school settings, frustration, anxiety, and failure are likely to result. Figure 13-22 is a list of preliminary interview questions, Figure 13-23 is a survey of transition needs, and Figure 13-24 is a work personality profile.

Career Assessment

Career assessment involves evaluating a broad range of practical life skills (vocational competencies, social behaviors, functional academics, and daily life skills) that are part of living and working as an adult, usually started in the elementary grades. (See Figure 13-25 for a career development checklist, Figure 13-26 for a job environment cluster assessment; and Figure 13-27 for a career education checklist.

Work-Sample Analysis

Work samples are used to evaluate specific and general work skills, traits, and characteristics. They may be produced by students as they work individually, in a cooperative group, or on a whole-class project. Work samples can simulate vocational/work-setting tasks that assess students' capability and involve tasks, materials, tools, and equipment taken from real jobs or job clusters that are used to measure vocational interest and potential (Venn, 2004). When work samples are standardized, or norm-referenced, variables such as students' production rates can be compared with the rates of typical workers in competitive employment (Venn, 2004). Teacher-made work samples are generally authentic, simulated examples of work experiences. They emphasize performance skills and are used to identify strengths and weaknesses. The purpose of

Figure 13–23 Survey of Transition Needs

Statement of Transition Needs

Student Name: _____ School Name: _____

DOB:_____ Age:_____ Grade:_____ Projected Year of Graduation:_____IEP/ITP Date:_____

Employment	**Statement of Transition Needs**
1. Knows job requirements and demands.	_____
2. Makes informed choices among occupational alternatives.	_____
3. Knows how to get a job.	_____
4. Demonstrates general job skills and work attitudes.	_____
5. Has the specific job skills.	_____

Future Education/Training

6. Knows how to gain entry into a community
   employment training program. _____
7. Knows how to gain entry into a GED program. _____
8. Knows how to gain entry into a vocational/technical school. _____
9. Knows how to gain entry into a college or university. _____
10. Can succeed in a postsecondary program. _____

Daily Living

11. Maintains personal grooming and hygiene. _____
12. Knows how to locate a place to live. _____
13. Knows how to set up living arrangements. _____
14. Performs everyday household tasks. _____
15. Manages own money. _____
16. Uses local transportation systems. _____

Leisure Activities

17. Performs indoor leisure activities. _____
18. Performs outdoor leisure activities. _____
19. Uses settings that provide entertainment. _____

Community Participation

20. Knows his or her basic legal rights. _____
21. Participates as an active citizen. _____
22. Makes legal decisions affecting his or her life. _____
23. Locates community services and resources. _____
24. Uses services and resources successfully. _____
25. Knows how to obtain financial services. _____

Health

26. Maintains good physical health. _____
27. Addresses physical problems. _____
28. Maintains good mental health. _____
29. Addresses mental health problems. _____
30. Knows how the reproductive system works. _____
31. Makes informed choices regarding sexual behavior. _____

Figure 13–23 *(Continued)*

Self-Determination	Statement of Transition Needs
32. Recognizes and accepts own strengths and limitations.	_____
33. Expresses feeling and ideas appropriately.	_____
34. Expresses feelings and ideas to others confidently.	_____
35. Sets personal goals.	_____
36. Makes personal decisions.	_____

Communication

37. Has needed speaking skills.	_____
38. Has needed listening skills.	_____
39. Has needed reading skills.	_____
40. Has needed writing skills.	_____

Interpersonal Relationships

41. Gets along well with family members.	_____
42. Knowledgeable of and possesses skills of parenting.	_____
43. Establishes and maintains friendships.	_____
44. Knowledgeable of appropriate social behavior in a variety of settings.	_____
45. Possess skills for getting along with coworkers.	_____
46. Possesses skills for getting along with supervisor.	_____

Copyright: PRO-ED from Informal Assessments for Transition Planning by G. M. Clark, J. R. Patton, & L. R. Moulton Appendix A—pages 151–153.

Figure 13–24 Work Personality Profile

Please describe the client's observed work performance using the five options listed below to complete the 58 behavioral items.

    4 = a definite strength, an employability asset
    3 = adequate performance, not a particular strength
    2 = performance inconsistent, potentially an employability problem
    1 = a problem area, will definitely limit the person's chances for employment
    X = no opportunity to observe the behavior

_____ 1. Sufficiently alert and aware
_____ 2. Learns new assignments quickly
_____ 3. Works steadily during entire work period
_____ 4. Accepts changes in work assignments
_____ 5. Needs virtually no direct supervision
_____ 6. Requests help in an appropriate fashion
_____ 7. Approaches supervisory personnel with confidence
_____ 8. Is appropriately friendly with supervisor
_____ 9. Shows pride in group effort
_____ 10. Shows interest in what others are doing

Figure 13–24 *(Continued)*

_____	11.	Expresses likes and dislikes appropriately
_____	12.	Initiates work-related activities on time
_____	13.	Accepts work assignments with instructions from supervisor without arguing
_____	14.	Improves performance when shown how
_____	15.	Works at routine jobs without resistance
_____	16.	Expresses willingness to try new assignments
_____	17.	Carries out assigned tasks without prompting
_____	18.	Asks for further instructions if task is not clear
_____	19.	Accepts correction without becoming upset
_____	20.	Discusses personal problems with supervisor only if work related
_____	21.	Accepts assignment for group tasks
_____	22.	Seeks out coworkers to be friends
_____	23.	Responds when others initiate conversation
_____	24.	Conforms to rules and regulations
_____	25.	Maintains satisfactory personal hygiene habits
_____	26.	Changes work methods when instructed to do so
_____	27.	Pays attention to details while working
_____	28.	Maintains productivity despite change in routine
_____	29.	Recognizes own mistakes
_____	30.	Asks for help when having difficulty with tasks
_____	31.	Comfortable with supervisor
_____	32.	Gets along with staff
_____	33.	Works comfortably in group tasks
_____	34.	Appears comfortable in social interactions
_____	35.	Initiates conversations with others
_____	36.	Displays good judgment in use of obscenities and vulgarities
_____	37.	Arrives appropriately dressed for work
_____	38.	Maintains improved work procedures after correction
_____	39.	Maintains work pace even if distractions occur
_____	40.	Performs satisfactorily on tasks that require variety and change
_____	41.	Initiates action to correct own mistakes
_____	42.	Performance remains stable in supervisor's presence
_____	43.	Supportive of others in group tasks
_____	44.	Joins social groups when they are available
_____	45.	Listens while other person speaks, avoids interrupting
_____	46.	Expresses pleasure in accomplishment
_____	47.	Listens to instructions or corrections attentively
_____	48.	Moves from job to job easily
_____	49.	Needs less than average amount of supervision
_____	50.	Offers assistance to coworkers when appropriate
_____	51.	Is sought out frequently by coworkers
_____	52.	Expresses positive feelings, such as praise, liking for others
_____	53.	Displays good judgment in playing practical jokes or "horsing around"
_____	54.	Transfers previously learned skills to new tasks
_____	55.	Handles problems with only occasional help
_____	56.	Assumes assigned role in group tasks
_____	57.	Expresses negative feelings appropriately, such as anger, fear, sadness
_____	58.	Controls temper

Source: "The Work Personality Profile," by R. T. Roessler and B. Bolton, 1986, *Vocational Evaluation and Work Adjustment Bulletin*, 18(1), pp. 8–11. Copyright 1986 by Vocational Evaluation and Work Adjustment Bulletin. Reprinted with permission.

Figure 13–25   Career Development Checklist

	Yes	No
Career Awareness		
• Can identify parents' and other family members' jobs	____	____
• Can describe what parents and others do on their jobs	____	____
• Can name and describe at least 10 different occupations	____	____
• Can describe how people get jobs	____	____
• Can describe at least three jobs to investigate	____	____
• Can discuss what happens if adults cannot or do not work	____	____
• Can identify why people have to get along with each other to work	____	____
Career Exploration		
• Can discern the difference between a job and a career	____	____
• Can identify three ways to find out about different occupations	____	____
• Can state at least three things they want in a job	____	____
• Can identify the steps in finding a job	____	____
• Can identify at least three careers they want to explore	____	____
• Can state preferences for indoor vs. outdoor work, solitary work vs. working with others, and working with their hands and tools/machines vs. working strictly with their minds	____	____
• Can discuss why interviews are important	____	____
• Can identify their strengths, abilities, skills, learning styles, and special needs regarding work or specific jobs	____	____
Career Preparation		
• Can identify career/vocational courses they want to take in school	____	____
• Can describe the educational and work requirements of specific careers and jobs	____	____
• Can identify where education and training can be obtained	____	____
• Can explain steps in acquiring the skills necessary to enter a chosen field or job	____	____
• Can describe entry-level skills, course or job requirements, and exit-level competencies to succeed in courses	____	____
• Can identify community and educational options and alternatives to gaining education and employment in a chosen field	____	____
• Can identify the worker characteristics and skills for working with others that are required in a chosen field or job	____	____
Career Assimilation		
• Can identify steps to take to advance in their place of employment	____	____
• Can identify educational benefits and ways of gaining additional training through their employment	____	____
• Can explain fields that are related to their current work in which they could transfer	____	____

Source: Assess for Success: Handbook on Transition Assessment, by P. Stilington, P. Neubert, W. Begun, R. Lombard, & P. Leconte, 1996. Copyright © 1996 by The Council for Exceptional Children. Reprinted with permission.

Figure 13–26   Demands of the Job—Environmental Clusters

Directions:

Step 1: For each environmental cluster, have the respondent rate each descriptor and mark on the rating scale as indicated.
   For example:
   Sit—What percentage of the time must the participant sit on the job?
   Identify and Set Goals—How critical for success is the ability to identify and set goals on the job? If needed, use comment area for additional notes.

Step 2: Note probability of possible **Accommodations/Modifications** in the environment for each descriptor. If needed, use comment area for additional notes.

Step 3: Note possible environmental **Supports,** if needed, use comment area for additional notes.

General Work Behaviors (Attitudes)

	Not Critical	Mildly Critical	Somewhat Critical	Critical	NA	Low Prob.	2	3	High Prob.	Supports/People
1. Attendance										
2. Punctuality										
3. Grooming/hygiene										
4. Attends to task (concentration)										
5. Work pace										
6. Organization										
7. Works independently										
8. Follows directions										
9. Flexibility (changes in job routine)										
10. Adheres to rules and safety										
11. Self-aware; monitors errors										
12. Identifies and sets goals										
13. Information retrieval and use (thinks on feet)										
14. Prioritizes tasks										

Comments:

Physical Demands of the Job

	Not Critical	Mildly Critical	Somewhat Critical	Critical	NA	Low Prob.	2	3	High Prob.	Supports/People
1. Sitting (% of job time)										
2. Standing/walking (% of job time)										
3. Strength										
4. Eye-hand coordination/manual dexterity										
5. Vision										
6. Hearing										
7. Work hours										

Comments:

Figure 13–26 *(Continued)*

Working Conditions (Physical)

	Not Critical	Mildly Critical	Somewhat Critical	Critical	NA	Accommodations/ Modifications Low Prob.	2	3	High Prob.	Supports/ People
1. Inside										
2. Variation in environmental temperature										
3. Presence of fumes, dust, odor in the air										
4. Mechanical hazards										
5. Noise										
6. Wet/damp										
7. Presence of dirt in environment										
8. Varied lighting										
9. Frequent changes/multiple placements on the job										

Comments:

Educational Demands

	Not Critical	Mildly Critical	Somewhat Critical	Critical	NA	Accommodations/ Modifications Low Prob.	2	3	High Prob.	Supports/ People
1. Educational requirement										
2. Specialized job-related vocabulary										
3. Reading comprehension										
4. Writing										
5. Math computation										
6. Attention to visual detail										
7. Oral communication—receptive (listening, remembering, understanding)										
8. Oral communication—expressive (speaking)										
9. Problem solving										
10. Computer skills										
11. Use of specialized equipment										

Comments:

Social Interaction on the job

	Not Critical	Mildly Critical	Somewhat Critical	Critical	NA	Accommodations/ Modifications Low Prob.	2	3	High Prob.	Supports/ People
1. Interacts with others (coworkers, customers)										
2. Interacts with supervisors										

Figure 13–26 *(Continued)*

Social Interaction on the job *(Continued)*	Not Critical	Mildly Critical	Somewhat Critical	Critical	NA	Low Prob.	2	3	High Prob.	Supports/ People
						Accommodations/ Modifications				
3. Asks for assistance										
4. Accepts and uses feedback										
5. Group work/team work										
6. Takes supervision from more than one supervisor/coworker										
Comments:										

Source: "Environmental Assessment" by M. Waintrup and P. Kelley, in *Functional Assessment in Transition and Rehabilitation for Adolescents and Adults with Learning Disabilities* (pp. 59–62), by M. Bullis and C. Davis (Eds.), 1999, Austin ,TX: PRO-ED; Copyright 1999 by PRO-ED, Inc. Reprinted with permission.

Figure 13–27   Career Education Checklist

Exploration Phase

Enter the date of evaluation in the boxes at the right.

Self	Seldom	Sometimes	Most of the Time
1. Can express his/her personal interests			
2. Knows how s/he feels about him/herself and how this affects him/her			
3. Aware of physical strengths and abilities			
Interpersonal Relations			
1. Displays appropriate emotional characteristics when interacting with others			
2. Knows what others think of him/her			
3. Understands and appreciates different characteristics in different people			
4. Knows that one will interact in different groups in different situations			
Self and Society			
1. Able to verbalize his/her own personal values			
2. Understands that people need to work if society is to survive			
3. Understands that the world is changing and jobs are changing			
Decision Making			
1. Has some long-term goals regarding a career			
2. Knows his/her abilities, qualities, values, and hopes			
3. Takes responsibilities for his/her decisions			
4. Matches his/her personal characteristics with possible career choices			
5. Understands what s/he needs to know for various career choices			
Economics			
1. Knows difference between consumers and producers			
2. Understands how supply and demand affects work world			

Figure 13–27 *(Continued)*

Economics *(Continued)*	Seldom	Sometimes	Most of the Time
3. Understands how world of work (income, hours, etc.) affects lifestyle of individuals			
4. Understands the concept of fringe benefits, insurance, etc.			
5. Understands minimum wage and hour laws, social security, and federal and state income tax			
Occupational Knowledge			
1. Knows how to use education as aid in developing skills for occupations			
2. Explores a wide range of occupations			
3. Knows what skills and education are needed for various jobs			
4. Knows general concept of what needs to be done to advance in various jobs			
5. Understands various working conditions with various jobs			
6. Understands role of employer, employee, manager, etc.			
7. Understands law of supply and demand as it applies to obtaining a job			
8. Understands how to seek employment			
Work Attitudes and Behaviors			
1. Displays behavior appropriate for school community			
2. Understands how working at a job integrates one into the community			
3. Understands that personal satisfaction is gained from work and leisure			
4. Understands that social recognition is related to work			
5. Understands monetary rewards come from work			
6. Understands that one may change jobs as one gets older and matures			

Source: Career/Transition Planning Forms, AEA 4, by AEA Education Agency 4, n.d., Sioux Center, IA: Author. Copyright by AEA Education Agency 4. Reprinted with permission.

work samples is to evaluate specific work-study skills before placement in college, vocational training, or work settings. They are used for career exploration and to assess work habits. They can help to determine how well students can work independently, follow directions, and complete assigned tasks. They can also ascertain the quality of the final product and students' physical coordination, dexterity, and strength.

Self-Determination Assessment

Self-determination assessment focuses on the four essential characteristics conceptualized by Wehmeyer (2001), including assessing whether (1) the person acted autonomously, (2) the behavior is self-regulated, (3) the person initiated and responded to the event, and (4) the person acted in a self-realizing manner. Self-determination emerges across one's lifespan as children and adults learn the skills, attitudes, and abilities necessary to act as the primary causal agent in their life and to make choices and decisions regarding one's quality of life, free from undue external influence or interference (Wehmeyer, 2001, p. 7). Research has demonstrated a positive relationship between self-determination and improved postschool outcomes (Wehmeyer & Schwartz, 1998). (See Figures 13–28 for a self-determination skill checklist.)

Figure 13–28   Self-Determination Skills Checklist

Does the student:

Choice-making Skills

- identify interests and preferences?
- select an option based on interests and preferences?

Problem-solving Skills

- identify and define a problem?
- generate potential solutions?

Decision-making Skills

- reflect on and evaluate the options?
- select between options and make a choice?

Goal-setting and Attainment Skills

- define and articulate a goal?
- identify current status in relation to the goal?
- develop an action plan?
- evaluate progress toward achieving the goal?

Self-regulation Skills

- problem solve?
- employ self-management strategies (e.g., anger control)?

Self-advocacy Skills

- advocate on his or her own behalf?
- recognize basic rights and responsibilities (knowledge)?
- use self-advocacy skills?
- be an effective team member (at individual/system level)?

Self-awareness and Self-knowledge Skills

- know one's strengths and limitations?
- identify common psychological/physical needs of people?
- recognize differences among people?
- understand how one's actions influence others?

Self-efficacy Skills

- believe in ability to successfully engage in a specific behavior within a certain context?

Source: Powers, Turner A.; Westwood, D.; Matuszewski, JU.; Wilson, R.; Phillips, A., 2001; Wehmeyer & Schwartz, 1998 in TEC, 2004, Jan, pp. 11.

In order to determine whether and how the student's level of self-determination and the potential work or study program and environment will facilitate self-determination, assessment should focus on the following questions (Brolin & Loyd, 2004):

Does the student

- believe he or she can control outcomes?
- believe he or she can be effective?
- know his or her strengths and weaknesses?
- have a positive self-concept?
- have good self-esteem?

Does the program

- provide curricula appropriate for career choice?
- encourage choice and preferences?
- promote interactions with peers without disabilities?

- provide access to good role models?
- facilitate experiences in which success is assured?
- allow control in decision making?
- promote goal setting?
- foster social problem-solving?
- support and encourage self-advocacy?
- encourage independence in locating and using sources of assistance?
- provide opportunities to develop and evaluate alternatives?
- promote an awareness of how behavior affects others?
- provide opportunities to accept and give praise and criticism?

Checklists and Rating Scales

Once the postsecondary options have been decided and specific skills needed for the program or job setting have been determined through an ecological or career performance assessment, a checklist or rating scale needs to be developed. (See Figures 13–29 and Figure 13–30.) These tools provide a scope and sequence of required skills. The series of skills needed for the new setting can be developed directly from students' IEP goals and objectives. The checklist can be used to denote progress and skill mastery.

Performance Assessment

Performance assessments "require students to generate rather than choose a response; [they] require students to actively accomplish complex and significant tasks while bringing to bear prior knowledge, recent learning, and relevant skills to solve problems" (Herman, Aschbacher, & Winters, 1992, p. 2). Using this method, assessment is not separate from learning, the two are integrally linked (Thoma & Held, 2002). (See Figure 13–31 for examples of authentic independent living and job-related performance assessment tasks.)

Portfolios

Portfolios provide a record of students' performance and progress in skill development over time and represent their interests, goals, and work output. The contents of a vocational or career-related portfolio generally include samples of student work completed in natural settings under authentic conditions. Students can actively participate in the compilation of their portfolios by being involved in selecting the items that are included. (See Figure 13–32.) Students can also be involved in self-evaluation by rating and maintaining checklists to monitor their competency in particular areas. They can use their portfolios to document their accomplishments when applying to a college or vocational training program or when being interviewed by a prospective employer. (Figure 13–33 lists items that could be included in a secondary-level vocational portfolio.)

Curriculum-Based Vocational Assessment

Curriculum-based vocational assessment (CBVA) is used to evaluate acquisition of vocational and related skills embedded within content and applied courses. It is based on ongoing performance and course content in the classroom or in community work experience activities (Bisconer, Strodden, & Porter, 1993). This method of assessment is structured on vocational skill development and concurrent work experience, as well as employment-related academic skills taught in school.

Figure 13–29   Postsecondary Personal Skills Checklist

	Yes	No	NA
Work-Study Skills			
• Works independently	_____	_____	_____
• Maintains attention to work tasks	_____	_____	_____
• Follows directions accurately	_____	_____	_____
• Organizes materials well	_____	_____	_____
• Budgets time wisely	_____	_____	_____
• Has regular attendance	_____	_____	_____
• Arrives to appointments and class on time	_____	_____	_____
• Arrives prepared with needed materials	_____	_____	_____
• Plans for short- and long-term assignments	_____	_____	_____
• Completes tasks within allotted time	_____	_____	_____
• Meets work deadlines	_____	_____	_____
• Uses test-preparation and test-taking skills	_____	_____	_____
• Uses outlining and note-taking skills	_____	_____	_____
• Proofreads work before submission	_____	_____	_____
• Completes tasks accurately	_____	_____	_____
• Begins tasks after instructions are given	_____	_____	_____
• Prioritizes assignments	_____	_____	_____
• Performs tasks in front of others	_____	_____	_____
• Perseveres rather than giving up	_____	_____	_____
• Follows routine or schedule	_____	_____	_____
• Makes transitions smoothly from task to task	_____	_____	_____
• Seeks assistance in an appropriate manner	_____	_____	_____
• Knows who to go to for help	_____	_____	_____
• Adjusts to changes; is flexible	_____	_____	_____
• Uses free time constructively	_____	_____	_____
Social/Affective Skills			
• Asks appropriate questions	_____	_____	_____
• Interprets feedback appropriately	_____	_____	_____
• Interacts well in group discussions	_____	_____	_____
• Gets along with coworkers and classmates	_____	_____	_____
• Relates appropriately to authority figures	_____	_____	_____
• Demonstrates healthy self-concept	_____	_____	_____
• Takes constructive criticism	_____	_____	_____
• Deals with frustration appropriately	_____	_____	_____
• Takes personal responsibility	_____	_____	_____
• Maintains a level of interest, motivation	_____	_____	_____
• Accepts individual differences	_____	_____	_____
• Relates to community members	_____	_____	_____
Interpersonal Skills			
• Dresses and grooms appropriately for the setting	_____	_____	_____
• Is self-motivated to learn, to take on tasks	_____	_____	_____
• Demonstrates a positive self-attitude	_____	_____	_____
• Adapts to change in routine and environment	_____	_____	_____
• Demonstrates ethical behavior			

Figure 13–29 (*Continued*)

	Yes	No	NA
• Accepts consequences for own behavior	____	____	____
• Accepts constructive criticism	____	____	____
• Takes responsibility for personal actions and items	____	____	____
• Controls impulsivity	____	____	____
• Maintains good hygiene	____	____	____
• Cooperates in group tasks	____	____	____
• Demonstrates positive attitude toward others	____	____	____
• Requests help appropriately	____	____	____
• Reads body clues	____	____	____
• Shows respect for others' feelings and property	____	____	____
• Accepts authority	____	____	____
• Complies with rules	____	____	____
• Copes with feelings of anger, frustration, stress	____	____	____
• Greets others pleasantly	____	____	____
• Recognizes and helps those in need	____	____	____
• Does not interrupt others	____	____	____
• Demonstrates good manners	____	____	____
• Is not easily distracted	____	____	____
• Interacts well with authority	____	____	____
• Plans and directs own life course	____	____	____
• Makes decisions	____	____	____

Communication Skills

	Yes	No	NA
• Expresses feelings, communicates verbally	____	____	____
• Listens to speaker, does not interrupt	____	____	____
• Contributes to group discussions	____	____	____
• Initiates or terminates conversations	____	____	____
• Listens to and interprets orally presented information	____	____	____

Figure 13–30 Functional Skills Rating Scale

Is the student able to:		Ratings			

Cognition/Information Processing Skills

• sequence information?	1	2	3	4	5
• understand abstract concepts?	1	2	3	4	5
• reason abstractly?	1	2	3	4	5
• retain information (short-term)?	1	2	3	4	5
• retain information (long-term)?	1	2	3	4	5
• organize and process information?	1	2	3	4	5
• make associations?	1	2	3	4	5
• make generalizations?	1	2	3	4	5
• apply metacognitive strategies?	1	2	3	4	5

Language Skills

• speak intelligibly?	1	2	3	4	5
• grasp verbal information?	1	2	3	4	5

Figure 13–30 *(Continued)*

• use appropriate vocabulary?	1	2	3	4	5
• understand words in context?	1	2	3	4	5
• express self clearly and precisely?	1	2	3	4	5
• speak with correct sentence structure?	1	2	3	4	5
• write clearly and precisely?	1	2	3	4	5
• use correct sentence structure?	1	2	3	4	5
• use correct spelling, grammar, punctuation?	1	2	3	4	5

Academic Skills

• read fluently with comprehension?	1	2	3	4	5
• express thoughts in writing?	1	2	3	4	5
• solve basic math computation and word problems?	1	2	3	4	5
• use correct spelling, grammar, punctuation?	1	2	3	4	5
• write legibly?	1	2	3	4	5

Environmental Adaptation Skills

• follow safety precautions?	1	2	3	4	5
• deal calmly with emergencies?	1	2	3	4	5
• move appropriately around surroundings?	1	2	3	4	5
• care appropriately for things in the environment?	1	2	3	4	5
• locate and return items used?	1	2	3	4	5
• take responsibility for assigned work?	1	2	3	4	5
• enter and leave premises appropriately?	1	2	3	4	5

Rating Scale: 1 = Never observed; 2 = Occasionally observed; 3 = Observed about half the time; 4 = Often observed; 5 = Always observed

---

Figure 13–31   Independent Living and Employment Performance Assessment Activities

- Develop a personal budget
- Double a recipe
- Use newspapers or catalogs to comparison shop for a refrigerator
- Plan the travel route from home to a potential job site
- Make menus for a week and a list of the needed grocery items
- Design a teen recreation center
- Write classified ads
- Role-play an interview with potential employers
- Interview the manager of a company
- Tape, edit, and produce a video of workers on the job

Figure 13–32   Career Portfolio Rating Sale

Directions: Evaluate the student, using the rating scale on the right. Circle the appropriate number to indicate the degree of competency. The rating for each task should reflect job readiness rather than the grade given in the class.

Employability Skills (Competencies that will enable the individual to obtain and retain a job)

The student can: **SCALE**

1. Establish realistic career goals/choices.	N	1	2	3	4
2. Display a positive attitude toward work (work ethic).	N	1	2	3	4

Figure 13–32 *(Continued)*

3.	Demonstrate a good record of attendance.	N	1	2	3	4
4.	Display punctuality at school, work, and following breaks.	N	1	2	3	4
5.	Display a pride in work.	N	1	2	3	4
6.	Demonstrate honesty.	N	1	2	3	4
7.	Demonstrate dependability.	N	1	2	3	4
8.	Observe and follow classroom/work rules and regulations.	N	1	2	3	4
9.	Display initiative (e.g., begin work without being asked, assume additional responsibility, help others voluntarily).	N	1	2	3	4
10.	Work at a consistent pace.	N	1	2	3	4
11.	Manage time appropriately.	N	1	2	3	4
12.	Demonstrate work stability (remain on the job/task until completed).	N	1	2	3	4
13.	Work effectively under pressure or within time limits.	N	1	2	3	4
14.	Keep work area clean.	N	1	2	3	4
15.	Display respect for other people.	N	1	2	3	4
16.	Show respect for property of others.	N	1	2	3	4
17.	Seek help when needed.	N	1	2	3	4
18.	React appropriately to constructive criticism.	N	1	2	3	4
19.	Accept praise appropriately.	N	1	2	3	4
20.	Assume responsibility for own actions/behaviors.	N	1	2	3	4
21.	Demonstrate appropriate reactions to own mistakes (e.g., acceptance, correction).	N	1	2	3	4
22.	Demonstrate problem-solving skills (e.g., identify problem, list possible solutions, select solution, evaluate results).	N	1	2	3	4
23.	Demonstrate willingness to learn new skills/information.	N	1	2	3	4
24.	Demonstrate adaptability to changing situations.	N	1	2	3	4
25.	Follow safety regulations.	N	1	2	3	4
26.	Respond appropriately to classroom and/or job-related emergencies.	N	1	2	3	4
27.	Practice good hygiene/grooming.	N	1	2	3	4
28.	Dress appropriately for work/specific job.	N	1	2	3	4
29.	Correctly complete a job application.	N	1	2	3	4
30.	Demonstrate appropriate job interviewing skills.	N	1	2	3	4
31.	Demonstrate the ability to complete a job resume.	N	1	2	3	4

Name of student: _____

Name of rater: _____

Date: _____

Source: Transition Planning: Developing a Career Portfolio for Students with Disabilities, by M. Sarkees-Wircenski and J. L. Wircenski, 1994, Cancer Development for Exceptional Individuals 17(2), p. 208. Copyright 1994 by Division on Career Development and Transition, The Council for Exceptional Children.

Figure 13–33 Suggestions for Secondary-Level Vocational Portfolio Entries

- Resumes
- Business projects
- Personal essays
- Aptitude/Achievement test results
- Reports of simulated work experiences
- Behavior rating scales
- Teachers' narrative progress reports
- Photographs of work products
- Sample business forms
- Artwork, creative pieces
- Audiotapes of practice interviews
- Interest surveys
- Videotapes of job role-playing
- Work-study skill checklists
- References from volunteer work
- CD-ROMs/disks of projects

ONLINE SUPPORTS

National Information Center for Children and Youth with Disabilities, http://www.nichcy.org

Assessing Students for Workplace Readiness, http://vocserve.berkeley. edu/centerFicus/cf15.html

Vocational Evaluation and Work Adjustment Association http://www.fairaccess.org/ vewaa_policy.htm

CBVA can also be used for programmatic evaluation of the curriculum and vocational instructional areas by charting students' progress through regular probing to determine specific skill mastery. It is a useful analytical tool used for measuring curricular impact on student outcomes and for providing information concerning students' strengths and weaknesses (Kohler, 1994). Based on CBVA results, students' programs can be adjusted for individual differences in progress.

SUMMARY POINTS

- Transitions are a normal aspect of human experience, occurring as individuals move through life. Some transitions are expected and planned for, others are unexpected, stressful, and life altering. Educational transitions are primarily passages from one academic grade, program, or experience to another.

- The main components of the transition process are assessment, planning, and follow-through.

- Research indicates that three factors influence students' transition experience: their skills and prior school-related experiences, their home lives, and classroom characteristics.

- The family assessment component in the IFSP is intended to determine the child's needs, the family's strengths and needs, and impact the child's disability has on family functioning and parent-child interactions.

- According to IDEA-2004, transition planning needs to begin no later than the first IEP in effect when the student is 16 years with a statement addressing appropriate transition assessments and transition services, and beginning no later than one year before the student reaches the age of majority, a statement informing the student of their rights.

- Play-based assessment involves observing children in a play environment where there are toys, dolls, and other interesting material and equipment that entice them to explore and initiate their own play actions and interactions. Arena assessment is a procedure in which family members and early childhood specialists collaborate in the assessment process. One member of the group interacts with the child while the other members record their observations and later discuss their observations.

- Person-centered assessment and planning focus on the unique and specific wants and needs of the student. This type of assessment is generally used as part of the transition planning process as students develop insight into who they are, who they want to be, where they want to go, and what they want to do with their lives.

- Situational assessment is the evaluation of students' work and job-related performance and functional skills under actual conditions in authentic environments, such as the job site.

Chapter Check-Ups

1. What does IDEA-2004 mandate regarding transition of the adolescent?
2. Discuss the issue of administering formal, standardized versus informal, more authentic assessment measures for transition at the early childhood level. What does the NAEYC advocate regarding developmental assessment?

3. Describe the key components that need to be the focus of assessment as students transition from (a) elementary to middle school; (b) middle to high school; (c) special to general education classes; and (d) hospital/rehabilitation/home after an illness and return to school.

4. How would a postsecondary student or employee qualify for "reasonable" accommodations? Based on your understanding of what is considered to be reasonable, describe an accommodation that would likely be considered as "unreasonable" and explain why.

5. Describe a situation in which a teacher might use an (a) audiotape and/or (b) a videotape as an assessment tool to record behavior.

Practical Application Assessment Activities

1. Interview employers of local establishments (e.g., grocery stores, fast food restaurants) to determine job prerequisites and responsibilities. Ask the employers what behaviors/skills are required for successful employment (e.g., cashier, cook, server). Identify how these required behaviors/skills can be assessed and monitored as part of the transition plan. Task analysis may be required.

2. Design a transition plan for a five-year-old preschooler who is physically disabled and visually impaired and is about to enter an inclusion kindergarten class.

3. Observe young children playing in small and large group activities (e.g., during playtime in a preschool class, at a birthday party). Identify the different stages of play you observe and describe the language and social interaction skills you note as they play.

4. Observe in a class for high school students who have cognitive and/or physical disabilities. Ask the academic teacher and the vocational education teacher about the types of learning, life and work-skill curricular activities in the students' programs. Also ask what types of aptitude, interest, and achievement tests are used as a basis for developing secondary transition plans.

Connection Between CEC, PRAXIS, and INTASC Standards and Chapter 13

The Council for Exceptional Children—Professional Standards

Council for Exceptional Children
The voice and vision of special education

Standard 3 Individual Learning Differences

1. Effects an exceptional condition can have on an individual's life.

2. Impact of learners' academic and social abilities, attitudes, interests, and values on instruction and career development.

3. Variations in beliefs, traditions, and values across and within cultures and their effects on relationships among individuals with exceptional learning needs, their family, and schooling.

Standard 4 Instructional Strategies

5. Use procedures to increase the individual's self-awareness, self-management, self-control, self-reliance, and self-esteem.

6. Use strategies that promote successful transitions for individuals with exceptional learning needs.

Standard 5 Learning Environments and Social Interactions

7. Strategies for preparing individuals to live harmoniously and productively in a culturally diverse world.

12. Identify realistic expectations for personal and social behavior in various settings.

13. Identify supports needed for integration into various program placements.

14. Design learning environments that encourage active participation in individual and group activities.

16. Use performance data and information from all stakeholders to make or suggest modifications in learning environments.

18. Teach self-advocacy.

19. Create an environment that encourages self-advocacy and increased independence.

Standard 7 Instructional Planning

7. Develop and implement comprehensive, longitudinal individualized programs in collaboration with team members.

8. Involve the individual and family in setting instructional goals and monitoring progress.

9. Use functional assessments to develop intervention plans.

10. Use task analysis.

12. Integrate affective, social, and life skills with academic curricula.

Standard 8 Assessment

1. Basic terminology used in assessment.

2. Legal provisions and ethical principles regarding assessment of individuals.

6. Gather relevant background information.

7. Administer nonbiased formal and informal assessments.

9. Develop or modify individualized assessment strategies.

10. Interpret information from formal and informal assessments.

11. Use assessment information in making eligibility, program, and placement decisions for individuals with exceptional learning needs, including those from culturally and/or linguistically diverse backgrounds.

12. Report assessment results to all stakeholders using effective communication skills.

13. Evaluate instruction and monitor progress of individuals with exceptional learning needs.

14. Create and maintain records.

Standard 10 Collaboration

2. Roles of individuals with exceptional learning needs, families, and school and community personnel in planning of an individualized program.

6. Collaborate with families and others in assessment of individuals with exceptional learning needs.

8. Assist individuals with exceptional learning needs and their families in becoming active participants in the educational team.

9. Plan and conduct collaborative conferences with individuals with exceptional learning needs and their families.
10. Collaborate with school personnel and community members in integrating individuals with exceptional learning needs into various settings.
11. Use group problem-solving skills to develop, implement, and evaluate collaborative activities.
13. Communicate with school personnel about the characteristics and needs of individuals.

PRAXIS Standards for Special Education

THE PRAXIS SERIES™

Standard 1 Understanding Exceptionalities

3. Basic concepts in special education, including definitions of all major categories and specific disabilities; causation and prevention of disability; the nature of behaviors, including frequency, duration, intensity, and degrees of severity; and classification of students with disabilities, including classifications as represented in IDEA and labeling of students.

Standard 2 Legal and Societal Issues

1. Federal laws and landmark legal cases related to special education.
2. Issues related to school, family, and/or community, such as teacher advocacy for students and families, including advocating for educational change and developing students' self-advocacy; family participation and support systems; public attitudes toward individuals with disabilities; and cultural and community influences.

Standard 3 Delivery of Services to Students with Disabilities

3. Assessment, including how to modify, construct, or select and conduct nondiscriminatory and appropriate informal and formal assessment procedures; how to interpret standardized and specialized assessment results; how to use evaluation result for various purposes, including monitoring instruction and IEP/ITP development; and how to prepare written reports and communicate findings to others.
4. Placement and program issues (including continuum of services; mainstreaming; integration; inclusion; least restrictive environment; noncategorical, categorical, and cross-categorical programs; related services; early intervention; community-based training; transition of students into and within special education placements; postschool transition; and access to assistive technology).

INTASC Standards for Teacher Education

Standard 8

The teacher understands and uses formal and informal assessment strategies to evaluate and ensure the continuous intellectual, social, and physical development of the learner.

Standard 10

The teacher fosters relationships with school colleagues, parents, and agencies in the larger community to support students' learning and well-being.

References

A Focus on Fluency Forum, San Francisco, CA. Retrieved September 1, 2004, from www.prel.org/programs/rel/fluency/Torgesen.ppt.

Abedi, J. (2000, April). *Confounding students' performance and their language background.* Paper presented at the meeting of the American Educational Research Association, New Orleans, LA.

Adams, M. R. (1988). Based on an article in *Speech News*, Baylor College Nedicine, November 1983.

Alberto, P. A., & Troutman, A. C. (2002). *Applied behavior analysis for teachers* (6th ed.). Upper Saddle River, NJ: Merrill/Prentice Hall.

Alliance Technical Assistance Alliance for Parent Centers (2001). *Evaluation: What does it mean for your child?* Minneapolis, MN: Pacer Center, Inc.

[The] Alliance (Technical Assistance Alliance for Parent Centers). (2001). *Evaluation: What does it mean for your child?* Minneapolis, MN: Pacer Center.

Allinder, R. M. (1996). When some is not better than none: Effects of differential implementation of curriculum-based measurement. *Exceptional Children, 62*(6), 525–535.

Alper, S., & Mills, K. (2001). Nonstandardized assessment in inclusive school settings. In A. S. Alper, D. L. Ryndak, & C. N. Schloss, (Eds.), *Alternate assessment of students with disabilities in inclusive settings*

(pp. 54–74). Needham Heights, MA: Allyn & Bacon.

Alper, S., Ryndak, D. L., & Schloss, C. N. (2001). *Alternate assessment of students with disabilities in inclusive settings.* Needham Heights, MA: Allyn & Bacon.

American Educational Research Association (AERA), American Psychological Association (APA), & National Council on Measurement in Education (NCME). (1999). *Standards for educational and psychological testing.* Washington, DC: AERA.

American Educational Research Association. (1999). *Standards for educational and psychological testing.* Washington, DC: American Psychological Association and National Council on Measurement in Education.

American Psychological Association. (1992). *Ethical principles of psychologists* (rev. ed.). Washington, DC: Author.

American Speech-Hearing-Language Association. (2004). Developmental language disorder. *Let's talk: For people with special communication needs, 70,* 1–2.

Anderson, E. (2002). School efforts on psychological outcomes during adolescence. *Journal of Educational Psychology, 94,* 795–809.

Anderson, N. E., & Olson, J. (1996, August). *Puerto Rico assessment of educational progress: 1996 PRAEP technical report.* Princeton, NJ: Educational Testing Service.

Anderson, N. J. (2002, April). *The role of metacognition in second language teaching and learning.* Center for Applied Linguistics Digest. Retrieved from January 2, 2004, from http://www.cal.org/resources/digest/0110anderson.html.

Anderson, R. (1998). Examining language loss in bilingual children. *The Multicultural Electronic Journal of Communication Disorders.* Retrieved June 5, 2002, from http://www.asha.ucf.edu/anderson.html.

Anderson, R. (2000). *The assessment of BICS/CALP: A developmental perspective.* http://home.earthlink.net/~psychron/ homepage.htm.

Anderson, V., & Roit, M. (1998). Reading as a gateway to language proficiency for language-minority students in elementary grades. In R. Gersten & R. Jiminez (Eds.), *Promoting language for culturally and linguistically diverse students* (pp. 42–56). Belmont, CA: Wadsworth.

Applegate, M. D., Quinn, K. B., & Applegate, A. (2004). *Critical Reading Inventory.* Upper Saddle River, NJ: Prentice Hall.

Armbruster, B. B., Lehr, F., & Osborn, J. (2001). *Put reading first: The research building blocks for teaching children to read. Kindergarten through grade 3.* Washington, DC: National Institute for Literacy.

Arter, J. & McTighe, J. (2001). *Scoring rubrics in the classroom: Using performance criteria for assessing* and improving student performance. Thousand Oaks, CA: Corwin Press.

Artiles, A. J., & Ortiz, A. A. (2002). English language learners with special education needs: Contexts and possibilities. In A. J. Artiles & A. A. Ortiz (Eds.), *English language learners with special education needs: Identification, assessment, and instruction* (pp. 3–27, 80–81). McHenry, IL: Center for Applied Linguistics and Delta Systems.

Ashlock, R. B. (2002). *Error patterns in computation* (8th ed.). Upper Saddle River, NJ: Merrill/Prentice Hall.

Audet, R. H., & Jordan, L. K. (2003). *Standards in the classroom: An implementation guide for teachers of science and mathematics.* Thousand Oaks, CA: Corwin Press.

Baca, L. M. (2002). Educating English language learners with special education needs: Trends and future directions. In A. J. Artiles & A. A. Ortiz (Eds.), *English language learners with special education needs: Identification, assessment, and instruction* (pp. 191–202). McHenry, IL: Center for Applied Linguistics and Delta Systems.

Ballard, J., Guthrie, P., McIntire, J. C., McLaughlin, M. J., Ortiz, A., & Thurlow, M. (1998). *IDEA Reauthorization: Focus on the IEP and Assessment* [Cassette Recording]. Reston, VA: Council for Exceptional Children.

Bank Street College of Education (1992, March). *News from the Center for Children and Technology and the Center for Technology in Education* 1(3) 1–6.

Bankson, N., Bernthal, J., & Hodson, B. (2004). *Speech sound disorders.* Rockville, MD: American Speech-Language-Hearing Association.

Barclay, K., & Benelli, C. (1996). Program evaluation through the eyes of a child. *Childhood Education, 72,* 91–96.

Bartel, N. R. (2004). *Teaching students with learning and behavior problems* (7th ed.). Austin, TX: Pro-Ed.

Bartel, N. R. (2004). Problems in mathematics achievement. In D. D. Hammill & N. R. Bartel (Eds.), *Teaching students with learning and behavior problems* (pp. 251–290). Austin, TX: Pro-Ed.

Beaty, J. (1997). *Observing development of the young child* (4th ed.). Upper Saddle River, NJ: Merrill/Prentice Hall.

Bender, W. N. (1998). *Learning disabilities: Characteristics, identification, and teaching strategies* (3rd ed.). Needham Heights, MA: Allyn & Bacon.

Betts, E. A. (1946). *Foundation of reading instruction.* New York: American Book.

Bialystok, E. (2001). *Bilingualism in development: Language, literacy and cognition.* Cambridge, MA: Cambridge University Press.

Bigge, J., & Stump, C. S. (1999). *Curriculum, assessment, and instruction for students with disabilities.* Belmont, CA: Wadsworth.

Bisconer, S. W., Strodden, R. A., & Porter, M. E. (1993). A psychometric evaluation of curriculum-based vocational assessment rating instruments used with students in mainstream vocational courses. *Career Development for Exceptional Individuals, 16,* 19–26.

Blalock, G., & Patton, J. R. (1996). Transition and students with learning disabilities: Creating sound futures. *Journal of Learning Disabilities, 29*(1), 7–16.

Bloom, B. (1956). *Taxonomy of educational goals: Handbook 1—Cognitive domain.* New York: McKay.

Bos, C. S., & Vaughn, S. (2002). *Strategies for teaching children with learning and behavior problems* (5th ed.). Boston: Allyn & Bacon.

Bos, C. S., & Vaughn, S. (2002). *Strategies for teaching students with learning and behavior problems* (4th ed.). Needham Heights, MA: Allyn & Bacon.

Bowe, F. (2005). *Teaching individuals with physical and multiple disabilities* (4th ed.). Upper Saddle River, NJ: Prentice Hall.

Bradley, D. F., & Calvin, M. B. (1998). Grading modified assignments: Equity or compromise? *Teaching Exceptional Children, 31*(2), 24–29.

Bredekamp, S., & Copple, C. (1997). *Developmentally appropriate practice in early childhood programs* (Rev.) Washington, DC: National Association for the Education of Young Children.

Brice, A. (2002). *The Hispanic child: Speech, language, culture and education.* Boston: Allyn & Bacon.

Bridges, L. (1995). *Assessment: Continuous learning.* Los Angeles: Galef Institute.

Brolin, D. E., & Loyd, R. J. (2004). *Career development and transition services: A functional life skills approach* (4th ed.). Upper Saddle River, NJ: Merrill/Prentice Hall.

Brown, W. H., Odom, S. L., & Holcombe, A. (1996). Observational assessment of young children's social behaviors with peers. *Early Childhood Research Quarterly, 11,* 19–41.

Bryant, B. R., & Rivera, D. P. (1995, November). *Cooperative learning: Teaching in an age of technology.* Paper presented at the meeting of the Learning Disabilities Association of Texas, Austin.

Bryant, D. P., Bryant, B. R., & Hammill, D. D. (2000). Characteristic behaviors of students with LD who have teacher-identified math weaknesses. *Journal of Learning Disabilities, 33,* 168–177, 199.

Bukowski, W. M., Sippola, L., Hoza, B., & Newcomb, A. F. (2000). Pages from a sociometric notebook: An analysis of nomination and rating scale measures of acceptance, rejection, and social preference. In A. H. N. Cillessen, & W. M. Bukowski, (Eds.), *Recent advances in the measurement of acceptance and rejection in the peer system* (pp. 11–26). San Francisco, CA: Jossey-Bass.

Bullis, M., & Davis, C. D. (1999). *Functional assessment in transition and rehabilitation for adolescents and adults with learning disorders.* Austin, TX: Pro-Ed.

Burnette, J. (2000, Fall). Improving results for culturally and linguistically diverse students. *Research Connections in Special Education, 7,* 1–2.

Burns, P. C., & Roe, B. D. (2002). *Informal Reading Inventory* (6th ed.). Boston: Houghton Mifflin.

Carlisle, J. (1999). Free recall as a test of reading comprehension for students with learning disabilities. *Learning Disability Quarterly, 22,* 11–12.

Carpenter, C. D., Ray, M. S., & Bloom, L. A. (1995). Portfolio assessment: Opportunities and challenges. *Intervention in School and Clinic, 31*(1), 34–41.

Carpenter, S. L., & King-Sears, M. E. (1998). Classroom assessment practices for instruction. In M. S. Rosenberg, L. O'Shea, & D. J. O'Shea, (Eds.), *Student teacher to master teacher* (2nd ed., pp. 89–121). Needham Heights, MA: Allyn & Bacon.

Catron, C. E., & Allen, J. (1999). *Early childhood curriculum* (2nd ed.). Upper Saddle River, NJ: Merrill/Prentice Hall.

Catron, C. E., & Allen, J. (1999). *Early childhood curriculum: A creative play model* (2nd ed). Upper Saddle River, NJ: Merrill/Prentice Hall.

Cegelka, P. T. (1995). An overview of effective education for students with learning problems. In P. T. Cegelka & W. H. Berdine (Eds.), *Effective instruction for students*

with learning difficulties, (pp. 1–17). Boston: Allyn & Bacon.

Center for Innovations in Special Education (1999). *Cultural and linguistic diversity and IDEA: An evaluation resource guide.* Columbia, MO: Author.

Center for Policy Options. (1993). *Outcomes-based accountability: Policy issues and options for students with disabilities.* Rockville, MD: Westat.

Center for the Improvement of Early Reading Achievement (2002). *Improving the reading of America's children: Concepts of prints, letter naming, and phonemic awareness.* Ann Arbor: University of Michigan.

Cho, S. J., Hudley, C., & Back, H. J. (2003). Cultural influences on ratings of self-perceived social, emotional, and academic adjustment for Korean American adolescents. *Assessment for Effective Intervention, 29*(1) 3–14.

Choate, J.S., Enright, B. E., Miller, L. J., Poteet, J.A., & Rakes, T.A. (1995). *Curriculum-based assessment and programming* (3rd ed.). Boston: Allyn & Bacon.

Clark, G. M. (1998). *Assessment for transitions planning.* Austin, TX: Pro-Ed.

Clay, M. (2000). *Running records for classroom teachers.* Westport, CT: Heinemann.

Clay, M. M. (1993). *An observation survey of early literacy achievement.* Portsmouth, NH: Heinemann.

Coalition of Essential Schools. (2002, May). Difference between rubrics and benchmarks. Retrieved from http://www.essentialschools.org/cs/resources/view/ces_res/164.

Cohen, L. G., & Spenciner, L. J. (1998). *Assessment of children and youth.* New York: Addison Wesley Longman.

Consortium of National Arts Education Associations. (1994). *The national visual arts standards.*

Reston, VA: National Art Education Association.

Conture, E. G. (2001). *Stuttering: Its nature, diagnosis and treatment.* Boston: Allyn & Bacon.

Council for Exceptional Children (2005). What's New in The New IDEA-2004. Arlington, VA. CEC.

Council for Exceptional Children (CEC). (2002). NABE recommendations regarding evaluation, eligibility and individual education programs. *Determining appropriate referrals of English language learners of special education: A self-assessment guide for principals.* Arlington, VA: Author.

Council for Exceptional Children (CEC). (2003, June/July). Strategies + technology = solutions for reading challenges. *CEC Today, 10*(1), 1–5.

Council for Exceptional Children, (2003). Strategies + technology = solutions for reading challenges. *CEC Today, 10*(1), 1–5.

Council for Exceptional Children. (1998). *IDEA-1997: Let's Make It Work.* Reston, VA: Author (Public Policy Unit).

Council for Exceptional Children. (2000, September). High stakes testing a mixed blessing for special students. *Today, 7*(2), 1–5.

Council for Exceptional Children. (2000). *Making assessment accommodations: A toolkit for educators.* Arlington, VA: Author.

Council for Exceptional Children. (2003, December 19). *New Regulations on No Child Left Behind's Annual Yearly Progress Requirements Give States and Districts More Flexibility, says CEC.* Retrieved January 15, 2004, from http://www.cec.sped.org.

Council of Chief State School Officers (1992). *Summary of recommendations and policy implications for improving the assessment and monitoring of students with limited English proficiency.* Retrieved

September 10, 2004, from http://www.state.vt.us/educ/ESL/htm/Step2/ proflevels2.html.

Coutinho, M. J., Oswald, D. P., & Best, A. M. (2002). The influence of socio demographics and gender on the disproportionate identification of minority students as having learning disabilities. *Remedial and Special Education, 23*(1), 49–60.

Cowen, E. L., Hightower, A. D., Pedro-Carroll, J. L., Work, W. C., Wyman, P. A., & Haffey, W. G. (1996). *School-based prevention for children at risk: The primary mental health project.* Washington, DC: American Psychological Association.

Coyne, M., Kame'enui, E., & Simmons, D. (2001). Prevention and intervention in beginning reading: Two complex systems. *Learning Disabilities Research and Practice, 16*(2), 627–73.

Crawford, D. B. (2000, April). *Making individualized educational programs (IEPs) easy: Using curriculum-based progress monitoring measures.* Paper presented at the Council for Exceptional Children Annual Convention, Vancouver, Canada.

Crowley, S. L., & Merrell, K. W. (2003). The structure of the school social behavior scales: A confirmatory factor analysis. *Assessment for Effective Intervention, 28*(2). 41–55.

Davis, M. D., Kilgo, J. L., & Gamel-McCormick, M. (1998). *Young children with special needs: A developmentally appropriate approach.* Boston: Allyn & Bacon.

Davis, M. D., Kilgo, J. L., & Gamel-McCormick, M. (1998). *Young children with special needs: A developmentally appropriate approach.* Needham Heights, MA: Allyn & Bacon.

deFur, S. H., & Patton, J. R. (1999). Special education, transition, and school-based services: Are they meant for each other? In S. H. deFur & J. R. Patton, (Eds.),

Transition and school-based services: Interdisciplinary perspectives for enhancing the transition process (pp. 15–50). Austin, TX: Pro-Ed.

Deno, S. (1985). The nature and development of curriculum-based measurement. *Preventing School Failure, 36*(2), 5–10.

Deno, S. (2004). *Curriculum-based measurement (CBM): Student assessment.*

Deno, S. L., Fuchs, L. Wesson, C., Tindal, G., Marston, D., & Kuehnle, K. (1981). *Procedures to develop and monitor progress on IEP goals.* Minneapolis: University of Minnesota, Institute for Research on Learning Disabilities.

Dens, S. L., & Mirkin, P. K. (1977). *Data-based program modification: A manual.* Reston, VA: Council for Exceptional Children.

Deshler, D. D., Ellis, E. S., & Lenz, B. K. (1996). *Teaching adolescents with learning disabilities: Strategies and methods* (2nd ed.). Denver, CO: Love Publishing.

DiCerbo, P. A. (2000). Introduction. In B. Antunez, P. A. DiCerbo, & K. Menken (Eds.), *Framing effective practice: Topics and issues in education of English language learners. A technical assistance synthesis* (pp. 1–2). Washington, DC: National Clearinghouse for Bilingual Education, Center for the Study of Language and Education, George Washington University.

Digest of Education Statistics. (2002). National Center for Education Statistics. Retrieved on September 20, 2004, from http://nces.ed.gov/programs/digest/d02/tables/dt055.asp.

Dole, R. (2004). Collaborating successfully with your school's physical therapist. *Teaching Exceptional Children, 36*(5).

Donovan, S., & Cross, C. (Eds.). (2002). *Minority students in special gifted education.*

Washington, DC: National Academy Press.

Dorough, D. K. & Rye, J. A. (1997, January). Mapping for understanding. *The Science Teacher*, 37–41.

Dorough, D. K., Rye, A. J., & Rubba, P. A. (1995, April). *Fifth- and sixth-grade student's explanations of global warming and ozone: Conceptions formed prior to classroom instruction.* Paper presented at the National Association for Research in Science Teaching annual meeting, San Francisco, CA.

Downing, J. E. & Demchak, M. A. (2002). First Steps: Determining individual abilities and how best to support students. In J. E. Downing (Ed.). *Including students with severe and multiple disabilities in typical classrooms: Practical strategies for teachers (2nd ed.).* Baltimore. MD: Paul H. Brookes.

Dunn, C. (1996). A status report on transition planning for individuals with learning disabilities. *Journal of Learning Disabilities, 29*(1), 31–39.

Education of the Handicapped Act Amendments of 1986, P. L. 99–457 [in 1990, the name of this act was changed to the Individuals with Disabilities Education Act (IDEA)].

Ehri, L. C. (1995). Phases of development in learning to read words by sight. *Journal of Research in Reading, 18,* 116–125.

Eisenson, J. (1990). Impairments and delays for spoken and written language in children. *Education, 109,* 419–423.

Ekwall, E. (1997). *Locating and correcting reading difficulties* (7th ed.). Upper Saddle River, NJ: Merrill/Prentice Hall.

Elliott, J., Thurlow, M., & Ysseldyke, J. (1996). *Assessment guidelines that maximize the participation of students with disabilities in large-scale assessments: Characteristics and considerations* (Synthesis

Report No.25). Minneapolis, MN: University of Minnesota, National Center on Educational Outcomes.

Elliott, J., Ysseldyke, J., Thurlow, M., & Erickson, R. (1998). What about assessment and accountability? Practical implications for educators. *Teaching Exceptional Children, 31*(1), 20-27.

Elliott, S. N., Malecki, C. K., & Demaray, M. K. (2001). New directions in social skills assessment and intervention for elementary and middle school students. *Exceptionality, 9*(1), 19-32.

Enciso, P. (2001). Taking our seats: The consequences of positioning in reading assessments. *Theory into Practice, 40*(3), 166-174.

Engel, B. (1990). An approach to assessment in early literacy. In C. Kamil (Ed.), *Achievement testing in the early grades: The games grown-ups play* (pp. 119-134). Washington, DC: National Association for the Education of Young Children.

Enguidanos, T., & Ruiz, N. T. (1997). Traigan sus vidas, yo traigo la mia: Shared reading for older, emergent readers in bilingual classrooms. In L. Denti & P. T. Cousins (Eds.), *New ways of looking at learning disabilities* (pp. 199-222). Denver, CO: Love.

Erickson, R. N., Thurlow, M. L., Thor, K. A., & Seyfarth, A. (1996). *State special education outcomes, 1995.* Minneapolis, MN: University of Minnesota, National Center on Educational Outcomes. (ERIC Document Reproduction Service No. ED385061).

Erickson, R., Thurlow, M. L., & Thor, K. (1995). *State special education outcomes. 1994.* Minneapolis, MN: University of Minnesota, National Center on Educational Outcomes. (ERIC Document Reproduction Service No. ED404799).

Erickson, R., Ysseldyke, J., Thurlow, M. & Elliott, J. (1998). Inclusive assessments and accountability systems: Tools of the trade in educational reform. *Teaching Exceptional Children, 31*(2), 4-9.

Espin, C. A., Busch, T., Shin, J., & Kruschwitz, R. (2001). Curriculum-based measures in the content areas: Validity of vocabulary-matching measures as indicators of performance in social studies. *Learning Disabilities Research and Practice, 16*(3), 142-151.

Evans, L. (2003). Helping your child manage text anxiety. *The Parent Letter: NYU Child Study Center, 1*(1), pp. 1-2.

Everson, J. M., & Reid, D. H. (1999). *Person-centered planning and outcome management.* Morganton, NC: Habilitative Management Consultants.

Farr, B. P., & Trumbull, E. (1997). *Assessment alternatives for diverse classrooms.* Norwood, MA: Christopher-Gordon.

Farr, R., & Tone, B. (1998). *Portfolio and performance assessment: Helping students evaluate their progress as readers and writers* (2nd ed.). Fort Worth, TX: Harcourt Brace.

Farris, P. J., & Cooper, S. M. (1997). *Elementary and middle school social studies: A whole language approach* (2nd ed.). Boston: McGraw Hill.

Fassler, R. (2001). Snow fighting with spring: Building on young English language learners' thinking. *Childhood Education, 78*(1), 25-29.

Fewster, S. & MacMillian P. D. (2002). School-based evidence for the validity of curriculum-based measurement of reading and writing. *Remedial and Special Education, 23*, 149-156.

Figueroa, R. A. (2000). *The role of limited English proficiency in special education identification and intervention.* Washington, DC: National Research Council.

Figueroa, R. A. (2002). Toward a new model of assessment. In A. J. Artiles & A. A. Ortiz (Eds.), *English language learners with special education needs: Identification, assessment, and instruction* (pp. 51-63). McHenry, IL: Center for Applied Linguistics and Delta Systems.

Figueroa, R. A., & Hernandez, S. (2002). *Testing Hispanic students in the United States: Technical and policy issues. For our nation on the fault line: Hispanic American education.* Washington, DC: President's Advisory Commission on Educational Excellence for Hispanic Americans.

Fleege, P. O., Chalesworth, R., Burts, D. C., & Hart, C. (1992). Stress begins in kindergarten: A look at behavior during standardized testing. *Journal of Research in Childhood Education, 7*(1), 20-26.

Flexer, R. W., & Luft, P. (2005). Transition assessment and postschool outcomes. In R. W. Flexer, T. J. Simmons, P. Luft, & R. M. Baer, (Eds.), *Transition planning for secondary students with disabilities,* (2nd ed., pp. 110-140). Upper Saddle River, NJ: Merrill/Prentice Hall.

Foorman, B. R., & Mehta, P. (2002, November). Definitions of fluency: Conceptual and methodological challenges. Power Point presentation at A Focus on Fluency Forum, San Francisco, CA.

Foorman, B. R., Francis, D. J., Davidson, K. C., Harm, M. W., & Griffin, J. (2002, April). *Variability in text features in six grade 1 basal reading programs.* Paper presented at the annual meeting of the American Educational Research Association, New Orleans.

Friend, M., & Bursuck, W. D. (2002). *Including students with special needs: A practical guide for classroom teachers* (3rd ed.). Boston, MA: Allyn & Bacon.

Frisby, C. (2001). Academic achievement. In L. Suzuki, J. G. Ponterotto, P. J. Meller (Eds.), *Handbook of multicultural assessment* (2nd ed.). San Franciso: Jossey-Bass.

Fry, E. B. (1977). Fry's readability graph: Clarification, validity, and extension to level 17. *Journal of Reading, 21*, 242-252.

Fuchs, D., Fuchs, L. S., Mathes, P. G., Lipsey, M. E., & Eaton, S. (2000). A meta-analysis of reading differences with and without the disabilities label: A brief report. *Learning Disabilities, 10*, 1-3.

Fuchs, D., Fuchs, L. S., Thompson, A., Al Otaiba, S., Yen, L., Yang, N. J., Braun, M., & O'Connor, R. E. (2001). Is reading important in reading-readiness programs? A randomized field trial with teachers as program implementers. *Journal of Educational Psychology, 93*, 251-267.

Fuchs, L. S. (1989). Evaluating solutions: Monitoring progress and revising intervention plans. In M. R. Shinn (Ed.), *Curriculum-based measurement: Assessing special children* (pp. 155-183). New York: Guilford.

Fuchs, L. S., & Deno, S. L. (1982). *Developing goals and objectives for educational programs.* Minneapolis: University of Minnesota.

Fuchs, L. S., & Deno, S. L. (1994). Must instructionally useful performance assessment be based in the curriculum? *Exceptional Children, 61*(1), 15-24.

Fuchs, L. S., Fuchs, D., Hamlett, C. L., Walz, L., & Germann, G. (1993). Formative evaluation of academic progress: How much growth can we expect? *School Psychology Review, 22*, 27-48.

Fuchs, L. S., Fuchs, D., Hamlett, C., Philips, N., & Bentz, J. (1994). Classwide curriculum-based measurement: Helping general educators meet the challenge of student diversity. *Exceptional Children, 60*(6), 518-537.

Fuchs, L. S., Hamlett, C. L., & Fuchs, D. (1997). *Monitoring basic skills progress: Basic reading* (2nd ed.) [Computer program]. Austin, TX: Pro-Ed.

Fuchs, L., & Fuchs, D. (2000). Analogue assessment of academic skills: Curriculum-based measurement and performance assessment. In E. Shapiro & T. Kratchowill (Eds.), *Behavioral assessment in schools*, 2nd ed., (pp. 168-201). New York: Guilford.

Fusco, E., & Fountain, G. (1992). Reflective teacher: Reflective learner. In A. L. Costa, J. A. Bellanca, & R. Fogarty (Eds.), *If minds matter: A forward to the future. Volume I* (pp. 239-255). Palatine, IL: IRI/Skylight Publishing, Inc.

Gandara, P. (1999). *Second language acquisition and academic achievement.* San Francisco: WestEd.

Garcia, S. B. (2002). Parent-professional collaboration in culturally sensitive assessment. In A. J. Artiles & A. A. Ortiz (Eds.), *English language learners with special education needs: Identification, assessment, and instruction* (pp. 87-103). McHenry, IL: Center for Applied Linguistics and Delta Systems.

Gentile, J. R., & Lalley, J. P. (2003). *Standards and mastery learning: Aligning teaching and assessment so all children can learn.* Thousand Oaks, CA: Corwin Press.

German, D. (2001). *It's on the tip of my tongue.* Chicago: Word Finding Materials.

Gillett, J. W. & Temple, C. (2000). *Understanding reading problems: Assessment and instruction* (56th ed). NY: Longman.

Ginsburg, H. P. (1997). Mathematics learning disabilities: A view from developmental psychology. *Journal of Learning Disabilities, 30*(1), 20-33.

Glynn, S. (1997, January). Drawing mental models. *The Science Teacher, 64*(1), 30-35.

Goldstein, B. (2000). *Cultural and linguistic diversity resource guide for speech language pathologists.* San Diego: Singular.

Good, R. H., & Kaminski, R. A. (2002). *Dynamic indicators of basic early literacy skills* (6th ed.). Eugene, OR: University of Oregon.

Goodman, K. S. (1973). Miscues: Windows on reading. In K. S. Goodman (Ed.), *Miscue analysis.* Urbana, IL: ERIC.

Goodman, Y. (1978, November). Kidwatching: An alternative to testing. *National Elementary Principal, 57*(4), 41-45.

Graham, S., Harris, K. R., & Fink, B. (2000). Is hand-writing causally related to learning to write? Treatment of handwriting problems in beginning writers. *Journal of Educational Psychology, 92*, 620-633.

Graves, A. W., Valles, E. C., & Rueda, R. (2000). Variations in interactive writing instruction: A study in four bilingual special education settings. *Learning Disabilities Research, 15*, 1-9.

Greenwood, C. R., & Rieth, H. J. (1994). Current dimensions of technology-based assessment in special education. *Exceptional Children, 61*(2), 105-113.

Gronlund, N. E. (1998). *Assessment of student achievement* (6th ed.). Needham Heights, MA: Allyn & Bacon.

Guerin, G. R., & Maier, A. S. (1983). *Informal assessment in education.* Palo Alto, CA: Mayfield.

Guernsey, T. F., & Klare, K. (1993). *Special education law.* Durham, NC: Carolina Academic Press.

Gullo, D. F. (1997). Assessing student learning through the analysis of pupil products. In B. Spodek & O. N. Saracho, (Eds.), *Issues in early childhood evaluation and assessment. Yearbook in Early Childhood Education* (Vol. 7, pp. 129-148). New York: Teachers College Press.

Gunning, T. G. (1998). *Assessing and correcting reading and writing difficulties.* Needham Heights, MA: Allyn & Bacon.

Haager, D., & Vaughn, S. (1995). Parent, teacher, peer, and self-reports of the social competence of students with learning disabilities. *Journal of Learning Disabilities, 28,* 205–215.

Hagie, M. U., Gallipo, P. L., & Svien, L. (2003). Traditional cultural versus traditional assessment for American Indian students: An investigation of potential test item bias. *Assessment for Effective Intervention, 29*(1), 15–25.

Hallahan, D. P. & Kauffman, J. K. (2003). *Exceptional learners: Introduction to special education* (9th ed). Boston: Allyn & Bacon.

Hallahan, D. P., & Kauffman, J. M. (2000). *Exceptional children: Introduction to special education* (8th ed.). Boston: Allyn & Bacon.

Hallahan, D. P., Kauffman, J. M., & Lloyd, J. W. (1999). *Introduction to learning disabilities.* Needham Heights, MA: Allyn & Bacon.

Hamiltan, C. & Shinn, M. R. (2003). Characteristics of word callers: an investigation of the accuracy of teachers' judgments of reading comprehension and oral reading skills. *School Psychology Review,* 32(2).

Hanson, R. (1997). Evaluating learning in science. *ASTA News: Alabama Science Teachers Association, 19,* 10–11.

Harris, H. L., & Coy, D. R. (2003). Helping students cope with test anxiety. *ERIC/CASS Digests,* (CG-03-06).

Harris, T. L., & Hodges, R. E., (1995). *The literacy dictionary.* Newark, DE: International Reading Association.

Hasbrouck, J. E., & Tindal, G. (1992). Curriculum-based oral reading fluency norms for students in grades 2 through 5. *Teaching Exceptional Children, 24,* 41–43.

Hasbrouck, J. E., Woldbeck, T., Ihnot, C., & Parker, R. I. (1999). One teacher's use of curriculum-based measurement: A changed opinion. *Learning Disabilities Research and Practice, 14,* 118–126.

Heiman, B. (1999, April). *Integrating technology and assessment.* Paper presented at the 1999 International Council for Exceptional Children Conference. Charlotte, NC.

Henderson, K. (2001, March). An overview of ADA, IDEA, and Section 504: Update 2001. *ERIC EC Digest* E606. Arlington, VA: The ERIC Clearinghouse on Disabilities and Gifted Children.

Herman, J. L., Aschbacher, P. R., & Winters, L. (1992). *A practical guide to alternative assessment.* Alexandria, VA: Association for Supervision and Curriculum Development.

Herman, J. L., Gearhart, M., & Aschbacher, P. R. (1996). Portfolios for classroom assessment: Design and implementation issues. In R. Calfee & P. Perfumo (Eds.), *Writing portfolios in the classroom: Policy and practice, promise and peril* (pp. 27–59). Mahwah, NJ: Lawrence Erlbaum.

Herman, J., Aschbacher, P., & Winters, L. (1992). *A practical guide to alternative assessment.* Alexandria, VA: Association for Supervision and Curriculum Development.

Heward, W. L. (2003). *Exceptional children: An introduction to special education* (7th ed.). Upper Saddle River, NJ: Merrill/Prentice Hall.

Hiebert, E. H. (2003, April). *The role of text in developing fluency: A comparison of two interventions.* Paper presented at the American Educational Research Association Conference, Chicago.

Hiebert, E. H., & Fisher, C. W. (2002, May). *Text matters in developing fluent reading.* Paper presented at the annual meeting of the International Reading Association, San Francisco.

Hillerich, R. I. (1978). *A writing vocabulary of elementary children.* (ERIC Document Reproduction Service No. ED 161 084).

Hook, P. E., & Jones, S. D. (2002). The importance of automaticity and fluency for efficient reading comprehension. *Perspectives* [International Dyslexia Association], *28*(1), 9–14.

Horn, E. A. (1926). *A basic writing vocabulary* (University of Iowa Monographs in Education, First Series No. 4). Iowa City, IA: University of Iowa.

Horton, L. W. (1970). Illegibilities in the cursive handwriting of sixth graders. *Elementary School Journal 70,* 446–450.

Horton, P. B., McConney, A., Gallo, M., Woods, A., Senn, G., & Hamelin, D. (1993). An investigation of the effectiveness of concept mapping as an instructional tool. *Science Education 77,* 95–111.

Howell, K. W, & Nolet, V. (2000). *Curriculum-based evaluation* (3rd ed.). Belmont, CA: Wadsworth/Thomson Learning.

Howell, K. W. & Nolet, V. (2000). *Curriculum-based evaluation: Teaching and decision making* (3rd ed.). Belmont, CA: Wadsworth.

Huefner, D. S. (2000). *Getting comfortable with special education law: A framework for working with children with disabilities.* Norwood, MA: Christopher Gordon.

Hughes, C. A. (1997). Memory and test-taking strategies. In D. D. Deshler, E. S. Ellis, & B. K. Lenz (Eds.). *Teaching adolescents with learning disabilities* (2nd ed., pp. 209–266). Denver, CO: Love Publishing.

IDEA '97 Final Regulations, Assistance to States for the Education of Children with Disabilities, 34 C.F.R. Part 300 (March 12, 1999).

Idol, L., & West, J. F. (1993). *Effective instruction of difficult-to-teach students.* Austin, TX: Pro-Ed.

Individuals with Disabilities Education Act (IDEA) Amendments of 1997, 20 U.S.C. §§1400 et seq.

Individuals with Disabilities Education Act (IDEA) Amendments of 1997, 20 U.S.C. §§1400 et seq. (Supp. 1996).

Individuals with Disabilities Education Act (IDEA) Amendments of 2004, Pub. L. No. 108-446.

Individuals with Disabilities Education Act (IDEA) Regulations, 34 C.F.R. §300.1–300.653 (1990). 34 C.F.R. §300.500 (3)(b) (1990). 34 C.F.R. §300.532(f) (1990). 34 C.F.R. §300.534 (1990). 34 C.F.R. §506(a) (1990).

Individuals with Disabilities Education Act, 20 U.S.C. §1400 et seq.

Irvin, J. L., Buehl, D. R., & Klemp, R. M. (2003). *Reading and the high school student: Strategies to enhance literacy.* Boston: Allyn & Bacon.

Janney, R., & Snell, M. E. (2000). *Teacher's guides to inclusive practices: Behavioral support.* Baltimore: Paul H. Brookes.

Jayanthi, M., Epstein, M. H., Polloway, E. A., & Bursuck, W. D. (1996). A national survey of general education teachers' perceptions of testing adaptations. *Journal of Special Education, 30*(1), 99–115.

Jefferies, S., Jefferies, T., & Mustain, W. "Why assess in PE?" *PE Central.* Retrieved on August 30, 2004, from http://www.pecentral.org/assessment/assessmentresearch.html.

Johns, J. L. (2001). *Basic reading inventory* (8th ed). Dubuque, IA: Kendall/Hunt Publishing.

Johns, J. L., & Lenski, S. D. (1997). *Improving reading: A handbook of strategies* (2nd ed.). Dubuque, IA: Kendall/Hunt.

Kame'enui, E. J., Carnine, D. W., Dixon, R. C., Simmons, D. C., &

Coyne, M. D. (Eds.). (2002). *Effective teaching strategies that accommodate diverse learners* (2nd ed.). Upper Saddle River, NJ: Merrill/Prentice Hall.

Karns, K., Fuchs, L., & Fuchs, D. (1995). Curriculum-based measurement: Facilitating individualized instruction and accommodating student diversity. *LD Forum, 20*(2), 16–19.

Kauffman, J., Mostert, M., Trent, S., & Hallahan, D. (1998). *Managing classroom behavior: A reflective case-based approach.* Boston: Allyn & Bacon.

Kaufman, A. S., & Kaufman, N. L. (1998). *Kaufman test of educational achievement.* Circle Pines, MI: American Guidance Service.

Kayser, H. (1995). Interpreters. In H. Kayser (Ed.), *Bilingual speech-language pathology: An Hispanic focus* (pp. 207–221). San Diego: Singular.

Kea, C. D., Campbell-Whatley, G. D., & Bratton, K. Culturally responsive assessment for African American students with learning and behavioral challenges. *Assessment for Effective Intervention, 29*(1), 27–38.

Kea, C. D., Cartledge, G., & Bowman, L. J. (2002). Interventions for African American learners with behavioral problems. In B. A. Ford & F. E. Obiakor (Eds.), *Creating successful learning environments for African American learners with exceptionalities* (pp. 79–94). Thousand Oaks, CA: Corwin Press.

Kim, A., & Yeh, J. (2002). *Stereotypes of Asian students. ERIC Digests.* (ERIC Document Reproduction Service No. ED462510).

Kindler, A. (2002). *What are the most common language groups for limited English proficient students?* (AskNCBE, No. 5). Washington, DC: National Clearinghouse for Bilingual Education. Retrieved March 10,

2005, from http://www.ncela.gwu.edu/expert/faq/05toplangs.htm.

King-Sears, M. E. (1998). *Curriculum-based assessment in special education.* San Diego: Singular Publishing Group.

King-Sears, M. E., Burgess, M., & Lawson, T. L. (1999, September/October). Applying curriculum-based assessment in inclusive settings. *Teaching Exceptional Children, 30*–38.

Kinsey, S. J. (2000). *The relationship between prosocial behaviors and academic achievement in the primary multiage classroom.* Unpublished doctoral dissertation. Loyola University, Chicago.

Knoff, H. M., Stollar, S. A., Johnson, J. J., & Chenneville, T. A. (1999). In E. V. Nuttall, I. Romero, & J. Kalesnik, *Assessing and screening preschoolers: Psychological and educational dimensions* (2nd ed.). Needham Heights, MA: Allyn & Bacon.

Kohler, P. D. (1994). On-the-job-training: A curricular approach to employment. *Career Development for Exceptional Individuals, 17,* 29–40.

Krajcik, J., Czerniak, C., & Berger, C. (1999) *Teaching children science: A project–based approach.* Boston: McGraw Hill.

Kuhn, M. R., & Stahl, S. A. (2003). Fluency: A review of developmental and remedial practices. *Journal of Educational Psychology, 95,* 3–21.

Kulm, G. (1994). *Mathematics assessment.* San Francisco: Jossey-Bass.

Kuska, A., Webster, E. J. D., & Elford, G. (1994). *Spelling in language arts.* Don Mills, Ontario, Canada: Thomas Nelson.

LaCelle-Peterson, M. W., & Rivera, C. (1994). Is it real for all kids? A framework for equitable assessment policies for English language learners. *Harvard Educational Review, 64*(1), 55–75.

Ladd, G. W. (2000). The fourth R: Relationships as risks and resources following children's transition to school. *American Educational Research Association Newsletter, 19*(1), 7, 9-11.

Langdon, H., & Saenz, T. (1996). Speech-language assessment of bilingual-bicultural students. In H. Langdon & T. Saenz (Eds.), *Language assessment and intervention with multicultural students: A guide for speech-language-hearing professionals* (pp. 3-30). Oceanside, CA: Academic Communication Associates.

LaParo, K. M., Pianta, R. C., & Cox, M. J. (2000). Teachers' reported transition practices for children transitioning into kindergarten and first grade. *Exceptional Children, 67*, 7-20.

Lawrence, M. (1994). The use of video technology in science teaching: A vehicle for alternative assessment. *Teaching and Change, 2*(1), 14-30.

Lederer, J. M. (2000). Reciprocal teaching of social studies in inclusive elementary classrooms. *Journal of Learning Disabilities, 33*(1), 91-106.

Lerner, J. (2003). *Learning disabilities: Theories, diagnosis, and teaching strategies.* Boston: Houghton Mifflin.

Lerner, J. (2003). *Learning disabilities: Theories, diagnosis, and teaching strategies* (9th ed.). Boston: Houghton Mifflin.

Lerner, J. (2004). *Learning disabilities: Theories, diagnosis, and teaching strategies* (9th ed.). Boston: Houghton Mifflin.

Leslie, L., & Caldwell, J. (2001). *Qualitative Reading Inventory-3,* Boston: Allyn & Bacon.

Lidz, C. S. (1997). Dynamic assessment approaches. In D. P. Flanagan, J. L. Genshaft, & P. L. Harrison (Eds.), *Contemporary intellectual assessment: Theories,*

tests, and issues (pp. 281-296). New York: Guilford Press.

Linn, R. L., & Gronlund, N. E. (2000). *Measurement and assessment in teaching* (8th ed.). Upper Saddle River, NJ: Merrill/Prentice Hall.

Linn, R. L., Baker, E. L., & Dunbar, S. B. (1991, November). Complex, performance-based assessment: Expectations and validation criteria. *Educational Researcher, 4*, 15-21.

Lipson, M. Y., & Wixson, K. K. (1997). *Assessment and instruction of reading and writing disability: An interactive approach* (2nd ed.). New York: Longman.

Lopez-Reyna, N. A., & Bay, M. (1997). Enriching assessment: Using varied assessments for diverse learners. *Teaching Exceptional Children, 29*(4), 33-37.

Losardo, A., & Notari-Syverson, A. (2001). *Alternative approaches to assessing young children.* Baltimore, MD: Brookes.

Lovett, M. W., Lacerenza, L., & Borden, S. L., Frijters, Steinbach, & DePalma (2000). Putting struggling readers on the PHAST track: A program to integrate phonological and strategy-based remedial reading instructions and maximize outcomes. *Journal of Learning Disabilities, 33,* 458-476.

Luftig, R. L. (1989). *Assessment of learners with special needs.* Boston: Allyn & Bacon.

Lynn, G. R., & Moats, L. (1997). Critical conceptual and methodological considerations in reading intervention research. *Journal of Learning Disabilities, 30,* 578-588.

Lyon, G. R., Fletcher, J. M., Shaywitz, S. E., Shaywitz, B. A., Torgesen, J. K., Wood, F. B., Schulte, A., & Olson, R. (2001). Rethinking learning disabilities. In C. E. Finn, A. J. Rotherham, & C. R. Hokanson, (Eds.), *Rethinking special education for a new century.*

Washington, DC: Thomas B. Fordham Foundation and Progressive Policy Institute.

Lyon, R. (1997). *Report on Learning Disabilities Research,* article adapted from testimony of Dr. Reid Lyon before the Committee on Education and the Workforce, U. S. House of Representatives, July 10, 1997.

Male, M. (2003). *Technology for inclusion: Meeting the special needs of all students* (3rd ed.). Needham Heights, MA: Allyn & Bacon.

Mann, P. H., Suiter, P. A., & McClung, R. M. (1992). *A guide to educating mainstreamed students* (4th ed.). Boston: Allyn & Bacon.

Manzo, A. V., & Manzo, U. C. (1995). *Teaching children to be literate: A reflective approach.* Orlando, FL: Harcourt Brace.

Marlarz, L., D'Arcangelo, M., & Kiernan, L. J. (1991). *Redesigning assessment: Facilitator's guide and videotape.* Alexandria: VA: Association for Supervision and Curriculum Development.

Mastropieri, M. A., & Scruggs, T. E. (1997). Best practices in promoting reading comprehension in students with learning disabilities: 1996 to 1997. *Remedial and Special Education, 18*, 197-213.

Mastropieri, M. A., & Scruggs, T. E. (1997). What's special about special education? A cautious view toward full inclusion. *Educational Forum, 61*, 206-211.

Mastropieri, M. A., & Scruggs, T. E. (2004). *The inclusive classroom: Strategies for effective instruction* (2nd ed.). Austin, TX: Pro-Ed.

Mastropieri, M. A., & Scruggs, T. E. (2004). *The inclusive classroom: Strategies for effective instruction* (2nd ed.). Upper Saddle River, NJ: Merrill/Prentice Hall.

Mastropieri, M. A., Scruggs, T. E., Bakken, J. P., & Wheldon, C. (1996). Reading comprehension: A synthesis of research in learning disabilities. In T. E. Scruggs & M. A. Mastropieri (Eds.), *Advances in learning and behavioral disabilities* (Vol. 10, Part B, pp. 201–223). Greenwich, CT: JAI Press.

Maurer, R. E. (1996). *Designing alternative assessments for interdisciplinary curriculum in middle and secondary schools.* Needham Heights, MA: Allyn & Bacon.

Maxwell, K. L., & Elder, S. K. (1999). Children's transition to kindergarten. *Young Children, 49*(6), 56–63.

McClellan, D. E., & Katz, L. G. (2001). Assessing young children's social competence. *ERIC Digest.* Champaign, IL: ERIC Clearinghouse on Elementary and Early Childhood Education. ED450953

McClellan, D. E., & Kinsey, S. (1999). Children's social behavior in relation to participation in mixed-age or same-age classrooms. Early Childhood Research & Practice [Online], 1(1). Available at http://ecrp.uiuc.edu/vlnl/vlvl.html.

McConnell, S. R. (2000). Assessment in early intervention and early childhood special education: Building on the past to project into our future. *Topics in Early Childhood Education, 20*(1), 43–48.

McDonnell, L. M., McLaughlin, M. J., & Morrison, P. (Eds.). (1997). *Educating one and all: Students with disabilities and standards-based reform.* Washington, DC: National Academy Press. (ERIC Document Reproduction Service No. ED409677).

McLoughlin, J. A., & Lewis, R. B. (2005). *Assessing special students* (6th ed.). Upper Saddle River, NJ: Merrill/Prentice Hall.

McLoughlin, J. A., & Lewis, R. B. (2005). *Assessing students with special needs* (5th ed.). Upper Saddle River, NJ: Merrill/Prentice Hall.

Meisels, S. (2001). Fusing assessment and intervention: Changing parents' and providers' views of young children. *Zero to Three, 21*(4), 4–10.

Meisinger, H., Schwanenflugel, P. J., Bradley, E., Kuhn, M. R., & Stahl, S. A. (2002). *Interaction quality during partner reading.* Paper presented at the annual meeting of the National Reading Conference, Miami, FL.

Menchetti, B. M., & Piland, V. C. (2001). Transition assessment and evaluation: Current methods and emerging alternatives. In S. Alper, D. L. Ryndak, & C. N. Schloss, (Eds.), *Alternate assessment of students with disabilities in inclusive settings,* (pp. 220–248). Boston: Allyn & Bacon.

Menon, S., & Hiebert, E. H. (2003, April). *A comparison of first graders' reading acquisition with little books and literature anthologies.* Paper presented at the annual meeting of the American Educational Research Association, Chicago.

Mercer, C. D. & Mercer, A. R. (2005). *Teaching students with learning problems* (7th ed.). Upper Saddle River, NJ: Merrill/Prentice Hall.

Mercer, C. D., & Pullen, P. C. (2005). *Students with learning disabilities* (6th ed.). Upper Saddle River, NJ: Merrill/ Prentice Hall.

Meyen, E. L., Vergason, G. A., & Whelan, R. J. (1996). *Strategies for teaching exceptional children in inclusive settings.* Denver, CO: Love.

Meyen, E. L., Vergason, G. A., & Whelan, R. J. (1996). *Strategies for teaching exceptional children in inclusive settings.* Denver, CO: Love.

Miller, L. L., & Felton, R. H. (2001). "It's one of them. . . . I don't know": Case study of a student with phonological, rapid naming, and word-finding deficits. *Journal of Special Education, 35*(3), 125–133.

Montague, M. (1997). Cognitive strategy instruction in mathematics for students with learning disabilities. *Journal of Learning Disabilities, 30*(2), 164–177.

Moon, M. S., & Inge, K. (2000). Vocational preparation and transition. In M. E. Snell & F. Brown, (Eds.), *Instruction of students with severe disabilities* (5th ed., pp. 591–628). Upper Saddle River, NJ: Merrill/Prentice Hall.

Morocco, C. C. (2001). Teaching for understanding with students with disabilities: New directions for research on access to the general education curriculum. *Learning Disabilities Quarterly, 24*(1), 5–13.

Moya, S. S., & O'Malley, J. M. (1994). A portfolio assessment model for ESL. *Journal of Educational Issues of Language Minority Students, 13,* 13–36.

Murdick, N., Gartin, B., & Crabtree, T. (2002). *Special education law.* Upper Saddle River, NJ: Merrill/Prentice Hall.

Muter, V., Hulme, C., & Taylor, S. (1998). Segmentation, not rhyming, predicts early progress in learning to read. *Journal of Experimental Child Psychology, 71,* 3–27.

Myers, C. L., McBride, S. L., & Peterson, C. A. (1996). Transdisciplinary, play-based assessment in early childhood special education: An examination of social validity. *Topics in Early Childhood, 16,* 102–126.

National Alliance of Black School Educators (NABSE), IDEA Local Implementation by Local Administrators & (ILIAD) Partnership. (2002). *Addressing over-representation of African-American students in special education: The prereferral intervention process, An administrator's guide.* Arlington, VA: Council for Exceptional Children; and Washington, DC: National Alliance of Black School Educators.

National Association for Sport & Physical Education (NASPE).

(1995). *Moving into the future: National standards for physical education*. Reston, VA: Author.

National Center for Educational Statistics. (2004). *The nation's report card*. Retrieved August 20, 2004, from http://nces.ed.gov/nationsreportcard/reading/.

National Council of Teachers of Math. (2000). *Principles and standards for school mathematics*. Reston, VA: Author.

National Council of Teachers of Mathematics. (1991). *Professional standards for teaching mathematics*. Reston, VA: Author.

National Education Association. (2002). Communicating with parents. *NEA Today, 20*(4), 10.

National Institute for Child Health and Human Development. (1999). *Keys to successful learning* (pp. 1–3). Washington, DC: Author.

National Institutes of Health. (2002). *Cancer rates and risks*. Bethesda, MD: National Cancer Institute.

National Reading Panel. (2000). *Teaching children to read: An evidence-based assessment of the scientific research literature on reading and its implications for reading instruction*. Washington, DC: National Institute of Child Health and Human Development.

National Research Council. (1996). *National science education standards*. Washington, DC: National Academy Press.

National Research Council. (1998). *Preventing reading difficulties in young children*. Washington, DC: National Academy of Sciences.

National Research Council. (1999). *Selecting instructional materials*. Washington, DC: National Academy Press.

Newcomer, P. L. (1999). *Standardized Reading Inventory*. Austin, TX: Pro-Ed.

Newland, T. E. (1932). An analytical study of the development of illegibilities in handwriting from the lower grades to adulthood. *Journal of Educational Research, 26*, 249–258.

Nitko, A. J. (2001). *Educational assessment of students* (3rd ed.) Upper Saddle River, NJ: Merrill/Prentice Hall.

Nolet, V. (1992). Classroom-based measurement and portfolio assessment. *Diagnostique, 18*(1), 5–26.

Northern Examining Association (1990). *Mathematics through problem solving*. Manchester, England: GCSE Syllabus.

Notari-Syverson, A., Losardo, A., & Young Sook, Lim (2003). Assessment of young children from culturally diverse backgrounds: A journey in progress. *Assessment for Effective Intervention, 29*(1) 39–51.

Nuttall, E. V., Romero, I., & Kalesnik, J. (1999). *Assessing and screening preschoolers: Psychological and educational dimensions* (2nd ed.). Needham Heights, MA: Allyn & Bacon.

O'Neil, R. E., Horner, R. H., Albin, R. W., Sprague, J. R., Storey, K., & Newton, N. S. (1997). *Functional assessment and program development for problem behavior: A practical handbook*. Pacific Grove, CA: Brooks/Cole.

Office of Civil Rights, U.S. Dept. of Education, OCR Senior Staff Memorandum, 19 IDELR 894 (OCR 1992).

Olson, J. F., & Goldstein, A. A. (1997). *Increasing the inclusion of students with disabilities and limited English proficiency in large-scale assessments: A summary of recent progress*. Washington, DC: U.S. Department of Education.

Ortiz, A. (2003). *English language learners with special needs: Effective instructional strategies*. Washington, DC: ERIC Clearinghouse on Languages and Linguistics. (Eric Document Reproduction Service No. ED469207).

Ortiz, A. A. & Yates, J. R. (2002). Considerations in the assessment of English language learners referred to special education. In A. J. Artiles & A. A. Ortiz (Eds.), *English language learners with special education needs: Identification, assessment, and instruction* (pp. 65–85). McHenry, IL: Center for Applied Linguistics and Delta Systems.

Ortiz, A. A., & Garcia, S. B. (1990). Using language assessment data for language and instructional planning for exceptional bilingual students. In A. Carrasquillo & R. Baecher (Eds.), *Teaching the bilingual special education student* (pp. 24–27). Norwood, NJ: Ablex.

Ortiz, A. A., & Graves, A. (2001). English language learners with literacy-related disabilities. *International Dyslexia Association Commemorative Booklet* (pp. 31–35).

Ortiz, A. A., & Yates, J. R. (2001). A framework for serving English language learners with disabilities. *Journal of Special Education Leadership, 14*(2), 72–80.

Osborn, J., Lehr, F., & Hiebert, E. H., (2003). *A focus on fluency*. Honolulu, HI: Pacific Resources for Education and Learning. Available at http://www.prel. org/products/re_/fluency-1.htm

Osborne, A. G. (1996). *Legal issues in special education*. Boston: Allyn & Bacon.

Overton, T. (2003). *Assessment in special education* (4th ed.). Upper Saddle River, NJ: Merrill/Prentice Hall.

Owens, K. D., & Sanders, R. L. (1998). Earth science assessments: Integrating creative arts, content knowledge, and critical thinking. *Science Scope, 22*(1), 44–47.

Paratore, J., Turpie, J., DiBiasio, M., & Sullivan, K. (1995). Shifting boundaries in home and school responsibilities: The construction of home-based literacy portfolios by immigrant parents and their children. *Research in the Teaching of English, 29,* 367–389.

Parker, R. C. (1993). *Language proficiency classification and instructional placement instrument: A diagnostic instrument for the proficient assessment of limited English proficient students.* Concord, NH: EEOO/New Hampshire Department of Education.

Patton, J. R., Polloway, E. A., & Cronin, M. E. (1994). *Science education for students with mild disabilities: A status report.* Austin, TX: Learning for Living. (ERIC Document Reproduction Service No. ED 370 329).

Pavri, S. (2001). Loneliness in children with disabilities: How teachers can help. *Teaching Exceptional Children, 33*(6), 52–58.

Pavri, S. (2002). Developmental delay or cultural difference? Developing effective child find practices for young children from culturally and linguistically diverse families. *Young Exceptional Children, 4*(4), 2–9.

Paxton, R. J. (1999). A deafening silence: History textbooks and the students who read them. *Review of Educational Research, 69*(3), 315–339.

PE Central Retrieved on Aug 30, 2004 from http://www.pecentral.org/assessment/assessmentresearch.htm or PE central. P. O. Box 10262, Blacksburg, VA. 24062. pec@pecentral.org.

Pellegrino, J. W., Jones, L. R., & Mitchell, K. J. (Eds.). (1999). *Grading the nation's report card: Evaluating NAEP and transforming the assessment of educational progress.* Washington, DC: National Academy Press.

Pena, E., Quinn, R., & Iglesias, A. (1992). The application of dynamic methods to language assessment: A non-biased procedure. *Journal of Special Education, 26*(3), 269–280.

Phillips, S. E. (1996). Legal defensibility of standards: Issues and policy perspectives. *Educational Measurement: Issues and Practice, 15*(2), 5–13, 19.

Pierangelo, R., & Giuliani, G. (1998). *Special educator's complete guide to 109 diagnostic tests.* West Nyack, NY: Center for Applied Research in Education.

Pierce, L. V. (2002). *Performance-based assessment: Promoting achievement for English language learners* (ERIC/CLL News Bulletin, 26, 1). Washington, DC: ERIC Clearinghouse on Languages and Linguistics.

Pisha, B., & Coyne, P. (2001). Will the courts go bibi? IDEA, 1997, the courts, and deaf education. *Exceptional Children, 67*(2), 187–198.

Plante, E., & Beeson, P. M. (1999). *Communication and communication disorders: A clinical introduction.* Needham Heights, MA: Allyn & Bacon.

Polloway, E. A., & Patton, J. R. (2000). *Strategies for teaching learners with special needs.* New York: Merrill/Prentice Hall.

Polloway, E. A., & Patton, J. R. (2000). *Strategies for teaching learners with special needs* (7th ed.). Upper Saddle River: NJ: Merrill-Prentice Hall.

Polloway, E. A., & Smith, T. (2000). *Language instruction for students with disabilities* (2nd ed.). Denver, CO: Love.

Prewitt, K. (2002, Winter). Demography, diversity, and democracy: The 2000 Census story. *Brookings Review* pp. 6–9. Washington, DC: Brookings Institute.

Puckett, M. B., & Black, J. K. (2000). *Authentic assessment of the young child* (2nd ed.). Upper Saddle River, NJ: Merrill/Prentice Hall.

Put reading first: The research building blocks for teaching children to read, (2001). Jessup, MD: National Institute for Literacy.

Reeves, D. B. (1998). *Making standards work.* Denver, CO: Center for Performance Assessment.

Rhodes, L. K., & Nathenson-Mejia, S. (1992). Anecdotal records: A powerful tool for ongoing literacy assessment. *The Reading Teacher, 45,* 502–509.

Richek, M. A., Caldwell, J. S., Jennings, J. H., & Lerner, J. W. (2000). *Reading problems: Assessment and teaching strategies* (4th ed.). Needham Heights, MA: Allyn & Bacon.

Richek, M., Caldwell, J., Jennings, J., & Lerner, J. (2002). *Reading problems: Assessment and teaching strategies.* Boston: Allyn & Bacon.

Rivera, D. P., & Smith, D. D. (1997). *Teaching students with learning and behavior problems* (3rd ed.). Needham Heights, MA: Allyn & Bacon.

Roberts, R., & Mather, N. (1997). Orthographic dyslexia: The neglected subtype. *Learning Disabilities Research and Practice, 12,* 236–250.

Robinson, R. L., & Crowe, T. A. (2001). Fluency and voice. In D. M. Ruscello (Ed.), *Tests and measurement in speech-language pathology* (pp. 163–183). Boston: Butterworth-Heinemann.

Roseberry-McKibbin, C. (2002). *Multicultural students with special language needs: Practical strategies for assessment and intervention* (2nd ed.). Oceanside, CA: Academic Communication Associates.

Roseberry-McKibbin, C., & Brice, A. (2004). Acquiring English as a second language: What's "normal," what's not. American Speech-Language-Hearing Association. Retrieved on January 12, 2004, from http://www.asha.org/public/speech/development/easl.htm.

Rothstein, L. (1998). Americans with Disabilities Act, Section 504, and adults with learning disabilities in adult education and transition to employment. In S. Vogel & S. Reder, (Eds.), *Learning disabilities, literacy, and adult education* (pp. 29-43). Baltimore: Paul H. Brookes.

Rothstein, L. L. (1999). *Special education law* (3rd ed.). New York: Longman.

Rourke, B. P., & Conway, J. (1997). Disabilities of arithmetic of arithmetic and mathematical reasoning: Perspectives from neurology and neuropsychology. *Journal of Learning Disabilities, 30*(1), 34-46.

Rous, B., & Hallam, R. A. (1998). Easing the transition to kindergarten. Assessment of social, behavioral, and functional skills in young children with disabilities. *Young Exceptional Children, 1*(4), 17-26.

Rubin, D. (2002). *Diagnosis and correction in reading instruction* (3rd ed). Needham Heights, MA: Allyn & Bacon.

Rug, L. (2001). *Running records*. Retrieved October 29, 2001, from http://24.72.1.100/lang/1998=99/running.htm.

Ruiz, N. T., & Figueroa, R. A. (1995). Learning-handicapped classroom with Latino students: The optimal learning environment project. *Education and Urban Society, 27*, 463-483.

Sabornie, E. J., & deBettencourt, L. U. (1997). *Teaching students with mild disabilities at the secondary level*. Upper Saddle River, NJ: Merrill/Prentice Hall.

Sabornie, E. J., & deBettencourt, L. U. (2004). *Teaching students with mild and high-incidence disabilities at the secondary level* (2nd ed.). Upper Saddle River, NJ: Merrill/Prentice Hall.

Salend, S. J. (1997). *Effective mainstreaming: Creating inclusive classrooms* (3rd ed.). New York: Macmillan.

Salend, S. J. (1998). Using portfolios to assess student performance. *Teaching Exceptional Children, 31*(2), 36-43.

Salend, S. J., & Garrick-Duhaney, L. M. (2002). Grading students in inclusive settings. *Teaching Exceptional Children, 34*(3), 8-15.

Salvia, J., & Ysseldyke, J. (2001). *Assessment in special and remedial education* (8th ed.). Boston: Houghton Mifflin.

Salvia, J., & Ysseldyke, J. (2004). *Assessment in special and inclusive education* (9th ed.). Boston: Houghton Mifflin.

Salvia, J., & Ysseldyke, J. E. (2004). *Assessment* (9th ed.). Boston: Houghton Mifflin.

Samuels, S. J. (1983). Diagnosing reading problems. *Topics in Learning and Learning Disabilities, 2*(4), 1-11.

Samuels, S. J. (1997). The method of repeated readings. *The Reading Teacher, 50*, 376-381. (Originally published in 1997 in *The Reading Teacher, 32*, 403-408).

Samuels, S. J. (1998). Decoding and automaticity: Helping poor readers become automatic at word recognition. *The Reading Teacher, 41*, 756-761.

Samuels, S. J. (2002). Reading fluency: Its development and assessment. In A. F. Farstrup & S. J. Samuels (Eds.), *What research has to say about reading instruction* (3rd ed., pp. 166-183). Newark, DE: International Reading Association.

Sanchez-Boyce, M. (2000). *The use of interpreters in special education assessments*. Unpublished doctoral dissertation, University of California at Davis.

Sargent, L. R. (1991). *Social skills for school and community*. Reston, VA: Division of Mental Retardation, Council for Exceptional Children (pp. 269-273).

Sattler, J. M. (1992). *Assessment of children* (3rd ed). San Diego: Sattler.

Sax, C. L., & Thoma, C. A. (2002). *Transition assessment: Wise practices for quality lives*. Baltimore: Brookes.

Scheiman, M. M., & Rouse, M. W. (Eds.). (1994). *Optometric management of learning-related visual problems*. St. Louis, MO: Mosby-Year Book.

Schmitt, M. C. (1990). A questionnaire to measure children's awareness of strategic reading processes. *The Reading Teacher, 43*(7), 454-461.

Schoenbrodt, L., Kumin, L., & Sloan, J. M. (1997). Learning disabilities existing concomitantly with communication disorder. *Journal of Learning Disabilities, 30*, 264-281.

Scott, P., & Raborn, D. (1996). Realizing the gifts of diversity among students with learning disabilities. *LD Forum, 21*(2), 10-18.

Seaman, J. A., DePauw, K. P., Morton, K. P., & Omoto, K. (2003). *Making connections: From theory to practice in adapted physical education*. Scottsdale, AZ: Holcomb Hathaway.

Section 504 of the Rehabilitation Act of 1973, 29 U.S.C. §§794 et seq. (1973).

Section 504 of the Rehabilitation Act of 1973 Regulations, 34 C.F.R. §104.3(j) (1973). 34 C.F.R. §104.35 (1973). 34 C.F.R. §104.44(a)(b)(c) (1990).

Seefeldt, C., & Barbour, N. (1998). *Early childhood education: An introduction* (4th ed.). Upper Saddle River, NJ: Prentice Hall.

Shafer, S. (1997). *Writing effective report card comments*. New York: Scholastic.

Shakrani, S. (1999). *Standardized achievement tests and English language learners: Validity and fairness*. Los Angeles: University of California, National Center for Research on Evaluation, Standards, and Student Testing.

Shanker, J. L. & Ekwall, E. E. (2003). Locating and correcting reading difficulties (8th ed.). Upper Saddle River, NJ: Merrill/Prentice Hall.

Shinn, M. R., Collins, V. L., & Gallagher, S. (1998). Curriculum-based measurement and problem solving assessment. In M. R. Shinn (Ed.), *Advanced applications of curriculum-based measurement* (pp. 143–174). New York: Guilford Press.

Shure, A., Cobb Morocco, C., Lyman DiGisi, L., & Yenkin, L. (1999, September/October). Pathways to planning: Improving student achievement in inclusive classrooms. *Teaching Exceptional Children*, 48–54.

Silvaroli, N. J., & Wheelock, W. H. (2000). *Classroom reading inventory* (9th ed.). New York: McGraw-Hill.

Silver, L. B. (2001, November 2001). What are learning disabilities? Retrieved April 10, 2004, from http://www. Idonline.org/il_indepth.

Sirvis, B. P., Doyle, M. B., & Alcouloumre, D. (2001). Assessment of students with physical and special health needs. In Alper, D. Rynak, & C. Sholoss (Eds.), *Alternate assessment of students with disabilities in inclusive settings*. (pp. 273–293). Boston: Allyn & Bacon.

Sitlington, P. I., Clark, G. M., & Kolstoe, O. P. (2000). *Transition education and services for adolescents with disabilities* (3rd ed.). Boston: Allyn & Bacon.

Sitlington, P. I., Neubert, D. A., Begun, W., Lombard, R. C., & Leconte, P. J. (1996). *Assess for success: Handbook on transition assessment*. Reston, VA: Council for Exceptional Children.

Sitlington, P. L., Neubert, D. A., & Leconte, P. J. (1997). Transition assessment: The position of the Division on Career Development and Transition. *Career Development for Exceptional Individuals, 20*(1), 69–79.

Slentz, K. (1997, January). *Evaluation and assessment in early childhood special education: Children who are linguistically diverse*. Olympia, WA: State Superintendent of Public Instruction.

Smith, D. D. (2001). *Introduction to special education: Teaching in an age of opportunity* (4th ed.). Boston: Allyn & Bacon.

Smith, S. W., & Kortering, L. J. (1996). Using computers to generate IEPs: Rethinking the process. *Journal of Special Education Technology, 13*(2) 80–81.

Snow, C. E., Burns, S., & Griffin, P. (Eds.). (1998). *Preventing reading difficulties in young children*. Washington, DC: National Academic Press.

Spache, G. D. (1981). *Diagnostic reading scales*. Monterey, CA: CTB McGraw-Hill.

Spandel, V. (1996). *Seeing with new eyes*. Portland, OR: Northwest Regional Educational Laboratory. Retrieved on November 30, 2004 from http://www.nwrel.org/assessment/toolkit98/six.html.

Spinelli, C. G. (1999). Breaking down barriers—Building strong foundations: Parents and teachers of exceptional students working together. *Learning Disabilities 9*(3), 123–130.

Spinelli, C. G. (2003). Educational and psychosocial implications affecting childhood cancer survivors: What educators need to know. *Physical Disabilities: Education and Related Services, 21*(2), 49–65.

Spinelli, C. G. (2004). Dealing with cancer in the classroom: The teacher's role and responsibilities. *Teaching Exceptional Children, 36*(4), 14–21.

Spinelli, C. S. (2001). Interactive teaching strategies and authentic curriculum and assessment: A model for effective classroom instruction. *Hong Kong Special Education Forum, 4*(1), 1–11.

Stahl, S. A., Heubach, K., & Cramond, B. (1996). *Fluency oriented reading instruction*. (NRRC Report No. 79). College Park, MD: National Reading Research Center.

Starkin, C. M., & Starkin, A. (1973). *Guides to decision making in computational math*. Bemidji, MN: Unique Curriculums Unlimited.

Stieglitz, E. L. (2002). *The Stieglitz informal reading inventory: Assessing reading behaviors from emergent to advanced*. Boston: Allyn & Bacon.

Stiggins, R. J. (1997). *Student-centered classroom assessment* (2nd ed.) Upper Saddle River, NJ: Merrill/Prentice Hall.

Stiggins, R. J. (2001). *Student-centered classroom assessment* (3rd ed.). Upper Saddle River, NJ: Merrill-Prentice Hall.

Sullivan, K. A., Lantz, P. J., & Zirkel, P. A. (2000). Leveling the playing field or leveling the players? Section 504, the Americans with Disabilities Act, and inter scholastic sports. *Journal of Special Education, 33*(4), pp. 258–267.

Suritsky, S. K., & Hughes, C. A. (1997). Note-taking strategy instruction. In D. D. Deshler, E. S. Ellis, & B. K. Lenz, (Eds.). *Teaching adolescents with learning disabilities* (2nd ed., pp. 267–312). Denver, CO: Love Publishing.

Swanson, S., & Howell, C. (1996). Test anxiety in adolescents with learning disabilities and behavior disorders. *Exceptional Children, 62*(5), 389–397.

Tannenbaum, J. (1996). *Practical ideas on alternative assessment for ESL students*. Washington, DC: ERIC Clearinghouse on Languages and Linguistics.

Taylor, R. L. (2003). *Assessment of exceptional students: Educational and psychological procedures* (6th ed.). Boston: Allyn & Bacon.

Teaching Diverse Learners. (2004). Providence, RI: The Northeast and Islands Regional Educational Laboratory. Retrieved on September 2, 2004, from http://www.alliance.brown.edu/tdl/.

Tharp, R. (1997). *From at-risk to excellence: Research, theory, and principles for practice*. Santa Cruz, CA: Center for Research on Education, Diversity, and Excellence.

Thoma, C. A., & Held, M. (2002). Measuring what's important: Using alternative assessments. In C. L. Sax & C. A. Thoma, (Eds.), *Transition assessment: Wise practices for quality lives*. Baltimore: Paul H. Brookes.

Thomas, W. P., & Collier, V. (1997, December). *School effectiveness for language minority students* (Resource Collection Series, No. 9). Washington, DC: National Clearinghouse for Bilingual Education. Retrieved April 20, 2002, from http://www.ncbe. gwu.edu/ncbepubs/resource/ effectiveness/index.htm.

Thompson, S., and Thurlow, M. (2001). *2001 State Special Outcomes: A Report on States Activities at the Beginning of a New Decade*. Available from the University of Minnesota, National Center on Educational Outcomes.

Thompson, S., Blount, A., & Thurlow, M. (2002). *A summary of research on the effects of test accommodations: 1999 through 2001*. Available from the University of Minnesota, National Center on Educational Outcomes, http://education. umn.edu/nceo/ OnlinePubs/Technical34. htm.

Thurlow, M. L., Elliott, J. L., & Ysseldyke, J. E. (1998). *Testing students with disabilities: Practical strategies for complying with district and state requirements*. Thousand Oaks, CA: Corwin Press.

Tindal, G. A. & Marston, D. B. (1990). *Classroom-based assessment: Evaluating instructional outcomes*. Columbus, OH: Merrill.

Tindal, G., Shinn, M. R., & Rodden-Nord, K. (1990). Contextually based school consultation: Influential variables. *Exceptional Children, 56*, 324-336.

Tompkins, G. E. (2002). *Language arts: Content and teaching strategies* (5th ed.). Upper Saddle River, NJ: Prentice Hall.

Torgesen, J. K., Rashotte, C. A., Alexander, A. W., Alexander, J., & McFee, K. (2002, November). *The challenge of fluent reading for older children with reading difficulties*. Retrieved August 15, 2004, from http://www.prel.org/ programs/rel/fluency/Torgesen. ppt.

Torgesen, J. K., Wagner, R. K., & Rashotte, C. A. (1997). Approaches to the prevention and remediation of phonologically based reading disabilities. In B. Blachman (Ed.), *Foundations of reading acquisition and dyslexia: Implications for early intervention* (pp. 287-304). Mahwah, NJ: Erlbaum.

Troia, G., Graham, S., & Harris, H. (1998). Teaching students with learning disabilities to mindfully plan when writing. *Exceptional Children, 65*(2), 235-252.

Turnbull, A., Turnbull, H. R., Smith, S., & Leal, D. (2002). *Exceptional lives: Special education in today's schools*. Upper Saddle River, NJ: Merill/Prentice Hall.

Turnbull, H. R. & Turnbull, A. (2000). *Free appropriate public education: The law and children with disabilities* (6th ed). Denver, CO: Love.

Twombly, E. (2001). Screening, assessment, curriculum planning and evaluation: Engaging parents in the process. *Zero to Three, 21*(4), 36-41.

U.S. Census Bureau. (n.d.). *Census 2000 supplementary survey: Profile of selected social characteristics*. Retrieved April 22, 2002, from http://factfinder. census. gov/home/en/c2ss.html.

U.S. Commission on Civil Rights (1997). *Equal educational opportunity and non-discrimination for students with disabilities: Federal enforcement of Section 504* (Vol. 2). (Equal educational opportunity project series). Washington, DC: Author.

U.S. Congress, Office of Technology Assessment. (1992, February). *Testing in American schools: Asking the right questions*. Washington, DC: U.S. Government Printing Office.

U.S. Department of Education. (1995). *The community action toolkit*. Washington, DC: Author.

U.S. Department of Education (1997). *19th Annual Report to Congress on the Implementation of the Individuals with Disabilities Education Act*. http.//www.ed. gov/offices/OSERS/OSEP/ osep97anlrpt/).

U.S. Department of Education (2000). *Nondiscrimination in high-stake testing: A resource guide*. Washington, DC: U.S. Department of Education, Office for Civil Rights.

Vallecorsa, A. L., deBettencourt, L. U., & Zigmond, N. (2000). *Students with mild disabilities in general education settings: A guide for special educators*. Upper Saddle River, NJ: Merrill/Prentice Hall.

Vallecorsa, A. L., deBettencourt, L. U., & Zigmond, N. (2001). *Students with mild disabilities in general education setting: A guide for special educators*. Upper Saddle River, NJ: Merrill/Prentice Hall.

Vavrus, L. (1990). Put portfolios to the test. *Instructor, 100*(1), 48-53.

Vellutino, F. R., Scalon, D. M., & Tanzman, M. S. (1994). Components of reading ability: Issues and problems in operationalizing word identification, phonological coding, and orthographic coding. In G. R. Lyon, (Ed.), *Frames of reference: Assessment of learning disabilities* (pp. 279-329). Baltimore: Paul H. Brookes.

Venn, J. (1994). *Assessment of students with special needs*. New York: Macmillan.

Venn, J. J. (2004). *Assessing students with special needs* (3rd ed.).

Upper Saddle River, NJ: Merrill/Prentice Hall.

Vermont Department of Education (2004). Retrieved July 28, 2004, from www.state.vt.us/educ/ESL/htm/Step2/health2.html.

Vogel, A. (1998). Adults with learning disabilities. In S. Vogel & S. Reder, (Eds.), *Learning disabilities, literacy, and adult education* (pp. 5-8). Baltimore: Paul H. Brookes.

Vygotsky, L. S. (1978). *Mind in society: The development of higher psychological processes.* In M. Cole, V. John-Steiner, S. Scribner, & E. Souberman (Eds. & Trans.). Cambridge, MA: Harvard University Press.

Watkins, C. R., & Schloss, C. N. (2001). Assessment in the referral process. In A. S. Alper, D. L. Ryndak, & C. N. Schloss, (Eds.), *Alternate assessment of students with disabilities in inclusive settings* (pp. 54-74). Needham Heights, MA: Allyn & Bacon.

Wechsler, D. (1997). *Wechsler adult intelligence scale* (3rd ed.). San Antonio, TX: Harcourt Assessments.

Wechsler, D. (2001). *Wechsler individual achievement test* (2nd ed.). San Antonio, TX: Harcourt Assessments.

Wechsler, D. (2002). *Wechsler preschool and primary scale of intelligence* (3rd ed.). San Antonio, TX: Harcourt Assessments.

Wechsler, D. (2003). *Wechsler intelligence scale for children* (4th ed.). San Antonio, TX: Harcourt Assessments.

Wechsler, D. (2003). *Wechsler intelligence scale for children* (4th ed., integrated.). San Antonio, TX: Harcourt Assessments.

Wehman, P. (1996). *Life beyond the classroom,* (2nd ed.). Baltimore: Paul H. Brookes.

Wehmeyer, M. L. (2001). Self-determination and transition. In P. Wehman (Ed.), *Life beyond the classroom: Transition strategies for young people with disabilities,* (3rd ed., pp. 35-60). Baltimore: Paul H. Brookes.

Wehmeyer, M. L., & Schywartz, M. (1998). The relationship between self-determiniation and quality of life for adults with mental retardation. *Education and Training in Mental Retardation and Developmental Disabilities, 33,* 3-12.

Wesson, C. L., & King, R. P. (1996). Portfolio assessment and special education students. *Teaching Exceptional Children, 28*(2), 44-48.

Westby, C., Burda, A., & Mehta, Z. (2003, April 29). Asking the right questions in the right ways: Strategies for ethnographic interviewing. *Asha, 8,* 4-5, 16-17.

Williams, C. W., & Hounshell, P. B. (1998). Enabling the learning disabled: Teaching strategies for challenged students. *The Science Teacher, 65*(1), 29-31.

Wilson, K., & Swanson, H. L. (2001). Are mathematics disabilities due to a domain-general or a domain-specific working memory deficit? *Journal of Learning Disabilities, 34*(3), 237-248.

Wilson, P. T. (1988). *Let's think about reading and reading instruction: A primer for tutors and teachers.* Dubuque, IA: Kendall/Hunt.

Witt, J. C., Elliott, S. N., Daly, E. J., Gresham, F. M., & Kramer, J. J. (1998). *Assessment of at-risk and special needs children* (2nd ed.). Boston: McGraw Hill.

Woodcock, R. W., McGrew, K. S., & Mather, N. (2001). *Woodcock-Johnson III.* Itasca, IL: Riverside.

Woods, J. J., & McCormick, K. M. (2002). Toward an integration of child- and family-centered practices in the assessment of preschool children: Welcoming the family. *Young Exceptional Children, 5*(3), 2-11.

Woods, M. L., & Moe, A. J. (2003). *Analytical Reading Inventory* (7th ed.). Upper Saddle River, NJ: Merrill/Prentice Hall.

Wright, J. (2004). *Curriculum-based measurement: A manual for teachers.* Retrieved June 10, 2004, from http://www.interventioncentral.org.

Yates, J. R., & Ortiz, A. (1998). Issues of culture and diversity affecting educators with disabilities: A change in demography is reshaping America. In R. J. Anderson, C. E. Keller, & J. M. Karp (Eds.), *Enhancing diversity: Educators with disabilities in the education enterprise.* Washington, DC: Gallaudet University Press.

Yell, M. M. (1999). Multiple choice to multiple rubrics: One teacher's journey to assessment. *Social Education, 65*(6), 326-329.

Yzquierdo, Z. A., Blalock, G., & Torres-Velasquez, D. (2004). Language-appropriate assessments for determining eligibility of English language learners for special education services. *Assessment for Effective Intervention, 29*(2), 17-30.

Zaner-Bloser Staff. (1996) *Evaluation scale.* Columbus, OH: Zaner-Bloser.

Zeffrino, T., & Eden, G. (2000). The neural basis of developmental dyslexia. *Annals of Dyslexia, 50,* 3-30.

Zeidner, M. (1998). *Test anxiety: The state of the art.* New York, NY: Plenum Press.

Zeno, S. M., Ivens, S. H., Millard, R. T., & Duvvuri, R. (1995). *The educator's word frequency guide.* New York: Touchstone Applied Science Associates.

Index